SOCIOLOGY AND RELIGION

A Book of Readings

NORMAN BIRNBAUM
Amherst College

GERTRUD LENZER
New York University

SOCIOLOGY

AND

RELIGION

A BOOK OF READINGS

PRENTICE-HALL, INC.   ENGLEWOOD CLIFFS, NEW JERSEY

SOCIOLOGY AND RELIGION

A Book of Readings

Birnbaum/Lenzer

© 1969 by Prentice-Hall, Inc., Englewood Cliffs, New Jersey

Library of Congress Catalog Card No. 68–28878

Printed in the United States of America

Current printing (last digit):

10 9 8 7 6 5 4 3 2

PRENTICE-HALL INTERNATIONAL, INC., *London*
PRENTICE-HALL OF AUSTRALIA, PTY. LTD., *Sydney*
PRENTICE-HALL OF CANADA, LTD., *Toronto*
PRENTICE-HALL OF INDIA PRIVATE LTD., *New Delhi*
PRENTICE-HALL OF JAPAN, INC., *Tokyo*

ACKNOWLEDGEMENTS

The authors wish to thank, in the first instance, the Warden and Fellows of Nuffield College of Oxford University. During the period in which Dr. Birnbaum held a Fellowship at the College, they enabled Dr. Lenzer to come to Oxford to work on the anthology. The authors also wish to thank Miss Jennie Bond of Nuffield College for invaluable secretarial assistance in this phase of their work. They also wish to thank those colleagues who were good enough to give permission to have their works reproduced here, and in particular Dr. Morioka, whose contribution was especially prepared for this volume.

CONTENTS

PART IV

**Religion in Transformation:
Discussion of the Present Situation**

SOCIOLOGY AND RELIGION

A Book of Readings

INTRODUCTION

The purpose of this brief introductory essay is twofold: to give the reader a guide to the development of the field, and to show that if sociology as a whole derives from the philosophy of history and political philosophy, the philosophical bases of the sociology of religion are no less pronounced. We give, therefore, a brief commentary on the development of the sociology of religion—intended to set the relevant texts in the context of general intellectual history.

No mode or discipline of thinking is without its precursors—this axiomatic statement is as relevant to the development of the sociology of religion as it is to the emergence of all the social sciences. One can find anticipations of the kind of thought that characterizes the sociology of religion in various locations of the historical past—in classical antiquity there are certain speculations of the pre-Socratics, as well as the views on religion elaborated by Lucretius. There is the nominalist tradition in medieval European philosophy and Muslim thought. And there are the skeptical reflections on religion of Machiavelli. Such instances, as well as others, may be regarded as anticipations of the kind of thinking that would one day result in the sociology of religion, but they cannot be regarded in themselves as substantively establishing such a discipline of study. That possibility only emerged at a particular moment in history —the end of the 17th century—when general and philosophical modes and categories of thought could be observed as undergoing a drastic shift in orientation. This shift is commonly, and accurately, referred to as secularization, the secularization of thought—or of spirituality itself, as Hegel was later to observe. That possibility came to its full realization with the development of the social sciences from the turn of the 18th century on and throughout the 19th century. It was then that secular thought organised itself into these new forms of inquiries. In a world in which all phenomena could be seen as man-made and without any transcendent originator or causation, the emergence of the social sciences in general and the sociology of religion in particular represented one of the most momentous developments in the process of secularization itself.

In his remarkable *Crise de la Conscience Européene,* Hazard observed that the radical discontinuity between seventeenth and eighteenth-century thought was enormous. The sociology of religion, then, had its origins in the general secularization of the European consciousness, as borne by the educated. Only this process of secularization allowed psychological distance from religious belief and practice sufficient to engender abstract formulations of the relationship between religion and society: the beginnings of systematic areligion and anti-religion provided ideological motivation for systematic reflection. It should be remembered, however, that even before that sort of thought about religion typified by the *Philosophes,* the relationship of religion to its historical setting had become the object of reflection. We may treat

1

Bossuet as an ecclesiastical apologist, yet the *Discours sur l'histoire universelle* (1681), in its insistence on the role of religion in history, took a position which made the later attacks of the Philosophes against religion easier (as in a different but parallel way did the philosophical and religious writings of Spinoza). If religion did indeed constitute an indispensable component of the social order, then a new social order could only be imagined without it. A somewhat modified incentive to think in the same terms was provided by Montesquieu: according to this anti-absolutistic thinker, the religious institutions and beliefs of a society constitute an indispensable component of its "esprit" or ethos. It followed that change in a society would demand an effort to change its religious institutions; moreover, whereas Bossuet was in favor of royal absolutism and depicted religion very positively, as its support and legitimation, Montesquieu was anti-absolutistic. He was discreet enough not to attack the Church as a buttress of absolutism, but the conclusion followed clearly enough. These political reflections on the generally legitimating role of religion in eighteenth-century Europe could not be used to attack religion until another sort of analysis had added a psychological dimension to the discussion: it remained to depict the psychological structures which generated, at the same time, belief and political consent.

David Hume's *Natural History of Religion* (1757) was written in the enlightened—compared with the contemporary Continent—atmosphere of a Scotland free of early Calvinist rigors. Hume himself was careful not to put his own religious scepticism (indeed agnosticism) in print in his lifetime: he did allow himself to publish his analysis of the basis of religious sentiments. These he attributed to inchoate psychological forces, chief amongst them being fear. He also depicted the evolution of religious beliefs and insisted on the elements common to fetishism, polytheism, and Christianity. The whole was done in a detached, indeed ironic tone, and concluded on a note of resigned ambiguity: the objects of religion were a mystery but was not the mystery part of the creator's design? Hume's style concealed what we now know was a negative intention; his French friends and contemporaries, the Encyclopedists, used less concealment, their irony was tinged with hostility, their anti-religious passion more open.

Before the Reformation, the development of nominalism contributed to the new view of faith later elaborated by the Reformers, its absolute separation from reason. Before the Enlightenment, the new empirical theory of knowledge did much to destroy the connection between faith and knowledge so laboriously reconstructed by European rationalism. Hume was in this tradition (was indeed in his theory of knowledge its most radical representative.) The general empirical temper generated by the new philosophy, combined with the obvious triumphs of the natural sciences, had devastating consequences for a rationalism become rigidified. An empirical method in the moral and historical sciences now seemed possible; in this respect the Encyclopedists were at one with the British empiricists. They proceeded, however, to use the evidence to construct a new conception of a natural reason: a doctrine of progress, to be accomplished as soon as the application of empirical method showed the fragility of received spiritual structures built upon errors, indeed lies, and domination.

The Encyclopedists held that religion was an obstacle to the progress of mankind.

Priests and the proponents of religion encouraged the darkest of fears and the crudest of superstitions, legitimated the worst of tyrannies: in the interest of maintaining the domination of those rulers who allied to the clerics and their equivalents claimed divine dispensation for their crimes, divine sanction for their rule. But if men, or more precisely ordinary men in a condition of social subjugation, were victimized by their own religious illusions, they had to have a capacity to acquire knowledge of truth, if the changes desired by the Philosophes were possible. Two elements, then, were required to complement the Philosophes' critique of religion: a theory of the psychological capacity of men to think, feel, and behave otherwise than in a condition of subjugation, and a theory of other moral possibilities in the world than those given by the *ancien régime*. This last in particular excited the interest of the Philosophes: in their ideas of natural law they gave expression to the view that men had a great potential for secular experience, since the world could be ordered (if the obscuring effect of religion were removed) in an equitable and perfected fashion. This, of course, was a positive notion of a secular utopia: we shall see, shortly, that secularization in the early sociology of religion could also assume a negative signifi-cance—as a condition of decomposition and degradation, as a denial of truth. The Encyclopedists with their irreligious convictions, it must be said, made common cause in certain respects with deists who held that God had endowed men with moral capacities to perceive moral and social truths not necessarily promulgated in explicit form by ecclesiastical institutions. The deistic doctrine contributed to a certain irenistic spirit: religious and human forms not exhausted by Christianity could now be deemed valuable, and worthy of enquiry.

The Enlightenment in its French form, then, opposed an abstract (and superior) reason to the concrete historical institutions it wished to change. There did develop a counter-current, a search for a new historical reason, not embodied in any one set of institutions but embodied in them all—if necessary, embodied in their very changes. We associate this current of thought with the beginnings of German historicism, with Herder, and above all, with Hegel. It is important, however, to see the connec-tions of this movement with the French Enlightenment. Perhaps the central figure in the relationship of the two is Kant (who, it will be recalled, failed to undertake his legendary daily walk only once—when reading Rousseau's *Confessions*). Kant attempted to derive a belief in God from other than empirical considerations, from the moral necessity intrinsic to any human action seeking to do good in a world empirically doomed to evil. More important for our immediate purposes, Kant attempted a derivation of man's moral nature not from empirical nature but from the abstract moral requirements of a moral mankind, from an hypothesized realm of moral ends or freedom. The subsequent preoccupation, above all in German thought, with concrete or historical reason is by no means unrelated to this Kantian hypothesis: we may understand it as the effort to determine the possibilities of freedom in the historical world. This led, inevitably, to an analysis of the historical role of religion, an enquiry into its embeddedness in social structure. If men actually lived in a moral world, a kingdom of ends set by themselves, it was necessary to distin-guish between these ends and a pseudo-morality, constituted by forces claiming a divine sanction they did not have. Meanwhile, it is plausible to regard Kant's search

for a purely human realm of morals and conduct as the transposition into philosophy of the religious ideas of one German Enlightenment thinker who took much
from France: Lessing, who held that precisely in the historical variety of religions
a positive human essence could be found.

Hegel himself, of course, has to be inserted in a tradition. As a university student,
he celebrated the French Revolution; his readings included the eighteenth-century
British social thinkers as well as the Philosophes. His immediate historicist predecessor in Germany was Herder, whose work he in turn seemed to have transposed onto
a more abstract and metahistorical plane.

Herder insisted on the historical distinctiveness of the national character, *Volksseele*—
in which religious belief, feelings and institutions colored and shaped distinctive
historical traditions. Hegel formalized this set of insights in his historical account
of the evolution of spirit. With respect to religion, he began on an entirely critical
note: the incorporation of Christianity, originally a spiritual protest against the
rigidified Synagogue, in the state emptied it of its own spiritual meaning. This was
the position of the younger Hegel: the elder one spiritualized his earlier appreciation of the historicity of religion, which became one of the central categories by
which spirit moved through history and was reconciled (after many splits and objecti-
fications) to itself. Hegel's thought never lost its historicity: its importance for us
lies in the cast it gave to German sociological thought generally and specifically to
its role in the formation of the religious thought of the young Hegelians.

In his *Life of Jesus* the young Hegelian Strauss held that Jesus was no doubt a
historic person, but that his divinity had been attributed to him on the basis of
prevailing religious conceptions (including mythic ones) in antiquity. Bauer carried
the argument further; he denied the historicity of Jesus. But his most important
contribution was perhaps his attack on Hegel for covert atheism: the spirit in Hegel's
system, Bauer argued, was an imperfectly secularized conception. God was active
in human history, for Hegel, only in the surrogate form of spirit—which tended
to be emptied, progressively, of specific theological content. Hegel, however, lacked
the courage to acknowledge his atheism. This cycle of criticism was completed by
Feuerbach, who in his *Essence of Christianity* declared that the prevalent notions of
God were in fact projections onto the universe of man's idealized image of himself.
What men worshipped, in other words, was not the supernatural but an idealized
conception of natural, human, possibility. It remained for Marx and Engels to draw
even more radical systematic conclusions from this series of discussions.

Completely immersed in the Hegelian tradition, the young Marx gradually detached
himself from it—a process facilitated both by his increasing social radicalism and
his contact with French thought in Paris. Engels' own encounter with Christianity
was if anything more direct: he came from a pietistic family and possessed a considerable religious education. Their early work concentrated on the political dimensions
of religion, its use or abuse as a means of moral and intellectual repression. In
this respect, they resembled their moral ancestors in the French Enlightenment.
But they came to see that the liberation of the citizen, to paraphrase Marx, did not
necessarily entail the liberation of the man: the connection between religion and

oppression was not only an outer one but had to be attributed to the psychological dimensions of the structure of history itself. History, and in particular recent history and the history of a capitalist society, was the history of class conflict: these, in turn, reflected a division of labor which affected spiritual life. The division of labor, and the consequent development of structures of exploitation through the market, subjugated men to the products of their own labor—which came to dominate them in the form of commodities and the laws governing their exchange. Men lived, therefore, in a condition of alienation: unable to control the consequences of their own work, unable in general to master their world, which became not theirs but an alien and oppressive environment. It was under these conditions that religion developed, or rather, that men required religious beliefs: religion expressed the condition of alienation (men worshipped supernatural entities which were in fact creations of their own fantasy) and at the same time a protest against it (positive images of a supernatural future were an implicit criticism of conditions on earth.) When Marx declared that for Germany religious criticism had ended and that political criticism had begun, he meant in effect that head-on attacks on religion were useless so long as the social condition which gave rise to religion persisted. This was part of the shift in emphasis in Marxist theory which led Marx and Engels to move from a statement of the theoretical presuppositions of human liberation to a consideration of its actual pre-conditions: from critical philosophy to revolutionary praxis. But despite that movement, the internal development of the Marxist sociology of religion continued. This consisted in a specification of the conditions of religious alienation, a deepening of the Marxist appreciation of the historical role of religion, including its positive aspects. Engels traced the history of religious evolution, and in his distinguished work on the German Peasants War, showed how in a religious epoch even revolutionary thoughts had to find religious expression. It must be said that the later works on religion of certain Marxists represented a regression, from a theoretical point of view: Bernstein treating the Reformation as an expression of class interests in a direct and mechanical sense makes a sad contrast with Engels. The revivification of the Marxist tradition had to wait until the twentieth century, under the influence of "bourgeois" thought. Let us, for the moment, turn our attention to the development of this last.

Marx's great forerunner, in the description of the peculiar characteristics of industrial society, was perhaps Saint-Simon. More convinced of its intrinsic moral potential, less systematic in any case (and visionary in a rather different sense than Marx), less devoted to the cause of human liberation and more to efficacy, discipline and the preservation of order and authority, he nevertheless had caught a glimpse of some of the new society's inner laws. In particular, he described a process of secularization which (in contradistinction to Marx) he supposed was taking place and which needed only to be brought to the attention of the elite to be completed. The "New Christianity" for Saint-Simon was the direct translation of a Christian moral and political vocabulary into the language of the new society, a language of production, technique and discipline. It will be seen that the element of human transcendence, so characteristic in Marx, was missing: but this was not alone a consequence of the absence of dialectical thinking in Saint-Simon but perhaps a cause of it. In any event, the full historical and sociological statement of a position anticipated in Saint-Simon waited upon Auguste Comte's Positive Philosophy.

Comte, Saint-Simon's associate, developed a panoramic vision of world history in which the emergence of a scientific mode of thought was a spiritual culmination of the evolution of humanity. Mankind and human society had passed through the stages of theology and metaphysics to arrive at the clarity and enlightenment of positivism: the highest triumph of positivism was to induce in mankind an appreciation of the inner meaning of its own history. This was, of course, an explicitly secularized account of the social evolution of religion—the more so, as the discussions of the inner structure and texture of the three phases, and in particular of the first two, showed that Comte was well aware of the variety and complexity of the relationship between belief, religious organization and the movement of society generally. For instance, he anticipated much of Tylor and Spencer in showing the particular relationships between the organization of cults of a polytheistic kind, the political power of the priesthood, and the general political division of society. Like Marx, he also anticipated Weber in showing an exact awareness of the connection between the Reformation's internalization of the monastic ethic and its consequences for work discipline in bourgeois society. Comte's image of human religious evolution was, of course, unilinear: he supposed that positivism had in fact relegated religion to the past. Interestingly enough, he made common cause with the political reactionaries of his day (Bonald, De Maistre) in insisting that familial authority—generally legitimized by religion, as he saw—was the critical element in the social stability he wished to restore to European society after the French Revolution. Comte was caught in a contradiction: the intrinsically rationalizing force of science could corrode traditional order, yet he wished to show that it could also legitimate a new, more lasting order. Like Marx's sketch for the future of mankind, Comte's was based on a gigantic leap of the imagination: yet the leap once achieved seemed to result in the sanctification of new tyrannies. The end of domination was not envisaged by Comte: perhaps his subsequent invention of a religion of humanity reflected his despair at finding freedom without God. At any rate, his central theses, that a society's order was defined and maintained by its religious and ideological conceptions, that science grew out of religion, that the maintenance and definition of a religious and ideological order is constitutive of the society itself, were to re-emerge in the nineteenth century—and at the beginning of the twentieth, the positivist and rationalist side being accentuated, in Durkheim himself.

Lammenais, whose extraordinary spiritual career—from ultra-Montanism to a schismatic Christian humanism and beyond—in some ways paralleled Comte's evolution, made no direct contribution to the formal sociology of religion. We do however see in his work and influence the beginnings of a change in theology itself, a response to the altered spiritual and social situation of a developing bourgeois and industrial society. The fact that Lammenais ended with social radicalism, whereas Comte (beginning with irreligion) was conservative, is in itself a chapter in the sociology of religion.

Meanwhile, in addition to these significant theoretical advances, the great work of nineteenth-century scholarship continued: studies of the great civilization complexes of the Orient, the beginnings of modern ethnology, archaeological and philological investigations into ancient culture. Just as the beginnings of these comparative studies had influenced the Enlightenment (and biblical and textual criticism before then had influenced the Reformation and critical theological scholarship generally), nineteenth-century social history in its evolutionary and comparative dimensions was of great influence on thinking about religion. A good instance of this conjunction of scholarly interests and systematic thought was the work of Fustel de Coulanges, whose studies of antique social organization dealt with the religious life of the antique city. The scholar was able to show that these cities were religious communities as well as kinship groupings and political units, indeed, that the separate aspects of their functioning were related and that membership in the religious community was a precondition of membership in the political one, that later Greek political conceptions represented a secularization of certain religious definitions of community.

The great mid-nineteenth century figures in this respect were, however, the British thinkers Tylor and Spencer. Tylor, who became the first professor of anthropology (ethnology) at Oxford, did his own anthropological field work—but in his *Primitive Culture* he presented an evolutionary account of the development of human culture which had a considerable focus on religion. His celebrated "minimal definition of religion" entailed a "belief in the existence of spiritual beings." Tylor traced the evolution of this belief in human society, from primitive fantasies about the movement of the individual soul in sleep and in death to the most complex of belief systems. His doctrine of animism has often been identified with the totality of his system (there is an intimation of this in Durkheim's critique), but a reading of the text corrects this impression. Rather, Tylor shows how religion, built historically on animistic foundations, changes with changes in the complexity of culture and of social institutions. He manifests as acute an appreciation of the political and social uses of religion as of its psychological aspects. Tylor greatly influenced, in turn, Herbert Spencer. This scholar utilised a vast amount of comparative information to depict the totality of the evolution of society. His work on "Ecclesiastical Institutions" is remarkable for the acuity of his perceptions into the political functions of religion as a mode of sacerdotal legitimation of power; indeed, his entire sociology is pervaded by a theory of consonance—the institutions of a society, according to Spencer, have to fit one another. This analysis of structural consonance had a spiritual or psychological correlate: the type of belief prevailing in society had to express the general institutional possibilities of action within it. Spencer envisaged society as undergoing a process of progressive differentiation, in the course of which ecclesiastical and political institutions gradually separated. Similarly, consciousness was divided: religious consciousness becoming gradually constricted until it was concentrated as a specific type in a specific institution, while scientific reasoning assumed command of the mind in larger areas of human function. Spencer held that religious consciousness as embodied in ecclesiastical institutions would—with the progress of the type of contractual and liberal society he termed "industrial"— disappear, to be replaced by a practically subliminal sense of the divinity, termed by Spencer, however, the "unknowable." By this he meant, apparently, that there was a purpose to evolution and its attendant spiritual differentiation. It is interesting that Spencer envisaged both the demise of formal religion and its retention in exceedingly attenuated philosophic form, which led Nietzsche to jest that it was very much like an English gentleman to portray God as "unknowable," and to keep his distance.

No greater contrast could be imagined than that between Spencer and Nietzsche. Both, however, were part of an evolutionary and empiricist temper: Nietzsche praised the British empirical philosophers for their attention to psychological fact, even if he preferred the speculative approach to spiritual problems manifested by the German idealist philosophers. Nietzsche's special contribution anticipated the great critical work of the twentieth century, and provided a curiously modern psychological analysis of certain types of religion. His great work in this respect was certainly the *Genealogie der Moral*: there, he treated Christianity as a religion of psychological resentment, born of a fundamental psychological structure already visible in the Old Testament. The doctrine that the first shall be last, of the heavenly reversal of earthly structures of power and privilege, of a positive valuation of asceticism and renunciation in this life, was a mode of psychological control over an oppressive historical environment. It suggested, however, that morality was in its Judaeo-Christian form a psychological derivative of a subjective reality. With this analysis, Nietzsche erected his own challenge to the claims of Christian ontology and ethics—showing, again, that a philosophical or metaphysical basis attaches to every ostensible phenomenology of religion.

Nietzsche himself remarked that the father of German philosophy was a Protestant pastor, and it is clear that the sources of his own attack on Christianity lay in the decomposition of Protestant theology itself. First, religion had been internalized, made a matter of feeling, a triumph of a human need (as with Schleiermacher). Then its institutional form had been decried, the impossibility of living a Christian life had been proclaimed (at least in this world)—as with Kierkegaard. Later, in genteel New England, the American psychologist and philosopher William James was to invent or discover the "will to believe"—a purely psychological explication of the religious phenomenon. It was Nietzsche's peculiar genius to have combined this psychological analysis (originally begun to buttress religion against the claims of reason) with a brutal critique of culture, and particularly of late culture, which did not spare religion. In so doing, he developed a comprehensive social psychological view of religion which is strikingly modern.

Meanwhile, the great work of comparative enquiry into religious structures proceeded. (Nietzsche himself was a professor of classical philology and a student of the great Church historian and chronicler of Pietism, Ritschl). Robertson Smith, a Semiticist in Scotland, extended the historical appreciation of the Old Testament by showing that the common meal in the setting of kinship group was a characteristic of the Semitic religions found amongst groups which bordered on the ancient Jews. Smith's work was to be taken up into the body of the sociology of religion in conjunction with that of Sir James Frazer, whose *Golden Bough* and *Totemism and Exogamy* were considerable contributions to a sociology of religion. In the first, Frazer discussed the rituals attendant upon the institution of divine kingship, the slaying of the divine king by his putative successor. In the second, the connection between totemic rituals and the existence of cohesive kin groupings, the ascription of exogamic prescriptions to those grouped about the same totemic object, was examined.

It is sometimes forgotten that Freud's great *Totem and Taboo* rested on these founda- ~ tions. Freud himself was agnostic, convinced (in the tradition of the secular enlightenment) that religion was an "illusion." He once said that he had been honored as a great Jewish thinker, whereas his only service to the Jews was not to have denied that he was one. Anthropologists have made light of the theory of the "primal horde" in Freud's work. They have forgotten that Freud intended this as metaphorical —as a demonstration of the basic psychic structure underlying the human ambivalence to authority, and of the religious expression that this took. Freud's account of the slaying of the primal father by the band of brothers, their violation of the endogamic prohibition by their possession of the women of the group, their celebration of the triumph and their incorporation of the father by the oral consumption of his remains, their subsequent crisis of mourning and guilt, the expression of these feelings in religious prohibitions on incest, the sublimated expression of the original meal (and original desire) in a totemic ritual, must be considered a new version of the social contract theory. For Freud saw in the agreement among the brothers to subjugate themselves (and their impulses) to social order the original-source of religion —thus repeating over a century later the Enlightenment view that religion was a mode of oppression. Freud, however, believed that impulse or instinctual renunciation was the necessary price of human culture—although he believed it best to face this truth unaided by religious illusion or consolation. At any rate, his critique of religion was of one piece with his analysis of it: the repressive aspects of religion, its dimension of fantasy (reconciliation with the repressive force), its compulsiveness all attested to its origin in needs—at once—of the human psyche and the social order. Of particular interest was Freud's view that the origins of the social order and of the human psyche in its civilized form were to be found in the original religious act, the reenactment of the primal crime. "The totemic feast, perhaps the first feast of mankind, can be thought of as the repetition and commemoration of this remarkable criminal act, with which so much began: social organization, moral rules, and religion." If we abstract from Freud's historiography, this remains: a systematic account of the psychic and social functions of religion, which may well have relevance for our understanding of the historical development of religion but which— apart from its character as a secular historical myth—provides insight into the structure of the psychic and social processes which underlie religion.

Nietzsche and Freud may be thought of as continuing a radical irreligious tradition in sociological thought, and as doing so by pointing to the existence of depths not explored by either their religious or irreligious predecessors. With Durkheim, we return to a line of development begun in the nineteenth century. Many of Durkheim's general ideas are already to be found in the work of Auguste Comte: the view that a society's cohesion depends upon the organization of its belief system, the theorem that social density and an increase in contacts accelerates the circulation of ideas and alters their quality, a conception of society as an articulated set of relationships, each sector of which imposed its own moral discipline on individuals as a means of attaining a morality for the whole. More, Durkheim's view of the evolution of religious sentiments, of the transformation of religion into science with social evolution, derives directly from Comte. (Back of Comte there may well stand, for Durkheim, Rousseau with his question about what can legitimate man's social bondage.) Durkheim's interests were those of a laicist defender of the Third French Republic in a period when political reaction and clericalism were allied: the development of a secular social morality which could replace religion as the mode and means of social cohesion in a rationalized society. This was the source of his concern for a sociological method in the moral sciences, the search for an objectively valid canon or organon of moral and social judgment in society. It is in this framework, and not alone as detached and analytical contributions to a social science, that his sociology of religion ought to be viewed.

˜ Durkheim's celebrated refutation of the doctrine of animism expounded by Tylor and Spencer was intended to show that the religious sentiment has its origins in the sentiment of respect and awe towards objective social power, the source of the individual's moral and economic substance. Its effect was to reduce the range of variation in religious structures, as proper objects for sociological enquiry, by insisting on the element common to each: a core of sociological or human meaning derived from the incorporation by the individual of social constraint as part of his own system of ideas, indeed, his own psyche. On this foundation was constructed Durkheim's interpretation of ritual: ritual served to create, express, and reinforce the cohesion of the group—without which society would decompose into its atomized units. Religion, in other terms, was almost entirely a product of the social life of the group and no psychological substratum more complex than the individual's need of society entered into it. It is true that Durkheim did not treat religion as an epiphenomenon—according to his analysis, there could be no societies without it, since the social bond was constituted largely by religion. Yet it was at this point that his ultimate philosophical and political intentions collided with the analytical means he had chosen to attain them.

The last section of the *Formes Elementaires de la Vie Religieuse* is in fact an account of the evolution of the human spirit and human culture in terms not dissimilar to Comte's: science develops out of religion, science is the consensus of modern societies, the mode of their integration in the pursuit of those ends attainable by what elsewhere Durkheim termed an organic solidarity. The insight that science rests on a consensus, no less than religion, is sound: but in the nature of the case, a scientific consensus is limited in quantitative extent and different in spiritual structure from a religious one. By insisting that science can have the compelling power of religion, Durkheim in effect de-sacralizes religion in precisely those periods when its strength (according to his previous analysis) was its sacredness. The sacralization of science, however desirable in terms of Durkheim's search for a secular morality, is not quite what Durkheim intended. Rather, the depiction of religion as in its sacral period a universal mode of discourse, itself an anticipation for science and logic, is precisely the depiction of religion rejected by Durkheim in the British when they attempted it. The insight and structure of Durkheim's sketch to the contrary notwithstanding, the ahistoricity of his method seems to account for its lack of coherence.

Durkheim's great contemporary in the sociology of religion was, no less than he, convinced of the ineluctable secularization of the world. But Max Weber worked in an intellectual tradition which gave primacy to historical development, to the study of structures in change. His sociology of religion, therefore, was attached to a conception of historical direction which allowed for great historical variation; its schematism was adapted to the phenomenology of the historical world itself. Weber described himself as "religiously unmusical," by which he meant that he was not a believer. He was, however, a (somewhat ironical) "Kulturprotestant," who regarded religion (not alone Protestantism) as a great historical force, despite the fact that contemporary social structure—in some measure an outgrowth of religious impulsions given to culture—was hostile to religion in its historical form. Weber's own philosophical and political interests were these. In opposition to the (vulgar) Marxism of German Social Democracy, he wished to show that ideas and ideologies were in fact autonomous forces in history. In opposition to the religionists, however, he wished to show that the dread force of what he termed rationalization allowed no religious revival: this, despite the fact that he was politically allied with the German Protestant group which can be described as ameliorative social Protestants, who wished to temper the internal rigors of German imperialism by founding or extending a social state in an authentic national community.

Weber's best known work in the sociology of religion is his early essay on *The Protestant Ethic and the Spirit of Capitalism*. In it, he argued that the Calvinist version of Protestantism induced in its believers a condition of doubt and anxiety over their chances of salvation, which impelled them in the direction of relentless and methodical work in the world in order to reduce that anxiety. Calvinism generally abjured the worship of the flesh and treated the world as neutral, as a place in which to work for the greater glory of God but which was itself not necessarily sacred. This allowed anti-traditional innovations in state, society and economy, encouraged the scientific investigation of reality, and indeed began that process of rationalization (in part) which was later to lead to the disenchantment of the world and full secularization. It is sometimes overlooked that Weber identified a specific social group as the bearers of Calvinism: the *petite* and intermediate (moyenne) bourgeoisie. It is also overlooked that Weber promulgated his version of Calvinism in conjunction with an analysis of the peculiarities of Lutheranism as a force in modern German history. Lutheranism, a consequence of Luther's attention to the inner certainty of salvation and his sanctification of earthly institutions, was traditional in its social emphases and consequences: it was responsible in part for the specific political attitudes of modern Germany, its devotion to an artisan spirit. In this respect, Weber drew upon the reflections of his Heidelberg colleague Ernst Troeltsch, and it is appropriate to interrupt our survey of Weber's work to consider, at this point, the influence upon him of Troeltsch.

Troeltsch began his career as a theologian and ended it as a professor of philosophy. The change represented a deep critique of institutionalized Christianity and of its then current doctrines: Troeltsch saw the liberating potentiality of Christianity as restricted by these, its earthly garments. This perception accounted for the fundamental distinction made in his *Social Teachings of the Christian Churches*: that between Church and Sect. The Church was all-embracing, an institution of universal grace obliged to live in the world by virtue of its universal claims. The Sect was selective, open only to those religiously qualified, and it aimed at the alteration of the world to make it more divine. Troeltsch traced this antithesis back to early Christian history, and examined its influence upon the very structure of the Reformation. He also expanded upon the distinction between Calvinism and Lutheranism with respect to modern European history: Troeltsch was critical of German imperialism and saw in Lutheranism's political consequences, for all of its positive sides (discipline and sobriety) something not entirely encouraging in German history. Troeltsch published his great work in 1912, after Weber's: the influences, however, seemed to be mutual.

If Troeltsch remained in the world of European Christianity, Weber looked beyond it. If the Protestant Ethic and western religious development generally were responsible for the peculiar characteristics of bourgeois and industrial consciousness and society, an investigation of other courses of development might show precisely how. Weber accordingly later in his life, embarked on studies of Ancient Judaism, China, and India (and began, at least, a project on Islam). The results were published posthumously in his *Religionssoziologie,* and in the section of *Wirtschaft und Gesellschaft* which bears the same title—as well as in the (also posthumous) *General Economic History.* The complexity, range, and penetration of Weber's insights practically defy summary. The following common elements may, however, be noted in his enquiry. Religion does not mechanically or automatically *reflect* a class position or a position of power, positive or negative. It does, however, constitute an interpretation of the historical situation of a given group—in response to what Weber termed the "metaphysical needs of the human spirit." That interpretation of course comprised the sociological elements which entered into the group's concrete problems of ethical and social comportment: a religious ethic from this point of view was a fusion of doctrinal prescriptions about the path to salvation and the concrete imperatives derived from a life situation.

Weber's concrete studies of the world religions involved him in detailed analyses of the social structures of a number of civilization complexes: nothing could be further from the truth than the vulgar view that Weber derived these from religious beliefs or ecclesiastical structures. Indeed, an exceedingly plausible case can be made out for the view that Weber became successively more "structural" as his studies progressed, that his attention came increasingly to focus on elements of social constraint as sources of religious belief. Indeed, in his final essay on the social source of Protestantism he ascribed it to the late medieval tradition of urban religiosity manifested by artisans and merchants whose work accustomed them to regularity and to moral regularity: to the notion of a reward, as well as to the self-government of the medieval commune. It will be seen that this explanation is a good deal more "structural," indeed Marxist, than those customarily associated with Weber's work.

The key to the understanding of Weber's sociology of religion, if any one key does exist, will be found in the philosophical or metaphysical dimensions of his view of history. His idea of "rationalisation" is extremely ambiguous, or at the least, multiple in its connotations. It can mean a given course of development by which any cultural system evolves, becomes internally consistent and organised and works out its own possibilities of development. It can also mean (as in the evolution of those bureaucratic structures of administration which he saw as characteristic for the west) the domination of one specific cultural element: the tendency to weigh ends and means rationally, to apply critical and universal standards of an abstract kind to the judgment of human action. It was this latter meaning he intended in connection with the development of western culture, and it was a total process of secularization which he described, in which the world was increasingly emptied of religious meaning. The charismatic excitement of other religions, even of earlier western Christian epochs, was denied to those who had to live in what he termed the "iron cage" of a modern and industrial culture. That this was the result of the religious development of the west was not the least of the historical paradoxes we had to deal with: for Weber, religion was in the last analysis an expression of the fact that we lived or that historical men lived in a plurality of value universes. The religious variations encountered in history bespoke common needs, but different experiences: there could hardly be a general sociology of religion, but rather a sociology of religious (and non-religious) structures. With Weber, the analytical refinement of positivistic method and the extreme penetration and range of the German historical school combined. With Weber, the modern theoretical development of the sociology of religion appeared to come to an end.

Are these appearances real? A brief examination of the recent past may help us to answer this question. Weber was followed in German social thought by the thinker who as a student frequented his home in Heidelberg, and who is now regarded as the most distinguished senior philosopher in the socialist bloc: Georg Lukacs. Lukacs' *Geschichte und Klassenbewusstsein,* repudiated by the author under party criticism but a work of immense influence, represented a return to the early Hegelian structure of Marxism. With respect to religion, Lukacs' work is most important for his reintroduction of the conception of reification into the Marxist discussion, whence it had disappeared with the positivistic and scientist versions of Marxism which concentrated on a theory of interests as determinants of ideology, including religion.

Perhaps the most immediate result of Weber's thought, however, was its gradual penetration into the sociology of the theologians. Bonhoeffer's doctrine of a religionless Christianity, of the Church dissolving itself to serve the world, clearly depends upon a prior sociological analysis which derives from Weber's view of secularization. Weber has had no such direct influence upon Catholicism, least of all French Catholicism. It may be said, however, that French Catholicism's recent sociological conception of community owes much to its contact with a Marxism deepened and indeed purified of positivistic accretions by its encounter with bourgeois sociology and philosophy, with Weber's historical sociology and the phenomenology of the German philosophers. This has detached a Catholicism in danger of becoming an appendage of a given social form from its fixation on these forms, has restored a doctrine of the historical movement and indeed progression towards God of human society, and has given a new theological meaning to a conception of alienation which was in the face of the rigidified theology of the early nineteenth-century anti-theological.

The contemporary sociology of religion, in its theoretic form, faces the problem of a fully secularized world; it seems paradoxical to be ending this discussion by asserting that the theologians seem to have done as well (if not better) than the sociologists in comprehending it. The reason for this condition may well lie in the perspectives each brings to the situation. The theological avant-garde expects no necessary reversal of the secularized historical structure: it seeks to apprehend it in its historical uniqueness. Contemporary sociology reached a point of great intensity of perception with Max Weber, though he was unable to find a praxis which would express his own farewell to bourgeois history. It has, nonetheless, been reduced to pure contemplation—a contemplation no less pure for having taken the form of positivistic categorization or a structuralist effort to find a pattern of eternal recurrence behind the variable appearances of history. This insistence of sociology on its freedom from values has in fact enslaved it to the surface of events, has pushed it towards seeking a pseudo-history for these events in constructed theories of their meaning—which apply to them categories abstracted from the general human and historical experience, and therefore curiously lifeless. It remains to be hoped that current efforts to renew the sociology of religion, by giving it a historical correction and by exploring the structures of secularization itself, will in fact be fruitful: there are, indeed, some encouraging signs. The exploration of secularization has led to a heightened appreciation of the historical role of religion in a multiplicity of contexts. The acceptance by the educated consciousness of religion not simply as a negative stage of development to be transcended but as an experience of immeasurable richness, opening the way to a new conception of human possibility, is not the least of the secular preconditions of a new sociology of religion.

One further series of considerations should be kept in mind as the following anthology of selections is read and analyzed. The development of the sociology of religion during the nineteenth century cannot be adequately understood as an isolated or altogether independent phenomenon. The sociology of religion is in its development to be understood as part of the study of social change; and the founders and developers of the sociology of religion were themselves among the most acute investigators of the processes and conflicts by which change comes about in societies. It is not difficult to understand why these two interests should coincide. The nineteenth century unfolds in the wake of the French Revolution; and nothing is more characteristic of that era—and of our own—than the consciousness of change, change in every area of existence. Questions of change served to mobilize the most diverse intellectual energies, and the various social and sociological theories express in both their methods and structures divergent attitudes towards these questions. Some attempt to understand change in an effort to insure its continuance, even its radical acceleration. Others have as their aim the effort of understanding change in order to counter it, or retard it, or to preserve those forms of social existence which were being threatened or eroded. Still others attempt a reconciliation, a balancing, as Comte said, of the forces of progress with the forces of order. The development of the sociology of religion embodies and recapitulates these different and often antagonistic solutions or explanations. In it we can see that what is problematical or at stake is not the truth or value of religion (in sociology, religion, unlike economics or politics, appears not to be an irreducible phenomenon, even though it is a phenomenon of great importance) but the truth and value of society itself.

Three additional general tendencies of thought may be suggested. These tendencies are associated with the traditions of French, English, and German social thought and theory. They may be very roughly differentiated as follows. The French tradition tends to place firmest emphasis on the functioning of the social group or unit as a whole, on its collective aspects; it tends as well to place much value on those processes which safeguard order, a natural corollary. The English tradition, with the notable exception of Spencer, tends to place primary emphasis on the individual person as the fundamental social unit; this tradition, unlike the French or German, tends not to produce large systematic sociological constructions; it tends on the whole to empirical, historical, and evolutionary studies of religion, and toward the empirical investigation by way of anthropology of the religious practices of primitive societies. The German tradition, diverse as it is, may be tentatively described as dialectical, radical, and historical in its major tendencies of thought; if a transcendent value is to be ascribed as attaching to this tradition, it is not the ordered collective of French thought, or the sacred individual of English social theory—it is the idea of humanity itself, humanity liberated or redeemed; sometimes this idea appears in the form of Truth or Reason, which suggests how highly theoretical this tradition of thought can sometimes become.

Something further should be said at this point about the two commanding figures in the modern sociology of religion, Max Weber and Emile Durkheim. It is commonly accepted that between them these two writers establish the sociology of religion as an independent discipline of study. There is no reason to argue with this view, but to it there must be added the awareness that Weber and Durkheim summed up and embodied in their writings the conflicting interpretations of both society and religion that had preoccupied most social theorists for a century. Both wrote in response to the stresses and conflicts produced by a rapidly changing, industrializing, and secularizing world; and both wrote in response as well to the challenges to that world contained in the writings of Marxist and socialist theorists. Although Weber attempted to modify or mitigate certain ultra-materialistic tendencies in Marxist thinking, his own studies of religion retained both the historical approach and something of the dialectic as well. The essential antagonism that he sees between charisma (the irrational forces which are at the foundations of religious experience and movements) and the processes of institutionalization, routinization, and rationalization preserves both the dialectical mode of thought and the critical cutting edge that so often accompanies it. Durkheim's procedures, on the other hand, move toward reducing or minimizing the role of conflict in both social theory and practice; his thinking is essentially ahistorical, and his notion of evolution is more formal than actual. He seeks in his sociology to isolate certain essential and permanent aspects of humanity and to demonstrate how these "universals" operate transhistorically.

Although historical studies in the sociology of religion continue to be made, it must also be said that Durkheim's influence is a chief influence to be found in the sociology of religion as it currently exists. The stress on collective operations, on ahistorical structures, and on structural-functional analyses in the sociology of religion today—as in sociology as a whole—all indicate the prevailing strength of his thinking. As far as the sociology of religion is concerned, this circumstance entails something of an irony. Since the development of the sociology of religion is inseparable from a context of concrete historical, religious, and political conditions and conflicts, there seems to be something oddly circumscribed about a sociology of religion whose major direction of effort is to define itself and regard its subject through ahistorical categories.

We have attempted to give selections which adequately represent the various sides of the classical discussion (in Sections I and II). In the subsequent sections, however (Sections III and IV), we have chosen to emphasize the continuation of a theoretic tradition which directly incorporates the problem of historical movement as the basic problem for sociological analysis. In Section III, we give historical studies covering a range of phenomena, but it will be seen that the first part deals with those revolutionary eruptions which often account for spiritual renewal, and that the second part deals with the institutionalization of change, its assimilation into relatively stable rhythms of religious life. In Section IV, we reproduce a number of studies which employ historical awareness as an instrument for the analysis of contemporary religious phenomena, including of course the problem of secularization. We have chosen this set of selections, and this emphasis, because there already exist valuable anthologies which reflect other viewpoints and intellectual concerns: the school of stuctural-functionalism, contemporary studies with the aid of quantitative techniques, and the anthropological tradition in the sociology of religion are all represented in existing texts. We hope that our own selections, and not least among them the first translations to appear in English from certain classical and contemporary European sociological texts, will serve further to familiarize English-speaking students with the European tradition of social thought and will as well remind them that a theoretic tradition which incorporates the movement of history itself is still very much alive. We also hope that this anthology may be of interest, not alone to sociologists, but to all concerned with the role of religion in human history.

The anthology concludes with an essay on the present situation of the sociology of religion by the *Doyen* of contemporary scholars in the field, Gabriel Le Bras of the Sorbonne. We have also appended a bibliography which indicates the intellectual sources from which we attempted to construct the anthology.

I

THE ORIGINS
OF
RELIGION

Historical, Genetic, and Evolutionary Analyses

David Hume

ORIGIN
OF RELIGION

If we would, therefore, indulge our curiosity, in inquiring concerning the origin of religion, we must turn our thoughts towards Polytheism, the primitive religion of uninstructed mankind.

Were men led into the apprehension of invisible, intelligent power, by a contemplation of the works of nature, they could never possibly entertain any conception but of one single being, who bestowed existence and order on this vast machine, and adjusted all its parts, according to one regular plan or connected system. For though to persons of a certain turn of mind, it may not appear altogether absurd, that several independent beings, endowed with superior wisdom, might conspire in the contrivance and execution of one regular plan,

From The Natural History of Religion, (1757), The Philosophical Works of David Hume. *Edinburgh and London :* 1826, IV, 441–49.

yet is this a merely arbitrary supposition, which, even if allowed possible, must be confessed neither to be supported by probability nor necessity.—All things in the universe are evidently of a piece. Every thing is adjusted to every thing. One design prevails throughout the whole. And this uniformity leads the mind to acknowledge one author; because the conception of different authors, without any distinction of attributes or operations, serves only to give perplexity to the imagination, without bestowing any satisfaction on the understanding. The statue of LAOCOON, as we learn from Pliny, was the work of three artists: But it is certain, that were we not told so, we should never have imagined, that a group of figures cut from one stone, and united in one plan, was not the work and contrivance of one statuary. To ascribe any single effect to the combination of several causes, is not surely a natural and obvious supposition.

On the other hand, if, leaving the works of nature, we trace the footsteps of Invisible Power in the various and contrary events of human life, we are necessarily led into polytheism, and to the acknowledgment of several limited and imperfect deities. Storms and tempests ruin what is nourished by the sun. The sun destroys what is fostered by the moisture of dews and rains. War may be favourable to a nation, whom the inclemency of the seasons afflicts with famine. Sickness and pestilence may depopulate a kingdom, amidst the most profuse plenty. The same nation is not, at the same time, equally successful by sea and by land. And a nation, which now triumphs over its enemies, may anon submit to their more prosperous arms. In short, the conduct of events, or what we call the plan of a particular Providence, is so full of variety and uncertainty, that, if we suppose it immediately ordered by any intelligent beings, we must acknowledge a contrariety in their designs and intentions, a constant combat of opposite powers, and a repentance or change of intention in the same power, from impotence or levity. Each nation had its tutelar deity. Each element is subjected to its invisible power or agent. The province of each god is separate from that of another. Nor are the operations of the same god always certain and invariable. To-day he protects: To-morrow he abandons us. Prayers and sacrifices, rites and ceremonies, well or ill performed, are the sources of his favour or enmity, and produce all the good or ill fortune which are to be found amongst mankind.

We may conclude, therefore, that, in all nations which have embraced polytheism, the first ideas of religion arose, not from a contemplation of the works of nature, but from a concern with regard to the events of life, and from the incessant hopes and fears which actuate the human mind. Accordingly we find, that all idolaters, having separated the provinces of their deities, have recourse to that invisible agent, to whose authority they are immediately subjected, and whose province it is to superintend that course of actions, in which they are, at any time, engaged. Juno is invoked at marriages; Lucina at births. Neptune receives the prayers of seamen; and Mars of warriors. The husbandman cultivates his field under the protection of Ceres; and the merchant acknowledges the authority of Mercury. Each natural event is supposed to be governed by some intelligent agent; and nothing prosperous or adverse can happen in life, which may not be the subject of peculiar prayers or thanksgivings.

It must necessarily, indeed, be allowed, that, in order to carry men's attention beyond the present course of things, or lead them into any inference concerning invisible intelligent power, they must be actuated by some passion which prompts their thought and reflection, some motive which urges their first inquiry. But what passion shall we here have recourse to, for explaining an effect of such mighty consequence? Not speculative curiosity, surely, or the pure love of truth. That motive is too refined for such gross apprehensions, and would lead men into inquiries concerning the frame of nature, a subject too large and comprehensive for their narrow capacities. No passions, therefore, can be supposed to work upon such barbarians, but the ordinary affections of human life; the anxious concern for happiness, the dread of future misery, the terror of death, the thirst of revenge, the appetite for food and other necessaries. Agitated by hopes and fears of this nature, especially the latter, men scrutinize, with a trembling curiosity, the course of future causes, and examine the various and contrary events of human life. And in this disordered scene, with eyes still more disordered and astonished, they see the first obscure traces of divinity.

We are placed in this world, as in a great theatre, where the true springs and causes of every event are entirely concealed from us; nor have we either sufficient wisdom to foresee, or power to prevent, those ills with which we are continually threatened. We hang in perpetual suspense between life and death, health and sickness, plenty and want, which are distributed amongst the human species by secret and unknown causes, whose operation is oft unexpected, and always unaccountable. These *unknown causes,* then, become the constant object of our hope and fear; and while the passions are kept in perpetual alarm by an anxious expectation of the events, the imagination is equally employed in forming ideas of those powers on which we have so entire a dependence. Could men anatomize nature, according to the most probable, at least the most intelligible philosophy, they would find that these causes are nothing but the particular fabric and structure of the minute parts of their own bodies and of external objects; and that, by a regular and constant machinery, all the events are produced, about which they are so much concerned. But this philosophy exceeds the comprehension of the ignorant multitude, who can only conceive the *unknown causes,* in a general and confused manner; though their imagination, perpetually employed on the same subject, must labour to form some particular and distinct idea of them. The more they consider these causes themselves, and the uncertainty of their operation, the less satisfaction do they meet with in their researches; and, however unwilling, they must at last have abandoned so arduous an attempt, were it not for a propensity in human nature, which leads into a system that gives them some satisfaction.

There is an universal tendency among mankind to conceive all beings like themselves, and to transfer to every object those qualities with which they are familiarly acquainted, and of which they are intimately conscious. We find human faces in the moon, armies in the clouds; and, by a natural propensity, if not corrected by experience and reflection, ascribe malice or good will to every thing that hurts or pleases us. Hence the frequency and beauty of the *prosopopœia* in poetry, where trees, mountains, and streams, are personified, and the inanimate parts of nature acquire sentiment and passion. And though these poetical figures and expressions gain not on the belief, they may serve, at least, to prove a certain tendency in the imagination, without which they could neither be beautiful nor natural. Nor is a river-god or hamadryad always taken for a mere poetical or imaginary personage, but may sometimes enter into the real creed of the ignorant vulgar; while each grove or field is represented as possessed of a particular *genius* or invisible power, which inhabits and protects it. Nay, philosophers cannot entirely exempt themselves from this natural frailty; but have oft ascribed to inanimate matter the horror of a *vacuum,* sympathies, antipathies, and other affections of human nature. The absurdity is not less, while we cast our eyes upwards; and, transferring, as is too usual, human passions and infirmities to the Deity, represent him as jealous and revengeful, capricious and partial, and, in short, a wicked and foolish man in every respect but his superior power and authority. No wonder, then, that mankind, being placed in such an absolute ignorance of causes, and being at the same time so anxious concerning their future fortune, should immediately acknowledge a dependence on invisible powers, possessed of sentiment and intelligence. The *unknown causes* which continually employ their thought, appearing always in the same aspect, are all apprehended to be of the same kind or species. Nor is it long before we ascribe to them thought, and reason, and passion, and sometimes even the limbs and figures of men, in order to bring them nearer to a resemblance with ourselves.

In proportion as any man's course of life is governed by accident, we always find that he increases in superstition, as may particularly be observed of gamesters and sailors, who, though of all mankind the least capable of serious reflection, abound most in frivolous and superstitious apprehensions. The gods, says Coriolanus in Dionysius, have an influence in every affair; but above all in war, where the event is so uncertain. All human life, especially before the institution of order and good government, being subject to fortuitous accidents, it is natural that superstition should prevail every where in barbarous ages, and put men on the most earnest inquiry concerning those invisible powers, who dispose of their happiness or misery. Ignorant of astronomy and the anatomy of plants and animals, and too little curious to observe the admirable adjustment of final causes, they remain still unacquainted with a first and a Supreme Creator, and with that infinitely Perfect Spirit, who alone, by his almighty will, bestowed order on the whole frame of nature. Such a magnificent idea is too big for their narrow conceptions, which can neither observe the beauty of the work, nor comprehend the grandeur of its author. They suppose their deities, however potent and invisible, to be nothing but a species of human creatures, perhaps raised from among mankind, and retaining all human passions and appetites, together with corporeal limbs and organs. Such limited beings, though masters of human fate, being each of them incapable of extending his influence every where, must be vastly multiplied, in order to answer that variety of events which happen over the whole face of nature. Thus every place is stored with a crowd of local deities; and thus polytheism has prevailed, and still prevails, among the greatest part of uninstructed mankind.

Any of the human affections may lead us into the notion of invisible, intelligent power; hope as well as fear, gratitude as well as affliction: But if we examine our own hearts, or observe what passes around us, we shall find that men are much oftener thrown on their knees by the melancholy than by the agreeable passions. Prosperity is easily received as our due, and few questions are asked concerning its cause or author. It begets cheerfulness, and activity, and alacrity, and a lively enjoyment of every social and sensual pleasure: And during this state of mind, men have little leisure or inclination to think of the unknown invisible regions. On the other hand, every disastrous accident alarms us, and sets us on inquiries concerning the principles whence it arose: Apprehensions spring up with regard to futurity: And the mind, sunk into diffidence, terror, and melancholy, has recourse to every method of appeasing those secret intelligent powers, on whom our fortune is supposed entirely to depend.

G. W. F. Hegel

MAGIC

The absolutely primary form of religion, to which we give the name of magic, consists in this, that the Spiritual is the ruling power over nature. This spiritual element does not yet exist, however, as Spirit; it is not yet found in its universality, but is merely the particular, contingent, empirical self-consciousness of man, which, although it is only mere passion, knows itself to be higher in its self-consciousness than nature—knows that it is a power ruling over nature.

Two different things are to be remarked here:—

1. In so far as immediate self-consciousness knows that this power lies within it, that it is the seat of this power, it at once marks itself off in that state in which it is such a power from its ordinary condition.

The man who is occupied with ordinary things has, when he goes about his simple business, *particular* objects before him. He then knows that he has to do with these only, as, for example, in fishing or the chase, and he limits his energies to these particular objects alone. But the consciousness of himself as a power over the *universal* power of nature, and over the vicissitudes or changes of nature, is something quite different from the consciousness of that ordinary manner of existence with its occupations and various activities.

Here the individual knows that he

From Lectures on the Philosophy of Religion (1840), London: 1895, I, 290–98.

must transplant himself into a higher state in order to have that power. This state is a gift belonging to particular persons, who have to learn by tradition all those means and ways by which such power can be exercised. A select number of individuals who are sensible of the presence of this sombre subjective quality within themselves, repair for instruction to the older ones.

2. This power is a direct power over nature in general, and is not to be likened to the indirect power, which we exercise by means of implements over natural objects in their separate forms. Such a power as this, which the educated man exercises over individual natural things, presupposes that he has receded from this world, that the world has acquired externality in relation to him,—an externality to which he concedes an independence relatively to himself, peculiar qualitative characteristics and laws; and it presupposes further that these things in their qualitative character are relative in regard to each other, standing in a manifold connection with one another.

This power, which gives the world a free standing in its qualitative character, is exercised by the educated man by means of his knowledge of the qualities of things, that is to say, of things as they are in regard to other things; another element thus makes its influence felt in them, and their weakness at once shows itself. He learns to know them on that weak side, and operates on them by so arming himself that he is able to attack them in their weakness and to compel them to submit to him.

For the accomplishment of this it is necessary that man should be free in himself. Not until he is himself free does he allow the external world, other people, and natural things to exist over against him as free. To the man who is not free, others are not free either.

On the other hand, any direct influence exercised by man, by means of his ideas, of his will, presupposes this mutual unfreedom, since power over external things is indeed attributed to man as representing what is Spiritual, but not as being a power which acts in a free manner, and which just on that account does not bring itself into relation to what is free, and as something which mediates; on the contrary, here the power over nature acts in a direct way. It thus is magic or sorcery.

As regards the external mode in which this idea actually appears, it is found in a form which implies that this magic is what is highest in the self-consciousness of those peoples. But in a subordinate way magic steals up to higher standpoints too, and insinuates itself into higher religions, and thus into the popular conception of witches, although in that form it is recognised as something which is partly impotent, and partly improper and godless.

There has been an inclination on the part of some (as, for example, in the Kantian philosophy) to consider prayer too as magic, because man seeks to make it effectual, not through mediation, but by starting direct from Spirit. The distinction here, however, is that man appeals to an absolute will, for which even the individual or unit is an object of care, and which can either grant the prayer or not, and which in so acting is determined by general purposes of good. Magic, however, in the general sense, simply amounts to this,—that man has

the mastery as he is in his natural state, as possessed of passions and desires.

Such is the general character of this primal and wholly immediate standpoint, namely, that the human consciousness, any definite human being, is recognised as the ruling power over nature in virtue of his own will. The natural has, however, by no means that wide range which it has in our idea of it. For here the greater part of nature still remains indifferent to man, or is just as he is accustomed to see it. Everything is stable. Earthquakes, thunderstorms, floods, animals, which threaten him with death, enemies, and the like, are another matter. To defend himself against these recourse is had to magic.

Such is the oldest mode of religion, the wildest, most barbarous form. It follows from what has been said that God is necessarily of a spiritual nature. This is His fundamental determination. Spiritual existence, in so far as it is an object for self-consciousness, is already a further advance, a differentiation of spirituality as that which is universal and as definite individual empirical self-consciousness; it is already a breaking off of the universal self-consciousness from the empirical spirituality of self-consciousness. At the beginning this does not yet exist.

The religion of nature as that of magic, begins from unfree freedom, so that the single or individual self-consciousness knows itself as something which is higher than natural things, and this knowledge is, to begin with, unmediated.

By recent travellers, such as Captain Parry, and before him Captain Ross, this religion has been found among the Esquimaux, wholly without the element of mediation and as the crudest consciousness. Among other peoples a mediation is already present.

Captain Parry says of them: "They are quite unaware that there is any other world; they live among rocks, ice and snow, upon rye, birds and fish, and do not know that nature exists in any other form. The English had an Esquimaux with them, who had lived some time in England, and he served as interpreter. Through him they obtained some knowledge regarding the people, and learned that they have not the slightest idea of Spirit, of a higher existence, of an essential substance as contrasted with their empirical mode of existence, of the immortality of the soul, of the everlasting duration of spirit, of the evil independent existence of the individual spirit. They know of no evil spirit, and they have, it is true, a great veneration for the sun and moon, but they do not adore them; they worship no image, no living creature. On the other hand, they have amongst them individuals whom they call Angekoks, magicians, conjurers. Those assert that they have it in their power to raise a storm, to create a calm, to bring whales near, &c., and say that they learnt these arts from old Angekoks. The people regard them with fear; in every family, however, there is at least one. A young Angekok wished to make the wind rise, and he proceeded to do it by dint of phrases and gestures. These phrases had no meaning and were directed toward no Supreme Being as a medium, but were addressed in an immediate way to the natural object over which the Angekok wished to exercise power; he required no aid from any one whatever. He was told of an omnipresent, all good, invisible Being who had made everything, and he asked where it lived, and when he was told it was everywhere, he at once became afraid, and wished to run away. On being asked where his people would go when they died, he replied that they would be buried; a long time ago an old man had once said that they would go to the moon, but it was long since any Esquimaux had believed that."

Thus they occupy the lowest stage of spiritual consciousness, but they possess the belief that self-consciousness is a mighty power over nature, without mediation, apart from any antithesis between that self-consciousness and a divine Being.

The English persuaded an Angekok to practise magic; this was done by means of dancing, so that he became frantic with the prodigious amount of exertion; he fell into a state of exhaustion, and gave forth phrases and sounds, his eyes rolling about all the while.

This religion of magic is very prevalent in Africa, as also among the Mongols and Chinese; here, however, it is no longer found in the absolute crudeness of its first form, but mediations already come in, which owe their origin to the fact that the Spiritual has begun to assume an objective form for self-consciousness.

In its first form this religion is more magic than religion; it is in Africa among the negroes that it prevails most extensively. It was already mentioned by Herodotus, and in recent times it has been found existing in a similar form. Yet the cases are but few in which such peoples appeal to their power over nature, for they use very little, and have few requirements, and, in judging of their conditions, we must forget the manifold needs which surround us, and the variously complicated modes we have of accomplishing our ends. Our information regarding the state of these peoples is for the most part derived from the missionaries of past times; the more recent accounts are, on the other hand, but scanty, and therefore some of the narratives of older date have to be received with suspicion, especially as missionaries are natural enemies of magic. The general facts, however, are undoubted, being established by a great variety of accounts.

The charge of avarice on the part of the priests must be abandoned here, as in the case of other religions. Offerings, gifts to the gods, become for the most part the share of the priests, but still you can only speak of avarice, and a people are only to be pitied on account of it, when they lay a great stress upon the possession of property. But to these peoples possessions are of no consequence; they know of no better use to which to put what they have than to give it away in this manner.

The character of this magic is more accurately shown by the mode and manner of its exercise. The magician retires to a hill, describes circles or figures in the sand, and utters magical words, makes signs toward the sky, blows toward the wind, sucks in his breath. A missionary who found himself at the head of a Portuguese army relates that the negroes who were their allies had brought a magician of this kind with them. A hurricane rendered his conjuring arts needful, and, in spite of the strong opposition of the missionary, they were resorted to. The magician appeared in a peculiar fantastical dress, looked up at the sky and the clouds, and afterwards chewed roots and murmured phrases. As the clouds drew nearer, he broke out into howls, made signs to the clouds, and spat towards the sky. The storm continuing notwithstanding, he waxed furious, shot arrows at the sky, threatened it with bad treatment, and thrust at the clouds with his knife.

The Schamans among the Mongols are very similar to these magicians. Wearing a fantastic dress, from which depend figures of metal and wood, they stupefy themselves with drink, and when in this state declare what is to happen and prophesy about the future.

In this sphere of magic the main principle is the direct domination of nature by means of the will, of self-consciousness —in other words, that Spirit is something of a higher kind than nature. However bad this magic may look

regarded in one aspect, still in another it is higher than a condition of dependence upon nature and fear of it.

It is to be observed here that there are negro peoples who have the belief that no man dies a natural death; that nature has not power over him, but that it is he who has power over nature. These are the Galla and Gaga tribes, which, as the most savage and most barbarous of conquerors, have repeatedly descended upon the coasts since the year 1542, pouring forth from the interior and inundating the whole country. These look upon man in the strength of his consciousness as too exalted to be capable of being killed by anything so obscure as the power of nature. What therefore takes place is, that sick people, in whose case magic has proved ineffectual, are put to death by their friends. In the same way the wild tribes of North America too killed their aged who had reached decrepitude, the meaning of which is unmistakable, namely, that man is not to perish by means of nature, but is to have due honour rendered to him at human hands. There is another people again who have the belief that everything would go to ruin if their highpriest were to die a natural death. He is therefore executed as soon as ever he becomes ill and weak; if a high-priest should notwithstanding die of some disease, they believe that some other person killed him by means of magic, and the magicians have to ascertain who the murderer was, when he is at once made away with. On the death of a king in particular, many persons are killed: according to a missionary of older days, it is the devil of the king who is slain.

Such, then, is the very first form of religion, which cannot indeed as yet be properly called religion. To religion essentially pertains the moment of objectivity, and this means that spiritual power shows itself as a mode of the Universal relatively to self-consciousness, for the individual, for the particular empirical consciousness. This objectivity is an essential characteristic, on which all depends. Not until it is present does religion begin, does a God exist, and even in the lowest condition there is at least a beginning of it. The mountain, the river, is not in its character as this particular mass of earth, as this particular water, the Divine, but as a mode of the existence of the Divine, of an essential, universal Being. But we do not yet find this in magic as such. It is the individual consciousness as this particular consciousness, and conse-quently the very negation of the Universal, which is what has the power here; not a god in the magician, but the magician himself is the conjurer and conqueror of nature. This is the religion of passion, which is still infinite for it-self, and therefore of sensuous particu-larity which is certain of itself. But in the religion of magic there is already also a distinguishing of the individual empirical consciousness of the person dealing in magic from that person in his character as representing the Univer-sal. It is owing to this that out of magic the religion of magic is developed.

Auguste Comte

THE PROGRESSIVE COURSE OF THE HUMAN MIND

A general statement of any system of philosophy may be either a sketch of a doctrine to be established, or a summary of a doctrine already established. If greater value belongs to the last, the first is still important, as characterizing from its origin the subject to be treated. In a case like the present, where the proposed study is vast and hitherto indeterminate, it is especially important that the field of research should be marked out with all possible accuracy. For this purpose, I will glance at the considerations which have originated this work, and which will be fully elaborated in the course of it.

In order to understand the true value

From The Positive Philosophy of Auguste Comte *(1830–1842),* London : 1896, I, 1–8.

and character of the Positive Philosophy, we must take a brief general view of the progressive course of the human mind, regarded as a whole; for no conception can be understood otherwise than through its history.

From the study of the development of human intelligence, in all directions, and through all times, the discovery arises of a great fundamental law, to which it is necessarily subject, and which has a solid foundation of proof, both in the facts of our organization and in our historical experience. The law is this:— that each of our leading conceptions,— each branch of our knowledge,—passes successively through three different theoretical conditions: the Theological, or fictitious; the Metaphysical, or abstract;

and the Scientific, or positive. In other words, the human mind, by its nature, employs in its progress three methods of philosophizing, the character of which is essentially different, and even radically opposed: viz., the theological method, the metaphysical, and the positive. Hence arise three philosophies, or general systems of conceptions on the aggregate of phenomena, each of which excludes the others. The first is the necessary point of departure of the human understanding; and the third is its fixed and definitive state. The second is merely a state of transition.

First stage: In the theological state, the human mind, seeking the essential nature of beings, the first and final causes (the origin and purpose) of all effects,—in short, Absolute knowledge,—supposes all phenomena to be produced by the immediate action of supernatural beings. Second Stage: In the metaphysical state, which is only a modification of the first, the mind supposes, instead of supernatural beings, abstract forces, veritable entities (that is, personified abstractions) inherent in all beings, and capable of producing all phenomena. What is called the explanation of phenomena is, in this stage, a mere reference of each to its proper entity.

Third stage: In the final, the positive state, the mind has given over the vain search after Absolute notions, the origin and destination of the universe, and the causes of phenomena, and applies itself to the study of their laws,—that is, their invariable relations of succession and resemblance. Reasoning and observation, duly combined, are the means of this knowledge. What is now understood when we speak of an explanation of facts is simply the establishment of a connection between single phenomena and some general facts, the number of which continually diminishes with the progress of science.

Ultimate point of each: The Theological system arrived at the highest perfection of which it is capable when it substituted the providential action of a single Being for the varied operations of the numerous divinities which had been before imagined. In the same way, in the last stage of the Metaphysical system, men substitute one great entity (Nature) as the cause of all phenomena, instead of the multitude of entities at first supposed. In the same way, again, the ultimate perfection of the Positive system would be (if such perfection could be hoped for) to represent all phenomena as particular aspects of a single general fact;—such as Gravitation, for instance.

The importance of the working of this general law will be established hereafter. At present, it must suffice to point out some of the grounds of it.

There is no science which, having attained the positive stage, does not bear marks of having passed through the others. Some time since it was (whatever it might be) composed, as we can now perceive, of metaphysical abstractions; and, further back in the course of time, it took its form from theological conceptions. We shall have only too much occasion to see, as we proceed, that our most advanced sciences still bear very evident marks of the two earlier periods through which they have passed.

The progress of the individual mind is not only an illustration, but an indirect evidence of that of the general mind. The point of departure of the individual and of the race being the same, the phases of the mind of a man correspond to the epochs of the mind of the race. Now, each of us is aware, if he looks back upon his own history, that he was a theologian in his childhood, a metaphysician in his youth, and a natural philosopher in his manhood. All men who are up to their age can verify this for themselves.

Besides the observation of facts, we have theoretical reasons in support of this law.

The most important of these reasons arises from the necessity that always exists for some theory to which to refer our facts, combined with the clear impossibility that, at the outset of human knowledge, men could have formed theories out of the observation of facts. All good intellects have repeated, since Bacon's time, that there can be no real knowledge but that which is based on observed facts. This is incontestible, in our present advanced stage; but, if we look back to the primitive stage of human knowledge, we shall see that it must have been otherwise then. If it is true that every theory must be based upon observed facts, it is equally true that facts cannot be observed without the guidance of some theory. Without such guidance, our facts would be desultory and fruitless; we could not retain them: for the most part we could not even perceive them.

Thus, between the necessity of observing facts in order to form a theory, and having a theory in order to observe facts, the human mind would have been entangled in a vicious circle, but for the natural opening afforded by Theological conceptions. This is the fundamental reason for the theological character of the primitive philosophy. This necessity is confirmed by the perfect suitability of the theological philosophy to the earliest researches of the human mind. It is remarkable that the most inaccessible questions,—those of the nature of beings, and the origin and purpose of phenomena, —should be the first to occur in a primitive state, while those which are really within our reach are regarded as almost unworthy of serious study. The reason is evident enough:—that experience alone can teach us the measure of our powers; and if men had not begun by an exaggerated estimate of what they can do, they would never have done all that they are capable of. Our organization requires this. At such a period there could have been no reception of a positive philosophy, whose function is to discover the laws of phenomena, and whose leading characteristic it is to regard as interdicted to human reason those sublime mysteries which theology explains, even to their minutest details, with the most attractive facility. It is just so under a practical view of the nature of the researches with which men first occupied themselves. Such inquiries offered the powerful charm of unlimited empire over the external world,—a world destined wholly for our use, and involved in every way with our existence. The theological philosophy, presenting this view, administered exactly the stimulus necessary to incite the human mind to the irksome labour without which it could make no progress. We can now scarcely conceive of such a state of things, our reason having become sufficiently mature to enter upon laborious scientific researches, without needing any such stimulus as wrought upon the imaginations of astrologers and alchemists. We have motive enough in the hope of discovering the laws of phenomena, with a view to the confirmation or rejection of a theory. But it could not be so in the earliest days; and it is to the chimeras of astrology and alchemy that we owe the long series of observations and experiments on which our positive science is based. Kepler felt this on behalf of astronomy, and Berthollet on behalf of chemistry. Thus was a spontaneous philosophy, the theological, the only possible beginning, method, and provisional system, out of which the Positive philosophy could grow. It is easy, after this, to perceive how Metaphysical methods and doctrines must have afforded the means of transition from the one to the other.

The human understanding, slow in its advance, could not step at once from the theological into the positive philosophy. The two are so radically opposed, that an intermediate system of conceptions has been necessary to render the transition possible. It is only in doing this, that Metaphysical conceptions have any utility whatever. In contemplating phenomena, men substitute for supernatural direction a corresponding entity. This entity may have been supposed to be derived from the supernatural action: but it is more easily lost sight of, leaving attention free for the facts themselves, till, at length, metaphysical agents have ceased to be anything more than the abstract names of phenomena. It is not easy to say by what other process than this our minds could have passed from supernatural considerations to natural; from the theological system to the positive.

The Law of human development being thus established, let us consider what is the proper nature of the Positive Philosophy. . . .

Our real business is to analyse accurately the circumstances of phenomena, and to connect them by the natural relations of succession and resemblance. The best illustration of this is in the case of the doctrine of Gravitation. We say that the general phenomena of the universe are *explained* by it, because it connects under one head the whole immense variety of astronomical facts; exhibiting the constant tendency of atoms towards each other in direct proportion to their masses, and in inverse proportion to the squares of their distances; whilst the general fact itself is a mere extension of one which is perfectly familiar to us, and which we therefore say that we know;—the weight of bodies on the surface of the earth. As to what weight and attraction are, we have nothing to do with that, for it is not a matter of knowledge at all. Theologians

and metaphysicians may imagine and refine about such questions; but positive philosophy rejects them. When any attempt has been made to explain them, it has ended only in saying that attraction is universal weight, and that weight is terrestrial attraction: that is, that the two orders of phenomena are identical; which is the point from which the question set out. Again, M. Fourier, in his fine series of researches on Heat, has given us all the most important and precise laws of the phenomena of heat, and many large and new truths, without once inquiring into its nature, as his predecessors had done when they disputed about calorific matter and the action of an universal ether. In treating his subject in the Positive method, he finds inexhaustible material for all his activity of research, without betaking himself to insoluble questions. Before ascertaining the stage which the Positive Philosophy has reached, we must bear in mind that the different kinds of our knowledge have passed through the three stages of progress at different rates, and have not therefore arrived at the same time. The rate of advance depends on the nature of the knowledge in question, so distinctly that, as we shall see hereafter, this consideration constitutes an accessory to the fundamental law of progress. Any kind of knowledge reaches the positive stage early in proportion to its generality, simplicity, and independence of other departments. Astronomical science, which is above all made up of facts that are general, simple, and independent of other sciences, arrived first; then terrestrial Physics; then Chemistry; and, at length, Physiology.

It is difficult to assign any precise date to this revolution in science. It may be said, like everything else, to have been always going on; and especially since the labours of Aristotle and the school of Alexandria; and then from the introduction of natural science into the West of Europe by the Arabs. But if we must fix upon some marked period, to serve as a rallying point, it must be that,—about two centuries ago,—when the human mind was astir under the precepts of Bacon, the conceptions of Descartes, and the discoveries of Galileo. Then it was that the spirit of the Positive philosophy rose up in opposition to that of the superstitious and scholastic systems which had hitherto obscured the true character of all science. Since that date, the progress of the Positive philosophy, and the decline of the other two, have been so marked that no rational mind now doubts that the revolution is destined to go on to its completion,—every branch of knowledge being, sooner or later, brought within the operation of Positive philosophy. This is not yet the case. Some are still lying outside: and not till they are brought in will the Positive philosophy possess that character of universality which is necessary to its definitive constitution.

In mentioning just now the four principal categories of phenomena,—astronomical, physical, chemical, and physiological,—there was an omission which will have been noticed. Nothing was said of Social phenomena. Though involved with the physiological, Social phenomena demand a distinct classification, both on account of their importance and of their difficulty. They are the most individual, the most complicated, the most dependent on all others; and therefore they must be the latest,—even if they had no special obstacle to encounter. This branch of science has not hitherto entered into the domain of Positive philosophy. Theological and metaphysical methods, exploded in other departments, are as yet exclusively applied, both in the way of inquiry and discussion, in all treatment of Social subjects, though the best minds are heartily weary of eternal disputes about divine right and the sovereignty of the people. This is the great, while it is evidently the only gap which has to be filled, to constitute, solid and entire, the Positive Philosophy. Now that the human mind has grasped celestial and terrestrial physics,—mechanical and chemical; organic physics, both vegetable and animal,—there remains one science, to fill up the series of sciences of observation,—Social physics. This is what men have now most need of: and this it is the principal aim of the present work to establish.

James George Frazer

MAGIC
AND RELIGION

From Chapter IV, "Magic and Religion" in abridged form, The Golden Bough. A Study in Magic and Religion, Abr. ed. London: Macmillan & Co., 1941, pp. 48–53; 54–55; 56–60. By permission of St. Martin's Press, Inc., Macmillan & Co., Ltd.; A. P. Watt & Son and Trinity College, Cambridge.

. . . In some cases of magic which have come before us we have seen that the operation of spirits is assumed, and that an attempt is made to win their favour by prayer and sacrifice. But these cases are on the whole exceptional; they exhibit magic tinged and alloyed with religion. Wherever sympathetic magic occurs in its pure unadulterated form, it assumes that in nature one event follows another necessarily and invariably without the intervention of any spiritual or personal agency. Thus its fundamental conception is identical with that of modern science; underlying the whole system is a faith, implicit but real and firm, in the order and uniformity of nature. The magician does not doubt that the same causes will always produce the same effects, that the performance of the proper ceremony, accompanied by the appropriate spell, will inevitably be attended by the desired result, unless, indeed, his incantations should chance to be thwarted and foiled by the more potent charms of another sorcerer. He supplicates no higher power: he sues the favour of no fickle and wayward being: he abases himself before no awful deity. Yet his power, great as he believes it to be, is by no means arbitrary and unlimited. He can wield it only so long as he strictly conforms to the rules of his art, or to what may be called the laws of nature as conceived by him. To neglect these rules, to break these laws in the smallest particular is to incur failure, and may even expose the unskilful practitioner himself to the utmost peril. If he claims a sovereignty over nature, it is a constitutional sovereignty rigorously limited in its scope and exercised in exact conformity with ancient usage. Thus the analogy between the magical and the scientific conceptions of the world is close. In both of them the succession of events is assumed to be perfectly regular and certain, being determined by immutable laws, the operation of which can be foreseen and calculated precisely; the elements of caprice, of chance, and of accident are banished from the course of nature. Both of them open up a seemingly boundless vista of possibilities to him who knows the causes of things and can touch the secret springs that set in motion the vast and intricate mechanism of the world. Hence the strong attrac-

tion which magic and science alike have exercised on the human mind; hence the powerful stimulus that both have given to the pursuit of knowledge. They lure the weary enquirer, the footsore seeker, on through the wilderness of disappointment in the present by their endless promises of the future: they take him up to the top of an exceeding high mountain and show him, beyond the dark clouds and rolling mists at his feet, a vision of the celestial city, far off, it may be, but radiant with unearthly splendour, bathed in the light of dreams.

The fatal flaw of magic lies not in its general assumption of a sequence of events determined by law, but in its total misconception of the nature of the particular laws which govern that sequence. If we analyse the various cases of sympathetic magic which have been passed in review in the preceding pages, and which may be taken as fair samples of the bulk, we shall find, as I have already indicated, that they are all mistaken applications of one or other of two great fundamental laws of thought, namely, the association of ideas by similarity and the association of ideas by contiguity in space or time. A mistaken association of similar ideas produces homoeopathic or imitative magic: a mistaken association of contiguous ideas produces contagious magic. The principles of association are excellent in themselves, and indeed absolutely essential to the working of the human mind. Legitimately applied they yield science; illegitimately applied they yield magic, the bastard sister of science. It is therefore a truism, almost a tautology, to say that all magic is necessarily false and barren; for were it ever to become true and fruitful, it would no longer be magic but science. From the earliest times man has been engaged in a search for general rules whereby to turn the order of natural phenomena to his own advantage, and in the long search he has scraped together a great hoard of such maxims, some of them golden and some of them mere dross. The true or golden rules constitute the body of applied science which we call the arts; the false are magic.

If magic is thus next of kin to science, we have still to enquire how it stands related to religion. But the view we take of that relation will necessarily be coloured by the idea which we have formed of the nature of religion itself; hence a writer may reasonably be expected to define his conception of religion before he proceeds to investigate its relation to magic. There is probably no subject in the world about which opinions differ so much as the nature of religion, and to frame a definition of it which would satisfy every one must obviously be impossible. All that a writer can do is, first, to say clearly what he means by religion, and afterwards to employ the word consistently in that sense throughout his work. By religion, then, I understand a propitiation or conciliation of powers superior to man which are believed to direct and control the course of nature and of human life. Thus defined, religion consists of two elements, a theoretical and a practical, namely, a belief in powers higher than man and an attempt to propitiate or please them. Of the two, belief clearly comes first, since we must believe in the existence of a divine being before we can attempt to please him. But unless the belief leads to a corresponding practice, it is not a religion but merely a theology; in the language of St. James, "faith, if it hath not works, is dead, being alone." In other words, no man is religious who does not govern his conduct in some measure by the fear or love of God. On the other hand, mere practice, divested of all religious belief, is also not religion. Two men may behave in exactly the same way, and yet one of them may be religious and the

other not. If the one acts from the love or fear of God, he is religious; if the other acts from the love or fear of man, he is moral or immoral according as his behaviour comports or conflicts with the general good. Hence belief and practice or, in theological language, faith and works are equally essential to religion, which cannot exist without both of them. But it is not necessary that religious practice should always take the form of a ritual; that is, it need not consist in the offering of sacrifice, the recitation of prayers, and other outward ceremonies. Its aim is to please the deity, and if the deity is one who delights in charity and mercy and purity more than in oblations of blood, the chanting of hymns, and the fumes of incense, his worshippers will best please him, not by prostrating themselves before him, by intoning his praises, and by filling his temples with costly gifts, but by being pure and merciful and charitable towards men, for in so doing they will imitate so far as human infirmity allows, the perfections of the divine nature. It was this ethical side of religion which the Hebrew prophets, inspired with a noble ideal of God's goodness and holiness, were never weary of inculcating. Thus Micah says: "He hath shewed thee, O man, what is good; and what doth the Lord require of thee, but to do justly, and to love mercy, and to walk humbly with thy God?" And at a later time much of the force by which Christianity conquered the world was drawn from the same high conception of God's moral nature and the duty laid on men of conforming themselves to it. "Pure religion and undefiled," says St. James, "before God and the Father is this, To visit the fatherless and widows in their affliction, and to keep himself unspotted from the world."

But if religion involves, first, a belief in superhuman beings who rule the world, and, second, an attempt to win their favour, it clearly assumes that the course of nature is to some extent elastic or variable, and that we can persuade or induce the mighty beings who control it to deflect, for our benefit, the current of events from the channel in which they would otherwise flow. Now this implied elasticity or variability of nature is directly opposed to the principles of magic as well as of science, both of which assume that the processes of nature are rigid and invariable in their operation, and that they can as little be turned from their course by persuasion and entreaty as by threats and intimidation. The distinction between the two conflicting views of the universe turns on their answer to the crucial question, are the forces which govern the world conscious and personal, or unconscious and impersonal? Religion, as a conciliation of the superhuman powers, assumes the former member of the alternative. For all conciliation implies that the being conciliated is a conscious or personal agent, that his conduct is in some measure uncertain, and that he can be prevailed upon to vary it in the desired direction by a judicious appeal to his interests, his appetites, or his emotions. Conciliation is never employed towards things which are regarded as inanimate, nor towards persons whose behaviour in the particular circumstances is known to be determined with absolute certainty. Thus in so far as religion assumes the world to be directed by conscious agents who may be turned from their purpose by persuasion, it stands in fundamental antagonism to magic as well as to science, both of which take for granted that the course of nature is determined, not by the passions or caprice of personal beings, but by the operation of immutable laws acting mechanically. In magic, indeed, the assumption is only implicit, but in science it is explicit. It is true that magic often deals with spirits, which are personal agents of the kind assumed by religion;

but whenever it does so in its proper form, it treats them exactly in the same fashion as it treats inanimate agents, that is, it constrains or coerces instead of conciliating or propitiating them as religion would do. Thus it assumes that all personal beings, whether human or divine, are in the last resort subject to those impersonal forces which control all things, but which nevertheless can be turned to account by any one who knows how to manipulate them by the appropriate ceremonies and spells. In ancient Egypt, for example, the magicians claimed the power of compelling even the highest gods to do their bidding, and actually threatened them with destruction in case of disobedience. Sometimes, without going quite so far as that, the wizard declared that he would scatter the bones of Osiris or reveal his sacred legend, if the god proved contumacious. Similarly in India at the present day the great Hindoo trinity itself of Brahma, Vishnu, and Siva is subject to the sorcerers, who, by means of their spells, exercise such an ascendancy over the mightiest deities, that these are bound submissively to execute on earth below, or in heaven above, whatever commands their masters the magicians may please to issue. There is a saying everywhere current in India: "The whole universe is subject to the gods; the gods are subject to the spells (*mantras*); the spells to the Brahmans; therefore the Brahmans are our gods."

This radical conflict of principle between magic and religion sufficiently explains the relentless hostility with which in history the priest has often pursued the magician. The haughty self-sufficiency of the magician, his arrogant demeanour towards the higher powers, and his unabashed claim to exercise a sway like theirs could not but revolt the priest, to whom, with his awful sense of the divine majesty, and his humble prostration in presence of it, such claims and such a demeanour must have appeared an impious and blasphemous usurpation of prerogatives that belong to God alone. And sometimes, we may suspect, lower motives concurred to whet the edge of the priest's hostility. He professed to be the proper medium, the true intercessor between God and man, and no doubt his interests as well as his feelings were often injured by a rival practitioner, who preached a surer and smoother road to fortune than the rugged and slippery path of divine favour.

Yet this antagonism, familiar as it is to us, seems to have made its appearance comparatively late in the history of religion. At an earlier stage the functions of priest and sorcerer were often combined or, to speak perhaps more correctly, were not yet differentiated from each other. To serve his purpose man wooed the good-will of gods or spirits by prayer and sacrifice, while at the same time he had recourse to ceremonies and forms of words which he hoped would of themselves bring about the desired result without the help of god or devil. In short, he performed religious and magical rites simultaneously; he uttered prayers and incantations almost in the same breath, knowing or recking little of the theoretical inconsistency of his behaviour, so long as by hook or crook he contrived to get what he wanted. Instances of this fusion or confusion of magic with religion have already met us in the practices of Melanesians and of other peoples.

The same confusion of magic and religion has survived among peoples that have risen to higher levels of culture. It was rife in ancient India and ancient Egypt; it is by no means extinct among European peasantry at the present day. With regard to ancient India we are told by an eminent Sanscrit scholar that "the sacrificial ritual at the earliest period of which we have detailed information is pervaded with practices that breathe the spirit of the most primitive magic." Speaking of the importance of magic in the East, and especially in Egypt, Professor Maspero remarks that "we ought not to attach to the word magic the degrading idea which it almost inevitably calls up in the mind of a modern. Ancient magic was the very foundation of religion. The faithful who desired to obtain some favour from a god had no chance of succeeding except by laying hands on the deity, and this arrest could only be effected by means of a certain number of rites, sacrifices, prayers, and chants, which the god himself had revealed, and which obliged him to do what was demanded of him.". . .

Yet though magic is thus found to fuse and amalgamate with religion in many ages and in many lands, there are some grounds for thinking that this fusion is not primitive, and that there was a time when man trusted to magic alone for the satisfaction of such wants as transcended his immediate animal cravings. In the first place a consideration of the fundamental notions of magic and religion may incline us to surmise that magic is older than religion in the history of humanity. We have seen that on the one hand magic is nothing but a mistaken application of the very simplest and most elementary processes of the mind, namely the association of ideas by virtue of resemblance or contiguity; and that on the other hand religion assumes the operation of conscious or personal agents, superior to man, behind the visible screen of nature. Obviously the conception of personal agents is more complex than a simple recognition of the similarity or contiguity of ideas; and a theory which assumes that the course of nature is determined by conscious agents is more abstruse and recondite, and requires for its apprehension a far higher degree of intelligence and reflection, than the view that things succeed each other simply by reason of their contiguity or resemblance. The very beasts associate the ideas of things that are like each other or that have been found together in their experience; and they could hardly survive for a day if they ceased to do so. But who attributes to the animals a belief that the phenomena of nature are worked by a multitude of invisible animals or by one enormous and prodigiously strong animal behind the scenes? It is probably no injustice to the brutes to assume that the honour of devising a theory of this latter sort must be reserved for human reason. Thus, if magic be deduced immediately from elementary processes of reasoning, and be, in fact, an error into which the mind falls almost spontaneously, while religion rests on conceptions which the merely animal intelligence can hardly be supposed to have yet attained to, it becomes probable that magic arose before religion in the evolution of our race, and that man essayed to bend nature to his wishes by the sheer force of spells and enchantments before he strove to coax and mollify a coy, capricious, or irascible deity by the soft insinuation of prayer and sacrifice.

The conclusion which we have thus reached deductively from a consideration of the fundamental ideas of magic and religion is confirmed inductively by the observation that among the aborigines of Australia, the rudest savages as to whom we possess accurate information, magic is universally practised, whereas religion in the sense of a propitiation or conciliation of the higher powers seems to be nearly unknown. Roughly speaking, all men in Australia are magicians, but not one is a priest; everybody fancies he can influence his fellows or the course of nature by sympathetic magic, but nobody dreams of propitiating gods by prayer and sacrifice. . . .

If an Age of Religion has thus everywhere, as I venture to surmise, been preceded by an Age of Magic, it is natural that we should enquire what causes have led mankind, or rather a portion of them, to abandon magic as a principle of faith and practice and to betake themselves to religion instead. When we reflect upon the multitude, the variety, and the complexity of the facts to be explained, and the scantiness of our information regarding them, we shall be ready to acknowledge that a full and satisfactory solution of so profound a problem is hardly to be hoped for, and that the most we can do in the present state of our knowledge is to hazard a more or less plausible conjecture. With all due diffidence, then, I would suggest that a tardy recognition of the inherent falsehood and barrenness of magic set the more thoughtful part of mankind to cast about for a truer theory of nature and a more fruitful method of turning her resources to account. The shrewder intelligences must in time have come to perceive that magical ceremonies and incantations did not really effect the results which they were designed to produce, and which the majority of their simpler fellows still believed that they did actually produce. This great discovery of the inefficacy of magic must have wrought a radical though probably slow revolution in the minds of those who had the sagacity to make it. The discovery amounted to this, that men for the first time recognised their inability to manipulate at pleasure certain natural forces which hitherto they had believed to be completely within their control. It was a confession of human ignorance and weakness. Man saw that he had taken for causes what were no causes, and that all his efforts to work by means of these imaginary causes had been vain. His painful toil had been wasted, his curious ingenuity had been squandered to no purpose. He had been pulling at strings to which nothing was attached; he had been marching, as he thought, straight to the goal, while in reality he had only been treading in a narrow circle. Not that the effects which he had striven so hard to produce did not continue to manifest themselves. They were still produced, but not by him. The rain still fell on the thirsty ground: the sun still pursued his daily, and the moon her nightly journey across the sky: the silent procession of the seasons still moved in light and shadow, in cloud and sunshine across the earth: men were still born to labour and sorrow, and still, after a brief sojourn here, were gathered to their fathers in the long home hereafter. All things indeed went on as before, yet all seemed different to him from whose eyes the old scales had fallen. For he could no longer cherish the pleasing illusion that it was he who guided the earth and the heaven in their courses, and that they would cease to perform their great revolutions were he to take his feeble hand from the wheel. In the death of his enemies and his friends he no longer saw a proof of the resistless potency of his own or of hostile enchantments; he now knew that friends and foes alike had succumbed to a force stronger than any that he could wield, and in obedience to a destiny which he was powerless to control.

Thus cut adrift from his ancient moorings and left to toss on a troubled sea of doubt and uncertainty, his old happy confidence in himself and his powers rudely shaken, our primitive philosopher must have been sadly perplexed and agitated till he came to rest, as in a quiet haven after a tempestuous voyage, in a new system of faith and practice, which seemed to offer a solution of his harassing doubts and a substitute, however precarious, for that sovereignty over nature which he had reluctantly abdicated. If the great world went on its way without the help of him or his fellows, it must surely be because there were other beings, like himself, but far

stronger, who, unseen themselves, directed its course and brought about all the varied series of events which he had hitherto believed to be dependent on his own magic. It was they, as he now believed, and not he himself, who made the stormy wind to blow, the lightning to flash, and the thunder to roll; who had laid the foundations of the solid earth and set bounds to the restless sea that it might not pass; who caused all the glorious lights of heaven to shine; who gave the fowls of the air their meat and the wild beasts of the desert their prey; who bade the fruitful land to bring forth in abundance, the high hills to be clothed with forests, the bubbling springs to rise under the rocks in the valleys, and green pastures to grow by still waters; who breathed into man's nostrils and made him live, or turned him to destruction by famine and pestilence and war. To these mighty beings, whose handiwork he traced in all the gorgeous and varied pageantry of nature, man now addressed himself, humbly confessing his dependence on their invisible power, and beseeching them of their mercy to furnish him with all good things, to defend him from the perils and dangers by which our mortal life is compassed about on every hand, and finally to bring his immortal spirit, freed from the burden of the body, to some happier world, beyond the reach of pain and sorrow, where he might rest with them and with the spirits of good men in joy and felicity for ever.

In this, or some such way as this, the deeper minds may be conceived to have made the great transition from magic to religion. But even in them the change can hardly ever have been sudden; probably it proceeded very slowly, and required long ages for its more or less perfect accomplishment. For the recognition of man's powerlessness to influence the course of nature on a grand scale must have been gradual; he cannot have been shorn of the whole of his fancied dominion at a blow. Step by step he must have been driven back from his proud position; foot by foot he must have yielded, with a sigh, the ground which he had once viewed as his own. Now it would be the wind, now the rain, now the sunshine, now the thunder, that he confessed himself unable to wield at will; and as province after province of nature thus fell from his grasp, till what had once seemed a kingdom threatened to shrink into a prison, man must have been more and more profoundly impressed with a sense of his own helplessness and the might of the invisible beings by whom he believed himself to be surrounded. Thus religion, beginning as a slight and partial acknowledgment of powers superior to man, tends with the growth of knowledge to deepen into a confession of man's entire and absolute dependence on the divine; his old free bearing is exchanged for an attitude of lowliest prostration before the mysterious powers of the unseen, and his highest virtue is to submit his will to theirs: *In la sua volontade è nostra pace*. But this deepening sense of religion, this more perfect submission to the divine will in all things, affects only those higher intelligences who have breadth of view enough to comprehend the vastness of the universe and the littleness of man. Small minds cannot grasp great ideas; to their narrow comprehension, their purblind vision, nothing seems really great and important but themselves. Such minds hardly rise into religion at all. They are, indeed, drilled by their betters into an outward conformity with its precepts and a verbal profession of its tenets; but at heart they cling to their old magical superstitions, which may be discountenanced and forbidden, but cannot be eradicated by religion, so long as they have their roots deep down in the mental framework and

constitution of the great majority of mankind.

The reader may well be tempted to ask, How was it that intelligent men did not sooner detect the fallacy of magic? How could they continue to cherish expectations that were invariably doomed to disappointment? With what heart persist in playing venerable antics that led to nothing, and mumbling solemn balderdash that remained without effect? Why cling to beliefs which were so flatly contradicted by experience? How dare to repeat experiments that had failed so often? The answer seems to be that the fallacy was far from easy to detect, the failure by no means obvious, since in many, perhaps in most, cases the desired event did actually follow, at a longer or shorter interval, the performance of the rite which was designed to bring it about; and a mind of more than common acuteness was needed to perceive that, even in these cases, the rite was not necessarily the cause of the event. A ceremony intended to make the wind blow or the rain fall, or to work the death of an enemy, will always be followed, sooner or later, by the occurrence it is meant to bring to pass; and primitive man may be excused for regarding the occurrence as a direct result of the ceremony, and the best possible proof of its efficacy. Similarly, rites observed in the morning to help the sun to rise, and in spring to wake the dreaming earth from her winter sleep, will invariably appear to be crowned with success, at least within the temperate zones; for in these regions the sun lights his golden lamp in the east every morning, and year by year the vernal earth decks herself afresh with a rich mantle of green. Hence the practical savage, with his conservative instincts, might well turn a deaf ear to the subtleties of the theoretical doubter, the philosophic radical, who presumed to hint that sunrise and spring might not, after all, be direct consequences of the punctual performance of certain daily or yearly ceremonies, and that the sun might perhaps continue to rise and trees to blossom though the ceremonies were occasionally intermitted, or even discontinued altogether. These sceptical doubts would naturally be repelled by the other with scorn and indignation as airy reveries subversive of the faith and manifestly contradicted by experience. "Can anything be plainer," he might say, "than that I light my twopenny candle on earth and that the sun then kindles his great fire in heaven? I should be glad to know whether, when I have put on my green robe in spring, the trees do not afterwards do the same? These are facts patent to everybody, and on them I take my stand. I am a plain practical man, not one of your theorists and splitters of hairs and choppers of logic.

Theories and speculation and all that may be very well in their way, and I have not the least objection to your indulging in them, provided, of course, you do not put them in practice. But give me leave to stick to facts; then I know where I am." The fallacy of this reasoning is obvious to us, because it happens to deal with facts about which we have long made up our minds. But let an argument of precisely the same calibre be applied to matters which are still under debate, and it may be questioned whether a British audience would not applaud it as sound, and esteem the speaker who used it a safe man—not brilliant or showy, perhaps, but thoroughly sensible and hard-headed. If such reasonings could pass muster among ourselves, need we wonder that they long escaped detection by the savage?

Edward B. Tylor

ANIMISM

The first requisite in a systematic study of the religions of the lower races, is to lay down a rudimentary definition of religion. By requiring in this definition the belief in a supreme deity or of judgment after death, the adoration of idols or the practice of sacrifice, or other partially-diffused doctrines or rites, no doubt many tribes may be excluded from the category of religious. But such nar-

From Primitive Culture : Researches into the Development of Mythology, Philosophy, Religion, Language, Art, and Custom (1871) 3rd ed., revised. London: 1891, I, 424–29; 436; 440; 445–46; 448; 450–51; 457–58; 467; 469; 474–75; 476–79; 496–502. By permission of John Murray (Publishers) Ltd.

row definition has the fault of identifying religion rather with particular developments than with the deeper motive which underlies them. It seems best to fall back at once on this essential source, and simply to claim, as a minimum definition of Religion, the belief in Spiritual Beings. If this standard be applied to the descriptions of low races as to religion, the following results will appear. It cannot be positively asserted that every existing tribe recognizes the belief in spiritual beings, for the native condition of a considerable number is obscure in this respect, and from the rapid change or extinction they are undergoing, may ever remain so. It would be yet more unwarranted to set down every tribe mentioned in history, or known to us by the discovery of antiquarian relics, as necessarily having possessed the defined minimum of religion. Greater still would be the unwisdom of declaring such a rudimentary belief natural or instinctive in all human tribes of all times; for no evidence justifies the opinion that man, known to be capable of so vast an intellectual development, cannot have emerged from a non-religious condition, previous to that religious condition in which he happens at present to come with sufficient clearness within our range of knowledge. It is desirable, however, to take our basis of enquiry in observation rather than from speculation. Here, so far as I can judge from the immense mass of accessible evidence, we have to admit that the belief in spiritual beings appears among all low races with whom we have attained to thoroughly intimate acquaintance; whereas the assertion of absence of such belief must apply either to ancient tribes, or to more or less imperfectly described modern ones. The exact bearing of this state of things on the problem of the origin of religion may be thus briefly stated. Were it distinctly proved that non-religious savages exist or have existed, these might be at least plausibly claimed as representatives of the condition of Man before he arrived at the religious stage of culture. It is not desirable, however, that this argument should be put forward, for the asserted existence of the non-religious tribes in question rests, as we have seen, on evidence often mistaken and never conclusive. The argument for the natural evolution of religious ideas among mankind is not invalidated by the rejection of an ally too weak at present to give effectual help. Non-religious tribes may not exist in our day, but the fact bears no more decisively on the development of religion, than the impos-

sibility of finding a modern English village without scissors or books or lucifer-matches bears on the fact that there was a time when no such things existed in the land.

I purpose here, under the name of Animism, to investigate the deep-lying doctrine of Spiritual Beings, which embodies the very essence of Spiritualistic as opposed to Materialistic philosophy. Animism is not a new technical term, though now seldom used.[1] From its special relation to the doctrine of the soul, it will be seen to have a peculiar appropriateness to the view here taken of the mode in which theological ideas have been developed among mankind. The word Spiritualism, though it may be, and sometimes is, used in a general sense, has this obvious defect to us, that it has become the designation of a particular modern sect, who indeed hold extreme spiritualistic views, but cannot be taken as typical representatives of these views in the world at large. The sense of Spiritualism in its wider acceptation, the general belief in spiritual beings, is here given to Animism.

Animism characterizes tribes very low in the scale of humanity, and thence ascends, deeply modified in its transmission, but from first to last preserving an unbroken continuity, into the midst of high modern culture. Doctrines adverse to it, so largely held by individuals or schools, are usually due not to early lowness of civilization, but to later changes in the intellectual course, to divergence from, or rejection of, ancestral faiths; and such newer developments do not affect the present en-

[1]The term has been especially used to denote the doctrine of Stahl, the promulgator also of the phlogiston-theory. The Animism of Stahl is a revival and development in modern scientific shape of the classic theory identifying vital principle and soul. See his 'Theoria Medica Vera,' Halle, 1737; and the critical dissertation on his views, Lemoine, 'Le Vitalisme et l'Animisme de Stahl,' Paris, 1864.

quiry as to the fundamental religious condition of mankind. Animism is, in fact, the groundwork of the Philosophy of Religion, from that of savages up to that of civilized men. And although it may at first sight seem to afford but a bare and meagre definition of a minimum of religion, it will be found practically sufficient; for where the root is, the branches will generally be produced. It is habitually found that the theory of Animism divides into two great dogmas, forming parts of one consistent doctrine; first, concerning souls of individual creatures, capable of continued existence after the death or destruction of the body; second, concerning other spirits, upward to the rank of powerful deities. Spiritual beings are held to affect or control the events of the material world, and man's life here and hereafter; and it being considered that they hold intercourse with men, and receive pleasure or displeasure from human actions, the belief in their existence leads naturally, and it might almost be said inevitably, sooner or later to active reverence and propitiation. Thus Animism, in its full development, includes the belief in souls and in a future state, in controlling deities and subordinate spirits, these doctrines practically resulting in some kind of active worship. One great element of religion, that moral element which among the higher nations forms its most vital part, is indeed little represented in the religion of the lower races. It is not that these races have no moral sense or no moral standard, for both are strongly marked among them, if not in formal precept, at least in that traditional consensus of society which we call public opinion, according to which certain actions are held to be good or bad, right or wrong. It is that the conjunction of ethics and Animistic philosophy, so intimate and powerful in the higher culture, seems scarcely yet to have begun in the lower. I propose here hardly to touch upon the purely moral aspects of religion, but rather to study the animism of the world so far as it constitutes, as unquestionably it does constitute, an ancient and world-wide philosophy, of which belief is the theory and worship is the practice. Endeavouring to shape the materials for an enquiry hitherto strangely undervalued and neglected, it will now be my task to bring as clearly as may be into view the fundamental animism of the lower races, and in some slight and broken outline to trace its course into higher regions of civilization. Here let me state once and for all two principal conditions under which the present research is carried on. First, as to the religious doctrines and practices examined, these are treated as belonging to theological systems devised by human reason, without supernatural aid or revelation; in other words, as being developments of Natural Religion. Second, as to the connexion between similar ideas and rites in the religions of the savage and the civilized world. While dwelling at some length on doctrines and ceremonies of the lower races, and sometimes particularizing for special reasons the related doctrines and ceremonies of the higher nations, it has not seemed my proper task to work out in detail the problems thus suggested among the philosophies and creeds of Christendom. Such applications, extending farthest from the direct scope of a work on primitive culture, are briefly stated in general terms, or touched in slight allusion, or taken for granted without remark. Educated readers possess the information required to work out their general bearing on theology, while more technical discussion is left to philosophers and theologians specially occupied with such arguments.

The first branch of the subject to be considered is the doctrine of human and other Souls, an examination of which will occupy the rest of the present chapter. What the doctrine of the soul is among the lower races, may be explained in stating the animistic theory of its development. It seems as though thinking men, as yet at a low level of culture, were deeply impressed by two groups of biological problems. In the first place, what is it that makes the difference between a living body and a dead one; what causes waking, sleep, trance, disease, death? In the second place, what are those human shapes which appear in dreams and visions? Looking at these two groups of phenomena, the ancient savage philosophers probably made their first step by the obvious inference that every man has two things belonging to him, namely, a life and a phantom. These two are evidently in close connexion with the body, the life as enabling it to feel and think and act, the phantom as being its image or second self; both, also, are perceived to be things separable from the body, the life as able to go away and leave it insensible or dead, the phantom as appearing to people at a distance from it. The second step would seem also easy for savages to make, seeing how extremely difficult civilized men have found it to unmake. It is merely to combine the life and the phantom. As both belong to the body, why should they not also belong to one another, and be manifestations of one and the same soul? Let them then be considered as united, and the result is that well-known conception which may be described as an apparitional-soul, a ghost-soul. This, at any rate, corresponds with the actual conception of the personal soul or spirit among the lower races, which may be defined as follows: It is a thin unsubstantial human image, in its nature a sort of vapour, film, or shadow; the cause of life and thought in the individual it animates; independently possessing the personal consciousness and volition of its corporeal owner, past or present; capable of leaving the body far behind, to flash swiftly from place to place; mostly impalpable and invisible, yet also manifesting physical power, and especially appearing to men waking or asleep as a phantasm separate from the body of which it bears the likeness; continuing to exist and appear to men after the death of that body; able to enter into, possess, and act in the bodies of other men, of animals, and even of things. Though this definition is by no means of universal application, it has sufficient generality to be taken as a standard, modified by more or less divergence among any particular people. Far from these world-wide opinions being arbitrary or conventional products, it is seldom even justifiable to consider their uniformity among distant races as proving communication of any sort. They are doctrines answering in the most forcible way to the plain evidence of men's senses, as interpreted by a fairly consistent and rational primitive philosophy. So well, indeed, does primitive animism account for the facts of nature, that it has held its place into the higher levels of education. Though classic and mediæval philosophy modified it much, and modern philosophy has handled it yet more unsparingly, it has so far retained the traces of its original character, that heirlooms of primitive ages may be claimed in the existing psychology of the civilized world. . . .

The early animistic theory of vitality, regarding the functions of life as caused by the soul, offers to the savage mind an explanation of several bodily and mental conditions, as being effects of a departure of the soul or some of its constituent spirits. This theory holds a wide and strong position in savage biology. . . .

This same doctrine forms one side of the theory of dreams prevalent among the lower races. Certain of the Greenlanders, Cranz remarks, consider that the soul quits the body in the night and goes out hunting, dancing, and visiting; their dreams, which are frequent and lively, having brought them to this opinion. . . .

As we survey the immense series of dream-stories of similar types in patristic, mediæval, and modern literature, we may find it difficult enough to decide which are truth and which are fiction. But along the course of these myriad narratives of human phantoms appearing in dreams to cheer or torment, to warn or inform, or to demand fulfilment of their own desires, the problem of dream-apparitions may be traced in progress of gradual determination, from the earlier conviction that a disembodied soul really comes into the presence of the sleeper, toward the later opinion that such a phantasm is produced in the dreamer's mind without the perception of any external objective figure.

The evidence of visions corresponds with the evidence of dreams in their bearing on primitive theories of the soul, and the two classes of phenomena substantiate and supplement one another. Even in healthy waking life, the savage or barbarian has never learnt to make that rigid distinction between subjective and objective, between imagination and reality, to enforce which is one of the main results of scientific education. Still less, when disordered in body and mind he sees around him phantom human forms, can he distrust the evidence of his very senses. Thus it comes to pass that throughout the lower civilization men believe, with the most vivid and intense belief, in the objective reality of the human spectres which they see in sickness, exhaustion, or excitement. As will be hereafter noticed, one main reason of the practices of fasting, penance, narcotising by drugs, and other means of bringing in morbid exaltation, is that the patients may obtain the sight of spectral beings, from whom they look to gain spiritual knowledge and even worldly power. Human ghosts are among the principal of these phantasmal figures. There is no doubt that honest visionaries describe ghosts as they really appear to their perception, while even the impostors who pretend to see them conform to the descriptions thus established; . . .

Death is the event which, in all stages of culture, brings thought to bear most intensely, though not always most healthily, on the problems of psychology. The apparition of the disembodied soul has in all ages been thought to bear especial relation to its departure from its body at death. . . .

That the apparitional human soul bears the likeness of its fleshly body, is the principle implicitly accepted by all who believe it really and objectively present in dreams and visions. My own view is that nothing but dreams and visions could have ever put into men's minds such an idea as that of souls being ethereal images of bodies. It is thus habitually taken for granted in animistic philosophy, savage or civilized, that souls set free from the earthly body are recognized by a likeness to it which they still retain, whether as ghostly wanderers on earth or inhabitants of the world beyond the grave. Man's spirit, says Swedenborg, is his mind, which lives after death in complete human form, and this is the poet's dictum in 'In Memoriam:'

Eternal form shall still divide
The eternal soul from all beside;
And I shall know him when we meet.

This world-wide thought, coming into view here in a multitude of cases from all grades of culture, needs no collection of ordinary instances to illustrate it. But a quaint and special group of beliefs will serve to display the thoroughness with which the soul is thus conceived as an image of the body. As a consistent corollary to such an opinion, it is argued that the mutilation of the body will have a corresponding effect upon the soul, and very low savage races have philosophy enough to work out this idea. . . .

Among rude races, the original conception of the human soul seems to have been that of ethereality, or vaporous materiality, which has held so large a place in human thought ever since. In fact, the later metaphysical notion of immateriality could scarcely have conveyed any meaning to a savage. It is moreover to be noticed that, as to the whole nature and action of apparitional souls, the lower philosophy escapes various difficulties which down to modern times have perplexed metaphysicians and theologians of the civilized world. Considering the thin ethereal body of the soul to be itself sufficient and suitable for visibility, movement, and speech, the primitive animists required no additional hypotheses to account for these manifestations; they had no place for theories such as detailed by Calmet, as that immaterial souls have their own vaporous bodies provided for them by supernatural means to enable them to appear as spectres, or that they possess the power of condensing the circumambient air into phantom-like bodies to invest themselves in, or forming from it vocal instruments. It appears to have been within systematic schools of civilized philosophy that the transcendental definitions of the immaterial soul were obtained, by abstraction from the primitive conception of the ethereal-material soul, so as to reduce it from a physical to a metaphysical entity.

Departing from the body at the time of death, the soul or spirit is considered set free to linger near the tomb, to wander on earth or flit in the air, or to travel to the proper region of spirits—the world beyond the grave. . . . Men do not stop short at the persuasion that death releases the soul to a free and active existence, but they quite logically proceed to assist nature, by slaying men in order to liberate their souls for ghostly uses. Thus there arises one of the most wide-spread, distinct, and intelligible rites of animistic religion—that of funeral human sacrifice for the service of the dead. When a man of rank dies and his soul departs to its own place, wherever and whatever that place may be, it is a rational inference of early philosophy that the souls of attendants, slaves, and wives, put to death at his funeral, will make the same journey and continue their service in the next life, and the argument is frequently stretched further, to include the souls of new victims sacrificed in order that they may enter upon the same ghostly servitude. It will appear from the ethnography of this rite that it is not strongly marked in the very lowest levels of culture, but that, arising in the lower barbaric stage, it develops itself in the higher, and thenceforth continues or dwindles in survival. . . .

In now passing from the consideration of the souls of men to that of the souls of the lower animals, we have first to inform ourselves as to the savage man's idea, which is very different from the civilized man's, of the nature of these lower animals. A remarkable group of observances customary among rude tribes will bring this distinction sharply into view. Savages talk quite seriously to beasts alive or dead as they would to men alive or dead, offer them homage, ask pardon when it is their painful duty to hunt and kill them. . . .

The sense of an absolute psychical distinction between man and beast, so prevalent in the civilized world, is hardly to be found among the lower races. Men to whom the cries of beasts and birds seem like human language, and their actions guided as it were by human thought, logically enough allow the existence of souls to beasts, birds, and reptiles, as to men. The lower psychology cannot but recognize in beasts the very characteristics which it attributes to the human soul, namely, the phenomena of life and death, will and judgment, and the phantom seen in vision or in dream. As for believers, savage or civilized, in the great doctrine of metempsychosis, these not only consider that an animal may have a soul, but that this soul may have inhabited a human being, and thus the creature may be in fact their own ancestor or once familiar friend. A line of facts, arranged as waymarks along the course of civilization, will serve to indicate the history of opinion from savagery onward, as to the souls of animals during life and after death . . . .

Plants, partaking with animals the phenomena of life and death, health and sickness, not unnaturally have some kind of soul ascribed to them. In fact, the notion of a vegetable soul, common to plants and to the higher organisms possessing an animal soul in addition, was familiar to mediæval philosophy, and is not yet forgotten by naturalists, But in the lower ranges of culture, at least within one wide district of the world, the souls of plants are much more fully identified with the souls of animals. . . .

Thus far the details of the lower animistic philosophy are not very unfamiliar to modern students. The primitive view of the souls of men and beasts, as asserted or acted on in the lower and middle levels of culture, so far belongs to current civilized thought, that those who hold the doctrine to be false, and the practices based upon it futile, can nevertheless understand and sympathise with the lower nations to whom they are matters of the most sober and serious conviction. Nor is even the notion of a separable spirit or soul as the cause of life in plants too incongruous with ordinary ideas to be readily appreciable. But the theory of souls in the lower culture stretches beyond this limit, to take in a conception much stranger to modern thought. Certain high savage races distinctly hold, and a large proportion of other savage and barbarian races make a more or less close approach to, a theory of separable and surviving souls or spirits belonging to stocks and stones, weapons, boats, food, clothes, ornaments, and other objects which to us are not merely soulless but lifeless.

Yet, strange as such a notion may seem to us at first sight, if we place ourselves by an effort in the intellectual position of an uncultured tribe, and examine the theory of object-souls from their point of view, we shall hardly pronounce it irrational. In discussing the origin of myth, some account has already been given of the primitive stage of thought in which personality and life are ascribed not to men and beasts only, but to things. It has been shown how what we call inanimate objects—rivers, stones, trees, weapons, and so forth—are treated as living intelligent beings, talked to, propitiated, punished for the harm they do. Hume, whose 'Natural History of Religion' is perhaps more than any other work the source of modern opinions as to the development of religion, comments on the influence of this personifying stage of thought. 'There is an universal tendency among mankind to conceive all beings like themselves, and to transfer to every object those qualities with which they are familiarly acquainted, and of which they are intimately conscious. . . . The *unknown causes*, which continually employ their thought, appearing always in the same aspect, are all apprehended to be of the same kind or species. Nor is it long before we ascribe to them thought and reason, and passion, and sometimes even the limbs and figures of men, in order to bring them nearer to a resemblance with ourselves.' Auguste Comte has ventured to bring such a state of thought under terms of strict definition in his conception of the primary mental condition of mankind—a state of 'pure fetishism, constantly characterized by the free and direct exercise of our primitive tendency to conceive all external bodies soever, natural or artificial, as animated by a life essentially analogous to our own, with mere differences of intensity.[2] Our comprehension of the lower stages of mental culture depends much on the thoroughness with which we can appreciate this primitive, childlike conception, and in this our best guide may be the memory of our own childish days. He who recollects when there was still personality to him in posts and sticks, chairs and toys, may well understand how the infant philosophy of mankind could extend the notion of vitality to what modern science only recognises as lifeless things; thus one main part of the lower animistic doctrine as to souls of objects is accounted for. The doctrine requires for its full conception of a soul not only life, but also a phantom or apparitional spirit; this development, however, follows without difficulty, for the evidence of dreams and visions applies to the spirits of objects in much the same manner as to human ghosts. Everyone who has seen visions while light-headed in fever, everyone who has ever dreamt a dream, has seen the phantoms of objects as well as of persons. How then can we charge the savage with far-fetched absurdity for taking into his philosophy and religion an opinion which rests on the very evidence of his senses? The notion is implicitly recognised in his accounts of ghosts, which do not come naked, but clothed, and even armed; of course there must be spirits of garments and weapons, seeing that the spirits of men come bearing them. It will indeed place savage philosophy in no unfavourable light, if we compare this extreme animistic development of it with the popular opinion still surviving in civilized countries, as to ghosts and the nature of the human soul as connected with them. When the ghost of Hamlet's father appeared armed cap-a-pie,

Such was the very armour he had on,
When he the ambitious Norway combated.

And thus it is a habitual feature of the ghost-stories of the civilized, as of the savage world, that the ghost comes dressed, and even dressed in well-known clothing worn in life. Hearing as well as sight testifies to the phantoms of objects: the clanking of ghostly chains and the rustling of ghostly dresses are described in the literature of apparitions. Now by the savage theory, according to which the ghost and his clothes are alike real and objective, and by the modern scientific theory, according to which both ghost and garment are alike imaginary and subjective, the facts of apparitions are rationally met. But the modern vulgar who ignore or repudiate the notion of ghosts of things, while retaining the notion of ghosts of persons, have fallen into a hybrid state of opinion which has neither the logic of the savage nor of the civilized philosopher. . . .

Having thus surveyed at large the theory of spirits or souls of objects, it remains to point out what, to general students, may seem the most important consideration belonging to it, namely, its close relation to one of the most influential doctrines of civilized philosophy. The savage thinker, though occupying himself so much with the phenomena of life, sleep, disease, and death, seems to have taken for granted, as a matter of course, the ordinary operations of his own mind. It hardly occurred to him to think about the machinery of thinking. Metaphysics is a study which first assumes clear shape at a comparatively high level of intellectual culture. The metaphysical philosophy of thought taught in our modern European lecture-rooms is historically traced back to the speculative

---

[2]Hume, 'Nat. Hist. of Rel.,' sec. ii; Comte, 'Philosophie Positive,' vol. v., p. 30.

psychology of classic Greece. Now one doctrine which there comes into view is especially associated with the name of Democritus, the philosopher of Abdera, in the fifth century B.C. When Democritus propounded the great problem of metaphysics, 'How do we perceive external things?'—thus making, as Lewes says, an era in the history of philosophy, —he put forth, in answer to the question, a theory of thought. He explained the fact of perception by declaring that things are always throwing off images (εἴδωλα) of themselves, which images, assimilating to themselves the surrounding air, enter a recipient soul, and are thus perceived. Now, supposing Democritus to have been really the originator of this famed theory of ideas, how far is he to be considered its inventor? Writers on the history of philosophy are accustomed to treat the doctrine as actually made by the philosophical school which taught it. Yet the evidence here brought forward shows it to be really the savage doctrine of object-souls, turned to a new purpose as a method of explaining the phenomena of thought. Nor is the correspondence a mere coincidence, for at this point of junction between classic religion and classic philosophy the traces of historical continuity may still be discerned. To say that Democritus was an ancient Greek is to say that from his childhood he had looked on at the funeral ceremonies of his country, beholding the funeral sacrifices of garments and jewels and money and food and drink, rites which his mother and his nurse could tell him were performed in order that the phantasmal images of these objects might pass into the possession of forms shadowy like themselves, the souls of dead men. Thus Democritus, seeking a solution of his great problem of the nature of thought, found it by simply decanting into his metaphysics a surviving doctrine of primitive savage animism. This thought of the phantoms

or souls of things, if simply modified to form a philosophical theory of perception, would then and there become his doctrine of Ideas. Nor does even this fully represent the closeness of union which connects the savage doctrine of flitting object-souls with the Epicurean philosophy. Lucretius actually makes the theory of film-like images of things (simulacra, membranæ) account both for the apparitions which come to men in dreams, and the images which impress their minds in thinking. So unbroken is the continuity of philosophic speculation from savage to cultured thought. Such are the debts which civilized philosophy owes to primitive animism.

The doctrine of ideas, thus developed in the classic world, has, indeed, by no means held its course thenceforth unchanged through metaphysics, but has undergone transition somewhat like that of the doctrine of the soul itself. Ideas, fined down to the abstract forms or species of material objects, and applied to other than visible qualities, have at last come merely to denote subjects of thought. Yet to this day the old theory has not utterly died out, and the retention of the significant term 'idea' (ἰδέα, visible form) is accompanied by a similar retention of original meaning. It is still one of the tasks of the metaphysician to display and refute the old notion of ideas as being real images, and to replace it by more abstract conceptions. It is a striking instance that Dugald Stewart can cite from the works of Sir Isaac Newton the following distinct recognition of 'sensible species': 'Is not the sensorium of animals, the place where the sentient substance is present; and to which the sensible species of things are brought, through the nerves and brain, that there may be perceived by the mind present in that place?' Again, Dr. Reid states the original theory of ideas, while declaring that he conceives it 'to have no solid foundation, though it has been adopted very generally by philosophers. . . . This notion of our perceiving external objects, not immediately, but in certain images or species of them conveyed by the senses, seems to be the most ancient philosophical hypothesis we have on the subject of perception, and to have, with small variations, retained its authority to this day.' Granted that Dr. Reid exaggerated the extent to which metaphysicians have kept up the notion of ideas as real images of things, few will deny that it does linger much in modern minds, and that people who talk of ideas do often, in some hazy metaphorical way, think of sensible images. One of the shrewdest things ever said about either ideas or ghosts was Bishop Berkeley's retort upon Halley, who bantered him about his idealism. The bishop claimed the mathematician as an idealist also, his 'ultimate ratios' being ghosts of departed quantities, appearing when the terms that produced them vanished.

It remains to sum up in a few words the doctrine of souls, in the various phases it has assumed from first to last among mankind. In the attempt to trace its main course through the successive grades of man's intellectual history, the evidence seems to accord best with a theory of its development, somewhat to the following effect. At the lowest levels of culture of which we have clear knowledge, the notion of a ghost-soul animating man while in the body, and appearing in dream and vision out of the body, is found deeply ingrained. There is no reason to think that this belief was learnt by savage tribes from contact with higher races, nor that it is a relic of higher culture from which the savage tribes have degenerated; for what is here treated as the primitive animistic doctrine is thoroughly at home among savages, who appear to hold it on the very evidence of their senses, interpreted on the biological principle which seems to them most reasonable. We may now

and then hear the savage doctrines and practices concerning souls claimed as relics of a high religious culture pervading the primæval race of man. They are said to be traces of remote ancestral religion, kept up in scanty and perverted memory by tribes degraded from a nobler state. It is easy to see that such an explanation of some few facts, sundered from their connexion with the general array, may seem plausible to certain minds. But a large view of the subject can hardly leave such argument in possession. The animism of savages stands for and by itself; it explains its own origin. The animism of civilised men, while more appropriate to advanced knowledge, is in great measure only explicable as a developed product of the older and ruder system. It is the doctrines and rites of the lower races which are, according to their philosophy, results of point-blank natural evidence and acts of straightforward practical purpose. It is the doctrines and rites of the higher races which show survival of the old in the midst of the new, modification of the old to bring it into conformity with the new, abandonment of the old because it is no longer compatible with the new. Let us see at a glance in what general relation the doctrine of souls among savage tribes stands to the doctrine of souls among barbaric and cultured nations. Among races within the limits of savagery, the general doctrine of souls is found worked out with remarkable breadth and consistency. The souls of animals are recognized by a natural extension from the theory of human souls; the souls of trees and plants follow in some vague partial way; and the souls of inanimate objects expand the general category to its extremest boundary. Thenceforth, as we explore human thought onward from savage into barbarian and civilized life, we find a state of theory more conformed to positive science, but in itself less complete and consistent. Far on into civilization, men still act as though in some half-meant way they believed in souls or ghosts of objects, while nevertheless their knowledge of physical science is beyond so crude a philosophy. As to the doctrine of souls of plants, fragmentary evidence of the history of its breaking down in Asia had reached us. In our own day and country, the notion of souls of beasts is to be seen dying out. Animism, indeed, seems to be drawing in its outposts, and concentrating itself on its first and main position, the doctrine of the human soul. This doctrine has undergone extreme modification in the course of culture. It has outlived the almost total loss of one great argument attached to it—the objective reality of apparitional souls or ghosts seen in dreams and visions. The soul has given up its ethereal substance, and become an immaterial entity, 'the shadow of a shade.' Its theory is becoming separated from the investigations of biology and mental science, which now discuss the phenomena of life and thought, the senses and the intellect, the emotions and the will, on a ground-work of pure experience. There has arisen an intellectual product whose very existence is of the deepest significance, a 'psychology' which has no longer anything to do with 'soul.' The soul's place in modern thought is in the metaphysics of religion, and its especial office there is that of furnishing an intellectual side to the religious doctrine of the future life. Such are the alterations which have differenced the fundamental animistic belief in its course through successive periods of the world's culture. Yet it is evident that, notwithstanding all this profound change, the conception of the human soul is, as to its most essential nature, continuous from the philosophy of the savage thinker to that of the modern professor of theology. Its definition has remained from the first that of an animating, separable, surviving entity, the vehicle of individual personal existence. The theory of the soul is one principal part of a system of religious philosophy, which unites, in an unbroken line of mental connexion, the savage fetish-worshipper and the civilized Christian. The divisions which have separated the great religions of the world into intolerant and hostile sects are for the most part superficial in comparison with the deepest of all religious schisms, that which divides Animism from Materialism.

Herbert Spencer

ANCESTOR-WORSHIP, DEITIES AND RELIGIOUS DIFFERENTIATION

Taking the aggregate of human peoples—tribes, societies, nations—we find that nearly all of them, if not literally all,

From The Principles of Sociology (1877), 3rd ed., London and Edinburgh: 1885 I, §§ 153, 204, 207.

have a belief, vague or distinct, in a reviving other-self of the dead man. Within this class of peoples we find a class not quite so large, by the members of which the other-self of the dead man is supposed to exist for a time, or always, after death. Nearly as numerous is the class of peoples included in this, who show us ghost-propitiation at the funeral, and for a subsequent interval. Then comes the narrower class contained in the last—those more advanced peoples who, along with the belief in a ghost which permanently exists, show us a persistent ancestor-worship. Again, somewhat further restricted, though by no means small, we have a class of peoples whose worship of distinguished ancestors partially subordinates that of the undistinguished. And eventually, the subordination growing more decided, becomes marked where these distinguished ancestors were leaders of conquering races.

Even the words applied in more advanced societies to different orders of supernatural beings, indicate by their original community of meaning, that this has been the course of genesis. The fact cited above, that among the Tannese the word for a god means literally a dead man, is typical of facts everywhere found. Ghost, spirit, demon—names at first applied to the other-self without distinctions of character—come to be differently applied as ascribed differences of character arise: the shade of an enemy becomes a devil, and a friendly shade becomes a divinity. Where the conceptions have not developed far, there are no differentiated titles, and the distinctions made by us cannot be expressed. The early Spanish missionaries in America were inconvenienced by finding that the only native word they could use for God also meant devil. In Greek, δαιμων and θεος are interchangeable. By Æschylus, Agamemnon's children are represented as appealing to their father's ghost as to a god. So, too, with the Romans. Besides the unspecialized use of demon, which means an angel or genius, good or bad, we find the unspecialized use of *deus* for god and ghost. On

tombs the *manes* were called gods; and a law directs that "the rights of the *manes*-gods are to be kept sacred." Similarly with the Hebrews. Isaiah, representing himself as commanded to reject it, quotes a current belief implying such identification:—"And when they say unto you, 'Consult the ghost-seers and the wizards, that chirp and that mutter! Should not people consult their gods, even the dead on behalf of the living?'" When Saul goes to question the ghost of Samuel, the expression of the enchantress is—"I saw gods [*elohim*] ascending out of the earth": god and ghost being thus used as equivalents.[1] Even in our own day the kinship is traceable. The statement that God is a spirit, shows the application of a term which, otherwise applied, signifies a human soul. Only by its qualifying epithet is the meaning of Holy Ghost distinguished from the meaning of ghost in general. A divine being is still denoted by words that originally meant the breath which, deserting a man's body at death, was supposed to constitute the surviving part.

Do not these various evidences warrant the suspicion that from the ghost, once uniformly conceived, have arisen the variously-conceived supernatural beings? We may infer, *a priori*, that in conformity

[1] *Principles of Sociology*. First published 1877. Vol. I.

Concerning the first of these passages, which is given as rendered in *The Book of Isaiah* (1870), Cheyne (p. 38) explains that *gods* are spirits of departed national heroes. (In *The Prophecies of Isaiah* [1882] he varies the translation; especially by changing gods into god—a rendering of *elohim,* which agrees with accepted ideas much better than it agrees with the context.) Concerning the second passage the Speaker's Commentary says—"It is possible that *elohim* is here used in a general sense of a *supernatural* appearance, either angel or spirit." And Keunen remarks (I, p. 224) "There is no doubt that originally the higher beings, the objects of man's fear (*elóah*), were indicated by it (the name *elohîm*), so that this name too avails as an argument in favour of a former plurality of gods."

with the law of Evolution, there will develop many unlike conceptions out of conceptions originally alike. The spirits of the dead, forming, in a primitive tribe, an ideal group the members of which are but little distinguished from one another, will grow more and more distinguished. As societies advance, and as traditions, local and general, accumulate and complicate, these once-similar human souls, acquiring in the popular mind differences of character and importance, will diverge; until their original community of nature becomes scarcely recognizable.

Expecting, then, heterogeneous modifications of them, multiplying in thought as populations increase, ever spreading into more varied habitats, and tending continually to fill every place in Nature that can be occupied, let us now contemplate some of their most conspicuous types. . . .

* * *

Behind the supernatural being of this order, as behind supernatural beings of all other orders, we thus find that there has in every case been a human personality. Anything which transcends the ordinary, a savage thinks of as supernatural or divine: the remarkable man among the rest. This remarkable man may be simply the remotest ancestor remembered as the founder of the tribe; he may be a chief famed for strength and bravery; he may be a medicineman of great repute; he may be an inventor of something new. And then, instead of being a member of the tribe, he may be a superior stranger bringing arts and knowledge; or he may be one of a superior race predominating by conquest. Being at first one or other of these, regarded with awe during his life, he is regarded with increased awe after his death; and the propitiation of his ghost, becoming greater than the propitiation of ghosts which are less feared, develops into an established worship.

There is no exception then. Using the phrase ancestor-worship in its broadest sense as comprehending all worship of the dead, be they of the same blood or not, we conclude that ancestor-worship is the root of every religion. . . .

* * *

Integration is, in the first place, shown us by simple increase of mass. In extremely low tribes which have but faint and wavering beliefs in the doubles of the dead, there are no established groups of supposed supernatural beings. Among the more advanced, who hold that dead members of the tribe have temporary second lives, ghosts form an imagined assemblage which, though continually augmented, is continually dissolving away—a cluster which does not increase because the subtractions equal the additions. But when, later, there arises the belief that ghosts exist permanently, this cluster necessarily grows; and its growth becomes great in proportion both as the society enlarges and as traditions are longer preserved. Hence such a multiplication of supernatural beings that even the superior among them are scarcely numerable. Gomara tells us that "the gods of Mexico are said to number 2,000"; and with these must be joined the far more numerous demons, and spirits of undistinguished persons, recognized in every locality. A like immense growth was exhibited in ancient mythologies; and is now exhibited by the mythology of India, as well as that of Japan. Along with this increase of mass, goes increase of coherence. The superstitions of the primitive man are loose and inconsistent: different members of a tribe make different statements; and the same individual varies his interpretations as occasion suggests. But in course of time the beliefs are elaborated into a well-knit system. Further, the hypothesis to which the ghost-theory leads, initiated by anomalous occurrences, extends itself to all phenomena; so that the properties and actions of surrounding things, as well as the thoughts and feelings of men, are ascribed to unseen beings, who thus constitute a combined mechanism of causation.

While increasing in mass and in coherence, the supernatural aggregate increases in heterogeneity. Alike as ghosts are at first conceived to be, they become unlike as fast as the tribe grows, complicates, and begins to have a history: the ghost-fauna, almost homogeneous at the outset, differentiates. Originally, the only distinctions of good or bad among the doubles of the dead, are such as were shown by the living men; as are also the only unlikenesses of power. But there soon arise conceived contrasts in goodness between the ghosts of relatives and the ghosts of other persons; as well as stronger contrasts between friendly ghosts belonging to the tribe and malicious ghosts belonging to other tribes. When social ranks are established, there follow contrasts of rank and accompanying potency among supernatural beings; which, as legends expand, grow more and more marked. Eventually there is formed in this way a hierarchy of partially-deified ancestors, demigods, great gods, and among the great gods one who is supreme; while there is simultaneously formed a hierarchy of diabolical powers. Then come those further differentiations which specialize the functions and habitats of these supernatural beings; until each mythology has its major and minor presiding agents, from Apollo down to a dryad, from Thor down to a watersprite, from a Saint down to a fairy. So that out of the originally small and almost uniform aggregate of supernatural beings, there gradually comes an aggregate as multiform as it is vast.

Change from the indefinite to the definite is no less clearly displayed. That early stage in which men show fear of the dead and yet do not themselves

expect any future existence, shows us an extreme indefiniteness of the ghost-theory. Even after the ghost-theory is established the beliefs in the resulting supernatural beings, though strong, are indistinct. At the same time that Livingstone describes the people of Angola as "constantly deprecating the wrath of departed souls," he says that they "have half-developed ideas and traditions of something or other, they know not what." And kindred accounts of uncivilized races elsewhere, are given by various travellers. But with progress conceptions become clearer. The different kinds of supernatural beings grow more defined in their forms, dispositions, powers, habits; until, in developed mythologies, they are specifically, and even individually, distinguished by attributes precisely stated.

Undeniably, then, a system of superstitions evolves after the same manner as all other things. By continuous integration and differentiation, it is formed into an aggregate which, while increasing, passes from an indefinite incoherent homogeneity to a definite coherent heterogeneity. This correspondence is, indeed, inevitable. The law which is conformed to by the evolving human being, and which is consequently conformed to by the evolving human intelligence, is of necessity conformed to by all products of that intelligence. Showing itself in structures, and by implication in the functions of those structures, this law cannot but show itself in the concrete manifestations of those functions. Just as language, considered as an objective product, bears the impress of this subjective process; so, too, does that system of ideas concerning the nature of things which the mind gradually elaborates.

So that in fact the hypothesis of Evolution absorbs the antagonist hypotheses preceding it, and strengthens itself by assimilating their components.

Wilhelm Wundt

DEMONS, HEROES, GODS

In entering upon a consideration of the development of primitive myths, we are at once confronted by the old question disputed by mythologists, ethnologists, and students of religion, Where and when did religion originate? For is not religion always concerned with the supernatural? Now, in certain cases, even primitive man supplements the sensuous world in which he lives and whose impressions he has not so much as elaborated into abstract concepts, with supersensuous elements, though he himself, of course, is unaware of their supersensuous character. The question, therefore, lies near at hand: Is religion already present at this stage, or is there at most a potentiality of religion, the germ of its future development? If the latter should be true, where, then, does religion begin? Now, our interest in the history of myth-formation derives largely from the very fact that the problem is intimately bound up with that of the origin of religion. Merely in itself the origin of the myth might have relatively little interest for us. The question, however, as to how religion arose acquires its great importance through its connection with the two further questions as to whether or not religion is a necessary constituent of human consciousness and whether it is

From Elements of Folk Psychology (1912), London and New York: 1916, pp. 75; 81–84; 92–93; 364; 282–286. By permission of George Allen & Unwin Ltd.

an original possession or is the result of certain preconditions of mythological thought. . . .

In so far as the mythology of primitive man gains a permanent foothold and influence, it consists of a *belief in magic and demons*. There are, however, two motives which engender this belief and give form and colour to the ideas and emotions springing from them. These are *death* and *sickness*.

Death! There are doubtless few impressions that have so powerful an effect upon the man of nature; indeed, civilized man as well is still very greatly stirred by the phenomenon of death. Let his companion meet with death, and even the outward actions of a primitive man are significant. The moment a person dies, the immediate impulse of primitive man is to leave him lying where he is and to flee. The dead person is abandoned, and the place where he died continues to be avoided for a long time—if possible, until animals have devoured the corpse. Obviously the emotion of *fear* is regnant. Its immediate cause is apparently the unusual and fear-inspiring changes which death makes in the appearance of a man. The suspension of movements, the pallor of death, the sudden cessation of breathing—these are phenomena sufficient to cause the most extreme terror. But what is the nature of the ideas that associate themselves with this fearsome impression? The flight from the corpse is evidence that man's fears are primarily for himself. To tarry in the presence of a dead person exposes the living man to the danger of being himself overtaken by death. The source of this danger is evidently identical with that which has brought death to the recently deceased person himself. Primitive man cannot think of death except as the sudden departure from the dying person of that which originally brought life. Nevertheless, there is evidently bound up with this conception the further idea that powers of life are still resident in the body; the latter remains firmly associated in the mind of primitive man with the impression of life. Here, then, we have the original source of the contradictory idea of a something that generates life and is therefore independent of the body, while nevertheless being connected with it. So far as we can gain knowledge of the impression which death makes on the mind of primitive man, two disparate motives are indissolubly united. He regards life as something that, in part, continues in some mysterious manner to dwell within the corpse, and in part, hovers about, invisible, in its vicinity. For this reason, the dead person becomes to him a *demon*, an invisible being capable of seizing upon man, of overpowering or killing him, or of bringing sickness upon him. In addition to this primitive idea of demons, we also find the conception of a *corporeal soul,* meaning by this the belief that the body is the vehicle of life, and that, so long as it has not itself disappeared, it continues to harbour the life within itself. The corporeal soul is here still regarded as a unit, which may, by separating itself from the body, become a demon and pass over into another person. No certain traces are as yet to be found of belief in a breath or shadow-like soul. As will appear later, this is a characteristic feature of the transition from primitive to totemic culture. When some investigators report

that the soul is occasionally referred to by the Semangs of Malacca as a small bird that soars into the air at the death of a person, it is not improbable that we here have to do either with the Semangs of culture, who have undergone marked changes under Malayan influence, or with the presence of an isolated idea that belongs to a different cultural circle. For in no other case are ideas similar to that of the psyche to be found on the level of primitive culture. On the other hand, the burial customs of the Malays and of the mixed races living in the immediate vicinity of the primitive peoples of the Malay Peninsula, already exhibit a striking contrast to the flight of primitive man from the corpse.

The next group of ideas, those arising from the impression made by *sickness,* particularly by such sickness as attacks man suddenly, are also restricted to the conception of a corporeal soul. For, one of the most characteristic marks of this conception is that magical, demoniacal powers are believed to issue from the body of the dead person. These powers, however, are not, as occurs in the above case, regarded as embodied in any visible thing—such as the exhalations of the breath or an escaping animal—that separates itself from the person. On the contrary, the demon that leaves the corpse and attacks another person in the form of a fatal sickness, is invisible. He is purely the result of an association between the fear aroused by the occurrence of death and the fright caused by an unexpected attack of sickness. The dead person, therefore, continues to remain the seat of demoniacal powers; these he can repeatedly direct against the living persons who approach him. Primitive man believes that the demon may assume any form whatsoever within the body, and deceitful medicine-men take advantage of this in ostensibly removing the sickness in the form of a piece of wood or of a stone. But it is precisely these ideas that are totally unrelated to that of a psyche and its embodiments. Though the corpse is perhaps the earliest object that suggests sickness-demons, it is in no wise the only one. Indeed, the attack of sickness is in itself sufficient to arouse fear of a demon. Thus, the Semangs and Senoi distinguish a vast number of different sickness-demons. Such ideas of demons, however, as we find among the Malays and the Singhalese, where demons are regarded as counter-agents to sickness-magic and usually take the form of fantastical animal monsters, never occur except at a later cultural stage. Any resemblance of these demons to 'soul animals,' which are always actual animals, is confined to the fact that they have some similarity to animals. Obviously they are creations of the imagination, due to fear and terror. Their only difference from the monsters of similar origin that are projected into the outward world is that they are reduced to proportions which fit the dimensions of the human body.

Closely connected with the magic of sickness is counter-magic, an agency by which disease is removed or the attack of sickness-demons warded off. Hence, probably, the original formation of a special group of men, which, though not, of course, at the very first a fixed professional class, was nevertheless the precursor of the latter. Among the American Indians, these were the 'medicine-men'; the peoples of northern Asia called them 'shamans'—more generally expressed, they were magicians. . . .

The regularly recurring features of the primitive myth, however, have their source in the immediate environment and in the facts of personal experience, in fear and terror. Thus, it is not intelligence nor reflection as to the origin and interconnection of phenomena that gives rise to mythological thinking, but emotion; ideas are only the material which the latter elaborates. The idea of a corporeal soul, present in the corpse yet also capable of abandoning it and of becoming a dangerous demon, is a creation of the emotion of fear. The demons who possess the sick man and cause his death, or who depart from him in convalescence, are products of emotion. They are supersensible, as is the soul, because they are born purely of emotion. Nevertheless, they always tend to assume a sensible nature, being imaged either as men, or as external things, such as animals, plants, weapons, and implements. Only in the course of later development are the demons themselves equipped with relatively permanent qualities that differ from the characteristics of the vehicles in which they are regarded as embodied.

Thus, then, we utterly confuse primitive thinking with our own scientific standpoint when we explain it by the need for the interpretation of phenomena. Causality, in our sense of the word, does not exist for primitive man. If we would speak of causality at all on his level of experience, we may say only that he is governed by the causality of magic. This, however, receives its stamp, not from the laws that regulate the connection of ideas, but from the forces of emotion. The mythological causality of emotional magic is no less spasmodic and irregular than the logical causality arising out of the orderly sequence of perceptions and ideas is constant. That the former preceded the latter is, nevertheless, of great importance. For the causality of natural law, as we know it, would hardly have been possible had not magical causality prepared the way for it. Yet the later arose from the earlier just at that moment in which the attention of men ceased to be held by the unusual, the startling, and the fearful, and occupied itself with the orderly, the regular, and commonplace. . . .

*   *   *

Herewith we come to a question which will bring us closer to an answer respecting the origin of gods. By what characteristic marks is a mythological conception to be distinguished as that of an actual god? The question might also be stated in a more concrete form. What characteristics differentiate a god from a *demon,* who is not yet a god because he lacks personality, and from a *hero,* who is regarded by the age in which gods originate as somewhat approximating a god but as nevertheless still a man? Or, briefly expressed, how does the god differ from the demon and from the ideal man?...

The gods of this age are likewise patterned entirely after powerful human personalities. They are anthropomorphic in every respect—human beings of a higher order, whose qualities, though found only among men, are magnified to infinitude. Just as the hero is a man endowed with more than ordinary human capacities, so the god is a hero exalted above the measure of earthly heroes. This itself implies that the hero necessarily precedes the god, just as man antedates the hero. Any fairly detailed account of this period, therefore, must deal with the hero before considering the god. The god is created after the image of the hero, and not, as traditional mythology still believes, the hero after the image of the god. It would, indeed, be a strange procedure for man first to create the ideal conception of his god and only subsequently to transform this into human outlines, and thus produce the hero. In the advance from man to the anthropomorphic god, the hero would surely already have been encountered. This, of course, does not imply that gods may not occasionally be transformed into heroes; it simply means that in the development as a whole the hero must have preceded the god. The relation here is precisely the same as that found everywhere else in connection with the development and degeneration of mythological conceptions. The fact of sequence, however, must not be interpreted to mean that we can point to a time in which there were heroes but no gods. Hero and god belong together. Both reflect an effort to exalt human personality into the superhuman. In this process, no fixed line may be drawn separating the hero, whose activity still falls within the human sphere, from the god, who is exalted above it. In fact, the differences between hero and god are by no means merely quantitative, measurable in terms of the elevation above the plane of human characteristics; the differentiating marks are essentially *qualitative.* The hero remains human in all his thought and action. The god, on the other hand, possesses not merely human capacities raised to their highest power, but also characteristics which are lacking in man and therefore in the hero. Especially noteworthy among the latter is the ability through his own power to perform magical acts, and thus to interfere at will in the course of nature as well as in human life. True, the hero of saga and poetry also employs magical agencies. The means of magic which he controls, however, have been bestowed upon him by some strange demoniacal being, either by one of those demons which, in the form of a man, an animal, or a fantastic monster, are recognized even by the early mythical tales as magical beings, or by a god, who, as such, combines the highest qualities of the hero with those of the demon. The conception of an anthropomorphic god, therefore, results from a fusion of hero with demon. Of these, the hero is a new creation, originating in the mental life of this later age. He was long foreshadowed, however, first by the animal ancestor (especially in so far as the latter brought blessings and good fortune), and then by the subsequent cult of human ancestors. But the figure of the hero is not completely developed until the human personality enters into the very forefront of mythological thought; then, through regular transitions, the value placed on personal characteristics is enhanced until the ideal of the hero is reached. Doubtless the hero may still incidentally be associated with the ancestor, yet personality as such has now come so to dominate the interest of the age that in comparison with it the genealogical feature is but secondary.

Not so with the demon-idea. Though it has come down from very remote times and has assumed many forms as a result of varying cultural conditions, the demon has always remained a magic being, arousing now hope, now fear and terror. This was its nature up to the very time when the ideal of the hero arose. This new idea it then appropriated, just as it did, in earlier times, the ideas of a soul that survives the deceased, of the totem animal, of the ancestor, and of other mythological figures. The very nature of the demon has always been constituted by such incorporated elements. From this point of view, the god also is only a new form of demon. In its earlier forms, however, as spirit-demon, animal-demon, and, finally, even as ancestor-demon, the demon was an impersonal product of the emotions, and possessed characteristics which underwent constant transformations. When it became a hero, it for the first time rose to the level of a personal being. Through the enhancement of the qualities of the hero it was then elevated into the sphere of the superhuman. Thus it came to constitute a human ideal far transcending the hero. This accounts for the uniqueness of the god-conception, and for the fact that, though the god assumes the essential characteristics of the demon, the two are nevertheless more widely distinct than were any of the earlier forms of demon conceptions from those that anteceded them. The rise of the god-idea, therefore, ushers in a new epoch of religious development. Just because of the contrast between personal god and impersonal demon, this epoch may be designated as that of the *origin of religion,*

in the narrower and proper sense of the word. The various forms of pure demon-belief are preparatory to religion; religion itself begins with the belief in gods. The relation which the belief in demons sustains to the belief in gods is another evidence that the hero and god must be grouped together, for there can be no clearly marked temporal difference in the origin of these two ideals of personality. Just as soon as the figure of the human hero arises, it assimilates the demon-conception, which was already long in existence and which continually underwent changes as a result of the various ideas with which it came into contact. Alongside of the being that arose from this fusion, however, there continued also the hero in his purity, as well as the demon, whose various forms were at most crowded into the background by the appearance of the gods. To however great an extent, therefore, the age of heroes and gods may introduce a completely new spiritual movement that proves fundamental to all future culture and religion, it nevertheless also includes all the elements of previous development. These elements, moreover, are not merely present in forms that have been altered and in part completely changed by the processes of assimilation; side by side with such forms, there are always also the original elements, which may be traced back to the earliest beginnings of mythological thought. The dominant factor determining the character of this new age, however, is the *hero.* The ideal of human personality which the hero engenders in the folk consciousness conditions all further development, and especially the origin of the god. For this reason the 'age of heroes and gods' might also, and more briefly, be called the *heroic age.*

As the direct incarnation of the idea of personality, it is the hero about whom the new development of myth and religion centres. Similarly, the hero also stands in closest relation to the transformations that occur in all other departments of human life. Enormous changes in economic conditions and in the forms of life dependent upon them, new social institutions, with their reactions upon custom and law, transformations and creations in all branches of art—all give expression to the new development upon which this age has entered. Here also, just as at the beginning of the anteceding age, there are numerous reciprocal relations between these various factors. The hero and the god cannot be conceived apart from the *State,* whose founding marks the beginning of this period. Custom and law are just as much results of the new political society as they are themselves essential factors in its creation. Neither the State nor the worship of gods protected by it could survive apart from the great changes in economic life that took place at the beginning of this period, and that were further established and perfected in the course of time. Thus, here also each element reinforces every other; all the factors of life are in constant interaction. At the beginning of the totemic period, as we have seen, it was the new creations of mythological thought that constituted the centre from which radiated all the other elements of culture. At the beginning of the age of heroes and gods it is the creative power of the *religious* consciousness whose activities most accurately mirror the various spiritual achievements of the period.

Sigmund Freud

TOTEM
AND TABOO

If we call the celebration of the totem meal to our help, we shall be able to find an answer. One day[1] the brothers who had been driven out came together, killed and devoured their father and so made an end of the patriarchal horde. United, they had the courage to do and succeeded in

From Totem and Taboo (1913), The Standard Edition of the Complete Psychological Works of Sigmund Freud, London: 1955, XIII, 141–55. Authorized translation by James Strachey. By permission of W.W. Norton & Company, Inc. Copyright 1950 by Routledge & Kegan Paul Ltd.

[1] To avoid misunderstanding, I must ask the reader to take into account the final sentences of the following footnote as a corrective to this description.

doing what would have been impossible for them individually. (Some cultural advance, perhaps command over some new weapon, had given them a sense of superior strength.) Cannibal savages as they were, it goes without saying that they devoured their victim as well as killing him. The violent primal father had doubtless been the feared and envied model of each one of the company of brothers: and in the act of devouring him they accomplished their identification with him, and each of them acquired a portion of his strength. The totem meal, which is perhaps mankind's earliest festival, would thus be a repetition and a commemoration of this memorable and criminal deed, which was the beginning of so many things—of social organization, of moral restrictions and of religion.[2]

[2]This hypothesis, which has such a monstrous air, of the tyrannical father being overwhelmed and killed by a combination of his exiled sons, was also arrived at by Atkinson (1903, 220f.) as a direct implication of the state of affairs in Darwin's primal horde: "The patriarch had only one enemy whom he should dread . . . a youthful band of brothers living together in forced celibacy, or at most in polyandrous relation with some single female captive. A horde as yet weak in their impubescence they are, but they would, when strength was gained with time, inevitably wrench by combined attacks, renewed again and again, both wife and life from the paternal tyrant." Atkinson, who incidentally passed his whole life in New Caledonia and had unusual opportunities for studying the natives, also pointed out that the conditions which Darwin assumed to prevail in the primal horde may easily be observed in herds of wild oxen and horses and regularly lead to the killing of the father of the herd. (Ibid., 222f.) He further supposed that, after the father had been disposed of, the horde would be disintegrated by a bitter struggle between the victorious sons. Thus any new organization of society would be precluded: they would be "an ever-recurring violent succession to the solitary paternal tyrant, by sons whose parricidal hands were so soon again clenched in fratricidal strife." (Ibid., 228.) Atkinson, who had no psycho-analytic hints to help him and who was ignorant of Robertson Smith's studies, found a less violent transition from the primal horde to the next social stage, at which numbers of males live together in a peaceable community. He believed that through the intervention of maternal love the sons—to begin with only the youngest, but later others as well—were allowed to remain with the horde, and that in return for this toleration the sons acknowledged their father's sexual privilege by renouncing all claim to their mother and sisters. (Ibid., 231ff.)

Such is the highly remarkable theory put forward by Atkinson. In its essential feature it is in agreement with my own; but its divergence results in its failing to effect a correlation with many other issues. The lack of precision in what I have written in the text above, its abbreviation of the time factor and its compression of the whole subject-matter, may be attributed to the reserve necessitated by the nature of the topic. It would be as foolish to aim at exactitude in such questions as it would be unfair to insist upon certainty.

In order that these latter consequences may seem plausible, leaving their premises on one side, we need only suppose that the tumultuous mob of brothers were filled with the same contradictory feelings which we can see at work in the ambivalent father-complexes of our children and of our neurotic patients. They hated their father, who presented such a formidable obstacle to their craving for power and their sexual desires; but they loved and admired him too. After they had got rid of him, had satisfied their hatred and had put into effect their wish to identify themselves with him, the affection which had all this time been pushed under was bound to make itself felt.[3] It did so in the form of remorse. A sense of guilt made its appearance, which in this instance coincided with the remorse felt by the whole group. The dead father became stronger than the living one had been—for events took the course we so often see them follow in human affairs to this day. What had up to then been prevented by his actual existence was thenceforward prohibited by the sons themselves, in accordance with the psychological procedure so familiar to us in psycho-analyses under the name of "deferred obedience." They revoked their deed by forbidding the killing of the totem, the substitute for their father; and they renounced its fruits by resigning their claim to the women who had now been set free. They thus created out of their filial sense of guilt the two fundamental taboos of totemism, which for that very reason inevitably corresponded to the two repressed wishes of the Oedipus complex.

[3]This fresh emotional attitude must also have been assisted by the fact that the deed cannot have given complete satisfaction to those who did it. From one point of view it had been done in vain. Not one of the sons had in fact been able to put his original wish—of taking his father's place—into effect. And, as we know, failure is far more propitious for a moral reaction than satisfaction.

Whoever contravened those taboos became guilty of the only two crimes with which primitive society concerned itself.[4]

The two taboos of totemism with which human morality has its beginning are not on a par psychologically. The first of them, the law protecting the totem animal, is founded wholly on emotional motives: the father had actually been eliminated, and in no real sense could the deed be undone. But the second rule, the prohibition of incest, has a powerful practical basis as well. Sexual desires do not unite men but divide them. Though the brothers had banded together in order to overcome their father, they were all one another's rivals in regard to the women. Each of them would have wished, like his father, to have all the women to himself. The new organization would have collapsed in a struggle of all against all, for none of them was of such overmastering strength as to be able to take on his father's part with success. Thus the brothers had no alternative, if they were to live together, but—not, perhaps, until they had passed through many dangerous crises—to institute the law against incest, by which they all alike renounced the women whom they desired and who had been their chief motive for despatching their father. In this way they rescued the organization which had made them strong—and which may have been based on homosexual feelings and acts, originating perhaps during the period of their expulsion from the horde. Here, too, may perhaps have been the germ of the institution of matriarchy, described by Bachofen (1861), which was in turn replaced by the patriarchal organization of the family.

On the other hand, the claim of totemism to be regarded as a first attempt at a

religion is based on the first of these two taboos—that upon taking the life of the totem animal. The animal struck the sons as a natural and obvious substitute for their father; but the treatment of it which they found imposed on themselves expressed more than the need to exhibit their remorse. They could attempt, in their relation to this surrogate father, to allay their burning sense of guilt, to bring about a kind of reconciliation with their father. The totemic system was, as it were, a covenant with their father, in which he promised them everything that a childish imagination may expect from a father—protection, care and indulgence—while on their side they undertook to respect his life, that is to say, not to repeat the deed which had brought destruction on their real father. Totemism, moreover, contained an attempt at self-justification: "If our father had treated us in the way the totem does, we should never have felt tempted to kill him." In this fashion totemism helped to smooth things over and to make it possible to forget the event to which it owed its origin.

Features were thus brought into existence which continued thenceforward to have a determining influence on the nature of religion. Totemic religion arose from the filial sense of guilt, in an attempt to allay that feeling and to appease the father by deferred obedience to him. All later religions are seen to be attempts at solving the same problem. They vary according to the methods which they adopt; but all have the same end in view and are reactions to the same great event with which civilization began and which, since it occurred, has not allowed mankind a moment's rest.

There is another feature which was already present in totemism and which has been preserved unaltered in religion. The tension of ambivalence was evidently too great for any contrivance to be able to counteract it; or it is pos-

---

[4]"Murder and incest, or offences of a like kind against the sacred laws of blood, are in primitive society the only crimes of which the community as such takes cognizance." (Smith, 1894, 419.)

sible that psycho-logical conditions in general are unfavourable to getting rid of these antithetical emotions. However that may be, we find that the ambivalence implicit in the father-complex persists in totemism and in religions generally. Totemic religion not only comprised expressions of remorse and attempts at atonement, it also served as a remembrance of the triumph over the father. Satisfaction over that triumph led to the institution of the memorial festival of the totem meal, in which the restrictions of deferred obedience no longer held. Thus it became a duty to repeat the crime of parricide again and again in the sacrifice of the totem animal, whenever, as a result of the changing conditions of life, the cherished fruit of the crime—appropriation of the paternal attributes—threatened to disappear. We shall not be surprised to find that the element of filial rebelliousness also emerges, in the *later* products of religion, often in the strangest disguises and transformations.

Hitherto we have followed the developments of the *affectionate* current of feeling towards the father, transformed into remorse, as we find them in religion and in moral ordinances (which are not sharply distinguished in totemism). But we must not overlook the fact that it was in the main with the impulses that led to parricide that the victory lay. For a long time afterwards, the social fraternal feelings, which were the basis of the whole transformation, continued to exercise a profound influence on the development of society. They found expression in the sanctification of the blood tie, in the emphasis upon the solidarity of all life within the same clan. In thus guaranteeing one another's lives, the brothers were declaring that no one of them must be treated by another as their father was treated by them all jointly. They were precluding the possibility of a repetition of their father's fate. To the religiously-based prohibition

against killing the totem was now added the socially-based prohibition against fratricide. It was not until long afterwards that the prohibition ceased to be limited to members of the clan and assumed the simple form: "Thou shalt do no murder." The patriarchal horde was replaced in the first instance by the fraternal clan, whose existence was assured by the blood tie. Society was now based on complicity in the common crime; religion was based on the sense of guilt and the remorse attaching to it; while morality was based partly on the exigencies of this society and partly on the penance demanded by the sense of guilt.

Thus psycho-analysis, in contradiction to the more recent views of the totemic system but in agreement with the earlier ones, required us to assume that totemism and exogamy were intimately connected and had a simultaneous origin.

* * *

A great number of powerful motives restrain me from any attempt at picturing the further development of religions from their origin in totemism to their condition to-day. I will only follow two threads whose course I can trace with especial clarity as they run through the pattern; the theme of the totemic sacrifice and the relation of son to father.[5]

Robertson Smith has shown us that the ancient totem meal recurs in the original form of sacrifice. The meaning of the act is the same: sanctification through participation in a common meal. The sense of guilt, which can only be allayed by the solidarity of all the participants, also persists. What is new is the clan deity, in whose supposed presence the sacrifice is performed, who participates in the meal as though he were a clansman, and with whom those who consume the meal become identified. How does the

---

[5]Cf. the discussion by C. G. Jung (1912), which is governed by views differing in certain respects from mine.

god come to be in a situation to which he was originally a stranger?

The answer might be that in the meantime the concept of God had emerged—from some unknown source—and had taken control of the whole of religious life; and that, like everything else that was to survive, the totem meal had been obliged to find a point of contact with the new system. The psycho-analysis of individual human beings, however, teaches us with quite special insistence that the god of each of them is formed in the likeness of his father, that his personal relation to God depends on his relation to his father in the flesh and oscillates and changes along with that relation, and that at bottom God is nothing other than an exalted father. As in the case of totemism, psycho-analysis recommends us to have faith in the believers who call God their father, just as the totem was called the tribal ancestor. If psycho-analysis deserves any attention, then—without prejudice to any other sources or meanings of the concept of God, upon which psycho-analysis can throw no light—the paternal element in that concept must be a most important one. But in that case the father is represented twice over in the situation of primitive sacrifice: once as God and once as the totemic animal victim. And, even granting the restricted number of explanations open to psycho-analysis, one must ask whether this is possible and what sense it can have.

We know that there are a multiplicity of relations between the god and the sacred animal (the totem or the sacrificial victim). (1) Each god usually has an animal (and quite often several animals) sacred to him. (2) In the case of certain specially sacred sacrifices—"mystic" sacrifices—the victim was precisely the animal sacred to the god [Smith, 1894 (290)]. (3) The god was often worshipped in the shape of an animal (or, to look at it in another way, animals were worshipped

as gods) long after the age of totemism. (4) In myths the god often transforms himself into an animal, and frequently into the animal that is sacred to him.

It therefore seems plausible to suppose that the god himself was the totem animal, and that he developed out of it at a later stage of religious feeling. But we are relieved from the necessity for further discussion by the consideration that the totem is nothing other than a surrogate of the father. Thus, while the totem may be the *first* form of father-surrogate, the god will be a later one, in which the father has regained his human shape. A new creation such as this, derived from what constitutes the root of every form of religion—a longing for the father—might occur if in the process of time some fundamental change had taken place in man's relation to the father, and perhaps, too, in his relation to animals.

Signs of the occurrence of changes of this kind may easily be seen, even if we leave on one side the beginning of a mental estrangement from animals and the disrupting of totemism owing to domestication. . . . There was one factor in the state of affairs produced by the elimination of the father which was bound in the course of time to cause an enormous increase in the longing felt for him. Each single one of the brothers who had banded together for the purpose of killing their father was inspired by a wish to become like him and had given expression to it by incorporating parts of their father's surrogate in the totem meal. But, in consequence of the pressure exercised upon each participant by the fraternal clan as a whole, that wish could not be fulfilled. For the future no one could or might ever again attain the father's supreme power, even though that was what all of them had striven for. Thus after a long lapse of time their bitterness against their father, which had driven them to their deed, grew less, and their longing for him increased; and it became possible for an ideal to emerge which embodied the unlimited power of the primal father against whom they had once fought as well as their readiness to submit to him. As a result of decisive cultural changes, the original democratic equality that had prevailed among all the individual clansmen became untenable; and there developed at the same time an inclination, based on veneration felt for particular human individuals, to revive the ancient paternal ideal by creating gods. The notion of a man becoming a god or of a god dying strikes us to-day as shockingly presumptuous; but even in classical antiquity there was nothing revolting in it.[6] The elevation of the father who has once been murdered into a god from whom the clan claimed descent was a far more serious attempt at atonement than had been the ancient covenant with the totem.

I cannot suggest at what point in this process of development a place is to be found for the great mother-goddesses, who may perhaps in general have preceded the father-gods. It seems certain, however, that the change in attitude to the father was not restricted to the sphere of religion but that it extended in a consistent manner to that other side of human life which had been affected by the father's removal—to social organization. With the introduction of father-deities a fatherless society gradually changed into one organized on a patriarchal basis. The family was a restoration of the former primal horde and it gave back to fathers a large portion of their former rights. There were once more

[6]"To us moderns, for whom the breach which divides the human and the divine has deepened into an impassable gulf, such mimicry may appear impious, but it was otherwise with the ancients. To their thinking gods and men were akin, for many families traced their descent from a divinity, and the deification of a man probably seemed as little extraordinary to them as the canonization of a saint seems to a modern Catholic." (Frazer, 1911a, 2, 177f.)

fathers, but the social achievements of the fraternal clan had not been abandoned; and the gulf between the new fathers of a family and the unrestricted primal father of the horde was wide enough to guarantee the continuance of the religious craving, the persistence of an unappeased longing for the father.

We see, then, that in the scene of sacrifice before the god of the clan the father *is* in fact represented twice over— as the god and as the totemic animal victim. But in our attempts at understanding this situation we must beware of interpretations which seek to translate it in a two-dimensional fashion as though it were an allegory, and which in so doing forget its historical stratification. The twofold presence of the father corresponds to the two chronologically successive meanings of the scene. The ambivalent attitude towards the father has found a plastic expression in it, and so, too, has the victory of the son's affectionate emotions over his hostile ones. The scene of the father's vanquishment, of his greatest defeat, has become the stuff for the representation of his supreme triumph. The importance which is everywhere, without exception, ascribed to sacrifice lies in the fact that it offers satisfaction to the father for the outrage inflicted on him in the same act in which that deed is commemorated.

As time went on, the animal lost its sacred character, and the sacrifice lost its connection with the totem feast; it became a simple offering to the deity, an act of renunciation in favour of the god. God Himself had become so far exalted above mankind that He could only be approached through an intermediary—the priest. At the same time divine kings made their appearance in the social structure and introduced the patriarchal system into the state. It must be confessed that the revenge taken by the deposed and restored father was a harsh one: the dominance of authority was at its climax. The subjugated sons made use of the new situation in order to unburden themselves still further of their sense of guilt. They were no longer in any way responsible for the sacrifice as it now was. It was God Himself who demanded it and regulated it. This is the phase in which we find myths showing the god himself killing the animal which is sacred to him and which is in fact himself. Here we have the most extreme denial of the great crime which was the beginning of society and of the sense of guilt. But there is a second meaning to this last picture of sacrifice which is unmistakable. It expresses satisfaction at the earlier father-surrogate having been abandoned in favour of the superior concept of God. At this point the psycho-analytic interpretation of the scene coincides approximately with the allegorical, surface translation of it, which represents the god as overcoming the animal side of his own nature.[7]

Nevertheless it would be a mistake to suppose that the hostile impulses inherent in the father-complex were completely silenced during this period of revived paternal authority. On the contrary, the first phases of the dominance of the two new father-surrogates—gods and kings—show the most energetic signs of the ambivalence that remains a characteristic of religion.

In his great work, *The Golden Bough,* Frazer (1911*a*, 2, Chap. XVIII) puts forward the view that the earliest kings of the Latin tribes were foreigners who played the part of a god and were solemnly executed at a particular festival. The annual sacrifice (or, as a variant, self-sacrifice) of a god seems to have been an essential element in the Semitic religions. The ceremonials of human sacrifice, performed in the most different parts of the inhabited globe, leave very little doubt that the victims met their end as representatives of the deity; and these sacrificial rites can be traced into late times, with an inanimate effigy or puppet taking the place of the living human being. The theanthropic sacrifice of the god, into which it is unfortunately impossible for me to enter here as fully as into animal sacrifice, throws a searching retrospective light upon the meaning of the older forms of sacrifice. (Smith, 1894, 410f.) It confesses, with a frankness that could hardly be excelled, to the fact that the object of the act of sacrifice has always been the same—namely what is now worshipped as God, that is to say, the father. The problem of the relation between animal and human sacrifice thus admits of a simple solution. The original animal sacrifice was already a substitute for a human sacrifice—for the ceremonial killing of the father; so that, when the father-surrogate once more resumed its human shape, the animal sacrifice too could be changed back into a human sacrifice.

The memory of the first great act of sacrifice thus proved indestructible, in spite of every effort to forget it; and at the very point at which men sought to be at the farthest distance from the motives that led to it, its undistorted reproduction emerged in the form of the sacrifice of the god. I need not enlarge here upon the developments of religious thought which, in the shape of rationalizations, made this recurrence possible. Robertson Smith, who had no thought of our derivation of sacrifice from the great

---

[7]It is generally agreed that when, in mythologies, one generation of gods is overcome by another, what is denoted is the historical replacement of one religious system by a new one, whether as a result of foreign conquest or of psychological development. In the latter case myth approximates to what Silberer (1909) has described as "functional phenomena." (Cf. Freud, 1900*a*, *Standard Ed.,* 5, 503ff.) The view maintained by Jung (1912) that the god who kills the animal is a libidinal symbol implies a concept of libido other than that which has hitherto been employed and seems to me questionable from every point of view.

event in human prehistory, states that the ceremonies at the festivals in which the ancient Semites celebrated the death of a deity "were currently interpreted as the commemoration of a mythical tragedy" (*ibid.*, 413). "The mourning," he declares, "is not a spontaneous expression of sympathy with the divine tragedy, but obligatory and enforced by fear of supernatural anger. And a chief object of the mourners is to disclaim responsibility for the god's death—a point which has already come before us in connection with theanthropic sacrifices, such as the 'ox-murder at Athens.'" (*Ibid.*, 412.) It seems most probable that these "current interpretations" were correct and that the feelings of the celebrants were fully explained by the underlying situation.

Let us assume it to be a fact, then, that in the course of the later development of religions the two driving factors, the son's sense of guilt and the son's rebelliousness, never became extinct. Whatever attempt was made at solving the religious problem, whatever kind of reconciliation was effected between these two opposing mental forces, sooner or later broke down, under the combined influence, no doubt, of historical events, cultural changes and internal psychical modifications.

The son's efforts to put himself in the place of the father-god became ever more obvious. The introduction of agriculture increased the son's importance in the patriarchal family. He ventured upon new demonstrations of his incestuous libido, which found symbolic satisfaction in his cultivation of Mother Earth. Divine figures such as Attis, Adonis and Tammuz emerged, spirits of vegetation and at the same time youthful divinities enjoying the favours of mother goddesses and committing incest with their mother in defiance of their father. But the sense of guilt, which was not allayed by these creations, found expression in myths which granted only short lives to these youthful favourites of the mother-goddesses and decreed their punishment by emasculation or by the wrath of the father in the form of an animal. Adonis was killed by a wild boar, the sacred animal of Aphrodite; Attis, beloved of Cybele, perished by castration.[8] The mourning for these gods and the rejoicings over their resurrection passed over into the ritual of another son-deity who was destined to lasting success.

When Christianity first penetrated into the ancient world it met with competition from the religion of Mithras and for a time it was doubtful which of the two deities would gain the victory. In spite of the halo of light surrounding his form, the youthful Persian god remains obscure to us. We may perhaps infer from the sculptures of Mithras slaying a bull that he represented a son who was alone in sacrificing his father and thus redeemed his brothers from their burden of complicity in the deed. There was an alternative method of allaying their guilt and

[8]Fear of castration plays an extremely large part, in the case of the youthful neurotics whom we come across, as an interference in their relations with their father. The illuminating instance reported by Ferenczi (1913*a*) has shown us how a little boy took as his totem the beast that had pecked at his little penis. When our (Jewish) children come to hear of ritual circumcision, they equate it with castration. The parallel in social psychology to this reaction by children has not yet been worked out, so far as I am aware. In primaeval times and in primitive races, where circumcision is so frequent, it is performed at the age of initiation into manhood and it is at that age that its significance is to be found; it was only as a secondary development that it was shifted back to the early years of life. It is of very great interest to find that among primitive peoples circumcision is combined with cutting the hair and knocking out teeth or is replaced by them, and that our children, who cannot possibly have any knowledge of this, in fact treat these two operations, in the anxiety with which they react to them, as equivalents of castration.

this was first adopted by Christ. He sacrificed his own life and so redeemed the company of brothers from original sin.

The doctrine of original sin was of Orphic origin. It formed a part of the mysteries, and spread from them to the schools of philosophy of ancient Greece. (Reinach, 1905–12, 2, 75ff.) Mankind, it was said, were descended from the Titans, who had killed the young Dionysus-Zagreus and had torn him to pieces. The burden of this crime weighed on them. A fragment of Anaximander relates how the unity of the world was broken by a primaeval sin,[9] and that whatever issued from it must bear the punishment. The tumultuous mobbing, the killing and the tearing in pieces by the Titans reminds us clearly enough of the totemic sacrifice described by St. Nilus (*ibid.*, 2, 93)— as, for the matter of that, do many other ancient myths, including, for instance, that of the death of Orpheus himself. Nevertheless, there is a disturbing difference in the fact of the murder having been committed on a *youthful* god.

There can be no doubt that in the Christian myth the original sin was one against God the Father. If, however, Christ redeemed mankind from the burden of original sin by the sacrifice of his own life, we are driven to conclude that the sin was a murder. The law of talion, which is so deeply rooted in human feelings, lays it down that a murder can only be expiated by the sacrifice of another life: self-sacrifice points back to bloodguilt.[10] And if this sacrifice of a life brought about atonement with God the Father, the crime to be expiated can only have been the murder of the father.

In the Christian doctrine, therefore, men were acknowledging in the most undisguised manner the guilty primaeval deed, since they found the fullest atonement for it in the sacrifice of this one son. Atonement with the father was all the more complete since the sacrifice was accompanied by a total renunciation of the women on whose account the rebellion against the father was started. But at that point the inexorable psychological law of ambivalence stepped in. The very deed in which the son offered the greatest possible atonement to the father brought him at the same time to the attainment of his wishes *against* the father. He himself became God, beside, or, more correctly, in place of, the father. A son-religion displaced the father-religion. As a sign of this substitution the ancient totem meal was revived in the form of communion, in which the company of brothers consumed the flesh and blood of the son— no longer the father—obtained sanctity thereby and identified themselves with him. Thus we can trace through the ages the identity of the totem meal with animal sacrifice, with theanthropic human sacrifice and with the Christian Eucharist, and we can recognize in all these rituals the effect of the crime by which men were so deeply weighed down but of which they must none the less feel so proud. The Christian communion, however, is essentially a fresh elimination of the father, a repetition of the guilty deed. We can see the full justice of Frazer's pronouncement that "the Christian communion has absorbed within itself a sacrament which is doubtless far older than Christianity."[11]

---

[9] *Une sorte de péché proethnique* (Reinach, 1905–12, 2, 76).

[10] We find that impulses to suicide in a neurotic turn out regularly to be self-punishments for wishes for someone else's death.

[11] Frazer (1912, 2, 51). No one familiar with the literature of the subject will imagine that the derivation of Christian communion from the totem meal is an idea originating from the author of the present essay.

Robert N. Bellah

RELIGIOUS EVOLUTION

"Time in its aging course teaches all things."
—Aeschylus: *Prometheus Bound*

THOUGH one can name precursors as far back as Herodotus, the systematically scientific study of religion begins only in the second half of the 19th century. According to Chantepie de la Saussaye, the two preconditions for this emergence were that religion had become by the time of Hegel the object of comprehensive philosophical speculation and that history by the time of Buckle had been enlarged to include the history of civilization and culture in general.[1] In its early phases, partly under the influence of Darwinism, the science of religion was dominated by an evolutionary tendency already implicit in Hegelian philosophy and early 19th century historiography. The grandfathers of modern sociology, Comte and Spencer, contributed to the strongly evolutionary approach to the study of religion as, with many reservations, did Durkheim and Weber.

But by the third decade of the 20th century the evolutionary wave was in full retreat both in the general field of science

From *"Religious Evolution,"* American Sociological Review, XXIX (1964), No. 3, 358–74. A number of statements abbreviated here are qualified or expanded in the original version. By permission of the author and the American Sociological Association.

[1] Chantepie de la Saussaye, *Manuel d'Histoire des Religions,* French translation directed by H. Hubert and I. Levy, Paris: Colin, 1904, author's introduction.

of religion and in the sociology of religion in particular. Of course, this was only one aspect of the general retreat of evolutionary thought in social science, but nowhere did the retreat go further nor the intensity of the opposition to evolution go deeper than in the field of religion. . . .

Evolution at any system level I define as a process of increasing differentiation and complexity of organization which endows the organism, social system or whatever the unit in question may be, with greater capacity to adapt to its environment so that it is in some sense more autonomous relative to its environment than were its less complex ancestors. I do not assume that evolution is inevitable, irreversible or must follow any single particular course. Nor do I assume that simpler forms cannot prosper and survive alongside more complex forms. What I mean by evolution, then, is nothing metaphysical but the simple empirical generalization that more complex forms develop from less complex forms and that the properties and possibilities of more complex forms differ from those of less complex forms.

A brief handy definition of religion is considerably more difficult than a definition of evolution. . . . So, for limited purposes only, let me define religion as a set of symbolic forms and acts which relate man to the ultimate conditions of his existence. . . . Everything already exists in some sense in the religious symbol system of the most primitive man; it would be hard to find anything later that is not "foreshadowed" there, as for example, the monotheistic God is foreshadowed in the high gods of some primitive peoples. Yet just as obviously the two cannot be equated. Not only in their idea of God but in many other ways the monotheistic religions of Judaism, Christianity and Islam involve a much more differentiated symbolization of, and produce a much more complex relation to, the ultimate conditions of human existence than do primitive religions. At least the existence of that kind of difference is the thesis I wish to develop. . . .

Having defined the ground rules under which I am operating let me now step back from the subject of religious evolution and look first at a few of the massive facts of human religious history. The first of these facts is the emergence in the first millenium B.C. all across the Old World, at least in centers of high culture, of the phenomenon of religious rejection of the world characterized by an extremely negative evaluation of man and society and the exaltation of another realm of reality as alone true and infinitely valuable. This theme emerges in Greece through a long development into Plato's classic formulation in the Phaedo that the body is the tomb or prison of the soul and that only by disentanglement from the body and all things worldly can the soul unify itself with the unimaginably different world of the divine. A very different formulation is found in Israel, but there too the world is profoundly devalued in the face of the transcendent God with whom alone is there any refuge or comfort. In India we find perhaps the most radical of all versions of world rejection, culminating in the great image of the Buddha, that the world is a burning house and man's urgent need is a way to escape from it. In China, Taoist ascetics urged the transvaluation of all the accepted values and withdrawal from human society, which they condemned as unnatural and perverse.

Nor was this a brief or passing phenomenon. For over 2000 years great pulses of world rejection spread over the civilized world. The *Qur'an* compares this present world to vegetation after rain, whose growth rejoices the unbeliever, but it quickly withers away and becomes as straw.[2] Men prefer life in the present world but the life to come is infinitely superior—it alone is everlasting.[3] Even in Japan, usually so innocently world accepting, Shōtoku Taishi declared that the world is a lie and only the Buddha is true, and in the Kamakura period the conviction that the world is hell led to orgies of religious suicide by seekers after Amida's paradise.[4] And it is hardly necessary to quote Revelations or Augustine for comparable Christian sentiments. I do not deny that there are profound differences among these various rejections of the world; Max Weber has written a great essay on the different directions of world rejection and their consequences for human action.[5] But for the moment I want to concentrate on the fact that they were all in some sense rejections and that world rejection is characteristic of a long and important period of religious history. I want to insist on this fact because I want to contrast it with an equally striking fact—namely the virtual absence of world rejection in primitive religions, in religion prior to the first millenium B.C., and in the modern world.[6]

[2]*Qur'an* 57, 19–20.
[3]*Qur'an* 87, 16–17.
[4]On these developments, see Ienaga Saburo, *Nihon Shisōshi ni okeru Hitei no Ronri no Hattatsu* (The Development of the Logic of Negation in the History of Japanese Thought), Tokyo: 1940.
[5]Max Weber, "Religious Rejections of the World and Their Directions," in Hans H. Gerth and C. Wright Mills (eds.), *From Max Weber,* New York: Oxford University Press, 1946.
[6]One might argue that the much discussed modern phenomenon of alienation is the same as world rejection. The concept of alienation has too many uses to receive full discussion here, but

Primitive religions are on the whole oriented to a single cosmos—they know nothing of a wholly different world relative to which the actual world is utterly devoid of value. They are concerned with the maintenance of personal, social and cosmic harmony and with attaining specific goods—rain, harvest, children, health—as men have always been. But the overriding goal of salvation that dominates the world-rejecting religions is almost absent in primitive religion, and life after death tends to be a shadowy semi-existence in some vaguely designated place in the single world.

World rejection is no more characteristic of the modern world than it is of primitive religion. Not only in the United States but through much of Asia there is at the moment something of a religious revival, but nowhere is this associated with a great new outburst of world rejection. In Asia apologists, even for religions with a long tradition of world rejection, are much more interested in showing the compatibility of their religions with the developing modern world than in totally rejecting it. And it is hardly necessary to point out that the American religious revival stems from motives quite opposite to world rejection.

One could attempt to account for this sequence of presence and absence of world rejection as a dominant religious theme without ever raising the issue of religious evolution, but I think I can account for these and many other facts of the historical development of religion in terms of a scheme of religious evolution. . . .

The scheme is based on several presuppositions, the most basic of which I have already referred to: namely, that religious symbolization of what Geertz calls "the general order of existence"[7] tends to change over time, at least in some instances, in the direction of more differentiated, comprehensive, and in Weber's sense, more rationalized formulations. A second assumption is that conceptions of religious action, of the nature of the religious actor, of religious organization and of the place of religion in the society tend to change in ways systematically related to the changes in symbolization. A third assumption is that these several changes in the sphere of religion, which constitute what I mean by religious evolution, are related to a variety of other dimensions of change in other social spheres which define the general process of sociocultural evolution.

Now, for heuristic purposes at least, it is also useful to assume a series of stages which may be regarded as relatively stable crystallizations of roughly the same order of complexity along a number of different dimensions. I shall use five stages which, for want of better terminology, I shall call primitive, archaic, historic, early modern and modern. These stages are ideal types derived from a theoretical formulation of the most generally observable historical regularities; they are meant to have a temporal reference but only in a very general sense.

Of course the scheme itself is not intended as an adequate description of historical reality. Particular lines of religious development cannot simply be forced into the terms of the scheme. In reality there may be compromise formations involving elements from two stages which I have for theoretical reasons discriminated; earlier stages may, as I have already suggested, strikingly foreshadow later developments; and more

it usually implies estrangement from or rejection of only selected aspects of the empirical world. In the contemporary world a really radical alienation from the whole of empirical reality would be discussed more in terms of psychosis than religion.

[7]Clifford Geertz, "Religion as a Cultural System," unpublished, 1963.

developed may regress to less developed stages. And of course no stage is ever completely abandoned; all earlier stages continue to coexist with and often within later ones. . . .

Primitive Religion

My description of a primitive stage of religion is a theoretical abstraction, but it is heavily indebted to the work of Lévy-Bruhl and Stanner for its main features.[8]

The *religious symbol system* at the primitive level is characterized by Lévy-Bruhl as "*le monde mythique,*" and Stanner directly translates the Australians' own word for it as "the Dreaming." The Dreaming is a time out of time, or in Stanner's words, "everywhen," inhabited by ancestral figures, some human, some animal.[9] Though they are often of heroic proportions and have capacities beyond those of ordinary men as well as being the progenitors and creators of many particular things in the world, they are not gods, for they do not control the world and are not worshipped.[10]

Two main features of this mythical

world of primitive religion are important for the purposes of the present theoretical scheme. The first is the very high degree to which the mythical world is related to the detailed features of the actual world. Not only is every clan and local group defined in terms of the ancestral progenitors and the mythical events of settlement, but virtually every mountain, rock and tree is explained in terms of the actions of mythical beings. All human action is prefigured in the Dreaming, including crimes and folly, so that actual existence and the paradigmatic myths are related in the most intimate possible way. The second main feature, not unrelated to the extreme particularity of the mythical material, is the fluidity of its organization. . . . The fluid structure of the myth is almost consciously indicated by the Australians in their use of the word Dreaming: this is not purely metaphorical, for as Ronald Berndt has shown in a careful study, men do actually have a propensity to dream during the periods of cult performance. Through the dreams they reshape the cult symbolism for private psychic ends and what is even more interesting, dreams may actually lead to a reinterpretation in myth which in turn causes a ritual innovation.[11] Both the particularity and the fluidity, then, help account for the hovering closeness of the world of myth to the actual world. A sense of gap, that things are not all they might be, is there but it is hardly experienced as tragic and is indeed on the verge of being comic.[12]

Primitive *religious action* is characterized not, as we have said, by worship, nor, as we shall see, by sacrifice, but by identification, "participation," acting-out. Just as the primitive symbol system is myth *par excellence,* so primitive religious action

[8]Of Stanner's publications the most relevant are a series of articles published under the general title "On Aboriginal Religion" in *Oceania,* 30 to 33 (1959–1963), and "The Dreaming" in T.A.G. Hungerford (ed.), *Australian Signpost,* Melbourne: Cheshire, 1956, and reprinted in William Lessa and Evon Z. Vogt (eds.), *Reader in Comparative Religion,* Evanston, Illinois: Row, Peterson, 1958. (References to "The Dreaming" are to the Lessa and Vogt volume.) Outside the Australian culture area the new world provides the most examples of the type of religion I call primitive. Navaho religion, for example, conforms closely to the type.

[9]"The Dreaming," p. 514.

[10]This is a controversial point. For extensive bibliography see Mircea Eliade, *Patterns in Comparative Religion,* New York: Sheed and Ward, 1958, p. 112. Eliade tends to accept the notion of high gods in Australia, but Stanner says of the two figures most often cited as high gods: "Not even by straining can one see in such culture heroes as Baiame and Darumulum the true hint of a Yahveh, jealous, omniscient and omnipotent." "The Dreaming," p. 518.

[11]Ronald Berndt, *Kunapipi,* Melbourne: Cheshire, 1951, pp. 71–84.

[12]Stanner, "On Aboriginal Religion I," *Oceania,* 30 (December, 1959), p. 126; Godfrey Lienhardt, *Divinity and Experience,* London: Oxford University Press, 1961, p. 53.

is ritual *par excellence*. In the ritual the participants become identified with the mythical beings they represent. The mythical beings are not addressed or propitiated or beseeched. The distance between man and mythical being, which was at best slight, disappears altogether in the moment of ritual when everywhen becomes now. There are no priests and no congregation, no mediating representative roles and no spectators. All present are involved in the ritual action itself and have become one with the myth. . . .

At the primitive level *religious organization* as a separate social structure does not exist. Church and society are one. Religious roles tend to be fused with other roles, and differentiations along lines of age, sex and kin group are important. While women are not as excluded from the religious life as male ethnographers once believed, their ritual life is to some degree separate and focused on particularly feminine life crises.[13] In most primitive societies age is an important criterion for leadership in the ceremonial life. Ceremonies are often handed down in particular moieties and clans, as is only natural when the myths are so largely concerned with ancestors. Specialized shamans or medicine men are found in some tribes but are not a necessary feature of primitive religion.

As for the *social implications* of primitive religion, Durkheim's analysis seems still to be largely acceptable.[14] The ritual life does reinforce the solidarity of the society and serves to induct the young into the norms of tribal behavior. We should not forget the innovative aspects of primitive religion, that particular myths and ceremonies are in a process of constant revision and alteration, and that in the face of severe historic crisis rather remarkable reformulations of primitive material can be made.[15] Yet on the whole the religious life is the strongest reinforcement of the basic tenet of Australian philosophy, namely that life, as Stanner puts it, is a "one possibility thing." The very fluidity and flexibility of primitive religion is a barrier to radical innovation. Primitive religion gives little leverage from which to change the world.

Archaic Religion

For purposes of the present conceptual scheme, as I have indicated, I am using primitive religion in an unusually restricted sense. Much that is usually classified as primitive religion would fall in my second category, archaic religion, which includes the religious systems of much of Africa and Polynesia and some of the New World, as well as the earliest religious systems of the ancient Middle East, India and China. The characteristic feature of archaic religion is the emergence of true cult with the complex of gods, priests, worship, sacrifice and in some cases divine or priestly kingship. The myth and ritual complex characteristic of primitive religion continues within the structure of archaic religion, but it is systematized and elaborated in new ways.

In the archaic *religious symbol system* mythical beings are much more definitely characterized. Instead of being great paradigmatic figures with whom men in ritual identify but with whom they do not really interact, the mythical beings are more objectified, conceived as actively and sometimes willfully controlling the natural and human world, and as beings with whom men must deal in a definite and purposive way—in a word they have become gods. Relations among the gods are a matter of considerable speculation

[13]Catherine Berndt, *Women's Changing Ceremonies in Northern Australia,* Paris: Herman, 1950.

[14]Emile Durkheim, *The Elementary Forms of the Religious Life,* Glencoe, Illinois: The Free Press, 1947.

[15]Anthony Wallace, "Revitalization Movements," *American Anthropologist,* 58 (April, 1956), pp. 264–279.

and systematization, so that definite principles of organization, especially hierarchies of control, are established. The basic world view is still, like the primitives', monistic. There is still only one world with gods dominating particular parts of it, especially important being the high gods of the heavenly regions whose vision, knowledge and power may be conceived as very extensive indeed.[16] But though the world is one it is far more differentiated, especially in a hierarchical way, than was the monistic world view of the primitives: archaic religions tend to elaborate a vast cosmology in which all things divine and natural have a place. Much of the particularity and fluidity characteristic of primitive myth is still to be found in archaic religious thinking. But where priestly roles have become well established a relatively stable symbolic structure may be worked out and transmitted over an extended period of time. Especially where at least craft literacy[17] has been attained, the mythical tradition may become the object of critical reflection and innovative speculation which can lead to new developments beyond the nature of archaic religion.

Archaic *religious action* takes the form of cult in which the distinction between men as subjects and gods as objects is much more definite than in primitive religion. Because the division is sharper the need for a communication system through which gods and men can interact is much more acute. Worship and especially sacrifice are precisely such communication systems, as Henri Hubert and Marcel Mauss so brilliantly established in their great essay on sacrifice.[18] There is no space here for a technical analysis of the sacrificial process;[19] suffice it to say that a double identification of priest and victim with both gods and men effects a transformation of motives comparable to that referred to in the discussion of primitive religious action. The main difference is that instead of a relatively passive identification in an all-encompassing ritual action, the sacrificial process, no matter how stereotyped, permits the human communicants a greater element of intentionality and entails more uncertainty relative to the divine response. Through this more differentiated form of religious action a new degree of freedom as well, perhaps, as an increased burden of anxiety enters the relations between man and the ultimate conditions of his existence.

Archaic *religious organization* is still by and large merged with other social structures, but the proliferation of functionally and hierarchically differentiated groups leads to a multiplication of cults, since every group in archaic society tends to have its cultic aspect. The emergence of a two-class system, itself related to the increasing density of population made possible by agriculture, has its religious aspect. The upper-status group, which tends to monopolize political and military power, usually claims a superior religious status as well. Noble families are proud of their divine descent and often have special priestly functions. The divine king who is the chief link between his people and the gods is only the extreme case of the general tendency of archaic societies. Specialized priesthoods attached to cult centers may differentiate

[16]Raffaele Pettazzoni, *The All-Knowing God,* London: Methuen, 1956.

[17]By "craft literacy" I mean the situation in which literacy is limited to specially trained scribes and is not a capacity generally shared by the upper-status group. For an interesting discussion, see Eric Havelock, *Preface to Plato,* Cambridge: Harvard University Press, 1963.

[18]Henri Hubert and Marcel Mauss, "Essai sur la nature et la fonction du Sacrifice," *L'Année Sociologique,* 2 (1899).

[19]Two outstanding recent empirical studies are E. E. Evans-Pritchard, *Nuer Religion,* London: Oxford, 1956, esp. chs. 8 through 11, and Godfrey Lienhardt, *op. cit.,* esp. chs. 7 and 8.

out but are usually kept subordinate to the political elite, which at this stage never completely divests itself of religious leadership. Occasionally priesthoods at cult centers located interstitially relative to political units—for example, Delphi in ancient Greece—may come to exercise a certain independence.

The most significant limitation on archaic religious organization is the failure to develop differentiated religious collectivities including adherents as well as priests. The cult centers provide facilities for sacrifice and worship to an essentially transient clientele which is not itself organized as a collectivity, even though the priesthood itself may be rather tightly organized. The appearance of mystery cults and related religious confraternities in the ancient world is usually related to a reorganization of the religious symbol and action systems which indicates a transition to the next main type of religious structure.

The *social implications* of archaic religion are to some extent similar to those of primitive religion. The individual and his society are seen as merged in a natural-divine cosmos. Traditional social structures and social practices are considered to be grounded in the divinely instituted cosmic order and there is little tension between religious demand and social conformity. Indeed, social conformity is at every point reinforced with religious sanction. Nevertheless the very notion of well characterized gods acting over against men with a certain freedom introduces an element of openness that is less apparent at the primitive level. The struggle between rival groups may be interpreted as the struggle between rival deities or as a deity's change of favor from one group to another. Through the problems posed by religious rationalization of political change new modes of religious thinking may open up. This is clearly an important aspect of the early history of Israel, and it occurred in many

other cases as well. The Greek preoccupation with the relation of the gods to the events of the Trojan War gave rise to a continuous deepening of religious thought from Homer to Euripides. In ancient China the attempt of the Chou to rationalize their conquest of the Shang led to an entirely new conception of the relation between human merit and divine favor. The breakdown of internal order led to messianic expectations of the coming of a savior king in such distant areas as Egypt on the one hand and Chou-period China on the other. These are but a few of the ways in which the problems of maintaining archaic religious symbolization in increasingly complex societies drove toward solutions that began to place the archaic pattern itself in jeopardy.

Historic Religion

The next stage in this theoretical scheme is called historic simply because the religions included are all relatively recent; they emerged in societies that were more or less literate and so have fallen chiefly under the discipline of history rather than that of archaeology or ethnography. The criterion that distinguishes the historic religions from the archaic is that the historic religions are all in some sense transcendental. The cosmological monism of the earlier stage is now more or less completely broken through and an entirely different realm of universal reality, having for religious man the highest value, is proclaimed. The discovery of an entirely different realm of religious reality seems to imply a derogation of the value of the given empirical cosmos: at any rate the world rejection discussed above is, in this stage for the first time, a general characteristic of the religious system.

The *symbol systems* of the historic religions differ greatly among themselves but share the element of transcendentalism which sets them off from the archaic religions; in this sense they are all dualistic. The strong emphasis on hierarchical ordering characteristic of archaic religions continues to be stressed in most of the historic religions. Not only is the supernatural realm "above" this world in terms of both value and control but both the supernatural and earthly worlds are themselves organized in terms of a religiously legitimated hierarchy. For the masses, at least, the new dualism is above all expressed in the difference between this world and the life after death. Religious concern, focused on this life in primitive and archaic religions, now tends to focus on life in the other realm, which may be either infinitely superior or, under certain circumstances, with the emergence of various conceptions of hell, infinitely worse. Under these circumstances the religious goal of salvation (or enlightenment, release and so forth) is for the first time the central religious preoccupation.

In one sense historic religions represent a great "demythologization" relative to archaic religions. The notion of the one God who has neither court nor relatives, who has no myth himself and who is the sole creator and ruler of the universe, the notion of self-subsistent being, or of release from the cycle of birth and rebirth, are all enormous simplifications of the ramified cosmologies of archaic religions. Yet all the historic religions have, to use Voegelin's term, mortgages imposed on them by the historical circumstances of their origin. All of them contain, in suspension as it were, elements of archaic cosmology alongside their transcendental assertions. Nonetheless, relative to earlier forms the historic religions are all universalistic. From the point of view of these religions a man is no longer defined chiefly in terms of what tribe or clan he comes from or what particular god he serves but

rather as a being capable of salvation. That is to say that it is for the first time possible to conceive of man as such.

Religious action in the historic religions is thus above all action necessary for salvation. Even where elements of ritual and sacrifice remain prominent they take on a new significance. In primitive ritual the individual is put in harmony with the natural divine cosmos. His mistakes are overcome through symbolization as part of the total pattern. Through sacrifice archaic man can make up for his failures to fulfill his obligations to men or gods. He can atone for particular acts of unfaithfulness. But historic religion convicts man of a basic flaw far more serious than those conceived of by earlier religions. According to Buddhism, man's very nature is greed and anger from which he must seek a total escape. For the Hebrew prophets, man's sin is not particular wicked deeds but his profound heedlessness of God, and only a turn to complete obedience will be acceptable to the Lord. For Muhammad the *kafir* is not, as we usually translate, the "unbeliever" but rather the ungrateful man who is careless of the divine compassion. For him, only Islam, willing submission to the will of God, can bring salvation.

The identity diffusion characteristic of both primitive and archaic religions is radically challenged by the historic religious symbolization, which leads for the first time to a clearly structured conception of the self. Devaluation of the empirical world and the empirical self highlights the conception of a responsible self, a core self or a true self, deeper than the flux of everyday experience, facing a reality over against itself, a reality which has a consistency belied by the fluctuations of mere sensory impressions.[20] Primitive man can only ac-

[20]Buddhism, with its doctrine of the ultimate non-existence of the self, seems to be an exception to this generalization, but for practical and

cept the world in its manifold givenness. Archaic man can through sacrifice fulfill his religious obligations and attain peace with the gods. But the historic religions promise man for the first time that he can understand the fundamental structure of reality and through salvation participate actively in it. The opportunity is far greater than before but so is the risk of failure.

Perhaps partly because of the profound risks involved the ideal of the religious life in the historic religions tends to be one of separation from the world. Even when, as in the case of Judaism and Islam, the religion enjoins types of worldly participation that are considered unacceptable or at least doubtful in some other historic religions, the devout are still set apart from ordinary worldlings by the massive collections of rules and obligations to which they must adhere. The early Christian solution, which, unlike the Buddhist, did allow the full possibility of salvation to the layman, nevertheless in its notion of a special state of religious perfection idealized religious withdrawal from the world. In fact the standard for lay piety tended to be closeness of approximation to the life of the religious.

Historic religion is associated with the emergence of differentiated religious collectivities as the chief characteristic of its *religious organization*. The profound dualism with respect to the conception of

reality is also expressed in the social realm. The single religio-political hierarchy of archaic society tends to split into two at least partially independent hierarchies, one political and one religious. Together with the notion of a transcendent realm beyond the natural cosmos comes a new religious elite that claims direct relation to the transmundane world. Even though notions of divine kingship linger on for a very long time in various compromise forms, it is no longer possible for a divine king to monopolize religious leadership. With the emergence of a religious elite alongside the political one the problem of legitimizing political power enters a new phase. Legitimation now rests upon a delicate balance of forces between the political and religious leadership. But the differentiation between religious and political that exists most clearly at the level of leadership tends also to be pushed down into the masses so that the roles of believer and subject become distinct. Even where, as in the case of Islam, this distinction was not supported by religious norms, it was soon recognized as an actuality.

The emergence of the historic religions is part of a general shift from the two-class system of the archaic period to the four-class system characteristic of all the great historic civilizations up to modern times: a political-military elite, a cultural-religious elite, a rural lower-status group (peasantry) and an urban lower-status group (merchants and artisans). Closely associated with the new religious developments was the growth of literacy among the elite groups and in the upper segments of the urban lower class. Other social changes, such as the growth in the market resulting from the first widespread use of coinage, the development of bureaucracy and law as well as new levels of urbanization, are less directly associated with religion but are part of the same great transformation that got underway in the first millenium

---

ethical purposes, at least, a distinction between the true self and the empirical self is made by all schools of Buddhism. Some schools of Mahayana Buddhism give a metaphysical basis to a notion of "basic self" or "great self" as opposed to the merely selfish self caught up in transience and desire. Further it would seem that *nirvana,* defined negatively so as rigorously to exclude any possibility of transience or change, serves fundamentally as an identity symbol. Of course the social and psychological consequences of this kind of identity symbol are very different from those following from other types of identity symbolization.

B.C. The distinction between religious and political elites applies to some extent to the two great lower strata. From the point of view of the historic religions the peasantry long remained relatively intractable and were often considered religiously second-class citizens, their predilection for cosmological symbolization rendering them always to some degree religiously suspect. The notion of the peasant as truly religious is a fairly modern idea. On the contrary it was the townsman who was much more likely to be numbered among the devout, and Max Weber has pointed out the great fecundity of the urban middle strata in religious innovations throughout the several great historical traditions.[21] Such groups developed new symbolizations that sometimes threatened the structure of the historic religions in their early form, and in the one case where a new stage of religious symbolization was finally achieved they made important contributions.

The *social implications* of the historic religions are implicit in the remarks on religious organization. The differentiation of a religious elite brought a new level of tension and a new possibility of conflict and change onto the social scene. Whether the confrontation was between Israelite prophet and king, Islamic ulama and sultan, Christian pope and emperor or even between Confucian scholar-official and his ruler, it implied that political acts could be judged in terms of standards that the political authorities could not finally control. . . . Religion, then, provided the ideology and social cohesion for many rebellions and reform movements in the historic civilizations, and consequently played a more dynamic and especially a more purposive role in social change than had previously been possible. On the other hand, we should not forget that in most of the

historic civilizations for long periods of time religion performed the functions we have noted from the beginning: legitimation and reinforcement of the existing social order.

Early Modern Religion

. . . The defining characteristic of early modern religion is the collapse of the hierarchical structuring of both this and the other world. The dualism of the historic religions remains as a feature of early modern religion but takes on a new significance in the context of more direct confrontation between the two worlds. Under the new circumstances salvation is not to be found in any kind of withdrawal from the world but in the midst of worldly activities. Of course elements of this existed in the historic religions from the beginning, but on the whole the historic religions as institutionalized had offered a mediated salvation. Either conformity to religious law, or participation in a sacramental system or performance of mystical exercises was necessary for salvation. All of these to some extent involved a turning away from the world. Further, in the religious two-class systems characteristic of the institutionalized historic religions the upper-status groups, the Christian monks or Sufi shaykhs or Buddhist ascetics, could through their pure acts and personal charisma store up a fund of grace that could then be shared with the less worthy. In this way too salvation was mediated rather than immediate. What the Reformation did was in principle, with the usual reservations and mortgages to the past, break through the whole mediated system of salvation and declare salvation potentially available to any man no matter what his station or calling might be.

Since immediate salvation seems implicit in all the historic religions it is not

[21]Max Weber, *The Sociology of Religion,* Boston: Beacon, 1963, pp. 95–98, etc.

surprising that similar reform movements exist in other traditions, notably Shinran Shonin's version of Pure Land Buddhism but also certain tendencies in Islam, Buddhism, Taosim and Confucianism. But the Protestant Reformation is the only attempt that was successfully institutionalized. In the case of Taoism and Confucianism the mortgage of archaic symbolization was so heavy that what seemed a new breakthrough easily became regressive. In the other cases, notably in the case of the Jōdo Shinshū, the radical implications were not sustained and a religion of mediated salvation soon reasserted itself. Religious movements of early modern type may be emerging in a number of the great traditions today, perhaps even in the Vatican Council, and there are also secular movements with features strongly analogous to what I call early modern religion. . . .

Early modern *religious symbolism* concentrates on the direct relation between the individual and transcendent reality. A great deal of the cosmological baggage of medieval Christianity is dropped as superstition. The fundamentally ritualist interpretation of the sacrament of the Eucharist as a re-enactment of the paradigmatic sacrifice is replaced with the anti-ritualist interpretation of the Eucharist as a commemoration of a once-and-for-all historical event. . . .

Religious action was now conceived to be identical with the whole of life. Special ascetic and devotional practices were dropped as well as the monastic roles that specialized in them and instead the service of God became a total demand in every walk of life. The stress was on faith, an internal quality of the person, rather than on particular acts clearly marked "religious." In this respect the process of identity unification that I have designated as a central feature of the historic religions advanced still further. The complex requirements for the attainment of salvation in the historic religions, though ideally they encouraged identity unification, could themselves become a new form of identity diffusion, as Luther and Shinran were aware. Assertion of the capacity for faith as an already received gift made it possible to undercut that difficulty. It also made it necessary to accept the ambiguity of human ethical life and the fact that salvation comes in spite of sin, not in its absolute absence. With the acceptance of the world not as it is but as a valid arena in which to work out the divine command, and with the acceptance of the self as capable of faith in spite of sin, the Reformation made it possible to turn away from world rejection in a way not possible in the historic religions. All of this was possible, however, only within the structure of a rigid orthodoxy and a tight though voluntaristic religious group.

I have already noted that early modern religion abandoned hierarchy as an essential dimension of its religious symbol system.[22] It did the same in its *religious organization*. Not only did it reject papal authority, but it also rejected the old form of the religious distinction between two levels of relative religious perfection. This was replaced with a new kind of religious two-class system: the division between elect and reprobates. The new form differed from the old one in that the elect were really a vanguard

[22]God, of course, remains hierarchically superior to man, but the complex stratified structure of which purgatory, saints, angels, and so on, are elements is eliminated. Also, the strong reassertion of covenant thinking brought a kind of formal equality into the God-man relation without eliminating the element of hierarchy. Strictly speaking then, early modern (and modern) religion does not abandon the idea of hierarchy as such, but retains it in a much more flexible form, relative to particular contexts, and closely related to new emphases on equality. What is abandoned is rather a single overarching hierarchy, summed up in the symbol of the great chain of being.

group in the fulfillment of the divine
plan rather than a qualitative religious
elite. . . . In fact the Reformation is part
of the general process of social change in
which the four-class system of peasant
societies began to break up in Europe.
Especially in the Anglo-Saxon world,
Protestantism greatly contributed to its
replacement by a more flexible multi-
centered mode of social organization
based more on contract and voluntary
association. Both church and state lost
some of the reified significance they had
in medieval times and later on the continent. The roles of church member and
citizen were but two among several.
Both church and state had their delimited spheres of authority, but with the
full institutionalization of the common
law neither had a right to dominate each
other or the whole of society. Nonetheless, the church acted for a long time as a
sort of cultural and ethical holding company, and many developments in philosophy, literature and social welfare took
their initiative from clerical or church
groups. . . .[23]

Whereas in most of the historic
civilizations religion stands as virtually
the only stable challenger to the
dominance of the political elite, in the
emerging early modern society religious
impulses give rise to a variety of institutional structures, from the beginning or
very soon becoming fully secular, which
stand beside and to some extent compete

with and limit the state. The direct
religious response to political and moral
problems does not disappear but the
impact of religious orientations on society
is also mediated by a variety of worldly
institutions in which religious values have
been expressed. . . .

In the early modern stage for the first
time pressures to social change in the
direction of greater realization of religious values are actually institutionalized
as part of the structure of the society
itself. The self-revising social order expressed in a voluntaristic and democratic
society can be seen as just such an outcome. The earliest phase of this development, especially the several examples of
Calvinist commonwealths, was voluntaristic only within the elect vanguard
group and otherwise was often illiberal
and even dictatorial. The transition toward a more completely democratic
society was complex and subject to many
blockages. Close analogies to the early
modern situation occur in many of the
contemporary developing countries,
which are trying for the first time to
construct social systems with a built-in
tendency to change in the direction of
greater value realization. The leadership
of these countries varies widely between
several kinds of vanguard revolutionary
movements with distinctly illiberal
proclivities to elites committed to the
implementation of a later, more democratic, model of Western political society.

[23]Of course, important developments in
modern culture stemming from the recovery of
Classical art and philosophy in the Renaissance
took place outside the main stream of religious
development. However, the deep interrelations
between religious and secular components of the
Renaissance should not be overlooked. Certainly the clergy in the Anglo-Saxon world were
among the foremost guardians of the Classical
tradition in literature and thought. The most
tangible expression of this was the close relation
of higher education to the church, a relation
which was not seriously weakened until the late
19th century in America.

Modern Religion

I am not sure whether in the long run
what I call early modern religion will
appear as a stage with the same degree of
distinctness as the others I have distinguished or whether it will appear only as
a transitional phase, but I am reasonably
sure that, even though we must speak
from the midst of it, the modern situation
represents a stage of religious develop-

ment in many ways profoundly different from that of historic religion. The central feature of the change is the collapse of the dualism that was so crucial to all the historic religions.

It is difficult to speak of a *modern religious symbol system*. It is indeed an open question whether there can be a religious symbol system analogous to any of the preceding ones in the modern situation, which is characterized by a deepening analysis of the very nature of symbolization itself. At the highest intellectual level I would trace the fundamental break with traditional historic symbolization to the work of Kant. By revealing the problematic nature of the traditional metaphysical basis of all the religions and by indicating that it is not so much a question of two worlds as it is of as many worlds as there are modes of apprehending them, he placed the whole religious problem in a new light. However simple the immediate result of his grounding religion in the structure of ethical life rather than in a metaphysics claiming cognitive adequacy, it nonetheless pointed decisively in the direction that modern religion would go. The entire modern analysis of religion, including much of the most important recent theology, though rejecting Kant's narrowly rational ethics, has been forced to ground religion in the structure of the human situation itself. In this respect the present paper is a symptom of the modern religious situation as well as an analysis of it. In the world view that has emerged from the tremendous intellectual advances of the last two centuries there is simply no room for a hierarchic dualistic religious symbol system of the classical historic type. This is not to be interpreted as a return to primitive monism: it is not that a single world has replaced a double one but that an infinitely multiplex one has replaced the simple duplex structure. It is not that life has become again a "one possibility thing" but that it has become an infinite possibility thing. The analysis of modern man as secular, materialistic, dehumanized and in the deepest sense areligious seems to me fundamentally misguided, for such a judgment is based on standards that cannot adequately gauge the modern temper.

Though it is central to the problems of modern religion, space forbids a review of the development of the modern analysis of religion on its scholarly and scientific side. I shall confine myself to some brief comments on directions of development within Protestant theology. In many respects Schliermacher is the key figure in early 19th century theology who saw the deeper implications of the Kantian breakthrough. The development of "liberal theology" in the later 19th century, partly on the basis of Schliermacher's beginnings, tended to fall back into Kant's overly rational limitations. Against this, Barth's reassertion of the power of the traditional symbolism was bound to produce a vigorous response, but unfortunately, due to Barth's own profound ambiguity on the ultimate status of dogma, the consequences were in part simply a regressive reassertion of the adequacy of the early modern theological formulation. By the middle of the 20th century, however, the deeper implications of Schliermacher's attempt were being developed in various ways by such diverse figures as Tillich, Bultmann and Bonhoeffer.[24] Tillich's assertion of "ecstatic naturalism," Bultmann's program of "demythologization" and Bonhoeffer's search for a "religionless Christianity," though they cannot be simply equated with each other are

[24]Paul Tillich, *The Courage to Be,* New Haven: Yale, 1952; Karl Jaspers and Rudolf Bultmann, *Myth and Christianity,* New York: Noonday, 1958; Dietrich Bonhoeffer, *Letters and Papers from Prison,* London: SCM Press, 1954. Numerous other works of these three theologians could be cited.

efforts to come to terms with the modern situation. Even on the Catholic side the situation is beginning to be recognized.

Interestingly enough, indications of the same general search for an entirely new mode of religious symbolization, though mostly confined to the Protestant West, also appear in that most developed of the non-Western countries, Japan. Uchimura Kanzō's non-church Christianity was a relatively early indication of a search for new directions and is being developed even further today. Even more interesting perhaps is the emergence of a similar development out of the Jōdo Shinshū tradition, at least in the person of Ienaga Saburo.[25] This example indeed suggests that highly "modern" implications exist in more than one strand of Mahayana Buddhism and perhaps several of the other great traditions as well. Although in my opinion these implications were never developed sufficiently to dominate a historical epoch as they did in the West in the last two centuries, they may well prove decisive in the future of these religions.

So far what I have been saying applies mainly to intellectuals, but at least some evidence indicates that changes are also occurring at the level of mass religiosity.[26] Behind the 96 per cent of Americans who

claim to believe in God[27] there are many instances of a massive reinterpretation that leaves Tillich, Bultmann and Bonhoeffer far behind. In fact, for many churchgoers the obligation of doctrinal orthodoxy sits lightly indeed, and the idea that all creedal statements must receive a personal reinterpretation is widely accepted. The dualistic world view certainly persists in the minds of many of the devout, but just as surely many others have developed elaborate and often pseudo-scientific rationalizations to bring their faith in its experienced validity into some kind of cognitive harmony with the 20th century world. The wave of popular response that some of the newer theology seems to be eliciting is another indication that not only the intellectuals find themselves in a new religious situation.[28]

To concentrate on the church in a discussion of the modern religious situation is already misleading, for it is precisely the characteristic of the new situation that the great problem of religion as I have defined it, the symbolization of man's relation to the ultimate conditions of his existence, is no longer the monopoly of any groups explicitly labeled religious. However much the development of Western Christianity may have led up to and in a sense created the modern religious situation, it just as obviously is no longer in control of it. Not only has any obligation of doctrinal orthodoxy been abandoned by the leading edge of modern culture, but every fixed position

---

[25]Robert N. Bellah, "Ienaga Saburo and the Search for Meaning in Modern Japan," in Marius Jansen (ed.), *Japanese Attitudes toward Modernization,* Princeton: Princeton University Press, 1965.

[26]There are a few scattered studies such as Gordon Allport, James Gillespie and Jacqueline Young, "The Religion of the Post-War College Student," *The Journal of Psychology,* 25 (January, 1948), pp. 3–33, but the subject does not lend itself well to investigation via questionnaires and brief interviews. Richard V. McCann in his Harvard doctoral dissertation, "The Nature and Varieties of Religious Change," 1955, utilized a much subtler approach involving depth interviewing and discovered a great deal of innovative reinterpretation in people from all walks of life. Unfortunately lack of control of sampling makes it impossible to generalize his results.

[27]Will Herberg, *Protestant, Catholic, Jew,* Garden City: Doubleday, 1955, p. 72.

[28]Bishop J.A.T. Robinson's *Honest to God,* Philadelphia: Westminster, 1963, which states in straightforward language the positions of some of the recent Protestant theologians mentioned above, has sold (by November, 1963) over 300,000 copies in England and over 71,000 in the United States with another 50,000 on order, and this in the first few months after publication. (Reported in *Christianity and Crisis,* 23 [November 11, 1963], p. 201.)

has become open to question in the process of making sense out of man and his situation. This involves a profounder commitment to the process I have been calling religious symbolization than ever before. The historic religions discovered the self; the early modern religion found a doctrinal basis on which to accept the self in all its empirical ambiguity; modern religion is beginning to understand the laws of the self's own existence and so to help man take responsibility for his own fate.

This statement is not intended to imply a simple liberal optimism, for the modern analysis of man has also disclosed the depths of the limitations imposed by man's situation. Nevertheless, the fundamental symbolization of modern man and his situation is that of a dynamic multidimensional self capable, within limits, of continual self-transformation and capable, again within limits, of remaking the world including the very symbolic forms with which he deals with it, even the forms that state the unalterable conditions of his own existence. Such a statement should not be taken to mean that I expect, even less that I advocate, some ghastly religion of social science. Rather I expect traditional religious symbolism to be maintained and developed in new directions, but with growing awareness that it is symbolism and that man in the last analysis is responsible for the choice of his symbolism. Naturally, continuation of the symbolization characteristic of earlier stages without any reinterpretation is to be expected among many in the modern world, just as it has occurred in every previous period.

Religious action in the modern period is, I think, clearly a continuation of tendencies already evident in the early modern stage. Now less than ever can man's search for meaning be confined to the church. But with the collapse of a clearly defined doctrinal orthodoxy and a religiously supported objective system of moral standards, religious action in the world becomes more demanding than ever. The search for adequate standards of action, which is at the same time a search for personal maturity and social relevance, is in itself the heart of the modern quest for salvation, if I may divest that word of its dualistic associations. How the specifically religious bodies are to adjust their time honored practices of worship and devotion to modern conditions is of growing concern in religious circles. Such diverse movements as the liturgical revival, pastoral psychology and renewed emphasis on social action are all efforts to meet the present need. Few of these trends have gotten much beyond the experimental but we can expect the experiments to continue.

In the modern situation as I have defined it, one might almost be tempted to see in Thomas Paine's "My mind is my church," or Thomas Jefferson's "I am a sect myself" the typical expression of *religious organization* in the near future. Nonetheless it seems unlikely that collective symbolization of the great inescapabilities of life will soon disappear. Of course the "free intellectual" will continue to exist as he has for millenia but such a solution can hardly be very general. Private voluntary religious association in the West achieved full legitimation for the first time in the early modern situation, but in the early stages especially, discipline and control within these groups was very intense. The tendency in more recent periods has been to continue the basic pattern but with a much more open and flexible pattern of membership. In accord with general trends I have already discussed, standards of doctrinal orthodoxy and attempts to enforce moral purity have largely been dropped. The assumption in most of the major Protestant denominations is that the church member can be considered responsible for himself. This trend seems likely to continue, with an increasingly fluid type of organization in which many special purpose subgroups form and disband. Rather than interpreting these trends as significant of indifference and secularization, I see in them the increasing acceptance of the notion that each individual must work out his own ultimate solutions and that the most the church can do is provide him a favorable environment for doing so, without imposing on him a prefabricated set of answers.[29] And it will be increasingly realized that answers to religious questions can validly be sought in various spheres of "secular" art and thought.

Here I can only suggest what I take to be the main *social implication* of the modern religious situation. Early modern society, to a considerable degree under religious pressure, developed, as we have seen, the notion of a self-revising social system in the form of a democratic society. But at least in the early phase of that development social flexibility was balanced against doctrinal (Protestant orthodoxy) and characterological (Puritan personality) rigidities. In a sense those rigidities were necessary to allow the flexibility to emerge in the social system, but it is the chief characteristic of the more recent modern phase that culture and personality themselves have come to be viewed as endlessly revisable. This has been characterized as a collapse of meaning and a failure of moral standards. No doubt the possibilities for pathological distortion in the modern situation are enormous. It remains to be seen whether the freedom modern society implies at the cultural and personality as well as the social level can be stably institutionalized in large-scale societies.

[29]The great Protestant stress on thinking for oneself in matters of religion is documented in Gerhard Lenski, *The Religious Factor,* Garden City, New York: Doubleday, 1961, pp. 270–273.

Yet the very situation that has been characterized as one of the collapse of meaning and the failure of moral standards can also, and I would argue more fruitfully, be viewed as one offering unprecedented opportunities for creative innovation in every sphere of human action.

Conclusion

The schematic presentation of the stages of religious evolution just concluded is based on the proposition that at each stage the freedom of personality and society has increased relative to the environing conditions. Freedom has increased because at each successive stage the relation of man to the conditions of his existence has been conceived as more complex, more open and more subject to change and development. The distinction between conditions that are really ultimate and those that are alterable becomes increasingly clear though never complete. Of course this scheme of religious evolution has implied at almost every point a general theory of social evolution, which has had to remain largely implicit.

Let me suggest in closing, as a modest effort at empirical testing, how the evolutionary scheme may help to explain the facts of alternating world acceptance and rejection which were noted near the beginning of the paper. I have argued that the world acceptance of the primitive and archaic levels is largely to be explained as the only possible response to a reality that invades the self to such an extent that the symbolizations of self and world are only very partially separate. The great wave of world rejection of the historic religions I have interpreted as a major advance in what Lienhardt calls "the differentiation between experience of the self and of the world which acts upon it." Only by withdrawing cathexis from the myriad objects of empirical reality could consciousness of a centered self in relation to an encompassing reality emerge. Early modern religion made it possible to maintain the centered self without denying the multifold empirical reality and so made world rejection in the classical sense unnecessary. In the modern phase knowledge of the laws of the formation of the self, as well as much more about the structure of the world, has opened up almost unlimited new directions of exploration and development. World rejection marks the beginning of a clear objectification of the social order and sharp criticism of it. In the earlier world-accepting phases religious conceptions and social order were so fused that it was almost impossible to criticize the latter from the point of view of the former. In the later phases the possibility of remaking the world to conform to value demands has served in a very different way to mute the extremes of world rejection. The world acceptance of the last two stages is shown in this analysis to have a profoundly different significance from that of the first two.

Construction of a wide-ranging evolutionary scheme like the one presented in this paper is an extremely risky enterprise. Nevertheless such efforts are justifiable if, by throwing light on perplexing developmental problems they contribute to modern man's efforts at self interpretation.

II

THE ESSENCE
OF
RELIGION

Religion as an Expression
of Historical, Social, and Personal Actualities

SECTION ONE

Religion as a Force of Historical and Social Stability: Its Discovery and Critique

Ludwig Feuerbach

THE TRUTH
OF RELIGION

WHAT we have hitherto been maintaining generally, even with regard to sensational impressions, of the relation between subject and object, applies especially to the relation between the subject and the religious object.

In the perceptions of the senses consciousness of the object is distinguishable from consciousness of self; but in religion, consciousness of the object and self-consciousness coincide. The object of the senses is out of man, the religious object is within him, and therefore as little forsakes him as his self-consciousness or his conscience; it is the intimate, the closest object. "God," says Augustine, for example, "is nearer, more related to us, and therefore more easily known by us, than sensible, corporeal things." The object of the senses is in itself indif-

From The Essence of Christianity (1841), London: 1854, pp. 12–14, 24–27, 29–31.

ferent—independent of the disposition or of the judgment; but the object of religion is a selected object; the most excellent, the first, the supreme being; it essentially presupposes a critical judgment, a discrimination between the divine and the non-divine, between that which is worthy of adoration and that which is not worthy. And here may be applied, without any limitation, the proposition: the object of any subject is nothing else than the subject's own nature taken objectively. Such as are a man's thoughts and dispositions, such is his God; so much worth as a man has, so much and no more has his God. Consciousness of God is self-consciousness, knowledge of God is self-knowledge. By his God thou knowest the man, and by the man his God; the two are identical. Whatever is God to a man, that is his heart and soul; and conversely, God is the manifested inward nature, the expressed self of a man,—religion the solemn unveiling of a man's hidden treasures, the revelation of his intimate thoughts, the open confession of his love-secrets.

But when religion—consciousness of God—is designated as the self-consciousness of man, this is not to be understood as affirming that the religious man is directly aware of this identity; for, on the contrary, ignorance of it is fundamental to the peculiar nature of religion. To preclude this misconception, it is better to say, religion is man's earliest and also indirect form of self-knowledge. Hence, religion everywhere precedes philosophy, as in the history of the race, so also in that of the individual. Man first of all sees his nature as if *out of* himself, before he finds it in himself. His own nature is in the first instance contemplated by him as that of another being. Religion is the childlike condition of humanity; but the child sees his nature—man—out of himself; in childhood a man is an object to himself, under the form of another man. Hence the historical progress of religion consists in this: that what by an earlier religion was regarded as objective, is now recognised as subjective; that is, what was formerly contemplated and worshipped as God is now perceived to be something *human*. What was at first religion becomes at a later period idolatry; man is seen to have adored his own nature. Man has given objectivity to himself, but has not recognised the object as his own nature: a later religion takes this forward step; every advance in religion is therefore a deeper self-knowledge. But every particular religion, while it pronounces its predecessors idolatrous, excepts itself—and necessarily so, otherwise it would no longer be religion—from the fate, the common nature of all religions; it imputes only to other religions what is the fault, if fault it be, of religion in general. Because it has a different object, a different tenour, because it has transcended the ideas of preceding religions, it er-

roneously supposes itself exalted above the necessary eternal laws which constitute the essence of religion—it fancies its object, its ideas, to be superhuman. But the essence of religion, thus hidden from the religious, is evident to the thinker, by whom religion is viewed objectively, which it cannot be by its votaries. And it is our task to show that the antithesis of divine and human is altogether illusory, that it is nothing else than the antithesis between the human nature in general, and the human individual: that, consequently, the object and contents of the Christian religion are altogether human.

Religion, at least the Christian, is the relation of man to himself, or more correctly to his own nature (*i.e.*, his subjective nature); but a relation to it, viewed as a nature apart from his own. The divine being is nothing else than the human being, or, rather the human nature purified, freed from the limits of the individual man, made objective—*i.e.*, contemplated and revered as another, a distinct being. All the attributes of the divine nature are, therefore, attributes of the human nature.

In relation to the attributes, the predicates, of the Divine Being, this is admitted without hesitation, but by no means in relation to the subject of these predicates. The negation of the subject is held to be irreligion, nay, atheism; though not so the negation of the predicates. But that which has no predicates or qualities, has no effect upon me; that which has no effect upon me, has no existence for me. To deny all the qualities of a being is equivalent to denying the being himself. A being without qualities is one which cannot become an object to the mind; and such a being is virtually non-existent. Where man deprives God of all qualities, God is no longer anything more to him than a negative being. To the truly religious man, God is not a being without qualities, because to him he is a positive, real being. The theory that God cannot be defined, and consequently cannot be known by man, is therefore the offspring of recent times, a product of modern unbelief. . . .

Now, when it is shown that what the subject is, lies entirely in the attributes of the subject; that is, that the predicate is the true subject; it is also proved that if the divine predicates are attributes of the human nature, the subject of those predicates is also of the human nature. But the divine predicates are partly general, partly personal. The general predicates are the metaphysical, but these serve only as external points of support to religion; they are not the characteristic definitions of religion. It is the personal predicates alone which constitute the essence of religion—in which the Divine Being is the object of religion. Such are, for example, that God is a Person, that he is the moral Law-giver, the Father of mankind, the Holy One, the Just, the Good, the Merciful. It is however at once clear, or it will at least be clear in the sequel, with regard to these and other definitions, that, especially as applied to a personality, they are purely human definitions, and that consequently man in religion—in his relation to God—is in relation to his own nature; for to the religious sentiment these predicates are not mere conceptions, mere images, which man forms of God, to be distinguished from that which God is in himself, but truths, facts, realities. Religion knows nothing of anthropomorphisms; to it they are not anthropomorphisms. It is the very essence of religion, that to it these definitions express the nature of God. They are pronounced to be images only by the understanding, which reflects on religion, and which while defending them yet before its own tribunal denies them. But to the religious sentiment God is a real Father, real Love and Mercy; for to it he is a real, living, personal being, and therefore his attributes are also

living and personal. Nay, the definitions which are the most sufficing to the religious sentiment, are precisely those which give the most offence to the understanding, and which in the process of reflection on religion it denies. Religion is essentially emotion; hence, objectively also, emotion is to it necessarily of a divine nature. Even anger appears to it an emotion not unworthy of God, provided only there be a religious motive at the foundation of this anger.

But here it is also essential to observe, and this phenomenon is an extremely remarkable one, characterising the very core of religion, that in proportion as the divine subject is in reality human, the greater is the apparent difference between God and man; that is, the more, by reflection on religion, by theology, is the identity of the divine and human denied, and the human, considered as such, is depreciated. The reason of this is, that as what is positive in the conception of the divine being can only be human, the conception of man, as an object of consciousness can only be negative. To enrich God, man must become poor; that God may be all, man must be nothing. But he desires to be nothing in himself, because what he takes from himself is not lost to him, since it is preserved in God. Man has his being in God; why then should he have it in himself? Where is the necessity of positing the same thing twice, of having it twice? What man withdraws from himself, what he renounces in himself, he only enjoys in an incomparably higher and fuller measure in God. . . .

And thus, in reality, whatever religion consciously denies—always supposing that what is denied by it is something essential, true, and consequently incapable of being ultimately denied—it unconsciously restores in God. Thus, in religion man denies his reason; of himself he knows nothing of God, his thoughts are only worldly, earthly; he can only believe what God reveals to him. But on this account the thoughts of God are human, earthly thoughts: like man, He has plans in His mind, he accommodates himself to circumstances and grades of intelligence, like a tutor with his pupils; he calculates closely the effect of his gifts and revelations; he observes man in all his doings; he knows all things, even the most earthly, the commonest, the most trivial. In brief, man in relation to God denies his own knowledge, his own thoughts, that he may place them in God. Man gives up his personality; but in return, God, the Almighty, infinite, unlimited being, is a person; he denies human dignity, the human *ego;* but in return God is to him a selfish, egoistical being, who in all things seeks only Himself, his own honour, his own ends; he represents God as simply seeking the satisfaction of his own selfishness, while yet He frowns on that of every other being; his God is the very luxury of egoism. Religion further denies goodness as a quality of human nature; man is wicked, corrupt, incapable of good; but on the other hand, God is only good— the Good Being. Man's nature demands as an object goodness, personified as God; but is it not hereby declared that goodness is an essential tendency of man? If my heart is wicked, my understanding perverted, how can I perceive and feel the holy to be holy, the good to be good? . . .

Man—this is the mystery of religion— projects his being into objectivity, and then again makes himself an object to this projected image of himself thus converted into a subject; he thinks of himself, is an object to himself, but as the object of an object, of another being than himself. Thus here. Man is an object to God. That man is good or evil is not indifferent to God; no! He has a lively, profound interest in man's being good; he wills that man should be good, happy —for without goodness there is no

happiness. Thus the religious man virtually retracts the nothingness of human activity, by making his dispositions and actions an object to God, by making man the end of God—for that which is an object to the mind is an end in action; by making the divine activity a means of human salvation. God acts, that man may be good and happy. Thus man, while he is apparently humiliated to the lowest degree, is in truth exalted to the highest. Thus, in and through God, man has in view himself alone. It is true that man places the aim of his action in God, but God has no other aim of action than the moral and eternal salvation of man: thus man has in fact no other aim than himself. The divine activity is not distinct from the human.

How could the divine activity work on me as its object, nay, work in me, if it were essentially different from me; how could it have a human aim, the aim of ameliorating and blessing man, if it were not itself human? Does not the purpose determine the nature of the act? When man makes his moral improvement an aim to himself, he has divine resolutions, divine projects; but also, when God seeks the salvation of man, He has human ends and a human mode of activity, corresponding to these ends. Thus in God man has only his own activity as an object. But, for the very reason that he regards his own activity as objective, goodness only as an object, he necessarily receives the impulse, the motive, not from himself, but from this object. He contemplates his nature as external to himself, and this nature as goodness; thus it is self-evident, it is mere tautology to say, that the impulse to good comes only from thence where he places the good.

God is the highest subjectivity of man abstracted from himself; hence man can do nothing of himself, all goodness comes from God. The more subjective God is, the more completely does man divest himself of his subjectivity, because God is, *per se,* his relinquished self, the possession of which he however again vindicates to himself. As the action of the arteries drives the blood into the extremities, and the action of the veins brings it back again, as life in general consists in a perpetual systole and diastole; so is it in religion. In the religious systole man propels his own nature from himself, he throws himself outward; in the religious diastole he receives the rejected nature into his heart again. God alone is the being who acts of himself,— this is the force of repulsion in religion; God is the being who acts in me, with me, through me, upon me, for me, is the principle of my salvation, of my good dispositions and actions, consequently my own good principle and nature,— this is the force of attraction in religion.

The course of religious development which has been generally indicated, consists specifically in this, that man abstracts more and more from God, and attributes more and more to himself. This is especially apparent in the belief in revelation. That which to a later age or a cultured people is given by nature or reason, is to an earlier age, or to a yet uncultured people, given by God. Every tendency of man, however natural —even the impulse to cleanliness, was conceived by the Israelites as a positive divine ordinance. From this example we again see that God is lowered, is conceived more entirely on the type of ordinary humanity, in proportion as man detracts from himself. How can the self-humiliation of man go further than when he disclaims the capability of fulfilling spontaneously the requirements of common decency? The Christian religion, on the other hand, distinguished the impulses and passions of man according to their quality, their character; it represented only good emotions, good dispositions, good thoughts, as revelations, operations—that is, as dispositions, feelings, thoughts,—of God; for what God reveals is a quality of God himself: that of which the heart is full, overflows the lips, as is the effect such is the cause, as the revelation, such the being who reveals himself. A God who reveals himself in good dispositions is a God whose essential attribute is only moral perfection. The Christian religion distinguishes inward moral purity from external physical purity; the Israelites identified the two. In relation to the Israelitish religion, the Christian religion is one of criticism and freedom. The Israelite trusted himself to do nothing except what was commanded by God; he was without will even in external things; the authority of religion extended itself even to his food. The Christian religion, on the other hand, in all these external things, made man dependent on himself, *i.e.,* placed in man what the Israelite placed out of himself, in God. Israel is the most complete presentation of positivism in religion. In relation to the Israelite, the Christian is an *esprit fort,* a free-thinker. Thus do things change. What yesterday was still religion, is no longer such to-day; and what to-day is atheism, to-morrow will be religion.

Karl Marx

THESES ON FEUERBACH

The chief defect of all hitherto existing materialism—that of Feuerbach included—is that the thing [*Gegenstand*], reality, sensuousness, is conceived only in the form of the *object* [*Objekt*] or of *contemplation* [*Anschauung*], but not as *human sensuous activity, practice,* not subjectively. Hence it happened that the *active* side, in contradistinction to materialism, was developed by idealism—but only abstractly, since, of course, idealism does not know real, sensuous activity as such. Feuerbach wants sensuous objects, really differentiated from the thought-objects, but he does not conceive human activity itself *as objective* [*gegenständliche*] activity. Hence, in the *Essence of Christianity,* he regards the theoretical attitude as the only genuinely human attitude, while practice is conceived and fixed only in its dirty-judaical form of appearance. Hence he does not grasp the significance of "revolutionary," of "practical-critical," activity.

The question whether objective [*gegenständliche*] truth can be attributed to human thinking is not a question of theory but a *practical* question. In practice man must prove the truth, that is, the reality and power, the this-sidedness [*Diesseitigkeit*] of his thinking. The dispute over the reality or non-reality of thinking which is isolated from practice is a purely *scholastic* question.

"*Theses on Feuerbach*" (1845), in K. Marx and F. Engels, On Religion. Moscow: 1957, pp. 69–72. By permission of Lawrence & Wishart Ltd., London.

The materialist doctrine that men are products of circumstances and upbringing, and that, therefore, changed men are products of other circumstances and changed upbringing, forgets that it is men that change circumstances and that the educator himself needs educating. Hence, this doctrine necessarily arrives at dividing society into two parts, of which one is superior to society (in Robert Owen, for example).

The coincidence of the changing of circumstances and of human activity can be conceived and rationally understood only as *revolutionizing practice.*

Feuerbach starts out from the fact of religious self-alienation, the duplication of the world into a religious, imaginary world and a real one. His work consists in the dissolution of the religious world into its secular basis. He overlooks the fact that after this work is completed the chief thing still remains to be done. For the fact that the secular foundation detaches itself from itself and establishes itself in the clouds as an independent realm is really only to be explained by the self-cleavage and self-contradictoriness of this secular basis. The latter must itself, therefore, first be understood in its contradiction, and then revolutionized in practice by the removal of the contradiction. Thus, for instance, once the earthly family is discovered to be the secret of the holy family, the former must then itself be criticized in theory and revolutionized in practice.

Feuerbach, not satisfied with *abstract thinking,* appeals to *sensuous contemplation;* but he does not conceive sensuousness as *practical,* human-sensuous activity.

Feuerbach resolves the religious essence into the *human* essence. But the human essence is no abstraction inherent in each single individual. In its reality it is the ensemble of the social relations.

Feuerbach, who does not enter upon a criticism of this real essence, is consequently compelled:

1. To abstract from the historical process and to fix the religious sentiment [*Gemüt*] as something by itself and to presuppose an abstract—*isolated*—human individual.

2. The human essence, therefore, can with him be comprehended only as "genius," as an internal, dumb generality which merely *naturally* unites the many individuals.

Feuerbach, consequently, does not see that the "religious sentiment" is itself a *social product,* and that the abstract individual whom he analyzes belongs in reality to a particular form of society.

Social life is essentially *practical.* All mysteries which mislead theory to mysticism find their rational solution in human practice and in the comprehension of this practice.

The highest point attained by *contemplative* materialism, that is, materialism which does not understand sensuousness as practical activity, is the contemplation of single individuals in "civil society."

The standpoint of the old materialism is "civil" society; the standpoint of the new is *human* society, or socialized humanity.

The philosophers have only *interpreted* the world, in various ways; the point, however, is to *change* it.

Karl Marx

RELIGIOUS ILLUSION
AND THE
TASK OF HISTORY

For Germany the *criticism of religion* is in the main complete, and criticism of religion is the premise of all criticism.

From "Contribution to the Critique of Hegel's Philosophy of Right" (1884), in K. Marx and F. Engels, On Religion. Moscow: 1957, pp. 41–42, 50–52. Permission of Lawrence & Wishart Ltd., London.

The *profane* existence of error, is discredited after its *heavenly oratio pro aris et focis*[1] has been rejected. Man, who looked for a superman in the fantastic reality of heaven and found nothing there but the

[1] Speech for the altars and hearths.—Ed.

reflexion of himself, will no longer be disposed to find but the *semblance* of himself, the non-human [*Unmensch*] where he seeks and must seek his true reality.

The basis of irreligious criticism is: *Man makes religion, religion does not make man.* In other words, religion is the self-consciousness and self-feeling of man who has either not yet found himself or has already lost himself again. But *man* is no abstract being squatting outside the world. Man is *the world of man,* the state, society. This state, this society, produce religion, *a reversed world-consciousness,* because they are a *reversed world.* Religion is the general theory of that world, its encyclopaedic compendium, its logic in a popular form, its spiritualistic *point d'honneur,* its enthusiasm, its moral sanction, its solemn completion, its universal ground for consolation and justification. It is the *fantastic realization* of the human essence because the *human essence* has no true reality. The struggle against religion is therefore mediately the fight against *the other world,* of which religion is the spiritual *aroma.*

Religious distress is at the same time the *expression* of real distress and the *protest* against real distress. Religion is the sigh of the oppressed creature, the heart of a heartless world, just as it is the spirit of a spiritless situation. It is the *opium* of the people.

The abolition of religion as the *illusory* happiness of the people is required for their *real* happiness. The demand to give up the illusions about its condition is the *demand to give up a condition which needs illusions.* The criticism of religion is therefore *in embryo the criticism of the vale of woe,* the *halo* of which is religion.

Criticism has plucked the imaginary flowers from the chain not so that man will wear the chain without any fantasy or consolation but so that he will shake off the chain and cull the living flower. The criticism of religion disillusions man

to make him think and act and shape his reality like a man who has been disillusioned and has come to reason, so that he will revolve round himself and therefore round his true sun. Religion is only the illusory sun which revolves round man as long as he does not revolve round himself.

The task of history, therefore, once the *world beyond the truth* has disappeared, is to establish the *truth of this world.* The immediate *task of philosophy,* which is at the service of history, once the *saintly form* of human self-alienation has been unmasked, is to unmask self-alienation in its *unholy forms.* Thus the criticism of heaven turns into the criticism of the earth, the *criticism of religion* into the *criticism of right* and the *criticism of theology* into the *criticism of politics....*

The weapon of criticism cannot, of course, replace criticism of the weapon, material force must be overthrown by material force; but theory also becomes a material force as soon as it has gripped the masses. Theory is capable of gripping the masses as soon as it demonstrates *ad hominem,* and it demonstrates *ad hominem* as soon as it becomes radical. To be radical is to grasp the root of the matter. But for the man the root is man himself. The evident proof of the radicalism of German theory, and hence of its practical energy, is that it proceeds from a resolute *positive* abolition of religion. The criticism of religion ends with the teaching that *man is the highest essence for man,* hence with the *categoric imperative to overthrow all relations* in which man is a debased, enslaved, abandoned, despicable essence, relations which cannot be better described than by the cry of a Frenchman when it was planned to introduce a tax on dogs: Poor dogs! They want to treat you as human beings!

Even historically, theoretical emancipation has specific practical significance for Germany. For Germany's *revolutionary* past is theoretical, it is the *Reformation.* As the revolution then began in the brain of the *monk,* so now it begins in the brain of the *philosopher.*

Luther, we grant, overcame bondage out of *devotion* by replacing it by bondage out of *conviction.* He shattered faith in authority because he restored the authority of faith. He turned priests into laymen because he turned laymen into priests. He freed man from outer religiosity because he made religiosity the inner man. He freed the body from chains because he enchained the heart.

But if Protestantism was not the true solution of the problem it was at least the true setting of it. It was no longer a case of the layman's struggle against the *priest outside himself* but of his struggle against *his own priest inside himself,* his *priestly nature.* And if the Protestant transformation of the German laymen into priests emancipated the lay popes, the *princes,* with the whole of their priestly clique, the privileged and philistines, the philosophical transformation of priestly Germans into men will emancipate the *people.* But *secularization* will not stop at the *confiscation of church estates* set in motion mainly by hypocritical Prussia any more than emancipation stops at princes. The Peasant War, the most radical fact of German history, came to grief because of theology. Today, when theology itself has come to grief, the most unfree fact of German history, our *status quo,* will be shattered against philosophy. On the eve of the Reformation official Germany was the most unconditional slave of Rome. On the eve of its revolution it is the unconditional slave of less than Rome, of Prussia and Austria, of country junkers and philistines.

Meanwhile, a major difficulty seems to stand in the way of a *radical* German revolution.

For revolutions require a *passive* element, a *material* basis. Theory is fulfilled in a people only insofar as it is the fulfilment of the needs of that people. But will the monstrous discrepancy between the demands of German thought and the answers of German reality find a corresponding discrepancy between civil society and the state and between civil society and itself? Will the theoretical needs be immediate practical needs? It is not enough for thought to strive for realization, reality must itself strive towards thought.

But Germany did not rise to the intermediary stage of political emancipation at the same time as the modern nations. It has not yet reached in practice the stages which it has surpassed in theory. How can it do a *somersault,* not only over its own limitations, but at the same time over the limitations of the modern nations, over limitations which it must in reality feel and strive for as for emancipation from its real limitations? Only a revolution of radical needs can be a radical revolution and it seems that precisely the preconditions and ground for such needs are lacking.

If Germany has accompanied the development of the modern nations only with the abstract activity of thought without taking an effective share in the real struggle of that development, it has, on the other hand, shared the *sufferings* of that development, without sharing in its enjoyment or its partial satisfaction. To the abstract activity on the one hand corresponds the abstract suffering on the other. That is why Germany will one day find itself on the level of European decadence before ever having been on the level of European emancipation. It will be comparable to a *fetish worshipper* pining away with the diseases of Christianity.

John Stuart Mill

UTILITY
OF RELIGION

It has sometimes been remarked how much has been written, both by friends and enemies, concerning the truth of religion, and how little, at least in the way of discussion or controversy, concerning its usefulness. This, however, might have been expected; for the truth, in matters which so deeply affect us, is our first concernment. If religion, or any particular form of it, is true, its usefulness follows without other proof. If to know authentically in what order of things, under what government of the universe it is our destiny to live, were not useful, it is difficult to imagine what could be considered so. Whether a person is in a pleasant or in an unpleasant place, a palace or a prison, it cannot be otherwise than useful to him to know where he is. So long, therefore, as men accepted the teachings of their religion as positive facts, no more a matter of doubt than their own existence or the existence of the objects around them, to ask the use of believing it could not possibly occur to them. The utility of religion did not need to be asserted until the arguments for its truth had in a great measure ceased to convince. People must either have ceased to believe, or have ceased to rely on the belief of others, before they could take that inferior ground of defence without a consciousness of lowering what they were endeav-

From Nature, the Utility of Religion, Theism, Being Three Essays on Religion, London: 1874, pp. 69–71; 76; 77–82; 84–88.

ouring to raise. An argument for the utility of religion is an appeal to unbelievers, to induce them to practise a well meant hypocrisy, or to semi-believers to make them avert their eyes from what might possibly shake their unstable belief, or finally to persons in general to abstain from expressing any doubts they may feel, since a fabric of immense importance to mankind is so insecure at its foundations, that men must hold their breath in its neighbourhood for fear of blowing it down.

In the present period of history, however, we seem to have arrived at a time when, among the arguments for and against religion, those which relate to its usefulness assume an important place. We are in an age of weak beliefs, and in which such belief as men have is much more determined by their wish to believe than by any mental appreciation of evidence. The wish to believe does not arise only from selfish but often from the most disinterested feelings; and though it cannot produce the unwavering and perfect reliance which once existed, it fences round all that remains of the impressions of early education; it often causes direct misgivings to fade away by disuse; and above all, it induces people to continue laying out their lives according to doctrines which have lost part of their hold on the mind, and to maintain towards the world the same, or a rather more demonstrative attitude of belief, than they thought it necessary to exhibit when their personal conviction was more complete.

If religious belief be indeed so necessary to mankind, as we are continually assured that it is, there is great reason to lament, that the intellectual grounds of it should require to be backed by moral bribery or subornation of the understanding. Such a state of things is most uncomfortable even for those who may, without actual insincerity, describe themselves as believers; and still worse as regards those who, having consciously ceased to find the evidences of religion convincing, are withheld from saying so lest they should aid in doing an irreparable injury to mankind. It is a most painful position to a conscientious and cultivated mind, to be drawn in contrary directions by the two noblest of all objects of pursuit, truth, and the general good. . . . This essential portion of the inquiry into the temporal usefulness of religion, is the subject of the present Essay. . . .

The inquiry divides itself into two parts, corresponding to the double aspect of the subject; its social, and its individual aspect. What does religion do for society, and what for the individual? What amount of benefit to social interests, in the ordinary sense of the phrase, arises from religious belief? And what influence has it in improving and ennobling individual human nature? . . .

To speak first, then, of religious belief as an instrument of social good. We must commence by drawing a distinction most commonly overlooked. It is usual to credit religion *as such* with the whole of the power inherent in *any* system of moral duties inculcated by education and enforced by opinion. Undoubtedly mankind would be in a deplorable state if no principles or precepts of justice, veracity, beneficence, were taught publicly or privately, and if these virtues were not encouraged, and the opposite vices repressed, by the praise and blame, the favourable and unfavourable sentiments, of mankind. And since nearly everything of this sort which does take place, takes place in the name of religion; since almost all who are taught any morality whatever, have it taught to them *as* religion, and inculcated on them through life principally in that character; the effect which the teaching produces as teaching, it is supposed to produce as religious teaching, and religion receives the credit of all the influence in human affairs which belongs to any generally accepted system of rules for the guidance and government of human life. . . .

Consider first, the enormous influence of authority on the human mind. I am now speaking of involuntary influence; effect on men's conviction, on their persuasion, on their involuntary sentiments. Authority is the evidence on which the mass of mankind believe everything which they are said to know, except facts of which their own senses have taken cognizance. It is the evidence on which even the wisest receive all those truths of science, or facts in history or in life, of which they have not personally examined the proofs. Over the immense majority of human beings, the general concurrence of mankind, in any matter of opinion, is all powerful. Whatever is thus certified to them, they believe with a fulness of assurance which they do not accord even to the evidence of their senses when the general opinion of mankind stands in opposition to it. When, therefore, any rule of life and duty, whether grounded or not on religion, has conspicuously received the general assent, it obtains a hold on the belief of every individual, stronger than it would have even if he had arrived at it by the inherent force of his own understanding. If Novalis could say, not without a real meaning, "My belief has gained infinitely to me from the moment when one other human being has begun to believe the same," how much more when it is not one other person, but all the human beings whom one knows of. Some may urge it as an objection, that no scheme of morality has this universal assent, and that none, therefore, can be indebted to this source for whatever power it possesses over the mind. So far as relates to the present age, the assertion is true, and strengthens the argument which it might at first seem to controvert; for exactly in proportion as the received systems of belief have been contested, and it has become known that they have many dissentients, their hold on the general belief has been loosened, and their practical influence on conduct has declined: and since this has happened to them notwithstanding the religious sanction which attached to them, there can be no stronger evidence that they were powerful not as religion, but as beliefs generally accepted by mankind. To find people who believe their religion as a person believes that fire will burn his hand when thrust into it, we must seek them in those Oriental countries where Europeans do not yet predominate, or in the European world when it was still universally Catholic. Men often disobeyed their religion in those times, because their human passions and appetites were too strong for it, or because the religion itself afforded means of indulgence to breaches of its obligations; but though they disobeyed, they, for the most part, did not doubt. There was in those days an absolute and unquestioning completeness of belief, never since general in Europe.

Such being the empire exercised over mankind by simple authority, the mere belief and testimony of their fellow creatures; consider next how tremendous is the power of education; how unspeakable is the effect of bringing people up from infancy in a belief, and in habits founded on it. Consider also that in all countries, and from the earliest ages down to the present, not merely those who are called, in a restricted sense of the term, the educated, but all or nearly all who have been brought up by parents, or by any one interested in them, have been taught from their earliest years some kind of religious belief, and some precepts as the commands of the heavenly powers to them and to mankind. And as it cannot be imagined that the commands of God are to young children anything more than the commands of their parents, it is reasonable to think that any system of social duty which mankind might adopt, even though divorced from religion, would have the same advantage of being inculcated from childhood, and would have it hereafter much more perfectly than any doctrine has it at present, society being far more disposed than formerly to take pains for the moral tuition of those numerous classes whose education it has hitherto left very much to chance. Now it is especially characteristic of the impressions of early education, that they possess what it is so much more difficult for later convictions to obtain—command over the feelings. We see daily how powerful a hold these first impressions retain over the feelings even of those, who have given up the opinions which they were early taught. While on the other hand, it is only persons of a much higher degree of natural sensibility and intellect combined than it is at all common to meet with, whose feelings entwine themselves with anything like the same force round opinions which they have adopted from their own investigations later in life; and even when they do, we may say with truth that it is because the strong sense of moral duty, the sincerity, courage and self-devotion which enabled them to do so, were themselves the fruits of early impressions.

The power of education is almost boundless: there is not one natural inclination which it is not strong enough to coerce, and, if needful, to destroy by disuse. . . .

We have now considered two powers, that of authority, and that of early education, which operate through men's involuntary beliefs, feelings and desires, and which religion has hitherto held as its almost exclusive appanage. Let us now consider a third power which operates directly on their actions, whether their involuntary sentiments are carried with it or not. This is the power of public opinion; of the praise and blame, the favour and disfavour, of their fellow creatures; and is a source of strength inherent in any system of moral belief which is generally adopted, whether connected with religion or not.

Men are so much accustomed to give to the motives that decide their actions, more flattering names than justly belong to them, that they are generally quite unconscious how much those parts of their conduct which they most pride themselves on (as well as some which they are ashamed of), are determined by the motive of public opinion. Of course public opinion for the most part enjoins the same things which are enjoined by the received social morality; that morality being, in truth, the summary of the conduct which each one of the multitude, whether he himself observes it with any strictness or not, desires that others should observe towards him. People are therefore easily able to flatter themselves that they are acting from the motive of conscience when they are doing in obedience to the inferior motive, things which their conscience approves. We continually see how great is the power of opinion in opposition to conscience; how men "follow a multitude to do evil;" how often opinion induces them to do what their conscience disapproves, and still oftener prevents them from doing what it commands. But when the motive of public opinion acts in the same direction with conscience, which, since it has usually itself made the conscience in the first instance, it for the most part naturally does; it is then, of all motives which operate on the bulk of mankind, the most overpowering.

The names of all the strongest passions (except the merely animal ones) manifested by human nature, are each of them a name for some one part only of the motive derived from what I here call public opinion. The love of glory; the love of praise; the love of admiration; the love of respect and deference; even the love of sympathy, are portions of its attractive power. Vanity is a vituperative name for its attractive influence generally, when considered excessive in degree. The fear of shame, the dread of ill repute or of being disliked or hated, are the direct and simple forms of its deterring power. But the deterring force of the unfavourable sentiments of mankind does not consist solely in the painfulness of knowing oneself to be the object of those sentiments; it includes all the penalties which they can inflict: exclusion from social intercourse and from the innumerable good offices which human beings require from one another; the forfeiture of all that is called success in life; often the great diminution or total loss of means of subsistence; positive ill offices of various kinds, sufficient to render life miserable, and reaching in some states of society as far as actual persecution to death. And again the attractive, or impelling influence of public opinion, includes the whole range of what is commonly meant by ambition: for, except in times of lawless military violence, the objects of social ambition can only be attained by means of the good opinion and favourable disposition of our fellow-creatures; nor, in nine cases out of ten, would those objects be even desired, were it not for the power they confer over the sentiments of mankind. Even the pleasure of self-approbation, in the great majority, is mainly dependent on the opinion of others. Such is the involuntary influence of authority on ordinary minds, that persons must be of a better than ordinary mould to be capable of a full assurance that they are in the right, when the world, that is, when *their* world, thinks them wrong: nor is there, to most men, any proof so demonstrative of their own virtue or talent as that people in general seem to believe in it. Through all departments of human affairs, regard for the sentiments of our fellow-creatures is in one shape or other, in nearly all characters, the pervading motive. And we ought to note that this motive is naturally strongest in the most sensitive natures, which are the most promising material for the formation of great virtues. How far its power reaches is known by too familiar experience to require either proof or illustration here. When once the means of living have been obtained, the far greater part of the remaining labour and effort which takes place on the earth, has for its object to acquire the respect or the favourable regard of mankind; to be looked up to, or at all events, not to be looked down upon by them. The industrial and commercial activity which advance civilization, the frivolity, prodigality, and selfish thirst of aggrandizement which retard it, flow equally from that source. While as an instance of the power exercised by the terrors derived from public opinion, we know how many murders have been committed merely to remove a witness who knew and was likely to disclose some secret that would bring disgrace upon his murderer.

Any one who fairly and impartially considers the subject, will see reason to believe that those great effects on human conduct, which are commonly ascribed to motives derived directly from religion, have mostly for their proximate cause the influence of human opinion. Religion has been powerful not by its intrinsic force, but because it has wielded that additional and more mighty power. The effect of religion has been immense in giving a direction to public opinion: which has, in many most important respects, been wholly determined by it. But without the sanctions superadded by public opinion, its own proper sanctions have never, save in exceptional characters, or in peculiar moods of mind, exercised a very potent influence, after the times had gone by, in which divine agency was supposed habitually to employ temporal rewards and punishments. When a man firmly believed that if he violated the sacredness of a particular sanctuary he would be struck dead on the spot, or smitten suddenly with a mortal disease, he doubtless took care not to incur the penalty: but when any one had had the courage to defy the danger, and escaped with impunity, the spell was broken. . . .

Friedrich Nietzsche

THE PRINCIPLE
OF RESENTMENT

Above all, there is no exception
(though there are opportunities for
exceptions) to this rule, that the idea of
political superiority always resolves
itself into the idea of psychological
superiority, in those cases where the
highest caste is at the same time the
priestly caste, and in accordance with its
general characteristics confers on itself
the privilege of a title which alludes
specifically to its priestly function. It is
in these cases, for instance, that "clean"
and "unclean" confront each other for
the first time as badges of class distinction; here again there develops a "good"
and a "bad," in a sense which has ceased
to be merely social. Moreover, care
should be taken not to take these ideas of
"clean" and "unclean" too seriously,
too broadly, or too symbolically: all the
ideas of ancient man have, on the contrary, got to be understood in their
initial stages, in a sense which is, to an
almost inconceivable extent, crude, coarse,
physical, and narrow, and above all
essentially *unsymbolical*. The "clean
man" is originally only a man who washes
himself, who abstains from certain foods
which are conducive to skin diseases,
who does not sleep with the unclean
women of the lower classes, who has a
horror of blood—not more, not much
more! On the other hand, the very

From The Genealogy of Morals (1887), Edinburgh
and London: 1910, pp. 26–31; 34–35; 38–40; 50–51;
161–169; 180–185.

nature of a priestly aristocracy shows the
reasons why just at such an early juncture
there should ensue a really dangerous
sharpening and intensification of opposed
values: it is, in fact, through these opposed values that gulfs are cleft in the
social plane, which a veritable Achilles
of free thought would shudder to cross.
There is from the outset a certain *diseased
taint* in such sacerdotal aristocracies, and
in the habits which prevail in such societies—habits which, *averse* as they are to
action, constitute a compound of introspection and explosive emotionalism,
as a result of which there appears that
introspective morbidity and neurasthenia,
which adheres almost inevitably to all
priests at all times: with regard, however,
to the remedy which they themselves
have invented for this disease—the
philosopher has no option but to state,
that it has proved itself in its effects a
hundred times more dangerous than the
disease, from which it should have been
the deliverer. Humanity itself is still
diseased from the effects of the naïvetés
of this priestly cure. Take, for instance,
certain kinds of diet (abstention from
flesh), fasts, sexual continence, flight into
the wilderness (a kind of Weir-Mitchell
isolation, though of course without that
system of excessive feeding and fattening
which is the most efficient antidote to
all the hysteria of the ascetic ideal);
consider too the whole metaphysic of
the priests, with its war on the senses, its
enervation, its hair-splitting; consider its

self-hypnotism on the fakir and Brahman principles (it uses Brahman as a glass disc and obsession), and that climax which we can understand only too well of an unusual satiety with its panacea of *nothingness* (or God:—the demand for a *unio mystica* with God is the demand of the Buddhist for nothingness, Nirvana—and nothing else!). In sacerdotal societies *every* element is on a more dangerous scale, not merely cures and remedies, but also pride, revenge, cunning, exaltation, love, ambition, virtue, morbidity:—further, it can fairly be stated that it is on the soil of this *essentially dangerous* form of human society, the sacerdotal form, that man really becomes for the first time an *interesting animal,* that it is in this form that the soul of man has in a higher sense attained *depths* and become *evil*—and those are the two fundamental forms of the superiority which up to the present man has exhibited over every other animal.

The reader will have already surmised with what ease the priestly mode of valuation can branch off from the knightly aristocratic mode, and then develop into the very antithesis of the latter: special impetus is given to this opposition, by every occasion when the castes of the priests and warriors confront each other with mutual jealousy and cannot agree over the prize. The knightly-aristocratic "values" are based on a careful cult of the physical, on a flowering, rich, and even effervescing healthiness, that goes considerably beyond what is necessary for maintaining life, on war, adventure, the chase, the dance, the tourney—on everything, in fact, which is contained in strong, free, and joyous action. The priestly-aristocratic mode of valuation is—we have seen—based on other hypotheses: it is bad enough for this class when it is a question of war! Yet the priests are, as is notorious, *the worst enemies*—why? Because they are the weakest. Their weakness causes their hate to expand into a monstrous and sinister shape, a shape which is most crafty and most poisonous. The really great haters in the history of the world have always been priests, who are also the cleverest haters—in comparison with the cleverness of priestly revenge, every other piece of cleverness is practically negligible. Human history would be too fatuous for anything were is not for the cleverness imported into it by the weak—take at once the most important instance. All the world's efforts against the "aristocrats," the "mighty," the "masters," the "holders of power," are negligible by comparison with what has been accomplished against those classes by *the Jews*—the Jews, that priestly nation which eventually realised that the one method of effecting satisfaction on its enemies and tyrants was by means of a radical transvaluation of values, which was at the same time an act of the *cleverest revenge.* Yet the method was only appropriate to a nation of priests, to a nation of the most jealously nursed priestly revengefulness. It was the Jews who, in opposition to the aristocratic equation (good = aristocratic = beautiful = happy = loved by the gods), dared with a terrifying logic to suggest the contrary equation, and indeed to maintain with the teeth of the most profound hatred (the hatred of weakness) this contrary equation, namely "the wretched are alone the good; the poor, the weak, the lowly, are alone the good; the suffering, the needy, the sick, the loathsome, are the only ones who are pious, the only ones who are blessed, for them alone is salvation—but you, on the other hand, you aristocrats, you men of power, you are to all eternity the evil, the horrible, the covetous, the insatiate, the godless; eternally also shall you be the unblessed, the cursed, the damned!" We know who it was who reaped the heritage of this Jewish transvaluation. In the context of the monstrous and inordinately fateful initiative which the Jews have exhibited in connection with this most fundamental of all declarations of war, I remember the passage which came to my pen on another occasion (*Beyond Good and Evil*, Aph. 95)—that it was, in fact, with the Jews that the *revolt of the slaves* begins in the sphere *of morals;* that revolt which has behind it a history of two millennia, and which at the present day has only moved out of our sight, because it—has achieved victory. . . .

The revolt of the slaves in morals begins in the very principle of *resentment* becoming creative and giving birth to values—a resentment experienced by creatures who, deprived as they are of the proper outlet of action, are forced to find their compensation in an imaginary revenge. While every aristocratic morality springs from a triumphant affirmation of its own demands, the slave morality says "no" from the very outset to what is "outside itself," "different from itself," and "not itself": and this "no" is its creative deed. This volte-face of the valuing standpoint—this *inevitable* gravitation to the objective instead of back to the subjective—is typical of "resentment": the slave-morality requires as the condition of its existence an external and objective world, to employ physiological terminology, it requires objective stimuli to be capable of action at all—its action is fundamentally a reaction. The contrary is the case when we come to the aristocrat's system of values: it acts and grows spontaneously, it merely seeks its antithesis in order to pronounce a more grateful and exultant "yes" to its own self;—its negative conception, "low," "vulgar," "bad," is merely a pale late-born foil in comparison with its positive and fundamental conception (saturated as it is with life and passion), of "we aristocrats, we good ones, we beautiful ones, we happy ones."
..
The method of this man is quite con-trary to that of the aristocratic man, who conceives the root idea "good" spontaneously and straight away, that is to say, out of himself, and from that material then creates for himself a concept of "bad!" This "bad" of aristocratic origin and that "evil" out of the cauldron of unsatisfied hatred—the former an imitation, an "extra," an additional nuance; the latter, on the other hand, the original, the beginning, the essential act in the conception of a slave-morality —these two words "bad" and "evil," how great a difference do they mark, in spite of the fact that they have an identical contrary in the idea "good." But the idea "good" is *not* the same: much rather let the question be asked, "Who is really evil according to the meaning of the morality of resentment?" In all sternness let it be answered thus:—*just* the good man of the other morality, just the aristocrat, the powerful one, the one who rules, but who is distorted by the venomous eye of resentfulness, into a new colour, a new signification, a new appearance. This particular point we would be the last to deny: the man who learnt to know those "good" ones only as enemies, learnt at the same time not to know them only as "*evil enemies,*" and the same men who *inter pares* were kept so rigorously in bounds through convention, respect, custom, and gratitude, though much more through mutual vigilance and jealousy *inter pares,* these men who in their relations with each other find so many new ways of manifesting consideration, self-control, delicacy, loyalty, pride, and friendship, these men are in reference to what is outside their circle (where the foreign element, a *foreign* country, begins), not much better than beasts of prey, which have been let loose. They enjoy there freedom from all social control, they feel that in the wilderness they can give vent with impunity to that tension which is produced by enclosure and

imprisonment in the peace of society, they *revert* to the innocence of the beast-of-prey conscience, like jubilant monsters, who perhaps come from a ghastly bout of murder, arson, rape and torture, with bravado and a moral equanimity, as though merely some wild student's prank had been played, perfectly convinced that the poets have now an ample theme to sing and celebrate.... These weaklings!—they also forsooth, wish to be strong some time; there is no doubt about it, some time *their* kingdom also must come—"the kingdom of God" is their name for it, as has been mentioned: —they are so meek in everything! Yet in order to experience *that* kingdom it is necessary to live long, to live beyond death,—yes *eternal* life is necessary so that one can make up for ever for that earthly life "in faith," "in love," "in hope." Make up for what? Make up by what? Dante, as it seems to me, made a crass mistake when with awe-inspiring ingenuity he placed that inscription over the gate of his hell, "Me too made eternal love": at any rate the following inscription would have a much better right to stand over the gate of the Christian Paradise and its "eternal blessedness"— "Me too made eternal hate"—granted of course that a truth may rightly stand over the gate to a lie! For what is the blessedness of that Paradise? Possibly we could quickly surmise it; but it is better that it should be explicitly attested by an authority who in such matters is not to be disparaged, Thomas of Aquinas, the great teacher and saint. *"Beati in regno celesti,"* says he, as gently as a lamb, *"videbunt poenas damnatorum, ut beatitude illis magis complaceat."* ...

If you have understood in all their depths—and I demand that you should *grasp them profoundly* and understand them profoundly—the reasons for the impossibility of its being the business of the healthy to nurse the sick, to make the

sick healthy, it follows that you have grasped this further necessity—the necessity of doctors and nurses who *themselves are sick*. And now we have and hold with both our hands the essence of the ascetic priest. The ascetic priest must be accepted by us as the predestined saviour, herdsman, and champion of the sick herd: thereby do we first understand his awful historic mission. The *lordship over sufferers* is his kingdom, to that points his instinct, in that he finds his own special art, his master-skill, his kind of happiness. He must himself be sick, his kind of happiness. He must be kith and kin to the sick and the abortions so as to understand them, so as to arrive at an understanding with them; but he must also be strong, even more master of himself than of others, impregnable, forsooth, in his will for power, so as to acquire the trust and the awe of the weak, so that he can be their hold, bulwark, prop, compulsion, overseer, tyrant, god. He has to protect them, protect his herds—*against* whom? Against the healthy, doubtless also against the envy towards the healthy. He must be the natural adversary and *scorner* of every rough, stormy, reinless, hard, violently-predatory health and power. The priest is the first form of the more delicate animal that scorns more easily than it hates. He will not be spared the waging of war with the beasts of prey, a war of guile (or "spirit") rather than of force, as is self-evident—he will in certain cases find it necessary to conjure up out of himself, or at any rate to represent practically a new type of the beast of prey—a new animal monstrosity in which the polar bear, the supple, cold, crouching panther, and, not least important, the fox, are joined together in a trinity as fascinating as it is fearsome. If necessity exacts it, then will he come on the scene with bearish seriousness, venerable, wise, cold, full of treacherous superiority, as the herald and mouthpiece of mysterious powers, sometimes going among even the other kind of beasts of prey, determined as he is to sow on their soil, wherever he can, suffering, discord, self-contradiction, and only too sure of his art, always to be lord of *sufferers* at all times. He brings with him, doubtless, salve and balsam; but before he can play the physician he must first wound; so, while he soothes the pain which the wound makes, *he at the same time poisons the wound*. Well versed is he in this above all things, is this wizard and wild beast tamer, in whose vicinity everything healthy must needs become ill, and everything ill must needs become tame. He protects, in sooth, his sick herd well enough, does this strange herdsman; he protects them also against themselves, against the sparks (even in the centre of the herd) of wickedness, knavery, malice, and all the other ills that the plaguey and the sick are heir to; he fights with cunning, hardness, and stealth against anarchy and against the ever imminent break-up inside the herd, where *resentment,* that most dangerous blasting-stuff and explosive, ever accumulates and accumulates. Getting rid of this blasting-stuff in such a way that it does not blow up the herd and the herdsman, that is his real feat, his supreme utility; if you wish to comprise in the shortest formula the value of the priestly life, it would be correct to say the priest is the *diverter of the course of resentment.* Every sufferer, in fact, searches instinctively for a cause of his suffering; to put it more exactly, a doer,—to put it still more precisely, a sentient *responsible* doer, in brief, something living, on which, either actually or in *effigie*, he can on any pretext vent his emotions. For the venting of emotions is the sufferer's greatest attempt at alleviation, that is to say, *stupefaction*, his mechanically desired narcotic against pain of any kind. It is in this phenomenon alone that is found, according to my judgment, the real physiological cause of resentment, revenge, and their family is to be found— that is, in a demand for the *deadening of pain through emotion:* this cause is generally, but in my view very erroneously, looked for in the defensive parry of a bare protective principle of reaction, of a "reflex movement" in the case of any sudden hurt and danger, after the manner that a decapitated frog still moves in order to get away from a corrosive acid. But the difference is fundamental. In one case the object is to prevent being hurt any more; in the other case the object is to *deaden* a racking, insidious, nearly unbearable pain by a more violent emotion of any kind whatsoever, and at any rate for the time being to drive it out of the consciousness—for this purpose an emotion is needed, as wild an emotion as possible, and to excite that emotion some excuse or other is needed. "It must be somebody's fault that I feel bad"—this kind of reasoning is peculiar to all invalids, and is but the more pronounced, the more ignorant they remain of the real cause of their feeling bad, the physiological cause (the cause may lie in a disease of the *nervus sympathicus,* or in an excessive secretion of bile, or in want of sulphate and phosphate of potash in the blood, or in pressure in the bowels which stops the circulation of the blood, or in degeneration of the ovaries, and so forth). All sufferers have an awful resourcefulness and ingenuity in finding excuses for painful emotions; they even enjoy their jealousy, their broodings over base actions and apparent injuries, they burrow through the intestines of their past and present in their search for obscure mysteries, wherein they will be at liberty to wallow in a torturing suspicion and get drunk on the venom of their own malice—they tear open the oldest wounds, they make themselves bleed from the scars which have long been healed, they make evil-doers out of friends, wife, child, and everything which is nearest to them. "I suffer: it must be somebody's fault"—so thinks every sick sheep. But his herdsman, the ascetic priest, says to him, "Quite so, my sheep, it must be the fault of some one; but thou thyself art that some one, it is all the fault of thyself alone—*it is the fault of thyself alone against thyself*": that is bold enough, false enough, but one thing is at least attained; thereby, as I have said, the course of resentment is—*diverted*.

You can see now what the remedial instinct of life has at least *tried* to effect, according to my conception, through the ascetic priest, and the purpose for which he had to employ a temporary tyranny of such paradoxical and anomalous ideas as "guilt," "sin," "sinfulness," "corruption," "damnation." What was done was to make the sick *harmless* up to a certain point, to destroy the incurable by means of themselves, to turn the milder cases severely on to themselves, to give their resentment a backward direction ("man needs but one thing"), and to *exploit* similarly the bad instincts of all sufferers with a view to self-discipline, self-surveillance, self-mastery. It is obvious that there can be no question at all in the case of a "medication" of this kind, a mere emotional medication, of any real *healing* of the sick in the physiological sense; it cannot even for a moment be asserted that in this connection the instinct of life has taken healing as its goal and purpose. On the one hand, a kind of congestion and organisation of the sick (the word "Church" is the most popular name for it); on the other, a kind of provisional safeguarding of the comparatively healthy, the more perfect specimens, the cleavage of a *rift* between healthy and sick—for a long time that was all! and it was much! it was *very* much!

I am proceeding, as you see, in this essay, from an hypothesis which, as far as such readers as I want are concerned, does not require to be proved; the hypothesis that "sinfulness" in man is not an actual fact, but rather merely the interpretation of a fact, of a physiological discomfort,—a discomfort seen through a moral religious perspective which is no longer binding upon us. The fact therefore, that any one feels "guilty," "sinful," is certainly not yet any proof that he is right in feeling so, any more than any one is healthy simply because he feels healthy. Remember the celebrated witch-ordeals: in those days the most acute and humane judges had no doubt but that in these cases they were confronted with guilt,—the "witches" *themselves had no doubt on the point,*—and yet the guilt was lacking. Let me elaborate this hypothesis: I do not for a minute accept the very "pain in the soul" as a real fact, but only as an explanation (a casual explanation) of facts that could not hitherto be precisely formulated; I regard it therefore as something as yet absolutely in the air and devoid of scientific cogency—just a nice fat word in the place of a lean note of interrogation. When any one fails to get rid of his "pain in the soul," the cause is, speaking crudely, to be found *not* in his "soul" but more probably in his stomach (speaking crudely, I repeat, but by no means wishing thereby that you should listen to me or understand me in a crude spirit). A strong and well-constituted man digests his experiences (deeds and misdeeds all included) just as he digests his meats, even when he has some tough morsels to swallow. If he fails to "relieve" himself" of an experience, this kind of indigestion is quite as much physiological as the other indigestion—and indeed in more ways than one, simply one of the results of the other. You can adopt such a theory, and yet *entre nous* be nevertheless the strongest opponent of all materialism.

But is he really a *physician,* this ascetic priest? We already understand why we are scarcely allowed to call him a phyician, however much he likes to feel a "saviour" and let himself be worshipped as a saviour.[1] It is only the actual suffering, the discomfort of the sufferer, which he combats, *not* its cause, not the actual state of sickness—this needs must constitute our most radical objection to priestly medication. But just once put yourself into that point of view, of which the priests have a monopoly, you will find it hard to exhaust your amazement, at what from that standpoint he has completely seen, sought, and found. The *mitigation* of suffering, every kind of "consoling"—all this manifests itself as his very genius: with what ingenuity has he interpreted his mission of consoler, with what aplomb and audacity has he chosen weapons necessary for the part. Christianity in particular should be dubbed a great treasure-chamber of ingenious consolations,—such a store of refreshing, soothing, deadening drugs has it accumulated within itself; so many of the most dangerous and daring expedients has it hazarded; with such sublety, refinement, Oriental refinement, has it divined what emotional stimulants can conquer, at any rate for a time, the deep depression, the leaden fatigue, the black melancholy of physiological cripples—for, speaking generally, all religions are mainly concerned with fighting a certain fatigue and heaviness that has infected everything. . . .

But you will soon understand me. Putting it shortly, there is reason enough, is there not, for us psychologists nowadays never getting away from a certain mistrust of our *own selves*? Probably even we ourselves are still "too good" for our work; probably, whatever contempt we feel for this popular craze for morality, we ourselves are perhaps none the less its victims, prey, and slaves; probably it infects even *us*. Of what was

[1] In the German text "Heiland." This has the double meaning of "healer" and "saviour."

that diplomat warning us, when he said to his colleagues: "Let us especially mistrust our first impulses, gentlemen! *they are almost always good*"? So should nowadays every psychologist talk to his colleagues. And thus we get back to our problem, which in point of fact does require from us a certain severity, a certain mistrust especially against "first impulses." *The ascetic ideal in the service of projected emotional excess:*—he who remembers the previous essay will already partially anticipate the essential meaning compressed into these above ten words. The thorough unswitching of the human soul, the plunging of it into terror, frost, ardour, rapture, so as to free it, as through some lightning shock, from all the smallness and pettiness of unhappiness, depression, and discomfort: what ways lead to *this* goal? And which of these ways does so most safely? . . . At bottom all great emotions have this power, provided that they find a sudden outlet—emotions such as rage, fear, lust, revenge, hope, triumph, despair, cruelty; and, in sooth, the ascetic priest has had no scruples in taking into his service the whole pack of hounds that rage in the human kennel, unleashing now these and now those, with the same constant object of waking man out of his protracted melancholy, of chasing away, at any rate for a time, his dull pain, his shrinking misery, but always under the sanction of a religious interpretation and justification. This emotional excess has subsequently to be *paid for,* this is self-evident—it makes the ill more ill—and therefore this kind of remedy for pain is according to modern standards a "guilty" kind. The dictates of fairness, however, require that we should all the more emphasise the fact that this remedy is applied with a *good conscience,* that the ascetic priest has prescribed it in the most implicit belief in its utility and indispensability;—often enough almost collapsing in the presence of the pain which he created;—that we should similarly emphasise the fact that the violent physiological revenges of such excesses, even perhaps the mental disturbances, are not absolutely inconsistent with the general tenor of this kind of remedy; this remedy, which, as we have shown previously, is *not* for the purpose of healing diseases, but of fighting the unhappiness of that depression, the alleviation and deadening of which was its object. The object was consequently achieved. The keynote by which the ascetic priest was enabled to get every kind of agonising and ecstatic music to play on the fibres of the human soul— was, as everyone knows, the exploitation of the feeling of "guilt." I have already indicated in the previous essay the origin of this feeling—as a piece of animal psychology and nothing else: we were thus confronted with the feeling of "guilt," in its crude state, as it were. It was first in the hands of the priest, real artist that he was in the feeling of guilt, that it took shape—oh, what a shape! "Sin"—for that is the name of the new priestly version of the animal "bad-conscience" (the inverted cruelty)— has up to the present been the greatest event in the history of the diseased soul: in "sin" we find the most perilous and fatal masterpiece of religious interpretation. Imagine man, suffering from himself, some way or other but at any rate physiologically, perhaps like an animal shut up in a cage, not clear as to the why and the wherefore! imagine him in his desire for reasons—reasons bring relief—in his desire again for remedies, narcotics at last, consulting one, who knows even the occult—and see, lo and behold, he gets a hint from his wizard, the ascetic priest, his *first* hint on the "cause" of his trouble: he must search for it *in himself,* in his guiltiness, in a piece of the past, he must understand his very suffering as a *state of punishment.*

He has heard, he has understood, has the unfortunate: he is now in the plight of a hen round which a line has been drawn. He never gets out of the circle of lines. The sick man has been turned into "the sinner"—and now for a few thousand years we never get away from the sight of this new invalid, of a "sinner"—shall we ever get away from it?— wherever we just look, everywhere the hypnotic gaze of the sinner always moving in one direction (in the direction of guilt, the *only* cause of suffering); everywhere the evil conscience, this "greuliche thier,"[2] to use Luther's language; everywhere rumination over the past, a distorted view of action, the gaze of the "green-eyed monster" turned on all action; everywhere the wilful misunderstanding of suffering, its transvaluation into feelings of guilt, fear of retribution; everywhere the scourge, the hairy shirt, the starving body, contrition; everywhere the sinner breaking himself on the ghastly wheel of a restless and morbidly eager conscience; everywhere mute pain, extreme fear, the agony of a tortured heart, the spasms of an unknown happiness, the shriek for "redemption." In point of fact, thanks to this system of procedure, the old depression, dullness, and fatigue were absolutely conquered, life itself became *very* interesting again, awake, eternally awake, sleepless, glowing, burnt away, exhausted and yet not tired—such was the figure cut by man, "the sinner," who was initiated into these mysteries. This grand old wizard of an ascetic priest fighting with depression—he had clearly triumphed, *his* kingdom had come: men no longer grumbled at pain, men *panted* after pain: "*More pain!* More pain!" So for centuries on end shrieked the demand of his acolytes and initiates. Every emotional excess which hurt; everything which broke, overthrew, crushed,

[2]"Horrible beast."

transported, ravished; the mystery of torture-chambers, the ingenuity of hell itself—all this was now discovered, divined, exploited, all this was at the service of the wizard, all this served to promote the triumph of his ideal, the ascetic ideal. "*My kingdom is not of this world*," quoth he, both at the beginning and at the end: had he still the right to talk like that? Goethe has maintained that there are only thirty-six tragic situations: we would infer from that, did we not know otherwise, that Goethe was no ascetic priest. He—knows more.

SECTION TWO

The Analysis of Religion as an Expression of Social Differentiation and Integration

Fustel de Coulanges

RELIGION AS
THE CONSTITUENT PRINCIPLE
OF THE ANCIENT FAMILY AND CITY

IF we transport ourselves in thought to those ancient generations of men, we find in each house an altar, and around this altar the family assembled. The family meets every morning to address its first prayers to the sacred fire, and in the evening to invoke it for a last time. In the course of the day the members are once more assembled near the fire for the meal, of which they partake piously after prayer and libation. In all these religious acts, hymns, which their fathers have handed down, are sung in common by the family.

Outside the house, near at hand, in a neighboring field, there is a tomb—the

From The Ancient City: A Study of the Religion, Laws, and Institutions of Greece and Rome, 4th ed., Boston & New York: 1882, pp. 49–51; 51–52; 76; 77–80; 146–148; 149–150; 155; 157–158; 167–169; 169–170; 175–176; 231–232; 235; 237–238; 258–262; 268–273; 519–529.

second home of this family. There several generations of ancestors repose together; death has not separated them. They remain grouped in this second existence, and continue to form an indissoluble family.

Between the living part and the dead part of the family there is only this distance of a few steps which separates the house from the tomb. On certain days, which are determined for each one by his domestic religion, the living assemble near their ancestors; they offer them the funeral meal, pour out milk and wine to them, lay out cakes and fruits, or burn the flesh of a victim to them. In exchange for these offerings they ask protection; they call these ancestors their gods, and ask them to render the fields fertile, the house prosperous, and their hearts virtuous.

Generation alone was not the foundaion of the ancient family. What proves his is, that the sister did not bear the ame relation to the family as the brother; hat the emancipated son and the married daughter ceased completely to form a part of the family; and, in fine, several other important provisions of the Greek and Roman laws, that we shall have occasion to examine farther along.

Nor is the family principle natural affection. For Greek and Roman law makes no account of this sentiment. The sentiment may exist in the heart, but it s not in the law. The father may have affection for his daughter, but he cannot will her property. The laws of succession—that is to say, those laws which most faithfully reflect the ideas that men had of the family—are in open contradiction both with the order of birth and with natural affection. . . .

The members of the ancient family were united by something more powerful than birth, affection, or physical strength; this was the religion of the sacred fire, and of dead ancestors. This caused the family to form a single body, both in this life and in the next. The ancient family was a religious rather than natural association; and we shall see presently that the wife was counted in the family only after the sacred ceremony of marriage had initiated her into the worship; that the son was no longer counted in it when he had renounced the worship, or had been emancipated; that, on the other hand, an adopted son was counted a real son, because, though he had not the ties of blood, he had something better—a community of worship; that the heir who refused to adopt the worship of this family had no right to the succession; and, finally, that relationship and the right of inheritance were governed not by birth, but by the rights of participation in the worship, such as religion had established them. Religion, it is true, did not create the family; but certainly it gave the family

its rules; and hence it comes that the constitution of the ancient family was so different from what it would have been if it had owed its foundation to natural affection.

The ancient Greek language has a very significant word to designate a family. It is ἐπίστιον, a word which signifies, literally, *that which is near a hearth.* A family was a group of persons whom religion permitted to invoke the same sacred fire, and to offer the funeral repast to the same ancestors.

The Right of Property

Here is an institution of the ancients of which we must not form an idea from anything that we see around us. The ancients founded the right of property on principles different from those of the present generation; as a result, the laws by which they guaranteed it are sensibly different from ours . . . the nations of Greece and Italy, from the earliest antiquity, always held to the idea of private property. We do not find an age when the soil was common among them; nor do we find anything that resembles the annual allotment of land which was in vogue among the Germans. And here we note a remarkable fact. While the races that do not accord to the individual a property in the soil, allow him at least a right to the fruits of his labor,—that is to say, to his harvest,—precisely the contrary custom prevailed among the Greeks. In many cities the citizens were required to store their crops in common, or at least the greater part, and to consume them in common. The individual, therefore, was not the master of the corn which he had gathered; but, at the same time, by a singular contradiction, he had an absolute property in the soil. To him the land was more than the harvest. It appears that among the Greeks the conception of private property was developed exactly contrary to what appears to be the natural order. It was not applied to the harvest first, and to the soil afterwards, but followed the inverse order.

There are three things which, from the most ancient times, we find founded and solidly established in these Greek and Italian societies: the domestic religion; the family; and the right of property—three things which had in the beginning a manifest religion, and which appear to have been inseparable. The idea of private property existed in the religion itself. Every family had its hearth and its ancestors. These gods could be adored only by this family, and protected it alone. They were its property.

Now between these gods and the soil, men of the early ages saw a mysterious relation. Let us first take the hearth. This altar is the symbol of a sedentary life; its name indicates this. It must be placed upon the ground; once established, it cannot be moved. The god of the family wishes to have a fixed abode; materially, it is difficult to transport the stone on which he shines; religiously, this is more difficult still, and is permitted to a man only when hard necessity presses him, when an enemy is pursuing him, or when the soil cannot support him. When they establish the hearth, it is with the thought and hope that it will always remain in the same spot. The god is installed there not for a day, not for the life of one man merely, but for as long a time as this family shall endure, and there remains any one to support its fire by sacrifices. Thus the sacred fire takes possession of the soil, and makes it its own. It is the god's property.

And the family, which through duty and religion remains grouped around its altar, is as much fixed to the soil as the altar itself. The idea of domicile follows naturally. The family is attached to the altar, the altar is attached to the soil; an intimate relation, therefore, is established between the soil and the family. There

must be his permanent home, which he will not dream of quitting, unless an unforeseen necessity constrains him to it. Like the hearth, it will always occupy this spot. This spot belongs to it, is its property, the property not simply of a man, but of a family, whose different members must, one after another, be born and die here.

Let us follow the idea of the ancients. Two sacred fires represent two distinct divinities, who are never united or confounded; this is so true, that even intermarriage between two families does not establish an alliance between their gods. The sacred fire must be isolated—that is to say, completely separated from all that is not of itself; the stranger must not approach it at the moment when the ceremonies of the worship are performed, or even be in sight of it. It is for this reason that these gods are called the concealed gods, $\mu \acute{\nu} \chi \iota o \iota$, or the interior gods, *Penates*. In order that this religious rule may be well observed, there must be an enclosure around this hearth at a certain distance. It did not matter whether this enclosure was a hedge, a wall of wood, or one of stone. Whatever it was, it marked the limit which separated the domain of one sacred fire from that of another. This enclosure was deemed sacred. It was an impious act to pass it. The god watched over it, and kept it under his care. They, therefore, applied to this god the epithet of $\xi \rho \chi \epsilon \hat{\iota} o \zeta$. This enclosure, traced and protected by religion, was the most certain emblem, the most undoubted mark of the right of property. . . .

THE FAMILY (GENS) WAS AT FIRST THE ONLY FORM OF SOCIETY

What we have seen of the family, its domestic religion, the gods which it had created for itself, the laws that it had established, the right of primogeniture on which it had been founded, its unity, its development from age to age until the formation of the gens, its justice, its priesthood, its internal government,— carries us forcibly, in thought, towards a primitive epoch, when the family was independent of all superior power, and when the city did not yet exist.

When we examine the domestic religion, those gods who belonged only to one family and exercised their providence only within the walls of one house, this worship which was secret, this religion which would not be propagated, this antique morality which prescribed the isolation of families,—it is clear that beliefs of this nature could not have taken root in the minds of men, except in an age when larger societies were not yet formed. If the religious sentiment was satisfied with so narrow a conception of the divine, it was because human associations were then narrow in proportion. The time when men believed only in the domestic gods was the time when there existed only families. It is quite true that this belief might have subsisted afterwards, and even for a long time, when cities and nations existed. Man does not easily free himself from opinions that have once exercised a strong influence over him. This belief might endure, therefore, even when it was in disaccord with the social state. What is there, indeed, more contradictory than to live in civil society and to have particular gods in each family? But it is clear that this contradiction did not always exist, and that at the epoch when this belief was established in the mind, and became powerful enough to form a religion, it corresponded exactly with the social state of man. Now, the only social state that is in accord with such a belief is that in which the family lives independent and isolated. . . .

Let us place ourselves, in thought, therefore, in the midst of those ancient generations whose traces have not been entirely effaced, and who delegated their beliefs and their laws to subsequent ages. Each family has its religion, its gods, its priesthood. Religious isolation is a law with it; its ceremonies are secret. In death even, or in the existence that follows it, families do not mingle; each one continues to live apart in the tomb, from which the stranger is excluded. Every family has also its property, that is to say, its lot of land, which is inseparably attached to it by its religion; its gods— *Termini*—guard the enclosure, and its Manes keep it in their care. Isolation of property is so obligatory that two domains cannot be contiguous, but a band of soil must be left between them which must be neutral ground, and must remain inviolable. Finally, every family has its chief, as a nation would have its king. It has its laws, which, doubtless, are unwritten, but which religious faith engraves in the heart of every man. It has its court of justice, above which there is no other that one can appeal to. Whatever man really needs for his material or moral life the family possesses within itself. It needs nothing from without; it is an organized state, a society that suffices for itself.

But this family of the ancient ages is not reduced to the proportions of the modern family. In larger societies the family separates and decreases. But in the absence of every other social organization, it extends, develops, and ramifies without becoming divided. Several younger branches remain grouped around an older one, near the one sacred fire and the common tomb. . . .

The religious idea and human society went on, therefore, expanding at the same time.

The domestic religion forbade two families to mingle and unite; but it was possible for several families, without sacrificing anything of their special religions, to join, at least, for the celebration of another worship which might have been common to all of them. And this is what happened. A certain number of families formed a group, called, in the Greek language, a phratria, in the Latin, a curia. Did there exist the tie of birth between the families of the same group? This cannot be affirmed. It is clear, however, that this new association was not formed without a certain enlargement of religious ideas. Even at the moment when they united, these families conceived the idea of a divinity superior to that of the household, one who was common to all, and who watched over the entire group. They raised an altar to him, lighted a sacred fire, and founded a worship. . . .

Every phratry or cury had a chief, a curion, or phratriarch, whose principal function was to preside at the sacrifices. Perhaps his attributes were at first more extensive. The phratry had its assemblies and its tribunal, and could pass decrees. In it, as well as in the family, there were a god, a worship, a priesthood, a legal tribunal, and a government. It was a small society that was modelled exactly upon the family.

The association naturally continued to increase, and after the same fashion; several phratries, or curies, were grouped together, and formed a tribe.

This new circle also had its religion; in each tribe there were an altar and a protecting divinity.

The god of the tribe was generally of the same nature as that of the phratry, or that of the family. It was a man deified, a *hero*. From him the tribe took its name. The Greeks called him the *eponymous hero*. He had his annual festal day. The principal part of the religious ceremony was a repast, of which the entire tribe partook.

The tribe, like the phratry, held assemblies and passed decrees, to which all the members were obliged to submit. It had a chief, *tribunus*. From what remains to us of the tribe we see that, originally, it was constituted to be an independent society, and as if there ha[d] been no other social power above it.

The City Formed

The tribe, like the family and th[e] phratry, was established as an indepe[n]dent body, since it had a special worshi[p] from which the stranger was exclude[d] Once formed, no new family could b[e] admitted to it. No more could tw[o] tribes be fused into one; their religion wa[s] opposed to this. But just as sever[al] phratries were united in a tribe, sever[al] tribes might associate together, on co[n]dition that the religion of each should b[e] respected. The day on which this allianc[e] took place the city existed.

It is of little account to seek the caus[e] which determined several neighborin[g] tribes to unite. Sometimes it was volu[n]tary; sometimes it was imposed by th[e] superior force of a tribe, or by the powe[r]ful will of a man. What is certain is, tha[t] the bond of the new association was sti[ll] a religion. The tribes that united to for[m] a city never failed to light a sacred fir[e] and to adopt a common religion.

Thus human society, in this race, d[id] not enlarge like a circle, which increas[e] on all sides, gaining little by little. The[re] were, on the contrary, small group[s] which, having been long establishe[d] were finally joined together in larg[e] ones. Several families formed the phr[a]try, several phratries the tribe, sever[al] tribes the city. Family, phratry, trib[e] city, were, moreover, societies exact[ly] similar to each other, which were forme[d] one after the other by a series of feder[a]tions.

We must remark, also, that when th[e] different groups became thus associate[d] none of them lost its individuality, or i[ts] independence. Although several famili[es] were united in a phratry, each one [of] them remained constituted just as it ha[d] been when separate. Nothing was changed in it, neither worship nor priesthood, nor property nor internal justice. Curies afterwards became associated, but each retained its worship, its assemblies, its festivals, its chief. From the tribe men passed to the city; but the tribe was not dissolved on that account, and each of them continued to form a body, very much as if the city had not existed. In religion there subsisted a multitude of subordinate worships, above which was established one common to all; in politics, numerous little governments continued to act, while above them a common government was founded.

The city was a confederation. Hence it was obliged, as least for several centuries, to respect the religious and civil independence of the tribes, curies, and families, and had not the right, at first, to interfere in the private affairs of each of these little bodies. It had nothing to do in the interior of a family; it was not the judge of what passed there; it left to the father the right and duty of judging his wife, his son, and his client. It is for this reason that private law, which had been fixed at the time when families were isolated, could subsist in the city, and was modified only at a very late period. . .

Thus the city was not an assemblage of individuals; it was a confederation of several groups, which were established before it, and which it permitted to remain. We see, in the Athenian orators, that every Athenian formed a portion of four distinct societies at the same time; he was a member of a family, of a phratry, of a tribe, and of a city. He did not enter at the same time and the same day into all these four, like a Frenchman, who at the moment of his birth belongs at once to a family, a commune, a department, and a country. The phratry and the tribe are not administrative divisions.

A man enters at different times into these four societies, and ascends, so to speak, from one to the other. First, the child is admitted into the family by the religious ceremony, which takes place six days after his birth. Some years later he enters the phratry by a new ceremony, which we have already described. Finally, at the age of sixteen or eighteen, he is presented for admission into the city. On that day, in the presence of an altar, and before the smoking flesh of a victim, he pronounces an oath, by which he binds himself, among other things, always to respect the religion of the city. From that day he is initiated into the public worship, and becomes a citizen. If we observe this young Athenian rising, step by step, from worship to worship, we have a symbol of the degrees through which human association has passed. The course which this young man is constrained to follow, is that which society first followed. . . .

Such was the origin of cities among the ancients. This study was necessary to give us a correct idea of the nature and institutions of the city. But here we must make a reservation. If the first cities were formed of a confederation of little societies previously established, this is not saying that all the cities known to us were formed in the same manner. The municipal organization once discovered, it was not necessary for each new city to pass over the same long and difficult route. It might often happen that they followed the inverse order. When a chief, quitting a city already organized, went to found another, he took with him commonly only a small number of his fellow-citizens. He associated with them a multitude of other men who came from different parts, and might even belong to different races. But this chief never failed to organize the new state after the model of the one he had just quitted. Consequently he divided his people into tribes

and phratries. Each of these little associations had an altar, sacrifices, and festivals; each even invented an ancient hero,
whom it honored with its worship, and
from whom, with the lapse of time, it
believed itself to have been descended.

It often happened, too, that the men of
some country lived without laws and
without order, either because no one
had ever been able to establish a social
organization there, as in Arcadia, or
because it had been corrupted and dissolved by too rapid revolutions, as at
Cyrene and Thurii. If a legislator undertook to establish order among these men,
he never failed to commence by dividing
them into tribes and phratries, as if this
were the only type of society. In each of
these organizations he named an eponymous hero, established sacrifices, and
inaugurated traditions. This was always
the manner of commencing, if he wished
to found a regular society. Thus Plato
did when he imagined a model city.

Government of the City. The King.

RELIGIOUS AUTHORITY OF THE KING

We should not picture to ourselves a
city, at its foundation, deliberating on
the form of government that it will
adopt, devising and discussing its laws,
and preparing its institutions. It was not
thus that laws were made and that
governments were established. The
political institutions of the city were born
with the city itself and on the same day
with it. Every member of the city carried
them within himself, for the germ of
them was in each man's belief and religion.

Religion prescribed that the hearth
should always have a supreme priest.
It did not permit the sacerdotal authority
to be divided. The domestic hearth had a

high priest, who was the father of the
family; the hearth of the cury, had its
curio, or phratriarch; every tribe, in the
same manner, had its religious chief,
whom the Athenians called the king of
the tribe. It was also necessary that the
city religion should have its supreme
priest.

This priest of the public hearth bore
the name of king. Sometimes they gave
him other titles. As he was especially the
priest of the prytaneum, the Greeks
preferred to call him the prytane; sometimes also they called him the archon.
Under these different names of king,
prytane, and archon we are to see a
personage who is, above all, the chief of
the worship. He keeps up the fire, offers
the sacrifice, pronounces the prayer,
and presides at the religious repasts.

It may be worth while to offer proof
that the ancient kings of Greece and
Italy were priests. In Aristotle we read,
"The care of the public sacrifices of the
city belongs, according to religious
custom, not to special priests, but to
those men who derive their dignity from
the hearth, and who in one place are
called kings, in another prytanes, and in a
third archons." . . .

POLITICAL AUTHORITY OF THE KING

Just as in the family the authority was
inherent in the priesthood, and the father,
as head of the domestic worship, was at
the same time judge and master, so the
high priest of the city was at the same
time its political chief. The altar—to
borrow an expression of Aristotle—
conferred dignity and power upon him.
There is nothing to surprise us in this
confusion of the priesthood and the civil
power. We find it at the beginning of
almost all societies, either because during
the infancy of a people nothing but
religion will command their obedience.

or because our nature feels the need of not submitting to any other power than that of a moral idea. . . .

It was not force, then, that created chiefs and kings in those ancient cities. It would not be correct to say that the first man who was king there was a lucky soldier. Authority flowed from the worship of the sacred fire. Religion created the king in the city, as it had made the family chief in the house. A belief, an unquestionable and imperious belief, declared that the hereditary priest of the hearth was the depositary of the holy duties and the guardian of the gods. How could one hesitate to obey such a man? A king was a sacred being; βασιλεις ξεροξ, says Pindar. Men saw in him, not a complete god, but at least "the most powerful man to call down the anger of the gods;" the man without whose aid no prayer was heard, no sacrifice accepted.

This royalty, semi-religious, semi-political, was established in all cities, from their foundation, without effort on the part of the kings, without resistance on the part of the subjects. We do not see at the origin of the ancient nations those fluctuations and struggles which mark the painful establishment of modern societies. We know how long a time was necessary, after the fall of the Roman empire, to restore the rules of a regular society. Europe saw, during several centuries, opposing principles dispute for the government of the people, and the people at times rejecting all social organization. No such spectacle was seen in ancient Greece, or in ancient Italy; their history does not commence with conflicts: revolutions appeared only at the close.

Among these populations, society formed slowly and by degrees, while passing from the family to the tribe, and from the tribe to the city, but without shock and without a struggle. Royalty was established quite naturally, in the family first, in the city later. It was not devised in the imagination of a few; it grew out of a necessity that was manifest to the eyes of all. During long ages it was peaceable, honored, and obeyed. The kings had no need of material force; they had neither army nor treasury; but, sustained by a faith that had a powerful influence over the mind, their authority was sacred and inviolable. . . .

The Citizen and the Stranger

The citizen was recognized by the fact that he had a part in the religion of the city, and it was from this participation that he derived all his civil and political rights. If he renounced the worship, he renounced the rights. We have already spoken of the public meals, which were the principal ceremony of the national worship. Now, at Sparta, one who did not join in these, even if it was not his fault, ceased at once to be counted among the citizens. At Athens, one who did not take part in the festivals of the national gods lost the rights of a citizen. At Rome, it was necessary to have been present at the sacred ceremony of the lustration, in order to enjoy political rights. The man who had not taken part in this—that is to say, who had not joined in the common prayer and the sacrifice—lost his citizenship until the next lustration.

If we wished to give an exact definition of a citizen, we should say that it was a man who had the religion of the city. The stranger, on the contrary, is one who has not access to the worship, one whom the gods of the city do not protect, and who has not even the right to invoke them. For these national gods do not wish to receive prayers and offering except from citizens; they repulse the stranger; entrance into their temples is forbidden to him, and his presence during the sacrifice is a sacrilege. Evidence of this ancient sentiment of repulsion has remained in one of the principal rites of Roman worship. The pontiff, when he sacrifices in the open air, must have his head veiled: "For before the sacred fires in the religious act which is offered to the national gods, the face of a stranger must not appear to the pontiff; the auspices would be disturbed." A sacred object which fell for a moment into the hands of a stranger at once became profane. It could not recover its religious character except by an expiatory ceremony. If the enemy seized upon a city, and the citizens succeeded in recovering it, above all things it was important that the temples should be purified and all the fires extinguished and rekindled. The presence of the stranger had defiled them.

Thus religion established between the citizen and the stranger a profound and ineffaceable distinction. This same religion, so long as it held its sway over the minds of men, forbade the right of citizenship to be granted to a stranger. In the time of Herodotus, Sparta had accorded it to no one except a prophet; and even for this the formal command of the oracle was necessary. Athens granted it sometimes; but with what precautions! First, it was necessary that the united people should vote by secret ballot for the admission of the stranger. Even this was nothing as yet; nine days afterwards a second assembly had to confirm the previous vote, and in this second case six thousand votes were required in favor of the admission—a number which will appear enormous when we recollect that it was very rare for an Athenian assembly to comprise so many citizens. After this a vote of the senate was required to confirm the decision of this double assembly. Finally, any citizen could oppose a sort of veto, and attack the decree as contrary to the ancient laws. Certainly there was no other public act where the legislator was surrounded with so many difficulties

and precautions as that which conferred upon a stranger the title of citizen. The formalities to go through were not near so great in declaring war, or in passing a new law. Why should these men oppose so many obstacles to a stranger who wished to become a citizen? Assuredly they did not fear that in the political assemblies his vote would turn the balance. Demosthenes gives us the true motive and the true thought of the Athenians: "It is because the purity of the sacrifices must be preserved." To exclude the stranger was to "watch over the sacred ceremonies." To admit a stranger among the citizens was "to give him a part in the religion and in the sacrifices." Now for such an act the people did not consider themselves entirely free, and were seized with religious scruples; for they knew that the national gods were disposed to repulse the stranger, and that the sacrifices would perhaps be rendered useless by the presence of the newcomer. The gift of the rights of a citizen to a stranger was a real violation of the fundamental principles of the national religion; and it is for this reason that, in the beginning, the city was so sparing of it. We must also note that the man admitted to citizenship with so much difficulty could be neither archon nor priest. The city, indeed, permitted him to take part in its worship, but as to presiding at it, that would have been too much.

No one could become a citizen at Athens if he was a citizen in another city; for it was a religious impossibility to be at the same time a member of two cities, as it also was to be a member of two families. One could not have two religions at the same time.

The participation in the worship carried with it the possession of rights. As the citizen might assist in the sacrifice which preceded the assembly, he could also vote at the assembly. As he could perform the sacrifices in the name of the city, he might be a prytane and an archon. Having the religion of the city, he might claim rights under its laws, and perform all the ceremonies of legal procedure.

The stranger, on the contrary, having no part in the religion, had none in the law. If he entered the sacred enclosure which the priests had traced for the assembly, he was punished with death. The laws of the city did not exist for him. If he had committed a crime, he was treated as a slave, and punished without process of law, the city owing him no legal protection. When men arrived at that stage that they felt the need of having laws for the stranger, it was necessary to establish an exceptional tribunal. At Rome, in order to judge the alien, the pretor had to become an alien himself—*prætor peregrinus*. At Athens the judge of foreigners was the polemarch— that is to say, the magistrate who was charged with the cares of war, and of all transactions with the enemy. . . .

The Municipal Spirit

What we have already seen of ancient institutions, and above all of ancient beliefs, has enabled us to obtain an idea of the profound gulf which always separated two cities. However near they might be to each other, they always formed two completely separate societies. Between them there was much more than the distance which separates two cities to-day, much more than the frontier which separates two states; their gods were not the same, or their ceremonies, or their prayers. The worship of one city was forbidden to men of a neighboring city. The belief was, that the gods of one city rejected the homage and prayers of any one who was not their own citizen.

These ancient beliefs, it is true, were modified and softened in the course of time; but they had been in their full vigor at the time when these societies were formed, and these societies always preserved the impression of them.

Two facts we can easily understand: first, that this religion, peculiar to each city, must have established the city in a very strong and almost unchangeable manner; it is, indeed, marvellous how long this social organization lasted, in spite of all its faults and all its chances of ruin; second, that the effect of this religion, during long ages, must have been to render it impossible to establish any other social form than the city.

Every city, even by the requirements of its religion, was independent. It was necessary that each should have its particular code, since each had its own religion, and the law flowed from the religion. Each was required to have its sovereign tribunal, and there could be no judicial tribunal superior to that of the city. Each had its religious festivals and its calendar; the months and the year could not be the same in two cities, as the series of religious acts was different. Each had its own money, which at first was marked with its religious emblem. Each had its weights and measures. It was not admitted that there could be anything common between two cities. The line of demarcation was so profound that one hardly imagined marriage possible between the inhabitants of two different cities. Such a union always appeared strange, and was long considered illegal. The legislation of Rome and that of Athens were visibly averse to admitting it. Nearly everywhere children born of such a marriage were confounded with bastards, and deprived of the rights of citizens. To make a marriage legal between inhabitants of two cities, it was necessary that there should be between those cities a particular convention—*jus connubii*.

Every city had about its territory a line of sacred bounds. This was the horizon of its national religion and of its gods. Beyond these bounds other gods reigned, and another worship was practised.

The most salient characteristic of the history of Greece and of Italy, before the Roman conquest, is the excessive division of property and the spirit of isolation in each city. Greece never succeeded in forming a single state; nor did the Latin or the Etruscan cities, or the Samnite tribes, succeed in forming a compact body. The incurable division of the Greeks has been attributed to the nature of their country, and we are told that the mountains which intersect each other establish natural lines of demarcation among men. But there were no mountains between Thebes and Platæa, between Argos and Sparta, between Sybaris and Crotona. There were none between the cities of Latium, or between the twelve cities of Etruria. Doubtless physical nature has some influence upon the history of a people, but the beliefs of men have a much more powerful one. In ancient times there was something more impassable than mountains between two neighboring cities, there were the series of sacred bounds, the difference of worship, and the hatred of the gods towards the foreigner.

For this reason the ancients were never able to establish, or even to conceive of, any other social organization than the city. Neither the Greeks, nor the Latins, nor even the Romans, for a very long time, ever had a thought that several cities might be united, and live on an equal footing under the same government. There might, indeed, be an alliance, or a temporary association, in view of some advantage to be gained, or some danger to be repelled; but there was never a complete union; for religion made of every city a body which could never be joined to another. Isolation was the law of the city.

With the beliefs and the religious usages which we have seen, how could several cities ever have become united in

one state? Men did not understand human association, and it did not appear regular, unless it was founded upon religion. The symbol of this association was a sacred repast partaken of in common. A few thousand citizens might indeed literally unite around the same prytaneum, recite the same prayer, and partake of the same sacred dishes. But how attempt, with these usages, to make a single state of entire Greece? How could men hold the public repasts, and perform all the sacred ceremonies, in which every citizen was bound to take a part? Where would they locate the prytaneum? How would they perform the annual lustration of the citizens? What would become of the inviolable limits which had from the beginning marked out the territory of the city, and which separated it forever from the rest of the earth's surface? What would become of all the local worships, the city divinities, and the heroes who inhabited every canton? Athens had within her limits the hero Œdipus, the enemy of Thebes: how unite Athens and Thebes in the same worship and under the same government?

When these superstitions became weakened (and this did not happen till a late period, in common minds), it was too late to establish a new form of state. The division had become consecrated by custom, by interest, by inveterate hatreds, and by the memory of past struggles. Men could no longer return to the past.

Every city held fast to its *autonomy:* this was the name they gave to an assemblage which comprised their worship, their laws, their government, and their entire religious and political independence.

It was easier for a city to subject another than to annex it. Victory might make slaves of all the inhabitants of a conquered city, but they could not be made citizens of the victorious city. To join two cities in a single state, to unite the conquered population with the victors, and associate them under the same government, is what was never seen among the ancients, with one exception, of which we shall speak presently. If Sparta conquered Messenia, it was not to make of the Spartans and Messenians a single people. The Spartans expelled the whole race of the vanquished, and took their lands. Athens proceeded in the same manner with Salamis, Ægina, and Melos.

The thought of removing the conquered to the city of the victors could not enter the mind of any one. The city possessed gods, hymns, festivals, and laws, which were its precious patrimony, and it took good care not to share these with the vanquished. It had not even the right to do this. Could Athens admit that a citizen of Ægina might enter the temple of Athene Polias? that he might offer his worship to Theseus? that he might take part in the sacred repasts? that, as a prytane, he might keep up the public fire? Religion forbade it. The conquered population of the isle of Ægina could not, therefore, form a single state with the population of Athens. Not having the same gods, the Æginetans and the Athenians could not have the same laws or the same magistrates.

But might not Athens, at any rate, leaving the conquered city intact, send magistrates within its walls to govern it? It was absolutely contrary to the principles of the ancients to place any man over a city, who was not a citizen of it. Indeed, the magistrate was a religious chief, and his principal function was to sacrifice in the name of the city. The foreigner, who had not the right to offer the sacrifice, could not therefore be a magistrate. Having no religious function, he had not in the eyes of men any regular authority. Sparta attempted to place its harmosts in the cities, but these men were not magistrates; they did not act as judges, or appear in the assemblies.

Having no regular relation with the people of the cities, they could not maintain themselves there for any great length of time.

Every conqueror, consequently, had only the alternative of destroying a subdued city and occupying its territory, or of leaving it entirely independent. There was no middle course. Either the city ceased to exist, or it was a sovereign state. So long as it retained its worship, it retained its government; it lost the one only by losing the other; and then it existed no longer. This absolute independence of the ancient city could only cease when the belief on which it was founded had completely disappeared. After these ideas had been transformed and several revolutions had passed over these antique societies, then men might come to have an idea of, and to establish, a larger state, governed by other rules. But for this it was necessary that men should discover other principles and other social bonds than those of the ancient ages.

Christianity Changes the Conditions of Government

The victory of Christianity marks the end of ancient society. With the new religion this social transformation, which we saw begun six or seven centuries earlier, was completed.

To understand how much the principles and the essential rules of politics were then changed, we need only recollect that ancient society had been established by an old religion whose principal dogma was that every god protected exclusively a single family or a single city, and existed only for that. This was the time of the domestic gods and the city-protecting divinities. This religion had produced laws; the relations among men—property, inheritance, legal proceedings—all were regulated, not by the principles of natural equity, but by the dogmas of this religion, and with a view to the requirements of its worship. It was this religion that had established a government among men; that of the father in the family; that of the king or magistrate in the city. All had come from religion, —that is to say, from the opinion that man had entertained of the divinity. Religion, law, and government were confounded, and had been but a single thing under three different aspects.

We have sought to place in a clear light this social system of the ancients, where religion was absolute master, both in public and private life; where the state was a religious community, the king a pontiff, the magistrate a priest, and the law a sacred formula; where patriotism was piety, and exile excommunication; where individual liberty was unknown; where man was enslaved to the state through his soul, his body, and his property; where the notions of law and of duty, of justice and of affection, were bounded within the limits of the city; where human association was necessarily confined within a certain circumference around a prytaneum; and where men saw no possibility of founding larger societies. Such were the characteristic traits of the Greek and Italian cities during the first period of their history.

But little by little, as we have seen, society became modified. Changes took place in government and in laws at the same time as in religious ideas. Already, in the fifth century which preceded Christianity, the alliance was no longer so close between religion on the one hand and law and politics on the other. The efforts of the oppressed classes, the overthrow of the sacerdotal class, the labors of philosophers, the progress of thought, had unsettled the ancient principles of human association. Men had made incessant efforts to free themselves from the thraldom of this old religion, in which

they could no longer believe; law and politics, as well as morals, in the course of time were freed from its fetters.

But this species of divorce came from the disappearance of the ancient religion; if law and politics began to be a little more independent, it was because men ceased to have religious beliefs. If society was no longer governed by religion, it was especially because this religion no longer had any power. But there came a day when the religious sentiment recovered life and vigor, and when, under the Christian form, belief regained its empire over the soul. Were men not then destined to see the reappearance of the ancient confusion of government and the priesthood, of faith and the law?

With Christianity not only was the religious sentiment revived, but it assumed a higher and less material expression. Whilst previously men had made for themselves gods of the human soul, or of the great forces of nature, they now began to look upon God as really foreign by his essence, from human nature on the one hand, and from the world on the other. The divine Being was placed outside and above physical nature. Whilst previously every man had made a god for himself, and there were as many of them as there were families and cities, God now appeared as a unique, immense, universal being, alone animating the worlds, alone able to supply the need of adoration that is in man. Religion, instead of being, as formerly among the nations of Greece and Italy, little more than an assemblage of practices, a series of rites which men repeated without having any idea of them, a succession of formulas which often were no longer understood because the language had grown old, a tradition which had been transmitted from age to age, and which owed its sacred character to its antiquity alone,—was now a collection of doctrines, and a great object proposed to faith. It was no longer exterior; it took up its abode especially in the thoughts of man. It was no longer matter; it became spirit. Christianity changed the nature and the form of adoration. Man no longer offered God food and drink. Prayer was no longer a form of incantation; it was an act of faith and a humble petition. The soul sustained another relation with the divinity; the fear of the gods was replaced by the love of God.

Christianity introduced other new ideas. It was not the domestic religion of any family, the national religion of any city, or of any race. It belonged neither to a caste nor to a corporation. From its first appearance it called to itself the whole human race. Christ said to his disciples, "Go ye into all the world, and preach the gospel to every creature."

This principle was so extraordinary, and so unexpected, that the first disciples hesitated for a moment; we may see in the Acts of the Apostles that several of them refused at first to propagate the new doctrine outside the nation with which it had originated. These disciples thought, like the ancient Jews, that the God of the Jews would not accept adoration from foreigners; like the Romans and the Greeks of ancient times, they believed that every race had its god, that to propagate the name and worship of this god was to give up one's own good and special protector, and that such a work was contrary at the same time to duty and to interest. But Peter replied to these disciples, "God gave the gentiles the like gift as he did unto us." St. Paul loved to repeat this grand principle on all occasions, and in every kind of form. "God had opened the door of faith unto the gentiles." "Is he the God of the Jews, only? Is he not also of the gentiles?" "We are all baptized into one body, whether we be Jews or gentiles."

In all this there was something quite new. For, everywhere, in the first ages of humanity, the divinity had been imagined as attaching himself especially to one race. The Jews had believed in the God of the Jews; the Athenians in the Athenian Pallas; the Romans in Jupiter Capitolinus. The right to practise a worship had been a privilege.

The foreigner had been repulsed from the temple; one not a Jew could not enter the temple of the Jews; the Lacedæmonian had not the right to invoke the Athenian Pallas. It is just to say, that, in the five centuries which preceded Christianity, all who thought were struggling against these narrow rules. Philosophy had often taught, since Anaxagoras, that the god of the universe received the homage of all men, without distinction. The religion of Eleusis had admitted the initiated from all cities. The religion of Cybele, of Serapis, and some others, had accepted, without distinction, worshippers from all nations. The Jews had begun to admit the foreigner to their religion; the Greeks and the Romans had admitted him into their cities. Christianity, coming after all this progress in thought and institutions, presented to the adoration of all men a single God, a universal God, a God who belonged to all, who had no chosen people, and who made no distinction in races, families, or states.

For this God there were no longer strangers. The stranger no longer profaned the temple, no longer tainted the sacrifice by his presence. The temple was open to all who believed in God. The priesthood ceased to be hereditary, because religion was no longer a patrimony. The worship was no longer kept secret; the rites, the prayers, the dogmas were no longer concealed. On the contrary, there was thenceforth religious instruction, which was not only given, but which was offered, which was carried to those who were the farthest away, and which sought out the most indifferent.

The spirit of propagandism replaced the law of exclusion.

From this great consequences flowed, as well for the relations between nations as for the government of states.

Between nations religion no longer commanded hatred; it no longer made it the citizen's duty to detest the foreigner; its very essence, on the contrary, was to teach him that towards the stranger, towards the enemy, he owed the duties of justice, and even of benevolence. The barriers between nations or races were thus thrown down; the *pomœrium* disappeared. "Christ," says the apostle, "hath broken down the middle wall of partition between us." "But now are they many members," he also says, "yet but one body." "There is neither Greek nor Jew, circumcision nor uncircumcision, Barbarian, Scythian, bond nor free: but Christ is all, and in all."

The people were also taught that they were all descended from the same common father. With the unity of God, the unity of the human race also appeared to men's minds; and it was thenceforth a religious necessity to forbid men to hate each other.

As to the government of the state, we cannot say that Christianity essentially altered that, precisely because it did not occupy itself with the state. In the ancient ages, religion and the state made but one; every people adored its own god, and every god governed his own people; the same code regulated the relations among men, and their duties towards the gods of the city. Religion then governed the state, and designated its chiefs by the voice of the lot, or by that of the auspices. The state, in its turn, interfered with the domain of the conscience, and punished every infraction of the rites and the worship of the city. Instead of this, Christ teaches that his kingdom is not of this world. He separates religion from government. Religion, being no longer of the earth, now interferes the least pos-

sible in terrestrial affairs. Christ adds, "Render to Cæsar the things that are Cæsar's, and to God the things that are God's." It is the first time that God and the state are so clearly distinguished. For Cæsar at that period was still the *pontifex maximus,* the chief and the principal organ of the Roman religion; he was the guardian and the interpreter of beliefs. He held the worship and the dogmas in his hands. Even his person was sacred and divine, for it was a peculiarity of the policy of the emperors that, wishing to recover the attributes of ancient royalty, they were careful not to forget the divine character which antiquity had attached to the king-pontiffs and to the priest-founders. But now Christ breaks the alliance which paganism and the empire wished to renew. He proclaims that religion is no longer the state, and that to obey Cæsar is no longer the same thing as to obey God.

Christianity completes the overthrow of the local worship; it extinguishes the prytanea, and completely destroys the city-protecting divinities. It does more; it refuses to assume the empire which these worships had exercised over civil society. It professes that between the state and itself there is nothing in common. It separates what all antiquity had confounded. We may remark, moreover, that during three centuries the new religion lived entirely beyond the action of the state; it knew how to dispense with state protection, and even to struggle against it. These three centuries established an abyss between the domain of the government and the domain of religion; and, as the recollection of this period could not be effaced, it followed that this distinction became a plain and incontestable truth, which the efforts even of a part of the clergy could not eradicate.

This principle was fertile in great results. On the one hand, politics became definitively freed from the strict rules which the ancient religion had traced, and could govern men without having to bend to sacred usages, without consulting the auspices or the oracles, without conforming all acts to the beliefs and requirements of a worship. Political action was freer; no other authority than that of the moral law now impeded it. On the other hand, if the state was more completely master in certain things, its action was also more limited. A complete half of man had been freed from its control. Christianity taught that only a part of man belonged to society; that he was bound to it by his body and by his material interests; that when subject to a tyrant, it was his duty to submit; that as a citizen of a republic, he ought to give his life for it, but that, in what related to his soul, he was free, and was bound only to God.

Stoicism had already marked this separation; it had restored man to himself, and had founded liberty of conscience. But that which was merely the effort of the energy of a courageous sect, Christianity made a universal and unchangeable rule for succeeding generations; what was only the consolation of a few, it made the common good of humanity.

If, now, we recollect what has been said above on the omnipotence of the states among the ancients,—if we bear in mind how far the city, in the name of its sacred character and of religion, which was inherent in it, exercised an absolute empire,—we shall see that this new principle was the source whence individual liberty flowed.

The mind once freed, the greatest difficulty was overcome, and liberty was compatible with social order.

Sentiments and manners, as well as politics, were then changed. The idea which men had of the duties of the citizen were modified. The first duty no longer consisted in giving one's time, one's strength, one's life to the state. Politics and war were no longer the whole of man;

all the virtues were no longer comprised in patriotism, for the soul no longer had a country. Man felt that he had other obligations besides that of living and dying for the city. Christianity distinguished the private from the public virtues. By giving less honor to the latter, it elevated the former; it placed God, the family, the human individual above country, the neighbor above the city.

Law was also changed in its nature. Among all ancient nations law had been subject to, and had received all its rules from, religion. Among the Persians, the Hindus, the Jews, the Greeks, the Italians, and the Gauls, the law had been contained in the sacred books or in religious traditions, and thus every religion had made laws after its own image. Christianity is the first religion that did not claim to be the source of law. It occupied itself with duties of men, not with their interests. Men saw it regulate neither the laws of property, nor the order of succession, nor obligations, nor legal proceedings. It placed itself outside the law, and outside all things purely terrestrial. Law was independent; it could draw its rules from nature, from the human conscience, from the powerful idea of the just that is in men's minds. It could develop in complete liberty; could be reformed and improved without obstacle; could follow the progress of morals, and could conform itself to the interests and social needs of every generation.

The happy influence of the new idea is easily seen in the history of Roman law. During several centuries preceding the triumph of Christianity, Roman law had already been striving to disengage itself from religion, and to approach natural equity; but it proceeded only by shifts and devices, which enervated and enfeebled its moral authority. The work of regenerating legislation, announced by the Stoic philosophers, pursued by the noble efforts of Roman jurisconsults. outlined by the artifices and expedients of the pretor, could not completely succeed except by favor of the independence which the new religion allowed to the law. We can see, as Christianity gained ground, that the Roman codes admitted new rules no longer by subterfuges, but openly and without hesitation. The domestic penates having been overthrown, and the sacred fires extinguished, the ancient constitution of the family disappeared forever, and with it the rules that had flowed from this source. The father had lost the absolute authority which his priesthood had formerly given him, and preserved only that which nature itself had conferred upon him for the good of the child. The wife, whom the old religion placed in a position inferior to the husband, became morally his equal. The laws of property were essentially altered; the sacred landmarks disap-

peared from the fields; the right of property no longer flowed from religion, but from labor; its acquisition became easier, and the formalities of the ancient law were definitively abolished.

Thus, by the single fact that the family no longer had its domestic religion, its constitution and its laws were transformed; so, too, from the single fact that the state no longer had its official religion, the rules for the government of men were forever changed.

Our study must end at this limit, which separates ancient from modern polities. We have written the history of a belief. It was established, and human society was constituted. It was modified, and society underwent a series of revolutions. It disappeared, and society changed its character. Such was the law of ancient times.

Herbert Spencer

AN ECCLESIASTICAL SYSTEM
AS
A SOCIAL BOND

Once more we must return to the religious idea and the religious sentiment in their rudimentary forms, to find an explanation of the part played by ecclesiastical systems in social development.

Though ancestor-worship has died out, there survive among us certain of the conceptions and feelings appropriate to it, and certain resulting observances,

From The Principles of Sociology (1877), London and Edinburgh: 1885, III (Part VI), §§ 622, 626, 627.

which enable us to understand its original effects, and the original effects of those cults immediately derived from it. I refer more especially to the behaviour of descendants after the death of a parent or grandparent. Three traits, of which we shall presently see the significance, may be noted.

When a funeral takes place, natural affection and usage supporting it, prompt the assembling of the family or clan: of children especially, of other relations to a considerable extent, and in a measure of friends. All, by taking part in the ceremony, join in that expression of respect which constituted the original worship and still remains a qualified form of worship. The burial of a progenitor consequently becomes an occasion on which, more than on any other, there is a revival of the thoughts and feelings appropriate to relationship, and a strengthening of the bonds among kindred.

An incidental result which is still more significant, not unfrequently occurs. If antagonisms among members of the family exist, they are not allowed to show themselves. Being possessed by a common sentiment towards the dead, and in so far made to sympathize, those who have been at enmity have their animosities to some extent mitigated; and not uncommonly reconciliations are effected. So that beyond a strengthening of the family-group by the gathering together of its members, there is a strengthening of it caused by the healing of breaches.

One more co-operative influence exists. The injunctions of the deceased are made known; and when these have reference to family-differences, obedience to them furthers harmony. Though it is true that directions concerning the distribution of property often initiate new quarrels, yet in respect of pre-existing quarrels, the known wish of the dying man that they should be ended, is influential in causing compromise or forgiveness; and if there has been a desire on his part that some particular course or policy should be pursued after his death, this desire, even orally expressed, tends very much to become a law to his descendants, and so to produce unity of action among them.

If in our days these influences still have considerable power, they must have had great power in days when there was a vivid conception of ancestral ghosts as liable to be made angry by disregard of their wishes, and able to punish the disobedient. Evidently the family-cult in

primitive times, must have greatly tended to maintain the family bond: alike by causing periodic assemblings for sacrifice, by repressing dissensions, and by producing conformity to the same injunctions.

Rising as we do from the ordinary father to the patriarch heading numerous families, propitiation of whose ghost is imperative on all of them, and thence to some head of kindred clans who, leading them to conquest, becomes after death a local chief god, above all others feared and obeyed; we may expect to find in the cults everywhere derived from ancestor-worship, the same influence which ancestor-worship in its simple original form shows us. We shall not be disappointed. Even concerning peoples so rude as the Ostyaks, we find the remark that "the use of the same consecrated spot, or the same priest, is also a bond of union"; and higher races yield still clearer evidence. . . .

The general influence of Ecclesiastical Institutions is conservative in a double sense. In several ways they maintain and strengthen social bonds, and so conserve the social aggregate; and they do this in large measure by conserving beliefs, sentiments, and usages which, evolved during earlier stages of the society, are shown by its survival to have had an approximate fitness to the requirements, and are likely still to have it in great measure. Elsewhere (*Study of Sociology*, Chap. V) I have, for another purpose, exemplified the extreme resistance to change offered by Ecclesiastical Institutions, and this more especially in respect of all things pertaining to the ecclesiastical organization itself. . . .

Again, then, the ghost-theory yields us the needful clue. As, before, we found that all religious observances may be traced back to funeral observances; so here, we find these influences which ecclesiastical institutions exert, have their germs in the influences exerted by the feelings entertained towards the dead. The burial of a late parent is an occasion on which the members of the family gather together and become bound by a renewed sense of kinship; on which any antagonism among them is temporarily or permanently extinguished; and on which they are further united by being subject in common to the deceased man's wishes, and made, in so far, to act in concert. The sentiment of filial piety thus manifesting itself, enlarges in its sphere when the deceased man is the patriarch, or the founder of the tribe, or the hero of the race. But be it in worship of a god or funeral of a parent, we ever see the same three influences—strengthening of union, suspension of hostilities, reinforcement of transmitted commands. In both cases the process of integration is in several ways furthered.

Thus, looking at it generally, we may say that ecclesiasticism stands for the principle of social continuity. Above all other agencies it is that which conduces to cohesion; not only between the coexisting parts of a nation, but also between its present generation and its past generations. In both ways it helps to maintain the individuality of the society. Or, changing somewhat the point of view, we may say that ecclesiasticism, embodying in its primitive form the rule of the dead over the living, and sanctifying in its more advanced forms the authority of the past over the present, has for its function to preserve in force the organized product of earlier experiences *versus* the modifying effects of more recent experiences. Evidently this organized product of past experiences is not without credentials. The life of the society has, up to the time being, been maintained under it; and hence a perennial reason for resistance to deviation. If we consider that habitually the chief or ruler, propitiation of whose ghost originates a local cult, acquired his position through successes of one or other kind, we must infer that obedience to the commands emanating from him, and maintenance of the usages he initiated, is, on the average of cases, conducive to social prosperity so long as conditions remain the same; and that therefore this intense conservatism of ecclesiastical institutions is not without a justification.

Even irrespective of the relative fitness of the inherited cult to the inherited social circumstances, there is an advantage in, if not indeed a necessity for, acceptance of traditional beliefs, and consequent conformity to the resulting customs and rules. For before an assemblage of men can become organized, the men must be held together, and kept ever in presence of the conditions to which they have to become adapted; and that they may be thus held, the coercive influence of their traditional beliefs must be strong. So great are the obstacles which the anti-social traits of the savage offer to that social cohesion which is the first condition to social progress, that he can be kept within the needful bonds only by a sentiment prompting absolute submission—submission to secular rule reinforced by that sacred rule which is at first in unison with it. And hence, as I have before pointed out, the truth that in whatever place arising—Egypt, Assyria, Peru, Mexico, China—social evolution throughout all its earlier stages has been accompanied not only by extreme subordination to living kings, but also by elaborate worships of the deities originating from dead kings.

W. Robertson Smith

RELIGION
AND NATURAL SOCIETY

We have seen that ancient faiths must be looked on as matters of institution rather than of dogma or formulated belief, and that the system of an antique religion was part of the social order under which its adherents lived; so that the word "system" must here be taken in a practical sense as when we speak of a political system, and not in the sense of an organised body of ideas or theological opinions. Broadly speaking, religion was made up of a series of acts and observances, the correct performance of which was necessary or desirable to secure the favour of the gods or to avert their anger; and in these observances every member of society had a share, marked out for him either in virtue of his being born within a certain family and community, or in virtue of the station, within the family and community, that he had come to hold in the course of his life. A man did not choose his religion or frame it for himself; it came to him as part of the general scheme of social obligations and ordinances laid upon him, as a matter of course, by his position in the family and in the nation. Individual men were more or less religious, as men now are more or less patriotic; that is, they discharged their religious duties with a greater or less degree of zeal according to their

From The Religion of the Semites: The Fundamental Institutions (1889), 2nd & enlarged ed., New York: 1894, pp. 28–31; 39–42; 239–40; 263–68; 287–89.

character and temperament; but there was no such thing as an absolutely irreligious man. A certain amount of religion was required of everybody; for the due performance of religious acts was a social obligation in which every one had his appointed share. Of intolerance in the modern sense of the word ancient society knew nothing; it never persecuted a man into particular beliefs for the good of his own soul. Religion did not exist for the saving of souls but for the preservation and welfare of society, and in all that was necessary to this end every man had to take his part, or break with the domestic and political community to which he belonged.

Perhaps the simplest way of putting the state of the case is this. Every human being, without choice on his own part, but simply in virtue of his birth and upbringing, becomes a member of what we call a *natural* society. He belongs, that is, to a certain family and a certain nation, and this membership lays upon him definite obligations and duties which he is called upon to fulfil as a matter of course, and on pain of social penalties and disabilities, while at the same time it confers upon him certain social rights and advantages. In this respect the ancient and modern worlds are alike; but there is this important difference, that the tribal or national societies of the ancient world were not strictly natural in the modern sense of the word, for the gods had their part and place in them equally with men. The circle into which a man was born was not simply a group of kinsfolk and fellow-citizens, but embraced also certain divine beings, the gods of the family and of the state, which to the ancient mind were as much a part of the particular community with which they stood connected as the human members of the social circle. The relation between the gods of antiquity and their worshippers was expressed in the language of human relationship, and this language was not taken in a figurative sense but with strict literality. If a god was spoken of as father and his worshippers as his offspring, the meaning was that the worshippers were literally of his stock, that he and they made up one natural family with reciprocal family duties to one another. Or, again, if the god was addressed as king, and the worshippers called themselves his servants, they meant that the supreme guidance of the state was actually in his hands, and accordingly the organisation of the state included provision for consulting his will and obtaining his direction in all weighty matters, and also provision for approaching him as king with due homage and tribute.

Thus a man was born into a fixed relation to certain gods as surely as he was born into relation to his fellowmen; and his religion, that is, the part of conduct which was determined by his relation to the gods, was simply one side of the general scheme of conduct prescribed for him by his position as a member of society. There was no separation between the spheres of religion and of ordinary life. Every social act had a reference to the gods as well as to men, for the social body was not made up of men only, but of gods and men.

This account of the position of religion in the social system holds good, I believe, for all parts and races of the ancient world in the earlier stages of

their history. The causes of so remarkable a uniformity lie hidden in the mists of prehistoric time, but must plainly have been of a general kind, operating on all parts of mankind without distinction of race and local environment; for in every region of the world, as soon as we find a nation or tribe emerging from prehistoric darkness into the light of authentic history, we find also that its religion conforms to the general type which has just been indicated. As time rolls on and society advances, modifications take place. In religion as in other matters the transition from the antique to the modern type of life is not sudden and unprepared, but is gradually led up to by a continuous distintegration of the old structure of society, accompanied by the growth of new ideas and institutions. . . .

*   *   *

Thus far we have looked only at the general fact, that in a Semitic community men and their gods formed a social and political as well as a religious whole. But to make our conceptions more concrete we must consider what place in this whole was occupied by the divine element of the social partnership. And here we find that the two leading conceptions of the relation of the god to his people are those of fatherhood and of kingship. We have learned to look on Semitic society as built up on two bases— on kinship, which is the foundation of the system of clans or gentes, and on the union of kins, living intermingled or side by side, and bound together by common interests, which is the foundation of the state. We now see that the clan and the state are both represented in religion: as father the god belongs to the family or clan, as king he belongs to the state; and in each sphere of the social order he holds the position of highest dignity. Both these conceptions deserve to be looked at and illustrated in some detail.

The relation of a father to his children

has a moral as well as a physical aspect, and each of these must be taken into account in considering what the fatherhood of the tribal deity meant in ancient religion. In the physical aspect the father is the being to whom the child owes his life, and through whom he traces kinship with the other members of his family or clan. The antique conception of kinship is participation in one blood, which passes from parent to child and circulates in the veins of every member of the family. The unity of the family or clan is viewed as a physical unity, for the blood is the life,— an idea familiar to us from the Old Testament,[1]—and it is the same blood and therefore the same life that is shared by every descendant of the common ancestor. The idea that the race has a life of its own, of which individual lives are only parts, is expressed even more clearly by picturing the race as a tree, of which the ancestor is the root or stem and the descendants the branches. This figure is used by all the Semites, and is very common both in the Old Testament and in the Arabian poets.

The moral aspect of fatherhood, again, lies in the social relations and obligations which flow from the physical relationship—in the sanctity of the tie of blood which binds together the whole family, and in the particular modification of this tie in the case of parent and child, the parent protecting and nourishing the child, while the child owes obedience and service to his parent.

In Christianity, and already in the spiritual religion of the Hebrews, the idea of divine fatherhood is entirely dissociated from the physical basis of natural fatherhood. Man was created in the image of God, but he was not begotten; Godsonship is not a thing of nature but a thing of grace. In the Old Testament, Israel is Jehovah's son, and Jehovah is his father who created him;[2] but this creation is not a physical act, it refers to the series of gracious deeds by which Israel was shaped into a nation. And so, though it may be said of the Israelites as a whole, "Ye are the children of Jehovah your God,"[3] this sonship is national, not personal, and the individual Israelite has not the right to call himself Jehovah's son.

But in heathen religions the fatherhood of the gods is physical fatherhood. Among the Greeks, for example, the idea that the gods fashioned men out of clay, as potters fashion images, is relatively modern. The older conception is that the races of men have gods for their ancestors, or are the children of the earth, the common mother of gods and men, so that men are really of the stock or kin of the gods.[4] That the same conception was familiar to the older Semites appears from the Bible. Jeremiah describes idolaters as saying to a stock, Thou art my father; and to a stone, Thou hast brought me forth.[5] . . .

*   *   *

I have already had occasion in another connection to shew by a variety of evidences that the earliest Semites, like primitive men of other races, drew no sharp line of distinction between the nature of gods, of men, and of beasts, and had no difficulty in admitting a real kinship between (a) gods and men, (b) gods and sacred animals, (c) families of

---

[1]Gen. ix. 4; Deut. xii. 23. Among the Arabs also *nafs* is used of the life-blood. When a man dies a natural death his life departs through the nostrils (*māta ḥatfa anfihi*), but when he is slain in battle "his life flows on the spear point" (Ḥamāsa, p. 52). Similarly *lā nafsa lahu sāïlatun* means *lā dama lahu yajrī* (Miṣbāḥ, s.v.). To the use of *nafs* in the sense of blood, the Arabian philologists refer such expressions as *nifās*, childbirth; nafsā, puerpera. The use of *nafisat* or *nufisat* in the sense of *ḥāḍat* (Bokhārī, i. 72, 1. 10) appears to justify their explanation.

[2]Hos. xi. 1; Deut. xxxii. 6.

[3]Deut. xiv. 1.

[4]See details and references in Preller-Robert, *Griechische Mythol.* (1887) i. 78 *sqq.*

[5]Jer. ii. 27.

men and families of beasts. As regards the third of these points, the direct evidence is fragmentary and sporadic; it is sufficient to prove that the idea of kinship between races of men and races of beasts was not foreign to the Semites, but it is not sufficient to prove that such a belief was widely prevalent, or to justify us in taking it as one of the fundamental principles on which Semitic ritual was founded. But it must be remembered that the three points are so connected that if any two of them are established, the third necessarily follows. Now, as regards (*a*), it is not disputed that the kinship of gods with their worshippers is a fundamental doctrine of Semitic religion; it appears so widely and in so many forms and applications, that we cannot look upon it otherwise than as one of the first and most universal principles of ancient faith. Again, as regards (*b*), a belief in sacred animals, which are treated with the reverence due to divine beings, is an essential element in the most widespread and important Semitic cults. All the great deities of the northern Semites had their sacred animals, and were themselves worshipped in animal form, or in association with animal symbols, down to a late date; and that this association implied a veritable unity of kind between animals and gods is placed beyond doubt, on the one hand, by the fact that the sacred animals, *e.g.* the doves and fish of Atargatis, were reverenced with divine honours; and, on the other hand, by theogonic myths, such as that which makes the dove-goddess be born from an egg, and transformation myths, such as that of Bambyce, where it was believed that the fish-goddess and her son had actually been transformed into fish.[6]

[6]Examples of the evidence on this head have been given above; a fuller account of it will fall to be given in a future course of lectures. Meantime the reader may refer to *Kinship*, chap. vii. I may here, however, add a general argument which seems to deserve attention. We have seen (*supra*, p. 142 *sqq.*) that holiness is not based on

Now if kinship between the gods and their worshippers, on the one hand, and kinship between the gods and certain kinds of animals, on the other, are deep-seated principles of Semitic religion, manifesting themselves in all parts of the sacred institutions of the race, we must necessarily conclude that kinship between families of men and animal kinds was an idea equally deep-seated, and we shall expect to find that sacred animals, wherever they occur, will be treated with the regard which men pay to their kinsfolk.

Indeed in a religion based on kinship, where the god and his worshippers are of one stock, the principle of sanctity and that of kinship are identical. The sanctity of a kinsman's life and the sanctity of the godhead are not two things, but one; for ultimately the only thing that is sacred is the common tribal life, or the common blood which is identified with the life. Whatever being partakes in this life is holy, and its holiness may be described indifferently, as participation in the divine life and nature, or as participation in the kindred blood.

Thus the conjecture that sacrificial animals were originally treated as kinsmen, is simply equivalent to the conjecture that sacrifices were drawn from animals of a holy kind, whose lives were ordinarily protected by religious scruples and sanctions; and in support of this position a great mass of evidence can be adduced, not merely for Semitic sacrifice, but for ancient sacrifice generally. . . .

*   *   *

the idea of property. Holy animals, and holy things generally, are primarily conceived, not as belonging to the deity, but as being themselves instinct with divine power or life. Thus a holy animal is one which has a divine life; and if it be holy to a particular god, the meaning must be that its life and his are somehow bound up together. From what is known of primitive ways of thought we may infer that this means that the sacred animal is akin to the god, for all valid and permanent relation between individuals is conceived as kinship.

Now, if we put aside the *piacula* and whole burnt-offerings, it appears that, according to the Levitical ritual, the distinction between oblations in which the worshipper shared, and oblations which were wholly given over to the deity to be consumed on the altar or by the priests, corresponds to the distinction between animal and vegetable offerings. The animal victim was presented at the altar and devoted by the imposition of hands, but the greater part of the flesh was returned to the worshipper, to be eaten by him under special rules. It could be eaten only by persons ceremonially clean, *i.e.*, fit to approach the deity; and if the food was not consumed on the same day, or in certain cases within two days, the remainder had to be burned.[7] The plain meaning of these rules is that the flesh is not common but holy,[8] and that the act of eating it is a part of the service, which is to be completed before men break up from the sanctuary.[9] The *zébaḥ,* therefore, is not a mere attenuated offering, in which man grudges to give up the whole victim to his God. On the contrary, the central significance of the rite lies in the act of communion between God and man, when the worshipper is admitted to eat of the same holy flesh of which a part is laid upon the altar as "the food of the deity." But with the *minḥa* nothing of this kind occurs; the whole consecrated offering is retained by the deity, and the worshipper's part in the service is completed as soon as he has made over his gift. In short, while the *zébaḥ* turns on an act of communion between the deity and his worshippers, the *minḥa* (as its name denotes) is simply a tribute. . . .

* * *

In acts of worship we expect to find the

[7]Lev. vii. 15 *sqq.*, xix. 6, xxii. 30.
[8]Hag. ii. 12; cf. Jer. xi. 15, LXX.
[9]The old sacrificial feasts occupy but a single day (1 Sam. ix.), or at most two days (1 Sam. xx. 27).

religious ideal expressed in its purest form, and we cannot easily think well of a type of religion whose ritual culminates in a jovial feast. It seems that such a faith sought nothing higher than a condition of physical *bien être,* and in one sense this judgment is just. The good things desired of the gods were the blessings of earthly life, not spiritual but carnal things. But Semitic heathenism was redeemed from mere materialism by the fact that religion was not the affair of the individual but of the community. The ideal was earthly, but it was not selfish. In rejoicing before his god a man rejoiced with and for the welfare of his kindred, his neighbours and his country, and, in renewing by a solemn act of worship the bond that united him to his god, he also renewed the bonds of family, social and national obligation. We have seen that the compact between the god and the community of his worshippers was not held to pledge the deity to make the private cares of each member of the community his own. The gods had their favourites no doubt, for whom they were prepared to do many things that they were not bound to do; but no man could approach his god in a purely personal matter with that spirit of absolute confidence which I have described as characteristic of antique religions; it was the community, and not the individual, that was sure of the permanent and unfailing help of its deity. It was a national not a personal providence that was taught by ancient religion. So much was this the case that in purely personal concerns the ancients were very apt to turn, not to the recognised religion of the family or of the state, but to magical superstitions. The gods watched over a man's civic life, they gave him his share in public benefits, the annual largess of the harvest and the vintage, national peace or victory over enemies, and so forth, but they were not sure helpers in every private need, and above all they would not help him in matters that were against the interests of the community as a whole. There was therefore a whole region of possible needs and desires for which religion could and would do nothing; and if supernatural help was sought in such things it had to be sought through magical ceremonies, designed to purchase or constrain the favour of demoniac powers with which the public religion had nothing to do. Not only did these magical superstitions lie outside religion, but in all well-ordered states they were regarded as illicit. A man had no right to enter into private relations with supernatural powers that might help him at the expense of the community to which he belonged. In his relations to the unseen he was bound always to think and act with and for the community, and not for himself alone.

With this it accords that every complete act of worship—for a mere vow was not a complete act till it was fulfilled by presenting a sacrifice—had a public or quasi-public character. Most sacrifices were offered on fixed occasions, at the great communal or national feasts, but even a private offering was not complete without guests, and the surplus of sacrificial flesh was not sold but distributed with an open hand.[10] Thus every act of worship expressed the idea that man does not live for himself only but for his fellows, and that this partnership of social interests is the sphere over which the gods preside and on which they bestow their assured blessing.

The ethical significance which thus appertains to the sacrificial meal, viewed as a social act, received particular emphasis from certain ancient customs and ideas connected with eating and drinking. According to antique ideas, those who eat and drink together are by this very act tied to one another by a bond of friendship and mutual obligation. Hence

when we find that in ancient religions all the ordinary functions of worship are summed up in the sacrificial meal, and that the ordinary intercourse between gods and men has no other form, we are to remember that the act of eating and drinking together is the solemn and stated expression of the fact that all who share the meal are brethren, and that the duties of friendship and brotherhood are implicitly acknowledged in their common act. By admitting man to his table the god admits him to his friendship; but this favour is extended to no man in his mere private capacity; he is received as one of a community, to eat and drink along with his fellows, and in the same measure as the act of worship cements the bond between him and his god, it cements also the bond between him and his brethren in the common faith.

We have now reached a point in our discussion at which it is possible to form some general estimate of the ethical value of the type of religion which has been described. The power of religion over life is twofold, lying partly in its association with particular precepts of conduct, to which it supplies a supernatural sanction, but mainly in its influence on the general tone and temper of men's minds, which it elevates to higher courage and purpose, and raises above a brutal servitude to the physical wants of the moment, by teaching men that their lives and happiness are not the mere sport of the blind forces of nature, but are watched over and cared for by a higher power. As a spring of action this influence is more potent than the fear of supernatural sanctions, for it is stimulative, while the other is only regulative. But to produce a moral effect on life the two must go together; a man's actions must be not only supported by the feeling that the divine help is with him, but regulated by the conviction that that help will not accompany him except on the right path. In ancient religion, as it appears among

[10]In Greece, in later times, sacrificial flesh was exposed for sale (1 Cor. x. 25).

the Semites, the confident assurance of divine help belongs, not to each man in his private concerns, but to the community in its public functions and public aims; and it is this assurance that is expressed in public acts of worship, where all the members of the community meet together to eat and drink at the table of their god, and so renew the sense that he and they are altogether at one. Now, if we look at the whole community of worshippers as absolutely one, personify them and think of them as a single individual, it is plain that the effect of this type of religion must be regarded as merely stimulative and not regulative. When the community is at one with itself and at one with its god, it may, for anything that religion has to say, do exactly what it pleases towards all who are outside it. Its friends are the god's friends, its enemies the god's enemies; it takes its god with it in whatever it chooses to do. As the ancient communities of religion are tribes or nations, this is as much as to say that, properly speaking, ancient religion has no influence on intertribal or international morality—in such matters the god simply goes with his own nation or his own tribe. So long as we consider the tribe or nation of common religion as a single subject, the influence of religion is limited to an increase of the national self-confidence— a quality very useful in the continual struggle for life that was waged between ancient communities, but which beyond this has no moral value.

But the case is very different when we look at the religious community as made up of a multitude of individuals, each of whom has private as well as public purposes and desires. In this aspect it is the regulative influence of ancient religion that is predominant, for the good things which religion holds forth are promised to the individual only in so far as he lives in and for the community. The conception of man's chief good set forth in the social act of sacrificial worship is the happiness of the individual in the happiness of the community, and thus the whole force of ancient religion is directed, so far as the individual is concerned, to maintain the civil virtues of loyalty and devotion to a man's fellows at a pitch of confident enthusiasm, to teach him to set his highest good in the prosperity of the society of which he is a member, not doubting that in so doing he has the divine power on his side and has given his life to a cause that cannot fail. This devotion to the common weal was, as every one knows, the mainspring of ancient morality and the source of all the heroic virtues of which ancient history presents so many illustrious examples. In ancient society, therefore, the religious ideal expressed in the act of social worship and the ethical ideal which governed the conduct of daily life were wholly at one, and all morality—as morality was then understood—was consecrated and enforced by religious motives and sanctions.

These observations are fully applicable only to the typical form of ancient religion, when it was still strictly tribal or national. When nationality and religion began to fall apart, certain worships assumed a character more or less cosmopolitan. Even in heathenism, therefore, in its more advanced forms, the gods, or at least certain gods, are in some measure the guardians of universal morality, and not merely of communal loyalty. But what was thus gained in comprehensiveness was lost in intensity and strength of religious feeling, and the advance towards ethical universalism, which was made with feeble and uncertain steps, was never sufficient to make up for the decline of the old heroic virtues that were fostered by the narrower type of national faith.

Emile Durkheim

RELIGION
AS A COLLECTIVE
REPRESENTATION

IN this book we propose to study the most primitive and simple religion which is actually known, to make an analysis of it, and to attempt an explanation of it. A religious system may be said to be the most primitive which we can observe when it fulfils the two following conditions: in the first place, when it is found in a society whose organization is surpassed by no others in simplicity;[1] and secondly, when it is possible to explain it without making use of any element borrowed from a previous religion.

We shall set ourselves to describe the organization of this system with all the exactness and fidelity that an ethnographer or an historian could give it. But our task will not be limited to that: sociology raises other problems than history or ethnography. It does not seek to know the passed forms of civilization with the sole end of knowing them and

From The Elementary Forms of the Religious Life (1912). New York: 1961, pp. 13, 15, 17, 19–21, 236–40, 251–55, 261. By permission of George Allen & Unwin Ltd. and The Macmillan Company. Copyright 1915 by George Allen & Unwin Ltd.

[1]In the same way, we shall say of these societies that they are primitive, and we shall call the men of these societies primitives. Undoubtedly the expression lacks precision, but that is hardly evitable, and besides, when we have taken pains to fix the meaning, it is not inconvenient.

reconstructing them. But rather, like every positive science, it has as its object the explanation of some actual reality which is near to us, and which consequently is capable of affecting our ideas and our acts: this reality is man, and more precisely, the man of to-day, for there is nothing which we are more interested in knowing. Then we are not going to study a very archaic religion simply for the pleasure of telling its peculiarities and its singularities. If we have taken it as the subject of our research, it is because it has seemed to us better adapted than any other to lead to an understanding of the religious nature of man, that is to say, to show us an essential and permanent aspect of humanity. . . .

But why give them [primitive religions] a sort of prerogative? Why choose them in preference to all others as the subject of our study?—It is merely for reasons of method. . . . At the foundation of all systems of beliefs and of all cults there ought necessarily to be a certain number of fundamental representations or conceptions and of ritual attitudes which, in spite of the diversity of forms which they have taken, have the same objective significance and fulfil the same functions everywhere. These are the permanent elements which constitute that which is permanent and human in religion; they form all the objective contents of the idea which is expressed when one speaks of *religion* in general. How is it possible to pick them out?

Surely it is not by observing the complex religions which appear in the course of history. Every one of these is made up of such a variety of elements that it is very difficult to distinguish what is secondary from what is principal, the essential from the accessory....Primitive religions do not merely aid us in disengaging the constituent elements of religion; they also have the great advantage that they facilitate the explanation of it. Since the facts there are simpler, the relations between them are more apparent. The reasons with which men account for their acts have not yet been elaborated and denatured by studied reflection; they are nearer and more closely related to the motives which have really determined these acts. In order to understand an hallucination perfectly, and give it its most appropriate treatment, a physician must know its original point of departure. Now this event is proportionately easier to find if he can observe it near its beginnings. The longer the disease is allowed to develop, the more it evades observation; that is because all sorts of interpretations have intervened as it advanced, which tend to force the original state into the background, and across which it is frequently difficult to find the initial one. Between a systematized hallucination and the first impressions which gave it birth, the distance is often considerable. It is the same thing with religious thought. In proportion as it progresses in history, the causes which called it into existence, though remaining active, are no longer perceived, except across a vast scheme of interpretations which quite transform them. Popular mythologies and subtle theologies have done their work: they have superimposed upon the primitive sentiments others

which are quite different, and which, though holding to the first, of which they are an elaborated form, only allow their true nature to appear very imperfectly. The psychological gap between the cause and the effect, between the apparent cause and the effective cause, has become more considerable and more difficult for the mind to leap. The remainder of this book will be an illustration and a verification of this remark on method. It will be seen how, in the primitive religions, the religious fact still visibly carries the mark of its origins: it would have been wellnigh impossible to infer them merely from the study of the more developed religions.

The study which we are undertaking is therefore a way of taking up again, *but under new conditions,* the old problem of the origin of religion. To be sure, if by origin we are to understand the very first beginning, the question has nothing scientific about it, and should be resolutely discarded. There was no given moment when religion began to exist, and there is consequently no need of finding a means of transporting ourselves thither in thought. Like every human institution, religion did not commence anywhere. Therefore, all speculations of this sort are justly discredited; they can only consist in subjective and arbitrary constructions which are subject to no sort of control. But the problem which we raise is quite another one. What we want to do is to find a means of discerning the ever-present causes upon which the most essential forms of religious thought and practice depend. Now for the reasons which were just set forth, these causes are proportionately more easily observable as the societies where they are observed are less complicated. That is why we try to get as near as possible to the origins.[2] It is not that we ascribe particular virtues to the lower religions.

On the contrary, they are rudimentary and gross; we cannot make of them a sort of model which later religions only have to reproduce. But even their grossness makes them instructive, for they thus become convenient for experiments, as in them, the facts and their relations are easily seen. In order to discover the laws of the phenomena which he studies, the physicist tries to simplify these latter and rid them of their secondary characteristics. For that which concerns institutions, nature spontaneously makes the same sort of simplifications at the beginning of history. We merely wish to put these to profit. . . .

*   *   *

Thus the totem is before all a symbol, a material expression of something else. But of what?

From the analysis to which we have been giving our attention, it is evident that it expresses and symbolizes two different sorts of things. In the first place, it is the outward and visible form of what we have called the totemic principle or god. But it is also the symbol of the determined society called the clan. It is its flag; it is the sign by which each clan distinguishes itself from the others, the visible mark of its personality, a mark borne by everything which is a part of the clan under any title whatsoever, men, beasts or things. So if it is at once the symbol of the god and of the society, is that not because the god and the society are only one? How could the emblem of the group have been able to become the figure of this quasi-divinity, if the group and the divinity were two distinct reali-

ties? The god of the clan, the totemic principle, can therefore be nothing else than the clan itself, personified and represented to the imagination under the visible form of the animal or vegetable which serves as totem.

But how has this apotheosis been possible, and how did it happen to take place in this fashion?

In a general way, it is unquestionable that a society has all that is necessary to arouse the sensation of the divine in minds, merely by the power that it has over them; for to its members it is what a god is to his worshippers. In fact, a god is, first of all, a being whom men think of as superior to themselves, and upon whom they feel that they depend. Whether it be a conscious personality, such as Zeus or Jahveh, or merely abstract forces such as those in play in totemism, the worshipper, in the one case as in the other, believes himself held to certain manners of acting which are imposed upon him by the nature of the sacred principle with which he feels that he is in communion. Now society also gives us the sensation of a perpetual dependence. Since it has a nature which is peculiar to itself and different from our individual nature, it pursues ends which are likewise special to it; but, as it cannot attain them except through our intermediacy, it imperiously demands our aid. It requires that, forgetful of our own interest, we make ourselves its servitors, and it submits us to every sort of inconvenience, privation and sacrifice, without which social life would be impossible. It is because of this that at every instant we are obliged to submit ourselves to rules of conduct and of thought which we have neither made nor desired, and which are sometimes even contrary to our most fundamental inclinations and instincts.

Even if society were unable to obtain these concessions and sacrifices from us except by a material constraint, it might awaken in us only the idea of a physical

[2]It is seen that we give a wholly relative sense to this word "origins," just as to the word "primitive." By it we do not mean an absolute beginning, but the most simple social condition that is actually known or that beyond which we cannot go at present. When we speak of the origins or of the commencement of religious history or thought, it is in this sense that our statements should be understood.

rce to which we must give way of necessity, instead of that of a moral ower such as religions adore. But as a natter of fact, the empire which it holds ver consciences is due much less to the hysical supremacy of which it has the rivilege than to the moral authority vith which it is invested. If we yield to s orders, it is not merely because it is trong enough to triumph over our esistance; it is primarily because it is the bject of a venerable respect.

We say that an object, whether individual or collective, inspires respect when he representation expressing it in the nind is gifted with such a force that it utomatically causes or inhibits actions, *ithout regard for any consideration relative o their useful or injurious effects.* When we bey somebody because of the moral uthority which we recognize in him, ve follow out his opinions, not because hey seem wise, but because a certain sort of physical energy is imminent in the dea that we form of this person, which onquers our will and inclines it in the ndicated direction. Respect is the emoion which we experience when we feel his interior and wholly spiritual pressure operating upon us. Then we are not determined by the advantages or inconveniences of the attitude which is prescribed or recommended to us; it is by the way n which we represent to ourselves the person recommending or prescribing it. This is why commands generally take a hort, peremptory form leaving no place or hesitation; it is because, in so far as it s a command and goes by its own force, t excludes all idea of deliberation or calculation; it gets its efficacy from the ntensity of the mental state in which it is placed. It is this intensity which creates what is called a moral ascendancy.

Now the ways of action to which ociety is strongly enough attached to mpose them upon its members, are, by hat very fact, marked with a distinctive ign provocative of respect. Since they are elaborated in common, the vigour with which they have been thought of by each particular mind is retained in all the other minds, and reciprocally. The representations which express them within each of us have an intensity which no purely private states of consciousness could ever attain; for they have the strength of the innumerable individual representations which have served to form each of them. It is society who speaks through the mouths of those who affirm them in our presence; it is society whom we hear in hearing them; and the voice of all has an accent which that of one alone could never have. The very violence with which society reacts, by way of blame or material suppression, against every attempted dissidence, contributes to strengthening its empire by manifesting the common conviction through this burst of ardour. In a word, when something is the object of such a state of opinion, the representation which each individual has of it gains a power of action from its origins and the conditions in which it was born, which even those feel who do not submit themselves to it. It tends to repel the representations which contradict it, and it keeps them at a distance; on the other hand, it commands those acts which will realize it, and it does so, not by a material coercion or by the perspective of something of this sort, but by the simple radiation of the mental energy which it contains. It has an efficacy coming solely from its psychical properties, and it is by just this sign that moral authority is recognized. So opinion, primarily a social thing, is a source of authority, and it might even be asked whether all authority is not the daughter of opinion.[3] It may be objected that science is often the antagonist of opinion, whose errors it combats and rectifies.

[3]This is the case at least with all moral authority recognized as such by the group as a whole.

But it cannot succeed in this task if it does not have sufficient authority, and it can obtain this authority only from opinion itself. If a people did not have faith in science, all the scientific demonstrations in the world would be without any influence whatsoever over their minds. Even to-day, if science happened to resist a very strong current of public opinion, it would risk losing its credit there.[4]

Since it is in spiritual ways that social pressure exercises itself, it could not fail to give men the idea that outside themselves there exist one or several powers, both moral and, at the same time, efficacious, upon which they depend. They must think of these powers, at least in part, as outside themselves, for these address them in a tone of command and sometimes even order them to do violence to their most natural inclinations. It is undoubtedly true that if they were

[4]We hope that this analysis and those which follow will put an end to an inexact interpretation of our thought, from which more than one misunderstanding has resulted. Since we have made constraint the *outward sign* by which social facts can be the most easily recognized and distinguished from the facts of individual psychology, it has been assumed that according to our opinion, physical constraint is the essential thing for social life. As a matter of fact, we have never considered it more than the material and apparent expression of an interior and profound fact which is wholly ideal: this is *moral authority*. The problem of sociology—if we can speak of *a* sociological problem—consists in seeking, among the different forms of external constraint, the different sorts of moral authority corresponding to them and in discovering the causes which have determined these latter. The particular question which we are treating in this present work has as its principal object, the discovery of the form under which that particular variety of moral authority which is inherent in all that is religious has been born, and out of what elements it is made. It will be seen presently that even if we do make social pressure one of the distinctive characteristics of sociological phenomena, we do not mean to say that it is the only one. We shall show another aspect of the collective life, nearly opposite to the preceding one, but none the less real.

able to see that these influences which they feel emanate from society, then the mythological system of interpretation would never be born. But social action follows ways that are too circuitous and obscure, and employs psychical mechanisms that are too complex to allow the ordinary observer to see when it comes. As long as scientific analysis does not come to teach it to them, men know well that they are acted upon, but they do not know by whom. So they must invent by themselves the idea of these powers with which they feel themselves in connection, and from that, we are able to catch a glimpse of the way by which they were led to represent them under forms that are really foreign to their nature and to transfigure them by thought. . . .

But the explanation is still incomplete. We have shown how the clan, by the manner in which it acts upon its members, awakens within them the idea of external forces which dominate them and exalt them; but we must still demand how it happens that these forces are thought of under the form of totems, that is to say, in the shape of an animal or plant.

It is because this animal or plant has given its name to the clan and serves it as emblem. In fact, it is a well-known law that the sentiments aroused in us by something spontaneously attach themselves to the symbol which represents them. For us, black is a sign of mourning; it also suggests sad impressions and ideas. This transference of sentiments comes simply from the fact that the idea of a thing and the idea of its symbol are closely united in our minds; the result is that the emotions provoked by the one extend contagiously to the other. But this contagion, which takes place in every case to a certain degree, is much more complete and more marked when the symbol is something simple, definite and easily representable, while the thing itself, owing to its dimensions, the number of its parts and the complexity of heir arrangement, is difficult to hold in the mind. For we are unable to consider n abstract entity, which we can represent only laboriously and confusedly, the ource of the strong sentiments which we eel. We cannot explain them to ourselves except by connecting them to some concrete object of whose reality we are vividly aware. Then if the thing itself does not fulfil this condition, it cannot serve as the accepted basis of the sentiments elt, even though it may be what really aroused them. Then some sign takes its place; it is to this that we connect the emotions it excites. It is this which is loved, feared, respected; it is to this that we are grateful; it is for this that we sacrifice ourselves. The soldier who dies or his flag, dies for his country; but as a matter of fact, in his own consciousness, it is the flag that has the first place. It sometimes happens that this even directly determines action. Whether one isolated standard remains in the hands of the enemy or not does not determine the fate of the country, yet the soldier allows himself to be killed to regain it. He loses sight of the fact that the flag is only a sign, and that it has no value in itself, but only brings to mind the reality that it represents; it is treated as if it were this reality itself.

Now the totem is the flag of the clan. It is therefore natural that the impressions aroused by the clan in individual minds—impressions of dependence and of increased vitality—should fix themselves to the idea of the totem rather than that of the clan: for the clan is too complex a reality to be represented clearly in all its complex unity by such rudimentary intelligences. More than that, the primitive does not even see that these impressions come to him from the group. He does not know that the coming together of a number of men associated in the same life results in disengaging new energies, which transform each of them. All that he knows is that he is raised above himself and that he sees a different life from the one he ordinarily leads. However, he must connect these sensations to some external object as their cause. Now what does he see about him? On every side those things which appeal to his senses and strike his imagination are the numerous images of the totem. They are the waninga and the nurtunja, which are symbols of the sacred being. They are churinga and bullroarers, upon which are generally carved combinations of lines having the same significance. They are the decorations covering the different parts of his body, which are totemic marks. How could this image, repeated everywhere and in all sorts of forms, fail to stand out with exceptional relief in his mind? Placed thus in the centre of the scene, it becomes representative. The sentiments experienced fix themselves upon it, for it is the only concrete object upon which they can fix themselves. It continues to bring them to mind and to evoke them even after the assembly has dissolved, for it survives the assembly, being carved upon the instruments of the cult, upon the sides of rocks, upon bucklers, etc. By it, the emotions experienced are perpetually sustained and revived. Everything happens just as if they inspired them directly. It is still more natural to attribute them to it for, since they are common to the group, they can be associated only with something that is equally common to all. Now the totemic emblem is the only thing satisfying this condition. By definition, it is common to all. During the ceremony, it is the centre of all regards. While generations change, it remains the same; it is the permanent element of the social life. So it is from it that those mysterious forces seem to emanate with which men feel that they are related, and thus they have been led to represent these forces under the form of the animate or inanimate being whose name the clan bears.

When this point is once established, we

are in a position to understand all that is essential in the totemic beliefs.

Since religious force is nothing other than the collective and anonymous force of the clan, and since this can be represented in the mind only in the form of the totem, the totemic emblem is like the visible body of the god. Therefore, it is from it that those kindly and dreadful actions seem to emanate, which the cult seeks to provoke or prevent; consequently, it is to it that the cult is addressed. This is the explanation of why it holds the first place in the series of sacred things.

But the clan, like every other sort of society, can live only in and through the individual consciousnesses that compose it. So if religious force, in so far as it is conceived as incorporated in the totemic emblem, appears to be outside of the individuals and to be endowed with a sort of transcendence over them, it, like the clan of which it is the symbol, can be realized only in and through them; in this sense, it is imminent in them and they necessarily represent it as such. They feel it present and active within them, for it is this which raises them to a superior life. This is why men have believed that they contain within them a principle comparable to the one residing in the totem, and consequently, why they have attributed a sacred character to themselves, but one less marked than that of the emblem. It is because the emblem is the pre-eminent source of the religious life; the man participates in it only indirectly, as he is well aware; he takes into account the fact that the force that transports him into the world of sacred things is not inherent in him, but comes to him from the outside.

But for still another reason, the animals or vegetables of the totemic species should have the same character and even to a higher degree. If the totemic principle is nothing else than the clan, it is the clan thought of under the material form of the totemic emblem; now this form is also that of the concrete beings whose name the clan bears. Owing to th resemblance, they could not fail to evok sentiments analogous to those aroused b the emblem itself. Since the latter is th object of a religious respect, they to should inspire respect of the same so and appear to be sacred. Having extern forms so nearly identical, it would b impossible for the native not to attribut to them forces of the same nature. It i therefore forbidden to kill or eat th totemic animal, since its flesh is believe to have the positive virtues resulting fro the rites; it is because it resembles th emblem of the clan, that is to say, it is i its own image. And since the anim naturally resembles the emblem mor than the man does, it is placed on superior rank in the hierarchy of sacre things. Between these two beings ther is undoubtedly a close relationship, fo they both partake of the same essence both incarnate something of the totemi principle. However, since the princip itself is conceived under an animal form the animal seems to incarnate it mor fully than the man. Therefore, if me consider it and treat it as a brother, it i at least as an elder brother.[5]

But even if the totemic principle has it preferred seat in a determined species o animal or vegetable, it cannot remai localized there. A sacred character is to high degree contagious; it therefor spreads out from the totemic being t everything that is closely or remotel connected with it. The religious senti ments inspired by the animal are com

[5]Thus we see that this fraternity is the logica consequence of totemism, rather than its basis Men have not imagined their duties towards th animals of the totemic species because the regarded them as kindred, but have imagined th kinship to explain the nature of the beliefs an rites of which they were the object. The anima was considered a relative of the man because i was a sacred being like the man, but it wa not treated as a sacred being because it wa regarded as a relative.

municated to the substances upon which it is nourished and which serve to make or remake its flesh and blood, to the things that resemble it, and to the different beings with which it has constant relations. Thus, little by little, sub-totems are attached to the totems and from the cosmological systems expressed by the primitive classifications. At last, the world is divided up among the totemic principles of each tribe.

We are now able to explain the origin of the ambiguity of religious forces as they appear in history, and how they are physical as well as human, moral as well as material. They are moral powers because they are made up entirely of the impressions this moral being, the group, arouses in those other moral beings, its individual members; they do not translate the manner in which physical things affect our senses, but the way in which the collective consciousness acts upon individual consciousnesses. Their authority is only one form of the moral ascendancy of society over its members. But, on the other hand, since they are conceived of under material forms, they could not fail to be regarded as closely related to material things.[6] Therefore they dominate the two worlds. Their residence is in men, but at the same time they are the vital principles of things. They animate minds and discipline them, but it is also they who make plants grow and animals reproduce. It is this double nature which has enabled religion to be like the womb from which come all the leading germs of human civilization. Since it has been made to embrace all of

reality, the physical world as well as the moral one, the forces that move bodies as well as those that move minds have been conceived in a religious form. That is how the most diverse methods and practices, both those that make possible the continuation of the moral life (law, morals, beaux-arts) and those serving the material life (the natural, technical and practical sciences), are either directly or indirectly derived from religion. . . .[7]

We are now able to understand how the totemic principle, and in general, every religious force, comes to be outside of the object in which it resides. It is because the idea of it is in no way made up of the impressions directly produced by this thing upon our senses or minds. Religious force is only the sentiment inspired by the group in its members, but projected outside of the consciousnesses that experience them, and objectified. To be objectified, they are fixed upon some object which thus becomes sacred; but any object might fulfil this function. In principle, there are none whose nature predestines them to it to the exclusion of all others; but also there are none that are necessarily impossible. Everything depends upon the circumstances which lead the sentiment creating religious ideas to establish itself here or there, upon this point or upon that one. Therefore, the sacred character assumed by an object is not implied in the intrinsic properties of this latter: *it is added to them.* The world of religious things is not one particular aspect of empirical nature; *it is superimposed upon it.*

---

[6] At the bottom of this conception there is a well-founded and persistent sentiment. Modern science also tends more and more to admit that the duality of man and nature does not exclude their unity, and that physical and moral forces, though distinct, are closely related. We undoubtedly have a different conception of this unity and relationship than the primitive, but beneath these different symbols, the truth affirmed by the two is the same.

[7] We say that this derivation is sometimes indirect because of the industrial methods which, in a large number of cases, seem to be derived from religion through the intermediacy of magic (see Hubert and Mauss, *Théorie générale de la Magie, Année Sociol.,* VII, pp. 144ff.); for, as we believe, magic forces are only a special form of religious forces. We shall have occasion to return to this point several times.

Bronislaw Malinowski

THE PUBLIC
AND THE INDIVIDUAL CHARACTER
OF RELIGION

Religion

THE festive and public character of the ceremonies of cult is a conspicuous feature of religion in general. Most sacred acts happen in a congregation; indeed, the solemn conclave of the faithful united in prayer, sacrifice, supplication, or thanksgiving is the very prototype of a religious ceremony. Religion needs the community as a whole so that its members may worship in common its sacred things and its divinities, and society needs religion for the maintenance of moral law and order.

In primitive societies the public character of worship, the give-and-take between religious faith and social organization, is at least as pronounced as in higher cultures. It is sufficient to glance over our previous inventory of religious phenomena to see that ceremonies at birth, rites of initiation, mortuary attentions to the dead, burial, the acts of mourning and commemoration, sacrifice and totemic ritual, are one and all public and collective, frequently affecting the tribe as a whole and absorbing all its

From "Magic, Science and Religion" (1925) in Joseph Needham, ed., Magic, Science and Religion and Other Essays, Boston and Glencoe: 1948, pp. 35–50, 59–64, 66–71. By permission of the Society for Promoting Christian Knowledge.

energies for the time being. This public character, the gathering together of big numbers, is especially pronounced in the annual or periodical feasts held at times of plenty, at harvest or at the height of the hunting or fishing season. Such feasts allow the people to indulge in their gay mood, to enjoy the abundance of crops and quarry, to meet their friends and relatives, to muster the whole community in full force, and to do all this in a mood of happiness and harmony. At times during such festivals visits of the departed take place: the spirits of ancestors and dead relatives return and receive offerings and sacrificial libations, mingle with the survivors in the acts of cult and in the rejoicings of the feast. Or the dead, even if they do not actually revisit the survivors, are commemorated by them, usually in the form of ancestor cult. Again, such festivities being frequently held, embody the ritual of garnered crops and other cults of vegetation. But whatever the other issues of such festivities, there can be no doubt that religion demands the existence of seasonal, periodical feasts with a big concourse of people, with rejoicings and festive apparel, with an abundance of food, and with relaxation of rules and taboos. The members of the tribe come together, and they relax the usual restrictions, specially the barriers of conventional reserve in social and in sexual intercourse. The appetites are provided for, indeed pandered to, and there is a common participation in the pleasures, a display to everyone of all that is good, the sharing of it in a universal mood of generosity. To the interest in plenty of material goods there is joined the interest in the multitude of people, in the congregation, in the tribe as a body.

With these facts of periodical festive gathering a number of other distinctly social elements must be ranged: the tribal character of almost all religious ceremonies, the social universality of moral rules, the contagion of sin, the importance of sheer convention and tradition in primitive religion and morals, above all the identification of the whole tribe as a social unit with its religion; that is, the absence of any religious sectarianism, dissension, or heterodoxy in primitive creed.

Society as the Substance of God

All these facts, especially the last one, show that religion is a tribal affair, and we are reminded of the famous dictum of Robertson Smith, that primitive religion is the concern of the community rather than of the individual. This exaggerated view contains a great deal of truth, but, in science, to recognize where the truth lies, on the one hand, and to unearth it and bring it fully to light, on the other, are by no means the same. Robertson Smith did not do much more in this matter, in fact, than set forth the important problem: why is it that primitive man performs his ceremonies in public? What is the relation between society and the truth revealed by religion and worshipped in it?

To these questions, some modern anthropologists, as we know, give a trenchant, apparently conclusive, and exceedingly simple answer. Professor Durkheim and his followers maintain that religion is social for all its Entities, its God or Gods, the Stuff all things religious are made of, are nothing more nor less than Society divinized.

This theory seems very well to explain the public nature of cult, the inspiration and comfort drawn by man, the social animal, from congregation, the intolerance shown by religion, especially in its early manifestations, the cogency of morals and other similar facts. It also satisfies our modern democratic bias, which in social science appears as a tendency to explain all by "collective" rather than by "individual forces." This, the theory which makes *vox populi vox Dei* appear as a sober, scientific truth, must surely be congenial to modern man.

Yet, upon reflection, critical misgivings, and very serious ones at that, arise. Everyone who has experienced religion deeply and sincerely knows that the strongest religious moments come in solitude, in turning away from the world, in concentration and in mental detachment, and not in the distraction of a crowd. Can primitive religion be so entirely devoid of the inspiration of solitude? No one who knows savages at first-hand or from a careful study of literature will have any doubts. Such facts as the seclusion of novices at initiation, their individual, personal struggles during the ordeal, the communion with spirits, divinities, and powers in lonely spots, all these show us primitive religion frequently lived through in solitude. Again, as we have seen before, the belief in immortality cannot be explained without the consideration of the religious frame of mind of the individual, who faces his own pending death in fear and sorrow. Primitive religion does not entirely lack its prophets, seers, soothsayers and interpreters of belief. All such facts, though they certainly do not prove that religion is exclusively individual, make it difficult to understand how it can be regarded as *the Social* pure and simple.

And again, the essence of morals, as opposed to legal or customary rules, is that they are enforced by conscience. The savage does not keep his taboo for fear of social punishment or of public opinion. He abstains from breaking it partly because he fears the direct evil consequences flowing from the will of a divinity, or from the forces of the sacred, but mainly because his personal responsibility and conscience forbid him doing it. The forbidden totem animal, incestuous or forbidden intercourse, the tabooed action or food, are directly abhorrent to him. I have seen and felt savages shrink from an illicit action with the same horror and disgust with which the religious Christian will shrink from the committing of what he considers sin. Now this mental attitude is undoubtedly due in part to the influence of society in so far as the particular prohibition is branded as horrible and disgusting by tradition. But it works in the individual and through forces of the individual mind. It is, therefore, neither exclusively social nor individual, but a mixture of both.

Professor Durkheim tries to establish his striking theory that Society is the raw material of Godhead by an analysis of primitive tribal festivities. He studies especially the seasonal ceremonies of the Central Australians. In these "the great collective effervescence during the periods of concentration" causes all the phenomena of their religion, and "the religious idea is born out of their effervescence." Professor Durkheim lays thus the emphasis on emotional ebullition, on exaltation, on the increased power which every individual feels when part of such a gathering. Yet but a little reflection is sufficient to show that even in primitive societies the heightening of emotions and the lifting of the individual out of himself are by no means restricted to gatherings and to crowd phenomena. The lover near his sweetheart, the darin. adventurer conquering his fears in th. face of real danger, the hunter at grip with a wild animal, the craftsman achiev ing a masterpiece, whether he be savag or civilized, will under such condition feel altered, uplifted, endowed wit higher forces. And there can be no doub that from many of these solitary exper ences where man feels the foreboding of death, the pangs of anxiety, the exalta tion of bliss, there flows a great deal o religious inspiration. Though most cere monies are carried out in public, mucl of religious revelation takes place i solitude.

On the other hand there are in primi tive societies collective acts with a much effervescence and passion as an religious ceremony can possibly have yet without the slightest religious color ing. Collective work in the gardens, a I have seen it in Melanesia, when me become carried away with emulation and zest for work, singing rhythmic songs uttering shouts of joy and slogans o competitive challenge, is full of thi "collective effervescence." But it i entirely profane, and society which "reveals itself" in this as in any othe public performance assumes no divine grandeur or godlike appearance. A battle a sailing regatta, one of the big triba gatherings for trading purposes, an Australian lay-corrobboree, a village brawl, are all from the social as well as from the psychological point of view essentially examples of crowd efferves cence. Yet no religion is generated on any of these occasions. Thus the *collective* and the *religious,* though impinging on each other, are by no means coextensive, and while a great deal of belief and religious inspiration must be traced back to solitary experiences of man, there is much concourse and effervescence which has no religious meaning or religious consequence.

If we extend yet further the definition
f "society" and regard it as a permanent
ntity, continuous through tradition and
ulture, each generation brought up by
s predecessor and moulded into its
keness by the social heritage of civili-
ation—can we not regard then Society
the prototype of Godhead? Even thus
ie facts of primitive life will remain
bellious to this theory. For tradition
omprises the sum-total of social norms
nd customs, rules of art and knowledge,
junctions, precepts, legends and myths,
nd part of this only is religious, while the
est is essentially profane. As we have
en in the second section of this essay,
rimitive man's empirical and rational
nowledge of nature, which is the foun-
ation of his arts and crafts, of his
conomic enterprises and of his con-
ructive abilities, forms an autonomous
omain of social tradition. Society as the
eeper of lay tradition, of the profane,
annot be the religious principle or
Divinity, for the place of this latter is
rithin the domain of the sacred only.
Ve have found, moreover, that one of
ne chief tasks of primitive religion,
specially in the performance of initiation
eremonies and tribal mysteries, is to
icralize the religious part of tradition.
: is clear, therefore, that religion cannot
erive all its sanctity from that source
rhich itself is made sacred by religion.

It is in fact only by a clever play on
rords and by a double-edged sophistica-
on of the argument that "society" can
e identified with the Divine and the
acred. If, indeed, we set equal the *social*
o the *moral* and widen this concept so
nat it covers all belief, all rules of con-
uct, all dictates of conscience; if, fur-
her, we personify the Moral Force and
egard it as a Collective Soul, then the
dentification of Society with Godhead
eeds not much dialectical skill to be
efended. But since the moral rules are
nly one part of the traditional heritage
f man, since morality is not identical

with the Power or Being from which it
is believed to spring, since finally the
metaphysical concept of "Collective Soul"
is barren in anthropology, we have to
reject the sociological theory of religion.

To sum up, the views of Durkheim
and his school cannot be accepted. First
of all, in primitive societies religion
arises to a great extent from purely
individual sources. Secondly, society as a
crowd is by no means always given to the
production of religious beliefs or even to
religious states of mind, while collective
effervescence is often of an entirely
secular nature. Thirdly, tradition, the
sum-total of certain rules and cultural
achievements, embraces, and in primitive
societies keeps in a tight grip, both
Profane and Sacred. Finally, the personification of society, the conception of
a "Collective Soul," is without any
foundation in fact, and is against the
sound methods of social science.

The Moral Efficiency of Savage Beliefs

With all this, in order to do justice to
Robertson Smith, Durkheim, and their
school, we have to admit that they have
brought out a number of relevant features of primitive religion. Above all,
by the very exaggeration of the sociological aspect of primitive faith they have
set forth a number of most important
questions: Why are most religious acts
in primitive societies performed collectively and in public? What is the part of
society in the establishment of the rules of
moral conduct? Why are not only morality but also belief, mythology, and all
sacred tradition compulsory to all the
members of a primitive tribe? In other
words, why is there only one body of
religious beliefs in each tribe, and why is
no difference of opinion ever tolerated?

To give an answer to these questions
we have to go back to our survey of

religious phenomena, to recall some of our conclusions there arrived at, and especially to fix our attention upon the technique by which belief is expressed and morals established in primitive religion.

Let us start with the religious act par excellence, the ceremonial of death. Here the call to religion arises out of an individual crisis, the death which threatens man or woman. Never does an individual need the comfort of belief and ritual so much as in the sacrament of the viaticum, in the last comforts given to him at the final stage of his life's journey—acts which are well-nigh universal in all primitive religions. These acts are directed against the overwhelming fear, against the corroding doubt, from which the savage is no more free than the civilized man. These acts confirm his hope that there is a hereafter, that it is not worse than present life; indeed, better. All the ritual expresses that belief, that emotional attitude which the dying man requires, which is the greatest comfort he can have in his supreme conflict. And this affirmation has behind it weight of numbers and the pomp of solemn ritual. For in all savage societies, death, as we have seen, compels the whole community to forgather, to attend to the dying, and to carry out the duties towards him. These duties do not, of course, develop any emotional sympathy with the dying—this would lead merely to a disintegrating panic. On the contrary, the line of ritual conduct opposes and contradicts some of the strongest emotions to which the dying man might become a prey. The whole conduct of the group, in fact, expresses the hope of salvation and immortality; that is, it expresses only one among the conflicting emotions of the individual.

After death, though the main actor has made his exit, the tragedy is not at an end. There are the bereaved ones, and these, savage or civilized, suffer alike,

and are thrown into a dangerous menta chaos. We have given an analysis of thi already, and found that, torn betwee fear and piety, reverence and horro love and disgust, they are in a state c mind which might lead to mental disinte gration. Out of this, religion lifts th individual by what could be called spir tual co-operation in the sacred mortuar rites. We have seen that in these rite there is expressed the dogma of con tinuity after death, as well as the mora attitude towards the departed. Th corpse, and with it the person of the dea one, is a potential object of horror as wel as of tender love. Religion confirms th second part of this double attitude b making the dead body into an object o sacred duties. The bond of union be tween the recently dead and the survivor is maintained, a fact of immense impor tance for the continuity of culture and for the safe keeping of tradition. In al this we see that the whole communit carries out the biddings of religiou tradition, but that these are again enacted for the benefit of a few individuals only the bereaved ones, that they arise from personal conflict and are a solution of thi conflict. It must also be remembered tha what the survivor goes through on suc an occasion prepares him for his own death. The belief in immortality, which he has lived through and practised in th case of his mother or father, makes him realize more clearly his own future life

In all this we have to make a clea distinction between the belief and the ethics of the ritual on the one hand, and on the other the means of enforcing them the technique by which the individual is made to receive his religious comfort The saving belief in spiritual continuity after death is already contained in the individual mind; it is not created by society. The sum-total of innate ten dencies, known usually as "the instinct of self-preservation," is at the root of this belief. The faith in immortality is, as we have seen, closely connected with the difficulty of facing one's own annihilation or that of a near and beloved person. This tendency makes the idea of the final disappearance of human personality odious, intolerable, socially destructive. Yet this idea and the fear of it always lurk in individual experience, and religion can remove it only by its negation in ritual.

Whether this is achieved by a Providence directly guiding human history, or by a process of natural selection in which a culture which evolves a belief and a ritual of immortality will survive and spread—this is a problem of theology or metaphysics. The anthropologist has done enough when he has shown the value of a certain phenomenon for social integrity and for the continuity of culture. In any case we see that what religion does in this matter is to select one out of the two alternatives suggested to man by his instinctive endowment.

This selection once made, however, society is indispensable for its enactment. The bereaved member of the group, himself overwhelmed by sorrow and fear, is incapable of relying on his own forces. He would be unable by his single effort to apply the dogma to his own case. Here the group steps in. The other members, untouched by the calamity, not torn mentally by the metaphysical dilemma, can respond to the crisis along the lines dictated by the religious order. Thus they bring consolation to the stricken one and lead him through the comforting experiences of religious ceremony. It is always easy to bear the misfortunes of others. The whole group, in which the majority are untouched by the pangs of fear and horror, can thus help the afflicted minority. Going through the religious ceremonies, the bereaved emerges changed by the revelation of immortality, communion with the beloved, the order of the next world. Religion commands in acts of cult, the group executes the command.

But, as we have seen, the comfort of ritual is not artificial, not manufactured for the occasion. It is but the result of the two conflicting tendencies which exist in man's innate emotional reaction to death: the religious attitude consists merely in the selection and ritual affirmation of one of these alternatives—the hope in a future life. And here the public concourse gives the emphasis, the powerful testimony to the belief. Public pomp and ceremony take effect through the contagiousness of faith, through the dignity of unanimous consent, the impressiveness of collective behavior. A multitude enacting as one an earnest and dignified ceremony invariably carries away even the disinterested observer, still more the affected participant.

But the distinction between social collaboration as the only technique necessary for the enactment of a belief on the one hand, and the creation of the belief or self-revelation of society on the other, must be emphatically pointed out. The community proclaims a number of definite truths and gives moral comfort to its members, but it does not give them the vague and empty assertion of its own divinity.

In another type of religious ritual, in the ceremonies of initiation, we found that the ritual establishes the existence of some power or personality from which tribal law is derived, and which is responsible for the moral rules imparted to the novice. To make the belief impressive, strong, and grandiose, there is the pomp of the ceremony and the hardships of preparation and ordeal. An unforgettable experience, unique in the life of the individual, is created, and by this he learns the doctrines of tribal tradition and the rules of its morality. The whole tribe is mobilized and all its authority set in motion to bear witness to the power and reality of the things revealed.

Here again, as at the death, we have to do with a crisis in the individual life, and a mental conflict associated with it. At puberty, the youth has to test his physical power, to cope with his sexual maturity, to take up his place in the tribe. This brings him promises, prerogatives, and temptations, and at the same time imposes burdens upon him. The right solution of the conflict lies in his compliance with tradition, in his submission to the sexual morality of his tribe and to the burdens of manhood, and that is accomplished in the ceremonies of initiation.

The public character of these ceremonies avails both to establish the greatness of the ultimate law-giver and to achieve homogeneity and uniformity in the teaching of morals. Thus they become a form of condensed education of a religious character. As in all schooling, the principles imparted are merely selected, fixed, emphasized out of what there is in the individual endowment. Here again publicity is a matter of technique, while the contents of what is taught are not invented by society but exist in the individual.

In other cults again, such as harvest festivals, totemic gatherings, first-fruit offerings and ceremonial display of food, we find religion sacralizing abundance and security and establishing the attitude of reverence towards the beneficent forces without. Here again the publicity of the cult is necessary as the only technique suitable for the establishment of the value of food, accumulation and abundance. The display to all, the admiration of all, the rivalry between any two producers, are the means by which value is created. For every value, religious and economic, must possess universal currency. But here again we find only the selection and emphasis of one of the two possible individual reactions. Accumulated food can either be squandered or preserved. It can either be an incentive to immediate heedless consumption and light-hearted carelessness about the

future, or else it can stimulate man to devising means of hoarding the treasure and of using it for culturally higher purposes. Religion sets its stamp on the culturally valuable attitude and enforces it by public enactment.

The public character of such feasts subserves another sociologically important function. The members of every group which forms a cultural unit must come in contact with each other from time to time, but besides its beneficent possibility of strengthening social ties, such contact is also fraught with the danger of friction. The danger is greater when people meet in times of stress, dearth, and hunger, when their appetite is unsatisfied and their sexual desires ready to flare up. A festive tribal gathering at times of plenty, when everyone is in a mood of harmony with nature and consequently with each other, takes on, therefore, the character of a meeting in a moral atmosphere. I mean an atmosphere of general harmony and benevolence. The occurrence of occasional licence at such gatherings and the relaxation of the rules of sex and of certain strictures of etiquette are probably due to the same cause. All motives for quarrel and disagreement must be eliminated or else a big tribal gathering could not peacefully come to an end. The moral value of harmony and good will is thus shown to be higher than the mere negative taboos which curb the principal human instincts. There is no virtue higher than charity, and in primitive religions as well as in higher it covers a multitude of sins; nay, it outweighs them.

It is, perhaps, unnecessary to go in detail over all the other types of religious acts. Totemism, the religion of the clan, which affirms the common descent from or affinity with the totemic animal, and claims the clan's collective power to control its supply and impresses upon all the clan members a joint totemic taboo and a reverential attitude towards the totemic species, must obviously culminate in public ceremonies and have a distinctly social character. Ancestor cult, the aim of which is to unite into one band of worshippers the family, the sib or the tribe, must bring them together in public ceremonies by its very nature, or else it would fail to fulfil its function. Tutelary spirits of local groups, tribes, or cities; departmental gods; professional or local divinities must one and all—by their very definition—be worshipped by village, tribe, town, profession, or body politic.

In cults which stand on the borderline between magic and religion, such as the Intichuma ceremonies, public garden rites, ceremonies of fishing and hunting, the necessity of performance in public is obvious, for these ceremonies, clearly distinguishable from any practical activities which they inaugurate or accompany, are yet their counterpart. To the co-operation in practical enterprise there corresponds the ceremony in common. Only by uniting the group of workers in an act of worship do they fulfil their cultural function.

In fact, instead of going concretely into all the types of religious ceremony, we might have established our thesis by an abstract argument: since religion centers round vital acts, and since all these command public interest of joint co-operative groups, every religious ceremony must be public and carried out by groups. All crises of life, all important enterprises, arouse the public interest of primitive communities, and they all have their ceremonies, magical or religious. The same social body of men which unites for the enterprise or is brought together by the critical event performs also the ceremonial act. Such an abstract argument, however, correct though it be, would not have allowed us to get a real insight into the mechanism of public enactment of religious acts such as we have gained by our concrete description.

Social and Individual Contributions in Primitive Religion

We are forced therefore to the conclusion that publicity is the indispensable technique of religious revelation in primitive communities, but that society is neither the author of religious truths, nor still less its self-revealed subject. The necessity of the public *mise en scène* of dogma and collective enunciation of moral truths is due to several causes. Let us sum them up.

First of all, social co-operation is needed to surround the unveiling of things sacred and of supernatural beings with solemn grandeur. The community whole-heartedly engaged in performing the forms of the ritual creates the atmosphere of homogeneous belief. In this collective action, those who at the moment least need the comfort of belief, the affirmation of the truth, help along those who are in need of it. The evil, disintegrating forces of destiny are thus distributed by a system of mutual insurance in spiritual misfortune and stress. In bereavement, at the crisis of puberty, during impending danger and evil, at times when prosperity might be used well or badly—religion standardizes the right way of thinking and acting and society takes up the verdict and repeats it in unison.

In the second place, public performance of religious dogma is indispensable for the maintenance of morals in primitive communities. Every article of faith, as we have seen, wields a moral influence. Now morals, in order to be active at all, must be universal. The endurance of social ties, the mutuality of services and obligations, the possibility of co-operation, are based in any society on the fact that every member knows what is expected of him; that, in short, there is a universal standard of conduct. No rule of morals can work unless it is anticipated and unless it can be counted upon. In primitive societies, where law, as enforced by judgments and penalties, is almost completely absent, the automatic, self-acting moral rule is of the greatest importance for forming the very foundations of primitive organization and culture. This is possible only in a society where there is no private teaching of morals, no personal codes of conduct and honor, no ethical schools, no differences of moral opinion. The teaching of morals must be open, public, and universal.

Thirdly and finally, the transmission and the conservation of sacred tradition entails publicity, or at least collectiveness of performance. It is essential to every religion that its dogma should be considered and treated as absolutely inalterable and inviolable. The believer must be firmly convinced that what he is led to accept as truth is held in safe-keeping, handed on exactly as it has been received, placed above any possibility of falsification or alteration. Every religion must have its tangible, reliable safeguards by which the authenticity of its tradition is guaranteed. In higher religions, we know the extreme importance of the authenticity of holy writings, the supreme concern about the purity of the text and the truth of interpretation. The native races have to rely on human memory. Yet, without books or inscriptions, without bodies of theologians, they are not less concerned about the purity of their texts, not less well safeguarded against alteration and misstatement. There is only one factor which can prevent the constant breaking of the sacred thread: the participation of a number of people in the safe-keeping of tradition. The public enactment of myth among certain tribes, the official recitals of sacred stories on certain occasions, the embodiment of parts of belief in sacred ceremonies, the guardianship of parts of tradition given

to special bodies of men: secret societies, totemic clans, highest-age grades—all these are means of safeguarding the doctrine of primitive religions. We see that wherever this doctrine is not quite public in the tribe there is a special type of social organization serving the purpose of its keeping.

These considerations explain also the orthodoxy of primitive religions, and excuse their intolerance. In a primitive community, not only the morals but also the dogmas have to be identical for all members. As long as savage creeds have been regarded as idle superstitions, as make-believe, as childish or diseased fancies, or at best crude philosophic speculations, it was difficult to understand why the savage clung to them so obstinately, so faithfully. But once we see that every canon of the savage's belief is a live force to him, that his doctrine is the very cement of social fabric—for all his morality is derived from it, all his social cohesion and his mental composure—it is easy to understand that he cannot afford to be tolerant. And it is clear also that once you begin to play ducks and drakes with his "superstitions," you destroy all his morality, without much chance of giving him another instead.

We see thus clearly the need for the prominently overt and collective nature of religious acts and for the universality of moral principles, and we also realize clearly why this is much more prominent in primitive religions than in civilized ones. Public participation and social interest in matters religious are thus explicable by clear, concrete, empirical reasons, and there is no room for an Entity, revealing itself in artful disguise to its worshippers, mystified and misled in the very act of revelation. The fact is that the social share in religious enactment is a condition necessary but not sufficient, and that without the analysis of the individual mind, we cannot take one step in the understanding of religion. . . .

Magic

Let us realize once more the type of situation in which we find magic. Man, engaged in a series of practical activities, comes to a gap; the hunter is disappointed by his quarry, the sailor misses propitious winds, the canoe-builder has to deal with some material of which he is never certain that it will stand the strain, or the healthy person suddenly feels his strength failing. What does man do naturally under such conditions, setting aside all magic, belief and ritual? Forsaken by his knowledge, baffled by his past experience and by his technical skill, he realizes his impotence. Yet his desire grips him only the more strongly; his anxiety, his fears and hopes, induce a tension in his organism which drives him to some sort of activity. Whether he be savage or civilized, whether in possession of magic or entirely ignorant of its existence, passive inaction, the only thing dictated by reason, is the last thing in which he can acquiesce. His nervous system and his whole organism drive him to some substitute activity. Obsessed by the idea of the desired end, he sees it and feels it. His organism reproduces the acts suggested by the anticipations of hope, dictated by the emotion of passion so strongly felt.

The man under the sway of impotent fury or dominated by thwarted hate spontaneously clenches his fist and carries out imaginary thrusts at his enemy, muttering imprecations, casting words of hatred and anger against him. The lover aching for his unattainable or irresponsive beauty sees her in his visions, addresses her, and entreats and commands her favors, feeling himself accepted, pressing her to his bosom in his dreams. The anxious fisherman or hunter sees in his imagination the quarry enmeshed in the nets, the animal attained by the spear; he utters their names, describes in words his visions of the magnificent catch, he even breaks out into gestures of mimic representation of what he desires. The man lost at night in the woods or the jungle, beset by superstitious fear, sees around him the haunting demons, addresses them, tries to ward off, to frighten them, or shrinks from them in fear, like an animal which attempts to save itself by feigning death.

These reactions to overwhelming emotion or obsessive desire are natural responses of man to such a situation, based on a universal psycho-physiological mechanism. They engender what could be called extended expressions of emotion in act and in word, the threatening gestures of impotent anger and its maledictions, the spontaneous enactment of the desired end in a practical impasse, the passionate fondling gestures of the lover, and so on. All these spontaneous acts and spontaneous works make man forecast the images of the wished-for results, or express his passion in uncontrollable gestures, or break out into words which give vent to desire and anticipate its end.

And what is the purely intellectual process, the conviction formed during such a free outburst of emotion in words and deeds? First there surges a clear image of the desired end, of the hated person, of the feared danger or ghost. And each image is blended with its specific passion, which drives us to assume an active attitude towards that image. When passion reaches the breaking point at which man loses control over himself, the words which he utters, his blind behaviour, allow the pent-up physiological tension to flow over. But over all this outburst presides the image of the end. It supplies the motive-force of the reaction, it apparently organizes and directs words and acts towards a definite purpose. The substitute action in which the passion finds its vent, and which is due to impotence, has subjectively all the value of a real action, to which emotion would, if not impeded, naturally have led.

As the tension spends itself in these words and gestures the obsessing visions fade away, the desired end seems nearer satisfaction, we regain our balance, once more at harmony with life. And we remain with a conviction that the words of malediction and the gestures of fury have travelled towards the hated person and hit their target; that the imploration of love, the visionary embraces, cannot have remained unanswered, that the visionary attainment of success in our pursuit cannot have been without a beneficial influence on the pending issue. In the case of fear, as the emotion which has led us to frenzied behavior gradually subsides, we feel that it is this behavior that has driven away the terrors. In brief, a strong emotional experience, which spends itself in a purely subjective flow of images, words, and acts of behavior, leaves a very deep conviction of its reality, as if of some practical and positive achievement, as if of something done by a power revealed to man. This power, born of mental and physiological obsession, seems to get hold of us from outside, and to primitive man, or to the credulous and untutored mind of all ages, the spontaneous spell, the spontaneous rite, and the spontaneous belief in their efficiency must appear as a direct revelation from some external and no doubt impersonal sources.

When we compare this spontaneous ritual and verbiage of overflowing passion or desire with traditionally fixed magical ritual and with the principles embodied in magical spells and sub-

stances, the striking resemblance of the two products shows that they are not independent of each other. Magical ritual, most of the principles of magic, most of its spells and substances, have been revealed to man in those passionate experiences which assail him in the impasses of his instinctive life and of his practical pursuits, in those gaps and breaches left in the ever-imperfect wall of culture which he erects between himself and the besetting temptations and dangers of his destiny. In this I think we have to recognize not only one of the sources but the very fountainhead of magical belief.

To most types of magical ritual, therefore, there corresponds a spontaneous ritual of emotional expression or of a forecast of the desired end. To most features of magical spell, to the commands, invocations, metaphors, there corresponds a natural flow of words, in malediction, in entreaty, in exorcism, and in the descriptions of unfulfilled wishes. To every belief in magical efficiency there can be laid in parallel one of those illusions of subjective experience, transient in the mind of the civilized rationalist, though even there never quite absent, but powerful and convincing to the simple man in every culture, and, above all, to the primitive savage mind.

Thus the foundations of magical belief and practice are not taken from the air, but are due to a number of experiences actually lived through, in which man receives the revelation of his power to attain the desired end. We must now ask: What is the relation between the promises contained in such experience and their fulfilment in real life? Plausible though the fallacious claims of magic might be to primitive man, how is it that they have remained so long unexposed?

The answer to this is that, first, it is a well-known fact that in human memory the testimony of a positive case always overshadows the negative one. One gain easily outweighs several losses. Thus the instances which affirm magic always loom far more conspicuously than those which deny it. But there are other facts which endorse by a real or apparent testimony the claims of magic. We have seen that magical ritual must have originated from a revelation in a real experience. But the man who from such an experience conceived, formulated, and gave to his tribesmen the nucleus of a new magical performance—acting, be it remembered, in perfect good faith—must have been a man of genius. The men who inherited and wielded his magic after him, no doubt always building it out and developing it, while believing that they were simply following up the tradition, must have been always men of great intelligence, energy, and power of enterprise. They would be the men successful in all emergencies. It is an empirical fact that in all savage societies magic and outstanding personality go hand in hand. Thus magic also coincides with personal success, skill, courage, and mental power. No wonder that it is considered a source of success.

This personal renown of the magician and its importance in enhancing the belief about the efficiency of magic are the cause of an interesting phenomenon: what may be called the *current mythology* of magic. Round every big magician there arises a halo made up of stories about his wonderful curse or kills, his catches, his victories, his conquests in love. In every savage society such stories form the backbone of belief in magic, for, supported as they are by the emotional experiences which everyone has had himself, the running chronicle of magical miracles establishes its claims beyond any doubt or cavil. Every eminent practitioner, besides his traditional claim, besides the filiation with his predecessors, makes his personal warrant of wonder-working.

Thus myth is not a dead product of past ages, merely surviving as an idle narrative. It is a living force, constantly producing new phenomena, constantly surrounding magic by new testimonies. Magic moves in the glory of past tradition, but it also creates its atmosphere of ever-nascent myth. As there is the body of legends already fixed, standardized, and constituting the folk-lore of the tribe, so there is always a stream of narratives in kind to those of the mythological time. Magic is the bridge between the golden age of primeval craft and the wonder-working power of to-day. Hence the formulas are full of mythical allusions, which, when uttered, unchain the powers of the past and cast them into the present. . . .

Magic, Science, and Religion

We are now in a position to state more fully the relation between magic and science already outlined above. Magic is akin to science in that it always has a definite aim intimately associated with human instincts, needs, and pursuits. The magic art is directed towards the attainment of practical aims. Like the other arts and crafts, it is also governed by a theory, by a system of principles which dictate the manner in which the act has to be performed in order to be effective. In analyzing magical spells, rites, and substances we have found that there are a number of general principles which govern them. Both science and magic develop a special technique. In magic, as in the other arts, man can undo what he has done or mend the damage which he has wrought. In fact, in magic the quantative equivalents of black and white seem to be much more exact and the effects of witchcraft much more completely eradicated by counter-witchcraft than is possible in any practical art or craft. Thus both magic and science show certain similarities, and, with Sir James Frazer, we can appropriately call magic a pseudo-science.

And the spurious character of this pseudo-science is not hard to detect. Science, even as represented by the primitive knowledge of savage man, is based on the normal universal experience of everyday life, experience won in man's struggle with nature for his subsistence and safety, founded on observation, fixed by reason. Magic is based on specific experience of emotional states in which man observes not nature but himself, in which the truth is revealed not by reason but by the play of emotions upon the human organism. Science is founded on the conviction that experience, effort, and reason are valid; magic on the belief that hope cannot fail nor desire deceive. The theories of knowledge are dictated by logic, those of magic by the association of ideas under the influence of desire. As a matter of empirical fact the body of rational knowledge and the body of magical lore are incorporated each in a different tradition, in a different social setting and in a different type of activity, and all these differences are clearly recognized by the savages. The one constitutes the domain of the profane; the other, hedged round by observances, mysteries, and taboos, makes up half of the domain of the sacred.

Both magic and religion arise and function in situations of emotional stress: crises of life, lacunae in important pursuits, death and initiation into tribal mysteries, unhappy love and unsatisfied hate. Both magic and religion open up escapes from such situations and such impasses as offer no empirical way out except by ritual and belief into the domain of the supernatural. This domain embraces, in religion, beliefs in ghosts, spirits, the primitive forebodings of providence, the guardians of tribal mysteries; in magic, the primeval force and virtue of magic. Both magic and religion are based strictly on mythological tradition, and they also both exist in the atmosphere of the miraculous, in a constant revelation of their wonder-working power. They both are surrounded by taboos and observances which mark off their acts from those of the profane world.

Now what distinguishes magic from religion? We have taken for our starting-point a most definite and tangible distinction: we have defined, within the domain of the sacred, magic as a practical art consisting of acts which are only means to a definite end expected to follow later on; religion as a body of self-contained acts being themselves the fulfillment of their purpose. We can now follow up this difference into its deeper layers. The practical art of magic has its limited, circumscribed technique: spell, rite, and the condition of the performer form always its trite trinity. Religion, with its complex aspects and purposes, has no such simple technique, and its unity can be seen neither in the form of its acts nor even in the uniformity of its subject-matter, but rather in the function which it fulfils and in the value of its belief and ritual. Again, the belief in magic, corresponding to its plain practical nature, is extremely simple. It is always the affirmation of man's power to cause certain definite effects by a definite spell and rite. In religion, on the other hand, we have a whole supernatural world of faith: the pantheon of spirits and demons, the benevolent powers of totem, guardian spirit, tribal all-father, the vision of the future life, create a second supernatural reality for primitive man. The mythology of religion is also more varied and complex as well as more creative. It usually centers round the various tenets of belief, and it develops them into cosnogonies, tales of culture-heroes, accounts of the doings of gods and demigods. In magic, important as it is, mythology is an ever-recurrent boasting about man's primeval achievements.

Magic, the specific art for specific ends, has in every one of its forms come once into the possession of man, and it had to be handed over in direct filiation from generation to generation. Hence it remains from the earliest times in the hands of specialists, and the first profession of mankind is that of a wizard or witch. Religion, on the other hand, in primitive conditions is an affair of all, in which everyone takes an active and equivalent part. Every member of the tribe has to go through initiation, and then himself initiates others. Everyone wails, mourns, digs the grave and commemorates, and in due time everyone has his turn in being mourned and commemorated. Spirits are for all, and everyone becomes a spirit. The only specialization in religion—that is, early spiritualistic mediumism—is not a profession but a personal gift. One more difference between magic and religion is the play of black and white in witchcraft, while religion in its primitive stages has but little of the contrast between good and evil, between the beneficent and malevolent powers. This is due also to the practical character of magic, which aims at direct quantitative results, while early religion, though essentially moral, has to deal with fateful, irremediable happenings and supernatural forces and beings, so that the undoing of things done by man does not enter into it. The maxim that fear first made gods in the universe is certainly not true in the light of anthropology.

In order to grasp the difference between religion and magic and to gain a clear vision of the three-cornered constellation of magic, religion, and science, let us briefly realize the cultural function of each. The function of primitive knowledge and its value have been assessed already and indeed are not difficult to grasp. By acquainting man with his surroundings, by allowing him to use the forces of nature and science, primitive knowledge bestows on man an immense biological advantage, setting him far above all the rest of creation. The function of religion and its value we have learned to understand in the survey of savage creeds and cults given above. We have shown there that religious faith establishes, fixes, and enhances all valuable mental attitudes, such as reverence for tradition, harmony with environment, courage and confidence in the struggle with difficulties and at the prospect of death. This belief, embodied and maintained by cult and ceremonial, has an immense biological value, and so reveals to primitive man truth in the wider, pragmatic sense of the word.

What is the cultural function of magic? We have seen that all the instincts and emotions, all practical activities, lead man into impasses where gaps in his knowledge and the limitations of his early power of observation and reason betray him at a crucial moment. Human organism reacts to this in spontaneous outbursts, in which rudimentary modes of behavior and rudimentary beliefs in their efficiency are engendered. Magic fixes upon these beliefs and rudimentary rites and standardizes them into permanent traditional forms. Thus magic supplies primitive man with a number of ready-made ritual acts and beliefs, with a definite mental and practical technique which serves to bridge over the dangerous gaps in every important pursuit or critical situation. It enables man to carry out with confidence his important tasks, to maintain his poise and his mental integrity in fits of anger, in the throes of hate, of unrequited love, of despair and anxiety. The function of magic is to ritualize man's optimism, to enhance his faith in the victory of hope over fear. Magic expresses the greater value for man of confidence over doubt, of steadfastness over vacillation, of optimism over pessimism.

Looking from far and above, from our high places of safety in developed civilization, it is easy to see all the crudity and irrelevance of magic. But without its power and guidance early man could not have mastered his practical difficulties as he has done, nor could man have advanced to the higher stages of culture. Hence the universal occurrence of magic in primitive societies and its enormous sway. Hence do we find magic an invariable adjunct of all important activities. I think we must see in it the embodiment of the sublime folly of hope, which has yet been the best school of man's character.[1]

[1]*Bibliographical Note.* The most important works on Primitive Religion, Magic and Knowledge, referred to in the text, directly or implicitly, are: E.B. Tylor, *Primitive Culture,* 4th ed., 2 vols., 1903; J.F. McLennan, *Studies in Ancient History,* 1886; W. Robertson Smith, *Lectures on the Religion of the Semites,* 1889; A. Lang, *The Making of Religion,* 1889, and *Magic and Religion,* 1901. These, though out of date as regards material and some of their conclusions, are still inspiring and deserve study. Entirely fresh and representing the most modern points of view are the classical works of J.G. Frazer, *The Golden Bough,* 3rd ed., in 12 vols., 1911–14 (also abridged edition, 1 vol.); *Totemism and Exogamy,* 4 vols., 1910; *Folk-Lore in the Old Testament,* 3 vols., 1919; *The Belief in Immortality and the Worship of the Dead,* so far 3 vols., 1913–24. With Frazer's works should be read the two excellent contributions of E. Crawley, *The Mystic Rose,* 1902 (out of print, new edition forthcoming), and *The Tree of Life,* 1905. Also on the subject of the history of morals, the two extremely important works: E. Westermarck, *The Origin and Development of the Moral Ideas,* 2 vols., 1905, and L.T. Hobhouse, *Morals in Evolution,* 2nd ed., 1915. Further: D.G. Brinton, *Religions of Primitive Peoples,* 1899; K. Th. Preuss, *Der Ursprung der Religion und Kunst,* 1904 (in "Globus," serially); R.R. Marett, *The Threshold of Religion,* 1909; H. Hubert et M. Mauss, *Mélanges d'histoire des religions,* 1909; A. van Gennep, *Les Rites de passage,* 1909; J. Harrison, *Themis,* 1910–12; I. King, *The Development of Religion,* 1910; W. Schmidt, *Der Ursprung der Gottesidee,* 1912; E. Durkheim, *Les Formes élémentaires de la Vie religieuse,* 1912 (also English translation); P. Ehrenreich, *Die Allgemeine Mythologie,* 1910; R.H. Lowie, *Primitive Religion,* 1925. An encyclopedic survey of facts and opinions will be found in Wilh. Wundt's voluminous *Volkerpsychologie,* 1904 ff.; J. Hastings' *Encyclopedia of Religion and Ethics* is excellent and indispensable to the serious student. Primitive Knowledge in particular is discussed by Lévy-Bruhl in *Les fonctions mentales dans les sociétées inférieures,* 1910; F. Boas, *The Mind of Primitive Man,* 1910; R. Thurnwald, *Psychologie des Primitiven Menschen,* in the *Handbuch der vergl. Psychol.,* edited by G. Kafka, 1922; A.A. Goldenwasser, *Early Civilization,* 1923. Cf. also R.H. Lowie, *Primitive Society,* 1920; and A.L. Kroeber, *Anthropology,* 1923. For fuller information upon the natives of Melanesia, who loom largely in the foregoing descriptions, cf. R.H. Codrington, *The Melanesians,* 1891; C.G. Seligman, *The Melanesians of British New Guinea,* 1910; R. Thurnwald, *Forschungen auf den Solomoninseln und Bismarckarchipel,* 2 vols., 1912, and *Die Gemeinde der Bánaro,* 1921; B. Malinowski, *The Natives of Mailu,* 1915 (in Trans. of the R. Soc. of S. Australia, vol. xxxix); *Boloma,* article in the Journ. of the R. Anthrop. Institute, 1916; *Argonauts of the Western Pacific,* 1922; and three articles in *Psyche,* III., 2; IV., 4; V., 3, 1923–25.

Claude Lévi-Strauss

TOTEMISM

Radcliffe-Brown's second theory of totemism appeared twenty-two years after the first, without the author emphasizing its novelty, in the Huxley Memorial Lecture for 1951 entitled "The Comparative Method in Social Anthropology." In fact, Radcliffe-Brown offers it as an example of this comparative method which alone will permit anthropology to formulate "general propositions." This is the same way in which the first theory was introduced. There is thus a methodological continuity between the one and the other. But the resemblance ends there.

The Australian tribes of the Darling River, in New South Wales, are divided into matrilineal exogamous moieties called Eaglehawk and Crow. A historical explanation for such a social system may be sought, e.g., that two hostile peoples once decided to make peace, and to secure it agreed that thenceforth the men of one group should marry women of the other, and reciprocally. But as we know nothing about the past of the tribes in question, this kind of explanation is condemned to remain gratuitous and conjectural.

Let us see rather whether similar institutions exist elsewhere. The Haida, of the Queen Charlotte Islands in British Columbia, are divided into matrilineal exogamous moieties called Eagle and Raven. A Haida myth tells how, at the beginning of time, the eagle was the

master of all the water on the earth, which he kept in a water-tight basket. The raven stole the basket, but as he flew with it over the island the water spilled on to the earth, thus creating the lakes and rivers from which the birds have since drunk and where came the salmon on which men chiefly live.

The eponymous birds of these Australian and American moieties thus belong to very similar, and symmetrically opposed, species. Moreover, there is an Australian myth which very much resembles the one just related. In this, the eaglehawk formerly kept the water in a well that he kept closed with a large stone, and which he lifted when he wanted to drink. The crow discovered this subterfuge, and wanting to have a drink himself, lifted the stone: he scratched his head, which was full of lice, over the water, and forgot to replace the stone. All the water ran away, forming the rivers of eastern Australia, and the lice changed into the fish which the natives eat. Ought we then to imagine, in the spirit of historical reconstruction, that there were formerly connections between Australia and America, in order to explain these analogies?

This would be to forget that Australian exogamous moieties—both matrilineal and patrilineal—are frequently designated by the names of birds, and that consequently, in Australia itself, the Darling River tribes are merely an illustration of a general situation. The white cockatoo is opposed to the crow in Western Australia, and white cockatoo to black cockatoo in Victoria. Bird totems are also very widespread in Melanesia, e.g., the moieties of certain tribes of New Ireland are named after the sea-eagle and the fish-hawk. To generalize further, we may compare the facts recounted earlier in connection with sexual totemism (and no longer with moieties), which also employs bird or animal designations: in eastern Australia the bat is the masculine totem, the night owl the feminine; in the northern part of New South Wales the totems are respectively the bat and the tree-creeper (*Climacteris sp.*). Finally, it happens that the Australian dualism is also applied to generations, i.e., an individual is placed in the same category as his grandfather and his grandson, while his father and his son are assigned to the opposite category. The moieties by generations thus formed are usually not given names. But where they are, they may be known by the names of birds, e.g., in western Australia, as kingfisher and bee-eater, or little red bird and little black bird:

> Our question "Why all these birds?" is thus widened in its scope. It is not only the exogamous moieties, but also dual divisions of other kinds that are identified by connection with a pair of birds. It is, however, not always a question of birds. In Australia the moieties may be associated with other pairs of animals, with two species of kangaroo in one part, with two species of bee in another. In California one moiety is associated with the coyote and the other with the wild cat.

The comparative method consists precisely in integrating a particular phenomenon into a larger whole, which the progress of the comparison makes more and more general. In conclusion, we are confronted with the following problem: how may it be explained that social groups, or segments of society, should be distinguished from each other by the association of each with a particular natural species? This, which is the very problem of totemism, includes two

others: how does each society see the relationship between human beings and the other natural species (a problem which is external to totemism, as the Andaman example show); and how does it come about, on the other hand, that social groups should be identified by means of emblems or symbols, or by emblematic or symbolic objects? This second problem lies equally outside the framework of totemism, since in this regard the same role may be vested, according to the type of community considered, in a flag, a coat of arms, a saint, or an animal species.

So far, Radcliffe-Brown's analysis has reproduced that which he formulated in 1929, which corresponds closely, as we have seen, with that of Boas. But his address of 1951 makes an innovation in declaring that this is not enough, for there remains an unresolved problem. Even if we assume that we can offer a satisfactory explanation of the "totemic" predilection for animal species, we still have to try to understand why any particular species is selected rather than another:

> What is the principle by which such pairs as eaglehawk and crow, eagle and raven, coyote and wild cat are chosen as representing the moieties of the dual division? The reason for asking this question is not idle curiosity. We may, it can be held, suppose that an understanding of the principle in question will give us an important insight into the way in which the natives themselves think about the dual division as a part of their social structure. In other words, instead of asking "Why all these birds?" we can ask "Why particularly eaglehawk and crow, and other pairs?"

This step is decisive. It brings about a reintegration of content with form, and thus opens the way to a genuine structural analysis, equally far removed from formalism and from functionalism. For it is indeed a structural analysis which Radcliffe-Brown undertakes, consolidating institutions with representations on the one hand, and interpreting in conjunction all the variants of the same myth on the other.

This myth, which is known from many parts of Australia, has to do with two protagonists, whose conflicts are the principal theme of the story. One version from Western Australia is about Eaglehawk and Crow. The former is mother's brother to Crow, and his potential father-in-law also because of the preferential marriage with the mother's brother's daughter. A father-in-law, real or potential, has the right to demand presents of food from his son-in-law and nephew, and Eaglehawk accordingly tells Crow to bring him a wallaby. After a successful hunt, Crow succumbs to temptation: he eats the animal and pretends to return empty-handed. But the uncle refuses to believe him, and questions him about his distended belly. Crow answers that to stay the pangs of his hunger he had filled his belly with the gum from the acacia. Still disbelieving him, Eaglehawk tickles his nephew until he vomits the meat. As a punishment, he throws him into the fire and keeps him there until his eyes are red and his feathers are blackened, while he emits in his pain the cry which is henceforth to be characteristic. Eaglehawk pronounces that Crow shall never again be a hunter, and that he will be reduced to stealing game. This is the way things have been ever since.

It is impossible, Radcliffe-Brown continues, to understand this myth without reference to the ethnographic context. The Australian aborigine thinks of himself as a "meat-eater," and the eaglehawk and crow, which are carnivorous birds, are his main rivals. When the natives go hunting by lighting bush-fires, the eaglehawks quickly appear and join in the hunt: they also are hunters. Perching not far from the camp fires, the crows await their chance to steal from the feast. Myths of this type may be compared with others, the structure of which is similar, although they are concerned with different animals. For example, the aborigines who inhabit the region where South Australia joins Victoria say that the kangaroo and the wombat (another marsupial, but smaller), which are the principal game, were once friends. One day Wombat began to make a "house" for himself (the animal lives in a burrow in the ground), and Kangaroo jeered at him and thus annoyed him. But when, for the very first time, rain began to fall, and Wombat sheltered in his house, he refused to make room for Kangaroo, claiming that it was too small for two. Furious, Kangaroo struck Wombat on the head with a big stone, flattening his skull; and Wombat, in riposte threw a spear at Kangaroo which fixed itself at the base of the backbone. This is the way things have been ever since: the wombat has a flat skull and lives in a burrow; the kangaroo has a tail and lives in the open:

This is, of course, a "just-so" story which you may think is childish. It amuses the listeners when it is told with the suitable dramatic expressions. But if we examine some dozens of these tales we find that they have a single theme. The resemblances and differences of animal species are translated into terms of friendship and conflict, solidarity and opposition. In other words the world of animal life is represented in terms of social relations similar to those of human society.

To arrive at this end, the natural species are classed in pairs of opposites, and this is possible only on condition that the species chosen have in common at least one characteristic which permits them to be compared.

The principle is clear in the case of the eaglehawk and crow, which are the two main carnivorous birds, though they differ from each other in that one is a bird of prey and the other a carrion-eater. But how are we to interpret the pair bat/night owl? Radcliffe-Brown admits that at first he was misled by the fact that both fly about at night. However, in one part of New South Wales it is the tree-creeper, a diurnal bird, which is opposed to the bat; it is the feminine totem, and a myth relates that it is this bird which taught women to climb trees.

Encouraged by this first explanation supplied by his informant, Radcliffe-Brown then asked, "What resemblance is there between the bat and the tree-creeper?" The native, obviously surprised by such ignorance, answered, "But of course they both live in holes in trees." This is also the case with the night owl and the nightjar. To eat meat, or to live in trees, is the common feature of the pair considered and presents a point of comparison with the human condition.* But there is also an opposition within the pair, underlying the similarity: while both of the birds are carnivorous, one is a "hunter" and the other is a "thief." While they are members of the same species, cockatoos differ in color, being white or black; birds which similarly live in holes in trees are distinguished as diurnal and nocturnal, and so on.

Consequently, the division eaglehawk/crow among the Darling River tribes, with which we began, is seen at the end of the analysis to be no more than "one particular example of a widespread type of the application of a certain structural principle," a principle consisting of the

union of opposites. The alleged totemism is no more than a particular expression, by means of a special nomenclature formed of animal and plant names (in a certain code, as we should say today), which is its sole distinctive characteristic, of correlations and oppositions which may be formalized in other ways, e.g., among certain tribes of North and South America, by oppositions of the type sky/earth, war/peace, upstream/downstream, red/white, etc. The most general model of this, and the most systematic application, is to be found perhaps in China, in the opposition of the two principles of Yang and Yin, as male and female, day and night, summer and winter, the union of which results in an organized totality (*tao*) such as the conjugal pair, the day, or the year. Totemism is thus reduced to a particular fashion of formulating a general problem, viz., how to make opposition, instead of being an obstacle to integration, serve rather to produce it.

Radcliffe-Brown's demonstration ends decisively the dilemma in which the adversaries as well as the proponents of totemism have been trapped because they could assign only two roles to living species, viz., that of a natural stimulus, or that of an arbitrary pretext. The animals in totemism cease to be solely or principally creatures which are feared, admired, or envied: their perceptible reality permits the embodiment of ideas and relations conceived by speculative thought on the basis of empirical observations. We can understand, too, that natural species are chosen not because they are "good to eat" but because they are "good to think."

The gap between this thesis and its predecessor is so great that we should like to know whether Radcliffe-Brown appreciated it. The answer is perhaps to be found in the notes of lectures he

---

*As we have gone a little beyond Radcliffe-Brown's account it may be asked in what respect the life of birds which live in holes in trees recalls the human condition. There is at least one Australian tribe, as a matter of fact, which names its moieties after the parts of a tree: "In the Ngeumba tribe Gwaimudthen is divided into nhurai (butt) and wangue (middle), while Gwaigulir is equivalent to winggo (top). These names refer to different portions of the shadow of a tree and refer to the positions taken up in camping. . . ." (Thomas, 1906, p. 152).

delivered in South Africa, and in the unpublished manuscript of an address on Australian cosmology, the last occasions for the expression of his thought before he died in 1953. He was not the man to admit with good grace that he might change his mind, or to recognize possible influences. Yet it is difficult not to remark, in this respect, that the ten years which preceded his Huxley Memorial Lecture were marked by the drawing together of anthropology and structural linguistics. For those who took part in this enterprise it is tempting at least to think that this may have found an echo in Radcliffe-Brown's thought. The ideas of opposition and correlation, and that of pair of opposites, have a long history; but it is structural linguistics and subsequently structural anthropology which rehabilitated them in the vocabulary of the humane sciences. It is striking to meet them, with all their implications, in the writings of Radcliffe-Brown, who, as we have seen, was led by them to abandon his earlier positions, which were still stamped with the mark of naturalism and empiricism. This departure, nevertheless, was not made without hesitation, and at one point Radcliffe-Brown seems uncertain about the scope of his thesis and the extent of its application beyond the area of the Australian facts: "The Australian idea of what is here called 'opposition' is a particular application of that association by contrariety that is a universal feature of human thinking, so that we think by pairs of contraries, upwards and downwards, strong and weak, black and white. But the Australian conception of 'opposition' combines the idea of a pair of contraries with that of a pair of opponents."

It is certainly the case that one consequence of modern structuralism (not, however, clearly enunciated) ought to be to rescue associational psychology from the discredit into which it has fallen.

Associationism had the great merit of sketching the contours of this elementary logic, which is like the least common denominator of all thought, and its only failure was not to recognize that it was an original logic, a direct expression of the structure of the mind (and behind the mind, probably, of the brain), and not an inert product of the action of the environment on an amorphous consciousness. But, contrary to what Radcliffe-Brown tends still to believe, it is this logic of oppositions and correlations, exclusions and inclusions, compatibilities and incompatibilities, which explains the laws of association, not the reverse. A renovated associationism would have to be based on a system of operations which would not be without similarity to Boolean algebra. As Radcliffe-Brown's very conclusions demonstrate, his analysis of Australian facts guides him beyond a simple ethnographic generalization—to the laws of language, and even of thought.

Nor is this all. We have already remarked that Radcliffe-Brown understood that in a structural analysis it is impossible to dissociate form from content. The form is not outside, but inside. In order to perceive the rationale of animal designations they must be envisaged concretely, for we are not free to trace a boundary on the far side of which purely arbitrary considerations would reign. Meaning is not decreed: if it is not everywhere it is nowhere. It is true that our limited knowledge often prevents us from pursuing it to its last retreats; for instance, Radcliffe-Brown does not explain why certain Australian tribes conceptualize the affinity between animal life and the human condition by analogy with carnivorous tastes while other tribes frame it in terms of common habitat. But his analysis implicitly presupposes that this difference itself is also meaningful, and that if we were better informed we should be able to correlate it with other differences, to be discovered between the respective beliefs of two groups, between their techniques, or between the relations of each to its environment.

In fact, the method adopted by Radcliffe-Brown is as sound as the interpretations which it suggests to him. Each level of social reality appears to him as an indispensable complement, without which it would be impossible to understand the other levels. Customs lead to beliefs, and these lead to techniques, but the different levels do not simply reflect each other. They react dialectically among themselves in such a way that we cannot hope to understand one of them without first evaluating, through their respective relations of opposition and correlation, *institutions, representations,* and *situations.* In every one of its practical undertakings, anthropology thus does no more than assert a homology of structure between human thought in action and the human object to which it is applied. The methodological integration of essence and form reflects, in its own way, a more necessary integration—that between method and reality.

SECTION THREE

Religion as an Expression
of Personal or Psychic Actualities

Friedrich Nietzsche

THE ORIGIN OF
THE
BAD CONSCIENCE

At this juncture I cannot avoid trying to give a tentative and provisional expression to my own hypothesis concerning the origin of the bad conscience; it is difficult to make it fully appreciated, and it requires continuous meditation, attention, and digestion. I regard the bad conscience as the serious illness which man was bound to contract under the stress of the most radical change which he has ever experienced—that change, when he found himself finally imprisoned within the pale of society and of peace.

Just like the plight of the water-animals, when they were compelled either to become land-animals or to perish, so was the plight of these half-animals,

From The Genealogy of Morals (1887), Edinburgh and London: 1910, pp. 99–102; 106–110.

perfectly adapted as they were to the savage life of war, prowling, and adventure—suddenly all their instincts were rendered worthless and "switched off." Henceforward they had to walk on their feet—"carry themselves," whereas heretofore they had been carried by the water: a terrible heaviness oppressed them. They found themselves clumsy in obeying the simplest directions, confronted with this new and unknown world they no longer had their old guides—the regulative instincts that had led them unconsciously to safety—they were reduced, were those unhappy creatures, to thinking, inferring, calculating, putting together causes and results, reduced to that poorest and most erratic organ of theirs, their "consciousness." I do not believe there was ever in the world such a feeling of misery, such a leaden

165

discomfort—further, those old instincts had not immediately ceased their demands! Only it was difficult and rarely possible to gratify them: speaking broadly, they were compelled to satisfy themselves by new and, as it were, hole-and-corner methods. All instincts which do not find a vent without, *turn inwards* —this is what I mean by the growing "internalisation" of man: consequently we have the first growth in man, of what subsequently was called his soul. The whole inner world, originally as thin as if it had been stretched between two layers of skin, burst apart and expanded proportionately, and obtained depth, breadth, and height, when man's external outlet became *obstructed*. These terrible bulwarks, with which the social organisation protected itself against the old instincts of freedom (punishments belong pre-eminently to these bulwarks), brought it about that all those instincts of wild, free, prowling man became turned backwards *against man himself*. Enmity, cruelty, the delight in persecution, in surprises, change, destruction— the turning of all these instincts against their own possessors: this is the origin of the "bad conscience." It was man, who, lacking external enemies and obstacles, and imprisoned as he was in the oppressive narrowness and monotony of custom, in his own impatience lacerated, persecuted, gnawed, frightened, and ill-treated himself; it was this animal in the hands of the tamer, which beat itself against the bars of its cage; it was this being who, pining and yearning for that desert home of which it has been deprived, was compelled to create out of its own self, an adventure, a torture-chamber, a hazardous and perilous desert—it was this fool, this homesick and desperate prisoner—who invented the "bad conscience." But thereby he introduced that most grave and sinister illness, from which mankind has not yet recovered, the suffering of man from the disease called man, as the result of a violent breaking from his animal past, the result, as it were, of a spasmodic plunge into a new environment and new conditions of existence, the result of a declaration of war against the old instincts, which up to that time had been the staple of his power, his joy, his formidableness. Let us immediately add that this fact of an animal ego turning against itself, taking part against itself, produced in the world so novel, profound, unheard-of, problematic, inconsistent, and *pregnant* a phenomenon, that the aspect of the world was radically altered thereby. In sooth, only divine spectators could have appreciated the drama that then began, and whose end baffles conjecture as yet—a drama too subtle, too wonderful, too paradoxical to warrant its undergoing a nonsensical and unheeded performance on some random grotesque planet! Henceforth man is to be counted as one of the most unexpected and sensational lucky shots in the game of the "big baby" of Heracleitus, whether he be called Zeus or Chance—he awakens on his behalf the interest, excitement, hope, almost the confidence, of his being the harbinger and forerunner of something, of man being no end, but only a stage, an interlude, a bridge, a great promise. . . .

Undoubtedly the bad conscience is an illness, but an illness like pregnancy is an illness. If we search out the conditions under which this illness reaches its most terrible and sublime zenith, we shall see what really first brought about its entry into the world. But to do this we must take a long breath, and we must first of all go back once again to an earlier point of view. The relation at civil law of the ower to his creditor (which has already been discussed in detail), has been interpreted once again (and indeed in a manner which historically is exceedingly remarkable and suspicious) into a relationship, which is perhaps more incomprehensible to us moderns than to any other era; that is, into the relationship of the *existing* generation to its *ancestors*. Within the original tribal association—we are talking of primitive times—each living generation recognises a legal obligation towards the earlier generation, and particularly towards the earliest, which founded the family (and this is something much more than a mere sentimental obligation, the existence of which, during the longest period of man's history, is by no means indisputable). There prevails in them the conviction that it is only thanks to sacrifices and efforts of their ancestors, that the race *persists* at all—and that this has to be *paid back* to them by sacrifices and services. Thus is recognised the *owing* of a debt, which accumulates continually by reason of these ancestors never ceasing in their subsequent life as potent spirits to secure by their power new privileges and advantages to the race. Gratis, perchance? But there is no gratis for that raw and "mean-souled" age. What return can be made?—Sacrifice (at first, nourishment, in its crudest sense), festivals, temples, tributes of veneration, above all, obedience—since all customs are, quâ works of the ancestors, equally their precepts and commands —are the ancestors ever given enough? This suspicion remains and grows: from time to time it extorts a great wholesale ransom, something monstrous in the way of repayment of the creditor (the notorious sacrifice of the first-born, for example, blood, human blood in any case). The *fear* of ancestors and their power, the consciousness of owing debts to them, necessarily increases, according to this kind of logic, in the exact proportion that the race itself increases, that the race itself becomes more victorious, more independent, more honoured, more feared. This, and not the contrary, is the fact. Each step towards race decay, all disastrous events. all symptoms of degeneration, of approaching disintegration, always *diminish* the fear of the founders' spirit, and whittle away the idea of his sagacity, providence, and potent presence. Conceive this crude kind of logic carried to its climax: it follows that the ancestors of the *most powerful* races must, through the growing fear that they exercise on the imaginations, grow themselves into monstrous dimensions, and become relegated to the gloom of a divine mystery that transcends imagination—the ancestor becomes at last necessarily transfigured into a *god*. Perhaps this is the very origin of the gods, that is, an origin from *fear!* And those who feel bound to add, "but from piety also," will have difficulty in maintaining this theory, with regard to the primeval and longest period of the human race. And of course this is even more the case as regards the *middle* period, the formative period of the aristocratic races—the aristocratic races which have given back with interest to their founders, the ancestors (heroes, gods), all those qualities which in the meanwhile have appeared in themselves, that is, the aristocratic qualities. We will later on glance again at the ennobling and promotion of the gods (which of course is totally distinct from their "sanctification"): let us now provisionally follow to its end the course of the whole of this development of the consciousness of "owing."

According to the teaching of history, the consciousness of owing debts to the deity by no means came to an end with the decay of the clan organisation of society; just as mankind has inherited the ideas of "good" and "bad" from the race-nobility (together with its fundamental tendency towards establishing social distinctions), so with the heritage of the racial and tribal gods it has also inherited the incubus of debts as yet unpaid and the desire to discharge them. The transition is effected by those large populations of slaves and bondsmen, who, whether through compulsion or through submission and *"mimicry,"* have accommodated themselves to the religion of their masters; through this channel these inherited tendencies inundate the world. The feeling of owing a debt to the deity has grown continuously for several centuries, always in the same proportion in which the idea of God and the consciousness of God have grown and become exalted among mankind. (The whole history of ethnic fights, victories, reconciliations, amalgamations, everything, in fact, which precedes the eventual classing of all the social elements in each great race-synthesis, are mirrored in the hotch-potch genealogy of their gods, in the legends of their fights, victories, and reconciliations. Progress towards universal empires invariably means progress towards universal deities; despotism, with its subjugation of the independent nobility, always paves the way for some system or other of monotheism.) The appearance of the Christian god, as the record god up to this time, has for that very reason brought equally into the world the record amount of guilt consciousness. Granted that we have gradually started on the *reverse* movement, there is no little probability in the deduction, based on the continuous decay in the belief in the Christian god, to the effect that there also already exists a considerable decay in the human consciousness of owing (ought); in fact, we cannot shut our eyes to the prospect of the complete and eventual triumph of atheism freeing mankind from all this feeling of obligation to their origin, their *causa prima*. Atheism and a kind of second innocence complement and supplement each other.

Sigmund Freud

OBSESSIVE ACTIONS AND RELIGIOUS PRACTICES

I am certainly not the first person to have been struck by the resemblance between what are called obsessive actions in sufferers from nervous affections and the observances by means of which believers give expression to their piety.

From "Obsessive Actions and Religious Practices" (1907), The Standard Edition of the Complete Psychological Works of Sigmund Freud, London: 1959, IX, 117–20; 122–27. By permission of Basic Books, Inc., Publishers and The Hogarth Press Ltd.

The term "ceremonial," which has been applied to some of these obsessive actions, is evidence of this. The resemblance, however, seems to me to be more than a superficial one, so that an insight into the origin of neurotic ceremonial may embolden us to draw inferences by analogy about the psychological processes of religious life.

People who carry out obsessive actions or ceremonials belong to the same class as those who suffer from obsessive thinking, obsessive ideas, obsessive impulses and the like. Taken together, these form a particular clinical entity, to which the name of "obsessional neurosis" ("*Zwangs-neurose*") is customarily applied.[1] But one should not attempt to deduce the character of the illness from its name; for, strictly speaking, other kinds of morbid mental phenomena have an equal claim to possessing what are spoken of as "obsessional" characteristics. In place of a definition we must for the time being be content with obtaining a detailed knowledge of these states, since we have not yet been able to arrive at a criterion of obsessional neuroses; it probably lies very deep, although we seem to sense its presence everywhere in the manifestations of the illness.

Neurotic ceremonials consist in making small adjustments to particular everyday actions, small additions or restrictions or arrangements, which have always to be carried out in the same, or in a methodically varied, manner. These activities give the impression of being mere formalities, and they seem quite meaningless to us. Nor do they appear otherwise to the patient himself; yet he is incapable of giving them up, for any deviation from the ceremonial is visited by intolerable anxiety, which obliges him at once to make his omission good. Just as trivial as the ceremonial actions themselves are the occasions and activities which are embellished, encumbered and in any case prolonged by the ceremonial—for instance, dressing and undressing, going to bed or satisfying bodily needs. The performance of a ceremonial can

be described by replacing it, as it were, by a series of unwritten laws. For instance, to take the case of the bed ceremonial: the chair must stand in a particular place beside the bed; the clothes must lie upon it folded in a particular order; the blanket must be tucked in at the bottom and the sheet smoothed out; the pillows must be arranged in such and such a manner, and the subject's own body must lie in a precisely defined position. Only after all this may he go to sleep. Thus in slight cases the ceremonial seems to be no more than an exaggeration of an orderly procedure that is customary and justifiable; but the special conscientiousness with which it is carried out and the anxiety which follows upon its neglect stamp the ceremonial as a "sacred act." Any interruption of it is for the most part badly tolerated, and the presence of other people during its performance is almost always ruled out.

Any activities whatever may become obsessive actions in the wider sense of the term if they are elaborated by small additions or given a rhythmic character by means of pauses and repetitions. We shall not expect to find a sharp distinction between "ceremonials" and "obsessive actions." As a rule obsessive actions have grown out of ceremonials. Besides these two, prohibitions and hindrances (abulias) make up the content of the disorder; these, in fact, only continue the work of the obsessive actions, inasmuch as some things are completely forbidden to the patient and others only allowed subject to his following a prescribed ceremonial.

It is remarkable that both compulsions and prohibitions (having to do something and having *not* to do something) apply in the first instance only to the subject's solitary activities and for a long time leave his social behaviour unaffected. Sufferers from this illness are consequently able to treat their affliction

---

[1]See Löwenfeld (1904). According to that author the term "*Zwangsvorstellung*" ("obsessional idea" or simply "obsession") was introduced by Krafft-Ebing in 1867. The concept (and the term) "obsessional neurosis" originated on the same authority, from Freud himself. His first published use of it was in his first paper on anxiety neurosis (1895*b*).

as a private matter and keep it concealed for many years. And, indeed, many more people suffer from these forms of obsessional neurosis than doctors hear of. For many sufferers, too, concealment is made easier from the fact that they are quite well able to fulfil their social duties during a part of the day, once they have devoted a number of hours to their secret doings, hidden from view like Melusine.[2]

It is easy to see where the resemblances lie between neurotic ceremonials and the sacred acts of religious ritual: in the qualms of conscience brought on by their neglect, in their complete isolation from all other actions (shown in the prohibition against interruption) and in the conscientiousness with which they are carried out in every detail. But the differences are equally obvious, and a few of them are so glaring that they make the comparison a sacrilege: the greater individual variability of (neurotic) ceremonial actions in contrast to the stereotyped character of rituals (prayer, turning to the East, etc.), their private nature as opposed to the public and communal character of religious observances, above all, however, the fact that, while the minutiae of religious ceremonial are full of significance and have a symbolic meaning, those of neurotics seem foolish and senseless. In this respect an obsessional neurosis presents a travesty, half comic and half tragic, of a private religion. But it is precisely this sharpest difference between neurotic and religious ceremonial which disappears when, with the help of the psychoanalytic technique of investigation, one penetrates to the true meaning of obsessive actions.[3] In the course of such an investigation the appearance which

[2] A beautiful woman in mediaeval legend, who led a secret existence as a water-nymph.
[3] See the collection of my shorter papers on the theory of the neuroses published in 1906 (*Standard Ed.* 3).

obsessive actions afford of being foolish and senseless is completely effaced, and the reason for their having that appearance is explained. It is found that the obsessive actions are perfectly significant in every detail, that they serve important interests of the personality and that they give expression to experiences that are still operative and to thoughts that are cathected with affect. They do this in two ways, either by direct or by symbolic representation; and they are consequently to be interpreted either historically or symbolically.

*   *   *

The same is true of ceremonials in the strict sense, only that the evidence for this would require a more circumstantial presentation. I am quite aware of how far our explanations of obsessive actions are apparently taking us from the sphere of religious thought. It is one of the conditions of the illness that the person who is obeying a compulsion carries it out without understanding its meaning—or at any rate its chief meaning. It is only thanks to the efforts of psychoanalytic treatment that he becomes conscious of the meaning of his obsessive action and, with it, of the motives that are impelling him to it. We express this important fact by saying that the obsessive action serves to express *unconscious* motives and ideas. In this, we seem to find a further departure from religious practices; but we must remember that as a rule the ordinary pious individual, too, performs a ceremonial without concerning himself with its significance, although priests and scientific investigators may be familiar with the —mostly symbolic—meaning of the ritual. In all believers, however, the motives which impel them to religious practices are unknown to them or are represented in consciousness by others which are advanced in their place.

Analysis of obsessive actions has already given us some sort of an insight into their causes and into the chain of motives which bring them into effect. We may say that the sufferer from compulsions and prohibitions behaves as if he were dominated by a sense of guilt, of which, however, he knows nothing, so that we must call it an unconscious sense of guilt, in spite of the apparent contradiction in terms.[4] This sense of guilt has its source in certain early mental events, but it is constantly being revived by renewed temptations which arise whenever there is a contemporary provocation. Moreover, it occasions a lurking sense of expectant anxiety, an expectation of misfortune, which is linked, through the idea of punishment, with the internal perception of the temptation. When the ceremonial is first being constructed, the patient is still conscious that he must do this or that lest some ill should befall, and as a rule the nature of the ill that is to be expected is still known to his consciousness. But what is already hidden from him is the connection—which is always demonstrable—between the occasion on which this expectant anxiety arises and the danger which it conjures up. Thus a ceremonial starts as an action for *defence* or *insurance, a protective measure.*

The sense of guilt of obsessional neurotics finds its counterpart in the protestations of pious people that they know that at heart they are miserable sinners; and the pious observances (such as prayers, invocations, etc.), with which such people preface every daily act, and in especial every unusual

undertaking, seem to have the value of defensive or protective measures.

A deeper insight into the mechanism of obsessional neurosis is gained if we take into account the primary fact which lies at the bottom of it. This is always *the repression of an instinctual impulse*[5] (a component of the sexual instinct) which was present in the subject's constitution and which was allowed to find expression for a while during his childhood but later succumbed to suppression. In the course of the repression of this instinct a special *conscientiousness* is created which is directed against the instinct's aims; but this psychical reaction-formation feels insecure and constantly threatened by the instinct which is lurking in the unconscious. The influence of the repressed instinct is felt as a temptation, and during the process of repression itself anxiety is generated, which gains control over the future in the form of *expectant* anxiety. The process of repression which leads to obsessional neurosis must be considered as one which is only partly successful and which increasingly threatens to fail. It may thus be compared to an unending conflict; fresh psychical efforts are continually required to counterbalance the forward pressure of the instinct.[6] Thus the ceremonial and obsessive actions arise partly as a defence against the temptation and partly as a protection against the ill which is expected. Against the temptation the protective measures seem soon to become inadequate; then the prohibitions come into play, with the purpose of keeping at a distance situations that give rise to temptation. Prohibitions take the place of obsessive actions, it

[4]The German word used here for "sense of guilt" is "*Schuldbewusstsein,*" literally "consciousness of guilt." This seems to be the earliest explicit appearance of the "unconscious sense of guilt" which was to play such an important part in Freud's later writings—e.g., at the beginning of the last chapter of *The Ego and the Id* (1923*b*). The way had been prepared for the notion, however, very much earlier, in Section II of the first paper on "The Neuro-Psychoses of Defence" (1894*a*).

[5]"*Triebregung.*" This appears to be Freud's first published use of what was to be one of his most used terms.

[6]This passage foreshadows the concept of "anticathexis," which is developed at length in Section IV of the paper on "The Unconscious" (1915*e*), *Standard Ed.,* 14, 180ff.

will be seen, just as a phobia is designed to avert a hysterical attack. Again, a ceremonial represents the sum of the conditions subject to which something that is not yet absolutely forbidden is permitted, just as the Church's marriage ceremony signifies for the believer a sanctioning of sexual enjoyment which would otherwise be sinful. A further characteristic of obsessional neurosis, as of all similar affections, is that its manifestations (its symptoms, including the obsessive actions) fulfil the condition of being a compromise between the warring forces of the mind. They thus always reproduce something of the pleasure which they are designed to prevent; they serve the repressed instinct no less than the agencies which are repressing it. As the illness progresses, indeed, actions which were originally mostly concerned with maintaining the defence come to approximate more and more to the proscribed actions through which the instinct was able to find expression in childhood.

Some features of this state of affairs may be seen in the sphere of religious life as well. The formation of a religion, too, seems to be based on the suppression, the renunciation, of certain instinctual impulses. These impulses, however, are not, as in the neuroses, exclusively components of the sexual instinct; they are self-seeking, socially harmful instincts, though, even so, they are usually not without a sexual component. A sense of guilt following upon continual temptation and an expectant anxiety in the form of fear of divine punishment have, after all, been familiar to us in the field of religion longer than in that of neurosis. Perhaps because of the admixture of sexual components, perhaps because of some general characteristics of the instincts, the suppression of instinct proves to be an inadequate and interminable process in religious life also. Indeed, complete backslidings into

sin are more common among pious people than among neurotics and these give rise to a new form of religious activity, namely acts of penance, which have their counterpart in obsessional neurosis.

We have noted as a curious and derogatory characteristic of obsessional neurosis that its ceremonials are concerned with the small actions of daily life and are expressed in foolish regulations and restrictions in connection with them. We cannot understand this remarkable feature of the clinical picture until we have realized that the mechanism of psychical *displacement*, which was first discovered by me in the construction of dreams,[7] dominates the mental processes of obsessional neurosis. It is already clear from the few examples of obsessive actions given above that their symbolism and the detail of their execution are brought about by a displacement from the actual, important thing on to a small one which takes its place—for instance, from a husband on to a chair.[8] It is this tendency to displacement which progressively changes the clinical picture and eventually succeeds in turning what is apparently the most trivial matter into something of the utmost importance and urgency. It cannot be denied that in the religious field as well there is a similar tendency to a displacement of psychical values, and in the same direction, so that the petty ceremonials of religious practice gradually become the essential thing and push aside the underlying thoughts. That is why religions are subject to reforms which work retroactively and aim at a re-establishment of the original balance of values.

[7]See *The Interpretation of Dreams* (1900a), Chapter VI, Section B (*Standard Ed.*, 4, 305ff.).

[8]Freud had already described this mechanism in his book on jokes (1905c), near the end of Section 11 of Chapter II. He often recurred to the point—for instance, in the "Rat Man" analysis (1909d), *Standard Ed.*, 10, 241, and in the metapsychological paper on repression (1915d), *ibid.*, 14, 157.

The character of compromise which obsessive actions possess in their capacity as neurotic symptoms is the character least easily detected in corresponding religious observances. Yet here, too, one is reminded of this feature of neuroses when one remembers how commonly all the acts which religion forbids—the expressions of the instincts it has suppressed—are committed precisely in the name of, and ostensibly for the sake of, religion.

In view of these similarities and analogies one might venture to regard obsessional neurosis as a pathological counterpart of the formation of a religion, and to describe that neurosis as an individual religiosity and religion as a universal obsessional neurosis. The most essential similarity would reside in the underlying renunciation of the activation of instincts that are constitutionally present; and the chief difference would lie in the nature of those instincts, which in the neurosis are exclusively sexual in their origin, while in religion they spring from egoistic sources.

A progressive renunciation of constitutional instincts, whose activation might afford the ego primary pleasure, appears to be one of the foundations of the development of human civilization.[9] Some part of this instinctual repression is effected by its religions, in that they require the individual to sacrifice his instinctual pleasure to the Deity: "Vengeance is mine, saith the Lord." In the development of the ancient religions one seems to discern that many things which mankind had renounced as "iniquities" had been surrendered to the Deity and were still permitted in his name, so that the handing over to him of bad and socially harmful instincts was the means by which man freed himself from their domination. For this reason, it is surely no accident that all the attributes of man, along with the misdeeds that follow from them, were to an unlimited amount ascribed to the ancient gods. Nor is it a contradiction of this that nevertheless man was not permitted to justify his own iniquities by appealing to divine example.

[9]This idea was expanded by Freud in the paper on sexual ethics written about a year later (1908d), pp. 186ff. below.

Erik H. Erikson

RELIGION AND THE CRISIS OF IDENTITY

From Young Man Luther, New York: 1958, pp. 13–16; 21–22; 253–63. By permission of W. W. Norton & Company, Inc. and Faber and Faber Ltd. Copyright © 1958, 1962 by Erik H. Erikson.

The literature on Luther, and by Luther, is stupendous in volume. Yet it adds up to very few reliable data on his childhood and youth. His role in history, and above all his personality, remain ambiguous on a grandiose scale. Luther has been both vilified and sanctified, and both by sincere and proven scholars, who have spent a good portion, if not all, of their lifetimes reconstructing him from the raw data—only to create, whenever they tried to encompass him with a formula, a superhuman or a suprahuman robot, a man who could never have breathed or moved or least of all spoken as Luther spoke. In writing this book, did I intend to do better?

Soeren Kierkegaard—the one man who could judge Luther with the compassionate objectivity of a kindred *homo religiosus*—once made a remark which sums up the problem which I felt I could approach with the means at my disposal. He wrote in his diary: "Luther ... is a patient of exceeding import for Christendom" (*en for Christenheden yderst vigtig Patient*). In quoting this statement out of context, I do not mean to imply that Kierkegaard intended to call Luther a patient in the sense of a clinical "case"; rather, he saw in him a religious attitude (patienthood) exemplified in an archetypal and immensely influential way. In taking this statement as a kind of motto for this book, we do not narrow our perspective to the clinical; we expand our clinical perspective to include a life style of patienthood as a sense of imposed suffering, of an intense need for cure, and (as Kierkegaard adds) a "passion for expressing and describing one's suffering."

Kierkegaard's point was that Luther overdid this subjective, this "patient," side of life, and in his old age failed to reach "a doctor's commanding view" (*Laegen's Overskuelse*). The last question we must leave open for the present.

"A patient." ... I expected to have access to this wider meaning of patienthood from my work with gifted but acutely disturbed young people. I did not wish merely to reduce young Luther to his diagnosis (which, within limits, could be done rather convincingly); I wished to delineate in his life (as I had done in the lives of young contem-

poraries) one of those life crises which make conscious or unconscious, diagnosed or unofficial, patients out of people until they find a cure—and this often means a cause.

I have called the major crisis of adolescence the *identity crisis;* it occurs in that period of the life cycle when each youth must forge for himself some central perspective and direction, some working unity, out of the effective remnants of his childhood and the hopes of his anticipated adulthood; he must detect some meaningful resemblance between what he has come to see in himself and what his sharpened awareness tells him others judge and expect him to be. This sounds dangerously like common sense; like all health, however, it is a matter of course only to those who possess it, and appears as a most complex achievement to those who have tasted its absence. Only in ill health does one realize the intricacy of the body; and only in a crisis, individual or historical, does it become obvious what a sensitive combination of interrelated factors the human personality is—a combination of capacities created in the distant past and of opportunities divined in the present; a combination of totally unconscious preconditions developed in individual growth and of social conditions created and recreated in the precarious interplay of generations. In some young people, in some classes, at some periods in history, this crisis will be minimal; in other people, classes, and periods, the crisis will be clearly marked off as a critical period, a kind of "second birth," apt to be aggravated either by widespread neuroticisms or by pervasive ideological unrest. Some young individuals will succumb to this crisis in all manner of neurotic, psychotic, or delinquent behavior; others will resolve it through participation in ideological movements passionately concerned with religion or politics, nature or art. Still others, al-

hough suffering and deviating danger-
usly through what appears to be a
rolonged adolescence, eventually come
o contribute an original bit to an emerg-
ng style of life: the very danger which
hey have sensed has forced them to
nobilize capacities to see and say, to
ream and plan, to design and construct,
n new ways.

Luther, so it seems, at one time was a
ather endangered young man, beset
vith a syndrome of conflicts whose
utline we have learned to recognize,
nd whose components to analyse. He
ound a spiritual solution, not without
he well-timed help of a therapeutically
clever superior in the Augustinian order.
His solution roughly bridged a political
nd psychological vacuum which history
ad created in a significant portion of
Western Christendom. Such coincidence,
further coinciding with the deployment
f highly specific personal gifts, makes
or historical "greatness." We will
ollow Luther through the crisis of his
outh, and the unfolding of his gifts,
o the first manifestation of his originality
s a thinker, namely, to the emergence of
new theology, apparently not imme-
iately perceived as a radical innovation
ither by him or his listeners, in his first
lectures on the Psalms (1513). What
appened to him after he had acquired
historical identity is more than another
hapter; for even half of the man is too
nuch for one book. The difference be-
ween the young and the old Luther is
o marked, and the second, the sturdy
rator, so exclusive a Luther-image to
nost readers, that I will speak of
"Martin" when I report on Luther's
arly years, which according to common
sage in the Luther literature include
is twenties; and of "Luther" where and
vhen he has become the leader of
Lutherans, seduced by history into look-
ng back on his past as upon a mytholog-
cal autobiography.

Kierkegaard's remark has a second

part: "... of very great import for
Christendom." This calls for an investigation of how the individual "case" became
an important, an historic "event," and
for formulations concerning the spiritual
and political identity crisis of Northern
Christendom in Luther's time. True,
I could have avoided those methodological uncertainties and impurities which
will undoubtedly occur by sticking to
my accustomed job of writing a case
history, and leaving the historical event
to those who, in turn, would consider
the case a mere accessory to the event.
But we clinicians have learned in recent
years that we cannot lift a case history
out of history, even as we suspect that
historians, when they try to separate the
logic of the historic event from that of
the life histories which intersect in it,
leave a number of vital historical problems
unattended. So we may have to risk
that bit of impurity which is inherent in
the hyphen of the psycho-historical as
well as of all other hyphenated approaches. They are the compost heap of
today's interdisciplinary efforts, which
may help to fertilize new fields, and to
produce future flowers of new methodological clarity.

Human nature can best be studied in
the state of conflict; and human conflict
comes to the detailed attention of interested recorders mainly under special
circumstances. One such circumstance
is the clinical encounter, in which the
suffering, for the sake of securing help,
have no other choice than to become case
histories; and another special circumstance is history, where extraordinary
beings, by their own self-centered ma-
neuvers and through the prodding of the
charismatic hunger of mankind, become
(auto) biographies. Clinical as well as
historical scholars have much to learn by
going back and forth between these two
kinds of recorded history. Luther, always
instructive, forces on the workers in
both fields a special awareness. He

indulged himself as he grew older in florid self-revelations of a kind which can make a clinical biographer feel that he is dealing with a client. If the clinician should indulge himself in this feeling, however, he will soon find out that the imaginary client has been dealing with him: for Luther is one of those autobiographers with a histrionic flair who can make enthusiastic use even of their neurotic suffering, matching selected memories with the clues given to them by their avid public to create their own official identities. . . .

Religion elaborates on what feels profoundly true even though it is not demonstrable: it translates into significant words, images, and codes the exceeding darkness which surrounds man's existence, and the light which pervades it beyond all desert or comprehension. Religion will occupy our attention [here] primarily as a source of ideologies for those who seek identities. In depicting the identity struggle of a *young* great man I am not as concerned with the validity of the dogmas which laid claim to him, or of the philosophies which influenced his systematic thought, as I am with the spiritual and intellectual milieu which the isms of his time—and these isms *had* to be religious—offered to his passionate search.

My focus, then, is on the "ideological." In modern history, this word has assumed a specifically political connotation, referring to totalitarian systems of thought which distort historical truth by methods ranging from fanatic self-deception to shrewd falsification and cold propaganda. Karl Mannheim has analyzed this word and the processes for which it stands from the sociological point of view. In this book, *ideology* will mean an unconscious tendency underlying religious and scientific as well as political thought: the tendency at a given time to make facts amenable to ideas, and ideas to

facts, in order to create a world image convincing enough to support the collective and the individual sense of identity. Far from being arbitrary or consciously manageable (although it is as exploitable as all of man's unconscious strivings), the total perspective created by ideological simplification reveals its strength by the dominance it exerts on the seeming logic of historical events, and by its influence on the identity formation of individuals (and thus on their "ego-strength"). In this sense, this is a book on identity and ideology.

In some periods of his history, and in some phases of his life cycle, man needs (until we invent something better) a new ideological orientation as surely and as sorely as he must have air and food. I will not be ashamed then, even as I analyze what is analyzable, to display sympathy and empathy with a young man who (by no means lovable all of the time) faced the problems of human *existence* in the most forward terms of his era. I will use the word *existential* in this simplest connotation, mindful that no school of thought has any monopoly on it. . . .

*   *   *

Let us consider, then, what we may call the metabolism of generations.

Each human life begins at a given evolutionary stage and level of tradition, bringing to its environment a capital of patterns and energies; these are used to grow on, and to grow into the social process with, and also as contributions to this process. Each new being is received into a style of life prepared by tradition and held together by tradition, and at the same time disintegrating because of the very nature of tradition. We say that tradition "molds" the individual, "channels" his drives. But the social process does not mold a new being merely to housebreak him; it molds generations in order to be remolded, to be reinvigorated, by them. Therefore, society can never afford merely to suppress drives or to guide their sublimation. It must also support the primary function of every individual ego, which is to transform instinctual energy into patterns of action, into character, into style—in short, into an identity with a core of integrity which is to be derived from and also contributed to the tradition. There is an optimum ego synthesis to which the individual aspires; and there is an optimum societal metabolism for which societies and cultures strive. In describing the interdependence of individual aspiration and of societal striving, we describe something indispensable to human life.

In an earlier book, I indicated a program of studies which might account for the dovetailing of the stages of individual life and of basic human institutions. The present book circumscribes for only one of these stages—the identity crisis—its intrinsic relation to the process of ideological rejuvenation in a period of history when organized religion dominated ideologies.

In discussing the identity crisis, we have, at least implicitly, presented some of the attributes of any psychosocial crisis. At a given age, a human being, by dint of his physical, intellectual and emotional growth, becomes ready and eager to face a new life task, that is, a set of choices and tests which are in some traditional way prescribed and prepared for him by his society's structure. A new life task presents a *crisis* whose outcome can be a successful graduation, or alternatively, an impairment of the life cycle which will aggravate future crises. Each crisis prepares the next, as one step leads to another; and each crisis also lays one more cornerstone for the adult personality. I will enumerate all these crises (more thoroughly treated elsewhere) to remind us, in summary, of certain issues in Luther's life; and also to suggest a developmental root for

the basic human values of faith, will, conscience, and reason—all necessary in rudimentary form for the identity which crowns childhood.

The first crisis is the one of early infancy. How this crisis is met decides whether a man's innermost mood will be determined more by basic trust or by basic mistrust. The outcome of this crisis—apart from accidents of heredity, gestation, and birth—depends largely on the quality of maternal care, that is, on the consistency and mutuality which guide the mother's ministrations and give a certain predictability and hopefulness to the baby's original cosmos of urgent and bewildering body feelings. The ratio and relation of basic trust to basic mistrust established during early infancy determines much of the individual's capacity for simple faith, and consequently also determines his future contribution to his society's store of faith—which, in turn, will feed into a future mother's ability to trust the world in which she teaches trust to newcomers. In this first stage we can assume that a historical process is already at work; history writing should therefore chart the influence of historical events on growing generations to be able to judge the quality of their future contribution to history. As for little Martin, I have drawn conclusions about that earliest time when his mother could still claim the baby, and when he was still all hers, inferring that she must have provided him with a font of basic trust on which he was able to draw in his fight for a primary faith present before all will, conscience, and reason, a faith which is "the soul's virginity."

The first crisis corresponds roughly to what Freud has described as orality; the second corresponds to anality. An awareness of these correspondences is essential for a true understanding of the dynamics involved.

The second crisis, that of infancy, develops the infantile sources of what later becomes a human being's will, in its variations of willpower and wilfulness. The resolution of this crisis will determine whether an individual is apt to be dominated by a sense of autonomy, or by a sense of shame and doubt. The social limitations imposed on intensified wilfulness inevitably create doubt about the justice governing the relations of grown and growing people. The way this doubt is met by the grown-ups determines much of a man's future ability to combine an unimpaired will with ready self-discipline, rebellion with responsibility.

The interpretation is plausible that Martin was driven early out of the trust stage, out from "under his mother's skirts," by a jealously ambitious father who tried to make him precociously independent from women, and sober and reliable in his work. Hans succeeded, but not without storing in the boy violent doubts of the father's justification and sincerity; a lifelong shame over the persisting gap between his own precocious conscience and his actual inner state; and a deep nostalgia for a situation of infantile trust. His theological solution—spiritual return to a faith which is there before all doubt, combined with a political submission to those who by necessity must wield the sword of secular law—seems to fit perfectly his personal need for compromise. While this analysis does not explain either the ideological power or the theological consistency of his solution, it does illustrate that ontogenetic experience is an indispensable link and transformer between one stage of history and the next. This link is a psychological one, and the energy transformed and the process of transformation are both charted by the psychoanalytic method.

Freud formulated these matters in dynamic terms. Few men before him gave more genuine expression to those experiences which are on the borderline between the psychological and the theological than Luther, who gleaned from these experiences a religious gain formulated in theological terms. Luther described states of badness which in many forms pervade human existence from childhood. For instance, his description of shame, an emotion first experienced when the infant stands naked in space and feels belittled: "He is put to sin and shame before God . . . this shame is now a thousand times greater, that a man must blush in the presence of God. For this means that there is no corner or hole in the whole of creation into which a man might creep, not even in hell, but he must let himself be exposed to the gaze of the whole creation, and stand in the open with all his shame, as a bad conscience feels when it is really struck. . . ." Or his description of doubt, an emotion first experienced when the child feels singled out by demands whose rationale he does not comprehend: "When he is tormented in *Anfechtung* it seems to him that he is alone: God is angry only with him, and irreconcilably angry against him: then he alone is a sinner and all the others are in the right, and they work against him at God's orders. There is nothing left for him but this unspeakable sighing through which, without knowing it, he is supported by the Spirit and cries 'Why does God pick on me alone?' "

Luther was a man who would not settle for an easy appeasement of these feelings on any level, from childhood through youth to his manhood, or in any segment of life. His often impulsive and intuitive formulations transparently display the infantile struggle at the bottom of the lifelong emotional issue.

His basic contribution was a living reformulation of faith. This marks him as a theologian of the first order; it also indicates his struggle with the ontogenetically earliest and most basic problems of life. He saw as his life's work a new elineation of faith and will, of religion nd the law: for it is clear that organized eligiosity, in circumstances where faith 1 a world order is monopolized by eligion, is the institution which tries to ive dogmatic permanence to a reaffirnation of that basic trust—and a renewed ictory over that basic mistrust—with vhich each human being emerges from arly infancy. In this way organized reli-;ion cements the faith which will support uture generations. Established law tries o formulate obligations and privileges, estraints and freedoms, in such a way hat man can submit to law and order vith a minimum of doubt and with little oss of face, and as an autonomous agent of order can teach the rudiments of liscipline to his young. The relation of faith and law, of course, is an eternal uman problem, whether it appears in juestions of church and state, mysti-ism and daily morality, or existential loneliness and political commitment.

The third crisis, that of initiative rersus guilt, is part of what Freud decribed as the central complex of the amily, namely, the Oedipus complex. t involves a lasting unconscious associa-ion of sensual freedom with the body of he mother and the administrations eceived from her hand; a lasting associa-ion of cruel prohibition with the inter-erence of the dangerous father; and the onsequences of these associations for ove and hate in reality and in phantasy. I will not discuss here the cultural elativity of Freud's observations nor the lated origin of his term; but I assume that hose who do wish to quibble about all his will feel the obligation to advance ystematic propositions about family, :hildhood, and society which come :loser to the core, rather than go back to he periphery, of the riddle which Freud vas the first to penetrate.) We have eviewed the strong indications of an :specially heavy interference by Hans Luder with Martin's attachment to his

mother, who, it is suggested, secretly provided for him what Goethe openly acknowledged as his mother's gift— "*Die Frohnatur, die Lust zu fabulieren*": gaiety and the pleasure of confabulation. We have indicated how this gift, which later emerged in Luther's poetry, became guilt-laden and was broken to harness by an education designed to make a precocious student of the boy. We have also traced its relationship to Luther's lifelong burden of excessive guilt. Here is one of Luther's descriptions of that guilt: "And this is the worst of all these ills, that the conscience cannot run away from itself, but it is always present to itself and knows all the terrors of the creature which such things bring even in this present life, because the ungodly man is like a raging sea. The third and greatest of all these horrors and the worst of all ills is to have a judge." He also said, "For this is the nature of a guilty conscience, to fly and to be terrified, even when all is safe and prosperous, to convert all into peril and death."

The stage of initiative, associated with Freud's phallic stage of psycho-sexuality, ties man's budding will to phantasy, play, games, and early work, and thus to the mutual delineation of unlimited imagination and aspiration and limiting, threatening conscience. As far as society is concerned, this is vitally related to the occupational and technological ideals perceived by the child; for the child can manage the fact that there is no return to the mother as a mother and no competition with the father as a father only to the degree to which a future career outside of the narrower family can at least be envisaged in ideal future occupations: these he learns to imitate in play, and to anticipate in school. We can surmise that for little Martin the father's own occupation was early precluded from anticipatory phantasy, and that a life of scholarly duty was obediently and sadly envisaged instead. This precocious severity of obedience later made it impossible for young Martin to anticipate any career but that of unlimited study for its own sake, as we have seen in following his path of obedience—in disobedience.

In the fourth stage, the child becomes able and eager to learn systematically, and to collaborate with others. The resolution of this stage decides much of the ratio between a sense of industry or work completion, and a sense of tool-inferiority, and prepares a man for the essential ingredients of the ethos as well as the rationale of his technology. He wants to know the *reason* for things, and is provided, at least, with rationalizations. He learns to use whatever simplest techniques and tools will prepare him most generally for the tasks of his culture. In Martin's case, the tool was literacy, Latin literacy, and we saw how he was molded by it—and how later he remolded, with the help of printing, his nation's literary habits. With a vengeance he could claim to have taught German even to his enemies.

But he achieved this only after a protracted identity crisis which is the main subject of this book. Whoever is hard put to feel identical with one set of people and ideas must that much more violently repudiate another set; and whenever an identity, once established, meets further crises, the danger of irrational repudiation of otherness and temporarily even of one's own identity increases.

I have already briefly mentioned the three crises which follow the crisis of identity; they concern problems of intimacy, generativity, and integrity. The crisis of intimacy in a monk is naturally distorted in its heterosexual core. What identity diffusion is to identity—its alternative and danger—isolation is to intimacy. In a monk this too is subject to particular rules, since

a monk seeks intentional and organized isolation, and submits all intimacy to prayer and confession.

Luther's intimacy crisis seems to have been fully experienced and resolved only on the Wartburg; that is, after his lectures had established him as a lecturer, and his speech at Worms as an orator of universal stamp. On the Wartburg he wrote *De Votis Monasticis,* obviously determined to take care of his sexual needs as soon as a dignified solution could be found. But the intimacy crisis is by no means only a sexual, or for that matter, a heterosexual, one: Luther, once free, wrote to men friends about his emotional life, including his sexuality, with a frankness clearly denoting a need to share intimacies with them. The most famous example, perhaps, is a letter written at a time when the tragicomedy of these priests' belated marriages to runaway nuns was in full swing. Luther had made a match between Spalatin and an ex-nun, a relative of Staupitz. In the letter, he wished Spalatin luck for the wedding night, and promised to think of him during a parallel performance to be arranged in his own marital bed.

Also on the Wartburg, Luther developed, with his translation of the Bible, a supreme ability to reach into the homes of his nation; as a preacher and a table talker he demonstrated his ability and his need to be intimate for the rest of his life. One could write a book about Luther on this theme alone; and perhaps in such a book all but the most wrathful utterances would be found to be communications exquisitely tuned to the recipient.

Owing to his prolonged identity crisis, and also to delayed sexual intimacy, intimacy and generativity were fused in Luther's life. We have given an account of the time when his generativity reached its crisis, namely, when within a short period he became both a father, and a leader of a wide following which began to disperse his teachings in any number of avaricious, rebellious, and mystical directions. Luther then tasted fully the danger of this stage, which paradoxically is felt by creative people more deeply than by others, namely, a sense of *stagnation,* experienced by him in manic-depressive form. As he recovered, he proceeded with the building of the edifice of his theology; yet he responded to the needs of his parishioners and students, including his princes, to the very end. Only his occasional outbursts expressed that fury of repudiation which was mental hygiene to him, but which set a lasting bad example to his people.

We now come to the last, the integrity crisis which again leads man to the portals of nothingness, or at any rate to the station of *having been.* I have described it thus:

Only he who in some way has taken care of things and people and has adapted himself to the triumphs and disappointments adherent to being, by necessity, the originator of others and the generator of things and ideas—only he may gradually grow the fruit of these seven stages. I know no better word for it than ego integrity. Lacking a clear definition, I shall point to a few constituents of this state of mind. It is the ego's accrued assurance of its proclivity for order and meaning. It is a post-narcissistic love of the human ego—not of the self—as an experience which conveys some world order and some spiritual sense, no matter how dearly paid for. It is the acceptance of one's one and only life cycle as something that had to be and that, by necessity, permitted of no substitutions: it thus means a new, a different, love of one's parents. It is a comradeship with the ordering ways of distant times and different pursuits, as expressed in the simple products and sayings of such times and pursuits. Although aware of the relativity of all the various life styles which have given meaning to human striving, the possessor of integrity is ready to defend the dignity of his own life style against all physical and economic threats. For he knows that an individual life is the accidental coincidence of but one life cycle with but one segment of history; and that for him all human integrity stands or falls with the one style of integrity of which he partakes. The style of integrity developed by his culture or civilization thus becomes the "patrimony of his soul," the seal of his moral paternity of himself ("... *pero el honor/Es patrimonio del alma*": Calderon). Before this final solution, death loses its sting.

This integrity crisis, last in the lives of ordinary men, is a lifelong and chronic crisis in a *homo religiosus.* He is always older, or in early years suddenly becomes older, than his playmates or even his parents and teachers, and focuses in a precocious way on what it takes others a lifetime to gain a mere inkling of: the questions of how to escape corruption in living and how in death to give meaning to life. Because he experiences a breakthrough to the last problems so early in his life maybe such a man had better become a martyr and seal his message with an early death; or else become a hermit in a solitude which anticipates the Beyond. We know little of Jesus of Nazareth as a young man, but we certainly cannot even begin to imagine him as middle-aged.

This short cut between the youthful crisis of identity and the mature one of integrity makes the religionist's problem of individual identity the same as the problem of existential identity. To some extent this problem is only an exaggeration of an abortive trait not uncommon in late adolescence. One may say that the religious leader becomes a professional in dealing with the kind of scruples which prove transitory in many all-too-serious postadolescents who later grow out of it, go to pieces over it, or find an intellectual or artistic medium which can stand between them and nothingness.

The late adolescent crisis, in addition to anticipating the more mature crises, can at the same time hark back to the very earliest crisis of life—trust or mistrust toward existence as such. This concentration in the cataclysm of the adolescent identity crisis of both first and last crises in the human life may well explain why religiously and artistically creative men often seem to be suffering from a barely compensated psychosis, and yet later prove superhumanly gifted in conveying a total meaning for man's life; while malignant disturbances in late adolescence often display precocious wisdom and usurped integrity. The chosen young man extends the problem of his identity to the borders of existence in the known universe; other human beings bend all their efforts to adopt and fulfill the departmentalized identities which they find prepared in their communities. He can permit himself to face as permanent the trust problem which drives others in whom it remains or becomes dominant into denial, despair, and psychosis. He acts as if mankind were starting all over with his own beginning as an individual, conscious of his singularity as well as his humanity; others hide in the folds of whatever tradition they are part of because of membership, occupation, or special interests. To him, history ends as well as starts with him; others must look to their memories, to legends, or to books to find models for the present and the future in what their predecessors have said and done. No wonder that he is something of an old man (a *philosophus,* and a sad one) when his age-mates are young, or that he remains something of a child when they age with finality. The name Lao-tse, I understand, means just that.

The danger of a reformer of the first order, however, lies in the nature of his influence on the masses. In our own day we have seen this in the life and influence of Gandhi. He, too, believed in the power of prayer; when he fasted and prayed, the masses and even the English held their breath. Because prayer gave them the power to say what would be heard by the lowliest and the highest, both Gandhi and Luther believed that they could count on the restraining as well as the arousing power of the Word. In such hope great religionists are supported—one could say they are seduced —by the fact that all people, because of their common undercurrent of existential anxiety, at cyclic intervals and during crises feel an intense need for a rejuvenation of trust which will give new meaning to their limited and perverted exercise of will, conscience, reason, and identity. But the best of them will fall asleep at Gethsemane; and the worst will accept the new faith only as a sanction for anarchic destructiveness or political guile. If faith can move mountains, let it move obstacles out of *their* way. But maybe the masses also sense that he who aspires to spiritual power, even though he speaks of renunciation, has an account to settle with an inner authority. He may disavow their rebellion, but he is a rebel. He may say in the deepest humility, as Luther said, that "his mouth is Christ's mouth"; his nerve is still the nerve of a usurper. So for a while the world may be worse for having had a vision of being better. From the oldest Zen poem to the most recent psychological formulation, it is clear that "the conflict between right and wrong is the sickness of the mind."

The great human question is to what extent early child training must or must not exploit man's early helplessness and moral sensitivity to the degree that a deep sense of evil and of guilt become unavoidable; for such a sense in the end can only result in clandestine commitment to evil in the name of higher values. Religionists, of course, assume that because a sense of evil dominated them even as they combated it, it belongs not only to man's "nature," but is God's plan, even God's gift to him. The answer to this assumption is that not only do child training systems differ in their exploitation of basic mistrust, shame, doubt, and guilt—so do religions. The trouble comes, first, from the mortal fear that instinctual forces would run wild if they were not dominated by a negative conscience; and second, from trying to formulate man's optimum as negative morality, to be reinforced by rigid institutions. In this formulation all man's erstwhile fears of the forces and demons of nature are reprojected onto his inner forces, and onto the child, whose dormant energies are alternatively vilified as potentially criminal, or romanticized as altogether angelic. Because man needs a disciplined conscience, he thinks he must have a bad one; and he assumes that he has a good conscience when, at times, he has an easy one. The answer to all this does not lie in attempts to avoid or to deny one or the other sense of badness in children altogether; the denial of the unavoidable can only deepen a sense of secret, unmanageable evil. The answer lies in man's capacity to create order which will give his children a disciplined as well as a tolerant conscience, and a world within which to act affirmatively. . . .

Transition: Modern Efforts
at a Theoretical Synthesis

Max Weber

CHARISMA:
ITS REVOLUTIONARY CHARACTER
AND ITS TRANSFORMATION

The Nature and Impact of Charisma

THE SOCIOLOGICAL NATURE OF CHARISMATIC AUTHORITY

Bureaucracy and patriarchalism are antagonistic in many respects, but they share *continuity* as one of their most important characteristics. In this sense both are structures of everyday life. Patriarchalism, in particular, is rooted in the need to meet ongoing, routine demands, and hence has its first locus in the *economy,* to be precise, in those of its branches which are concerned with normal want satisfaction. The patriarch is the natural leader in matters of every-

From Max Weber, Economy and Society, (1922), Guenther Roth and Claus Wittich, eds. Totowa, N.J.: Bedminster Press, 1968, pp. 1111–1123, 1133–1141, 1159–1162. Copyright © 1968 Bedminster Press Incorporated. Reprinted by permission.

day life. In this respect, bureaucracy is merely the rational counterpart of patriarchalism. Bureaucracy, too, is a permanent structure and, with its system of rational rules, oriented toward the satisfaction of calculable needs with ordinary, everyday means.

All *extra*ordinary needs, i.e., those which *transcend* the sphere of everyday economic routines, have always been satisfied in an entirely heterogeneous manner: on a *charismatic* basis. The further we go back into history, the more strongly does this statement hold. It means the following: that the "natural" leaders in moments of distress—whether psychic, physical, economic, ethical, religious, or political—were neither appointed officeholders nor "professionals" in the present-day sense (i.e., persons performing against compensation a "profession" based on training and special expertise), but rather the bearers of specific gifts of body and mind that were considered "supernatural" (in the sense that not everybody could have access to them).

The term "charisma" in this context must be used in a completely value-free sense. The heroic ecstasy of the Nordic berserk, the legendary Irish folk hero Cuchulain or the Homeric Achilles was a manic seizure; the berserk, for example, bit into his shield and all about himself, like a mad dog, before rushing off in bloodthirsty frenzy; for a long time his seizure was said to have been artificially induced through drugs. In Byzantium, a number of such "blond beasts" were kept just like war elephants in ancient times. The ecstasis of the Shamans is linked to constitutional epilepsy, the possession and testing of which proves the charismatic qualification. For us, both forms of ecstasy are not edifying; neither is the kind of revelation found in the Holy Book of the Mormons; if we were to evaluate this revelation, we would perhaps be forced to call it a rank swindle. However, sociology is not concerned with such value judgments. Important is that the head of the Mormons and those "heroes" and "magicians" proved their charisma in the eyes of their adherents. They practiced their arts, and they exercised their authority, by virtue of this gift ("charisma") and, where the idea of God had already been clearly established, by virtue of the Divine mission inherent in their ability. This was true of doctors and prophets just as much as of judges, military leaders, or the leaders of great hunting expeditions.

It is to Rudolf Sohm's credit that he worked out the sociological character of this kind of domination (*Gewaltstruktur*); however, since he developed this category with regard to one historically important case—the rise of the ecclesiastic authority of the early Christian church—his treatment was bound to be one-sided from the viewpoint of historical diversity. In principle, these phenomena are universal, even though they are often most evident in the religious realm.

In radical contrast to bureaucratic organization, charisma knows no formal and regulated appointment or dismissal, no career, advancement or salary, no supervisory or appeals body, no local or purely technical jurisdiction, and no permanent institutions in the manner of bureaucratic agencies, which are independent of the incumbents and their personal charisma. Charisma is self-determined and sets its own limits. Its bearer seizes the task for which he is destined and demands that others obey and follow him by virtue of his mission. If those to whom he feels sent do not recognize him, his claim collapses; if they recognize it, he is their master as long as he "proves" himself. However, he does not derive his claims from the will of his followers, in the manner of an election; rather, it is their *duty* to recognize his charisma. Chinese theory makes the emperor's right to govern dependent upon popular consent, but this is just as little an instance of popular sovereignty as is the necessity of the prophet's "recognition" by the believers in the early Christian congregation. In the Chinese case this is simply the recognition of the charismatic character of the royal office, which requires his *personal* qualification and effectiveness. As a rule, charisma is a highly individual quality. This implies that the mission and the power of its bearer is qualitatively delimited from within, not by an external order. Normally, the mission is directed to a local, ethnic, social, political, vocational or some other group, and that means that it also finds its limits at the edges of these groups.

As in all other respects, charismatic domination is also the opposite of bureaucracy in regard to its economic substructure. Bureaucracy depends on continuous income, at least *a potiori* on a money economy and tax money, but charisma lives in, not off, this world. This must be understood properly. Frequently charisma abhors the owning and making of money—witness Saint Francis and many of his kind. But this is not the rule. In our value-free sense of the term, an ingenious pirate may be a charismatic ruler, and the charismatic political heroes are out for booty—especially money. The point is that charisma rejects as undignified all methodical rational acquisition, in fact, all rational economic conduct. This accounts also for its radical difference from the patriarchal structure, which rests upon an orderly household. In its pure form charisma is never a source of private income; it is neither utilized for the exchange of services nor is it exercized for pay, and it does not know orderly taxation to meet the material demands of its mission; rather, if it has a peaceful purpose, it receives the requisite means through sponsors or through honorific gifts, dues and other voluntary contributions of its own following. In the case of charismatic warriors, the booty is both means and end of the mission. In contrast to all patriarchal forms of domination, pure charisma is opposed to all systematic economic activities; in fact, it is *the* strongest anti-economic force, even when it is after material possessions, as in the case of the charismatic warrior. For charisma is by nature not a continuous institution, but in its pure type the very opposite. In order to live up to their mission the master as well as his disciples and immediate following must be free of the ordinary worldly attachments and duties of occupational and family life. Those who have a share ($\kappa\lambda\widetilde{\eta}\rho o\varsigma$) in charisma must inevitably turn away from the world: witness the statute of the Jesuit order forbidding members to hold ecclesiastic offices; the prohibitions for members of other orders to own property, or for the order itself, as in the original rule of Saint Francis; the celibacy of priests and knights of an order; the actual adherence to the rule of celibacy on the part of numerous holders of prophetic or artistic charisma. According to the type of charisma and the conduct corresponding to it, the economic conditions of participation may contrast with one another. It is just as consistent for modern charismatic movements of artistic origin to consider "men of independent means" —in plain words, *rentiers*—the most qualified followers of the charismatic leader, as it was for the medieval monasteries to demand the economic opposite, the friar's vow of poverty.

FOUNDATIONS AND INSTABILITY OF CHARISMATIC AUTHORITY

Charismatic authority is naturally unstable. The holder may lose his charisma, he may feel "forsaken by his God," as Jesus did on the cross [cf. Ps 22: 1, Mat. 27: 46, Mark 15: 34]; it may appear to his followers that "his powers have left him." Then his mission comes to an end, and hope expects and searches for a new bearer; his followers abandon him, for pure charisma does not recognize any legitimacy other than one which flows from personal strength proven time and again. The charismatic hero derives his authority not from an established order and enactments, as if it were an official competence, and not from custom or feudal fealty, as under patrimonialism. He gains and retains it solely by proving his powers in practice. He must work miracles, if he wants to be a prophet. He must perform heroic deeds, if he wants to be a warlord. Most of all, his divine mission must prove itself by *bringing wellbeing* to his faithful followers; if they do not fare well, he obviously is not the god-sent master. It is clear that this very serious meaning of genuine charisma is radically different from the convenient pretensions of the present "divine right of kings," which harks back to the "inscrutable" will of the Lord, "to whom alone the monarch is responsible." The very opposite is true of the genuinely charismatic ruler, who is responsible to the ruled—responsible, that is, to prove that he is indeed the master willed by God.

For this reason a ruler such as the Chinese emperor, whose power still contains—in theory—important charismatic vestiges, may publicly accuse himself of his sins and insufficiencies, if his administration fails to banish the distress of the ruled, whether it is caused by floods or unsuccessful wars; we have witnessed this in China even during the last decades. If this penitence does not propitiate the gods, the ruler faces deposition and death, often enough as an expiatory sacrifice. This is the concrete meaning of Meng-tse's (Mencius') statement that the people's voice is God's voice (according to him, the *only* way in which God speaks): If the people withdraw their recognition, the master becomes a mere private person—this is explicitly stated—, and if he claims to be more, a usurper deserving of punishment. This state of affairs is also found under primitive conditions, without the pathos of these highly revolutionary phrases. Since all primitive authorities have inherent charismatic qualities, with the exception of patriarchalism in the strictest sense, the chief is often simply deserted if success is unfaithful to him.

THE REVOLUTIONARY NATURE OF CHARISMA

The mere fact of recognizing the personal mission of a charismatic master establishes his power. Whether it is more active or passive, this recognition derives from the surrender of the faithful to the extraordinary and unheard of, to what is alien to all regulation and tradition and therefore is viewed as divine—surrender which arises from distress or enthusiasm. Because of this mode of legitimation genuine charismatic domination knows no abstract laws and regulations and no formal adjudication. Its "objective" law flows from the highly personal experience of divine grace and god-like heroic strength and rejects all external order solely for the sake of glorifying genuine prophetic and heroic ethos. Hence, in a revolutionary and sovereign manner, charismatic domination transforms all values and breaks all traditional and rational norms: "It has been written..., but *I* say unto you. ..."

The specific form of charismatic adjudication is prophetic revelation, the oracle, or the Solomonic award of a charismatic sage, an award based on concrete and individual considerations which yet demand absolute validity. This is the realm proper of "*kadi*-justice" in the proverbial, not the historical sense (of the word). For the adjudication of the (historical) Islamic *kadi* is determined by sacred tradition and its interpretation, which frequently is extremely formalistic; rules are disregarded only when those other means of adjudication fail. Genuine charismatic justice does not refer to rules; in its pure type it is the most extreme contrast to formal and traditional prescription and maintains its autonomy toward the sacredness of tradition as much as toward rationalist deductions from abstract norms. We cannot compare here the recourse to the principle *aequum et bonum* in Roman law and the original meaning of "equity" in English law to charismatic justice in general and the theocratic *kadi*-justice of the Islam in particular. Both are products partly of a law that is already strongly rationalized and partly of abstract natural law; at any rate, the principle *ex fide bona* refers to standards of fairness in business relations and thus is just as little truly irrational justice as our own principle of "judicial discretion." By contrast, all adjudication which uses ordeals as evidence derives from charismatic justice. However, because such adjudication replaces personal charismatic authority by a regular procedure which formally determines the will of God, it belongs already to the realm of that depersonalization of charisma with which we will deal soon.

As we have seen, bureaucratic rationalization, too, often has been a major revolutionary force with regard to tradition. But it revolutionizes with *technical means,* in principle, as does every economic reorganization, "from without": It *first* changes the material and social orders and *through* them the people, by changing the conditions of adaptation, and perhaps the opportunities for adaptation, through a rational determination of means and ends. By contrast, the power of charisma rests upon the belief in revelation and heroes, upon the conviction that certain manifestations—whether they be of a religious, ethical, artistic, scientific, political or other kind—are important and valuable; it rests upon "heroism" of an ascetic, military, judicial, magical or whichever kind. Charismatic belief revolutionizes men "from within" and shapes material and social conditions according to its revolutionary will. Of course, this contrast must be correctly understood. In spite of vast differences, "ideas" have essentially the same psychological roots, whether they are religious, artistic, ethical, scientific or whatever else; this also applies to ideas about political and social organization. It is a time-bound, subjective value-judgment which would like to attribute some of these ideas to "reason" and others to "intuition" (or whatever other

distinctions may be used). The mathematical imagination of a Weyerstrass, for instance, is "intuition" in exactly the same sense as is that of any artist, prophet—or demagogue. But not here lies the difference. (Parenthetically, in the value sphere, which does not concern us here, all these kinds of ideas—including artistic intuition—have in common that to objectivate themselves, to prove their reality, they must signify a grasp on the demands of the "work" or, if you prefer, a being seized by them; they are not merely a subjective feeling or experience.) The decisive difference—and that is important for understanding the meaning of "rationalism"—is not inherent in the *creator* of ideas or of "works," or in his inner experience; rather, the difference is rooted in the manner in which the ruled and led experience and internalize these ideas. As we have shown earlier, rationalization proceeds in such a fashion that the broad masses of the led merely accept or adapt themselves to the external, technical resultants which are of practical significance for their interests (as we "learn" the multiplication table and as too many jurists "learn" the techniques of law), whereas the substance of the creator's ideas remain irrelevant to them. This is meant when we say that rationalization and rational organization revolutionize "from the outside," whereas charisma, if it has any specific effects at all, manifests its revolutionary power from within, from a central *metanoia* [change] of the followers' attitudes. The bureaucratic order merely replaces the belief in the sanctity of traditional norms by compliance with rationally determined rules and by the knowledge that these rules can be superseded by others, if one has the necessary power, and hence are not sacred. But charisma, in its most potent forms, disrupts rational rule as well as tradition altogether and overturns all notions of sanctity. Instead of reverence for customs that are ancient and hence sacred, it enforces the inner subjection to the unprecedented and absolutely unique and therefore Divine. In this purely empirical and value-free sense charisma is indeed the specifically creative revolutionary force of history.

RANGE OF EFFECTIVENESS

Both charismatic and patriarchal power rest on personal devotion to, and personal authority of, "natural" leaders, in contrast to the appointed leaders of the bureaucratic order, yet this basis is very different in the two cases. Just like the official, the patriarch benefits from devotion and authority as a bearer of norms, with the difference that these norms are not purposively established as are the laws and regulations of bureaucracy, but have been inviolable from times out of mind. The bearer of charisma enjoys loyalty and authority by virtue of a mission believed to be embodied in him; this mission has not necessarily and not always been revolutionary, but in its most charismatic forms it has inverted all value hierarchies and overthrown custom, law and tradition. In contrast to the charismatic structure that arises out of the anxiety and enthusiasm of an extraordinary situation, patriarchal power serves the demands of everyday life and persists in its function, as everyday life itself, in spite of all changes of its concrete holder and its environment. Both structures are found in all areas of life. Many of the old Teutonic armies fought in a patriarchal manner, each lineage group led by its head; the armies of *coloni* of ancient Oriental monarchs and the contingents of Frankish retainers, who took the field under their *seniores,* were patrimonial. The patriarch's religious function and domestic worship persist side by side with the official community cult, on the one hand, and the great movements of charismatic prophecy, which are almost always revolutionary, on the other. Whether we look at Teutonic or American Indian tribes, the charismatic hero who marches out with a voluntary following appears next to the chieftain of peace, who is responsible for the routine economic affairs of the community, and next to the popular levy, which is mobilized in the case of tribal warfare. In an official war of the whole tribe, too, the normal peace-time authorities are often replaced by a warlord who is proclaimed *ad hoc* "the leader of the army" *(Herzog),* since he proved himself a hero in military exploits.

In contrast to the revolutionary role of charisma, the traditional everyday needs in politics and religion are met by the patriarchal structure, which is based upon habituation, respect for tradition, piety toward parents and ancestors, and the servant's personal faithfulness. The same is true in the economic field. As an orderly round of activities which procures the material means of want satisfaction, the economy is the specific locus of patriarchal rulership and, with the rise of the enterprise in the course of rationalization, also of bureaucratic domination. However, charisma is by no means alien to the economy. Under primitive conditions charismatic features are frequently found in one economic branch, the relevance of which declined with the advance of material culture: hunting, which was organized like a military operation, even at a later stage, as can be seen from the Assyrian royal inscriptions. However, the antagonism between charisma and everyday life arises also in the capitalist economy, with the difference that charisma does not confront the household but the enterprise. An instance of grandiose robber capitalism and of a spoils-oriented following is provided by Henry Villard's exploits. [In 1889] he organized the famous "blind pool" in order to stage a stock exchange raid on the shares of the Northern Pacific Railroad; he asked the public for a loan of fifty million pounds without revealing his goal, and received it without security by virtue of his reputation. The structure and spirit of this robber capitalism differs radically from the rational management of an ordinary capitalist large-scale enterprise and is most similar to some age-old phenomena: the huge rapacious enterprises in the financial and colonial sphere, and "occasional trade" with its mixture of piracy and slave hunting. The double nature of what may be called the "capitalist spirit," and the specific character of modern routinized capitalism with its professional bureaucracy can be understood only if these two structural elements, which are ultimately different but everywhere intertwined, are conceptually distinguished.

THE SOCIAL STRUCTURE OF CHARISMATIC DOMINATION

It is true that the "purer" charismatic authority in our sense is, the less can it be understood as an organization in the usual sense: as an order of persons and things that function according to the means-ends scheme. However, charismatic authority does not imply an amorphous condition; it indicates rather a definite social structure with a staff and an apparatus of services and material means that is adapted to the mission of the leader. The personal staff constitutes a charismatic aristocracy composed of a select group of adherents who are united by discipleship and loyalty and chosen according to personal charismatic qualification. For the charismatic subject adequate material contributions are considered a dictate of conscience, although they are formally voluntary, unregulated and irregular; they are offered according to need and economic capacity. The more typical the charismatic structure, the less do

followers or disciples obtain their material sustenance and social position in the form of benefices, salaries or other kinds of orderly compensation, titles or ranks. Instead, insofar as the individual's maintenance is not already assured, the followers share in the use of those goods which the authoritarian leader receives as donation, booty or endowment and which he distributes among them without accounting or contractual fixation. Thus the followers may have a claim to be fed at the common table, to be clothed and to receive honorific gifts from the leader, and to share in the social, political or religious esteem and honor in which he himself is held. Any deviation from this pattern affects the "purity" of the charismatic structure and modifies it in the direction of other structures.

THE COMMUNIST WANT SATISFACTION OF THE CHARISMATIC COMMUNITY

Next to the household, charisma is thus the second important historical representative of *communism,* defined here as the absence of formal accountability in the *consumption* sphere, not as the rational organization of *production* for a common account (as under socialism). Every historical instance of communism in this sense has either a traditional, that means, patriarchal basis or the extraordinary foundation of charismatic belief; in the former case it is household communism, and only in this form has it been an everyday phenomenon; in the latter case it was, if fully developed, either the spoils communism of the camp or the monastery's communism of love with its variations and its degeneration into *caritas* and alms-giving. In various degrees of purity the spoils communism of the camp is found in all charismatic warriors' organizations, from the pirate state of the Ligurian islands to the Islamic state of the caliph Omar and the military orders of Christianity and of

Japanese Buddhism. In one form or another, the communism of love was paramount in all religions. It persists among the professional followers of the Divine: the monks. We also find it in numerous Pietist organizations—for example, among Labadie's followers—and in other high-strung religious groups of an exclusive character. The preservation of authentic heroism and saintliness appears to the adherents dependent upon the retention of a communist basis and the absence of the striving for individual property. And correctly so since charisma is basically an extraordinary and hence necessarily non-economic power, and its vitality is immediately endangered when everyday economic interests become predominant, as it threatens to happen everywhere. The first step in this direction is the prebend—an allowance replacing the old communist maintenance out of common provisions—, which has here its real origin. With all available means the charismatic leaders attempt to limit this disintegration. All warrior states retained remnants of charismatic communism—Sparta is a typical example—and tried to protect the heroic individual against the "temptation" posed by responsibility for property, rational acquisition and a family, just like the religious orders did. The adjustment between these charismatic remnants and the individual's economic interests, which arise with prebendalization and persist ever after, may take the most diverse forms. Invariably, however, the reign of genuine charisma comes to an end when it can no longer withhold the unqualified permission to found families and to engage in economic pursuits. Only the common danger of military life or the love ethos of an unworldly discipleship can preserve communism, which in turn is the only guarantor of the purity of charisma vis-à-vis everyday interests.

Every charisma is on the road from a turbulently emotional life that knows no economic rationality to a slow death by suffocation under the weight of material interests: every hour of its existence brings it nearer to this end.

The Genesis and Transformation of Charismatic Authority

THE ROUTINIZATION OF CHARISMA

Charismatic rulership in the typical sense described above always results from unusual, especially political or economic situations, or from extraordinary psychic, particularly religious states, or from both together. It arises from collective excitement produced by extraordinary events and from surrender to heroism of any kind. This alone is sufficient to warrant the conclusion that the faith of the leader himself and of his disciples in his charisma—be it of a prophetic or any other kind—is undiminished, consistent and effective only *in statu nascendi,* just as is true of the faithful devotion to him and his mission on the part of those to whom he considers himself sent. When the tide that lifted a charismatically led group out of everyday life flows back into the channels of workaday routines, at least the "pure" form of charismatic domination will wane and turn into an "institution"; it is then either mechanized, as it were, or imperceptibly displaced by other structures, or fused with them in the most diverse forms, so that it becomes a mere component of a concrete historical structure. In this case it is often transformed beyond recognition, and identifiable only on an analytical level.

Thus the pure type of charismatic rulership is in a very specific sense unstable, and all its modifications have basically one and the same cause: the desire to transform charisma and charismatic blessings from a unique, transitory gift of grace of extraordinary times and persons into a permanent possession of everyday life. This is desired usually by the master, always by his disciples, and most of all by his charismatic subjects. Inevitably, however, this changes the nature of the charismatic structure. The charismatic following of a war leader may be transformed into a state, the charismatic community of a prophet, artist, philosopher, ethical or scientific innovator may become a church, sect, academy or school, and the charismatic group which espouses certain cultural ideals may develop into a party or merely the staff of newspapers and periodicals. In every case charisma is henceforth exposed to the conditions of everyday life and to the powers dominating it, especially to the economic interests. . . . As soon as charismatic domination loses its personal foundation and the acutely emotional faith which distinguishes it from the traditional mold of everyday life, its alliance with tradition is the most obvious and often the only alternative, especially in periods in which the rationalization of organizational techniques (*Lebenstechnik*) is still incipient. In such an alliance the essence of charisma appears to be definitely abandoned, and this is indeed true insofar as its eminently revolutionary character is concerned. It is the basic feature of this ever recurring development that charisma is captured by the interest of all economic and social power holders in the *legitimation* of their possessions by a charismatic, and thus sacred, source of authority. Instead of upsetting everything that is traditional or based on legal acquisition (in the modern sense), as it does *in statu nascendi,* charisma becomes a legitimation for "acquired rights." In this function, which is alien to its essence, charisma becomes a part of everyday life; for the needs which it satisfies in this way are universal, especially for one general reason [the legitimation of leadership and succession]. . . .

CHARISMA AND THE PERSISTENT FORMS OF DOMINATION

As these examples show, charismatic domination is by no means limited to primitive stages of development, and the three basic types of domination cannot be placed into a simple evolutionary line: they in fact appear together in the most diverse combinations. It is the fate of charisma, however, to recede with the development of permanent institutional stuctures. . . .

When the manipulation of deities and demons becomes an object of a permanent cult, the charismatic prophet and magician turns into a priest. When wars become chronic and technological development necessitates the systematic training and recruitment of all able-bodied men, the charismatic war leader becomes a king. . . .

THE DEPERSONALIZATION OF CHARISMA: LINEAGE CHARISMA, "CLAN STATE" AND PRIMOGENITURE

Whatever we have said until now about the possible consequences of the routinization of charisma has not affected its strictly personal quality. However, we will now turn to phenomena whose common feature is a peculiar depersonalization of charisma. From a unique gift of grace charisma may be transformed into a quality that is either (a) transferable or (b) personally acquirable or (c) attached to the incumbent of an office or to an institutional structure regardless of the persons involved. We are justified in still speaking of charisma in this impersonal sense only because there always remains an extraordinary quality which is not accessible to everyone and which typically overshadows the charismatic subjects. It is for this very reason that charisma can fulfil its social function. However, since in this manner charisma becomes a component of everyday life and changes into a permanent structure, its essence and mode of operation are significantly transformed.

The most frequent case of a depersonalization of charisma is the belief in its transferability through blood ties. Thus the desires of the disciples or followers and of the charismatic subjects for the perpetuation of charisma are fulfilled in a most simple fashion. However, the notion of a truly individual inheritance was as alien here as it was originally to the household. Instead of individual inheritance we find the immortal household as property-holder vis-à-vis the succeeding generations. . . .

In historical times, however, the principle of house and lineage charisma has generally been adhered to far less consistently. As a rule, the most primitive and the highest stages of culture only know the charismatic privilege of the ruling dynasty and possibly of a very limited number of other powerful families. Under primitive conditions the charisma of the magician, rainmaker, medicine-man and priest, as long as it is not fused with political authority, is much less frequently tied to the charisma of a house; only the development of a regular cult gives rise to those charismatic blood ties between certain priestly positions and aristocratic lineage groups that occur often and in turn affect the hereditability of other types of charisma. As physiological blood ties gain increasing importance, deification sets in, at first of the ancestors and eventually also of the incumbent ruler, if the process is not interrupted; we shall return to some of its consequences. . . .

This has had probably even more far-reaching consequences than the fate of Alexander's family. In contrast to this role of heredity, almost all capable Roman emperors of the first three centuries ascended the throne by virtue of designation through adoption, not by virtue of blood relationship; and most of those who became emperors in the latter way weakened the office. The reasons for these divergent consequences are apparently connected with the difference between the political structure of a feudal state and that of an increasingly bureaucratized state that is dependent upon a standing army and its officers. We will not pursue this difference at this point.

OFFICE CHARISMA

Once the belief is established that charisma is bound to blood relationship, its meaning is altogether reversed. If originally a man was ennobled by virtue of his own actions, now only the deeds of his forefathers could legitimate him. Hence one became a member of the Roman nobility not by holding a nobilitating office, but because one's own ancestors had done so, and the office aristocracy delimited in this way endeavored to monopolize the offices. This reversal of genuine charisma into its exact opposite occurred everywhere according to the same pattern. The genuinely American (Puritan) mentality glorified the self-made man as the bearer of charisma and counted the heir for nothing, but this attitude is being reversed before our own eyes; now only descent—from the Pilgrim Fathers, Pocahontas and the Knickerbockers—or membership in the accepted families of "old" wealth is valued. The closing of the rolls of nobility, the tests of ancestry, the admission of the newly rich only as *gentes minores,* and similar phenomena are all equally an expression of the attempt to increase status by making it scarce. Economic motives are not only behind the monopolization of remunerative offices or of other connections with the state, but also behind the monopolization of the *connubium;* noble rank provides an advantage in the quest for the hands of rich heiresses and also increases the demand for one's own daughters.

In addition to the depersonalization of charisma in the form of inheritance, there are other historically important forms. First of all, charisma may be transferred through artificial, magical means instead of through blood relationship: The apostolic succession secured through episcopal ordination, the indelible charismatic qualification acquired through the priest's ordination, the king's coronation and anointment, and innumerable similar practices among primitive and civilized peoples all derive from this mode of transmission. Most of the time the symbol has become something merely formal, and in practice is less important than the conception often related to it—the linkage of charisma with the holding of an *office*, which itself is acquired by the laying on of hands, anointment, etc. Here we find that peculiar transformation of charisma into an institution: as permanent structures and traditions replace the belief in the revelation and heroism of charismatic personalities, charisma becomes part of an established social structure.

In the early Christian church the Bishop of Rome occupied an essentially charismatic position (originally together with the Roman *ecclesia*): The church of Rome acquired very early a specific authority and asserted it time and again against the intellectual superiority of the Hellenistic Orient, which produced almost all great church fathers, established the dogmas and held all ecumenical councils; this predominance lasted as long as the unity of the church was maintained on the basis of the firm belief that God would not permit the church of the world capital to err despite its much smaller intellectual endowment. This authority was nothing but charismatic; it was by no means a primacy in the modern sense of a definitive doctrinal authority (*Lehramt*), nor did it resemble universal jurisdic-

tional powers in the sense of an appellate function or even an episcopal jurisdiction in competition with the local powers. Such notions had not yet been developed. Moreover, just like any other charisma, this one too was at first considered a precarious gift of grace; at least one Bishop of Rome was anathematized by a Council. But on the whole this charisma was believed to be a Divine promise to the church. Even Innocent III at the height of his power did not invoke more than the rather general and vague belief in this promise; only the bureaucratized and intellectualized church of modern history turned it into a charisma of office and differentiated, as does every bureaucracy, between the office (*ex cathedra*) and the incumbent.

The charisma of office—the belief in the specific state of grace of a social institution—is by no means limited to the churches and even less to primitive conditions. Under modern conditions, too, it finds politically relevant expression in the attitudes of the subjects to the state. For these attitudes may vary considerably according to whether they are friendly or hostile to the charisma of office. The specific lack of respect of Puritanism for mundane affairs, its rejection of all idolization, eradicated all charismatic respect towards the powers-that-be in the areas of Puritan predominance. The conduct of an office appeared as a business like all others, the ruler and his officials as sinners like everyone else—strongly emphasized by Kuyper—and as no wiser than anyone else. Through God's inscrutable will they chanced upon their position and thus gained the power to fabricate laws, statutes, judgments and ordinances. Whoever shows the marks of damnation must of course be removed from a church office, but this principle is inapplicable and also dispensable with regard to state offices. As long as the secular powerholders do not directly violate conscience and God's honor, they are tolerated, for any change would merely replace them with others just as sinful and probably just as foolish. But they do not have any inwardly binding authority since they are merely parts of an order made by and for man. The office is functionally necessary, but it does not transcend its incumbent and cannot reflect upon him any dignity, such as is possessed, for example, by the lowest royal court (*königliches Amtsgericht*) according to normal German sentiment. . . .

Political and Hierocratic Domination

HIEROCRACY, THEOCRACY AND CAESAROPAPISM

At any rate, the relations between secular and ecclesiastic power differ greatly depending on whether we deal with 1) a ruler who is legitimated by priests, either as an incarnation or in the name of God, 2) a high priest who is also king—these are the two cases of hierocracy—or, finally, 3) a secular, caesaropapist ruler who exercises supreme authority in ecclesiastic matters by virtue of his autonomous legitimacy. Wherever hierocracy in this sense occurred—theocracy proper is limited to the second case—, it had far-reaching effects on the administrative structure. Hierocracy must forestall the rise of secular powers capable of emancipating themselves. Wherever a co-ordinate or subordinate royal position exists, hierocracy seeks to prevent the king from securing independent resources; it impedes the accumulation of the *thesauros* which was indispensable to all kings of early history, and the strengthening of his bodyguard in order to vitiate the establishment of an independent royal army—witness the early case of Josiah in Judah. Furthermore, hierocracy checks as much as possible the rise of an autonomous and

secular military nobility, since this would threaten its predominance, and therefore it frequently favors the (relatively) peaceful "bourgeoisie." The elective affinity between bourgeois and religious powers, which is typical of a certain stage in their development, may grow into a formal alliance against the feudal powers; this happened rather frequently in the Orient and also in Italy at the time of the struggle over lay investiture [11th century]. This opposition to political charisma has everywhere recommended hierocracy to conquerors as a means of domesticating a subject population. . . .

Everywhere state and society have been greatly influenced by the struggle between military and temple nobility, between royal and priestly following. This struggle did not always lead to an open conflict, but it produced distinctive features and differences, whether we refer to the relationship between the priestly and the warrior caste in India, the partly manifest and partly latent conflict between military nobility and priesthood in the oldest city-states of Mesopotamia, in Egypt and Palestine, or to the complete takeover of priestly positions by the secular nobility in the Hellenic polis and particularly in Rome. The clash of the two powers in medieval Europe and in the Islam resulted in the greatest differences between the cultural development of the Orient and the Occident.

The extreme opposite of any kind of hierocracy, caesaropapism—the complete subordination of priestly to secular power—, can nowhere be found in its pure type. Caesaropapist powers are wielded not only by the Chinese, Russian, Turkish and Persian ruler but also by the English and German ruler, who is the head of the church (*summus episcopus*), yet these powers are everywhere limited by autonomous ecclesiastic charisma. The Byzantine *basileus,* like the pharaoh, Indian and Chinese monarchs, and also the Protestant *summi episcopi,* attempted repeatedly, and mostly without success, to impose religious beliefs and norms of their own making. Such attempts were always extremely dangerous for them. In general, the subjugation of religious to royal authority was most successful when religious qualification still functioned as a magical charisma of its bearers and had not yet been rationalized into a bureaucratic apparatus with its own doctrinal system—two usually related phenomena; subjugation was feasible especially when ethics or salvation were not yet dominant in religious thought or had been abandoned again. But wherever they prevail, hierocracy is often invincible, and secular authority must compromise with it. By contrast, magic-ritual forces were controlled most thoroughly in the ancient polis, rather well by the feudal powers in Japan and the patrimonial ones in China, and at least reasonably well by the bureaucratic state in Byzantium and Russia. But wherever religious charisma developed a doctrinal system and an organizational apparatus, the caesaropapist state, too, contained a strong hierocratic admixture.

As a rule, priestly charisma compromised with the secular power, most of the time tacitly but sometimes also through a concordat. Thus the spheres of control were mutually guaranteed, and each power was permitted to exert certain influences in the other's realm in order to minimize collisions of interest; the secular authorities, for example, participated in the appointment of certain clerical officials, and the priests influenced the educational institutions of the state. These compromises also committed the two powers to mutual assistance. Examples of this kind are found in the ecclesiastic and secular organizations of the predominantly caesaropapist Carolingian empire, in the Holy Roman empire, which had

similar features under the Ottonian and early Salic rulers, and in the many Protestant countries that were largely caesaropapist. Under a different power distribution, such compromises also occurred in the areas of the Counter-Reformation, the Concordats and the Bulls of Circumscription. The secular ruler makes available to the priests the external means of enforcement for the maintenance of their power or at least for the collection of church taxes and other contributions. In return, the priests offer their religious sanctions in support of the ruler's legitimacy and for the domestication of the subjects. Powerful ecclesiastic reform movements, such as the Gregorian, attempted at times to negate completely the autonomous charisma of the political power, but they were not permanently successful. Similar to the [way in which the] doctrine of equal social rank [was adjusted by the nobility], the Catholic church today acknowledges the autonomy of political charisma by the very fact that it makes acceptance and submission a religious duty in the face of every government that indisputably holds *de facto* power, as long as such a regime does not despoil the church.

Some theocratic or caesaropapist elements tend to be present in every legitimate political power, since ultimately every charisma is akin to religious powers in that it claims at least some remnant of supernatural derivation; in one way or another, legitimate political power therefore always claims the "grace of God."

It should be clearly understood that the dominance of any of these systems does not depend upon the influence that religion in general exerts upon the life of a people. . . .

Only the manner in which social domination is organized varies greatly, and this has consequences for the course of religious development. . . .

Ernst Troeltsch

RELIGION, ECONOMICS, AND SOCIETY

"Religion and economics" is a theme that would have sounded very strange at an earlier date. "Philosophy and economics," "music and economics," "mathematics and economics" would have hardly been more surprising. Such a theme was altogether meaningless so long as religion was understood purely ideologically as dogma or doctrine or metaphysics or as a kind of moralism connected with certain conceptions about the cosmos. The scholars of the Enlightenment would have probably referred to the financial system of the Papacy, to the material interests of priests and pious rulers, with an understanding smile. They would, no doubt, have understood the theme merely as a matter of the very commonplace motives for things that were regarded as so sublime at the time. Thus Hume considered the Reformation to be the consequence of a dispute over the revenues derived from indulgences.

About the middle of the nineteenth century when, for the first time, the consequences of the capitalistic system collided openly with the ethical demands of Christianity, a much deeper understanding of the problem was born. But the problem appeared as a purely practical ethical one: how to overcome the devastating results of the Manchester

type of economic liberalism through Christian love and character-training. Kingsley, Maurice, and Carlyle raised the banner of Christian social reform and the Christian socialism of Stöcker and Friedrich Naumann followed them in Germany.

That is not the meaning of the question, however, as it is posed today. Nowadays the problem of the relation between religion and economics has a purely theoretical significance in connection with the history of religion and culture. Certainly the formulation of the problem is derived from the economic theory of the history of culture—generally designated quite wrongly as historical materialism—which spread from Karl Marx's great work to all formulations of historical problems. Of course, the problem had already been introduced by various historians, such as Karl Nitzsch, and had been largely answered by reference to political and legal history. Hence it has no necessary relationship with the socialist system as such. Actually the problem was partly generated by the process of refining and extending the investigation of historical causality, and partly impressed upon us by our contemporary experience of the overwhelming influence of economics on the whole of life. In political history the problem has become self-evident to us today, although its significance extends much further. It is only that in the history of politics and law the con-

From "Religion, Wirtschaft und Gesellschaft" (1913), Aufsätze zur Geistesgeschichte und Religionssoziologie, Tübingen: 1925, pp. 21-33. Translated by David Little; revised by Walter Bense. Copyright © 1968 by Beacon Press. By permission of the publisher.

nection with economic foundations becomes especially clear. The connection persists, however, even in the sphere of spiritual culture where it affects the religious and metaphysical world-views that constitute the spiritual center. The connection is largely unconscious and unintended, but connections of this sort are undoubtedly the strongest and most lasting in the life of the mind. It was not in vain that Karl Marx learned from Hegel, who was able to discern with artistic sensitivity and amazing precision the interweaving and intermingling of all the spiritual contents of a culture and to reconstruct their underlying motive forces. There is no question that, for understanding religion as a very practical, basic force in life, the focusing of attention on such connections can shed an extraordinary amount of light. It is perhaps no exaggeration to say that it is only in this way that a true understanding of religion and of its importance for life is made possible. We are thus made aware of a side of religion which of course had always been operative even before its theoretical elucidation but which had not entered the scientific consciousness; nor has it entered it, for the most part, even today.

Heretofore religion has been conceived, especially among Protestants, purely in terms of ideology and dogma. Catholics at least exhibited a deeper understanding for the cultic and institutional side of religion. Cultic and irrational factors in religion have been emphasized more and more strongly by ethnographic investigations; and, correspondingly, the purely dogmatic-ideological aspects have been progressively discounted. But the close relation of religion to social life and, since this relationship is largely conditioned by economic elements, the close relation of religion to economic life have been given far too little attention. The one exception is the brilliant work of Fustel de Coulanges, *La cité antique* (1864), although it has not found the following it deserves. Consequently, it is only the socialist history of culture and the influences that have radiated from it which have brought the problem widespread—though not yet universal—recognition.

The way in which the problem has been treated in socialist literature, as in Kautsky's work on the origins of Christianity, is largely to be blamed for the limited recognition of the problem. Despite several valuable insights, the dreary dogmatism of the familiar socialist reconstruction of history prevails. According to this view, purely economic conditions are the cause of class stratification, and each class is reflected in a metaphysic and a religion that protects its existence and interests. Christianity is then the utopian, otherworldly reflection of the unorganized, wretched, and helpless proletariat of late antiquity. This purely religious and therefore powerless organization of the proletariat, which was out of step with the social evolution of the time, was soon subjugated by the ruling classes. Through certain changes in its dogma and ethic, it was made to serve the interests of property and power. The original proletarian character of the Christian movement has been able to break through only occasionally. Now this reconstruction of the origin of Christianity rests wholly upon imagination. But even in the more refined and informed exposition of these events by Maurenbrecher, the derivation of the Christian religion from proletarian mass psychology is treated as a self-evident principle of historical causation. Accordingly, the gospel is interpreted in a completely unhistorical proletarian sense. Here too the theory of a one-sided dependence of religion on economically determined class conditions appears as a dogmatic presupposition: religion in its essence is a reflection of class conditions. Socialist literature does not attempt to explain or to prove this principle in the light of the general material of the history of religions. At bottom, it is simply a polemical weapon against Christianity. But the actual significance of this principle and the various changes it undergoes in the various stages of religious life can be shown only through an investigation covering the entire history of religion.[1]

The problem is very much more complicated. It should not be immediately tied to so comprehensive a question as the origin of religion. For this question cannot be resolved by purely historical and psychological means; it leads to all sorts of reconstructions that are far removed from the concrete and living reality of the problem that concerns us. Our problem must be related to life as it is actually lived in the religions familiar to us. Quite enough material will be found here for the treatment of this problem. The question of sources and origins, which is purely a matter for the philosophy of religion, can accordingly remain undiscussed. Our problem is rather: To what extent does life as it is actually lived in various religions show an inner and essential influence upon the religious element at the hands of economic life and the classes and stratification of society, which are to a large extent conditioned by economic factors? And again: To what extent do we find essential and inner influences of the religious element upon economic activity? The merely accidental and transitory contacts between religion and social life will have to be disregarded, or rather taken into consideration only insofar as inner and enduring relationships emerge from these contacts.

The concurrence of two lines of development which are entirely separate and independent of each other but touch at a certain point is not unusual in history. We would rather expect it in our sphere of investigation since both the forces now in contact, religion and economics, are originally almost completely strangers to each other. But once this is recognized, those accidental contacts which the pragmatism of the Enlightenment liked to stress must be excluded from our investigation. Although they represent an aspect of our problem which in practice is not unimportant, they are nevertheless merely transitory and remain, so to speak, external.

With this statement of the problem, it is presupposed that in those historical religions that have to be considered, the religious element that expresses itself in myth and cult, in the world of conceptions and of feeling, is something relatively independent, and only enters into relations with all sorts of economic interests but never coincides with them. This is true of all developed religions. The ethnographic and anthropological investigation of religion is not sufficiently oriented to this aspect of the question and therefore can provide no answers for it. For this reason these investigations must remain outside our consideration. We can afford to neglect them because we have before us matters which are not to be understood on the basis of the prehistoric primitive development of the spirit, but rather in terms of the com-

[1]So penetrating and sensitive a sociologist as Simmel has attempted in this general way to establish an understanding of the history of religion. He designates as the psychological root of religion the feeling of devotion that the individual members of a sociological collectivity feel toward its mysteriously present, all-pervasive "power." Simmel even derives the belief in miracles from the overwhelming incomprehensibility of such a "power." Religion properly so called is said to emerge only from the objectification of the religious-supernatural element embodied in this kind of group "power." Now, Simmel's notion is also no more than an ingenious fantasy that appropriates from Marxism an exalted estimation of the function of sociological collectivities without the exclusively Marxist emphasis upon economic foundations.

plexities of a culture already partially differentiated. In such a culture, there is always to be detected a tendency towards independence on the part of specifically religious life and thought and towards similar independence on the part of economic activity, which must be understood from the point of view of its practical purpose. The problem of the relationship between religion and economics can grow only out of a partly conscious, partly unconscious mutual influencing and interpenetration of both tendencies. But if these tendencies are essentially different from one another, then their contact cannot be direct. Religions are not economic ideals, nor are the forms and interests of economic life religious laws. The contacts are only mediate. The question then arises as to the nature of this mediating element. The answer is very simple. It consists of the great sociological forms of existence, which, on the one hand, are constantly being created by religion and once grounded therein, deeply affect all economic activity, or which, on the other hand, arise from economic causes, among others, and in turn draw the world of religious conceptions into their own purview.

Fustel has already formulated the questions with extraordinary clarity and pertinence. He points out that with the Indians, Greeks, and Romans the organizing force of religious worship of ancestors and of the dead supplies the foundations of the patriarchal family, of family and private law, of established private property in land, of the closed household or family economy, and of the legal position of women, children, and slaves. Once united with religion and sanctified by it, these forms of regulation exert an enormous force over practical life. According to their principles curiae and phratries are formed, and finally the city with completely analogous cultic forms; and in law and morals, in war and peace,

the entire life of the polis remains bound to a ritual system that has the greatest importance for all political and legal life and, consequently, for all economic activity as well. Here the strong, decisive initiative of religious thought and the sociological organization created by it is completely clear. Of course, one may readily ask whether this development of ancestor worship does not rather depend upon the process of transition to a sedentary and agricultural economy. In that case the initiative would still lie on the side of economic life, as supplying the conditions for the determinative line of development of ancestor worship. A comparison with the development of cultus among nomadic and half-nomadic peoples, such as the Tartars and the Mongols, would yield information on this point. With regard to the Israelites, the American sociologist Wallis has, in fact, shown how both the religious veneration of the wider kinship group's clan-god and the nomadic community that was supported by the clan-god permanently impressed upon the people of Israel the character of a conservative-primitive economic morality and a religion of kinship solidarity that stood opposed to the culture-religion of the city. The morality of brotherhood, primitive and semi-socialist in tendency and opposed to the culture of city and world empire, was then sublimated and interiorized by the prophets into the humanitarian religious morality that we encounter in the noblest laws and prophecies of the Old Testament.

These examples could easily be multiplied. The Indian caste system, which was related to religious presuppositions, determined the economic character of India. The Chinese family cult had the greatest significance for the social structure of the empire and for the type and direction of economic activity. It is clear that these relationships, which penetrate the entirety of the spirit and meaning of life deeply on both the religious and economic sides, are extraordinarily close and yet quite complicated and by no means immediate. As Fustel has pertinently stressed, it is a reciprocal relation that can be established only in each particular case and in which it is very difficult to determine the priority of one element or the other, since the events themselves are unconscious.

The same scholar shows no less clearly and graphically how the social order that is conditioned by the original sociological forces of the cult breaks down slowly under the impact of the rationalism of political and economic interests. This rationalism follows its own impulses as soon as there is a sufficient number of people whose needs are no longer satisfied by the older cultic social system. Using the Greeks and Romans as an example, Fustel describes the revolutions that were directed against the religious ordering and regulation of society, the rationalism of needs let loose in these revolutions, and the attempts at rational reconstructions of society. These attempts, in turn, produced repercussions in ethics and social philosophy, where they sought to create a new ethical ideal for themselves. One may add that such revolutions were relatively successful only in Greece and Rome, while everywhere else society and economy are still sociologically bound to the cultus, except in those areas where the universal religions predominate, which will be discussed in a moment. In this connection one ought to read the travel book of the American, Harry Franck, *Vagabond Journey Around the World*,[2] in which he sees society at its lowest levels. From his book one receives both the most vivid impression of the impact of these things on practical economic life, and at the same time astonishing examples of the religious apotheosis of the given social order.

[2] New York: Century Company, 1910.

The religious-political troubles of modern Japan are relevant here. Japan has accepted the European brand of economic rationalism, but is unable to integrate it with the cultic-sociological foundations of Japanese life. Hence, the religious experiments which at one time artificially seek to create a new religion of the state and the emperor; at another time they move in the direction of Christianity; and then again settle for an indifferent European atheism.

But it is not possible here to pursue this theme in all its vast breadth. It is rather necessary to concentrate on one specific point. Up to now we have touched upon only the ethnic religion of ancestor and state-worship; but the point to be considered is suggested by the fact that such religion by no means prevails exclusively. At certain points universal and spiritual religions have broken through which consist essentially of a conception of God, an ethos, an inner conviction, and a religious world-view, and which accordingly reproduce themselves in radically new sociological forms. Here the universal community of thought and conviction of a propagated religion replaces the cultic community of specific natural (or kinship) groups. Here the relationship between religion and economics is completely different. The role of universal religion is taken in the East by Buddhism and related movements and in the West by Judaism and its two great off-shoots, Christianity and Islam. Certainly these new religious formations did not come into being without a previous social and thus economic history which helped to condition them.

Suffice it to say that a new formulation of our problem emerges here. The religious idea here is itself ethical and metaphysical and comprises a point of view vis-à-vis social and economic life directly through its religious valuation of life, rather than indirectly through its sociological consequences. Of course, the point of view differs among the different religions we have mentioned. Buddhism regards as indifferent the old caste system, which was sanctioned by the cult, but it allows the system to continue and in general creates no independent religious community of its own. Hence its idea, which consists in absolute poverty, becomes fully operative only among those who are Buddhism's peculiar bearers, the monks. As for the rest of the people, Buddhism allows the social orders to exist as they are. It only hinders the emergence of every form of rationalized economic life that might possibly destroy it.

Among the western religions, Judaism, as is well known, has attained an enormous economic significance. This is true partly because of its belief in creation, which actively affirms the world, and because of its religious treatment of the virtues of industry, diligence, and temperance. But to a greater extent, the importance of economic life was born of Judaism's lot in the history of the world.[3] In Judaism, religion remains above all bound to an ethnic loyalty and its economic ethic and attitude have been influenced by the futuristic and this-worldly destiny of the chosen people. Here there is certainly no clean break between the religious and the social and economic spheres. Nor is there such a clean break in the case of Islam, which is inwardly bound, by the Koran and its system of law, to a primitive stage of social and economic organization. This fact explains the strength and success of its mission with less civilized races, but also its weakness and its hostility toward European economic practices, which are quite incompatible with the primitive nature of Islamic law and the decisions of the qadi courts.

[3]The latter has been underrated in Sombart's famous and rather illuminating book, just as the former has been exaggerated.

The actual separation of the religious inwardness and the religious community from all things social and economic has occurred only in Christianity. Even so, this separation does not mean a complete ascetic negation of the world, but rather, as in Judaism, an affirmation of the goodness of creation and the significance of the world as an arena of activity. Now this separation by no means provides a particularly clear solution to our problem. Rather, it contains the most difficult and most complicated articulation of the problem. We must consider especially the following points.

In the first place: when religion is so completely interiorized and spiritualized, it is indeed freed from involvement with social and economic life. Such freedom means, however, that it is all the more difficult to bring the determinative influence of the religious idea to bear directly on the world of secular life. The religious idea here remains at so high a level of ideality that it is helpless before the concrete relationships of life with their powerful configurations of interest. Specifically, this approach to religion implies that economic activity is left to develop, without any interference, its own rationalism of interests and utility in terms of a purely secular principle. Now the rationalism of economic and social life assumes, in the last analysis, the form of the economic struggle for survival; that is, of competition. Hence this type of religious ethic everywhere confronts the struggle for survival without being able to restrain it, since in this struggle only purely rational considerations are admitted. The world of religious ideas disposes of no direct means of its own by which it might organize or restrict economic life. Rather, religion has to rely on the rational means by which secular utilitarianism itself undertakes to regulate economic life. Religious sanctification of men's character and brotherly love cannot directly solve these problems of themselves. This fact was rightly recognized in the once widely discussed book by Benjamin Kidd (of England) entitled *Social Evolution,* for which the zoologist Weismann wrote a foreword. Kidd contrasts the rationalism of the struggle for survival as a purely rational principle with the religious principle of authority and order based on the higher principles of love. If Kidd is correct, then the solution of the problem is bound to consist in some means for pacifying or mitigating the struggle for survival, a means that religion can never produce out of its own resources. In order to grasp and fix rational or accidental forms of regulation over the struggle for survival, religion must rely on forces within that struggle that are favorable to and compatible with religion. It will always be a question of compromise with, and adjustment to, the actualities of life.

Secondly, the dominant religious idea in and of itself appears to be purely religious and ideological in nature. For here the starting point is no immediate cultic integration of the natural life, no coincidence of certain natural forms with cultic forms of community, but the ethical ideal. Yet the autonomy of this ideal is still very much qualified. The actual relationship is much more complicated than appears at first sight. In fact, the basic ideals are not at all so independent of the real and concrete foundation upon and with reference to which they arise. Jesus' own ideals were connected with the kind of economy, the climate, and the other conditions characteristic of Galilee. These same ideals could not have been produced in a large modern city. All the economic ideals of subsequent Christian ages have likewise been unconsciously and unintentionally colored by the soil from which they sprang. They always contain elements that pertain to the period and the situation, but since this relativity is

not consciously perceived, they are apotheosized into eternal truths, divine demands, or expositions of the Bible. Just as the Biblical world of ideas everywhere reveals the social and economic ground upon which it rests, so all later interpretations of the Bible are for their part conditioned by the commonplaces of their respective time and place. Catholics, Lutherans, Calvinists, sectarians, and mystics all read the Bible in the light of certain definite sociological presuppositions that they regard as self-evident and desire to see confirmed and controlled by the Bible. At the same time, of course, those actions that appear to be simply philosophical and rationalistic, or purely customary and conventional, are unconsciously conditioned by Christian presuppositions. A great deal of Christian spirit is contained in ostensibly wholly secular systems. The relationship must, of course, be established and elucidated from case to case. There are no general laws and formulas of progressive development here, to cater to the modern predilection for generalizations. There is an interplay of forces the results of which must be ascertained for every idea that dominates the economic and social life of great historical periods.

Thirdly, because of its pure inwardness and its high degree of religious autonomy, the Christian idea possesses no means whatsoever for direct action in the social sphere. Even the very idealistic ethical demands of Christianity are not in themselves such a means. Despite the fact that a direct and purely ideological influence is constantly being asserted, the main impact of the Christian idea does not obtain directly through the ethical demand itself, but rather indirectly through the forms of religious community created by this idea. These forms of community are based on dogmatic, cultic and purely religious ideas; they are never developed with a view to secular social goals. This is why they possess an organizing and binding power that is shared by no purely rationalistic social structure. With these potent sociological forms, then, they comprehend the whole of life and shape its spiritual and ethical commonplaces, in a manner analogous to the ancient ancestor and city cults noted by Fustel. Certainly there is contained in Catholicism and Protestantism something of the social soil from which they drew their vitality. Yet the purely religious and sociological organization of authority, institution, and individualism has determined the general cultural atmosphere to an even greater extent and only through that general atmosphere has it influenced the secular life socially and economically. Despite the apparent autonomy of the ideology of Christian ethics, the Marxist problem still remains, but in such a way that it signifies not only the dependence of religious on social factors, but also the dependence of social on religious factors. This mutual dependence cannot be made clear in individual cases by a general theory but only by a particular investigation of each case in question. Yet it becomes clear now that economic rationalism, when awakened to its potentially unlimited autonomy, rejects religious and sociological ties and strives to develop wholly independently of them.

Thus there are several reasons that ultimately require us to limit our investigation to the one religion with which we are intimately acquainted, our own: firstly, the immensity of the problem in the full breadth of its actual existence in the history of religion; secondly, the confinement, up to now, of scholarly recognition and observation of the problem to a few points; and thirdly, the necessity of examining the problem concretely in every case considered. It is not that our own religion is the only one that is practically relevant for our culture. It is rather that Christianity is intrinsically especially significant in this connection.

Christianity has grown up on the boundary line between the East and West out of the religiously motivated humanitarianism and hope of redemption that belonged to the prophets of Israel. Christianity attained the purest kind of religious inwardness and human relatedness because it was not bound to any natural or social conditions. At the same time it developed a radical hope of redemption which momentarily expected the realization of a situation corresponding to its ideals, i.e., the miraculous foundation of the kingdom of God. This ethos and hope of redemption were combined with the religious veneration of the one who proclaimed the kingdom of God. From this combination arose a new, purely religious and cultic human community, which finally was forced by the continued delay of the kingdom's coming to apply their ideal as the church's rule of life to the practical and continuing life of society and economics. The problem of the relationship between religion and economics arose at once, and has not yet been resolved.

Emile Durkheim

THE FALSE DICHOTOMY
OF REAL
AND IDEAL

Some reply that men have a natural faculty for idealizing, that is to say, of substituting for the real world another different one, to which they transport themselves by thought. But that is merely changing the terms of the problem; it is not resolving it or even advancing it. This systematic idealization is an essential characteristic of religions. Explaining them by an innate power of idealization is simply replacing one word by another which is the equivalent of the first; it is as if they said that men have made religions because they have a religious nature. Animals know only one world, the one which they perceive by experience, internal as well as external. Men alone have the faculty of conceiving the ideal, of adding something to the real. Now where does this singular privilege come from? Before making it an initial fact or a mysterious virtue which escapes science, we must be sure that it does not depend upon empirically determinable conditions.

The explanation of religion which we have proposed has precisely this advantage, that it gives an answer to this question. For our definition of the sacred is that it is something added to and above

From The Elementary Forms of the Religious Life (1912). New York: 1961, pp. 469–472, 474–479. By permission of George Allen & Unwin Ltd. and The Macmillan Company. Copyright 1915 by George Allen & Unwin Ltd.

the real: now the ideal answers to this same definition; we cannot explain one without explaining the other. In fact, we have seen that if collective life awakens religious thought on reaching a certain degree of intensity, it is because it brings about a state of effervescence which changes the conditions of psychic activity. Vital energies are over-excited, passions more active, sensations stronger; there are even some which are produced only at this moment. A man does not recognize himself; he feels himself transformed and consequently he transforms the environment which surrounds him. In order to account for the very particular impressions which he receives, he attributes to the things with which he is in most direct contact properties which they have not, exceptional powers and virtues which the objects of every-day experience do not possess. In a word, above the real world where his profane life passes he has placed another which, in one sense, does not exist except in thought, but to which he attributes a higher sort of dignity than to the first. Thus, from a double point of view it is an ideal world.

The formation of the ideal world is therefore not an irreducible fact which escapes science; it depends upon conditions which observation can touch; it is a natural product of social life. For a society to become conscious of itself and maintain at the necessary degree of intensity the sentiments which it thus attains, it must assemble and concentrate itself. Now this concentration brings about an exaltation of the mental life which takes form in a group of ideal conceptions where is portrayed the new life thus awakened; they correspond to this new set of psychical forces which is added to those which we have at our disposition for the daily tasks of existence. A society can neither create itself nor recreate itself without at the same time creating an ideal. This creation is not a sort of work of supererogation for it, by which it would complete itself, being already formed; it is the act by which it is periodically made and remade. Therefore when some oppose the ideal society to the real society, like two antagonists which would lead us in opposite directions, they materialize and oppose abstractions. The ideal society is not outside of the real society; it is a part of it. Far from being divided between them as between two poles which mutually repel each other, we cannot hold to one without holding to the other. For a society is not made up merely of the mass of individuals who compose it, the ground which they occupy, the things which they use and the movements which they perform, but above all is the idea which it forms of itself. It is undoubtedly true that it hesitates over the manner in which it ought to conceive itself; it feels itself drawn in divergent directions. But these conflicts which break forth are not between the ideal and reality, but between two different ideals, that of yesterday and that of to-day, that which has the authority of tradition and that which has the hope of the future. There is surely a place for investigating whence these ideals evolve; but whatever solution may be given to this problem, it still remains that all passes in the world of the ideal.

Thus the collective ideal which religion expresses is far from being due to a vague innate power of the individual, but it is rather at the school of collective life that the individual has learned to idealize. It is in assimilating the ideals elaborated by society that he has become capable of conceiving the ideal. It is society which, by leading him within its sphere of action, has made him acquire the need of raising himself above the world of experience and has at the same time furnished him with the means of conceiving another. For society has constructed this new world in constructing itself, since it is society which this expresses. Thus both with the individual and in the group, the faculty of idealizing has nothing mysterious about it. It is not a sort of luxury which a man could get along without, but a condition of his very existence. He could not be a social being, that is to say, he could not be a man, if he had not acquired it. It is true that in incarnating themselves in individuals, collective ideals tend to individualize themselves. Each understands them after his own fashion and marks them with his own stamp; he suppresses certain elements and adds others. Thus the personal ideal disengages itself from the social ideal in proportion as the individual personality develops itself and becomes an autonomous source of action. But if we wish to understand this aptitude, so singular in appearance, of living outside of reality, it is enough to connect it with the social conditions upon which it depends.

Therefore it is necessary to avoid seeing in this theory of religion a simple restatement of historical materialism: that would be misunderstanding our thought to an extreme degree. In showing that religion is something essentially social, we do not mean to say that it confines itself to translating into another language the material forms of society and its immediate vital necessities. It is true that we take it as evident that social life depends upon its material foundation and bears its mark, just as the mental life of an individual depends upon his nervous system and in fact his whole organism. But collective consciousness is something more than a mere epiphenomenon of its morphological basis, just as individual consciousness is something more than a simple efflorescence of the nervous system. In order that the former may appear, a synthesis *sui generis* of particular consciousnesses is required. Now this synthesis has the effect of disengaging a whole world of sentiments, ideas and images which, once born, obey laws all their own. They attract each other, repel each other, unite, divide themselves, and multiply, though these combinations are not commanded and necessitated by the condition of the underlying reality. The life thus brought into being even enjoys so great an independence that it sometimes indulges in manifestations with no purpose or utility of any sort, for the mere pleasure of affirming itself. We have shown that this is often precisely the case with ritual activity and mythological thought. . . .

Thus there is something eternal in religion which is destined to survive all the particular symbols in which religious thought has successively enveloped itself. There can be no society which does not feel the need of upholding and reaffirming at regular intervals the collective sentiments and the collective ideas which make its unity and its personality. Now this moral remaking cannot be achieved except by the means of reunions, assemblies and meetings where the individuals, being closely united to one another, reaffirm in common their common sentiments; hence come ceremonies which do not differ from regular religious ceremonies, either in their object, the results which they produce, or the processes employed to attain these results. What essential difference is there between an assembly of Christians celebrating the principal dates of the life of Christ, or of Jews remembering the exodus from Egypt or the promulgation of the decalogue, and a reunion of citizens commemorating the promulgation of a new moral or legal system or some great event in the national life?

If we find a little difficulty to-day in imagining what these feasts and ceremonies of the future could consist in, it is because we are going through a stage of transition and moral mediocrity. The great things of the past which filled our fathers with enthusiasm do not excite the same ardour in us, either because they have come into common usage to such an extent that we are unconscious of them, or else because they no longer answer to our actual aspirations; but as yet there is nothing to replace them. We can no longer impassionate ourselves for the principles in the name of which Christianity recommended to masters that they treat their slaves humanely, and, on the other hand, the idea which it has formed of human equality and fraternity seems to us to-day to leave too large a place for unjust inequalities. Its pity for the outcast seems to us too Platonic; we desire another which would be more practicable; but as yet we cannot clearly see what it should be nor how it could be realized in facts. In a word, the old gods are growing old or already dead, and others are not yet born. This is what rendered vain the attempt of Comte with the old historic souvenirs artificially revived: it is life itself, and not a dead past which can produce a living cult. But this state of incertitude and confused agitation cannot last for ever. A day will come when our societies will know again those hours of creative effervescence, in the course of which new ideas arise and new formulæ are found which serve for a while as a guide to humanity; and when these hours shall have been passed through once, men will spontaneously feel the need of reliving them from time to time in thought, that is to say, of keeping alive their memory by means of celebrations which regularly reproduce their fruits. We have already seen how the French Revolution established a whole cycle of holidays to keep the principles with which it was inspired in a state of perpetual youth. If this institution quickly fell away, it was because the revolutionary faith lasted but a moment, and deceptions and discouragements rapidly succeeded the first moments of enthusiasm. But though the work may have miscarried, it enables us to imagine what might have happened in other conditions; and everything leads us to believe that it will be taken up again sooner or later. There are no gospels which are immortal, but neither is there any reason for believing that humanity is incapable of inventing new ones. As to the question of what symbols this new faith will express itself with, whether they will resemble those of the past or not, and whether or not they will be more adequate for the reality which they seek to translate, that is something which surpasses the human faculty of foresight and which does not appertain to the principal question.

But feasts and rites, in a word, the cult, are not the whole religion. This is not merely a system of practices, but also a system of ideas whose object is to explain the world; we have seen that even the humblest have their cosmology. Whatever connection there may be between these two elements of the religious life, they are still quite different. The one is turned towards action, which it demands and regulates; the other is turned towards thought, which it enriches and organizes. Then they do not depend upon the same conditions, and consequently it may be asked if the second answers to necessities as universal and as permanent as the first.

When specific characteristics are attributed to religious thought, and when it is believed that its function is to express, by means peculiar to itself, an aspect of reality which evades ordinary knowledge as well as science, one naturally refuses to admit that religion can ever abandon its speculative rôle. But our analysis of the facts does not seem to have shown this specific quality of religion. The religion which we have just studied is one of those whose symbols are the most disconcerting for the reason. There all appears mysterious. These beings which belong to the most heterogeneous groups at the same time, who multiply without ceasing to be one, who divide without diminishing, all seem, at first view, to belong to an entirely different world from the one where we live; some have even gone so far as to say that the mind which constructed them ignored the laws of logic completely. Perhaps the contrast between reason and faith has never been more thorough. Then if there has ever been a moment in history when their heterogeneousness should have stood out clearly, it is here. But contrary to all appearances, as we have pointed out, the realities to which religious speculation is then applied are the same as those which later serve as the subject of reflection for philosophers: they are nature, man, society. The mystery which appears to surround them is wholly superficial and disappears before a more painstaking observation: it is enough merely to set aside the veil with which mythological imagination has covered them for them to appear such as they really are. Religion sets itself to translate these realities into an intelligible language which does not differ in nature from that employed by science; the attempt is made by both to connect things with each other, to establish internal relations between them, to classify them and to systematize them. We have even seen that the essential ideas of scientific logic are of religious origin. It is true that in order to utilize them, science gives them a new elaboration; it purges them of all accidental elements; in a general way, it brings a spirit of criticism into all its doings, which religion ignores; it surrounds itself with precautions to "escape precipitation and bias," and to hold aside the passions, prejudices and all subjective influences. But these perfectionings of of method are not enough to differentiate it from religion. In this regard, both pursue the same end; scientific thought is only a more perfect form of religious thought. Thus it seems natural that the second should progressively retire before the first, as this becomes better fitted to perform the task.

And there is no doubt that this regression has taken place in the course of history. Having left religion, science tends to substitute itself for this latter in all that which concerns the cognitive and intellectual functions. Christianity has already definitely consecrated this substitution in the order of material things. Seeing in matter that which is profane before all else, it readily left the knowledge of this to another discipline, *tradidit mundum hominum disputationi,* "He gave the world over to the disputes of men"; it is thus that the natural sciences have been able to establish themselves and make their authority recognized without very great difficulty. But it could not give up the world of souls so easily; for it is before all over souls that the god of the Christians aspires to reign. That is why the idea of submitting the psychic life to science produced the effect of a sort of profanation for a long time; even to-day it is repugnant to many minds. However, experimental and comparative psychology is founded and to-day we must reckon with it. But the world of the religious and moral life is still forbidden. The great majority of men continue to believe that here there is an order of things which the mind cannot penetrate except by very special ways. Hence comes the active resistance which is met with every time that someone tries to treat religious and moral phenomena scientifically. But in spite of these oppositions, these attempts are constantly repeated and this persistence even allows us to foresee that this final barrier will finally give way and that science will establish herself as mistress even in this reserved region.

That is what the conflict between science and religion really amounts to. It is said that science denies religion in principle. But religion exists; it is a system of given facts; in a word, it is a reality. How could science deny this reality? Also, in so far as religion is action, and in so far as it is a means of making men live, science could not take its place, for even if this expresses life, it does not create it; it may well seek to explain the faith, but by that very act it presupposes it. Thus there is no conflict except upon one limited point. Of the two functions which religion originally fulfilled, there is one, and only one, which tends to escape it more and more: that is its speculative function. That which science refuses to grant to religion is not its right to exist, but its right to dogmatize upon the nature of things and the special competence which it claims for itself for knowing man and the world. As a matter of fact, it does not know itself. It does not even know what it is made of, nor to what need it answers. It is itself a subject for science, so far is it from being able to make the law for science! And from another point of view, since there is no proper subject for religious speculation outside that reality to which scientific reflection is applied, it is evident that this former cannot play the same rôle in the future that it has played in the past.

However, it seems destined to transform itself rather than to disappear.

We have said that there is something

eternal in religion: it is the cult and the faith. Men cannot celebrate ceremonies for which they see no reason, nor can they accept a faith which they in no way understand. To spread itself or merely to maintain itself, it must be justified, that is to say, a theory must be made of it. A theory of this sort must undoubtedly be founded upon the different sciences, from the moment when these exist; first of all, upon the social sciences, for religious faith has its origin in society; then upon psychology, for society is a synthesis of human consciousnesses; and finally upon the sciences of nature, for man and society are a part of the universe and can be abstracted from it only artificially. But howsoever important these facts taken from the constituted sciences may be, they are not enough; for faith is before all else an impetus to action, while science, no matter how far it may be pushed, always remains at a distance from this. Science is fragmentary and incomplete; it advances but slowly and is never finished; but life cannot wait. The theories which are destined to make men live and act are therefore obliged to pass science and complete it prematurely. They are possible only when the practical exigencies and the vital necessities which we feel without distinctly conceiving them push thought in advance, beyond that which

science permits us to affirm. Thus religions, even the most rational and laicized, cannot and never will be able to dispense with a particular form of speculation which, though having the same subject as science itself, cannot be really scientific: the obscure intuitions of sensation and sentiment too often take the place of logical reasons. On one side, this speculation resembles that which we meet with in the religions of the past; but on another, it is different. While claiming and exercising the right of going beyond science, it must commence by knowing this and by inspiring itself with it. Ever since the authority of science was established, it must be reckoned with; one can go farther than it under the pressure of necessity, but he must take his direction from it. He can affirm nothing that it denies, deny nothing that it affirms, and establish nothing that is not directly or indirectly founded upon principles taken from it. From now on, the faith no longer exercises the same hegemony as formerly over the system of ideas that we may continue to call religion. A rival power rises up before it which, being born of it, ever after submits it to its criticism and control. And everything makes us foresee that this control will constantly become more extended and efficient, while no limit can be assigned to its future influence.

III

RELIGION
IN
TRANSFORMATION

Historical Studies

SECTION ONE

Revolutionary Transformation in Religion

Friedrich Engels

ON THE HISTORY
OF
EARLY CHRISTIANITY

The history of early Christianity has notable points of resemblance with the modern working-class movement. Like the latter, Christianity was originally a movement of oppressed people; it first appeared as the religion of slaves and emancipated slaves, of poor people deprived of all rights, of peoples subjugated or dispersed by Rome. Both Christianity and the workers' socialism preach forthcoming salvation from bondage and misery; Christianity places his salvation in a life beyond, after death, in heaven; socialism places it in this world, in a transformation of society. Both are persecuted and baited, their adherents are despised and made the objects of exclusive laws, the former as enemies of the human race, the latter as enemies of the state, enemies of religion, the family, social order. And in spite of all persecution, nay, even spurred on by it, they forge victoriously, irresistibly ahead. Three hundred years after its appearance Christianity was the recognised state religion in the Roman World Empire, and in barely sixty years socialism has won itself a position which makes its victory absolutely certain. . . .

The messages are but the introduction to the theme properly so-called of John's communication to the seven churches of Asia Minor and through them to the remaining reformed Judaism of the year 69, out of which Christianity later developed. And herewith we enter the innermost holy of holies of early Christianity.

From "On the History of Early Christianity" (1894–95) in K. Marx and F. Engels, On Religion. Moscow: 1957, pp. 313, 330–333. By permission of Lawrence and Wishart Ltd., London.

What kind of people were the first Christians recruited from? Mainly from the "labouring and burdened," the members of the lowest strata of the people, as becomes a revolutionary element. And what did they consist of? In the towns of impoverished free men, all sorts of people, like the "mean whites" of the southern slave states and the European beachcombers and adventurers in colonial and Chinese seaports, then of emancipated slaves and, above all, actual slaves; on the large estates in Italy, Sicily, and Africa of slaves, and in the rural districts of the provinces of small peasants who had fallen more and more into bondage through debt. There was absolutely no common road to emancipation for all these elements. For all of them paradise lay lost behind them; for the ruined free men it was the former *polis*, the town and the state at the same time, of which their forefathers had been free citizens; for the war-captive slaves the time of freedom before their subjugation and captivity; for the small peasants the abolished gentile social system and communal landownership. All that had been smitten down by the levelling iron first of conquering Rome. The largest social group that antiquity had attained was the tribe and the union of kindred tribes; among the barbarians grouping was based on alliances of families and among the town-founding Greeks and Italians on the *polis*, which consisted of one or more kindred tribes. Philip and Alexander gave the Hellenic peninsula political unity but that did not lead to the formation of a Greek nation. Nations became possible only through the downfall of Roman world domination. This domination had put an end once for all to the smaller unions; military might, Roman jurisdiction and the tax-collecting machinery completely dissolved the traditional inner organization. To the loss of independence and distinctive organization was added the forcible plunder by military and civil authorities who took the treasures of the subjugated away from them and then lent them back at usurious rates in order to extort still more out of them. The pressure of taxation and the need for money which it caused in regions dominated only or mainly by natural economy plunged the peasants into ever deeper bondage to the usurers, gave rise to great differences in fortune, making the rich richer and the poor completely destitute. Any resistance of isolated small tribes or towns to the gigantic Roman world power was hopeless. Where was the way out, salvation, for the enslaved, oppressed and impoverished, a way out common to all these groups of people whose interests were mutually alien or even opposed? And yet it had to be found if a great revolutionary movement was to embrace them all.

This way out was found. But not in this world. In the state in which things were it could only be a religious way out. Then a new world was disclosed. The continued life of the soul after the death of the body had gradually become a recognized article of faith throughout the Roman world. A kind of recompense or punishment of the deceased souls for their actions while on earth also received more and more general recognition. As far as recompense was concerned, admittedly, the prospects were not so good: antiquity was too spontaneously materialistic not to attribute infinitely greater value to life on earth than to life in the kingdom of shadows; to live on after death was considered by the Greeks rather as a misfortune. Then came Christianity, which took recompense and punishment in the world beyond seriously and created heaven and hell, and a way out was found which would lead the labouring and burdened from this vale of woe to eternal paradise. And in fact only with the prospect of a reward in the world beyond could the stoico-philonic renunciation of the world and ascetics be exalted to the basic moral principle of a new universal religion which would inspire the oppressed masses with enthusiasm.

But this heavenly paradise does not open to the faithful by the mere fact of their death. We shall see that the kingdom of God, the capital of which is the New Jerusalem, can only be conquered and opened after arduous struggles with the powers of hell. But in the imagination of the early Christians these struggles were immediately ahead. John describes his book at the very beginning as the revelation of "things which must *shortly* come to pass"; and immediately afterwards, I, 3, he declares "Blessed is he that readeth and that they hear the words of this prophecy . . . for *the time is at hand.*"

Henri Desroche

SOCIALISM AND THE SOCIOLOGY OF CHRISTIANITY

The first of the controversial questions which J. Wach ascribed to the tasks of the Sociology of 20th Century Religion is that of the possible antagonism between the polemic and the apologetic status which might have affected this science. "Just as Sociology came to represent for some an offensive weapon, others, on the defensive, wanted a 'religious,' 'Christian' or 'Protestant Sociology.' This was all the more delicately discussed as the study approached the subject of the great living religions." As long as people are occupied with subjects remaining outside their immediate interests and concerns, the difficulties do not seem so great. There is no reason why a Catholic, a Protestant and, for example, an intellectual with Marxist leanings should not be of one mind when studying the ceremonies of the American Indians, of Babylonian Mythology and of Buddhist Ethics. But the difficulties become much bigger when the subject comprises the causes of the Reformation or the structure of a sect. Despite these difficulties and by resorting to a provisionary methodological solution, J. Wach, basically a theologian, sought and advocated incessantly, a sociology of religion which would be a unified and unifying science, open to divergent ideologies. It would, therefore, be no more theological than anti-theological. We continue to think that while there is a Catholic philosophy of society and a Marxist philosophy of society, there can only be one religious sociology, which we can study from different points of view and develop in a variety of ways, but which would utilise only one set of criteria.

"Socialisme et sociologie du Christianisme," Cahiers Internationaux de Sociologie, XXI (1956), 149-67 [footnotes omitted]. Translated for this anthology by Judith Okely and Ann Duncan. By permission of Presses Universitaires de France and the translators.

The work of Wach is important enough for this modified optimism to be considered seriously, inclusively in the aspect it is proposed to examine here—that of ONE sociology of Christianity to which, in spite of, or rather because of, their ideologically divergent, if not contradictory premises, a religious sociology of irreligion just as much as an irreligious sociology of religion would contribute. Marxist sociology will be regarded as the prototype of the latter.

This eventuality has conflicted, on both sides at least, with innumerable monolithic or normative claims, which the pressing needs for a social or religious policy are still developing. On its own generally accepted level, this eventuality seems to be favored, however, by a whole series of methodological vicissitudes. Was it not, for example, the staggering blow delivered by Engels, with his thesis or hypothesis of the capitalist origin of Protestantism which provoked Max Weber's investigation into the possible origin or possible "Protestant" "spirit" of capitalism? And did not Engels' work also inspire, indirectly, W. Sombart's investigations into the incidence of Judaism, then Tawney's work? This galaxy of research remains one of the most *stimulating* factors in the subsequent development of every sociology of religion by focusing attention on non-religious factors in religion.

1. Socialism and Religious Genealogy

Are socialism in general and Marxism in particular open to classification in religious genealogy? The question is again rather confused by apologetic or polemic evaluations. Of the first type are those which claim for socialism a dignity and prestige equal to that normally reserved for a religion. Of the second type, apparently more and more frequently in occurrence, are those which either from a particular ecclesiastical standpoint denounce socialism's derivation from an ersatzreligion, or those which, from a generalised anti-ecclesiastical standpoint, deplore the monolithic conformism borrowed, so they claim, from the disciplines of authoritarian religions.

It is possible that the socialism of a convert might have appeared, or could appear to be the transfer of religious fervour into a social conviction. Although there has been an exchange of content, it is possible that some characteristics will remain—*either* the modes of depersonalisation: enthusiasm in conformity, the effervescence of a certain eschatology, exclusivism, certainties by proxy, intransigence, even something like an historical Manicheism. *Or*, on the other hand, modes of personalisation might survive: appetite for coherence, universalism, longing for the ideal of abnegation, devotion to a conviction, development of the scale of participation, etc. To be honest, the resources of social psychology are rather lacking in these respects. For, if the "transitions" from socialism to Christianity have promoted several voluntarily spectacular autobiographies or testimonials (the literary genre: "From Karl Marx to Jesus Christ"), the inverse process can hardly do more than establish itself statistically on the scale of countries like Italy or France (comparison between baptismal statistics and electoral statistics), just as long as the interior motivations of this process have never been the object of a serious study. This process can be interpreted in various ways, either a transfer or a break, or indeed some sort of process with a dual adherence.

For want of something better, the question of the possible place and rank of socialism in religious genealogy must then restrict itself to a more modest debate, however prejudicial, a debate which limits itself to Marxism as it appears in the official texts. Can this Marxism claim to be "religious?"

If one examines the classical sources, he reply to this question is undoubtedly negative. And the well informed commentators have often stressed this difference between the science of human society in Marx and Engels on the one hand and Feuerbach's or A. Comte's religion of humanity on the other. This difference is radical. Marxist-atheism remains resistant to all deification including that of Man. And to take an image of Engels, Marxist-humanism, wherein man is, however, the "supreme reason" for man, is no more a religion than chemistry is an alchemy. During the years 1840–1850, the Parisian reformists who shared the ideas of Louis Blanc, expressed themselves in this very same manner. They could only think of a man without religion as a monster and they said to him: "So atheism is your religion." When Feuerbach wanted to establish true religion on the basis of an essentially materialistic conception of nature, that meant in reality considering modern chemistry as being the true alchemy. If religion can exist without God, alchemy can very well exist without its philosopher's stone. Engels confirmed and retrospectively annotated as below the impressions of his 1844 encounters with the "communists" of the French school. He had recounted these impressions straight away in a memorandum in English, to the October number of the *New Moral World*. "On my return route via Paris," wrote Engels, "I visited a communist club of the mystical school. By the term 'god' they mean precisely what the people of Ham Common understand by 'love spirit.' Nevertheless they considered it a secondary question. On all the practical propositions they were in agreement with us, adding, . . . 'so atheism is your religion.' Religion, in French, signifies conviction, feeling, not worship."

Around the same period (of youth) and in similar articles sent to R. Owens journal, the "New Moral World" Engels often returned to that ambiguity of expression which tended to make communism pass for neo-religion. He knew the Icarians and made the following judicious remark about them: "While the English Socialists are generally opposed to Christianity and have to suffer all the prejudices of a really Christian people, the French Communists, although they belong to a nation notorious for its scepticism, are themselves Christian. One of their favourite axioms is: 'Christianity is Communism.' They try to prove this through the Bible, showing the communal way of life which the first Christians are said to have led, etc." He found the same trait in Weitling and his followers. "Weitling and his group are, in this respect, exactly like the Icarians in France and they claim that Christianity is Communism."

The beginnings of Marxism were, therefore, explicitly favoured by the religious or neo-religious atmosphere of the "new Christianities" in which Communism and Socialism seemed to be a substitute or rival religion. If Communism had to be a "religion," it was most likely at this time that it would have the greatest chance—or the greatest risk. The facts at this conjuncture are clear. In this phase, between the years 1844 and 1848, Marxism clarified itself, doubtless appearing as a break with the anti-social, therefore, anti-socialist Christianities, but just as much as a *rejection* of any religious mythicization of the new-born socialism. "All this," thought Engels, concerning the Icarians, "shows only that these good people are not the best Christians, although they pretend to be such: for if they were, they would know the Bible better and would discover that while several passages from the Bible are possibly favourable to Communism, nevertheless, the general spirit of its doctrines is utterly opposed to it, as furthermore, to every rational measure." The differentiation was to reach its final culmination with the circular against Kriege in 1845. It was also an indirect denunciation of Weitling, by its criticism of those who confuse *Communism* with *communion.* Other analogous prophecies were likewise discarded. From the beginning, Marxist Communism rejected not only every collusion but also every religious category. The Soviet refusal to recognise the recent claim by certain Russian Baptists to a Christian Communism, logically follows on this initial position. The continuity of this refusal, marked by many vicissitudes, invalidates every *criteriological* interpretation of Communism as a post-Christian or extra-Christian religion.

Yet this does not mean that Communism would not have any historical relations to Christianity. Indeed there is probably, first, a *typological* reference which Engels commented on in his study of primitive Christianity; moreover, it would be valid for many mass movements *in statu nascendi.* There is also, probably, a *genetic* relation but not that of "truths gone mad," any more than that invoked by ecclesiastical self-criticism of the type which believes it can reveal the causes of atheistic socialism in the a-social attitudes of the churchmen and of the nominally Christian ruling classes, and their responsibility for the fact that the churches seem to have lost the working class. The explanation has several times been recognised as too facile and on all accounts insufficient in itself to account for the facts. Rather, this genetic relation, if there must be a reference, must be sought in the secular and recorded evolution of the differentiations of Christianity. The Marxist classics have tried, more or less, if only by their *obiter dicta,* to set out these differentiations, beginning with "their" sociology of Christianity. Although these beginnings are fragmentary, it turns out that they make particular note of the religious repercussions of the great social revolutions in Europe over the centuries: those of the Chiliasts at the time of the medieval peasant risings, those of the Calixtans or the Taborites in the Bohemian uprising of the 15th century, those of Muenzer and his followers in the German peasants' revolt, those of the Levellers in the English Revolution, those of French deists during the intellectual crisis of the 18th century. Their overall analysis tends to indicate an *Aufhebung* of religion; that is, both a fulfillment and a suppression, a continuity and a discontinuity, continuity with a whole tradition which, with a marginal Christianity, had outlined the urgency and the conditions of a Kingdom of God on earth. A tradition which by its progress, its changes, its experiences, they considered to have developed a revolutionary set of possibilities. Discontinuity also with all the religious prehistory held by Engels to be largely bound up with the agrarian developments, of which the last to date— that of the German Muenzerians—is found to be linked at the same time to the first act in a bourgeois revolution. Engels' opinion of Muenzer is, moreover, significant of the dialectic of the continuous in the discontinuous. Besides, that opinion perhaps represents all the theory and progress of the "third age," from Joachim de Flore to the last part of Hegel's philosophy of religion—admittedly not ratified as axioms or precedents justifying new standards, but taken for granted as lessons from past experience in the assessment of present experience.

Moreover, the retrospective approach needs to be made precise. It is indeed completely different from the one (often borrowed by revivals) which think it can find the premises of a future religion in past disagreements. For, on the one hand, one does not find in Engels any nostalgia for early Christianity: on the contrary, he deems "every heresy which only sees a degeneracy in the development of the Church and its dogmas, reactionary in form." On the other hand, contrary to Carlyle, he holds that Christianity is the supreme religion, the highest and ultimate: *"if he* [Carlyle] *knew the nature of Christianity he would be aware that after this no other religion is possible. Not even pantheism."*

In view of this definition, one may wonder if these premises do not provide a plausible frame for investigation in which one could fix the exact genetic reference of Marxism to Christianity. This reference would, as a whole, be one of "Dissent," in a chain of cumulative effects (differentiation of the *religious* contents taking an a-clerical, a-dogmatic and a-theological form) but which would finally change their outward sign by going to the extreme (differentiation of the a-theist form with a nonreligious content.)

It would be a question from the start, of that tradition made apparent by E. Troeltsch in his exhumation of the "Sektentypus," or at least of the series in that tradition whose theological-sociological link occurs fairly regularly. By *theological* is meant: experience or ecclesiastical nostalgia for a universal ministry of the faithful, movement towards laicization (Bible reading in the vernacular, frequent communion, communion of both kinds, popular liturgy and the administration of certain sacraments). By *sociological* is meant types of claims directed towards the Church's wealth, before being directed towards feudal wealth. As for the change in the outward sign, one wonders if Marx himself did not furnish an outline in the famous and enigmatic text of his youth, where he seems to have grafted the development of the proletarian revolution onto the preceding revolution of the German Reformation. The forced dialectic of this early style gives a special edge to almost every word and for this reason makes any accurate translation difficult.

The two conflicting developments are clearer in their context and look like this:

The German Reformation
1. Transformation of the layman into priest;
2. Political emancipation of the ruling classes;
3. Expropriation of the Church's wealth (by secularisation).

The Proletarian Revolution
1. Transformation-into-man of this layman-turned-priest;
2. Political emancipation of the masses;
3. Expropriation of the whole of capitalist property.

This is only one indication, one of those very *obiter dicta* where one can glean the elements of an historical sociology of Christianity which would seem to have been that of the Marxist classics. Yet it begins an historical-ethical dialectic of "emancipation" where it is not impossible to see an eventually *economic* imperative of Communism ("expropriation of the expropriators") link up by a series of intermediary stages, which are typological at least, with an *initially religious* aspiration of a certain humanism. Among the oldest of enquiries into feudal property are to be found in fact those dating from the controversies aroused by the "literary" Franciscans and dissidents (Fraticelli). These centered around the *right to religious poverty* which became progressively the *duty of religious poverty* for the Church as a whole (i.e., in the views of Wycliffe and the Lollards); then the *absence* of *religious right to feudal property as a whole* (this appears already in a phase of Wycliffism, then more especially in the peasants' character, elaborated by Muenzer in his thesis based on the biblical texts which showed the priority for the Community's rights over those of the clerical or lay master); then, posterior to the Reformation policy of confiscating ecclesiastical property, the *absence of social rights,* first for *ecclesiastical property holders* (the question of clerical possessions during the French Revolution) then for feudal property holders (the night of August 4th); next the *social duty* with regard to individual capitalist property in detail (this is generally the theme of "utopian" French socialisms); and finally the *economic necessity for the expropriation of capitalist property as a whole. . . .*

Can one add to the religious effects of this socio-economic dialectic, the equally religious repercussions of the anthropological and cultural dialectic since the system of representation advocated throughout the differentiations of Christianity plays genetically with regard to *atheism* a similar and corresponding role to that played with regard to communism by the *property* systems advocated during the same differentations. Some of Marx's writings and more perhaps of Engels' would seem to suggest this. We will return later to the implication this supposition makes of a certain discontinuity in a probable continuity.

2. Theology and Secularisation

Several fundamental texts on "double gravitation" evoke a radical discontinuity between the mental and theological universe of Christianity and the mental and secularised universe of socialism. This discontinuity is, in fact, certain and makes the two universes foreign to each other, typologically at least. Does this typological discontinuity, therefore, exclude genetic continuities and methodological similarities? This question can at least be broached, if not resolved, by considering both the political and cultural aspects of the secularisation specifically implied by Marxist Socialism. In its first meaning, Marxist atheism implies essentially the establishment of an atheist state, in the sense that it should be a-Christian, that is to say, laicised or

lay. Or again, the completion in the realm of politics, of the process of secularisation already extensively undertaken in the other realms of human knowledge or action. "Only the grossest ignorance could maintain that the theory which consists in making the concept of the state autonomous is a new invention of contemporary philosophers. In politics, philosophy has only done what physics, mathematics, medicine and, indeed, many other sciences have accomplished in their own spheres. Bacon declared that theological physics was a virgin consecrated to God—and as a result, sterile; he freed physics from theology and it became fertile. You have no more business to ask a politician whether he is a believer than you have to ask a doctor. Copernicus had hardly completed his great discovery of the real solar system than they discovered the State's law of gravity. It was found that the State's centre of gravity lay in itself. And just as the different European governments, with the superficial character of a first experiment tried to apply this result to the system of political balance of power, men such as Machiavelli, Campanella and later Spinoza, Hugo Grotius and eventually Rousseau, Fichte and Hegel, began to look at the State realistically and to develop from it the natural laws, starting with reason and experience rather than theology. In the same way, Copernicus did not concern himself with the fact that Joshua had stopped the sun at Gideon and the moon in the valley of Ajalon. Modern philosophy has done nothing more than pursue a task begun by Heraclitus and Aristotle."

As a corollary to this widespread emergence of the human sciences to a position of autonomy, the claim of the secular, therefore a-theological and a-theist state, represented however in Marxist analysis, the final ripening of the contradictions in the Christian State. The era offered some examples, all the more flagrant since they coincided regionally—especially in France—with societies which had become or were becoming non-Christian in huge blocks. "The so-called Christian State has on the contrary a political attitude vis-à-vis religion and a religious attitude vis-à-vis politics. If it swallows all apparently political forms, it swallows religion equally as a matter of form."

After a century, the claim of this secular state as it became more specifically state and less and less formally Christian, seems to be pretty unspectacular. The most obstinate rebels know how to remain attached to the "thesis." But at the same time they cultivate, in practice, the "hypothesis" according to the current rule of interpretation of obstacles such as the Syllabus. And in other respects the defence of this secularity is based on a line which includes but also overlaps the sector of Marxist states or parties. Finally, the successive political experiments of the great modern nations from the American constitution right up to that of the U.S.S.R. passing naturally via the French Revolution, have demonstrated the justification and the benefits of this secularisation, namely: the termination of public compulsion to *cujus regio ejus religio* in spiritual matters, the end of discrimination in citizen's rights, liberty of conscience, rejection of positions of confessional monopolies (e.g. the ecclesiastical monopoly over the civic state), etc. All these reasons today render these claims more familiar and more plausible. An exception is made, of course, for countries where the majority of civil or civic rights remain, constitutionally or by agreement, subordinate to and limited by the prescriptions and prohibitions of an ecclesiastical law.

But the secularity of the state or of its services does not exhaust the political content of Marxist atheism. Marx, in analysing these "Free States of North America" where neither a state religion nor a majority religion existed, counts them together with France, amongst "the inventors of the rights of man." Marx says that these American States in a non-religious State, are at the same time "States favoured by religious feeling." He notes: "If in the countries whose political emancipation has been completed, we find not only the existence of, but the fresh and joyful existence of, religion, the proof is certain that the existence of religion in no way conflicts with the perfection of the State...." From this, two conclusions were possible: either, the *existence* of religion at State level is, therefore, not *necessary* for the vitality of religion on the social level; or else—and this is Marx's inference—the *suppression* of religion at State level is, therefore, not sufficient for the suppression of religion on the social level. The political suppression of every religious denomination in the midst of a State which is itself alien to religions, confessions or denomination, is comparable to the political abolition of private property in a state deciding that the electorate and eligibility for it are no longer linked to the census. In both cases, an evaporation of principle into the political "heavens" has as a counter balance a density which is correspondingly higher on the social plane. And finally the *unity* acquired theoretically has as a corollary a *separation* all the more marked in practice. "Man liberates himself politically from religion when he rejects its importance in *public law* and restricts it to *private law*. Religion is then no longer the essence of the community but the distinctive essence. The infinite atomisation of religion in North America, for example, gives it the outward appearance of a strictly private matter. Religion has been relegated to the region of private interests and, expelled from the community as such."

The non-religious and lay state has certainly ceased to function as a theological heaven for believers, but it has become a political heaven for its citizens. It has therefore become a supreme detour, a supreme mediator and, in this respect, a supreme and secular disguise for what constitutes the essence of religious alienation. "Religion is precisely the recognition of mankind via a detour and through a mediator." In other words, atheism implies a double suppression: not only of the role of the state in religion, but equally and above all of religion in the essence of the state. It is only on this condition that the *Aufhebung* of religion can have a role equivalent to the *Aufhebung* of private property.

Now this setting aside of ideas, ideologies, theological representation as so many mediations to overcome, and even the necessity of their rejection in the light of a new and superior degree of knowledge, are not in themselves, by any means novelties in the history of Christian differentiations. The whole branch of Left Wingers was animated by a similar demand so that it could concentrate itself and both attain and follow the famous "Inner Light." Engels would have been thrilled with a Joachimite and perhaps Amalrician theology of the Holy Spirit. Reference to this led Muenzer to include this Spirit in "the enthusiasm for reason." And had not the prince of scholastic theology, in stricter fashion, placed the negative way above all discussion on the divine names? Had he not demonstrated that it ended on a level where not only the representations and the definitions of God but also the very fact of declaring "He exists" lose their importance and significance? Moreover, it is this negative tradition via the current German mystic (Tauler?) which will probably touch Muenzerian thought.

It might seem dangerous to attempt to infer the origins of a whole system, beginning with an "Itinerary ad deum" of medieval type (Amaury de Bene, Joachim de Flore) right up to an atheism which is supposed to have dialectically outstripped every religion. And detailed information should be furnished on the possible nature of that continuity. One can at least offer the following: the formal discontinuity between Marxist atheism and Christian religion can only be properly understood in connection with a generic continuity and a differential process whose points of departure are found precisely in the ecclesiological crises related to or subsequent to the great agrarian or industrial revolutions. Certainly Engels' warnings should be taken into account: they close the door on an historical sociology of Christianity which would be "a simple appendix to the history of the Church." Engels' whole work has thoroughly elaborated the framework, if not the content, of a sociological genesis of the one or several Christianities. Certain questions posed by him have even remained, as we have already stated, at the centre of the most important subsequent studies in German on the sociology of this religion. This framework remains fundamental, it seems. The number and the complexity of the analyses that it stimulates or suggests could only appear useless to a crude atheism, in the sense that people have spoken of a crude Communism—one which is used to denounce a totalitarian suppression of all ownership of property just as of all mutual dependence amongst persons. The '40s offered several ostentatious examples of this. But just as socialism, "the science of society," presupposes analyses of situations incurred and of phases experienced by the regime of the ownership of material wealth, so also an atheism which wishes to be a "science of religion" presupposes some corresponding analyses of situations and phases experienced by the regime of the representation of spiritual wealth. From this point of view, the axiom "Religion is the opium of the people" with the propaganda or counter-propaganda significance given to it by isolation from its context, could not be retained as a theoretical *compendium* of Marxist thought, without over-simplification. The background to this thought on such a point is formed by the whole system of a sociology of knowledge and in particular by its sociology of ideologies. The framework and the first characteristics of this sociology of religious knowledge and ideologies are formed in particular by the many scattered fragments of Engels' work. It seems he was more concerned than Marx with this repercussion. Moreover he was less suspect and probably less facile than K. Kautsky who, for his part, devoted himself to an investigation of this sort. As for the method—under the circumstances essential to the projected discipline—it is regrettable that it had to seem like a pure and simple version of an objectivist positivism as if it thereby proposed an "historico-philosophical theory," more or less related to the law of the three stages and limiting the religious phenomena for all time and everywhere to be the elementary stage of the act of an evasive consciousness. In that case, the "reform of consciousness" would be little more than the substitution of one ideology for another. To transpose a phrase of Engels: now, at last, the necessary applications would hardly present any more difficulties than that of "solving a simple equation."

In fact this method, as it was proposed, does not seem to have been that. It does not claim to give irresistibly convincing schema in controversies over the abstract interpretation of the history of religions. The method is more closely related to something like a social psychoanalysis used for a concrete transformation of the religions in history, and thus awakening religious consciousness to the rational understanding of itself. An awakening attained in so far as the social conditions of existence became clear in the network of mental representations. After some examination this is at least what is suggested by the terms of Marx's manifesto, written in the form of a letter to A. Ruge, just when the *Annales franco-allemandes* had been founded: "The reform of consciousness consists solely in making the world aware of its own consciousness, awakening it from its own inward-looking phantasies and *explaining* its own actions to it. As is the case, moreover, with Feuerbach, in his criticism of religion, our aim can only be to invest religious and political questions with consciously human form.

Our slogan should, therefore, be: the reform of consciousness, not by dogmas but by the analysis of the mystical *consciousness* unintelligible to itself, whether it is apparent in either religion or politics. It will then be clear that for a very long time the world has possessed the dream of something of which it must now be conscious if it is to possess it in reality. It will be clear that it is not a question of some long caesura between the past and the future of the practical application (*Vollziehung*) of past ideas. Finally, it will be clear that humanity is not beginning a new task but is completing the former, only this time with the awareness of it.

"We can, therefore, sum up the trend of our paper in a single phrase: our era's own self-understanding (Critical philosophy) of its struggles and aspirations. This is a task for the world and for us. A confession (*Beichte*) is required, nothing more. To have its sins forgiven, humanity has only to declare what they are."

At the time when these lines were written, the radical nature of this "reform of consciousness" could appear contradictory to all theology. Not only is all thought engaged in this self-understanding offered for criticism and so, for the "overthrow" of every mode of religious thought, but also this social psychoanalysis (in which the procedure of the subsequent psychoanalysis is found likewise to be "reversed" in advance) is put forward in terms which tend to assume the fundamental and classical act of religion which the "metanoia" has always been. ". . . A confession is required, nothing more. . . ."

And yet just as in its negative function this "reform of consciousness," "self-explanation," "critical philosophy" is related to a whole preceding tradition, that of the "Realm of the Spirit" and of the Third Age, which Hegel takes up and rationalises in the last chapters of his Philosophy of Religion; so also its positive function, including here the subsequent complex idea of referring every religious representation to the expression of the conditions of social existence, must encounter or provoke, if not explicit adhesions, at least some connivances or parallels in the modes of rational approach to the religious achievement, including some still arising, more or less, directly from the theological position.

A symptomatic fact: Ruge records that between 1843 and 1844, he and Marx failed to find any French partners for the *Annales franco-allemandes.* This was precisely because the majority of French socialists, with the momentary exception of Proudhon, would not agree to the proposed religious criticism. This included men such as Leroux, Cabet, Louis Blanc and Lamennais. But several years later, in 1885, the idea of a Franco-German review was taken up again and, what is more, with an aim of religious criticism which was at least implicit, an achievement which was not without consequence for a whole tradition of rational explorations of religious facts, and for the subsequent constitution of the sciences of religion and for the *impact, in return, of those different sciences (exegesis, history, ethnology, psychology, sociology) on the corresponding fields of theological disciplines.*

This last methodological repercussion does not take by surprise the history of a discipline whose principal stages were marked by the integration of new rational instruments with each new cultural cycle. And one wonders if the methodological element in the change of emphasis suggested by the approach of Marxist socialism (and by the ensuing relativisation) would not be likely to offer a new rational instrument to theological expression itself.

As indeed people have often noticed and commented, rationalisation is not in itself unfamiliar to religious consciousness and "unintelligibility to itself" is only a starting point, in truth a source for demands for inner intelligibility on various levels in the hierarchy of consciousness:

spontaneous consciousness at the level of scriptural expression even though it may be an elementary catechesis;

hieratic consciousness at the level of dogmatic expression which, according to the individual case ratifies, selects, qualifies, sanctions and controls the reading of this scripture; and,

intellectualised consciousness at the level of classical theological expression, one which requires a *reddere rationem* of the raw products of the collective consciousness in primitive or later times, and so an expression which implies the confrontation of their respective contents with a mental universe. A key is needed to grasp its full meaning *(intellectus fidei),* a key which may pass from the elaborations of a gnosis to the conceptual tools of scholasticism or the strictest dialectic.

Finally, logical consciousness in an abstract but archetype phenomenology, such as Hegel's from which Marx and Engels received their first instruction in the subject. The totality of these methods thus seems to proclaim, define, defend and purify religious consciousness as an historical reality. We are in a theological movement which could be called *direct*.

But there comes a time when the endeavour of this religious consciousness bears less on the nature of its products than on the mechanism of its production; less on the content of its dogmas of creation than on the conditions of the creation of its dogmas; less on the way in which the gods make humanity live than on the way in which human beings live off their gods or make them live; less on the divine in the human than on the anthropology or the anthropomorphism of divinities or pantheons; less on the religious representations of historical reality than on the historical conditions of religious realities; less on the interpretation of a revelation by means of a subsequent tradition than by the retroactivity of this tradition in the constitution of this prior revelation; less on a theology of social history than on the social history of theological schools; less on the influx of churches upon cultures or civilisations than on the ebb of cultures and civilisations into the ecclesiastical life and institutions; less on the Christianisation of empires than on the imperialisation of Christianities; less on the absolute nature of an historical revelation than on the historical character or the "Historicisation" of these revelations of the absolute, etc. From this point on, religious consciousness *(whether or not it ceases to be religious is another question entirely)* is prey to demands for intelligibility of an order, perhaps complimentary, but in any case the inverse of the intelligibility offered by straight classical theology. This highly problematical point released by nineteenth century socialism can be studied in a very recent and highly commendable sociology of religion—that of J. Wach. The initial phrasing of the question which has been touched upon here was borrowed from him.

Karl Mannheim

THE FIRST FORM OF THE UTOPIAN MENTALITY : THE ORGIASTIC CHILIASM OF THE ANABAPTISTS

The decisive turning-point in modern history was, from the point of view of our problem, the moment in which "Chiliasm" joined forces with the active demands of the oppressed strata of society.[1] The very idea of the dawn of a

From Ideology and Utopia (1929), London: 1936, pp. 190–197. By permission of Routledge & Kegan Paul, Ltd. and Harcourt, Brace & World, Inc.

[1]To fix the beginning of a movement at a given point in the stream of historical events is

millenial kingdom on earth always contained a revolutionizing tendency, and

always hazardous and signifies a neglect of the forerunners of the movement. But the successful reconstruction of what is most essential in historical development depends upon the historian's ability to give the proper emphasis to those turning-points which are decisive in the articulation of phenomena. The fact that modern socialism often dates its origins from the time of the Anabaptists is in part evidence that the move-the church made every effort to paralyse this situationally transcendent idea with all the means at its command. These intermittently reviving doctrines reappeared again in Joachim of Flores among others, but in his case they were not as yet thought of as revolutionizing. In the Hussites, however, and then in Thomas Münzer[2] and the Anabaptists these ideas became transformed into the activistic movements of specific social strata. Longings which up to that time had been either unattached to a specific goal or concentrated upon other-worldly objectives suddenly took on a mundane complexion. They were now felt to be realizable—here and now—and infused social conduct with a singular zeal.

The "spiritualization of politics," which may be said to have begun at this turn in history, more or less affected all the currents of the time. The source of spiritual tension, however, was the emergence of the utopian mentality which originated in the oppressed strata of society. It is at this point that politics in the modern sense of the term begins, if

we here understand by politics a more or less conscious participation of all strata of society in the achievement of some mundane purpose, as contrasted with a fatalistic acceptance of events as they are, or of control from "above."[3]

The lower classes in the post-medieval period only very gradually assumed this motor function in the total social process and only bit by bit did they arrive at an awareness of their own social and political significance. Even though this stage is, as already indicated, still very far removed from the stage of "proletarian self-consciousness," it is nevertheless the starting point of the process gradually leading to it. Henceforth the oppressed classes in society tend in a more clearly discernible fashion to play a specific role in the dynamic development of the total social process. From this time on we get an increasing social differentiation of purposes and psychic attitudes.

This by no means implies that this most extreme form of the utopian mentality has been the only determining factor in history since that time. None the less its presence in the social realm has exerted an almost continual influence even upon antithetical mentalities. Even the opponents of this extreme form of utopian mentality oriented themselves, though unwittingly and unconsciously, with reference to it. The utopian vision aroused a contrary vision. The Chiliastic optimism of the revolutionaries ultimately gave birth to the formation of the conservative attitude of resignation and to the realistic attitude in politics.

---

ment led by Thomas Münzer is to be regarded as a step in the direction of modern revolutionary movements. It is obvious, of course, that we are not yet dealing here with class-conscious proletarians. Similarly, it must be readily granted that Münzer was a social revolutionary from religious motives. However, the sociologist must pay particular attention to this movement, because in it Chiliasm and the social revolution were structurally integrated.

[2]Of the literature concerning Münzer, we mention only K. Holl, "Luther und die Schwärmer" (*Gesammelte Aufsätze zur Kirchengeschichte,* Tübingen, 1927, pp. 420ff.*)*, where a wide range of citations bearing upon a single problem is admirably assembled. In the references that follow, we simply cite the passage in Holl without reprinting it in detail.

For a characterization of Chiliasm, cf. especially Bloch, E., *Thomas Münzer als Theologe der Revolution* (Munich, 1921). An inner affinity between Münzer and this author has made possible a very adequate exposition of the essence of the phenomenon of Chiliasm.

[3]Politics might, of course, be defined in a number of ways. In this case again we should keep in mind a statement made earlier: the definition is always related to its purpose and to the point of view of the observer. Our purpose here is the tracing of the relationship between the formation of the collective consciousness and political history, and consequently our definition, which selects certain facts, must be related to this formulation of the problem.

This situation was of great moment not only for politics but also for those spiritual strivings which had become fused with practical movements and which had abandoned their detached and aloof position. Orgiastic energies and ecstatic outbursts began to operate in a worldly setting, and tensions, previously transcending day to day life became explosive agents within it. The impossible gives birth to the possible, and the absolute interferes with the world and conditions actual events. This fundamental and most radical form of the modern utopia was fashioned out of a singular material. It corresponded to the spiritual fermentation and physical excitement of the peasants, of a stratum living closest to the earth. It was at the same time robustly material and highly spiritual.

Nothing would be more misleading than to try to understand these events from the point of view of the "history of ideas." "Ideas" did not drive these men to revolutionary deeds. Their actual outburst was conditioned by ecstatic-orgiastic energies. The reality-transcending elements in consciousness which here were aroused to an active utopian function were not "ideas." To see everything that occurred during this period as the work of "ideas" is an unconscious distortion produced during the liberal-humanitarian stage of utopian mentality. The history of ideas was the creation of an "idea-struck" age, which involuntarily reinterpreted the past in the light of its own central experiences. It was not "ideas" that impelled men during the Peasant Wars to revolutionary action. This eruption had its roots in much deeper-lying vital and elemental levels of the psyche.

If we are to come closer to an understanding of the true substance of Chiliasm and if we are to make it accessible to scientific comprehension, it is first of all necessary to distinguish from Chiliasm itself the images, symbols, and forms in which the Chiliastic mind thought. For nowhere else is our experience as valid as here, that what is already formed, and the expression things assume, tend to become detached from their origins and to go their own way independently of the motives that prompted them. The essential feature of Chiliasm is its tendency always to dissociate itself from its own images and symbols. It is precisely because the driving force of this utopia does not lie in the form of its external expression that a view of the phenomenon based upon the mere history of ideas fails to do it justice. Such a view constantly threatens to miss the essential point. If we use the methods of the history of ideas, we tend to put in place of the history of the substance of Chiliasm the history of frames of reference which have already been emptied of content, i.e. the history of mere Chiliastic ideas as such.[4] Likewise, the investigation of the careers of Chiliastic revolutionaries is apt to be misleading, since it is of the nature of Chiliastic experience to ebb in the course of time and to undergo an unremitting transformation in the course of the persons' experience. Hence, to adhere closely to the theme of investigation itself, we must seek out a method of research which will give a living view of the material and which will present it as if we were experiencing it ourselves. We must constantly ask ourselves whether the Chiliastic attitude itself is actually present in the forms of thought and experience with which we are dealing in a given case.

[4]In the conflict between Münzer and Luther there is evidence of the above-mentioned divergence between emphasis upon the substance of faith which can only be experienced and the "ideas" which symbolize it. According to Münzer, Luther is one who believes exclusively in the letter of the Scriptures. For Münzer, such faith is a "stolen, unexperienced, apish mimicry." Citations in Holl, p. 427.

The only true, perhaps the only direct, identifying characteristic of Chiliastic experience is absolute presentness. We always occupy some here and now on the spatial and temporal stage but, from the point of view of Chiliastic experience, the position that we occupy is only incidental. For the real Chiliast, the present becomes the breach through which what was previously inward bursts out suddenly, takes hold of the outer world and transforms it.

The mystic lives either in recollection of ecstasy, or in longing for it. His metaphors describe this ecstasy as a psychic situation which cannot be conceived of in spatial and temporal terms as a union with the closed world of the beyond. It is perhaps this same ecstatic substance which turns with the Chiliast into the immediate here and now, but not in order simply to delight in it, but in order to whip it up and to make it a part of himself. Thomas Münzer, the Chiliastic prophet, expressed himself as follows: "For that reason, all prophets should speak in this manner, 'Thus saith the Lord,' and not, 'Thus said the Lord,' as if it had occurred in the past rather than in the present."

The experience of the mystic is purely spiritual, and if there are some traces of sensual experience in his language it is because he has to express an inexpressible spiritual contact and can only find his symbols in the sensual analogies of everyday life. With the Chiliast, however, sensual experience is present in all its robustness, and is as inseparable from the spirituality in him as he is from his immediate present. It is as if through this immediate present he had first come into the world and entered into his own body.

To quote Münzer himself:—

"I seek only that you accept the living word in which I live and breathe, so that it should not come back to me empty. Take it to your hearts, I beseech you in the name of the red blood of Christ. I take an account of you and I wish to give you an account of myself. Can I not do this, may I be the child of temporal and eternal death. A higher pledge I cannot give you."

The Chiliast expects a union with the immediate present. Hence he is not preoccupied in his daily life with optimistic hopes for the future or romantic reminiscences. His attitude is characterized by a tense expectation. He is always on his toes awaiting the propitious moment and thus there is no inner articulation of time for him. He is not actually concerned with the millenium that is to come;[5] what is important for him is that it happened here and now, and that it arose from mundane existence, as a sudden swing over into another kind of existence. The promise of the future which is to come is not for him a reason for postponement, but merely a point of orientation, something external to the ordinary course of events from where he is on the lookout ready to take the leap.

Because of the peculiarity of its structure, medieval, feudal society did not know revolution in the modern sense.[6]

[5] On the sociology of the inward-turning of experience, and in general on the theory of the relationship of forms of experience and forms of political-public activity, it should be noted that, in the degree that Karlstadt and the South German Baptists fell away from Münzer, they turned more and more from the Chiliastic experience of immediacy towards prophetic experience and an optimistic hope for the future (cf. Holl, p. 458).

[6] One of the features of modern revolution already pointed out by Stahl is that it is no ordinary uprising against a certain oppressor but a striving for an upheaval against the whole existing social order in a thorough-going and systematic way. If this systematic aim is made the starting-point in the analysis and its historical and intellectual antecedents are sought out one arrives in this case also at Chiliasm. As unsystematic as Chiliasm may seem to be in other respects, in one phase it had a tendency towards abstract systematic orientation. Thus, for exam-

Since the earliest appearance of this form of political change, Chiliasm has always accompanied revolutionary outbursts and given them their spirit. When this spirit ebbs and deserts these movements, there remains behind in the world a naked mass-frenzy and a despiritualized fury. Chiliasm sees the revolution as a value in itself, not as an unavoidable means to a rationally set end, but as the only creative principle of the immediate present, as the longed-for realization of its aspirations in this world. "The will to destroy is a creative will," said Bakunin,[7] because of the Satan within him, the Satan of whom he loved to speak as working through contagion. That he was not fundamentally interested in the realization of a rationally thought-out world is betrayed by his statement: "I do not believe in constitutions or in laws. The best constitution would leave me dissatisfied. We need something different. Storm and vitality and a new lawless and consequently free world."

Whenever the ecstatic spirit wearies of broadened perspectives and imagery, we get a reappearance of the concrete promise of a better world, although it is in no way meant to be taken quite literally. For this mentality, promises of a better world removed in time and space are like uncashable cheques—their only function is to fix that point in the "world beyond events" of which we have spoken, and from which he, who is expectantly awaiting the propitious moment, can be assured of detachment from that which is merely in the process of becoming. Not being at one with whatever events transpire in the "evil" here and now, he awaits only the critical juncture of events and that moment when the external concatenation of circumstances coincides with the ecstatic restlessness of his soul.

Consequently, in observing the structure and course of development of the Chiliastic mentality, it is quite unimportant (although for the history of the variations in *motif,* it may be significant) that in place of a temporal utopia we get a spatial one, and that in the Age of Reason and Enlightenment the closed system of rational deduction comes to permeate the utopian outlook. In a certain sense the rational, axiomatic point of departure, the closed system of deductive procedure, and the internally balanced equilibrium of motives comprised in the body of axioms are quite as capable of insuring that inner coherence and isolation from the world as are the utopian dreams.

Furthermore, the remoteness from space and time of what is merely rationally correct and valid, is, in a certain sense, more likely to lead to the outside realm beyond experience than could be hoped for through these utopian dreams which are laden with the corporeal content of the world as it.

Nothing is more removed from actual events than the closed rational system. Under certain circumstances, nothing contains more irrational drive than a fully self-contained, intellectualitsic world-view. Nevertheless, in every formal rational system there is the danger that the Chiliastic-ecstatic element will ebb away behind the intellectual façade. Not every rational utopia, therefore, is tantamount to Chiliastic faith, and not every rational utopia in this sense represents a detachment and alienation from the world. The abstract nature of the rational utopia contradicts the

---

ple, Radványi has pointed out that Chiliasm did not attack individual persons, but only attacked and persecuted the evil principle active in individuals and institutions. (Cf. his unpublished dissertation, *Der Chiliasmus,* Heidelberg, 1923, p. 98.) Further citations in Holl, p. 454.

[7] We shall later show that the anarchism of the Bakunian variety comes closest in our opinion to continuing the Chiliastic outlook in the modern world.

intense emotional drive of a sensually alert Chiliastic faith in the complete and immediate present. Thus the rational utopian mentality although often born of the Chiliastic mentality may inadvertently become its prime antagonist, just as the liberal-humanitarian utopia tended more and more to turn against Chiliasm.

Franklin Hamlin Littell

THE SOCIAL BACKGROUND OF THE ANABAPTIST VIEW OF THE CHURCH

Myr ist geben alle gewallt ynn hymel vnd erden/ dar umb gehet hyn/ vnd leret alle volcker/ vnd teufft die ynn den namen des vaters vñ des sons vnd des heyligen geysts/ vnd leret sie halten/ alles was ich euch befolhen have/ vnd sihe/ ich byn bey euch alle tage/ bis ans ende der wellt. Matthew 28
Das Newe Testament Deudsch (Wittenberg, 1522)
Gehet hyn ynn alle wellt/ vnd predigt das Evangelion/ alle Creaturn/ wer do glaubt vnd taufft wird/ der wirt selig werden/ we aber nicht gleubt/ der wirt verdampt werden. Mark 16
Die erde ist des HERREN vnd was drinnen ist/
Der erdboden vnd was drauff wonet. Psalm 24.
Biblia/ das ist/ die gantze Heilige Schrift Deudsch (Wittenberg, 1534)

No texts appear more frequently than the above in the confessions of faith and court testimonies of the Anabaptists, and none show more clearly the degree to which Anabaptism was different in conviction and type from the intact and stable ways of magisterial Protestantism. The Anabaptists did not think of themselves as a minority witness, temporarily withdrawn until the Great Church should mend its ways. Neither did they accept the status of conventicles, little cells of piety, acting as a leaven within the great masses of baptized believers in the territorial churches. They believed that the Church of the Restitution, the True Church with its disciplined laymen, carried history. The Restitution which had occurred was full of meaning on the world map. The Anabaptists believed that they were forerunners of a time to come, in which the Lord would establish His people and His law throughout the earth.

It was the Holy Spirit who gathered and governed.

Therefore is such a people, community, assembly or Church gathered and led together by the Holy Spirit, which from henceforth ruleth, controlleth and ordereth everything in her. . . .
The children of God . . . become his children through the unifying Spirit. Thus, it is evident that the Church is gathered together by the Holy Spirit: also that she hath being and is kept in being by him, and that there is no other Church apart from that which the Holy Spirit buildeth and gathereth.[1]

[1]Peter Rideman, *Account of Our Religion, Doctrine and Faith* (London: Hodder & Stoughton/Plough Publishing House, 1950), pp. 38, 39.

From The Anabaptist View of the Church. Boston : 1958, pp. 109–133. By permission of Beacon Press.

The Spirit who gathered and governed was also a *sending* Spirit. "But after it had all been accomplished according to the Scriptures, and had been made new in Christ, He did not send out the scribes and Pharisees with Moses' law, but His disciples with His own doctrine, saying: Go ye into all the world. . . ."[2] Against the pattern of compulsion and territorial conformity, the radicals proposed to restore the New Testament missionary method of proclamation and letter-writing. Both revolutionaries and *Stille* had the missionary vision, although their understanding of the particulars of the approaching fulfillment differed greatly.[3]

No words of the Master were given more serious attention by His Anabaptist followers than the Great Commission. In the words of Menno Simons: "He sent out His messengers preaching this peace, His apostles who spread this grace abroad through the whole world, who shone as bright, burning torches before all men, so that they might lead me and all erring sinners into the right way. O Lord, not unto me, but unto Thee be praise and honor. Their words I love, their practices I follow."[4]

The form of the Commission seemed to sum up His whole teaching in a glorious program comprehending the whole world. The pilgrim, familiar seeker of the Middle Ages, was transformed in the fiery experience of the "evangelical Täufer"[5] into an effective evangelist and martyr. The pilgrim missioner, eschatological figure and personality type whose reappearance signified the breakthrough of the Age of the Spirit in Joachimitism,[6] became a characteristic type in the Anabaptist network of communities and congregations. His wandering footsteps and shedding of blood were a determined if not always systematic testimony to the influence of a lay mission which counted no cost too dear to him who would walk in the steps of the Crucified. . . .

Not only was a new historical significance given to the Great Commission, but its application was made relevant to the life of the ordinary layman. The missionary mandate was no longer the prerogative of special orders or selected professionals. The layman was no longer limited to remaining obediently in his appointed place and status.[7] The Commission applied to the most simple believer and claimed him as an evangelist. Until this time the ordinary Christian had looked largely to the higher authorities, both secular and religious, to make decisions of policy and to carry the weight of Christian statesmanship. In the Church of the Restitution, the world view was no longer restricted to the powerful and educated. In Anabaptist opinion, the craftsman might make a

---

[2]"Foundation of Christian Doctrine" (1539), in *Menno Simons, The Complete Writings of . . .* (Scottdale, Pennsylvania: Herald Press, 1956), pp. 103–226, 178.

[3]*Infra*, p. 133. See article by the author, "The Anabaptist Theology of Missions," XXI *MQR* (1947) 1: 5–17; Wilhelm Wiswedel, "Die alten Täufergemeinden und ihr missionarisches Wirken," 40 *ARG* (1943) 183–200, 45 *ARG* (1948) 115–32; Roland H. Bainton, "The Great Commission," VIII *Mennonite Life* (1953) 4: 183–89; Harold S. Bender, "Evangelism," *ME* (1956) II, 269–73.

[4]"Meditation on the Twenty-fifth Psalm" (c. 1537), *The Complete Writings of Menno Simons,* pp. 63–86, 71.

[5]This name has been given them by certain authors who rightly find the terms "Wiedertäufer" and "Täufer" inaccurate and restrictive. See Introduction, *supra.* "Evangelical Anabaptists" would seem best to indicate their overwhelming sense of mission. See Robert Friedmann, "Conception of the Anabaptists," IX *CH* (1940) 4: 341–65, 362.

[6]Ernst Benz, *Ecclesia Spiritualis* (Stuttgart: W. Kohlhammer Verlag, 1934), pp. 25–26.

[7]Contrast Butzer's position: "The Christians don't need to do anything else than what they've previously done; each stands up for the gospel in his appointed place, and the Kingdom of God will grow." Gustav Warneck, p. 18.

better missioner than the cultured man. Jesus himself preached to men in terms of their trade, not with many books. "For the common man can be better informed by [lessons from] the creatures than through writing."[8] When the missioner Hanss Schmidt was asked about his studies, he told the authorities: "I study with pick and flail."[9] For the Brethren that was honorable and sufficient, and it better equipped him to go forth into all lands "in order to gather the sheep of the Lord" and "to fish for men" than would participation in the wranglings of the philosophers.[10]

There lies a deeper meaning here, as well: from the peasant who plows his field for the planting, the faithful were to learn how God works His people in fulfilling His purpose.[11] In suffering and travail, His faithful are plowed for the Kingdom's sake. And the ordinary layman, the common man, can best proclaim the Gospel to common men. The domination of the outward, the material, the powerful, will give way before the calm speaking of the simple Christian whose only authority is the Gospel. And it will be the babes, the naive, who will come through where those wise and understanding "after the flesh" will fail.

Above all the Reformers resisted the "wandering" of the Anabaptists. Lutherans taught that each calling has divine blessing, and condemned the irresponsibility of those who cast loose from family and job to be missioners. They came, in their resistance to the corner preachers and radical congregations, to enforce tight authority in the

parish. Orderly ordination and calling to the ministry were vigorously championed against the Anabaptists, "for they cannot establish their calling."[12] Such separatists were the devil's apostles, for "no one can have a ministry outside and without command or calling."[13] "Whoever preaches without an appointment, that one is an enthusiast [*Schwärmer*]"[14]....

The gathering of voluntary religious associations[15] by a freely and comprehensively conceived evangel, sealed by believers' baptism, consituted in early times a challenge to the imperial power—and in the sixteenth century was a threat to magisterial Protestantism. The establishments sought to offset the winning power of the broadly conceived and energetically pursued mission by infant baptism. This bulwark of the standing order was introduced in the Roman Empire, according to Jakob Huter, as a

---

[8]*WtQ1938*, p. 95 (Hans Schlaffer).

[9]*WtQ1930*, #947 (Dec. 4, 1590), p. 658.

[10]*Beck*, p. 39, fn. 2 (instructions to Georg Zaunring).

[11]The Anabaptists said the *Schriftgelernten* ("scribes") have no *creütz*: they were as though the goldsmith only talked to the metal and didn't take it into his shop: *WtQ1938*, p. 74 (Leonhard Schiemer).

[12]"Ein Brieff D. Mart. Luthers Von den Schleichern und Winckelpredigern" (1532), *WA* XXX, 3: 519.

[13]*WA* XXX, 3: 521. The Anabaptist failure to stay put in fixed stations in life was the chief complaint of Theodor Beza (1519–1605), who also denied the continuing authority of the Great Commission: *ML* (1913) I, 215. Luther said that after the visit to the manger the shepherds went back to their flocks and didn't wander around in the woods like the Anabaptists; Georg Buchwald, *Predigten D. Martin Luthers* (Gütersloh: C. Bertelsmann Verlag, 1925–26), I, 175 (Dec. 26, 1528); again, II, 76 (Dec. 27, 1530).

[14]Gustav Warneck, "Mission unter den Heiden: 2, protestantische," *Real. —3* (1903) XIII, 130–31.

[15]"Freiwilligkeitskirche" was a term used by their enemies, in part justified by their championing of Erasmus against Luther in the controversy about the Free Will. See article by F.J. Wray, "Free Will," *ME* (1956) II, 387–89. Pilgram Marpeck and Peter Rideman were Augustinian, Hübmaier and Denck and Menno more Erasmian. "Freiwilligkeitskirche" also conveys their significance as voluntary religious associations in lands controlled by Roman Catholic and Protestant state churches; see *GHW/M*, p. 87.

blunt reaction of tyranny to the power of the Great Commission.[16]

The maintenance of infant baptism and compulsion in religion by the state churches of the Reformation placed them in the period before the Restitution, in the fallen time of the Great Church. The words of the New Testament were clear enough, and the example of the Early Church could hardly be misinterpreted. The Anabaptists looked out upon the known world as a great missionary territory, and they sought to evangelize on the comprehensive scale of the great heroes of the past.

The Heroic Prototype

In the life of the Anabaptist congregations the man of the Early Church reappeared. He was a hero with one supreme loyalty, to Christ his Master. He performed miracles. His persecutors sometimes died terrible deaths.[17] He strove to obey literally the counsels of perfection which were now binding upon every believer, and he lived "loose from the world" as a pilgrim, missioner, and martyr.

From prison a pilgrim of the faith wrote of his condition: "I am cut loose from all the world, from wife, from father, and mother and sister according to the flesh, and from all men; but that is right; Christ was also cut loose from all men and from his disciples; it is enough that I be as He was...."[18] This ascetic emphasis led to a glory in pilgrimage and a triumph in martyrdom. Scores of missioners traveled from Waldshut throughout Switzerland, from Zürich through the Tyrol and southern Germany, and finally, from Moravia as far as Venice, Amsterdam, and Krakow. Lay evangelists moved among the corner congregations, threading all Europe, and a chain of synods and free gatherings tied the movement together....

Economic Factors of Importance

No set of ideas can survive, nor can it even come to birth, except "in the fullness of time." In particular, the theoretical pattern must be related to

---

[16]*WtQ1938*, pp. 178–79 (Jakob Huter). See also p. 238: "There it stands, in the first place one shall preach, then comes believing, thirdly, those that believe, baptize (them). The children cannot believe, they know nothing of God, of Christ, therefore the baptism isn't used for them during childhood." (The Five Articles, c. 1547.) "Question. 'What do you hold concerning infant baptism?' Answer. 'I consider it nothing else than a human institution.' Qu. 'By what then will you prove, or establish your baptism?' Ans. 'By Mark xvi.'" Confession of an Anabaptist at Antwerp, 1551; T.J. van Braght, I, 436–37. Infant baptism is refuted on the basis of the text, "preach and baptize," for they must first have the faith; *WtQ1930*, #169 (April 9, 1557), p. 143. Permitting infant baptism indicates that the full values of mature decision are not known (Mark 16: 16!); *Egli*, #1201 (June 4, 1527), II, p. 547. The answer of Christ *De baptismo parvulorum* is Matt. 28, then Mark 16; *WtQ1934*, #228 (Hans Hechtlein, 1530), pp. 200–201. The two main influences launching Hans Hut on his great evangel seem to have been studying Matt. 28, Mark 16, and Acts 19: 1–7 on infant baptism, and Müntzer's "Hoch verursachte schutzrede..."; Wilhelm Neuser, *Hans Hut, Leben und Wirken* bis zum Nikolsburger Religionsgespräch (Berlin: Hermann Blanke, 1913), pp. 12–13, fn. 40; p. 15, fn. 63. Thomas von Imbroich, who greatly influenced Campanus, is recorded to have said (May 5, 1558): "They asked him why he did not have his children baptized? He answered: 'The Scripture teaches nothing of infant baptism; and they who will be baptized according to God's word must first be believers!'" T.J. van Braght, *op. cit.*, II, 139. Felix Manz, in his "Protestation und Schutzschrift" (1524), had informed the Town Council that infant baptism was introduced into the church artificially (kündtlich), while the true scriptural basis of baptism was the Great Commission; *WtQ: Zürich*, #16, pp. 23f.

[17]*Beck*, p. 67.

[18]*Beck*, #795 (August, 1525), p. 377.

large historic forces that create the atmosphere in which the intellectual movement can live and give concrete form to its internal drive. At the time of the Restitution there were certain given factors including important economic developments, which favored the emergence of a new solidarity and joined forces with the Anabaptist vision of religious reform to make a new style of Christian Community workable.

The sixteenth century was a time of social unrest and economic upheaval, of revolutionary dreams and attempted reforms. In an economy made fluid by commerce with Asia and wealth from America, craftsmen and peasants found themselves displaced. These were the chief classes to produce programs and centers of revolt, to respond most readily to the intense eschatology of the Melchiorites, and to go in goodly numbers to the Christian communist villages in Moravia. Though court records show that many who joined the colonies had had some substance, the Hutterite mission found ready response from the hungry and depressed as well as from the religiously dissatisfied.[19] Journeymen

without fixed place of residence or master were a common sight in this age as they wandered from city to city. If they were also Anabaptist in sympathies, they added to their testimony that Christ alone was "Master" (*vorsteer*). The Anabaptist craftsmen transformed social misfortune into a religious vehicle, and glorified in "living loose from the world."

Groups disjointed by a changing economy became wanderers in the land, their economic status and style of life throwing them into constant contact with the large numbers of religious expellees and persecutees. On the social side they were torn loose and dispossessed; on the religious side they were generally seekers if not adherents of some

---

[19]The effectiveness of the Hutterite missioners among the depressed classes is portrayed in #634, #667, #716, #721 in *WtQ1930*. It is Bossert's final conclusion that the Schwenckfelders won more preachers and women from the nobility, while the Anabaptists drew mostly from the peasants; p. xii. Accounts of those fleeing to Moravia, debts and small goods, indicate their station as tradespeople and craftsmen; #261 (Nov. 9, 1569), p. 249; #262 (Oct. 27, 1569), p. 250. Properties inventoried sometimes indicate a fair degree of prosperity; *WtQ1934*, #27 (1527), pp. 23–24. On the general problem of the relation of Anabaptism ("Handwerker Christentum"?) to social forces, see Georg Loesche, "Archivalische Beiträge zur Geschichte des Täufertums und des Protestantismus in Tirol und Voralberg." *47 Jahrbuch der Gesellschaft für die Geschichte des Protestantismus im ehemaligen und im neuen Österreich* (1926), p. 3. The flooding in of economic refugees accentuated the problems of organization within the

Moravian communities, and many new colonists returned to their former stations when conditions were better or when persecution threatened the life in Moravia. One motif may have been a kind of reaction against city life and commercial complexities, and idealization of "die Bedürfnislosigkeit"; Ernst Correll, pp. 61–62. A definite form of confession and submission was provided for those who returned, would promise obedience, and re-establish themselves in the fabric of a stable society; *WtQ1930*, #198 (June 27, 1559), p. 185. See also the case of Hans Volmar of Geradstatten, who after re-baptism went to Moravia and then returned and submitted; *WtQ1930*, #64, p. 44; also Christmann Schmidt of Diegenbach, who was banished on return, #70, p. 47. Konrad Wirtemberger of Zaisersweiher, who returned but refused to conform, was expelled and exiled; *WtQ1930*, #68, p. 46. Appollonia of Horrheim and husband came back from Moravia and submitted; *WtQ1930*, #73–74, p. 49. Very evidently the migration to Moravia was only an economic movement for many, and they found the life and discipline in the colonies too rigorous to bear. A fine new study on Anabaptism and economic groups is Paul Peachey, *Die soziale Herkunft der Schweizer Täufer in der Reformationszeit* (Karlsruhe: Heinrich Schneider, 1954). See article by Friedmann on "Economic History of the Hutterian Brethren," *ME* (1956) II, 143–45; also, Gerhard J. Neumann, "Nach und von Mähren," reprinted from *ARG* (1957) 1: 75–90.

Left Wing movement. Women imprisoned at Erlangen in 1527 reported that their husbands left, seeking the word of the Gospel where it might be found and consigning the children to their care. One journeyman said, "I will go and will search out the old and new faiths [to see] which is the true and best."[20]

The savage persecution loosed on the Anabaptist congregations threw hundreds more into the general currents of economic and religious unrest. Poor relief records show the travel of families toward Moravia. Most of them were, like Veit Frick, "a poor, unpromising people, that have to do their daily work and have many children."[21] Standard processes for confiscation of property and goods were worked out in the courts, and affected the most able craftsmen and farmers as well as those cast adrift by economic circumstances.[22] Whole families were uprooted, and many men traveled from city to city leaving families to fend for themselves.

Those able agriculturalists or handworkers, who were expelled from their former stations by religious persecution rather than by unrest, constitute a somewhat different phenomenon from the individual wanderers. But displacement for religious causes became increasingly important with the years. Such dissolution of social bonds was a permanent and inevitable function of religious territorial agreements like that of Augsburg, 1555. In the years of preparation and early ingathering, the individual wanderer was important. Later, under the impact of community life and discipline, the collective responsibility for the mission loomed large. The more responsible groups were concerned to maintain a sound and integreted economy within the fellowship of believers, and within the Hutterite communities real honor was tendered craftsmen in terms of their work.

But in the larger society there was a looseness of relationships toward job and family which the Reformers considered thoroughly irresponsible,[23] without realizing that it was at least as much a product of economic change and political repression as it was of radical religious separatism. They could not understand the apparent instability of one who "had a wife and four children, no home place and was the citizen of no city."[24] They hoped to carry over from medieval civilization those relation-

[20]*WtQ1934*, #12 (1527), p. 15. One of the men was Hans Ritter, who accompanied Hans Hut on many trips.

[21]*WtQ1930*, #231 (Feb. 5, 1563), p. 227; see poor relief records, pp. 231f. A General Rescript (July 13, 1538) mentioned journeymen going up and down in the land and wandering off to Moravia.

[22]*WtQ1930*, #241, pp. 234f. A typical process of confiscation against persons who had been in Moravia for some years included the following items: 1) Are there children, how old, and are they also Anabaptist? 2) If no other kin are eligible, who has a just claim to the goods and property? See #251 (Dec. 24, 1565): questions about goods and money of Anabaptists who had gone 28 years before to Moravia. See also #263 (Oct. 7, 1570): judgment on an estate; the daughter had married an Anabaptist and lived in Moravia, and her part was put in escrow.

[23]*WtQ1934*, p. 18. Proof was given by the authorities that a man should not wander, but stay with his wife and children; #150 (Feb. 1, 1529), pp. 143–46. Note Calvin's opposition to the "bare-footed evangel" of the Libertines, which was as much social as ecclesiastical; Karl Müller, "Calvin und die 'Libertiner,'" XL ZKG (1922) N.F. III: 83–129. Luther, himself a good *Hausvater,* stated the family as one of the orders of "natural" responsibility (*Schöpfungsordnungen*), against the wandering *Schwärmer* as well as against Roman celibacy.

[24]So was it reported of a wanderer examined by Johannes Brenz; *WtQ1930*, #169 (April 9, 1557), p. 146. A familiar phrase in court records was "wife and children not of his faith," which may have been due to the father's effort to protect them from the authorities but could have derived also from the fact that the father had traveled widely in guild circles and broken loose from the established religion.

ships which made for a stable society, and did not comprehend the fact that economic and religious change, coupled with the pluralism of religious persecutions which they themselves justified, made such stability impossible. To the religious radical, driven by persecution and the Lord's Commission, all such considerations were "worldly." We can almost hear the Anabaptist say to the authorities of the Great Church and the magistrates who tried to hold him fast in his "natural" responsibilities: "I no longer live, but Christ in me and the world crucified in me!"[25]

Just as economic displacement joined forces with the religious drive to make wandering and pilgrimage common, so the establishment of a planned economy in Moravia became the cornerstone and the surety for a consistent and planned missionary effort. The practice of Christian Community established in Moravia was intimately tied to Anabaptist evangelical operations in the German-speaking lands. The Great Commission itself seemed to argue for the kind of selflessness best expressed by a strong discipline of community or communism.[26] In all Anabaptist groups a communism of consumption functioned for the state of the evangel, and the Hutterite communities maintained their strongest internal discipline during the years of ardent missionary passion.[27] A base of operations was built which served the entire movement, and the most missionary minded were the congregations fraternally related to that economy.

Thus the Anabaptists developed a theology of suffering, transforming the persecuted remnant into a triumphant church, rich in historical significance and bringing the means of present salvation.[28] The idea of suffering became their moving power and hope in the Third Age, a refined and nonviolent parallel to the revolutionary conquest conceived by the radicals at Münster. "Suffering is the way, the door, and the means to God, the door into the sheep-stall."[29]

In baptism the believer learned that he was to leave all selfish concern—including private ownership—behind, and through the cross and suffering come to salvation. The internal significance of suffering is revealed in Anabaptist records of the uses of communism and the Ban. When threatened by the authorities, Hanss Schmidt said, Let the Lord's will be done: he had suffered all his life as a pilgrim loose from the world, and his brethren would take care of his wife and children.[30] (Here again communism's utility as a base of operations for the missionary work is clear.) Even the community's acceptance of responsibility for the education of children, in which the Hutterites made remarkable pedagogical contributions,[31] became a part of the realistic measures that made the sustaining of the mission possible. The cross of Christ *(Creutz christy)* and the communion of saints *(gemeinschaft der heilligen)* are the key ideas in Anabaptist thought at this level. Good and evil must be separated by a vigorous use of the Ban, so that the individual hero and the heroic community will be able to stand in time of trial. "For a Christian without

[25]*WtQ1938*, p. 214 (Ulrich Stadler).

[26]*WtQ1934*, #254 (April 30, 1531), p. 231: "di armen fruma leut auf apostolisch ire guter gemein halten," on the basis of the Great Commission.

[27]Ernst Correll, p. 18.

[28]Lydia Müller, *Der Kommunismus der mährischen Wiedertäufer* (Leipzig: M. Heinsius Nachf., 1927), p. 59. On a famous case of persecution at Schwäbisch-Gmünd, see "Wolfgang Esslinger," *ME* (1956) II, 252.

[29]*WtQ1938*, p. 155 (Huter).

[30]*WtQ1930*, #947 (Dec. 4, 1590), pp. 658–59, 662.

[31]On Hutterite educational contributions, see article by Friedmann, in *ME* (1956) II, 149–50; Wilhelm Wiswedel, "Das Schulwesen der Huterischen Bruder in Mähren," XXXVII *ARG* (1940) 1: 38–60.

suffering is like an untrained doctor, and like a house whose beam has not been hewn."[32] The internal organization of the community was a function of their capacity as pilgrims, missioners, and martyrs.

There is no doubt that the *Stille* consciously repudiated the revolutionaries' shift from weaponless warfare to the taking of the sword, but it is questionable whether all chiliastic thinking was purged.[33] And certainly there was a great surcharge of eschatological thinking, in which the missions method came to play a dominant part in the vision of the coming Kingdom on earth. The teleological necessity of suffering remained, and with it the *Täufer* sense of participating in the last scene of a world-shaking drama. When the last cup of blood had been shed, they might look for the Day of Victory. The quiet eschatology which became exclusive after Münster did not change the world view nor the expectation of a Kingdom on earth; *it changed the attitude to power*.[34] The

manner of the coming of the Kingdom was, for the nonresistant Anabaptists, the Pauline missions method rather than by the "slaying of the godless" and violent revolution. The willingness to suffer martyrdom[35] for the faith was their strength.[36]

The expectation of a coming Kingdom of God on earth, to which the faithful come through a welter of blood, can be seen to link the revolutionaries and the nonresistants.[37] The lack of historical concern in the secular sense, which is frequently noted in Anabaptist thinking,[38] was not truly nonhistorical, but rather it stemmed from a contempt for the traditional things upon which God had already passed judgment and which were soon to pass away. Their unconcern with present matters was rooted in a great vision of things to come. Hübmaier said that those who deny a visible church and say His Kingdom is not of this world are faced with the prayer, "Thy Kingdom come. . . ."[39]

---

[32] *WtQ1938*, p. 67 (Schiemer).

[33] *WtQ1938*, p. 154.

[34] Karl Holl, "Luther und die Schwärmer," section 7 of *Gesammelte Aufsatze zur Kirchengeschichte* (Tübingen: J.C.B. Mohr, 1923), I, 429. Also: "Dan warhaftig innerlich wort ist ewige und almechtige kraft Gottes gleichfermig in menschen wie in Gott, und vermag alle ding," *WtQ1938*, p. 214 (Stadler).

[35] See quotations of observers: *Beck*, p. xx.

[36] Otto Clemen, "Das Prager Manifest Thomas Münzers," XXX *ARG* (1933) 73–81, 75. It was with Joachim of Fiore that suffering became

eschatological, signifying in mysterious fashion an effective opposition to the Great Church: Ernst Benz, *op. cit.*, p. 298.

[37] It must be admitted that Menno and his associates represented to a degree a reaction against all eschatology. Nevertheless, they looked for the Thousand Years of Peace which should be ushered in with Christ's coming; *Beck*, p. xviii.

[38] John W. Johnson, "Balthazar Hubmaier and Baptist Historic Commitments," IX *Journal of Religion* (1929) 50–65, 54f.

[39] Article by Loserth, *ML* (1937) II, 353–63, 360.

Yonina Talmon

PURSUIT OF THE MILLENNIUM:
THE RELATION BETWEEN
RELIGIOUS AND SOCIAL CHANGE

MILLENARIAN movements have recently attracted the attention of scholars in different fields. Norman Cohn has studied the history of Millenarism in medieval and reformation Europe centering his attention mainly on France and Germany. Eric J. Hobsbawm devoted a considerable part of his analysis in *Primitive Rebels* to millenarian movements in Spain and Italy during the 19th and early 20th centuries. From Georges Balandier's studies we gain insight into several millenarian movements in Africa. Peter Worsley has examined and analysed the history of the millenarian movements which have proliferated in Melanesia during the last century. A more recent addition to this field is Bryan Wilson's book "Sects and Society" in which he deals with an ongoing millenarian movement in Britain. In time the movements studied range from the middle ages to the present day. The geographical spread is as great. Most important of all from a comparative point of view, these studies enable us to examine the millenarian movements in different historical settings and in different types of societies.[1]

Comparative analysis of millenarian movements has a number of distinct axes: (a) *Comparative analysis of different types of millenarian movements.* This is the main task of most of the studies discussed here. (b) *Comparative analysis of millenarian and non-millenarian religious movements.* Hobsbawm engages in such analysis when he compares the millenarian movements to the labour sects. This is the major task of Wilson's book which compares the millenarian Christadelphians to the mildly millenarian Elimites and to the non-millenarian Christian Scientists. He is concerned mainly with comparison of patterns of internal change in different types of religious sects. Comparative analysis between millenarian and non-millenarian religious groups figures to some extent in Balandier's and Worsley's studies as well. (c) *Comparative analysis of millenarian movements and non-religious political movements.* Elucidation of the relation between millenarism and modern revolutionary movements is a major theme in most of the studies in this field.

From "Pursuit of the Millennium: The Relation Between Religious and Social Change." Authorized reproduction in abridged form from the European Journal of Sociology, III (1962), 125–26, 130–48.

[1]N. Cohn, *The Pursuit of the Millennium* (New York 1957). E. J. Hobsbawm, *Primitive Rebels*

(Manchester 1959). G. Balandier, *Sociologie actuelle de l'Afrique Noire* (Paris 1955). P. Worsley, *The Trumpet Shall Sound* (London 1957). See also his "Rebellion and Revolution," *Science and Society,* XXV (1961), 26–27. B. R. Wilson, *Sects and Society* (Berkeley and Los Angeles 1961). Cf. also the special issues of *Archives de Sociologie des religions* on this problem, IV (1957) and V (1958).

The studies of millenarism discussed here present different approaches to the problem. There are considerable disagreements on basic theoretical as well as methodological matters. Yet, when juxtaposed and examined in relation to each other, it emerges that they have a certain continuity and common purpose. The most important underlying common denominator is the concern with the analysis of social change. Most of the scholars engaged in research in this field are not so much interested in millenarism as such but in the light that the study of such radical and potentially explosive religious movements may shed on the relation between religion and social change. Critical analysis of these studies reveals the development of a tentative typology and a cumulative growth of a body of hypotheses on the aetiology of origins and continuance of such movements. It seems worthwhile to elucidate and systematise the main findings and then relate them to the more general theoretical problem of analysis of change. . . .

Perhaps the most important thing about millenarism is its *attitude towards time*. It views time as a linear process which leads to a final future. There is a fullness of time and end of days which will bring about a decisive consummation of all history. The millennium is not necessarily limited to a thousand years; it symbolises the metahistorical future in which the world will be inhabited by a humanity liberated from all the limitations of human existence, redeemed from pain and transience, from fallibility and sin, thus becoming at once perfectly good and perfectly happy. The world will be utterly, completely and irrevocably changed. Radical millenarian movements regard the millennium as imminent and live in tense expectation and preparation for it.

Coupled with this emphasis on the apocalyptic future is the equally radical rejection of the present as totally evil and abysmally corrupt. The transition from the present into the final future is not a gradual process of progressive approximations to the final goal. It is a sudden and revolutionary leap onto a totally different level of existence. Sometimes this transformation is expected to occur suddenly and miraculously without a preparatory struggle. Yet more often than not we find that the new dispensation is born out of unprecedented cataclysms, disastrous upheavals and bloody calamities. The apocalyptic victory will be won by means of a prodigious and final struggle which will destroy the agents of corruption, purge the sinful world and prepare it for its final redemption. Millenarism is thus basically a merger between an historical and a non-historical conception of time. Historical change leads to a cessation of all change. Divine will is made manifest and realised in the historical process, yet its final consummation will come in a mythical millennium which is the end of all history.

Millenarism is a forward-looking, future-oriented religious ideology. However, while its attitude to the present is outrightly and radically negative, its attitude to the past is more ambivalent. The rejection of the present usually includes the near and often the more distant past as well. Millenarism usually has a strong anti-traditional component and preparation for the millennium has often entailed a ritualised overthrow of traditional norms. Primitive millenarian movements have engaged in a breaking of hallowed taboos and in a desecration of their most valued religious symbols, thus dissociating themselves from their traditional culture. Their main concern was often not the perpetuation or revival of their indigenous tradition but the birth of a new order. Yet this strong anti-past orientation is often mitigated when the millennium is envisaged as a return of a mythical golden age. When the mil-

lennium is regarded as a paradise regained, those elements of tradition which
are viewed as embedded in it, become
also components of the new order. By
establishing a connection between the
meta-historical past and the meta-historical future, the millenarian movement can be radically change-oriented
yet incorporate traditional elements in
its view of the final future.

Another important characteristic of
millenarian movements is their view of
salvation as a *merger of the spiritual with
the terrestrial*. The millenarian view of
salvation is transcendent and immanent
at the same time. The heavenly city is to
appear on earth. It is in this world that
the saints, the elect, or the chosen people
will experience the blessing, not as
ethereal saints. Millenarism offers not an
otherworldly hope but the fulfilment of
divine purpose in a new universe and a
new social order. This terrestrial emphasis
is more or less evident in all the millenarian movements. In its crudest and
more extreme form we encounter it in the
Cargo Cults. The core of these cults is a
belief that the culture hero, the devil or
the spirit of the dead will return in some
mechanical means of transportation such
as aeroplanes, lorries or ships, loaded
with a cargo of imported goods. The
cargo has been made in heaven for the
use of the natives, but the white men have
diverted it from them. The return of the
cargo to its rightful owners will bring
about an era of universal plenty and
happiness. The natives will be liberated
from alien domination once and for all
and will be completely exempt from all
the ills of human existence. Yet even in
such a down-to-earth and materialistic
conception of the millennium there is a
more or less strong spiritual ingredient.
The new order will be also a new moral
order based on justice, peace and cooperation.

Closely connected with the former
characteristic is the *collective orientation* of
millenarism. The aim of millenarian
movements is not only the salvation of
individual souls but the erection of a
heavenly city for a chosen people. The
millenarian message is directed to an
already existing group or calls for a
formation of new groups of elect. It
views these groups as divinely appointed
bearers of the good tiding and calls on
them to prepare for the imminent advent.
The group is more or less collectively
responsible and will enjoy the wonderful
future awaiting it as a group.

What is the *role of the group in bringing
about the advent*? There are many variations in this respect. Movements of this
type range from the fairly passive and
quietist on the one hand, to the extremely
activist and aggressive on the other.
There are certain elements in the millenarian ideology which work against an
outrightly active definition of the role of
the follower. The followers of these
movements are not makers of the revolution; they expect it to be brought about
miraculously from above. Ultimately,
initiative and actual power to bring
about change rest with divine powers.
All millenarian movements share a
fundamental vagueness about the actual
way in which the new order will be
brought about, expecting it to happen
somehow by direct divine intervention.
In many millenarian movements the part
of the people before the change is to
gather together, to watch the signs of the
inevitable advent, to engage in measures
of ritual preparation and purify themselves. Yet there is a strong activist
militant ingredient in the millenarian
ideology which more often than not
outweighs the passive elements in it.
Most of the radical millenarian movements define the role of the follower
much more actively. In such movements,
the believers have the power to hasten
and retard salvation. In some cases the
advent cannot come to pass without the
active help of the elect. Since the vision

of redemption is both transcendent and terrestrial, paving the way for it often entails the employment of both ritual and secular measures. Since the onset of the millennium is more often than not viewed as entailing a final struggle, the followers pit themselves against the powers of evil. The hope of a total and imminent salvation which will be brought about by divine powers with the active support and help of the elect throws such movements into spells of hectic and often rebellious activity. The millenarian vision instils in the movement a sense of extreme urgency and a dedication to an all-embracing purpose. Every minute and every deed count and everything must be sacrificed to the cause. The followers are driven to stake everything and spare nothing since their aim is no less than the final solution of all human problems. It would seem that the combination of the historical and the meta-historical in the millennial time conception, the vision of the unification of the transcendent and the terrestrial in a completely transformed and holy social order, the merger between individual and social destinies, coupled with a total rejection of the existing order and a view of an imminent final struggle have a powerful revolutionary potential. No wonder that in most of the movements described in these studies the millenarian ideology has precipitated and instigated active revolt against the established authorities. Comparative analysis seems to indicate that, generally speaking, the more extremely millenarian a movement is the more activist it is. As Worsley has pointed out, there seems to be a correlation between the time conception of each movement and its position in the *passivity-activity continuum*. Movements which view the millennium as imminent and have a total and vivid conception of redemption are, on the whole, much more activist than movements which expect it to happen at some remote date and consequently tend to have a more partial and rather pale conception of the millennium. It would seem that truly great expectations and a sense of immediacy enhance the orientation to active rebellion while postponement of the critical date and lesser expectation breed passivity and quietism.

This generalisation holds more or less true when examined in the material on pre-modern and primitive movements. It has to be modified to some extent with regard to such movements in modern societies. The Christadelphians have a radical millenarian ideology. They live in tense expectation of an imminent and total redemption. They rigorously oppose the social order as totally depraved and view its present difficulties with vindictiveness. Yet their attitudes are not translated into direct action against it. They defied the authorities in the matter of conscription to the army and stuck to their opposition to service in the armed forces. However, they did not oppose the authorities on other matters and did not engage in active rebellion against the established order. They have kept aloof from the world. Tense, impatient and vindictive, they await the divinely appointed time of its downfall. The same seems to be more or less true for other modern millenarian movements such as the Seventh Day Adventist and Jehovah's Witnesses.[2] Wilson hints that modern millenarian movements are less rebellious than their counterparts elsewhere mainly because there are very slender chances for successful rebellion in a modern society. He feels, however, that internal pressures towards militancy are so strong in such a movement that were a revolt at all feasible the Christadelphians would have pitted themselves

[2] Jehovah's Witnesses have a more extreme rejection of the existing social order and have engaged in a more active struggle against the authorities. Cf. R. Pike, *Jehovah's Witnesses* (London 1954), also H. H. Stroup, *The Jehovah's Witnesses* (New York 1945).

against the social order and tried to overthrow it.

Most millenarian movements are *messianic*. Redemption is brought about by a messiah who mediates between the divine and the human. Most important, of course, is the figure of Jesus, but there are other figures as well. In many of the medieval movements redemption is brought about by the sleeping monarch who comes to life again and rescues his people. In primitive societies, the messiah is the culture hero or a departed leader who was persecuted and put to death by the authorities. Often it is a multiple messiah seen in the form of the spirits of the dead ancestors. Another important mediator between the divine and the movement is the *leader*. Inspired leaders who claimed to be appointed by divine powers have played an extremely important role in these movements. Sometimes these prophetic figures move from mere prophecy to become messianic incarnations of divine leadership, but more often than not the figure of the messiah and the figure of the leader remain distinct. Leaders act as precursors of the messiah and as his prophets by announcing the good tidings. They develop their special brand of millenarism by emphasising millenarian elements in their traditional culture and by seizing upon millenarian elements in the cultures which impinge on them. They interpret the millennial traditions and vulgarise them, combining disparate elements and systematising. They supply their followers with secondary exegesis when their hopes fail to materialise. They teach the new ritual and preach the new moral code. They organise their followers and lead them in preparation for the advent.

Inspired and energetic leaders have played such an important role in some of the millenarian movements that when they lost their drive or died, the movements they initiated and organised disintegrated almost immediately. Yet it should be stressed that in many cases leaders function as a symbolic focus of identification rather than as sources of authority and initiative. In some regions, millenarism is an endemic force and when it reaches a flash-point it may seize upon any available figure. The initiative in such case comes primarily from the community which sometimes almost imposes the leadership position on its leader. Some of the leaders are in fact insignificant and their elevation to such a position seems to be accidental—they happened to be there and fulfilled an urgent need for a mediator.[3] That the function of leadership is sometimes primarily symbolic is clearly seen in the cases of movements with absent leaders. In some notable instances the influence of a leader and his integrating power have increased enormously after he left or was removed from his scene of operations. Death, imprisonment or mysterious absence have increased their stature and enhanced their authority. Only when absent did they begin to loom large as powerful prophetic figures.

Often there is also not just one charismatic leader but a multiple leadership. First, we find in a number of instances a division of leadership between the organiser who is concerned with practical matters and the inspired prophet. Secondly, the movements are sometimes based on loyalty to leaders on the local level and do not have an overall leadership. Moreover, the strong fissiparous tendencies which operate in most of these movements work against attempts at unification of leadership. Millenarian movements suffer from frequent cessation and fission partly because they base their recruitment of their leaders on inspiration. A revelatory basis of recruit-

[3]Cf. K. Burridge, *Mambu* (London 1960), pp. 203–207, 254–259; also his "Cargo cult activity in Tangu," *Oceania*, XXIV (1954), 241–244.

ment facilitates the emergence of numerous leaders and prophets since many may claim divine inspiration. That this is only a partial explanation is suggested by the fact that millenarian movements seem to suffer from fissiparous tendencies more than religious movements with an equally inspirational leadership. It seems that millenarian movements are particularly prone to fissions because they preach rebellion against authority and probably attract rebellious non-conformist and contentious people. The denial of authority seems to be a factor in perpetuating internecine strife. The fissiparous tendency is particularly strong in radical but non-active movements. The attempt to arouse and canalise rebellious feelings but to postpone active rebellion until some future occasion resulted in the case of the Christadelphians in the turning of rebelliousness inwards and in a proliferation of leaders.

Organisationally, millenarian movements vary from the amorphous and ephemeral movement with a cohesive core of leaders and ardent followers and a large ill-defined body of followers, to the fairly stable segregated and exclusive sect-like group. The organisational form of a more or less ephemeral movement is, however, more typical. This is no doubt closely related to the nature of the millenarian message. The promise of an imminent and total redemption awakes enthusiastic hopes and sweeps a large number of followers into the movement. However, its source of strength is also its source of weakness—by promising an imminent delivery and sometimes even fixing a definite date, it brings its own downfall. When the appointed day or period passes without any spectacular happenings or with not the right apocalyptic events, the movement faces a serious crisis which often disrupts and even disperses it completely.

The crisis of non-materialisation of the millennium is a severe one but it need not always lead to disruption.[4] In some notable cases the failures of prophecy did not cause disaffection and immediate disintegration. The commitment to the promise of a millennium was so intense that the shock of temporary disappointment could not shatter it. Paradoxically, non-materialization was followed in these cases by a burst of vigorous proselytizing activities and drew the believers together. These movements are sometimes able to develop a body of exegesis which accounts for the delay and keeps the hope alive. A frequent solution is the switch from a short-range radical millenarism to a long-range and more or less attenuated version of it. Another solution is refraining from fixing any definite date but still keeping the hope of a speedy delivery in full force. Wilson's study of the Christadelphians proves that such a solution is feasible and can work for a considerable length of time without serious modification of the original doctrine. Hobsbawm shows that radical millenarism has become a permanent though periodically dormant force in Andalusia for more than seventy years, suffering reversal after reversal yet flaring up again and again. The recurrent revival of the movement follows an almost cyclical pattern; the millennial outbursts follow one another after approximately a ten-year interval. Similar though not as cyclical patterns of disruption and revival can be observed in the medieval material as well as in Melanesia and Africa. Sometimes there is a hidden continuity between the different phases of the movement. When the millenarian movement suffers a reverse, it goes under cover. It remains underground until it sees a better chance for its struggle, repeatedly hiding or going out into the open but retaining its radical millenarism. It should be stressed,

[4]See L. Festinger, H. W. Riecken and S. Schachter, *When Prophecy Fails* (Minneapolis 1956).

however, that often there is hardly any
direct connection between what may
seem to be recurrent phases of the self-
same movement. Continuation of similar
conditions often breed similar yet independent reactions. In many cases, there
is no direct influence or any continuity
of either tradition or personnel between
the different movements.

Most millenarian movements are
highly emotional. With the exception of the
Christadelphians who discourage emotional release in any form and emphasise
exegesis, exhortation and doctrine, almost all the other movements involve
wild and very often frenzied emotional
display. In many instances we encounter
hysterical and paranoid phenomena—
mass possession, trances, fantasies. The
emotional tension manifests itself in
motor phenomena such as twitching,
shaking and convulsions which have
swiftly spread through wide areas.
Closely related to the high emotional
tension is a strong antinomian tendency.
Millenarian movements deliberately
break accepted taboos and overthrow
hallowed norms. They engage in many
ritualised forms of sin and sacrilege.
Sexual aberrations in the form of either
extreme asceticism or sexual excess are
very common as well. There is often
unbridled expression of aggression.
Members of such movements have swept
over the country, devastating, burning
and massacring on their way. Sometimes aggression is turned inwards: the
members destroy their own property and
even commit mass suicide.

What are the *conditions which give rise
to* such movements and in which *social
groups are they anchored?* The data clearly
support the frequently posited relationship between socio-economic conditions
and religious expression. Radical millenarism found support in all levels of
society at one time or another but
essentially it is a religion of the *deprived
groups*—oppressed peasants, the poorest

of the poor in cities and towns, populations of colonial countries. The millenarian hope usually flares up as a
reaction to particularly severe hardships
and suffering. Many of the outbursts of
millenarism took place against a background of disaster—plagues, devastating
fires, recurrent long droughts that were
the dire lot of the peasants, slumps that
caused widespread unemployment and
poverty and calamitous wars.[5] Repeated
historical experiences of disaster, living
under constant threat of hunger, illness
and untimely and cruel death led to
rejection not only of actual history but
of history as such. The fantastic hope of
total redemption was often born out of
abysmal despair.

Yet there is much more to it than just
that. The analysis clearly shows that the
development of millenarism cannot be
interpreted only in terms of an extremely
severe deprivation. The predisposing
factor was often not so much any particular hardship but a markedly *uneven
relation between expectations and the means
of their satisfaction.*[6] In Cohn's and
Hobsbawm's material it is predominantly
the inability to satisfy traditional expectations. In medieval Europe millenarism
affected mainly people who, because of
the pressure of surplus population were
cut off from the traditional order and
were unable to satisfy wants instilled in
them by it. The insidious onslaught of
the developing capitalistic order on a
backward and isolated peasant economy
created the same basic difficulty in Spain
and Italy centuries later, although there
it affected not only people who were cut

[5]See B. Barber, Acculturation and messianic
movements, *American Sociological Review,* VI
(1941), 663–668 and D. F. Aberle, The Prophet
Dance and reactions to white contact, *Southwestern J. of Anthropology,* XV (1959), 77–83.

[6]On the relation between deprivation and
frustration, see R. Linton, Nativistic Movements, *American Anthropologist,* VL (1943),
230–240. Cf. also R. Firth, The Theory of Cargo
Cult: A note on Tikopia, *Man* (1955), No. 142.

off from their rural base but the rural community as a whole. We encounter the same type of frustration in primitive societies as well but there it increasingly becomes not so much a problem of the lack of means to supply traditional wants but the development of a set of new expectations. The encounter with modern societies engenders enormously inflated expectations without a concomitant and adequate development of institutional means for their supply. This discrepancy creates a void which is often bridged by millenarian hope. That frustration may be much more important than actual hardship becomes evident when we consider the fact that millenarian unrest was caused in certain parts of New Guinea not by any direct contact with the white men. Though there were hardly any changes in the status quo indirect contacts brought about changed expectation and acute frustration. It should be stressed that in many cases millenarian outbursts were caused not by a deterioration of conditions but by a limited amelioration which raised new hopes and new expectations but left them largely unfulfilled.

The incongruity between ends and means is not the only source of frustration. Much of the deep dissatisfaction stems from incongruities and difficulties in the realm of *regulation of ends*. Quick change and encounter with radically different systems of values result in a more or less severe cultural disintegration. When the impinging cultural influences penetrate into the traditional setting and gain a foothold there they often undermine the effectiveness of traditional norms as guides of action. Even the most central traditional values cease to be self-evident and sacred. In many spheres there are contradictory claims and mutually exclusive obligations. Since conflicting claims tend to neutralise and annul each other, the impinging cultural influences often

weaken and even destroy the indigenous tradition without substituting a new system of values, thus causing confusion and anomie. When the alien culture is that of a more prestigious upper class or that of a colonial ruling class, it is often willingly or unwillingly, consciously or unconsciously, acknowledged as superior. This causes much self-doubt and even self-hatred.[7] Wilson stresses quite rightly that the sense of cultural deprivation and the quest for cultural reorientation are sometimes more important than economic frustration. Millenarism is often born out of the search for a tolerably coherent system of values, a new cultural identity and regained sense of dignity and self-respect.

Another important factor operative in the emergence of millenarism was found to be *social isolation* brought about by the disruption of traditional group ties. Cohn points out that millenarism did not appeal much to people who were firmly embedded in well-integrated kinship groupings and effectively organised and protected in cohesive local communities. The people most exposed to the new pressures and therefore more prone to millenarism were the mal-integrated and isolated who could find no assured and recognised place in cohesive primary groups. The importance of a breakdown of kinship and local groupings is a major theme in the analysis of pre-modern, modern and primitive societies as well.

Yet even the combination of such factors as severe deprivation, severe frustration and extreme isolation does not supply us with a full answer to our question. The most important contribution of Balandier, Worsley and Hobsbawm to this analysis lies in their insist-

---

[7]For the description and analysis of this aspect of the growth of millenarism, see K. Burridge, *op. cit.* pp. 246–254; also Z. W. Werblowsky, Messianism in Primitive Societies, *The Listener,* LXIV (1958), p. 684.

ence that millenarism is essentially a *pre-political phenomenon*. In primitive societies it appears mainly in so-called stateless segmentary societies which have rudimentary political institutions or lack any specialised political institutions altogether. When it appears in societies with fairly developed political institutions it appeals to strata which are politically passive and have no experience of political organisation and no access to political power. Instances of such non-political strata in societies with a more or less developed political structure are the peasants in feudal societies, the peasants in isolated and backward areas in modern societies, marginal and politically passive elements in the working class, recent immigrants and mal-integrated and politically inarticulate minority groups. Sometimes millenarism is post-political, appearing after the downfall of a fairly developed political system. The collapse of an entire political system by a crushing defeat and the shattering of tribal or national hopes have sometimes led to widespread millenarism. It is the lack of effective organisation, the absence of regular institutionalised ways of voicing their grievances and pressing their claims that pushes such groups to a millenarian solution. Not being able to cope with their difficulties by concerted political action, they turn to millenarism. According to this analysis, millenarism is born out of great distress coupled with political helplessness.

That the combination of all the necessary predisposing factors will actually lead to millenarism and not result in the development of other types of religious ideology is ultimately conditioned also by the type of prevalent religious beliefs. Clearly, religions in which history has no meaning whatsoever and religions which have a cyclical repetitive conception of time are not conducive to millenarism. Apocalyptic

eschatology is essentially alien to religions of a philosophical and mystical cast which turn the eye of the believer towards eternity where there is no movement and no process. This is certainly the case with some nature and cosmic religions which live in the framework of ever-recurring repetitive cycles of rise and decline.[8] Another important factor operative in this sphere is a "this-worldly" emphasis. Religions with a radical, other-worldly orientation which puts all the emphasis on the hereafter or on a purely spiritual and totally non-terrestrial salvation do not give rise to the vision of the kingdom of God on earth. This explains why there is apparently no apocalyptic tradition in Hinduism and why it has not occupied an important place in Buddhism.

On the whole, millenarism appeared mainly in countries which had direct or indirect contact with the Judeo-Christian messianic traditions. Christianity itself originally derived its initial élan from radical millenarism and, although the millenarian ideology was reinterpreted and relegated to a secondary position, it still played an important part in the history of Europe. The Christian missions were the most important agency for the worldwide spreading of millenarism. Several fundamentalist sects played a particularly important role in this process, but millenarism appeared also in cases where the main contact with it was mediated by less apocalyptic versions of Christianity. The millenarism is reinstated to its central position by a process of selection and reinterpretation.

When millenarism developed in primitive societies it was influenced by pre-existing religious concepts as well. Some primitive mythologies contain eminently suitable beliefs such as the expectation of the future return of the

[8]Cf. M. Eliade, *Le mythe de l'éternel retour* (Paris 1949).

culture hero or the idea of the return of all the dead as a prelude to a messianic era.[9] It should be stressed, however, that these themes appeared in a rather embryonic form and did not occupy a particularly important position in primitive mythology. They were developed, reinterpreted and elaborated into full-fledged millenarian conceptions only under the impact of the new situation and after the contact with Christianity. The pre-existing primitive conceptions affected the development of millenarism in yet another way. The prevalence of millenarism in Melanesia and the importance of expectations of cargo in its view of the millennium are, it would seem, due to the strong and almost exclusive emphasis which the indigenous religion puts on ritual activity oriented to the acquisition of material goods.

What are the *functions of millenarism?* How does it answer the needs of its followers and what does it contribute to the strata and societies where it appears? In this sphere we find different interpretations and different emphases. Cohn's approach to this particular problem is predominantly psychological. He regards millenarism as primarily an outlet for extreme anxiety and as a delusion of despair. He treats it as a collective paranoid fantasy born out of irrational fears and fantastic expectations. He feels that the megalomaniac view of oneself as wholly good, abominably persecuted yet assured of final triumph, the attribution of demonic power to the adversary, the inability to accept the ineluctable limitations of human existence, constitute the unmistakable syndrome of paranoia. The irrational and hysterical emotionality, the destructive and often suicidal activities seem to

him clear symptoms of mental illness. Hobsbawm and Worsley reject this psychological interpretation and press for a more sociological approach. Worsley strongly objects to the description of these movements as irrational and tries to prove that if we take into consideration the social conditions and the cultural milieu which gave rise to them they cease to be bizarre and fantastic and become fully understandable and not illogical reactions. The highly emotional and aggressive behaviour is related to the revolutionary nature of the movement which strives to overthrow the old order and establish a new one. The severing of old ties and the rejection of old norms demand an enormous effort and engender a deep sense of guilt, hence much of the hysteria and the aggression. Many of the antinomian manifestations are a deliberate overthrow of the accepted norms, not in order to throw overboard all morality but in order to create a new brotherhood and a new morality.[10] The paranoid manifestations stem from the contradictions inherent in the situation in which such movements appear and from the difficulties inherent in their revolutionary task and not so much from psychological aberrations of individual followers. Wilson treats the sociological and psychological interpretations as complementary but he too stresses the situational strains rather than the abnormality of the followers. Wilson supplies us here with a careful and balanced analysis of functions versus dysfunctions on three different levels. He distinguishes between the functions and dysfunctions of millenarism for the individual follower, for the movement and for society as a whole. By and large, he feels that millenarism has strong disruptive poten-

---

[9]M. I. Pereira de Queiroz, L'influence du milieu social interne sur les mouvements messianiques brésiliens, *Archives de sociologie des religions,* 5 (1958), pp. 3–29; ID., Classifications des messianismes brésiliens, *ibid.* pp. 111–120.

[10]The most sophisticated and rigorous analysis of the development and functions of antinomian ritual in a messianic movement will be found in G. Scholem, *Main Trends in Jewish Mysticism* (New York 1946), pp. 287–324.

tialities. While it supplies the individual followers with strong identification with a cohesive movement and gives him hope for imminent delivery, it creates serious difficulties in the sphere of canalisation of aggression. Such movements always face the crisis of non-materialisation and suffer from the turning of the aggression of its members inwards which manifests itself in numerous fissions. A millenarian movement can counteract more or less successfully the disintegrating tendencies inherent in its religious ideology for a long time but this is achieved at the cost of considerable malintegration from the point of view of the total society. Christadelphianism institutionalises deviant tendencies without being able to bring about actual change.

A far more positive evaluation of millenarism emerges from the studies of Balandier, Worsley and Hobsbawm. The main hypothesis which ·underlies these studies is that millenarism is an activating and unifying force in hitherto politically passive and segregated groups and that in recent and contemporary history it has been an important *precursor of political awakening and a forerunner of political organisation*. Such functions were performed also by other types of religious movements, but radical millenarism is much more potent in this respect. The main effect of the millenarian movement is to overcome divisions and join previously isolated or even hostile groups together. Though faced by the same common problems and sometimes even sharing the same culture, these groups cannot act as a unified force except on a localised and ad hoc basis. When confronted by crisis and by necessity to take concerted action, they are compelled to create a new unity which transcends kinship and local loyalties. Millenarism helps to draw into activity and organise masses of people on a large scale almost simultaneously. Conversion acts as a sudden overpower-

ing awakening. It brings about a new awareness and a change in men's attitude to life, shaking them out of their apathy. Since millenarism has a strong collective orientation and is also activity-centered, this conversion does not lead them only inwards to repentance and meditation but draws them outwards to involvement and activity in the movement. Millenarism usually evokes exceptionally intense commitment and fervour and, since exaltation eases communication, millenarism expands swiftly almost as if by contagion, crosscutting and breaking down local barriers. It widens the horizon of identification and participation and creates wider unities.

The revolutionary nature of millenarism makes it a very potent agent of change. It demands a fundamental transformation and not just improvement and reform. The radical versions of millenarism incite the followers to active anticipation of the advent and even to active revolt. It invests their struggle with the aura of a final cosmic drama. It interprets present difficulties as signs of the beginning of the end and views every small success as proof of invincibility and as portents of future triumph. It arouses truly great hopes and therefore can make equally great demands on its followers. By promising complete salvation, it is able to liberate formerly untapped energies and generate a supreme effort without which no major break with the existing order can be achieved.

Millenarism helps to bring about a breakthrough to the future. Yet its special efficacy lies also in its power to bridge future and past. We have already pointed out that inasmuch as the end of days is somehow connected with the mythical beginning, the vision of the apocalyptic future includes certain traditional elements.[11] Even the most anti-

---

[11]Cf. A. Wallace, Revitalisation Movements, *American Anthropologist*, LVIII, (1956), 264–280.

traditional version of millenarism is in fact a creative synthesis between the new and old. Even when rejecting and transcending the old, it reinstates important aspects of it. It constantly reinterprets such traditional elements and places them in a new context. It invests the old with new meanings while the new elements may often have traditional connotations. Even when it negates the content of tradition it does not invalidate the principles by which truth is traditionally sought and preserved.

While bridging the gap between future and past, millenarism also connects religion and politics. Operating in societies or in strata completely dominated by religion, millenarism couches its political message in the familiar and powerful language and images of traditional religion employing and revitalising its age old symbols. In such milieus recruitment to new political goals is often possible only when expressed in religious terms. In many cases it is also the only means of establishing cooperation between leaders and followers. Millenarism provides an important mechanism of recruitment of new leaders. It opens up new avenues of ascent and develops a set of new statuses. Although some of the new leaders derive their authority from their central or marginal position in the traditional order, more often than not their authority stems at least in part from their comparatively superior knowledge and greater experience in non-traditional spheres of activity and has no traditional legitimation. Millenarism helps them to establish their authority. Externalisation and sanctification of the source of authority puts the leader above sectional loyalties and helps him to avoid sectional discord. By projecting their authority to the supernatural sphere they objectify and legitimise it. Millenarism helps the leader in this respect in yet another way. It closes the gap which often develops

between a more "advanced" and more politically minded leader and the more traditional mass of his followers. In many cases he cannot hope to reach his followers and really communicate with them if he does not express his protest in popular and widely understood religious terms. In some cases, the movement is started by an "advanced" and politically minded leader, but when its political ideology reaches the masses, it is spontaneously interpreted in religious terms. The best example of such a process is the development of Amicalism described by Balandier.

The resort to a religious appeal is sincere and non-manipulative in most cases. During the first stages of reorganisation most of the leaders have got little experience in the political sphere and cannot express their striving except in a religious form. During later phases of development the resort to religion may sometimes become a conscious propagandist and organisational device. The leader clothes his political ideology in religious terms because he realises that this is the only way to mobilise the masses. He often emphasises the religious components of his ideology also for the purpose of hiding his real intentions from the authorities.

Millenarism is thus essentially a *connecting link* between pre-political and political movements. It lubricates the passage from premodern religious revolt to a full-fledged revolutionary movement. The process of transition can be actually traced in both primitive and recent premodern movements. There are two main distinct avenues of transition. In some cases the movements gradually change their nature, slowly becoming less ritualised and more secular in emphasis. These movements start to pay much more attention to purely political and economic goals. They attach far more importance to strategy and tactics and organise more effectively.

Yet they do not sever their ties with their millenarian tradition and continue to derive much of their revolutionary zeal from its promise of final salvation. Another major direction of development entails the complete absorption of the millenarian movement within a secular revolutionary movement.[12] When the millenarian movement fails to achieve its goals and disintegrates, its disappointed followers turn to secular revolutionism, embracing an extreme and militant version of either nationalist or socialist ideology. The millenarian movement serves in such cases as a kind of preparatory school for revolutionaries. When they "graduate" from it they are ready to go over to militant secular movements.

It should be stressed that the hypothesis which posits that millenarism functions as an integrating force and as forerunner of political action is borne out only in material on the contemporary history of Melanesia and Africa on the one hand and in the material on the recent history of Italy on the other. Most of the medieval movements were ephemeral outbursts and only a few of them had strong formative powers and lasting social consequences. Since they had little chance to change the massive structure of medieval society, most of these revolutionary revivals short-circuited and disappeared. Material on the American Indians suggests that radical millenarism has played a limited and largely disrup-

tive role there.[13] Any movement with a revolutionary potential was quickly suppressed, leaving an aftermath of disillusion and disorganisation.[14] The task of rehabilitating and integrating the Indians was performed mainly by reformist cults oriented to peaceful accommodation to the white society.[15] Membership in millenarian movements in modern societies functions more as a competing alternative to membership in militant secular movements rather than as a preparation for it. All these movements reject secular movements and enjoin on their members to keep away from them. It is clear that the actual functions which any millenarian movement performs in any given situation depend on the degree of differentiation between the religious and political sphere in the society in which it operates and on the chances it has to engage in active political action and carry out a successful revolution. Much work needs still to be done before we can arrive at generally valid generalisation in this sphere.

All the studies discussed here regard millenarism as in one sense or another a prototype of modern revolutionary movements.[16]

This is demonstrated and justified in four different ways:

a) Secular revolutionary movements differ greatly from other types of secular

[12]On the relations between millenarism and nationalist movements in primitive societies, see W. E. Mühlmann, Chiliasmus, Nativismus, Nationalismus, *Verhandlungen des 14. Deutschen Soziologentages* (Stuttgart 1959); G. Balandier, Messianismes et nationalismes en Afrique noire, *Cahiers internationaux de sociologie,* XIV (1953), 41–65; also J. Guiart, Naissance et avortement d'un messianisme, *Archives de sociologie des religions, 7* (1959), 3–44; ID., Cargo Cults and Modern Political Evolution in Melanesia, *South Pacific,* V (1951).

[13]See E. Vogt, The American Indian—Transition, Reformation and Accommodation, *American Anthropologist,* LVIII (1956), pp. 249–264.

[14]C. Du Bois, The 1870 Ghost Dance, *University of California Anthropological Records,* III (1939–1946), 1–152.

[15]Cf. G. Barnett, *Indian Shakers and Messianic Cults of the Pacific Northwest* (Carbondale 1957); see also S. Slotkin, *The Peyote Religion* (Glencoe 1958).

[16]It is significant that this is also a major theme in a number of recent studies on history of modern social and political ideas. See A. Salomon, *The Tyranny of Progress* (New York 1955), and J. L. Talmon, *Political Messianism* (London 1960).

political movements and have in a certain sense a semireligious character. Their world view is total and all embracing. It purports to solve basic problems of meaning and trace and interpret the unfolding of world history. The revolutionary ideology is a matter of ultimate concern and utmost seriousness; it demands from the followers unquestioning faith and unconditional loyalty. It is therefore all-pervasive and defines every aspect of life. Much like the great religious movements of the past, secular revolutionism has stirred deeply large masses of people evoking intense fervor and dedication to its cause.

b) There is an even more marked affinity between these political movements and millenarism. Secular revolutionism shares with millenarism the apocalyptic element—like millenarism it looks forward to a total and imminent realization of its ideals. Millenarism shares with secular revolutionism its collective and terrestrial emphasis as · well as the radical condemnation of the existing social order. Both the religious and secular versions of revolutionism reject gradual and peaceful improvement and prepare for a final decisive struggle. Millenarism has a more passive definition of the role of the follower, but, by and large, we find in both versions of revolutionism a potent merger between inevitability and freedom which assures the revolutionaries of their final triumph, yet endows them with some power to hasten or retard salvation.

c) There is in addition a partial similarity in the conditions which bring about such movements. Like millenarism, secular revolutionism is brought about by a combination of severe deprivation, acute frustration and disintegration of primary groups.

d) Last but not least, there are direct connections and a continuity of tradition between religious and secular revolu-

tionism. Cohn assumes such undercurrent of continuity without proving his contention systematically. Balandier, Worsley and Hobsbawm set about substantiating this thesis by actually tracing direct transitions from one to the other.[17]

To be sure, this type of analysis highlights similarities and glosses over differences which are, in many cases, as great and as important as the affinities. It is certainly a far cry, for instance, to equate communism and Nazism and treat them as one and the same thing for the purpose of comparison with millenarism. Cohn states repeatedly that differences between Nationalist and Socialist revolutionism are largely immaterial in this context. There is little to be gained from pushing such analogies too far. As noted above, the contention of direct continuity between religious and secular revolutionism was borne out only in part of the material. There is no doubt that in many cases religious and secular revolutionism are independent of each other. The affinities stem from the similarity of the predisposing factors and from the dynamics of the common revolutionary position rather than from any direct interchange of ideas or transfer of members from one to the other.

The analogy with modern revolutionism is employed for different purposes. Cohn uses it primarily in order to underline the essentially primitive, mythical and menacing nature of modern revolutionary movements. Worsley and Hobsbawm use it in order to uncover the modern elements in premodern movements. Behind this difference of approach there is a fundamentally different evalua-

[17]See also H. Desroche, Messianismes et utopies; note sur les origines du socialisme occidental, *Archives de sociologie des religions,* 8 (1959), pp. 31–46; Micromillénarismes et communautarisme en Amérique du Nord du xviiᵉ au xixᵉ siècle, *Archives de sociologie des religions,* 4 (1957), pp. 57–92.

tion of millenarism. Cohn views millenarism as a dangerous collective
madness, as an essentially irrational,
destructive and disruptive force. Both
Worsley and Hobsbawm stress its underlying realism and its inherent though
hidden rationality. They view it as a
primarily positive and constructive force.

So far we have summed up and analysed the main conclusions arrived at by
recent studies of millenarism. We shall
conclude this review by a short critical
examination of the theoretical assumptions on which these studies are based
and the wider theoretical implications of
their findings. There are different degrees
of involvement with theoretical problems here. Cohn is not at all concerned
with general problems of sociological
theory; he just makes a limited use of
certain analytical tools supplied to him
by sociology. He uses these analytical
tools competently and imaginatively, but
does not attempt to deal with his problems on a higher level of abstraction.
Balandier has a keen interest in the theory
of change, but he too is primarily concerned with the application of general
theory to his special case rather than with
the examination of what his study has
contributed to general theory. The other
studies dealt with here are more theoretically oriented. The main purpose of
Wilson's study is a critical examination of
certain general propositions on the
dynamics of sect development. He
specifies the conditions which facilitate
resistance to denominationalising tendencies and analyses the mechanisms
which help the established sect to
resist external and internal pressures and
preserve its initial ideology without
serious modifications. Hobsbawm's and
Worsley's attempts to deal with problems of change are less systematic but
far more ambitious. They examine the
relations between religious and social
change within a large-scale evolutionary

framework concentrating their attention
on the transition from premodern to
modern society.

The analytical tools used by Worsley
and Hobsbawm are mainly those forged
by Marxian sociology. This is by no
means a rigid and simplicist application
of Marxian theory. The theoretical
analysis is, on the whole, subtle and
flexible. It is often enriched and modified
by incorporation of modes of analysis
and ideas developed by non-Marxian
sociologists. If anything, these studies
prove that a neo-Marxian theory provides
powerful tools for the analysis of change.
These studies also make manifest, however, some of its inherent limitations. By
and large, religion is treated here as an
ideology which just expresses concrete
socio-economic interests rather than
moulds and directs them. It is primarily
an instrument in the political struggle.
Its "pie in the sky" or mystical versions
act as opiate to the people and help to
preserve the status quo. Its this-worldly,
activist and future-oriented versions act
as expressions of the drive towards
change. On the theoretical level, religion
is denied any independent causal significance and there is no adequate analysis
of internal, partly independent processes
in the religious sphere.[18] Both Hobsbawm and Worsley tend to deal with conditions and consequences of millenarism
rather than with development of its
doctrine and ritual. This is particularly
noticeable in Hobsbawm's book. Hobsbawm is not much concerned and rather
bored with the finer details of the
theological analysis of millenarism.
Sometimes he cannot hide his impatience
and distaste for the misplaced ingenuity

---

[18]The importance of treating religion as a
partly independent sphere is fully demonstrated
by G. Geertz, Ritual and Social Change: A
Javanese Example, *American Anthropologist,*
LIX (1957), 32–55. See also his *Religion of Java*
(Glencoe 1960).

that goes into building up elaborate universes of symbolism. Worlsey devotes a certain amount of attention to the symbols employed by the cargo cults and sometimes manages to supply us with a perceptive analysis of the different levels of meaning of these symbols but his treatment of this matter only occasionally approaches the subtlety of Cohn's analysis. Both Hobsbawm and Worsley recognize the influence of predisposing religious factors on the development of millenarism but tend to minimize their importance. Their analysis of the relation between hardship and deprivation is not quite balanced. They have a strong tendency to overemphasize the importance of severe hardship and disregard the frustrating effects of partial and discontinued amelioration. Their analysis is sometimes vitiated also by construing religion as an intentionally manipulated propagandist and organizational device. Now and then there is an almost imperceptible shift from imputation of latent functions by the investigator to imputation of semi-conscious distortion and disguise by the actors. Neither of the authors discussed here realizes the full implications of the fact that millenarism combines a historical with a mythical time conception. The assumption that a future orientation and a past orientation are mutually exclusive and incompatible vitiates Worsley's just criticism of the characterization of millenarian movements as "nativistic." Millenarian movements are forward-looking not backwards-looking movements, yet their vision of the future usually contains many reinterpreted elements of native tradition. It is precisely this combination of a radical revolutionary position with traditionalism which accounts for the widespread appeal of these movements. It is because these movements merge a future orientation with either an overt or covert past

orientation that they are such potent agents of change.

Both Worsley's and Hobsbawm's studies are based on evolutionary assumptions. A critical reappraisal of evolutionary theory is long due and it is therefore a pity that these assumptions are not clearly defined and are used rather uncritically.[19] In spite of the fact that Hobsbawm's book hinges on the distinction between the archaic and the modern forms of rebellion, he does not define these concepts clearly. Even the basic distinction between the contemporary in a historical sense and the contemporary or modern in a typological sense is left largely implicit. Both Worsley and Hobsbawm view religious movements in modern society as transitional phenomena destined to disappear soon. They feel that the full articulation and spread of processes of institutional differentiation and modernisation will lead to a quick decline and final disappearance not only of millenarism but of all other religious movements as well. This is tacitly assumed without proper discussion or proof.[20]

While their discussion of theoretical problems is at times vigorous and acute, they do not make full use or even discuss adequately all the available theoretical formulations in this field. Worsley's critical review of Max Weber's theories on the relation between religion and social change is squeezed in and put out of the way in a short appendix. His ambiguous and shifting use of the term rationality vitiates much of his otherwise useful criticism of Weber. The aversion to any

[19]For a critical re-evaluation of evolutionary theories, see S. F. Nadel, *The Principles of Social Anthropology* (Glencoe 1955), and S. Tax ed., *The Evolution of Man* (Chicago 1960).

[20]For a different interpretation of the place of religion in modern society, see T. Parsons, *Social Structure and Social Process* (Glencoe 1960), pp. 195–322.

type of formal sociology causes an almost complete disregard of Simmel's theory of conflict in spite of its relevance to the analysis.[21] K. Mannheim's analysis of utopianism[22] is overlooked and not mentioned at all. Mannheim's study has serious shortcomings, yet it provides many important insights and should not be totally ignored. Both studies would have gained much from a widening of their theoretical base and from a fuller and more critical examination of their assumptions.

The studies on millenarism have proved the fruitfulness of a comprehensive comparative and historical approach, yet it would seem that further progress in this field will be achieved primarily by means of theoretically oriented yet very detailed case studies. Further elaboration and specification of the hypotheses outlined here will be possible mainly on the basis of additional more sharply focused and more fully worked out case studies.

[21]For examination of the relevance of Simmel's theory of conflict in the study of change, see L. Coser, *The Functions of Social Conflict* (Glencoe 1956).

[22]K. Mannheim, *Ideology and Utopia* (New York 1936).

M. D. Chenu

MAN,
MASTER OF NATURE

It was not moreover the theologians who, in the Faculty, put forward this idea of the physical and spiritual interdependence of man and the universe, of this new balance between grace and nature. At least, they pronounced no laws about it until the Church had a life of its own, which was during the twelfth century, spiritually and pastorally, in new forms and circumstances. The great quarrel between monks and ordinary canons and then, beyond the canonical reform, the apostolic movements inspired strictly from the Gospels, implied not only new institutions but also entirely new attitudes in the dialectic between the world and the Gospel, all of which defined the inner tension of Christians.

"L'homme maître de la nature. Ars et natura," La théologie au douzième siècle, Paris: 1957, pp. 44–51. Translated for this anthology by Ann Duncan. By permission of Librairie Philosophique Joseph Vrin, Paris, and the translator.

There were two aspects to this return to the original *vita apostolica,* as distinct from monastic feudalism, since it called for Christians to be present in the world and had this effect. Instead of centering the perfect way of life round the monastic ideal, foreshadowing on earth the city of God, the aim was now to permeate and transform a world in which a new civilisation was emerging as the burden of feudalism was shaken off. So there were not only moral purifications, inspired by the will to reform already prevalent in the twelfth century, but also evangelical truths were channeled into a specific social economy. This was the meeting point of the Church and the world, accomplished in simple, clear-cut actions, which took full account of the qualities of a new type of man, rather than through Christianity, powerful as an institution but compromised for that very reason. It is not therefore surprising if in the following generations it was among the evangelicals that the theologians were recruited for this new Christianity in which reason itself, the quintessence of human nature, took part in constructing God's science on earth. Scholastic theology, as will be said later, is the highest application of the axiom: "Gratia non tollit naturam, sed perficit."

This new awareness, originating in an apostolic perception of the world, reflected the discovery of nature on the social life and its evolutions. Keeping to lay reality, and before analysing these repercussions,[1] let us continue our investigation on the modest level of earthly life. Man does not really encounter nature until he has taken possession of it and put it at his service: this is the very order of things—for the Christian, the order of creation as expressed in the first pages of the Bible. The twelfth century illustrates this stage of development.

In his history of technology, L. Mumford, reinstating the first efforts of humanity before the modern era, stresses the importance of the progress made during the Middle Ages and introduces his description by recalling the mutual dependence of artist and artisan in the growing awareness of nature.[2] "In the fresh naturalist sculptures of twelfth century churches, one can notice the first movement of the sleeper troubled by the morning light. The craftsman's interest in nature was at first confused; by slow degrees, the artist began to carve oak leaves or hawthorn branches delicately but at the same time continued to create strange monsters, gargoyles, fantastic or legendary beasts. Yet the interest in nature became progressively wider and more absorbing." We readily accept Mumford's suggestion, which is, moreover, supported by art historians: we consider the development of techniques to be the sign and means of a real and active discovery of nature; while at the same time man becomes to some extent more aware of himself, through this mastery over nature. This awareness is at first subconscious but is soon apparent in the interests aroused in the intellectual life by the physical influences of work, which also ensure a sensible balance in dialectical intoxication or the turning inwards to illusion.

In this aspect too, the twelfth century forms the pivot in mediaeval civilisation of a complete transformation in material conditions; it has been called a "technical revolution." Due to the explosion of feudalism and its exclusive policy as regards land holding; due to the economical and political emancipation of craftsmen in towns, organised in corporations; due to an active circulation of people and wealth in a market economy, the birth and extension of new techniques caused profound changes both in material and intellectual life; in certain modes of perception, of feeling and of representation. Did not Aristotle base his analysis of evolution and its factors on the analogy of the craftsman's creation?[3]

"Can objects made by man, shoes, cheese and other similar products, be considered as works of God?" Maître Gilbert wonders. This is a theological question and not a philosophical consideration in the manner of Aristotle: the naive appearance of his formula conceals one of the first conscious queries about the rôle of human economy in the religious world-plan; and this has more far-reaching implications than the answer—not without interest in itself— in which Gilbert makes a distinction in God's vast work of creation between natural operations, and the creations of

---

[1] Cf. *infra,* chap. X: *Monks, clerics and laymen. At the crossroads of the evangelical life.*

[2] L. Mumford, *Technique et civilisation,* Paris, 1936.

[3] On this analogy between τέχνη and φύσις, cf. *II Phys.,* 1, 139 a 32–36; 2, 194 a 21.

man, thus situated in the religious context of world "administration."[4]

This reflection is not inspired by circumstances but is conscious, organic religious metaphysic according to which *homo artifex* is defined with reference to the *opus Creatoris* and *opus naturae;* the first reference situates human activity in its religious context, the second gives it its earthly scope and significance. This analysis is based on Chalcidius' commentary on the *Timaeus* ch. 23 ("Omnia enim quae sunt vel opus Dei sunt, vel naturae, vel naturam imitantis hominis artificis"); but is extended to form a total vision of the world and definition of man, even the obligations for an economy.

Ostenso quod nihil est sine causa, subjungit quid contrahat effectus ex efficiente. Sciendum est enim quod omne opus vel est opus *creatoris,* vel est opus *nature,* vel *artificis* imitantis natura. Et est opus creatoris prima creatio sine prejacente materia, ut creatio elementorum vel spirituum, vel ea que vidimus fieri contra consuetum cursum nature, ut partum virginis, etc. Opus nature est quod similia nascantur ex similibus ex semine vel ex germine, quia est natura vis rebus insita similia de similibus operans. Opus artificis est opus hominis, quod prop-

ter indigentiam operatur, ut vestimenta contra frigus, domum contra intemperiem aeris; sed in omnibus que agit naturam imitatur; cum enim facit vestem, juxta naturalem membrorum dispositionem facit eam; in compositione vero domus consideret quod in planis remanet aqua putrefaciens ligna, ex convallibus vero descendit et mundificat; unde concavam, facit domum.[5]

In making this typically Carthusian distinction between three types of action, full importance must be given to the distinction between works properly divine,—creation and miracles,—and works of nature, also divine because of supreme causality but accomplished according to an autonomous order of things. The diffused spirituality of the Christian was at that time governed by the Augustinian representation of a universe where God's omnipotence was revealed just as much by flowerings in spring time as by the vegetation on Aaron's rod, by the production of wine from grapes as much as by the miracle of Cana, as well by the daily birth of children as by the resurrection of the dead. This religious blockage which undervalued the second causes had, deep down, a symbolic vision of the world, in which phenomena tended not to be explained by the immediate causes in favour of a meaning which could—legitimately—be given to them, with a sacred as well as poetic value, with reference to their ultimate fate. The various current neoplatonic ideas endowed these representations with the density of a high quality philosophical reflection, in spite of the infantilism they sometimes contained. The development of doctrines observed elsewhere here reappears.

[4] *Note super Johannem sec. mag. Gilb* [*ertum*], ms, London, Lambeth Palace 360, fol. 32 rb: "De artificialibus quaeritur utrum a Deo facta sunt, sicut caseus, et sotulares, et hujusmodi quae dicuntur esse opera hominis non Dei.—Omnia quidem a Deo facta sunt tanquam ab auctore; quaedam tamen ejus opera dicuntur, sicut sunt, illa quae per se operatur ita scil. quod nec naturae similitudine, nec alicujus ministerio, ut caelum et terram. Alia dicuntur opera naturae, quae a Deo ita creantur quod ad alterius similitudinem, et quod grana ex granis, et equis ex equo, et similia ex similibus. Alia quae hominis ministerio facit, hominum dicuntur. Unus ergo omnium auctor Deus, diversi tamen operandi rationes, et auctoritas et ministerii, quorum alterum homo dicitur auctor, alterum vero Deus. Similiter usualiter dici solet de aliquo divite quod multa fecit edificia, quae eadem singulariter fecit et carpentarius, sed alter auctoritate sola et jussu alter ministerio."

[5] Guillaume de Conches, *Glossa in Timaeum,* 28 a (publ Parent, p. 147). Cf. *Dragmaticon,* pub. Gratorolus, p. 31. This subject inspired even the Augustinian Robert de Melun, *Sententie,* I, 1, 21, pub. Martin, p. 224–227.: De distinctione operationum et de hoc quod alio quodam modo Deus hec operatur que opera nature dicuntur quam ipsa natura.

Jean de Salisbury, more of a sociologist, notes the place held in the City by the guilds of crafts, rural work or mechanical trades, whose growing specialisation, to the common good, prevented the legislator from formulating for each one the principles by which their innumerous functions should be controlled.[6] Alexander Neckham (†1217), successively a master of law, medicine and theology, aware of the various constructive methods of different branches of knowledge, composed, as well as his *De naturis rerum,* a sort of dictionary of tools and domestic implements, *De nominibus utensilium,* thus applying the contemporary taste for lexicography to mechanical things.[7]

The technical progress outstripped, both in volume and quality, the still primitive religious or professional conception of its rôle. The production of energy made astounding progress with the wider use of improved machines for controlling water power and producing circular movements: mills, hydraulic wheels (one horse instead of 25); windmills, which have first been traced in Europe as early as 1105;

reduction of power by hoisting apparatus; war industries, which disqualified the old cavalry (the Lateran Council in 1139 forbade the use of the recently introduced cross-bow). Methods of communication gave man more and more freedom: the invention of the yoke harness for oxen transformed rural life; the fixed rudder dates from 1180; the compass made large scale navigation possible and favoured trade in which the merchant classes were replacing the nobility which had been ousted, contributed to shift Mediterranean trade towards the Atlantic. In 1188, the bridge of Avignon was built, with eighteen stone arches. With the mechanical clock people began to make better use of time, as its regularity of which measured machine civilisation, since "the clock not only shows the passage of time but also synchronises human actions" (L. Mumford); the bells of the clock tower controlled urban life: machines were everywhere, giving a new environment to life, no longer commanded by human rhythm but by mechanical time. The lavish decoration of clocks expressed the startling effect of this innovation on people's minds.

In this mechanical world, man came out of his empirical confusion, depersonalised his actions, became aware of the objective density and articulation of things dominated by natural laws. Order is no longer just the schema of an aesthetic imagination or religious conviction; it is proven, supported by method: nature is comprehensible and predictable. Man's knowledge included the mastery of nature. The *quadrivium,* knowledge of *res,* had as much educative value as *trivium,* knowledge of *verba,* which created too many rhetoricians and dialecticians. Gilbert de la Porée advised students overly keen on dialectic "to learn the baker's trade." And were not the craftsmen of Chartres cathedral men

[6]Jean de Salisbury, *Polycraticus,* VI, c. 20: Qui sint pedes reipublicae et de cura eis impendenda (here we already have the image used by those who, among modern sociologists, support the organicist theory): "...In his [officiis] quidem agraicolarum ratio vertitur, qui terrae semper adhaerent, sive in sationalibus, sive in consitivis, sive in pascuis, sive in floreis agitentur. His etiam aggregantur multae species lanificii, artes ue mechanicae quae in ligno, ferro, aere metallisque variis consistunt...Haec autem tot sunt ut respublica non octipedes cancros, sed et centipedes pedum numerositate transcendat ...Tam variae figurae sunt ut nullus unquam officioruem scriptor in singulas species eorum specialia praecepta dederit."

[7]Alexander Neckham, *De nominibus utensilium,* pub., Wright, *A volume of vocabularies,* p. 96–119, and Scheller, in *Jahrbuch für englische und romanische Literatur,* VII, p. 58–74, 155–173. Cf. Ch. H. Haskins, *Studies in the history of mediaeval science,* 1924, p. 359–363.

of the same stature as Abelard?[8] Hugues de Saint-Victor gave a large place in his *Didascalion,* to the mechanical skills, "lanificium, armaturam, navigationem, agriculturam, venationem, medicinam, theatricam"* (leisure pursuits are not forgotten in this pleasant economy!);[9] and Godefroid de Saint-Victor, drawing up the list of trades by their social function, rejected the definition given them by an unfortunate etymology which none the less survived until Classical French: "Scientiae machanicae, idest moechiae seu adulterinae," that is, which adulterate the substance of man's spiritual dignity.[10]

This *homo artifex,* creator of forms, henceforward made a distinction between what is animate and what is mechanical; rid himself of the infantile imagery of animism and false deifications of the superhuman; the sacred things made profane by these uses had no authentic religious value. He was better acquainted with his rôle in the universe. The mediaevals were haunted by the automaton who would usefully dehumanise so many banal activities; but man's mastery over matter introduced this opaque and inert reality into an economy which, in its highest expression, in the new heavens and new earth, deified once and for all the universe of nature. Nicolas d'Amiens expressly professed this: he is not just making an *a priori* deduction. Formerly too, the Ionian thinkers and artisans, far from the gods of Hesiod, built a new cosmogony, in which nature was revealed by tools and intelligence.

Ars et natura: once again the twelfth century professors gained from Aristotle a much more mature philosophical development, which their dialectic did not use to the full.[11] But twelfth century thought, less hemmed in by the Faculty, had already realised to what extent art, by perfecting nature, could reveal man; and at the same time the discovery of nature was giving substance to a metaphysic of the universe and to new methods of thought. Hence a double struggle, immediately turned into a Christian theme, from Genesis to the Pauline mysticism, in a world of sin which man can no longer govern. Nature is coupled with history. Vigour is brought by the other branch of ambiguous Platonism, although again not without severe corrections. Augustine connects original sin with generation, Nature's main task, without mentioning its other manifestations.

By the very lifting of the pressures which were gradually making the notion of nature appear, we consciously gave way to a unilateral presentation of the spiritual and doctrinal currents of the twelfth century; but at each moment these same pressures were falling spontaneously and healthily on the "inner life" which, by virtue of its nature, the intel-

---

[8]Guillaume de Conches, according to Jean de Salisbury (*Metalog.,* III, 10, publ. Webb, p. 161) compared to the dialectician's art the work of a certain Ascelin, famous master-smith: "Hescelinus faber, sicut magister Willelmus referebat, illorum morem sequebatur, qui nihil in disputationibus certum appetunt, et sic rem fabrilem, sicut hii expediunt dialecticam, exercebat."

*Wool making, armament, navigation, agriculture, hunting, medicine, theatricals.

[9]Hugues de Saint-Victor, *Didascalion,* II, ch. 20–23. This moreover is the effect of his openness of mind and reading of the Classics, more than of observing the artisans of his time.

[10]Godefroid de Saint-Victor, *Microcosmus,* 55–57. Cf. Ph. Delhaye, *Le Microcosmus de Godefroid de Saint-Victor. Etude théologique,* Lille, 1951, p. 115, who notices the precise meaning of this technical humanism. M.-D. Chenu, *Arts "mécaniques" et oeuvres serviles,* in *Rev. sc. ph. th.,* 29 (1940), pp. 313–315, where the link between this conception of work and feudal serfdom is pointed out.

[11]These professors, both in arts and sciences, were moreover very aware of the deficiency of the arts and crafts with relation to nature's successes. Cf. in relation to Jean de Meung, G. Pare, *op. cit.,* pp. 65–68.

lectual and mechanical mastery of the macrocosm called into the microcosm. Saint Bernard hardly noticed this parallelism; but the Cistercian grace which Guillaume de Saint-Thierry had received benefited from an anthropological knowledge fostered, as well as by Augustine, by the cosmic sense of the Greeks; and his *Physica animae,* a treatise on God's image in man, deals not just with self-knowledge but, as the title says,[12] investigates the "physique" of the soul, preached by the naturalists and ecclesiastical doctors (Grégoire de Nysse, *De hominis opificio,* in Scot Erigène's translation).

Such investigations lack force but are very significant; they go on increasing and, what is more, with the advent of Avicenna at the end of the century, move to new territories, which seem for a moment as if the Persian philosopher must be the result of the combined pressures of Denys (Erigène), Augustine and Aristotle.[13] These investigations are significant: not only because they show the influx of heterogeneous sources, or the permanent and contrasting interactions of currents of thought, but because they indicate the internal link, in the authentic Christian spirit, of these two incongruous values: the discovery of nature and the *contemptus mundi.* The tension between them not only defines the state of the Christian in the world but also controls his theological work at the same time as his personal life. It is normal and inevitable that this tension finally produces different options in theological reflection as in spiritual awareness and apostolic duties. Several times Cîteaux publicly opposed the masters of Chartres and the *Porretani* pointed out the weaknesses of the Augustinian Pierre Lombard. When not yielding to

his myth of nature, Alain himself pronounced Augustine formulae on original sin. It is because man's *nature* alone cannot define man's existence and conduct; this nature is involved in the historic conditions, in *circumstances* as Augustine said, which a philosophy of essences, if it ignores history, ends up by neglecting since they cannot be deduced from nature.

Every "world philosophy" (Guillaume de Conches), it is true, tends legitimately to grasp its object in its entirety, and it would be erroneous as well as clumsy to arrange at the expense of this and for the pretended benefit of the religious soul, a zone of mystery, as a refuge for the sacred; profane sciences comprise the whole of nature. Yet all nature also conceals sacral qualities: it is the view point which changes; science and mysticism ought naturally to grant this to each other. To proclaim the values of Nature was indeed to put an end to a certain Christian conception of the universe, as it was to put an end to a certain form of Christianity, in order to fight the ideas and politics of the Holy Roman Empire.

During the twelve hundreds both aspects of this (intrinsically single) movement were developed simultaneously and Jean de Salisbury provided several prodromes in spite of his violent support of Thomas Becket. Laicism and scientism introduce a rather malignant fever into it, but it was in the end a healthy growing pain. On the portal of Chartres, Christ remained the saviour of creation.

Theology also reaped some benefit, in a rational development right in the heart of its faith. It is the same Alain de Lille, this authority on nature, who is also the theorist of "rules of theology," that is, of the method according to which the knowledge of faith, like every mental discipline, is organised and built, with the aid of internal principles which give

---

[12]The title of the second part of his *De natura corporis et animae.*

[13]Cf. for example, the conformist tendency of the *Liber de causis primis et secundis.* Cf. *infra.*

it the appearance and value of a science.[14] Alain does not juxtapose reason and faith any more than he does the sacred and the profane: he differentiates between them in order to unite them. "Non adversa, sed diversa sentimus,"[15] he makes Nature say, mindful of the supreme dignity of theology. Certain spiritual people were troubled by such confidence in reason; the century of Albert the Great, Bonaventure and Thomas Aquinas proved them wrong.

It seemed evident that, without detriment to the *contemptus mundi* of Cîteaux, or to the monastic theology which supported it, the greatness of the twelfth century also comprised—without alas! a genius having given it the most suitable expression, or put it in proper proportion—this *religious* discovery of the universe in nature which, to use the word of the thoroughly secular Jean de Meung, is the antechamber of God. Besides Alain de Lille died at Cîteaux—at the time when Saint Dominic was replacing the flagging Cistercians in the evangelical direction of a new civilisation, which was to be defined by Saint Thomas Aquinas in human and theological terms.

Friedrich Heer

MEDIEVAL POPULAR RELIGIOUS MOVEMENTS

Waldensians were persecuted along with Cathars, and accounted arch-heretics. But it had been Waldo's intention to preach against Catharism and counteract its influence; he never dreamed he was on the way to founding a sect. This typifies the tragedy of the Church's situation from the middle of the eleventh to the middle of the thirteenth century. While Christianity and the Church were still "open," the Gospel could for the first time penetrate deep into the minds and consciences of individuals, captivating people of every degree, noblemen, peasants, townsmen, simple village priests, men, women and children. Seized by the spirit, laymen and monks turned itinerant preachers, proclaiming a Christ who came not with a sword and power but in poverty, and whose habitation was not in episcopal palaces and cathedral chapters, nor in opulent ancient monastic communities, but in the open air, on the land, in the fields and in the hearts of those who received Him. The *Cristo de los campesinos* of the Spanish proletariat (frequently alluded to in the Spanish heresy hunts of the sixteenth century) was already being preached in the eleventh and twelfth centuries by the

From The Medieval World. London: 1962, pp. 158–166, 168–171. By permission of the publishers, Weidenfeld and Nicolson Ltd. and New American Library.

[14]Alain de Lille, *Theologicae regulae*, P.L., 210, 621–684.

[15]*Id., De planctu Naturae*, P.L., 200, 446: "Nec mirum si in his Theologia suam mihi familiaritatem non exhibet, quoniam in plerisquę non adversa sed diversa sentimus. Ego ratione fidem, illa fide comparat rationem; ego scio ut credam, illa credit ut sciat; ego consentio sciens, illa sentit consentiens."

inspired visionaries who initiated Europe's first revivalist movement.

There were numerous small groups of these "poor men of Christ" (as some of them called themselves) in southern and northern France, in Flanders, the Rhineland and northern Italy. They had no presentiment of what was to spring from their small beginnings. They regarded themselves as undisputed members of "holy Christianity" (in the eleventh and twelfth centuries "church" in popular parlance meant simply the church building).

One notices again and again that the fate of a group of religious revivalists seems to hinge on "accident"; that this should be so is one of history's grimmer secrets. Such a group may achieve ecclesiastical recognition as a reforming order or congregation, or as a group of laymen; or it may be caught up in the wake of denunciation and persecution and after a time become really "heretical." Forced out of the mainstream and pushed underground, such groups become infected with radicalism and are in danger of secularization; their range of vision contracts, and, equally damaging, they make common cause with the subterranean brotherhood already in existence all over Europe.

St Francis of Assisi has many admirers nowadays, among them pious Catholics, Protestants and non-Christians, attracted by his love for animals and all created things and by his pacifism. These pious, at times downright sentimental, devotees of the *Poverello* have rarely any notion of how close he came to the surrounding flames, which consumed some who stood nearest to him, his persecuted friends and brothers.

Let us recapitulate briefly some of the elements of early medieval popular piety which still retained their vigour: they were a provocation and a challenge, electrifying the atmosphere at the very moment when "awakened" men had come to realize how little of true Christianity the Christian world contained.

The sense of great joy and inward freedom which the early Church derived from its possession of the Good News (which every one could read for himself), and its sense of union with the resurrected Lord, had long since been overlaid by feelings of terror and estrangement. Men at their prayers no longer raised their arms and turned toward Christ, their rising sun, but folded their hands in the attitude of serfs, serfs of God and of their sin. Where formerly the priest had celebrated the Mass facing the people, in proof of his accessibility, now he turned his back on them and retreated to the fastnesses of the sanctuary, separated from the people's part of the church by a forbidding screen. Finally, the Mass was read in a tongue the people could not understand. As a prophylactic against spiritual harm the people concentrated on their love for a multitude of saints, invoked as the "friends of God," as advocates with power to heal, as channels of access to the dread and omnipotent majesty of God. Some of these saints were of mythical origin, others belonged to the ancestral kindred of important noble families. As late as the mid-twelfth century Pope Alexander III found it necessary to ask the Swedes to refrain from promptly honouring as saints "men who died in their cups" (at a sacral feast).

Mystery, the mystery of the Mass, ritual and liturgy, proliferated an outgrowth of the miraculous which eroded the edges of wholesome piety like a cancer. The supreme reality was no longer to be found in sober and sanctified participation in that mystery which proclaimed the transformation of mankind, "the putting on of the new man," but in the miraculous and marvellous. The mania for marvels was such that apparitions and visions were looked for, and found, on all sides; many of them were no doubt genuinely curious phenomena. Although in the twelfth century the fever for the marvellous found some relief through its eruption into literature, particularly the *roman courtois,* religion was still its chief field of action. We have already remarked on the critical attitude of the authors of *Reineke Fuchs* and the German *Tristan* towards the cult of the marvellous and spectacular.

This symptom, and the other manifestations of the headstrong growth and deformation of popular religious emotion, had two main underlying causes. First, Christ was no longer directly accessible to the people; direct contact with Him was first and foremost the privilege of monks and after them of the secular priesthood, who administered the power of Christ in the sacraments, particularly the Mass, which brought them daily into the presence of Christ the King, the great Lord of Heaven. Secondly, the Roman Church's veto on the translation of the Gospels and other religious texts into the vernacular was a most effective means of keeping the people at arm's length. The Greek Church, which had long been a missionary church, took an opposite view and had numerous translations of the Bible into vernacular languages to its credit: Coptic, Syriac, Old Latin, Ethiopian, Georgian, Armenian, Gothic and Old Slavonic. Byzantine missionaries were working among the Huns in their own language from early in the sixth century. The Roman Church, even to this day, has always jealously guarded the supremacy of Latin as the sacred tongue to the exclusion of all others. The price has been a heavy one. There was no "authorized" Christian translation of the Bible which could be read by the Berbers, the Celts or the Germanic peoples. The task of translating the Bible into the native languages would have presented no problem to the intellectual talent of the Church in Africa, the Church of Tertullian and Augustine. But it was not undertaken, and North Africa fell to Islam. From the twelfth century the Latin Church was starting to lose individual souls and entire peoples to religious movements which catered for their needs by translating the Bible and other religious literature into their own tongues. The later Middle Ages saw the defection first of England and Bohemia and later of Germany.

Catharism, the most powerful of the anti-Roman religious movements of the twelfth and thirteenth centuries, inherited from the Eastern Church and from Manichaeism the practice of conducting evangelistic work in the vernacular, with the assistance of vernacular texts. The record of the Manichees as translators equalled and indeed surpassed that of the Greeks. In the twelfth century they were assiduously carrying on this work in the West, having earlier produced translations into Asiatic languages, including Chinese, and into the African and Spanish Latin of late antiquity.

It was not until the twelfth century that popular religious movements began to be labelled by sympathizers and opponents as orthodox or heretical, "left" or "right." During the eleventh century, when the way for the full-scale movements was being prepared, accusations of heresy were at first levelled only at individual peasants and "illiterate" persons, and at certain clerics and noblemen. For example, about the year 1000 there was the case of a villager from Champagne called Leuthard; returning from the fields one day (perhaps, like Joan of Arc, he had had a vision there) he drove away his wife, dashed to pieces the crucifix in the church, refused to pay his tithe and declared he had no further use for the prophets of the Old Testament. In 1019 there were southern French 'heretics' at Orleans, who succeeded in winning over a section of the nobility and educated clergy in the entourage of the French king, Robert the Pious (996–1031), who was a patron of church reform. Unmasked by spies as "heretics," they went cheerfully to their deaths on December 28, 1022, the first people to be burned as heretics in the West. They were confident that the entire population of France, including the king, would soon be captivated by their teaching.

About 1028 a group of peasants, clerics and nobles with heretical leanings established themselves at the castle of Monteforte, between Turin and Genoa, under the protection of the countess. This group seems to have had something of the gay serenity characteristic of the Franciscans. They taught that God the Father created all, that Christ was not God, remote and terrible, but the soul of mankind, in whom God delighted, and that the Holy Ghost was the proper knowledge and understanding of Holy Writ. Offered the choice between the Cross as interpreted by the Church and the stake, they unhesitatingly chose the latter. The ecclesiastical chronicles of the period, whose testimony on this point can surely be accepted without reserve, frequently remark on the cheerful eagerness with which "heretics" went to their death; this must have been the fruit of the inward freedom and joy, the liberation and integration of the innermost depths of being which came from the novelty of living by the light of a personally experienced faith. The intoxicating sense of joy and freedom one finds among the earliest Franciscans and Jesuits had its roots in the same experience.

During the eleventh century the most powerful promoter of popular religious emotion was the Papacy itself. When the Pope was the greatest revolutionary of his day, men who would otherwise have been labelled heretics became his most devoted followers. The Patarene movement, which started at Milan and Florence in 1057, found an ally in the revolutionary Pope Gregory VII, at that time in conflict with the "simoniacal" episcopate, strongly aristocratic in complexion, who refused to co-operate in his reform of the Church. Gregory thus mobilized the people in defence of the "freedom of the Church," since he needed to protect his reforms from the dangerous embrace of a feudalized and Germanized Church. The people, in their longing for the "Christ of poverty," were themselves in conflict with their bishops and looked to the Papacy for aid. In 1077, for example, some fanatical Flemish laymen begged the Pope's protection against the Bishop of Cambrai, who had denounced them as heretics. In 1162 Flemish townsmen were again protesting to the Pope, Alexander III, on account of their condemnation as heretics by the Archbishop of Reims, who objected to their "apostolic" mode of life. In 1179 the same Pope embraced with brotherly affection Peter Waldo, driven by the threats of the Archbishop of Lyons to seek help from Rome.

Even so, Rome was too weak during the twelfth century to be capable of gathering these wayward souls into the Church, where they might have been protected and disciplined; the men and spiritual resources necessary for such a task were lacking. The problem was left increasingly to the bishops and the religious orders, old and new, whose view of the "innovators" was shot through with suspicion and dislike. The chief ground of complaint was the presumption of these "uneducated" men in preaching, and in reading and propagating translations of the Bible. Peter Waldo became a "heretic" because neither he nor his followers allowed themselves to be deterred from preaching. "The freedom of the Word of God" was for these visionaries a higher freedom than the "freedom of the Church."

Europe in the early twelfth century was swarming with hermits, wandering preachers and foot-loose monks. When they joined forces the resulting group might develop either into a new Order or Congregation, sealed with the blessing of the Church, or into a heretical sect. Robert of Arbrissel (already mentioned as the guest of Guillaume IX, the grandfather of Eleanor of Aquitaine and the first troubadour) was one such wanderer. He founded the congregation of Fontévrault, the place of refuge both of Eleanor herself and of the daughters of Peter Waldo.

Robert's foundation was an individual affair and there were other religious individualists about this time who formed the nucleus of a movement, sometimes large, sometimes small. They were particularly numerous in France and Flanders, though one finds them in northern Italy as well. They represented all ranks of society and included priests, monks, noblemen, smiths, artisans, peasants and urban patricians. The driving force behind all these manifestations of religious fervor was the urge to lead the apostolic life in imitation of the poverty and humility of Christ.

These twelfth-century "heretics" were convinced that their teaching was faithful to the teaching and spirit of the Gospels, while the Church, as it seemed to them, was in a state of apostasy, having denied God, Christ, the Holy Spirit and love itself; they were "true Christians." These "heretics" distinguished between "good" priests and "bad," from whom they refused to receive the sacraments. But their "anticlericalism" should not be misinterpreted. Even during the most "Catholic" periods, medieval society was sufficiently uninhibited and heterogeneous to tolerate very open criticism of the clergy, so that in this, as in other respects, the twelfth century "heretics" were in line with popular sentiment. If a few such groups did end by seeking for themselves a theoretical justification which took them further outside the Church of their own

time, they were driven to it in self-defence by persecution and the opposition of individual bishops.

It is interesting to notice that as time went on women of noble birth became prominent as patrons of religious heterodoxy, a cause which had found sympathizers among their menfolk from an early date. Women were tired of the masculine ascendency, they disliked being chattels in the marriage market and the objects of monkish suspicion and contempt. Looking for a way of escape from this oppression they found it in education, of the mind and of the spirit. Courtly culture and Catharism both flourished under the protection of noble ladies, above all the noble ladies of Provence.

The arrival of Catharism in western Europe during the twelfth century marked a dramatic turning-point in the fortunes of "heretics" of every sort. Catharism itself originated outside Europe, in the East, and was at bottom a non-Christian religion. Initially it penetrated southwestern Europe subterraneously; but when it came out into the open its success was rapid and it was suppressed only after a civil war lasting thirty years. Cathars first appeared in western Europe about 1140 and the last Cathars of southern France were burnt at the stake in 1323–24. Even then their spirit lived on. The Huguenots of the sixteenth and seventeenth centuries were led by a sure instinct to recognize the Cathars as their spiritual kin, and their church as a figure of the archetypal church. Bossuet, the champion of an integrated Catholicism under the aegis of the Sun King, did not hesitate to describe the Cathars as the precursors of the Huguenots, adherents of that devil's church which flaunted its permanent challenge to the Church of Rome.

The drama and tragedy of the Cathars was closely bound up with the tragedy which overtook courtly civilization in the South and the fate of popular religious movements as a whole in the thirteenth and fourteenth centuries; there were always enemies ready to link this or that group with the Cathars, which by definition made them anti-Christian. Waldensians and Cathars were burnt at the same stake, despite the initial great antagonism of the Waldensians towards Catharism; Franciscans who refused to accept Bonaventure's victory over Francis had the Cathar label attached to them indiscriminately.

Catharism represented the first attempt by an eastern non-Christian religion to gain a foothold in the West. It had its roots in Gnosticism, which was Greek, and in Manichaeism, which came from Persia and the Near East. *Cathari* in Greek means "the pure." Purity of spirit and its liberation from the evil world and from matter was the goal of the Greek mystery religions and of Manichaeism. The chief characteristic of Gnosticism was its confident belief in the power of a pure spirit to attain direct communion with the Godhead; the Manichees were distinguished by their belief in the distinct and infrangible boundary separating the "children of light" from the "children of darkness." This dualistic doctrine, which could be regarded as both optimistic and pessimistic, made its appearance in Bulgaria during the tenth century. The Bulgars were at the time suffering a triple oppression, from the Russians, the Byzantines and the Roman Church. Bulgar society was sharply divided. On the one hand was the wealthy aristocracy and the wealthy church, on the other the lesser aristocracy, the lower clergy and the peasants. It was to this second group that the village priest Bogomil addressed his message, which can be summed up briefly: "The world is evil, let us therefore live like the apostles, in penitence, prayer and inward recollection." If simplicity of life was the ideal, then all ecclesiastical magnificence and

secular might and riches were vanity. In this world the Christian could expect only blood and tears, since this world was the creation of Satan, God's elder son and Christ's brother, the "God" of Genesis and the Old Testament.

It is evident that Christian themes and non-Christian gnostic teachings were already starting to merge with each other. During the ninth century the Byzantine Emperors had forcibly transported to Thrace the adherents of two eastern gnostic sects, the Paulicians and the Messalians, who later joined up with the Bogomils, the "friends of God." After the conquest of the Bulgar kingdom by the Byzantines in 1018, the Empire was itself permeated by underground heterodoxy. In this affluent setting the Bogomils succeeded in gaining adherents among the higher nobility, a class much given to philosophizing and religious and intellectual enquiry, particularly into cosmological and philosophical subjects. Catharism was to have a similar attraction for the Provençal nobility in the twelfth century. The Bogomils even made some impression on the spiritually arid field of Byzantine monasticism. A split developed within the Bogomils themselves as a result of the extension of their activity into the alien political and intellectual climate of the Byzantine Empire. The old Bogomils styled themselves the Church of the "Bulgars," while the "new" Bogomils, taking their name from the Thracian district of Dragovitsa, became the "Dragovitsan" Church. When the Crusaders arrived in the Byzantine Empire in the early twelfth century they found the Emperor much taken up with the question of the expulsion of the Bogomils. Ejected from Byzantium (in 1110 and after 1140), the Bogomils wandered far and wide, carrying their teaching with them. Their missionary activity was deployed first in Serbia, Bosnia and Dalmatia, reaching Italy and France at a later date. In Bosnia Bogoıilism was for a time the state religion; uring the reign of Ban Kulin (1180–204) it was the ideological mainstay of ıe country's resistance to the expanıonist designs of Hungary, which dhered to the Papacy. In the Balkans, neasily wedged between the two great Churches and the two great Empires, etween West Rome and East Rome, the Bogomils managed to survive until the 'urks came to power in the fifteenth entury. Even this was not the end. As n underground movement, Bogomilism ivided into two branches: one was a adical and militant secret society, one of ıe roots of the secret fraternities of the ineteenth and early twentieth centuries which played their part in determining ıe course of the first and second world wars; the other branch was a pacifist rotherhood, equally radical, which from he sixteenth century joined forces with dealists from Western Europe in Tranylvania, Poland and Moravia, and from here penetrated into Russia. The last emaining Bogomil clan, in Herzegovina, ɔ said to have been converted to Islam n 1867. The whole character of the Balan underground, in its religious, politcal and intellectual aspects, can only ɔe understood in the light of Bogoʊilism, and the same can be said of the ınderground in Western Europe, where Bogomils were persecuted as "Cathars" nd "Bulgars" (the generic name for eretics of all sorts).

Bogomil teachings were introduced nto the Rhineland and northern France ɔy merchants, and perhaps also by lisillusioned Crusaders returning from he Second Crusade in 1149. Bogomils xpelled from Byzantium also congreʒated in these regions. This was the open" (some might say dangerously ɔpen) Europe of the twelfth century. The passage of these "heretics" to the West was "like a triumphal procession; hey were made welcome everywhere, with a well-nigh incredible enthusiasm."

The wealthy city of Cologne was particularly susceptible. Bernard of Clairvaux, the most eloquent champion of Western Christendom, fulminated against them unsupported and in vain. The main heads of his indictment were their pride and hypocrisy.

Catharism gained a hold on the region between the Rhine and the Pyrenees in just over two years. 'The harmony between their lives and their teaching had an intoxicating effect.' All classes of people were taken with the frenzy, all distinctions of rank were forgotten; Cathar adherents included both clergy and women. Europe was in the full flood of its first Revivalist movement.

Following Bogomil precedent, the Cathars founded bishoprics in the West. The first was in northern France, probably at Mont-Aimé in Champagne (*circa* 1150–60?). The next foundation, in the region of Albi in southern France, gave the movement a new name. Albigensian missions sent from France into Italy covered the whole country from Lombardy to Naples.

In 1162 a band of German Cathars led by a man named Gerhard arrived in England; they were probably peasants from the Rhineland and included women. They met with little success, and on the orders of an ecclesiastical Council held at Oxford they were branded on the forehead and expelled, accepting their fate with cheerful fortitude. The Assize of Clarendon of 1166, which has a clause against favouring heretics, is the first example of a secular heresy law to be found in medieval Europe. An English chronicler, commenting on the unsuccessful sortie of these heretics into England, remarks that this nameless movement had left its traces everywhere, in France, Spain and England, drifting and settling like the sands of the seashore. In 1210 there is again evidence of Catharism in England.

Catharism spread so quickly that even

its own leaders were unable to control it. The administrative and spiritual weaknesses arising from this over-rapid advance produced fissures and cleavages within the movement, which in consequence lost some of its momentum. Eastern heresiarchs, who had been anxiously watching the turn of events in the West, decided it was time to intervene. Nicetas, bishop of the strictly dualist Dragovitsan church of Constantinople, came to Lombardy, probably in 1167, and consecrated as bishop a man named Marcus, who was deacon of the Italian Cathar church. As a result, Italian Catharism became much more radical; hitherto the Cathars of Western Europe, following the "old Bogomils," had taught a modified form of dualism (Satan helped God to create the world). Nicetas converted not only the Italian but also the French Cathars to his doctrines, and at the Cathar Council held at Saint-Felix-de-Caraman near Toulouse in 1167 reconsecrated three Cathar bishops, the bishops of Northern France, Southern France and Lombardy. By sheer weight of personality, this Easterner had succeeded in bringing together under one authority most of the Cathars of Western Europe, and in persuading them to accept the radicalism of his own extreme doctrines. Catharism was now much less Christian and less Western in temper; Oriental and non-Christian elements replaced poverty and the apostolic way of life as its dominating features.

In his great address to the Cathar Council Nicetas had warned his Western brethren to remain in peace and harmony among themselves. But this was asking for too much. The peculiar genius of European medieval civilization was to reveal itself, having been momentarily suppressed, just as clearly in Catharism, the anti-Church, as within the bosom of the Church of Rome itself. Catholic Christianity was already accommodating a wide range of very disparate elements. This feat of coexistence, to later generations well-nigh inconceivable, was if anything surpassed by the Cathars of Western Europe. The Cathars hived off into a number of deviating groups; and the beliefs of ordinary members of Cathar congregations contained a wide range of Christian elements, some of them quite orthodox. The Cathars later even evolved their own brand of Scholasticism; and in the course of argument they came closer and closer to the position of their adversaries, until they were posing the same problems, formulated in the same way. Catharism, in short, was a rich mélange of material taken from Gospel Christianity and of other beliefs, which were of Manichaean and Gnostic origin.

Later in the twelfth century the Cathars started to make inroads on eastern Europe, reaching out from the episcopal cities of the Rhineland along the Danube to Passau and Vienna. The Cathar "paradise" was Italy and Provence. In Italy they had six churches, of which the Lombard was the largest and the Florentine, where they had their own theological academy at Poggibonsi, the most sophisticated. All ranks of society were represented, but scriveners and weavers, members of those "sedentary and meditative trades," formed an élite. Between the twelfth and nineteenth centuries, in fact, weavers would be a constant element as the intelligentsia of the proletariat and the champions of proletarian intellectualism; they were always well represented numerically in nonconformist movements, whether religious or political. In towns the majority of Cathar supporters were artisans and day labourers. In southern France and Provence the movement had aristocratic protection. Here the wealthy nobility carried on a running feud with the wealthy higher clergy and monastic houses, whose properties they found tempting; the petty aristocracy were attracted to heresy for the same reason. Feminine interest in Catharism was on a more elevated plane. Ladies who openly declared themselves Cathars included *grandes dames* such as the wives of Raymond VI of Toulouse and Raymond-Roger of Foix, kinswomen of Queen Eleanor, ladies of high rank such as the famous Blanche de Laurrac, and nuns of noble birth; some ladies even maintained Cathar priests as their domestic chaplains.

What was it that so attracted the men of the twelfth century to the teaching of the Cathars, with its characteristic mélange of Gnostic and Christian elements? The idea of "purity" must always have held pride of place. It was a fundamental conviction of Catharism that there was an irreconcilable antithesis between the soul of the pure man and the evil world. Proof that this view of the world still has its compelling attraction for people of great intelligence and purity of spirit is provided by the case of Simone Weil, one of the most spiritual and single-minded of modern French intellectuals. Her thirst for the absolute was inextinguishable; during the second world war she made a pilgrimage to Toulouse, where neo-Catharism was being preached. The "Pure" were required to cleanse the world and themselves of everything unspiritual, which was by definition "impure." The ghost of Catharism hovers about the cradle of all later purifiers: of all Puritans. One of the first things to need "purification" was the Bible. The Old Testament was subjected to close scrutiny, from which only thirteen prophets, the five books of Solomon and the Psalms (later a great favourite with the Huguenots) emerged to be received into the Cathar canon. Christ was not God; He and the Virgin were spirits of a high order, their physical bodies merely appearances. The souls of men were "fallen spirits," corrupted by Satan in Heaven and thereafter flung down to earth.

* * *

There was equal lack of uniformity in Cathar views concerning the good God. One of the last Cathars to teach in southern France held that nature itself was the good God, that earth, water, and wind were the true trinity. This was an extreme case. The general line of teaching was as follows. The history of the world was to be understood as the conflict between the two Gods, the evil and the good. All man's sufferings were rooted in his ignorance: the "children of darkness" were fighting the "children of light." Blinded by Satan, the "children of darkness" addressed their prayers to the evil God, to Jehovah, Baal, Jupiter and the God of the Roman Church—seen as an institution ambitious for power—and so fell deeper and deeper into the toils of enslaving matter. Mankind could be redeemed through "true knowledge," through recognition of the true and good God. Christ was a teacher sent by this good God. After his death, Satan brought into being the Satanic Church, the whore of Babylon, the Church of Rome, which was now persecuting the "Pure," the poor, the true followers of Christ, and would continue to do so until the end of the world. One current doctrine (it had also been held by some orthodox reformers in the eleventh century) which found favour among some Cathars and also among some other heterodox Christians had momentous implications: namely that from the time of Constantine the Roman Church had succumbed to material attractions and the lust for power, and was ruling in unholy alliance with the princes of this world. Neither the Church nor the secular princes had the right to persecute and judge "heretics," still less to condemn them to death. (This belief was shared by the Waldensians.) The capital punishment of criminals and heretics was plain murder. All wars and all

Crusades were sinful. Between the twelfth and the fifteenth centuries the Bogomil Church in Bosnia, true to its pacifist convictions, acted as peacemaker between the monarchy and the aristocracy, Catholics and Bogomils, Hungarians and Turks. Cathar propaganda against war and the Crusade was so effective that the Catholics were forced to reply; in their voluminous tracts justifying war and the Crusade as a means of "defending the social order" we find the theologians of the twelfth and thirteenth centuries using arguments similar to those of theologians in the twentieth.

This world is wicked and a man who seeks to be pure must renounce it. The "Perfect" (*perfecti*) renounced the flesh in all its forms, abstaining from sexual intercourse and marriage; they practised the severest asceticism, living as nomads, dedicated to poverty and preaching and wholly without resources. The people were fascinated by this Cathar élite, wondering if perhaps "true monks" had at last appeared to satisfy their yearnings. The Perfect demonstrated what men who lived by "pure spirit" could achieve. Behind the teaching and exegesis of the Perfect (they relied almost exclusively on the New Testament) lay a considerable wealth of learning, which was more than could be said of most popular Catholic teaching. Moreover the Bible and Cathar literature were offered to the people in the vernacular tongues, and here they need fear no rival.

The individual "Perfect" formed his whole life in accordance with the spirit, which became his understanding and his will. One consequence of this was that he acquired the right to bring about his own death, through suicide. The favourite method was the *endura* or voluntary fast. The glorification of suicide was something new in medieval Europe; in the region of Toulouse, where there were so many suicides of

the Perfect during the twelfth and thirteenth centuries, stoic and renaissance ideas were to come together during the sixteenth and seventeenth centuries to produce a similar phenomenon.

The radicalism of the "Church of the Pure" thus had an equal appeal for the masses and for the educated. The majority of those interested in the sect were content to lead more or less ordinary lives, looking on the Perfect as their ideal and aspiring to be accepted among them before death. The fascination of Cathar ritual was a particular source of anxiety to its opponents. Bernard of Clairvaux and other preachers denounced the Cathars for their furtiveness and secrecy "like criminals ashamed of the light,' they celebrated their "abominable liturgies" in city basements, in outhouses and cellars, in forests and woodland shacks It was said that in districts where they were particularly influential, such as Toulouse, Milan and Florence, they even used churches for their services. The shock for Bernard and those who later preached the Albigensian Crusade would have been still greater had they realized that in many essential features Cathar ritual reflected the practices of the early, pre-Constantine Church. The whole drama of the Albigensian Crusade, 1208–28, during which Catharism was all but annihilated, turns on this tremendous fact: the drastically altered Christianity which had emerged from centuries of barbarization, after exposure to late Roman, Celtic and Germanic influences, was now being confronted by a way of life and thought and worship so radical and fanatical that it came disturbingly close to reproducing the situation of the early Church. During its first four centuries Christianity had been in a state of chaotic ferment; it was a time when a hundred flowers bloomed (the metaphor comes from Clement of Alexandria), a time for the introduction of a variety of strains, classical, oriental, Hellenistic

Greek, and Christianity of all shades; even if they were in conflict, there was benefit to be gained from their cross-fertilization. During the "open" and sus-ceptible twelfth century there was a chance that Christian Europe might recapture this vitality.

William Haller

THE CALLING
OF THE SAINTS

Within two generations of the time when Thomas Cartwright was expelled from Cambridge for his advocacy of reform, the Puritan preachers had so increased in numbers and influence that the ruling powers in church and state had either to suppress them or give way before them. What is the explanation of their rise? Discontent in all classes of society, aggravated by the political incompetence of the first two Stuarts, supplied opportunity which the preachers knew how to turn to the advantage of their cause. But this fact, though important, does not by itself account for the role which Laud found the press and the Puritan pulpit so freely exercising when he rose to the primacy in 1633. The preachers could have made little of their opportunity if they had lacked ideas or the skill to persuade their public that their ideas offered sure remedy for the troubles of life. We must therefore next inquire what it was the preachers preached, how they preached and with what effect. In no other way can we truly understand the Puritan Revolution or those forces of thought and imagination

and that way of life which have so long prevailed among English-speaking people.

First of all we must endeavor to grasp the meaning of the central dogma of Puritanism as it applied to the life of men in the seventeenth century. This was a conception of an all-embracing determinism, theologically formulated as the doctrine of predestination. It is a conception which, especially in its postulates of an absolute human depravity and a purely arbitrary human redemption, has often seemed absurd to the common sense and abhorrent to the humanitarian sentiment of later generations. In these pages we are not concerned with such reactions. Believing in predestination, the Puritan preachers persuaded our forefathers to trust in nothing but God and the spirit within themselves and to defy the devil and all his minions. In doing this, they were not fools or clowns or bigots or pedants but academic intellectuals trained in the approved science and the accustomed arts of their time and addressing themselves to what they took to be the supreme need of the people of their time. With what ideas they could command they confronted the confusion and demoralization of a society which had been racked by the tremendous changes of the preceding century, and

From The Rise of Puritanism (1938). New York: 1957, pp. 83–88, 89–90, 91, 95–97, 98–99, 99–100, 111, 111–113, 117–119, 123–125. By permission of Columbia University Press.

with what skill and force of character they possessed they attempted to implant courage, discipline and order. They took the doctrine of predestination as their dialectical weapon because it seemed to them to offer the most rational assurance for restored confidence in the future of mankind.

That Puritan doctrine was indebted to Calvin hardly requires to be said, but we have proceeded only a little way toward understanding the Puritan preachers when we have said that they were Calvinists. As Englishmen, they were Calvinists with a difference. In Geneva and in Scotland, as compared to England, the triumph of the Calvinist reformers had been quick and complete. Hence in those countries they soon gained a relatively free hand to impose their formula upon the whole social structure. No such opportunity to re-establish order throughout the church fell to the English Calvinists. Uniformity of belief and discipline was actually obtainable in England only within the sect or independent congregation and at the price of separation from the rest of society. The non-conformists and dissenters, though too weak and few to enforce their will upon others, did manage precariously to get their way among themselves, and those of them who were able to escape to New England were able to protect themselves from disunion if they wished by again handing heretics over to the secular arm or by turning them out into the wilderness. Thus in Geneva, in Scotland, in Massachusetts, and under peculiar limitations among the English sects, Calvinists of one type or another were able to achieve a reformed society in which differences of opinion were checked and uniformity maintained. But throughout England, except under the handicap of persecution, they were permitted to do nothing of the kind. There they had to accommodate themselves year after year as best they could

to that peculiar condition which had been set up by the politic Elizabeth and which compelled Englishmen, the more surely the longer it endured, to the maintenance not of religious uniformity but of some sort and degree of toleration as the sine qua non of political security and economic prosperity. The reformers then, unless they were willing to risk ostracism, exile or persecution, had to refrain from too directly assailing the government or their fellow subjects. They were in no position to suppress the people who did not fall in with their ideas, and had to advance their ideas as best they could by the peaceful arts of persuasion. Hence the English Calvinists found that all they could do to advance their cause, though they were for some two generations permitted to do that, was to plead for it by the help of whatever gifts of mind and utterance they happened to possess. Under such conditions they produced, at any rate prior to 1640, no great public leaders, lawgivers and theologians of the stature of Knox and Calvin, but a host of popular propagandists who exploited as never before the potentialities of pulpit and press. Thus Calvinism in England did not lead to a swift reconstruction of the church but to the creation of a literature which expressed a way of life that eventually far transcended all ecclesiastical and even all religious bounds.

The history of Puritan thought in England is primarily the history of the setting forth of the basic doctrine of predestination in terms calculated to appeal to the English populace. It is at the same time necessarily a history of the effect of popular reaction upon the doctrine itself and upon the modes of its presentation. Strictly speaking, English Puritanism in the large may continue to be called Calvinistic chiefly as a matter of historical reference. Actually, the preachers, Calvinist though they were in varying degrees, referred as often to

St. Augustine as to the author of the *Institutes* but were chary on principle of citing any merely human authorities whatsoever. The French reformer's positive, clear, dogmatic intelligence supplied them with ideas but not on the whole with a model of discourse which they chose to imitate when they mounted the pulpit. The nature of the task to which they addressed themselves is exactly set forth by John Downame in his appropriately entitled *Guide to Godlynesse*:

> could find no one part of Divinity more profitable, in these times ... then that which consisteth more in experience and practice, then in theory and speculation; and more principally tendeth to the sanctification of the heart, then the informing of the judgement and the increasing of knowledge; and to the stirring up of all to the practice of that they know in the duties of a godly life, and in bringing foorth the fruits of faith in new obedience; then to fit them for discourse.

Calvin's most important effect upon the preachers was to send them posting back to scripture, particularly to the epistles of Paul, to Paul's life as recorded in Acts, and so to the gospels and to the rest of holy writ. Consequently there is less of the manner and spirit of Calvin in the preachers' lives and writings than of the apostle to the Gentiles. They were following the latter's example in essaying to adapt their teaching to the spiritual condition of all men who felt themselves excluded, aggrieved, hampered and oppressed by the special privileges, the vested interests, the class prejudices of the existing order. They offered to all such the comfort that he offers in every age to the unrecognized and disallowed. There is no respect of persons, Paul said, with God, no real difference between Jew and Gentile. This spiritual equalitarianism, implicit in every word the preachers spoke, seized upon the imaginations of men

who, no matter what their social rank, had reason to be discontented with the Stuart regime in church and state, and it thus became the central force of revolutionary Puritanism. Over against the inequalities of an indurated social system and an obsolete form of government, the people learned from preachers inspired by Paul to bear in mind the equality of all men before God and presently to draw the obvious practical inference that God before whom all men are leveled is sure in his own time to uplift the low and humble the great.

The famous doctrine of predestination, of salvation by faith alone, was for the Puritan classes but the rationalized statement of this sentiment, a clear dogma answering with irrefutable logic to men's emotional need for something by which to be convinced. The modern mind, inexpert in such modes of reasoning, turns away from the intricate dialectic by which the logic of predestination was upon occasion presented, and we may well do the same here. The preachers themselves asserted again and again that only so much doctrine was important to be understood as could be understood by men of least knowledge and capacity when set forth in plain English. What, therefore, is important for us to understand is less how learned doctors argued among themselves than what they succeeded in conveying to the people, not what their doctrine was but what it meant and did. Let us then disregard the technical treatises and systems of divinity, numerous though they were, and fasten our attention upon the popular sermons and tracts which the preachers offered to the common public in even greater abundance. First of all, we must note, they urged the people to base their understanding of the word of God upon Paul's Epistle to the Romans. If one began one's study of scripture at that point, William Perkins advised, and then went to the gospel of John, one had the key to the whole. Thomas Draxe is still more specific and more eloquent. The Epistle to the Romans, he says, is like to nothing less than paradise itself, enclosing "the Quintessence and perfection of saving Doctrine," and the eighth chapter, he goes on to say, is like a conduit conveying the waters of life; rather it is the tree of life in the midst of the garden.

Instructed by William Perkins, by Thomas Draxe, by John Downame, whose devotion to practical teaching we noted a few pages back, or by any one of a great number of eminent divines whom we shall have presently to consider, what did men learn from Paul? They learned that the will of God was revealed in the Bible, in the human heart and in nature. "For the invisible things of him from the creation of the world are clearly seen, being understood by the things that are made, even his eternal power and Godhead." The first revelation of God's will was in the law, and so long as man obeyed the law, he was happy. Disobeying it, he was inevitably and justly damned forever. No man from that time forth, since all are members one of another, could be justified under the law in the eyes of God. "For all have sinned, and come short of the glory of God." "There is none righteous, no, not one," and nothing that any man of his own motion is able to do can avail under the law to remove the universal imputation of sin. But now comes grace. By sin man surrendered his freedom, and so left it solely to God whether to save him or not as He might freely choose. God chose to do so in the person of his Son who, taking upon himself the nature of man, atoned once and for all for the sin of man. "Wherefore, as by one man sin entered into the world, and death by sin; and so death passed upon all men, for that all have sinned, . . . even so by the righteousness of one the free gift came upon all men unto justification of life." Therefore, though

the old Adam is still present in us imput ing sin to our members, so also may th new Adam be present imputing right eousness. We are saved, if we are saved not by satisfying the law, for that, whicl we could not do for ourselves, Chris accomplished for us, but by receivin; Christ into our spirits, by believing i him and in the sufficiency of his right eousness without help from us to aton« for all our sins, no matter how man» or how black.

But this led to a question of the utmos concern to the individual human soul. I every sinner therefore saved? If not then who are the elect and who are th« damned, and on what ground are they chosen or rejected? What can a man dc to be saved, and how can he win th« assurance of grace? Tremendous debate« expressing differences of thought tha· have long continued to trouble us unde» other terms raged over these points Even the devils in Milton's hell occupiec their leisure in disputes over "fixed fate free will, fore-knowledge absolute." Tc the orthodox the answer seemed clear. Not all men were saved. Multitudes were eternally damned. God alone determinec from the beginning who these should be. "For whom he did foreknow, he alsc did predestinate to be conformed to the image of his Son, that he might be the firstborn among many brethren." These alone and for no cause but God's free grace were predestined to be one with the redeemer. The rest remained under the law in the flesh, dead in spirit, at enmity with God. The manifestation of grace in the elect was faith. Those destined to be saved in Christ believed in his power and willingness to redeem. Those who believed evinced to themselves their faith and their redemption by making incessant war on sin in their own members. It was not that they could do no evil. They sinned again and again. But the evil which they did they hated. "For I delight in the law of God after the nward man: But I see another law in my members, warring against the law of my mind." The saint was a fighting, not an innocent, soul. He put on the whole armor of God and went forth to war against the sin that dwells in all flesh. This, so long as he kept it up, was the evidence of his election. The outcome need never be in doubt. He who never ceased fighting was sure to triumph in the end. That was predestined. "We are more than conquerors through him that loved us." Fascinated, the Puritan mind hung endlessly upon the facile but inscrutable phrases of the eighth chapter of Romans: "Moreover, whom he did predestinate, them he also called: and whom he called, them he also justified: and whom he justified, them he also glorified." . . .

The persuasive strength of the doctrine of predestination, as the Puritan preachers presented it, sprang not from its metaphysical but its moral validity. It could, men believed, be proved by inexorable logic out of scripture, but what really convinced them was its fruitfulness when applied to their own living situation. It was supremely apposite. It supplied a basis both practical and ideal for decision. It suggested an attitude and a line of conduct. Put to the test of experience, it applied and it worked. The concept of universal depravity, by leveling all superiority not of the spirit, enormously enhanced the self-respect of the ordinary man. If none were righteous, then one man was as good as another. God chose whom he would and the distinctions of this world counted for nothing. The concept of free grace still further heightened his confidence. If the only real aristocracy was the aristocracy created by God, then nothing really counted but character and inner worth. Only they were Jews who were Jews inwardly, and the true circumcision was not that of the body. If election were manifested not by

outward conformity to an imposed law but by the struggle of the spirit within against the weakness and disobedience of the flesh, then any man might find reason for hope within his own breast. If all this was predestined, then there could be no fear concerning the issue of life's ordeal. "If God be with us, who can be against us?" The triumph of the saints was foreordained. Therefore nothing they could desire was impossible for them to attain. Heaven was theirs already, and if presently they demanded possession of the earth as well, that was no more than human. . . .

Election, vocation, justification, sanctification, glorification, here was the perfect formula explaining what happened to every human soul born to be saved. It explained what happened to Paul, what might happen at any time to the very sinners who sat at the preacher's feet. The preacher could, of course, prove the formula to his own satisfaction beyond shadow of rational doubt. He could deduce it, that is, by an intellectual method which few of his hearers knew enough to question from premises which few men alive could critically examine. But it was far less important for his purposes to prove the formula than to demonstrate from observation and experience of life, as seen in himself, in the people about him and in the poetic narrative of scripture, precisely how it worked. In sermons and popular treatises almost beyond number, the Puritan preachers described the psychological pattern which exemplified the working of the formula, which all the saints were supposed to have exemplified and which every man who desired to be saved must hope would be exemplified again in his own case. As in later times men were taught to follow with patient observation the least workings of natural law in the external universe, men in the Puritan age were taught to follow by intense introspection the working of the law of predestination within their own souls. Theoretically, there was nothing they could do but watch, nothing they could of their own will do to induce or further the process of regeneration. They were only the witnesses of a drama which moved to its predetermined end according to a law they could do no more than marvel at. But the theatre of that drama was the human breast, and their own fate right up to the deathbed scene hung upon its outcome. They watched its unfolding, therefore, with the most absorbed attention. With the most anxious curiosity, they looked into their own most secret thoughts for signs that the grace of God was at its work of regeneration, and what they so urgently looked for they naturally saw. Seen by the light of the word, as they read it in the holy book and heard it expounded from the pulpit, their own lives fell under their gaze into the pattern set by Paul.

For their further prompting a flood of books soon came pouring forth from the shops of enterprising printers and booksellers. . . . The most powerful and lasting effect of the popularization of Pauline doctrine . . . was to arouse the most active widespread interest in the inner experience of every individual human being and an almost equally active and widespread activity in giving expression to that interest. Every man was either a convert or susceptible of conversion, and the inner life of any man, once converted, was fraught with daily possibilities for struggle and adventure. It followed that every man's state of spiritual health was the subject of acute concern to the man himself and of sympathetic curiosity to others. Naturally this gave occasion to the reporting and comparing of individual case histories, to the endless retailing of confession, reminiscence and anecdote. Out of such, shall we say, spiritual gossip arose a body of legend and a type of popular literature which was soon found to be quite as edifying and certainly as fascinating as the more formal tracts and sermons. The conditions for the development of such a form of expression were perfect—a generally accepted pattern and opportunities as abundant as life for variations upon a common theme. The devout Puritan turned his back on stage plays and romances, but only in order to look in his own heart and write what happened there. Speaking from the pulpit, the preacher did not as a rule supply explicit personal details, though his teaching was presumed to reflect personal experience. But outside the pulpit, the preacher—and of course common saints were encouraged to follow his example—was free to talk about himself and other people as much as he wished. Not only that, but he very generally kept a journal of his transactions with God and the devil or at least left written record of his conversion. The diary . . . became the Puritan substitute for the confessional, and though few diaries have actually been preserved intact, the substance of many and the fact of their having been kept are apparent in the mass of biographical writing which rapidly accumulated as the Puritan movement progressed.

For an understanding of the nature and purpose of these diaries, we can best turn to a little treatise, called *The Journal or Diary of a Thankful Christian,* published in 1656. It is by John Beadle, himself a preacher who had been "watered by the droppings of that great Elijah, that renowned man of God in his generation, Reverend Mr. Thomas Hooker." The state, says Beadle, has its "diurnals" of affairs, tradesmen keep their shop books, merchants their accounts, lawyers their books of precedents and physicians theirs of experiments, wary heads of households their records of daily disbursements and travelers theirs of things seen and endured. But Christians, who like stewards or factors must one day give strict account to their Lord, have even more to gain by keeping a journal. The godly man should "keep a strict account of his effectual calling." If possible, he should "set down the time when, the place where, and the person by whom he was converted." He should make note of all the men and means that God has at any time used for his good, especially the services of parents, schoolmasters and patrons. He will find it singularly useful to put into his diary "what Times we have lived in, what Minister we have lived under, what Callings we were of, what Wealth was bestowed on us, what places of Authority and Command were committed to us." Most important of all, the Christian should record all the mercies of Providence, all the answers vouchsafed by God to his prayers. "Indeed what is our whole life, but a continued deliverance? We are daily delivered, either from the violence of the creature, or the rage of men, or the treachery of our own hearts; either our houses are freed from firing, or goods from plundering, or our bodies from danger, or our names from reproaches, or our souls from snares." The Puritan faith invested the individual soul, the most trivial circumstances of the most commonplace existence, with the utmost significance. Why should not a man keep a record of matters in which God took so active an interest as he did in the petty moods and doings of any common sinner? . . .

The psychological function of the Puritan autobiography and diary was primarily the same as that of auricular confession. This should not be for us obscured by the fact that, owing to the circumstances of English life, the Puritan confession was imparted to paper and so sooner or later to one's friends and even to the general public in something which finally attained what can only be called literary form. The doctrine of salvation by faith alone became implanted in spiritual experience by a method of self-discipline the effect of which was to build up the self-respect and courage of the individual. When a man or a woman desired to be received into the outward communion of the elect, he or she had to make open acknowledgment of repentance and change of heart. Naturally there was satisfaction to be received and to be given in a specific account of full personal particulars. . . .

The test of the saint's conversion was, of course, to be seen in his perseverance in the faith, and faith must be continually active. Each day one sinned, each day one must repent, each day one must be reconciled afresh to God, and each day one must—or at any rate it was advised that one should—enter these circumstances in one's diary. It was of the very essence of Puritan self-discipline that whatsoever thoughts and actions the old Adam within had most desire to keep hidden, the very worst abominations of the heart, one must when one retired to one's private chamber at night draw forth into the light of conscience. To set them down in writing, albeit in secret "character," was a great help in this. They were the devil incarnate in man and could drag him down to hell. It was also of the essence of Puritan discipline that one should remember and record the good things that happened. These showed the saint that, bad as he was, God had not forsaken him, that God was still taking an intimate and loving interest in his affairs even when bestowing afflictions upon him. Having thus balanced his spiritual books, he could go to bed with a good conscience, sleep sound and wake with courage. Some of the biographies are nothing if not explicit in stating the point and in making plain the profit to be derived from such daily posting of one's accounts with God. . . .

We need not further multiply illustrations of the way in which the spiritual preachers lived their lives and also turned them into pious legend. Of no less importance is it to note that they composed according to the same pattern the lives of people they converted. Thus the experience of the commonest men came also to be dignified by the spirit into literary material no less worthy and interesting than that concerning the preachers themselves. . . . The account of Katherine Brettargh (1579–1601) is the picture of an almost incredibly perfect Puritan child and wife. "The Sabbath day was always dear and welcome to her, and though many times she went far for it, yet she would not be without the Ministery of the Word: And her heart was so tender, and full of compassion, that oftentimes she was perceived to hear Sermons, read, pray, and meditate, with tears." Married at twenty, she was the model helpmeet, bountiful to the poor, faithful to her program of daily prayer, reading and meditation. In two years she died, and her biographer spares us none of the horrors of her deathbed temptation, concluding though they do, as always, in the victory of the spirit.

In 1625 John Bruen (born 1560), her brother, died, and another preacher, William Hinde, wrote his life. It is a particularly rich and vivacious account of a Puritan Squire Allworthy, a pillar of the faith in the countryside and a benefactor of the faithful, painful preachers. In youth he was much given to "hawking, hunting, and such carnal delights." But he soon repented and then none more earnest than he in the good life. Early and late, in heat and cold, he would ride to hear sermons and bring home copies of what he heard. No wonder that, after thirty-six years of such practice, "he left to the heirs of his Family so many Volumnes of Manuscripts set up orderly in his Study, as is scarce credible." Naturally he also set up godly preachers in his neighborhood, even at

his own expense, "honoring God with his substance, by giving maintenance to such as were the Lords Labourers in his harvest." He ordered the painted windows which darkened his chapel with superstitious images to be torn down and the windows glazed again. He brought in so many preachers that "the Pipers, Fidlers, Bearwards, Players and Gamesters," who had been infesting the town of Tarvin on Sundays, fled and the place was filled instead by "multitudes of welaffected people." To be sure he fed solid creature meals to the godly upon these occasions, "so that at one of these times, he spent in his house a fat Beef and a half in the space of three dayes." He was much given to hospitality. "His house was the common Inn of Gods children that came neer him." There was no waste permitted, but a bountiful sufficiency obtained at his table, furnished as it was from "a great flight of Pigeons, a Warren of Conies, delicate Fishponds, besides other ordinary provision." Thus, especially in the "deer years," he filled the bellies of multitudes. But he was truly admired for his practice of religion, "insomuch that divers Gentlemen of the best rank desired to sojourn in his house, for their better information in the way of God." His servants profited no less. He employed only such as set their faces toward heaven, and he treated them as brothers in Christ. Consequently he had no man or maid who was idle or unprofitable. He was especially devoted to one old fellow, who, though he could not read, "had a good gift in prayer," knew the Bible, and kept a leather girdle he had invented as an aid to memory, "long and large, which went twice about him." It was divided into parts, one for each book, with points and thongs for chapters and knots for verses. "This he used instead of pen and ink in hearing Sermons." His master went often to barn or hopyard to confer with him, fed him from the high table when he grew old, and when he died kept his girdle, "and would merrily call it the Girdle of verity." Thus John Bruen lived his life according to the rule the preachers set, earned their gratitude, made a properly edifying end and left to one of them the materials with which to write a biography for the encouragement of other godly inclined gentlemen. He had many imitators and successors among those who had it in their power likewise to further the work of the Lord. . . .

Along with the sermons and treatises in which they anatomized the spiritual life and with the diaries and confessional biographies in which they and their proselytes depicted the workings of grace in particular cases, the preachers also took to setting forth the pattern of daily existence which the saint should follow. We have already seen that Richard Rogers and the preachers of his neighborhood, even while the Armada loomed off the Essex shore, were much occupied with the attempt to draw up a rule of life for their own and others' guidance. The results emerged in 1603 in the publication of Rogers' *Seven Treatises*. "I propound," says the author, "to helpe the frailtie of Gods children, . . . by setting before their eies as in a glasse, the infinite, secret, and deceitfull corruptions of the heart: from whence . . . sore and dangerous evils doe arise." But along with this, he proposes to give them a rule which will enable them to overcome and escape these dangers. He desires "to intreate and to aide my poore neighbours and brethren . . . if by many meanes I may be able hereby, to make the Christian way anything more easie and pleasant unto them, then many finde it: and to bring it into more price, then the most doe value it at." The saints have knowledge of "their wants, their infirmities, their corruptions, rebellions, hindrances & other discouragements." He will soon show them "how they may every day in the best manner, remedie, or at least

wise weaken and diminish them, and that they may also behold their liberties and prerogatives, which they have by Christ." Other writers, he says at the conclusion to his book, have set forth many good things for the instruction of their fellows. None has heretofore done what he has done, namely "driven at this one particular of daily directing a Christian."

It takes Rogers in the *Seven Treatises* just short of six hundred large quarto pages to depict all the perils and to prescribe all the duties of the Christian day. He writes plainly and not without abundance of homely illustration and particular application, but he has not yet learned that men can weary even of the plainest and most wholesome instruction if too long protracted. This lesson, however, was not wasted on the preachers. Many were the short and easy expositions of the Puritan code published by Rogers' successors. A typical example, one of the most frequently reprinted, was *A Garden of Spirituall Flowers*. This little manual was made up of brief plain statements of doctrine and of practical directions for godly living, culled and condensed from the writings of Rogers himself, from Richard Greenham, William Perkins and two less-known men. It tells one how to act like a saint and so rest assured that one has grace. It passes from "Short Rules sent by Master Richard Greenham to a Gentlewoman troubled in minde" to "A short Direction for the daily Exercise of a Christian, both on the Sabbath day, and also on the week dayes."

Let us glance for a moment at the ideal day of the elect, as described in *A Garden of Spirituall Flowers* and the many other popular presentations of the Puritan code. The saint is told to awake with God and pray. "And let this bee done solemnely upon thy knees (and not as many doe, lazing upon their beds) that it may bee done with a humble, pure, and sincere devotion." If he is the head of a household, he should be stirring early to call his family together for morning prayers. After breakfast he may betake himself to his ordinary calling and business, seeing that his family does likewise. There are "Rules for the behaving of [himself] Christian-like in imployment about [his] worldly businesse, and enjoying the benefit of the same." He must keep close watch upon his heart, words and deeds, and see that his time is not idly, carelessly or unprofitably spent. He must mind his own business and let other men mind theirs. "Be not a Tale-berer, nor a Tale-receiver: deale justly & uprightly with all men: let thy conversation be without covetousnesse, and without prodigalitie: serve the Lord in singlenesse of heart: be doing good, and abstaine from all appearance of evill." In the same spirit he is told how to bear himself in company and in solitude, in prosperity and in adversity. He is not to shun prosperity nor yet to set his heart upon it. If it comes, it will come as God's free gift and is to be used as such. He is not to fear the adversity which God may bestow for the strengthening of his spirit. Business done, he goes home and concludes the day by gathering his household once more about him. He reads to them from scripture, catechizes them, sings psalms and prays with them. Then he goes to his chamber to meditate and, as we have seen, to balance his spiritual accounts. And so to bed. For Sundays, he is given special directions. In church, whither he proceeds in the morning at the head of his family, he must keep his eyes fixed on the preacher, so that thoughts may not wander. He is advised to mark the speaker's text, observe how it is "divided," note the handling of each division, find the places in scripture alleged for proof, fold down the leaf at the appropriate passages so that he may review them at leisure. Then home again to discuss the sermon

with the family after dinner and back again to church to repeat the whole performance in the afternoon. If such a program seem preposterous to the man of the present day, he should remember that his forefathers even in the conduct of this world's business were concerned about their consciences. Perhaps the desire of later generations to escape from Puritanism has been at least in part a desire to do business with less hindrance from a scheme of life so insistent upon keeping the individual forever in mind of his moral responsibilities. . . .

One further aspect of the Puritan conception of the good life remains to be presented before we undertake to discuss the saga of the spiritual life set forth in the sermons. The preachers endeavored by precept and example to show how the elect, while living according to the code of saintliness, must use their gifts and opportunities in this life. The Puritan code was much more than a table of prohibitions. It was the program of an active, not a monastic or contemplative, life. The saints stripped themselves for battle, and only as the battle waxed hot and desperate did they degenerate into the fanatical iconoclasts of familiar tradition. Milton's lady scorned not the gifts that Comus offered her but the giver. "Worldly things," according to Sibbes, "are good in themselves, and given to sweeten our passage to Heaven," even to sweeten our "profession of Religion." We must use the world as our servant, not our master, take comfort in it but not set our hearts upon it or let ourselves be made "drunke with the cares below." All is, in other words, as we have grace to use it. "This world and the things thereof are all good, and were all made of God, for the benefit of his creature." John Dod, gathering his flock about him, opening his doors to all comers, sitting down at the head of a full table, talking himself thirsty, and calling for a draft of wine and beer mixed, was no bigoted ascetic, though he did disapprove of stage plays, dancing and card-playing. The saint had no reason to fear the world or run away from it. Rather he must go forth into it and do the will of God there. Rogers scorns the suggestion that, if men live according to the godly rule, they will neglect their necessary affairs "and so poverty grow upon the land." On the contrary, he says, he who goes about his work, not first attending upon God by faith, "goeth about it preposterously, & shal find his successe answerable." "He riddeth not most worke, who goeth to it most early, when his instruments which he should use in the performance of the same be blunt and dull." "Godlinesse hinders not mens labours, neither decaies the Common-wealth." There is a "godly thrift," a "Christian gaining" and a "lawfull prospering" which come to him who goes to work "with a minde which is at peace with God." Who cannot see that by the labor of such men "the Commonwealth . . . should flourish much more, having a certeine promise of blessing"?

The saint knows that he need not fear to lose a penny while he stops to say his prayers. He knows that whatever he has and whatever he gains in the course of business comes from God. His prime piece of capital, he knows, consists in the abilities and opportunities which God has bestowed upon him for doing the business of the world. They are his talent, and he never forgets by whom this was given or by whom and on what terms it will be exacted in return. This doctrine comes, of course, directly from the parable of the talents, "wherein," to use the words of Gabriel Powell, "is shewed, that no man, of what state or condition soever hee bee, is Lord of his owne riches or substance, but the steward and disposer of it, accountable unto God for all things." It is the theme of Milton's sonnet concerning the one talent which is death to hide. Our indi-

vidual abilities are not given us as rewards to be enjoyed—no sinner merits any favor from God. Nor does God grant them as necessary means to ends of his own—"God doth not need either man's work or his own gifts." They are bestowed as unconditioned occasions for service upon such as truly love their maker. Those who put their gifts to work, or, as Milton would have it, merely stand ready and waiting to do so, may feel assured that they please him. Those who do not may expect one day to hear the master chide. For, to quote Powell once more, "we must be accountable for the least farthing which we have received of God; after what manner we came by it, how and to what use we have bestowed and spent it."

No part of the Puritan code was more weighted with practical significance than this. Nothing in the postulates of Puritan doctrine up to this point was inconsistent with the stopping of Puritanism at mere pietism within self-centered groups of believers, and such pietistic groups did in fact spring up within the Puritan movement as among Protestants on the continent. But by insistence upon the moral aspects of the doctrine of the talent the preachers opened a wide door through which they drove their flocks out into the world to have their fill of experience. To be specific, they gave in this way to the general doctrine of God's calling a definite application. When God called his elect to repent and believe, he also called upon them to act. The gifts and opportunities, no matter how humble and narrow, with which the saint was invested were also part of his commission from God. Whatsoever we undertake in the exercise of our talents and in the spirit of faith is good. It is what God has called us to do. Woe unto us if we do not do it, and happy the man who responds to the vocation of his own abilities. God is strict about his business, but just. "They which are furnished with gifts for their callings, namely aptnesse and willingnesse, and are thereunto called or set apart by men" may rest assured that they are called by God. Moreover, when they walk in a calling lawful in itself and suited to their capacities, they are walking in his presence and under his special protection. This was a conviction destined to have disturbing results when authority attempted to rule that it was not lawful for a Milton to exercise his talent for instructing his fellow countrymen or a Lilburne his for trading in pamphlets, wool or soap. For the doctrine of the talent also taught that all "offices & callings which serve to preserve the good estate of any family, Church or common wealth, are lawfull & of God." Was not every man, since all were equal under the law of God, required to believe "that the

calling in which he is; is the particular calling in which God [would] bee served of him?" Any common man needed but to know in his heart that what he did he did sincerely as God's own work, and it followed that what he did was what God would have him do. His own conscience was the judge of his own conduct. "Common actions are as the doer is affected. A sincere man . . . is commanded to serve God in his calling as well as in the Church, and therefore he will not," indeed he cannot, "doe it negligently . . . He will not do it falsely, he will not prophane his calling." Common actions thus performed "with an eye to God" were all "good, and religious actions. For the Grace of God is a blessed Alcumist, where it toucheth it makes good, and religious." . . .

Franz Borkenau

THE NEW MORALITY
AND THE
NEW THEOLOGY

With the decomposition of the traditionalistic, estate-bound social order, established law and the political order became separated from the moral demands which the individual imposes upon himself. A larger scope for individual desire is now possible within the coarsely-woven web of an essentially prohibitive legal order. This area, freed

From Der Übergang vom feudalen zum bürgerlichen Weltbild. Paris: 1934, pp. 152–170. Translated for this anthology by Ann Harding. By permission of Frau Hilde Borkenau and Presses Universitaires de France.

from legal regulation, is not deprived of all structure. Rather, its emergence calls into being two new sorts of structure. The economic life of capitalism prevails in the area freed from legal regulation. It is not a product of egoism, of a fictitious purely egotistical human nature. As Max Weber has shown, its functioning requires a completely new ascetic attitude of the masses to the process of work. This can be attained neither by legalised forced labour, as in serfdom, nor by the tradition of an estate, sanctioning an unalterable quota of work. The problem of a new mass morality becomes acute, it becomes necessary to supplement the legally defined minimal moral performance with a maximal moral standard, whether sanctioned by religion or something else. Simultaneously, a new moral problem arises for that part of the upper stratum which does not participate directly in the capitalistic process of production. In the disintegration of estate conceptions of honor, the increasing prevalence of capitalistic behavior, the binding force of tradition dissolves; the question becomes how the uprooted individual is now to conduct himself as he confronts a new life.

We have already met this problem from time to time. In the concept of Natural Law the emphasis shifted from society to the individual, to the same degree as the "natural" social order disappeared. Torn out of his seemingly natural communal environment, the individual can no longer derive the meaning of his life (to use the term for the moment without further definition) from society, but has to seek it only in himself. As this process develops, the projection back onto nature of human problems becomes ever more pronounced. What on the one side seems to be the pre-history of the modern idea of nature seems to be, on the other, the emergence of a doctrine of the human individual. Man is to derive his life goal from his nature; there develops a philosophical anthropology (described in great detail by Dilthey). Ficino's teaching represents the first phase in the development of this new doctrine. For the first time, in the discussion between himself and Pomponazzi, the problem of the human soul is the center of attention; Ficino puts all his efforts into depicting its troubled course as cosmically meaningful. The direct relationship of the individual soul to the cosmos is propounded at the same time in the very same Florence where Machiavelli is the

first to presuppose the absence of any natural social order. Soon even this attempt to relate the soul to a cosmic order is abandoned. In the naturalism of Vives and Cardanos the most perfect individual, the *uomo universale,* himself becomes the meaning of his own life and therewith the meaning of the entire *genus.* This ideal, however, disappears just like the idea of an order based on natural law. In the collapse which the Counter-Reformation entailed for Italy, in the catastrophe of the wars of religion in France and the Netherlands, the style of life of the noble and fulfilled individual, sovereign amidst a disintegrating social order, becomes impossible. Instead of a conception of the individual as a nature-like unity, which was possibly perfect, appeared a soul delivered up to the unavoidable buffeting of fate. The idea of individual character loses the naive obviousness which it possessed in the Renaissance, and it finally comes to be seen that different and opposing natures struggle within the isolated individual.

Before this development reached the stage of Vives' conception of natural law, Calvinism, concerned with the other side of the problem of morality, the problem of mass morality, proclaimed its final result: the total depravity of individual human nature. It alone proclaims without any reservation the depravity of the world, the basic antagonism of duty and desire, the sphere of lawless, natural egoism, the contingency of success in its relation to action.

As we know, Calvin's attitude, generally favorable to capitalism, also had an effect on his explicit economic and political views, on his attitude towards interest, towards change of occupation, etc. As equally undeniable as this sympathetic relationship of Calvin to capitalism, is the affinity of the first Calvinist social strata for capitalism. The ideology of the Renaissance, however, was based on the social strata of financial and mercantile capital. But then these strata remained distant for a long time from the capitalist process of production, with which the developing Calvinist morality was above all concerned. It is one of the most important insights to result from all M. Weber's research that the first manufacturers to introduce capitalist methods systematically into the production process, did not come from the financial and merchant-bourgeoisie, but from rising artisans. The two strata of speculative financial capital and solid manufacturing capital felt bitter hostility for each other. Just as little as the manufacturing bourgeoisie developed from the monied aristocracy of the Renaissance did its ideology derive from their Renaissance aestheticism. On the other hand nothing is more certain than that in most countries—in addition to certain individuals of the high nobility, who took up the cause of the Reformation for political reasons—the mass of the lesser nobility were the first to fight for Calvinism in its first period: in Holland the "Geusen"; in France the lesser nobility, above all in the south and south-west, whom we find in all the battles of the Huguenot wars; the same is true for Scotland. In addition to the lesser nobility, and perhaps numerically stronger, the main supporters in France, as in Holland and England, were the artisans whose guild organization was disintegrating. There was also rather a strong influx of intellectuals, but only at the beginning, at any rate in France. But the development of these strata within the Calvinist confession took a basically different course. The artisans remained loyal everywhere; in the further course of development they became manufacturers or proletarians wherever the capitalist stage was reached. The manufacturers later combined with part of the banking elite and both together led the Calvinist communities. This fact

has been specially demonstrated for France. On the other hand the nobility maintained its leading role only as long as and in those places where no capitalist development took place, in Scotland until the 17th century and in Hungary. In Holland it remained loyal to the Calvinist cause, having become completely bourgeois. In England it never had a major share in the Calvinist movement. In France finally the nobility were defecting from the confession in large numbers since Henry IV, so that even before the evocation of the Edict of Nantes, not a single notable aristocrat belonged to their ranks. Thus Calvinism became, in the course of its development, a purely bourgeois confession; indeed in all three modern capitalist countries, in France, Holland and England, it became the bourgeois confession. The attitude of the different strata to it varied in the same measure as they were close to or distant from modern capitalism—that is to say the systematically working not primarily speculative form. This means, however, that Calvinism was originally the confession of strata which were developing towards manufacturing capitalism. Everywhere manufacturing capitalism took its recruits from the higher strata of the artisans and that part of the nobility which had turned bourgeois; it is these two groups which grew together to become the founding fathers of the Calvinist communities in a union that only seemed outwardly strange. There are only two ways out of the disintegration which monetary capital brings into all feudal structures: to sink into the misery of serfdom, cottage industry, a life of outlawry and vagrancy, or to rise into the capitalist class by means of the most austerely rational work.

Calvinism is in the first instance the confession of non-capitalist groups, who react to the capitalist process of disintegration with a movement of adjustment. They do not represent at first any unified class, but are rather a conglomeration of the most varied strata, which have been brought together by the same developmental tendency and which, in the course of this development, become more alike, that is to say more bourgeois. M. Weber's thesis, that the capitalist outlook of these strata preceded their capitalist form of life, is therefore right. But it is limited by the limitations of M. Weber's formulation. For it must first be investigated why these strata, who were not yet capitalist, assumed a capitalist ideology. Then it will become apparent that under the influence of the infiltration of monetary capital they developed in a direction which necessitated a much more thoroughly capitalized way of life, than had occurred ever before in history.

Since the discussion which M. Weber began on the relationship between protestantism and capitalism is of vital importance, something more must be said about the methodological side of the point in question. The result which M. Weber believes he obtains from empirical material is a priori completely given by the isolating causal methodology which he employs.

His approach is isolating in so far as he is only aware of historical facts and events, which are separated from one another, and which determine the course of history. Did the Calvinist work-morality precede the application of this morality in the capitalist production process? Most certainly! Therefore capitalism is essentially determined by religion. But it is just as certain that certain elements of natural science, for example the experiment, especially applied in art, that a shift in trade routes, more or less chance discoveries of precious metals etc., also preceded the development of modern capitalism. Was it brought about, not by the laws of development, by which feudalism dis-

integrated, but rather by wars, discoveries, inventions and new dogma? This is clearly not the case. All these elements assumed importance only in connection with the disintegration process of feudalism and were determined by it. Ideologies are certainly important in history, otherwise they would not arise. If one looks for their effects without seeking their causes—that is the essence of the isolating method—this will inevitably result in positive refutations of the materialist concept of history. There is, further, a very close connection between the isolating and the mechanistic-causal method. From the viewpoint of both methods it is a foregone conclusion that any attempt to trace back religious ideas to the production process has failed, if these ideas do not correspond exactly with the actual life of the class which confesses them. In what this correspondence should consist, remains here, as in all analogical thinking, unclear. It seems to be clear, however, in any case, that the supporters of a consequently capitalist religion must have been the class most advanced in the direction of capitalism. If that is not the case, then the attempted proof seems to have failed. This is quite wrong! The relationship between a religion and the class that supports it is almost never such, that the religion expresses the real conditions of life of this class. As a mere "reflection" it would be meaningless. New religions make possible difficult processes of adaptation, that is to say they direct energies towards a form of life which is not yet in existence. All ideological processes are developed by resolute people, who respond to outside influences not according to mechanical laws, but by means of spontaneous adaptation with the aim of self-preservation. Since history is constituted by the actions of beings gifted with spontaneity, there are in history, as distinct from the realm of mechanics, developmental tendencies.

These developmental tendencies arise regularly from the efforts of groups, to maintain themselves within a changing total society. The isolating-causal method which recognises only specific causal relationships, lacks all means to describe these relationships. Meanwhile it must have become clear, that in this polemic we oppose dialectical materialism, which is based on the categories of totality and objective tendency, to mechanistic thinking.

The transformation of the tendency to adapt to capitalism into Calvinist dogma proceeds in a very clear way. Calvinism contains, in so far as individual morality is concerned, two main points: the first is the assertion of the depravity of the world and the human being. It implies the proclamation of the antisocial egoism of the individual as the only earthly driving power, and the assertion of the contingency of performance and success. The second is decisive. The philosophy of the late Renaissance, too, stressed the central importance of the self-preservation of the isolated individual. The Calvinist concept of contingency prevents, however, any aesthetic or ethical interpretation of this egoism. For the Renaissance the egotistical life led to perfection, whether of the beautiful individual, or of the soul freed from the body. In contrast to this the basic concept of Calvinist dogma of free, basically arbitrary predestination contains the idea that no conduct of simply any kind whatsoever can give human existence an immanent aim: neither a divine one, for the connection between virtue and salvation is expressly denied, nor an earthly one, for that would be idolisation of the flesh. It is not by chance that the condemnation of every spontaneous pleasure as idolisation of the flesh is paramount in the ethical commandments of Calvinism. It excludes the possibility of an aesthetic view of the world. Here it can be seen very clearly how different social groups regard the same facts from different points

of view. The egoism of the isolated individual is basic for the Renaissance and Reformation. The former interpreted it as a context of harmonious beauty, not because the life of this period and stratum was filled with harmonious beauty—quite the contrary—but because it was attempting to develop in the direction of a landed rentier class, whose ideal of existence is an harmonious aestheticism, which despises the life of the masses. The Calvinists are also nothing but uprooted egoistical individuals, but they develop from this condition, in conscious opposition to the Renaissance, a life of irrational exertion. The monied bourgeoisie is the beneficiary of the disintegration process of feudalism; it must therefore idealise the new world. Those strata, however, which are uprooted by the disintegration, can only see the world in darkest colours.

But a second element has to be added to this consistent assertion of depravity if a capitalist morality is to arise. For the mere statement of depravity leaves yet another way open: to conduct oneself in a depraved world in accordance with it. We shall show, that this second possibility has also given rise to a theory. In order to demand a moral effort in a depraved world, a special religious doctrine is necessary. The content of this effort is not, in fact, referred to by the religious doctrine, or more exactly only formally. Within a capitalist economy there is only the way of life of the adventurer—which M. Weber has called political capitalism—and the struggle for victory in the competitive battle by means of rationalised, almost limitless effort. The Calvinist idea of proving oneself does not in itself contain, as M. Weber believes, a capitalist material attitude. For the way in which anyone proves himself successfully depends entirely on the milieu in which he lives. Unlimited effort as a means of proving oneself is employed only, where other forms of conduct lead to failure. That is not necessarily a capitalist economy; by way of exception this can take place in a society, whose members have been transplanted from a capitalist world into an initially non-capitalist one, as in New England, and who then continue their capitalist form of existence; above all it suffices for the working strata to be compelled to adapt to monetary (finance) capital. The idea of proving oneself leads, therefore, to the introduction of capitalist methods of work only under special economic conditions. But it must first of all be proclaimed in order to be effective in this direction. This Calvinism does: in order to be able to do it, it needs the terrifying figure of the Deus absconditus who rises behind the evil world. He demands irrational moral effort. Irrational in a threefold sense: unrelated to divine salvation, to success in work, and above all to individual happiness. As in Thomism the satisfaction of earthly instincts and supernatural salvation are united in the concept of the lex naturalis, so both are condemned together in Calvinism in the rejection of this idea and its replacement by the idea of proving oneself. The whole content of this idea is: unlimited moral effort, in full consciousness of the impossiblity of justifying it rationally in any direction. The idea of proving oneself is the last link of Calvinist morality, fully developed only in the 17th century. The point of departure of Calvinism is only the depravity of the world and an extremely rigoristic morality despite it. This moral rigorism makes Calvinism at once different in mood from Lutheranism. Predestined salvation through faith is common to both reformed confessions. But whilst Lutheranism from the very beginning stresses salvation by faith and by this means subjectively weakens the experience of depravity, Calvinism lays all its emphasis on the manifestation of faith through works. In a world which lacks every material norm of justice, this manifestation can only take the form of unlimited effort irrespective of its content. In so far as practical moral theology links the *certitudo salutatis* to the success of this effort, it draws expressly those consequences which are laid down from the very beginning in the doctrine.

Now it is clear why the developing manufacturing bourgeoisie can have no other ideology than an irrationalist-religious one. In a society where unlimited effort in competition has not yet become the inevitable claim of the instinct for self-preservation, it appears to the individual as entirely irrational. Two things are therefore needed to justify it: a conception of the depravity of the world in which rational conduct in the medieval sense is impossible, as well as the conception of a God, whose commands are irrational and who is according to human standards evil. To carry out the process of adaptation to capitalism, the artisan and minor aristocrat, besieged by monetary capital, need to make a spontaneous decision. This decision itself, though, has in no way religious content. But then the same decision must be given moral validity against others, and be proclaimed as the norm. The world is evil, the process of adaptation has nothing to do with the natural happiness of individuals. But all the same it must be set in action on all sides; against the catholic adherents of traditional forms of life, who hinder the adaptation, against atheist aestheticising high aristocrats and bankers, the deadly enemies of these strata, against the chiliastic anabaptist, who instead of adaptation to the evil world seeks the millennium. The decision of a limited stratum to renew its life, becomes an ideology which claims to be the norm, in this situation of a struggle with other moral claims. The norm of the capitalist process of production can only be an irrationalist-religious one, so long as it can not depend on the automatic functioning of the capitalist economy.

It must have been noticed that here we have put two elements of Calvinist dogma, the depravity of the world and moral rigorism, bluntly in the foreground, but have not mentioned at all the two doctrines which are regarded as typical of Calvinism: predestination and the absence of free will. We believe that with this order of rank we portray historical reality exactly. Predestination and the absence of free will are not as new as they appear, new is only the connection in which Calvinism regards them and which is determined by the concept of the evil world. In the initial stages they were of no central importance in the battle for the masses. Autin has rightly emphasised that the catholic masses were not repelled by these doctrines, but by the rejection of the worship of the saints, the sacraments and papal authority. All this affects the treasury of grace of the church, that is to say the belief, deeply rooted in all traditionalist forms of life, in the possibility of gaining salvation in this world and the next by precisely fixed, traditionally defined performances and consequently the possibility of making good the deficiencies in these performances through conventional penitence and supplication. That Calvinism denied this, that it rejected respectable moral comfort together with enthusiastic veneration and life-embracing ritual, provoked the masses to anger, not the absence of free will and predestination. There was equally little reason for theological objection to these two doctrines. As late as the 17th century a large portion of Catholic theologians espoused both doctrines. And there can be no doubt that they are in agreement with Thomism. Thomas quite definitely made salvation and condemnation of mankind dependent on the predetermination of God. He exempted one

group of phenomena from determination by providence: the contingent ones. God knows indeed the contingent beforehand, too, but he does not bring it about. Free human actions are the main realm of contingency. Predestination consists of the granting of supernatural grace, which removes the contingency of human actions; it is therefore always predestination to salvation. The punishment on the other hand consists in the fact that God leaves the human being to himself. Without supernatural grace it is impossible to gain salvation. Good works and the intercession of the saints do not change God's decision, they themselves are rather predetermined links of the chain, through which God's decision is realised. The exemption of "free actions" from predetermination is therefore merely formal. In the inevitability of salvation, or, respectively, damnation, the theory of Thomas has the same result as Calvin's. Thomas is far removed from that doctrine of the freedom of the will which prevails today within Catholicism under Jesuit influence. If he separates punishment from predestination and ascribes the guilt to free will, then he does it purely for the sake of theodicy. Calvin attributes the rejection of the reprobates to the activity of God, Thomas to his passive laissez-faire attitude. This is merely an apologetically important difference. For even according to Calvin nothing more is necessary for reprobation, than that God leaves man to his own depravity.

Therefore on the basis of our system of categories, we would expect that Thomas, like Calvin, would teach the absence of free human will, which must necessarily end in damnation if it is not turned to good through God's compelling grace. But Thomas teaches the opposite. In so far as the human will seems to him to be necessarily determined, then it is not determination for evil but for good. Even after the Fall man

is a being destined by nature for salvation. (Is not this theory, when compared
with Calvin's, a telling symptom of the
growing gloom that permeated the view
of the world in the three intermediate
centuries?) The "necessitas" of the
striving after salvation does not, according to Thomas, conflict with freedom.
It is the very nature of man. Thomas
opposes this positive freedom (which
in its form of necessity is identical with
the Calvinist absence of freedom, but in
its content, the good, is diametrically
opposed to the Calvinist inescapable
depravity) with a negative freedom as it
were, of two kinds: one referring to
understanding, the other to the instincts.
From the supreme evident truths all
other knowledge might be thought to
follow. But for us some truths are evident
and necessary, others contingent. So also
in the case of the will. Man necessarily
strives after the highest good, beatitudo,
but the relation of the secondary goods
to it is often not evident. There are,
therefore, necessary value judgments,
and those that are not. Corruption
through the Fall of man consists in the
fact that often the "appetitus sensualis"
does not obey reason. To overcome this
corruption requires supernatural grace.

The contrast between Thomas and
Calvin on this question rests therefore
not on a different conception of omnipotence and freedom, but on a different
estimation of man; this itself is inseparably connected with the difference of the
moral demands. The positive freedom
of Thomas, the necessary striving after
the good in which man realises his nature,
is denied by Calvin. It would be meaningless on the other hand to call the
inescapable urge in man for evil, "freedom." Freedom in "necessitas" is for
Thomas the realisation of man's own
nature; and the true nature of man
remains even for Calvin the striving after
God, as it existed before the Fall. The
immersion of man in sin is therefore

not freedom but bondage. The contrast
is even greater in the case of freedom of
choice. For Thomas this concept is not,
as first for the Jesuits and since Spinoza
mostly, constituted by the problem of
the necessary determination of man by
efficient causes; in any further discussion
it is of the greatest importance to remember this. That the will is free does not
mean for Thomas, that it acts without
external causes; for it is the "appetites"
which move it in each case. It means
rather that in the choice between these
"appetites," in certain cases no final
cause intervenes. The choice is free, in
so far as it is or appears indifferent from
the stand-point of the ration or beatitudo (both are identical in the result as
to what one chooses). That something
can appear indifferent without being so
is the result of the Fall. But this appearance would not be possible if there were
not really morally indifferent decisions.
Since Thomas regarded the world as
a whole as good, since he accepts all
natural instincts as reasonable, since
consequently the natural life is in itself
moral, then the minority of decisions by
far are the object of a moral problem.
According to his conception the will
has freedom of choice, in so far as the
choice is morally indifferent. We shall
find everywhere the strict connection
between the sphere of freedom of choice
and that of the morally indifferent, as well
as that between the recognition of the
adiaphoron and the optimistic opinion
of "natural" man. Thus it is the radical
denial of the adiaphoron which cause the
Reformation to deny freedom of choice.
For Luther and Calvin there is nothing
indifferent since the Fall corrupted man to
the very core, since everything that he
does is filled with carnal lust, and all
carnal lust is evil. It is in this basically
different estimation of life that the difference lies. For Thomas all natural lust
is good, as long as it is not sinful. For
the Reformers all lust was sinful because

it is natural. Naturally no reformer denied that the majority of actions are indifferent, from the point of view of positive divine and human law. But measured by the standard of human nature they all prove to be products of sin and in relation to the concrete commandment they are only in the sense that different sins can be indifferent to one another.

All this does not affect the modern version of the problem of the freedom of the will. Today we might say that the fact that all actions are evil, does not prevent a free choice between them. But this question never arises with Calvin. For Thomas the inner necessity of the final goal of the will lies in its integration in the ultimate meaningfulness of the hierarchy of the world. Whatever is not necessary in relation to that is not necessary at all but "contingent." Thus whatever is determined by purely external causes, even in the nonorganic world, is for him the contingent. For the Reformers the question remains exactly the same. It is true, human nature is no longer related to God in any comprehensible way. But now as ever no other kind of necessity can be conceived than that with which the members of a hierarchical order are directed towards God as its head, the idea of necessity developed in the feudal period; consequently the absence of this direction of the human life towards God does not mean freedom in the sense of the indifference of the will (an idea that was completely unknown to the modern world before the Jesuits), but an irresistible urge to remain far from God, absolute lack of freedom. In other words, Thomas sets the highest freedom of man in his necessary attachment to God. Calvin has exactly the same system of concepts; since according to him man in his nature is remote from God, he is imprisoned in the greatest servitude. The fact that equal value can be attached to the

different "carnal" actions makes it possible, to differentiate between the positively sinful and the merely generally corrupt as the basis of a practical morality, but it is of no significance for the problem of the freedom of the will. Even more: the question of the natural causal determinants of the will and their limitations—i.e. the real modern problem of the freedom of the will—lies, within this formulation of the question, not only not in the range of vision, but is even impossible. For if the will were simply not determinate then from this point of view a Luciferic independence would have to be ascribed to it. Then man, at the same time both evil and "free," would be a devil, equal to God in power. If, on the other hand, the thorough, causal determination of the decisions of the will, proceeding according to rules, were accepted, even the modest remainder of the theodicy in Calvinism would be impossible. For if the damnation of man took place according to, for us, visible and comprehensible rules, then the God who created the world would be nothing but an evil demon. This would make the moral rigorism, so important practically, impossible. For this presupposes a mysterious and yet certain relation between merit and salvation. Calvinist morality rests on the suspended balance between the doctrine of the depravity of man and that of the wise government of a mysterious God. These two doctrines can be linked only if every natural legitimate connection in human actions is excluded. It will be seen that here, too, there exists a consistent logical connection between the solutions of the problem: those schools which conceive the world and man as essentially good and therefore develop the theodicy from the comprehensible goodness of the world, attribute to God only a passive role in reprobation, since they make man responsible for his possible damnation; at the same time they teach the independence of the causae secundae, which are only indirectly dependent from God, and of their regular effects. The pessimistic schools on the other hand, emphasise the direct intervention of God everywhere, therefore deny the independent regularity of events in the world and stress the mystery of God's decree. The latter is the crucial point. The mysterious is the most important trait of Calvinist particular predestination.

The whole of Calvinist dogma in its contrast with Thomism is completely pervaded by the antagonism of optimism and pessimism or—expressed practically and morally—the recognition or rejection of the importance of good works for salvation. The whole Reformation is, in its very essence, above all the battle for a new mass morality, for this is—since the adaptation of the middle strata to monetary capital presupposes a changed moral attitude—the basic problem of developing capitalism. All philosophical problems are, as the example of Calvinism first shows, decisively determined by this question. We now have still to stress some special features of Calvinist mass morality.

The decisive force of Calvinism when compared to all other anthropological schools, is very largely due to the fact, that Calvinism alone does not know the problem of a double morality. All schools which have developed within Catholicism proceed, for reasons which have still to be discussed, from an assumed duality of mankind: on the one hand the masses who somehow or other must be adapted to the greatest possible exertion of powers, on the other hand the "wise," who by means of an understanding of the total relationship, preserve the possibility of a beautiful life, even in this capitalist world. For Calvinism this duality does not exist. The manufacturer and his workers are first of all formally subjected to the same claims of inner-worldly asceticism. Even the bourgeois has to renounce every comprehensible and meaningful form of life and place himself under the law of unlimited irrational effort. Although Calvinism is for the bourgeoisie an instrument of mass domestication, it is also at the same time an instrument of self-mastery. By this means it gains, when compared to the mystical doctrines for the "wise" which cannot be used for mass-domestication, the powerful superiority of the generally applicable; when compared with a doctrine such as Jesuitism, dedicated purely to domestication, however, it has the advantage of the powerful emotion of a genuine religious conviction, which is not only valid for others, but also for its supporters. It shares its general validity with Thomism, but is superior to it in its inseparable connection with the strongest developing economic power. Thus in the countries in which it prevailed, Calvinism solved the problem of mass morality and made capitalist conduct into something which was taken for granted. In this very feature lie the limitations of the development of theoretical thinking in these countries. We shall see how far all modern philosophical thinking especially is dependent on the fact, that the capitalist form of life remains problematical and needs rational justification. But Calvinism did not demand this, indeed it even excluded it as a result of its irrational assumptions. Naturally Calvinism itself could not answer all the questions that arise in a capitalist society concerning state, economy and technology. Calvinism condemned the conception that life was unified and ordered on the basis of religious principles and limited itself to the purely formal rule of proving oneself; in doing so it subjected all these spheres to a purely inner-worldly interpretation which was at the same time piece-meal. Natural philosophy becomes merely a series of systematised statements of technically important facts, law an interpretation of positive propositions, the economy the result of the accepted fiction of the homo oeconomicus. Thus Calvinism becomes the proclaimer of sober realism, of an empirical systematisation of the parts of human knowledge of the rejection of every unified rational world view. This greatly eases the ideological position of the bourgeoisie. Through this piece-meal, empirical outlook the main difficulty of every Calvinist ideology is circumvented: the impossibility of proving that the demands of capitalist life are in harmony with the drives, with the "nature" of man. Philosophy in the real sense, therefore, could develop within the Calvinist sphere only in the most narrow circles, among unbelievers like Hobbes and Spinoza. The apologetic philosophy on the other hand, which began to appear only towards the end of the 18th century, operated uncritically from Hume and Smith to Bentham and Spencer, with the fiction of the eternity and natural character of capitalist man.

Lucien Goldmann

THE HIDDEN GOD

What was the general condition of science and philosophy in the years during which Pascal wrote the *Pensées?* It was characterised by the triumph of philosophical rationalism and of the scientific and mechanistic attitude, which accompanied it. This mechanistic rationalism had not appeared suddenly on the intellectual scene° like Athene issuing ready armed from the head of Zeus, but owed its triumph to a long struggle against two scientific and philosophical positions that were still alive in the seventeenth century: the Aristotelian and Thomist concept of physics and philosophy, and the animistic philosophy of nature. In 1662, the year of Pascal's death, Thomism still dominated the teaching in most of the Schools, while Aristotelian physics was retreating only slowly before the findings of Galileo, Torricelli and Descartes.[1]

Thomistic Aristotelianism, the animistic philosophy of nature and mechanistic rationalism constitute three stages in the development of Western bourgeois thought, stages which it has successively transcended to reach the irrational tendency which characterises it today.

In the thirteenth century Thomism was the ideological expression of a movement of deep social change. The Third Estate had succeeded in inserting an urban and administrative section governed by 'reason' and secular law into the com-

From The Hidden God (1955). London: 1964, pp. 25–39. By permission of *Routledge & Kegan Paul Ltd.* and *Humanities Press Inc.*

[1]The excellent studies of Father Lenoble on Mersenne, and especially of Monsieur Koyré on Galileo, have thrown much light on the concrete aspects of this evolution.

pletely rural and decentralised hierarchy of the feudal system of the ninth and tenth centuries. The relationship between reason and faith in Thomism reflects and expresses both the real relationship between the Third Estate and the feudal nobility, on the one hand, and between the Church and the State on the other. At the end of the fifteenth century in Italy and Germany, after the discovery of America, and in the second half of the sixteenth century and the first half of the seventeenth in the other countries of Western Europe, the towns, the Third Estate and, later, the central state administration itself, all became sufficiently powerful to challenge the supremacy of the Church and of the feudal nobility. It was then that the Thomistic edifice, with its subordination of philosophy to theology and of reason to faith, and Aristotelian physics, with its subordination of the sublunary to the celestial world, were overthrown to make way for the Monistic and Pantheistic world of natural philosophy. But, as Monsieur Koyré has very intelligently pointed out, natural philosophy did not replace Thomism by a similarly precise and stable system. It abolished the miraculous intervention of the divinity by integrating it into the natural world, but once the possibility of supernatural interference had been destroyed, everything became both natural and possible. Nature had lost her rights, and the criterion which had enabled men to distinguish truth from error, fact from fiction, and the possible from the absurd, gradually became more difficult to discern. The man of bourgeois society, drunk with enthusiasm by the discovery of the external world, saw no limits to the future possibilities which lay open before him.

In the course of the sixteenth and seventeenth centuries the monarchical state gradually became firmly established

and the bourgeoisie became the economically ruling class, and at least the equivalent in power of the nobility, which tended to lose its real social functions and fall from being *noblesse d'épée* to being *noblesse de cour;* the bourgeoisie then organised the production of wealth and elaborated the doctrine of rationalism on the two fundamental planes of epistemology and of the physical sciences. At the time when Pascal was writing the *Pensées* both Aristotelianism and neo-Platonic animism had been put out of date; the development of capitalism had transcended them on the economic and social plane, while on the intellectual level they had been rendered completely unimportant by the work of a whole collection of more or less rigorous and scientific thinkers such as Borelli, Torricelli, Roberval and Fermat, and above all by that of the great precursors of modern science such as Galileo, Descartes and Huygens.[2]

In his youth Pascal had played an active part in the attempt to abolish one of the central pillars of Aristotelian physics: the idea that nature 'has a horror of the vacuum.' This makes it even more interesting to note that while the *Pensées* occasionally refer to Aristotelian physics, they in fact assume the struggle to have been won, and attribute very little importance to Aristotelian or neo-Platonic ideas. In fact, the only positions which Pascal thinks worth discussing are those of the two ideologies which

[2]Monsieur Koyré has also shown not only the important role played by the development of the animistic philosophy of nature in dealing the final blow to Aristotelianism but also—and this is more important—the long endeavour of thinkers in the field of mathematics and mechanics to constitute an image of the world which would be wholly free of any psychic or animistic element. One of the greatest pitfalls lay in the idea of attraction, which thinkers in the field of mechanics refused to accept because they saw it as a reversion to animism and to the attribution of psychic qualities to matter.

have just triumphed: scepticism and the mechanistic rationalism whose foremost representative was Descartes. It can be added that throughout this controversy Pascal never attempts to separate physics from morality and theology. He is not concerned with limited and partial experiments, but with world visions. Descartes is a worthy adversary, and even as he fought against him Pascal never ceased to respect him. The dialogue is conducted between minds of equal power.

What, in fact, had rationalism done? In the first place it had destroyed the two closely connected ideas of the community and the universe, and had replaced them by the totally different concepts of the isolated individual and of infinite space. In the history of the human mind this represented a twin conquest of immense importance: on the social plane the values to be recognised were those of justice and individual liberty; on the intellectual plane the system recognised as valid was that of mechanistic physics.

There were, however, other consequences: the triumph of the Third Estate replaced a hierarchical society in which each man knew and recognised the value of his own place compared to that of other people, by the concept of a collection of free, equal ánd isolated individuals, whose relationships were largely those of buyers and sellers.

It was, of course, a slow evolution, which had begun towards the end of the eleventh century, continued during the twelfth and thirteenth and was to be finally developed only during the nineteenth century, but which did, nevertheless, find a powerful intellectual, scientific, literary and philosophical expression in the seventeenth century. After the value of the individual had been affirmed in the now stoic, now epicurean, now sceptical but always

individualistic work of Montaigne both Descartes and Corneille affirm, i the seventeenth century, that the individual can be self-sufficient.[3] Long befor the time of Adam Smith and of Ricardo Descartes was already writing to Princes Elizabeth of Bohemia that:

God has so established the order of thing and has joined men together in so close society, that even if every man were to b concerned only with himself, and to show n charity towards others, he would still, in th normal course of events, be working o their behalf in everything that lay withi his power, provided that he acted prudently and, in particular, that he lived in a societ where morals and customs had not falle into corruption.[4]

It was again Descartes who, this time o a philosophical plane, formulated th first great manifesto of revolutionar and democratic rationalism: 'Commo sense is the most evenly distributed thing in the whole world . . . the ability t judge correctly, and to distinguish truth from error—which is what me properly call common sense or reason— is naturally equal in all men.'

The line which takes us from Descarte to the *Monadology* of Leibnitz, from *L Cid* to that literary monadology to which Balzac gave the title of *La Comédi humaine,* as well as to Fichte, Voltair and Valéry, is sinuous and complex but nevertheless real and unbroken.[5]

[3]The poet and playwright insist, as is natural on the truth of this as far as action is concerned the philosopher on its consequences in the realm of thought.
[4]Letter of October 6th, 1645.
[5]It goes without saying that a general state ment of this nature can never do more than bring out one particular aspect out of a multitude o others. The important thing is to avoid an misleading perspective. Thus, we know very wel that although the windowless and doorles Monad represents a continuation of the Car tesian ego, the fact that these Monads are organ ised in a hierarchical system constitutes a slip

Thus, as Western bourgeois and capi-
list society developed, the intellectual
ad affective value of the community
radually became less important as far
s men's actions and ideas were con-
erned, and was replaced by a self-
antred attitude which allowed considera-
ons of communal interest to play only
 small part by the side of private and
ersonal ones. The social and religious
aan of the Middle Ages was replaced
y the Cartesian and Fichtean Ego, the
oorless and windowless monad of
eibnitz, and the 'economic man' of the
assical economists.

This change of social attitudes was
aturally reflected on the plane of ethics
ad religion. Expressed crudely, it meant
aat when individualism carried its own
rinciples to their logical conclusion,
hics and religion ceased to play an
adependent part in determining human
ctions. The great seventeenth-century
ationalists, Descartes, Malebranche and
eibnitz, certainly still talk about moral-
y, and, with the possible exception of
pinoza, they still believe in God. But
aeir moral and religious attitudes are
aerely old bottles which their new vision
f the world has filled with completely
ew wine. This is so much the case that
e no longer find—as we do at other
eriods in history—that new religious
ad moral emotions and ideas have merely
een substituted for old ones. This time,

the change is far more radical, and Pascal
was perhaps the only thinker of this
generation to be completely aware of it.
What happened was that the older
ethical and Christian forms were
filled with a completely amoral and irreligious substance. This is obvious in the
case of Spinoza, whose ideas have been
well described as a form of theological
atheism, and who still uses the word
'God' in order to express a complete
refusal of any really transcendental
attitude, as well as giving the title of
'Ethics' to a work in which all considerations of human behaviour are based upon
the *conatus*, upon the egoism of the
modes which tend to persist in their
own being.[6]

This change is equally visible if we
limit ourselves to a study of French
thinkers. Descartes believed in God and
Malebranche was a priest: however, the
'God of the philosophers' is no longer
very real when placed by the side of
man's reason. The Cartesian God intervenes in the rational mechanism of the
world simply in order to keep it going
once it has been first started. As Pascal
remarked, his only function in Cartesian
philosophy is to 'give a little tap to
start the world off,' after which he has
nothing else to do. Even if we are more

[6]This is, naturally, only a partial and one-
sided view of this philosophy. For if, by its
refusal of any transcendence, Spinoza's philosophy marks the logical conclusion of Cartesian
rationalism and individualism it nevertheless
also represents, by the introduction of the idea
of totality, a move beyond this rationalistic individualism and a return to a genuinely religious
mode of thinking.

One of the most urgent—and the most difficult—tasks confronting the modern historian
of philosophy is to explain in comprehensible
terms this co-existence in the seventeenth century
of an extreme individualism and a form of pantheism within a philosophy which admits only
one real substance. (Goethe indicated that such
a problem existed in the famous scene between
Faust and the World Spirit.)

ing backward from the democratic system of
Descartes. This regression can, moreover, be
xplained by the fact that the German bour-
eoisie was much less advanced than the middle
ass in France. (Cf. Lucien Goldmann, *La
ommunauté humaine et l'univers chez Kant* [P.U.F.,
949].) However, it is natural that in a work
evoted primarily to Pascal and Racine any refer-
ace to other thinkers, such as Descartes or
eibnitz, cannot hope to give even a schemat-
ally complete image. All that can be done is to
efer to certain features or elements of their
ork which may enable us to understand the
uthors immediately under discussion.

just to Descartes and point out that his God establishes the laws of the world at the same moment that he brings it into being, and that he then proceeds to maintain it in existence, we can still see that Pascal was quite right to ignore this arbitrary creation of the eternal truths, since it goes against all the other principles of Cartesian rationalism. We can see that this is the case from the example of Malebranche, the most important and faithful of Descartes' disciples, who fifty years after his master's death took notice of this fact and abolished this function of the Cartesian divinity. For him, the idea of order comes before the creation of the world, and is necessarily identical with the very will of God. As Arnauld very rightly observed, Malebranche retains miracles and the particular instances of the will of God merely as vague acknowledgments of the Biblical texts from which they cannot be removed. Grace itself is made to fit into the rational system of immediate causes.

Although his book speaks of God from the first page to the last, Spinoza draws the final consequences of this change by dispensing with the creation of the world and with its deliberate maintenance in existence by God. The name of God still lingers on, but the content has entirely disappeared.

In the same way there is no room in any consistently individualistic mode of thought for a God who still retains any real functions, there is likewise no room for any system of genuine morality. Like any other world vision, both rationalistic and empiricist individualism can still retain certain rules of conduct which it may refer to as moral or ethical norms. But in fact, whether its ideal is one of power or one of prudence or wisdom, any thorough-going individualism will still need to deduce these rules either from the individual's mind or from his heart,

since by very definition individualism has abolished any supra-individual reality capable of guiding man and offering him genuinely transcendent norms.

This is not simply a verbal quibble happiness, pleasure or wisdom have nothing at all to do with the criteria of good and evil; they can be judged only by the qualitatively different standards of success and failure, knowledge and ignorance, etc., and neither these qualities nor the standards by which they are judged have any specifically moral significance. Actions can be judged as good or evil only by reference to an independent system of ethical criteria which transcends the individual and exists independently of him. These criteria may be theological or they may be social, but in either case there is something—God or the community— which stands outside and above the individual. It is the characteristic of rationalism, however, to abolish both God and the community, and it is this which explains why the rise of rationalism was accompanied by the disappearance of any external norm which might guide the individual in his life and actions. Good and evil become, in a rationalist context, merely a question of what is reasonable and what is absurd, moral virtue becomes the *virtù* of the Renaissance man, and this in turn changes into the prudence and *savoir-vivre* of the seventeenth-century *honnête homme*.

The rationalism which, when carried to its logical though extreme conclusion, sees men only as isolated individuals for whom other men exist only as objects, also carries out a similar change in man's way of looking at the external world. On the human level, it destroys the idea of community and replaces it by that of an infinitely large collection of reasonable individuals who are all equal and all interchangeable; on the level of the physical sciences, it destroys the idea f an orderly universe and replaces it by that of an infinite space which has neither limits nor individual qualities, and whose parts are both absolutely identical and completely interchangeable.

In the Aristotelian concept of space, as in the Thomistic idea of the community, each thing had its own place in the order of nature and tended to return to it: heavy bodies fell in order to reach the centre of the earth, light bodies rose because the natural place for them was above. Things were spoken to and judged by space, were told what to do and where to go, in exactly the same way as men were judged and directed by the community, and the language of space was, basically, the language of God. Cartesian rationalism changed the world, with the result that, as Henri Gouhier pointed out, 'the physics based upon clear ideas blew away all the "animal souls," "powers," and "principles" with which the scholastics had peopled nature: mechanistic physics offered man the means of conquering the world both by his intellect and by his technical skills, giving the scientist a universe that was intelligible and the artisan a universe subjected to the action of his tools.'[7] Both men and things became instruments, objects on which the thoughts and actions of the rational and reasonable individual could exercise their influence. The result was that once men, space and physical nature were reduced to the level of objects, they began to behave as objects. When confronted with the great problems of human existence they remained dumb. And God, deprived of the physical universe and of the conscience of man, the only two instruments by which He had been capable of communicating with man, departed from the world where He could no longer speak

[7]Cf. H. Gouhier, *Introduction aux 'Méditations cartésiennes' de Malebranche*, p. xxvii.

to the person He had made in His own image.

From a rationalist standpoint, there was nothing grave or disturbing about this. The man of Descartes and Corneille, like the man of the empiricists, needed no help from outside. He would have had no use for it. The rationalist was quite willing to see God as the author of the eternal truths, the creator and preserver of the world, and as the being who could—at least theoretically—perform infrequent miracles; but it was only on condition that this God did not interfere with the way men behaved, and, above all, that he refrained from casting doubt upon the absolute validity of human reason in the realms of both ethics and epistemology. Voltaire himself was prepared to build a chapel to a God who remained within such modest limits.

As far as their daily life was concerned, the rationalists were all the more ready to accept the God who manifested himself through the rational order and general laws of the world, since, during the seventeenth and eighteenth centuries, He also came to perform a very useful service: that of controlling the 'irrational' and dangerous reactions of the 'ignorant masses' who could neither understand nor appreciate the value of the consistently selfish and rational activity of economic man and of his social and political creations.

However, if in Descartes' time and in the course of the three centuries which followed him, victorious rationalism found no difficulty in eliminating the idea of the community and of specifically moral values from the economic and social behaviour of the individual, this was because, in spite of all the potential dangers which this involved, individualism had not yet revealed its final consequences.

As it gradually destroyed social life from the inside, rationalism was nevertheless still affecting a society which remained deeply imbued with values that men continued to respect emotionally and even to observe in practice, in spite of the way in which they contradicted the new ideas which were beginning to prevail. For a long time, the surviving remnants of Christianity and humanistic idealism continued to hide the dangers of a world which had no real moral values, and allowed man to celebrate the triumphs of scientific thought and technological progress as if these presented no problems. God had indeed left the world of men, but only a very small minority of the intellectuals in Western Europe realised that He had gone.

It is only in our own day that we have become conscious of this absence of valid ethical norms and of the terrible dangers which it involves. For if—in defiance of the God of enlightened rationalism—the ignorant masses have used political and trade-union action in order to impose some measure of control on the excesses of individualism in economic life, the absence of ethical forces capable of directing the use of scientific discoveries and of using them for the benefit of a genuine human community threatens to have unimaginable consequences.

Rationalism continued to grow and develop in this way in France until the twentieth century, but in the seventeenth it stood at a turning-point. It had then, thanks to the work of Descartes and Galileo, found a philosophical system and a system of mathematical physics which were unmistakably superior to the old Aristotelian framework. It was against this background that, in connection with other factors, the Jansenist attitude which found its most coherent expression in the great tragic works of Pascal and Racine was developed.

The nature of the tragic mind in seventeenth-century France can be characterised by two factors: the complete and exact understanding of the new world created by rationalistic individualism, together with all the invaluable and scientifically valid acquisitions which this offered to the human intellect; and at the same time, the complete refusal to accept this world as the only one in which man could live, move and have his being.

Reason is an important factor in human life, one of which man is justly proud and which he will never be able to give up; however, it by no means constitutes the whole man, and it should not and cannot be taken as a sufficient guide to human life. This is true on every plane, even on that of scientific research, where reason seems so preeminently at home. This is why, after the amoral and a-religious period of rationalism and empiricism, the tragic vision represents a return to morality and religion, of religion in the wider meaning of faith in a set of values which transcend the individual. However, the tragic vision never actually reaches the stage of offering either a set of ideas or an art which are capable, by offering a new community and a new universe, of taking the place of the atomistic and mechanistic universe set up by individual reason and, from this point of view, it must be considered as essentially a transitional phase. It accepts that the world of rationalist and empirical thought is definite and unchangeable—although it perceives the ambiguity and confusion which lie behind its apparent clarity—and can offer as a challenge to it only a new set of demands and a new scale of values.

However, the tragic vision is incapable of seeing itself in this historical perspective. It is essentially unhistorical, since it lacks the principal dimension of history which is the future. Refusal, in the

dical and absolute form which it
sumes in tragic thought, has only one
imension in time: the present. As
arcos pointed out:

> Thoughts of the future are a dangerous
> d clever temptation of the Evil One,
> ontrary to the spirit of the Gospel, and
> apable of ruining everything if not resisted;
> ey must be rejected without even a first
> ance, since God's word tells us not only
> take no thought for the morrow in things
> mporal but also in things spiritual, and it is
> ese which hang much more on His will.[8]

Rationalist thought and the tragic
ision share a common way of looking
t the problems of the community and
f the universe—or, rather, of the prob-
ms raised by the absence of any true
ommunity and universe, that is to say
e problems raised by society and by
pace. Both see the individual as unable
find either in the universe or in society
ny guiding or transcendant principle;
nd, for both of them, if harmony and
greement do exist in the realm of things
nd the society of men, this is merely
he result of the automatic interplay of
holly rational and selfish considera-
ions, in which each man consults only
is own interests. The difference between
hem lies in the fact that while rationalism
s prepared to accept this state of affairs
nd indeed regards it as basically desirable
—it shows its truly a-religious nature by
onsidering human reason as capable of
iscovering genuine truths, if only on
he plane of mathematics—the tragic
ision is intensely aware of the inade-
uacy of such a world view. It cannot
ccept a concept of human society and
f physical space in which no human
alue has any necessary and non-con-
ingent foundation, and in which all
on-values are both equally possible and
qually probable.

[8]Cf. Martin de Barcos, *Pensées* (B.H.F., fr.
2.988), pp. 351–2.

Mechanistic rationalism had, with
Descartes and Galileo, replaced the false
and imaginary concepts of Aristotelian
physics with a far more accurate notion
of space, which it looked upon as wholly
valid; it was this concept that was to
make possible all the immense technological progress of the future, and Descartes
considered that it would be possible, in a few years, to increase the span
of normal life. Good and evil had no
part to play in this concept, and the only
problems with which it confronted man
were those of success or failure on a
purely technical and scientific level. It
was, indeed, of the concept of space
first elaborated in the seventeenth century
that Poincaré rightly said that we must,
in order to understand it, make a clear
distinction between statements in the
indicative and statements in the imperative. This kind of space no longer had
any limits because it had lost all possible
human characteristics.

It was this same concept of space,
whose very infinity seemed to the rationalists to be a sign of the greatness of God,
since it revealed the existence of an
infinity which human reason could not
grasp, that inspired Pascal, as he foresaw
both the immense possibilities and the
immense dangers which it contained,
and saw the incompatibility between
such a concept and the existence of God,
to cry out in a phrase of equal accuracy
and power: 'The eternal silence of these
infinite spaces casts me into dread'
(fr. 206, E. 392).

This remark is linked to the most
important scientific discovery of seventeenth-century rationalism, that of geo-
metrically infinite space, and it places
by the side of it the silence of God.
In the infinite space of rational science
God falls silent, because in elaborating
this concept man has been obliged to
give up any genuinely ethical norm. The
central problem which tragic thought

and the tragic mind had to face, a problem which only dialectical thought can solve on both the moral and the scientific plane, was that of discovering whether there still was some means and some hope of reintegrating supra-individual values into this rational concept of space, which had now replaced for ever the Aristotelian and Thomist universe. The problem was whether man could still rediscover God; or, to express the same idea in a less ideological but identical form, whether man could rediscover the community and the universe.

Although it appears to speak solely of cosmological matters, fragment 206 (E. 392) in Pascal's *Pensées* also has a moral content; or, rather, it deals with the gulf that lies between physical and cosmological reality, on the one hand, and human reality on the other. It was this content that Lukàcs reformulated when, without in any way referring to Pascal, but nevertheless speaking of tragic man, he wrote:

He hopes that a judgment by God will illuminate the different struggles which he sees in the world before him, and will reveal the ultimate truth. But the world around him still follows the same path, indifferent to both questions and answers. No word comes from either created or natural things, and the race is not to the swift nor battle to the strong. The clear voice of the judgment of God no longer sounds out above the march of human destiny, for the voice which once gave life to all has now fallen silent. Man must live alone and by himself. The voice of the Judge has fallen silent for ever, and this is why man will always be vanquished, doomed to destruction in victory even more than in defeat.[9]

God's voice no longer speaks directly to man. This is one of the fundamental points of tragic thought. 'Vere tu es

Deus absconditus,' quotes Pascal. The hidden God.

However, this fragment also calls forth another remark which is valid for a large number of Pascal texts. It is that we should always give their exact and literal meaning to everything that Pascal writes, and should never try to whittle down the meaning of his *Pensées* in order to make them more accessible to Cartesian common sense. We must not allow ourselves to be held back by the fact that Pascal sometimes took fright at his own boldness, and tried to tone down the paradoxical nature of his ideas by writing a second version. (For example, he began by saying of Descartes—with complete accuracy—that 'too much light darkens the mind.' He then changed it to 'too much light dazzles the mind.')[10]

Deus absconditus. The hidden God. It is an idea which is fundamental in tragic thought in general and in Pascalian thought in particular. It is a paradoxical idea, in spite of the fact that certain fragments of the *Pensées* seem, at first sight, capable of being interpreted in a perfectly logical way. For example, fragment 559 (E. 319) could be interpreted as meaning: God has hidden himself from the sight of most men, but He is nevertheless visible to those to whom He has accorded Grace to see Him, since it reads:

Had there never appeared any sign of God, then this eternal privation would be ambiguous, and could just as well be caused by the complete absence of any Divine Principle as by man's unworthiness to know it; but since God shows himself intermittently but not always, then all ambiguity disappears. For if God has once appeared, then he must always exist. From which we are forced to conclude that God exists, and that men are unworthy of Him.

This interpretation would, however, be

---

[9]Georg von Lukàcs, *Die Seele und die Formen,* pp. 332–3.

[10]In fragment 72. Cf. Brunschvicg's edition of the *Pensées et Opuscules,* note 6 to p. 353.

unfaithful to Pascal's thought as a whole, since this never says 'Yes' *or* 'No' but always 'Yes' *and* 'No.' For Pascal, the hidden God is both present and absent, and not sometimes absent and sometimes present. He is always absent and always present.

Even in fragment 559, the essential argument lies in the words 'if God has once appeared, then He must always exist,' or, as an earlier and much stronger version put it: 'The eternal Being is for ever if He once has been.' What, then, is the meaning of the expression 'once appears' in fragment 559? For tragic thought, this represents an essential but constantly unrealised possibility. For at the very moment that God appears to man, then man ceases to be tragic. To see and hear God is to go beyond tragedy. For the Pascal who wrote fragment 559, God always exists but never appears, and this in spite of Pascal's own certainty —which I shall study when discussing the argument of the wager—that God can and may appear at every moment of man's life, although He never actually does so.

Even now, however, we have still not reached the real meaning of the hidden God. Always to be without ever appearing is, as far as Cartesian common sense is concerned, a logical and acceptable attitude, although common sense never actually goes so far as accepting it. But we must add that for Pascal, and for tragic man in general, this hidden God is present in a more real and more important way than any empirical and perceptible being, and that His is the only essential presence that exists. That God should be always absent and always present is the real centre of the tragic vision.

In 1910, again with no thought of Pascal in mind, Lukàcs began his essay in the following manner: 'Tragedy is a game, a game of man and of his destiny, a game which is watched by God. But God is nothing more than a spectator, and he never intervenes, either by word or deeds, in what the actors are doing. Only his eyes rest upon them.'[11] Lukàcs then went on to discuss the central problem of any tragic vision: can a man still live when the eye of God has lighted upon him? Is there not an unbridgeable gulf between human life and the divine presence?

For a rationalist, such a question is meaningless and absurd, for in the view of Descartes, Malebranche and Spinoza, God exists to guarantee the existence of order and the eternal truths, and to offer man a world open to his ideas and accessible to his instruments. This is why, full of confidence in man and human reason, these thinkers are also certain that God is present for the human soul.[12] The only difference lies in the fact that the God of the rationalists has no longer any personal reality for man, since all he does is to guarantee the harmony existing among the different monads or between human reason and the external world. He is no longer man's guardian and his guide, no longer the person that he can turn to for advice; he has become a general and universal rule which guarantees man's right to free himself from any external authority, and to follow where his strength and reason may guide him. But, at the same time, he

[11] *Loc. cit.,* p. 327.

[12] On this particular point rationalism marks a renewal of a genuine Augustinian tradition, and this in spite of the fact that it transforms it completely by making spirituality become mathematical reason. Jansenism, on the other hand, in spite of the protestations that its representatives made of Augustinian orthodoxy, constituted a break in the tradition. The Church, which always has had a remarkable flair for detecting heresy, was acting in a perfectly logical manner when it both condemned Jansenism and affirmed at the same time the orthodoxy of Saint Augustine.

leaves man alone in the face of a silent and static world of things and individuals.

The God of tragedy, the God of Racine, Pascal and Kant, is a wholly different being. Like the rationalists' God, he does indeed bring man no help from outside; but, unlike the rationalists' God, he offers man no guarantee of the validity of his own strength and powers of reasoning. Far from offering man anything, the God of tragedy judges man and makes demands on him; he forbids the slightest degree of compromise, and constantly reminds man—who lives in a universe where life is made possible only by approximations—that a true calling is one devoted to the quest for wholeness and authenticity. Or, to speak as Pascal does, this God demands that man should devote himself to the only true life, which is a life of absolute justice and absolute truth, a life which has nothing to do with the relative truth and relative justice of ordinary human existence. He is a God, in Lukàcs' words,

whose cruel and harsh tribunal knows neither pardon nor prescription, who mercilessly punishes the slightest hint of infidelity towards the quest for Essence; a God who, with blind rigidity, sweeps from the ranks of men all those who have, by the slightest gesture, made in the most fleeting and forgotten moment of time, shown that they are strangers to the world of Essences; a God whose merciless judgment can be softened by no riches and no splendid gifts offered by the soul, and in whose sight a long life, filled with the most glorious actions, is as nothing. Yet, at the same time, he is a God so full of smiling compassion that He forgives all the sins of daily life on the one condition that these have not offended against the innermost centre. Indeed, it would be wrong even to say that He forgives such sins; they pass unnoticed before His eyes, and His glance slips over them without being affected.[13]

He is a God whose judgments and scale of values are wholly different from

[13]Cf. Lukàcs, *Die Seele und die Formen*, pp. 338–39.

those of everyday life, and Lukàcs writes speaking of the tragic man who lives in the gaze of such a God, that 'many things disappear which earlier seemed to be the very pillars of his existence, while others, before scarcely visible, become his rock and resting place.' It was on similar thought that Pascal concluded the *Mystère de Jésus,* writing that 'we must perform little things as if they were great ones because of the majesty of Christ Jesus who does them in us and who lives our life; and we must do great things as if they were simple and easy, because of His omnipotence.'

Or, again, as Lukàcs writes,

Daily life is a confused and many-coloured anarchy, where nothing attains its perfect essence, and no clear dividing line separates the pure from the impure. Everything flows, everything is broken or destroyed, and nothing attains authenticity. For men love everything which is hazy and uncertain in life, and adore the soothing monotony of the Grand Perhaps. Everything clear and unambiguous makes them afraid, and their weakness and cowardice lead them to embrace every obstacle set up by the world and every gate that seems to bar their path. For what lies behind each rock too steep for them to climb is the unsuspected and ever unattainable paradise of their dreams. Their life is made up of hopes and desires, and everything which prevents them from fulfilling their destiny is easily and cheaply transformed into an internal richness of the soul. The man who leads an ordinary life never knows where the rivers which carry him along will lead to, since where nothing is ever achieved everything remains possible.

However [he adds], when a miracle occurs then something real is achieved. . . . A miracle is both the result and the starting point for a number of definite actions: in an unforeseeable manner, it forces itself into a man's life and makes it into a clear and unambiguous sum of things achieved. . . . It strips the soul of all the deceitful veils woven from brilliant moments and vague feelings rich with meaning; and, as the soul then shows itself with every feature carefully picked out, and with its most naked essence isible to the eye, it stands alone before God. And before God, only the miracle is real.

We can now see the meaning and importance for the tragic thinker or writer of the question: 'Can a man still live when the eye of God has lighted upon him?' And we can also see what is the only possible reply that can be given.

Romila Thapar

AŚOKA
AND BUDDHISM

The cult of Aśoka has been popular in twentieth-century India. During the last ten years it has increased considerably. Not only have Aśokan symbols been adopted by the Government of India, but much of modern Indian political thinking is being related to Aśokan ideas. As is the case with all heroes of the past, the modern delineation is not always historically accurate. The initial difficulty is that of distinguishing between the man and the statesman.

This confusion is frequent in recent studies on the emperor Aśoka, and is due in part to the circumstances in which the evidence about him became known. Prior to 1837, Aśoka was largely a mere name in the genealogies of Indian kings included in the ancient texts, the *Purānas*.[1] We are told that he belonged to the Mauryan dynasty, was the grandson of Candragupta, the founder of the dynasty and that he reigned for thirty-six years. Candragupta began his career *circa* 321 B.C. He was thus a near contemporary of Alexander of Macedon,

and is believed as a young man to have met Alexander during the latter's campaign in north-western India.[2] Further information about the first two Mauryan rulers is available from Greek and Latin sources[3] which describe the close relations between Candragupta Maurya and Seleucus Nicator, who on the death of Alexander, founded the Seleucid dynasty at Babylon. There is little reference to Aśoka and his work, in the post-Mauryan period. A few inscriptions of the twelfth century A.D. refer to him in a generally vague manner.

The emperor Aśoka in his lifetime issued a series of edicts and proclamations, which were inscribed on rock surfaces and on finely polished sandstone pillars throughout his vast empire. Most of these inscriptions are in *Brāhmi,* the earliest Indian script so far known to have been used for the writing of Sanskrit and Prākrit.[4] As the script developed and changed through the centuries, the ear-

[2]Plutarch, *Life of Alexander,* lxii.

[3]These accounts may be found in the works of the following writers: Strabo, Arrian, Megasthenes, Diodorus, Ptolemy and Pliny.

[4]A few inscriptions in the north-west of India are inscribed in *Kharosthi,* a script derived from the Persian Aramaic. In 1958 a bilingual inscription in Greek and Aramaic was discovered near Kandahar in Afghanistan.

From Past and Present, 18 (1960), 43–51. Reprinted in its entirety by permission of the publishers and the author.

[1]F. E. Pargiter, *Dynasties of the Kali Age* (London, 1931), pp. 26ff.

lier versions became archaic. As no systematic study of this script was maintained, it eventually became unreadable, and the inscriptions of Aśoka therefore made no impression on later writing of history. It was not until 1837 that they were deciphered by James Prinsep.

The emphasis on their Buddhist content came about in a curious way. In the inscriptions, the author is described as *Devānampiya Piyadassi rāja,* The Beloved of the Gods, the king Piyadassi. The king seldom used his personal name, Aśoka, and generally referred to himself by the above title. The identification of the king Piyadassi was made on the basis of a comparison with the Buddhist chronicles of Ceylon in which Aśoka is referred to as Piyadassi.[5] The discovery of an inscription in 1915 (and others more recently), containing both the title and the personal name, however confirmed the identification. It is clear from Aśoka's edicts that he was a Buddhist.[6] Buddhist sources from Ceylon, Tibet and China contain fairly detailed accounts of his life. The Aśokan edicts were therefore interpreted on the basis of information provided by these sources. It is indeed unfortunate that in reconstructing his life and activities these and other religious sources were regarded as reliable and complementary evidence to that of his own inscriptions. The Buddhist sources, naturally wishing to take advantage of the fact that Aśoka was a Buddhist, made him out to be a personification of piety, a picture which is not endorsed by his own inscriptions.

In the studies of Aśoka he is generally depicted as having been suddenly converted to Buddhism as a result of his remorse at the cruelty inflicted on the people of Kalinga during his campaign in that country, in the ninth year of his reign. Conformity to Buddhist ethics then appears to become the sole concern of the king's life. Smith (the first historian to write a monograph on Aśoka), has described him as a monk and monarch at the same time.[7] This approach, though not accepted literally by all historians, has nevertheless conditioned historical analysis of Aśoka's reign. Among the more extreme views is that of Fritz Kern, who tried to examine the inner springs of Aśoka's actions against the theological background of existence both in this world and the after life, as well as of what he believes to be a widespread desire on the part of Indians of this period to become ascetics and to escape from life by other means. He depicts at great length the supposed conflict in the mind of the king who wishes to free himself of earthly ties and yet is conscious of his responsibility as a ruler to society.[8] Aśoka was certainly attracted to Buddhism and became a practising Buddhist. But his was not an eccentric or sudden conversion as is clear from his own edicts. Buddhism in the context of society as it was then, was not just another religion. It was the result of a widespread movement towards change which affected many aspects of life from personal beliefs to social ideas. Any statesman with an understanding of the period would have had to come to terms with such an important new development.

The inscriptions are of two kinds. The smaller group consists of declarations of the king as a lay Buddhist to his church, The Buddhist *Samgha.*[9] These describe his own acceptance of Buddhism and his relationship with the *Samgha.* Here the somewhat intolerant and wholly credulous believer appears, as in one inscription where he proclaims in no

---

[5]*Dipavamsa,* ed. Oldenberg (Pali Texts Soc., 1879), vi. I.

[6]Jules Bloch, *Les Inscriptions d'Asoka* (Paris, 1950), pp. 145–6.

[7]V. Smith, *Asoka,* 3rd edn. (Oxford, 1920).

[8]Kern, *Asoka* (Bern, 1956).

[9]The literal meaning of *Samgha* is "society" or "assembly." It was the official title adopted for the Buddhist Order of monks.

uncertain terms that dissident monks and nuns must be expelled from the Order. Another inscription in a less fanatical vein speaks of the various scriptures with which all good Buddhists should be familiar. By far the most important inscriptions are those of the larger group which may be described as proclamations to the public at large. This group consists of the Major and Minor Rock Edicts and the Pillar Edicts.[10] These inscriptions explain his well-known policy of *Dhamma*. (*Dhamma* is the Prākrit form of the Sanskrit word *Dharma*, virtually untranslatable into English. It has been variously translated as Morality, Piety, Righteousness, etc. Since the precise nuance of the word cannot be conveyed, I prefer to keep it in the original.) It was in the conception of this policy, seen in the context of Mauryan India, that the true achievement of Aśoka lay. He did not see *Dhamma* as piety resulting from good deeds inspired by formal religious beliefs, but as an emphasis on social responsibility.

In the past historians have generally interpreted Aśoka's *Dhamma* almost as a synonym for Buddhism, suggesting thereby that Aśoka was concerned with making Buddhism a state religion. It is doubtful if this was his intention although he himself, as a firm believer in Buddhism, was convinced that it was the way to personal salvation. The policy of *Dhamma* was a policy of social responsibility. It aimed at building up an attitude of mind in which social behaviour, the behaviour of one person towards another, was considered of great importance. It was a plea for the recognition of the dignity of man, and for a humanistic spirit in the activities of society.

In examining this policy it is necessary to analyse the conditions which gave rise to it. It was in part a policy which was nurtured in the mind of Aśoka, but since he saw it largely as a solution to existing problems, it is in the light of these problems that its true value can be assessed. Aśoka's private beliefs and his immediate environment of course had their share in moulding the policy. As a family, the Mauryas did not conform to the accepted religion of most royal families of the time, Brahmanism. Candragupta is said to have been a Jaina, and Bindusāra the father of Aśoka favoured the Ājīvikas. Both of these were non-orthodox sects and if anything antagonistic to Brahmanical ideas. The teachings of Mahāvīra, who preached in the sixth century B.C. and who was a near contemporary of the Buddha, came to be called Jainism. It began as a protest against certain aspects of Brahmanism, the prevailing religion. There was a considerable stress on non-violence to the extent of insisting that even the accidental killing of minute insects was sinful. All creation was said to function in accordance with a universal law, thus the power of the gods (who were the prime movers of the universe in Brahmanical belief) was greatly reduced. In fact Mahāvīra rarely refers to the gods in this capacity which has led to Jainism being described as atheistic. The transmigration of souls was fundamental to Jaina thinking. Like the Buddhists, the Jainas also aimed at *Nirvāna,* or the "ceasing of being reborn." The Ājīvika movement was contemporary with Jainism. This again tended to be atheistic and maintained that the actions and events of one's life cannot be changed since they are predetermined by one's *karma* or destiny. This determinism was in conflict with the Brahmanical

---

[10]The first group consists of the Schism Edict, Bhabra Edict, Rummindei pillar inscription and the Nigalisegar pillar inscription. (Bloch, *op. cit.*, pp. 152–158.) The larger and more important group consists of the Major and Minor Rock Edicts and the Pillar Edicts. (Bloch, *op. cit.,* pp. 90–151, and pp. 161–172.)

belief that a man could improve his lot in his next life by being virtuous and conforming to Brahmanical laws in his present life. These were considered heretical beliefs, and it is therefore not surprising that Aśoka himself did not conform to Brahmanical theory and preferred to support the Buddhists.

The sixth century B.C. in India may be described as a century of questioning. The existence of a variety of sects concerned both with religious belief and philosophical speculation testifies to a period of vigorous debate and discussion. Not only were the existing values questioned but each newly developed theory was put through a severe test of criticism. The uncompromising materialism of the early Cārvākas battled with the metaphysical subtleties of the Upanisadic thinkers. The Brahmanical stronghold gradually built up through the later Vedic period (from *circa* 900 B.C. onwards), was being attacked by the new forces. The privileges of the priests were being questioned, so too the efficacy of the ceremonies and the rituals they performed. The caste system, which had begun to assume the features of its later rigidity, also came under attack, though often not in a direct way.[11] Generally the less fortunate of the four castes tended to favour the new sects as against their previous allegiance to Brahmanism. This was particularly the case with the third caste, the *vaisyas*.

Though technically included among the highly favoured twice-born (i. e. first with their natural birth and the second time on their initiation), in the practical matters of daily life they tended to be excluded from the privileges of the first two castes.[12]

Buddhism was, as it were, the spearhead of these dissident groups. It demanded a relaxing of the social rigidity encouraged by the caste system. As it did not favour the privileges of the upper castes, it had a tremendous appeal among the other sections of society.[13] The ritualistic side of Buddhism associated itself with the popular cults, such as those connected with tree-worship and the fertility cults.[14] The conception of the "Middle Way" propagated a code of ethics which took into consideration the practical necessities of daily life and did not demand the impossible. This must have provided a workable solution to the many who could not or did not have the leisure to find salvation through becoming ascetics in the best of Brahmanical traditions. Added to this was the fact that there was a large element of democracy in the organisation of Buddhist monasteries during this period.[15] Thus Brahmanism was seeking to establish itself with the rigidity in social ideas and emphasis on temporal control which were to characterise it in the early centuries A.D., while at the same time the dissident groups tried to keep back this force.

These religious and social trends were

[11]The caste system divides society into four main castes. The highest caste is that of the brahmans or priests. This is followed by the *ksatriyas*, the aristocracy, also referred to as the warrior caste. The third in rank are the *vaisyas* which included the merchants, landowners and the wealthier cultivators. The fourth caste was that of the *sūdras*, generally the poorer peasants and their counterparts in urban centres. Beyond this four-fold division were the outcastes and the untouchables who were considered impure owing to the nature of their professions. A Hindu is born into a particular caste and no amount of social or economic improvement can change the caste in a person's lifetime.

[12]*Aitereya Brāhmana* (Anandāsrama Sanskrit Ser., Poona 1896), vii. 20.

[13]Evidence for these attitudes is available from the *Jātaka* stories. These were current in the Buddhist period and later, and reveal a detailed picture of society at the time.

[14]This is clear from the incorporation of cult symbols in the earliest existing Buddhist art at the sites sacred to the religion such as Sanchi and Bharhut.

[15]The rules regarding the Order in the *Vinaya Pitaka* point to this.

elated to certain economic changes of fundamental nature which had occurred in the centuries immediately before the Mauryan period. The Aryan economy in northern India, a semi-nomadic pastoral economy during the early Vedic period (up to *circa* 900 B.C.), was changing to a settled agrarian village economy. This was the natural step after the forests had been cleared and agrarian village communities became the general pattern in the Ganges valley. However, these changes did not occur at a uniform pace throughout the sub-continent. Areas in the Deccan for instance remained at a pastoral stage for a longer period. The new economy in the northern region brought with it the institution of bureaucracy in the rural officers and the tax-collectors. The expansion of the agrarian economy at this stage accelerated the realisation that a single predominant economy facilitated the evaluation of taxes. There was also much to be gained from such an economy by those who governed, since it would permit more easily than any other the almost permanent fixing of taxation systems and tax rates. The predictability of revenue in the form of taxes created a feeling of economic security. These ideas are clearly expressed in a text on policy which dates from this period, the *Arthaśāstra*. It was written by Kautalya the minister of Candragupta. The author assumes that monarchy is the ideal form of government and elaborates in great detail on the processes of administration under such a system. State supervision of practically every activity is advised. The right of the state to tax all possible sources of income is claimed.

Together with the establishment of an agrarian economy, the pre-Mauryan period saw the opening up of trade on an extensive scale. This also resulted in the increasing importance of the *Vaisyas* who formed the majority of the traders and merchants. The material improvement of the *Vaisyas* through trade strengthened their position in urban life and fanned their resentment against the unjustified privileges of the upper castes. The establishment of guilds ushered in a new factor in urban society. City life came to depend on them to a high degree and the socially more favoured had now to contend with a new opposition. Trade developed internally, with neighbouring countries and with those across the seas. The penetration of Aryan culture into south India increased during this period and followed the various trade routes. These were usually along the river valleys. The volume of trade along the overland routes across modern Afghanistan and Persia to the Mediterranean ports, increased greatly. For the many Greek settlers along these routes, who were deserters from Alexander's army and others, this east-west trade became a highly lucrative business. Regular trade was also conducted between Broach on the west coast of India, and Babylon.[16] The communication of ideas must also have accompanied the trade in spices, textiles, precious stones and gold.

Up to a point these economic factors assisted in the evolution of the political pattern. The Mauryan period saw the imposition of imperial control over an extensive area of small kingdoms and republics. During the reign of Aśoka, the empire included almost the entire sub-continent of India and parts of Afghanistan. This imperial system was a comparatively new feature to Indian politics. The previous dynasty, the Nandas, had ruled an empire for a short period, but it was not nearly as extensive as that of the Mauryas, nor did it include

[16]These routes and trade connections are mentioned in a number of sources: *Arthaśāstra,* ed. G. Sastri (Trivandrum, 1924–5); Strabo, *Geography,* xv. I. 50; Rhys Davids, *Buddhist India* (London, 1903), pp. 103ff.; W.W. Tarn, *Hellenistic Civilisation* (London, 1927), pp. 211ff.

such a variety of peoples and cultures. The Mauryan empire was not restricted to the Ganges valley and its neighbourhood, where the population was either Aryan in culture or was acquainted with Aryan culture. It included more diverse elements, many of whom were thrown together for the first time. The hub of the empire was the highly Aryanised region of Magadha in modern Bihar. The extremities however were quite foreign to each other. The cosmopolitan Indo-Greek region of Gandhara in the northwest, belonged to an almost totally different culture from the Dravidian south. The size and scope of the imperial structure, together with the diversity of its constituents, led to the emergence of a political form that placed an overwhelming emphasis on governmental machinery and authority.

It would seem that the people of the Mauryan empire needed a focus or some common stand for all these conflicting or divergent forces, something that would draw them together and give them a feeling of unity. Such a focus would naturally have greater success if supported by the emperor, since the structure of Mauryan India invested control in the ruler at the centre. In fact the emperor himself was the author of a movement which aimed at this very object. In seeking a group of unifying principles, Aśoka concentrated on the fundamental aspects of each issue, and the result was his policy of *Dhamma*.

It is apparent that the principles of *Dhamma* were acceptable to people belonging to any religious sect.[17] The policy was not defined in terms of rules and regulations. It seems to have been deliberately left vague in details, and only the broad policy is given, which was to mould behaviour. Of the basic principles, the one on which Aśoka laid

---

[17]In this discussion of *Dhamma*, the sources are the Edicts mentioned in note 10 above.

most stress and which he repeated frequently was that of toleration. Toleration according to him was of two kinds: a toleration of people themselves and also a toleration of people's beliefs and ideas. He sums it up as follows:

. . . consideration towards slaves and servants, obedience to mother and father, generosity towards friends, acquaintances and relatives, and towards priests and monks. . . .

But the Beloved of the Gods does not consider gifts or honour to be as important as the advancement of the essential doctrine of all sects. . . . Its basis is the control of one's speech, so as not to extol one's own sect or disparage that of another on unsuitable occasions. . . . On each occasion one should honour another man's sect, for by doing so one increases the influence of one's own sect and benefits that of the other man; while by doing otherwise one dimishes the influence of one's own sect and harms the other man's. . . . Therefore concord is to be commended, so that men may hear one another's principles. . . .

Another principle fundamental to the practice of *Dhamma* was non-violence. Aśoka did not insist upon it as a religious precept like the Buddhists and Jainas, but because violence was not in keeping with social behaviour. The practice of non-violence consisted both in the renunciation of war and conquest by violence, and in a restraint on the killing of animals. But his was not a stubborn insistence on complete non-violence. He did recognise that there were occasions when violence might be unavoidable, as for instance when the more primitive forest tribes were troublesome to his officers. In a very moving passage on the general suffering, physical and mental, caused by war, he declares that in adhering to *Dhamma* he will not conquer by force in the future. Without doubting his sincere intentions in this matter, it may however be pointed out that there was little in the way of territory left for him to conquer in the sub-continent. He also states that he would prefer his descendants not to conquer by force, but if they should have to, then he hopes that it will be conducted with a maximum of mercy and clemency.

The policy of *Dhamma* also included measures which today would be described as "social welfare." The emperor claims that:

On the roads I have had banyan trees planted, which will give shade to beasts and men. I have had mango groves planted and I have had wells dug and rest houses built every nine miles. . . . And I have had many watering places made everywhere for the use of beasts and men. But this benefit is important, and indeed the world has enjoyed attention in many ways from former kings as well as from me. But I have done these things in order that my people might conform to *Dhamma*.

He attacked in no uncertain terms what he describes as "useless ceremonies and sacrifices," held as a result of superstitious beliefs, as for example those which were meant to ensure a safe journey or a quick recovery from an illness. These were the stock-in-trade of the lower order of priests who exploited their position in order to earn money on the side.

In order to implement this policy Aśoka instituted a category of officers known as the *Dhamma-mahāmattas* (the officers of *Dhamma*). They were responsible for publicising *Dhamma*, acting as the reporters of the king and more gen-erally for bringing the king and his government in touch with public opinion. They seem gradually to have developed into a type of priesthood of *Dhamma*, with extensive powers of interference in the lives of the people, thus to a degree nullifying their very purpose. They were also sent on missions to neighbouring countries and to various Hellenic kingdoms in the west. Aśoka was so convinced of the success of his *Dhamma* and of his attempts at encouraging Indian society to adjust itself to the changes, that he appears to have believed that his own efforts might be of help to other rulers elsewhere.

Despite the fact that the reign of Aśoka brought thirty years of peace, and marked material prosperity (as is evident from archaeological remains), nevertheless Aśoka did not succeed in attempting to unite the empire or produce large scale enthusiasm for *Dhamma*. The reasons for this are many. Some may be attributed to his own faults, such as his early over-enthusiasm and his later self-complacency. Others lay outside the scope of *Dhamma* and must be sought in the pattern of Indian polity. In evaluating his contribution it can certainly be said to his credit that he understood the problems of his age, i.e., the need for a unifying factor in a society composed of units at various levels of development. It is unfortunate that his solution, the policy of *Dhamma*, was too vague, and perhaps too idealistic.

Ernst Troeltsch

THE THREE TYPES
OF
CHRISTIAN COMMUNITY

It has become clear how little the Gospel and the Primitive Church shaped the religious community itself from a uniform point of view. The Gospel of Jesus was a free personal piety, with a strong impulse towards profound intimacy and spiritual fellowship and communion, but without any tendency towards the organization of a cult, or towards the creation of a religious community. Only when faith in Jesus, the Risen and Exalted Lord, became the central point of worship in a new religious community did the necessity for organization arise. From the very beginning there appeared the three main types of the sociological development of Christian thought: the Church, the sect, and mysticism.

The Church is an institution which has been endowed with grace and salvation as the result of the work of Redemption; it is able to receive the masses, and to adjust itself to the world, because, to a certain extent, it can afford to ignore the need for subjective holiness for the sake of the objective treasures of grace and of redemption.

The sect is a voluntary society, composed of strict and definite Christian believers bound to each other by the fact

From The Social Teaching of the Christian Churches (1912). London : George Allen & Unwin Ltd. and New York : The Macmillan Company, 1931, pp. 993–994; pp. 997–1002. By permission.

that all have experienced "the new birth." These "believers" live apart from the world, are limited to small groups, emphasize the law instead of grace, and in varying degrees within their own circle set up the Christian order, based on love; all this is done in preparation for and expectation of the coming Kingdom of God.

Mysticism means that the world of ideas which had hardened into formal worship and doctrine is transformed into a purely personal and inward experience; this leads to the formation of groups on a purely personal basis, with no permanent form, which also tend to weaken the significance of forms of worship, doctrine, and the historical element.

From the beginning these three forms were foreshadowed, and all down the centuries to the present day, wherever religion is dominant, they still appear alongside of one another, while among themselves they are strangely and variously interwoven and interconnected. The churches alone have the power to stir the masses in any real and lasting way. When mass movements take place the sects draw closer to the churches. Mysticism has an affinity with the autonomy of science, and it forms a refuge for the religious life of the cultured classes; in sections of the population which are untouched by science it leads to extravagant and emotional forms of piety, but in spite of that it forms a welcome complement to the Church and the Sects. . . .

The diversity of ideas which the Christian conception of truth contains is evident in these three different types of religion, and this explains the complicated and inconsistent relation of Christianity to the authority of the State and to the idea of toleration.

The aim of the Church is to be the Church of the people and of the masses; it therefore transfers all divine and sacred character from individuals to the objective organ of redemption, with its divine endowment of grace and truth. The Church possesses a redeeming energy which is directly miraculous, and in contrast to all other kinds of human power. Thus it possesses an absolute directly divine truth and doctrinal authority over against all human subjectivity. In its very nature such truths must be uniform and universally authoritative. Thus in the Church itself this unchangeable truth is justified, and indeed bound to maintain its supremacy over pastors and teachers, and also over the laity. Every idealistic attempt to ascribe this development of the truth to the inward miraculous power of the Church itself, without compulsion, breaks down in the practical impossibility of carrying it through, and simply results in a return to compulsion. This attitude of compulsion must, however, finally express itself externally, because errors and customs which dishonour God ought not to be tolerated, and because it is not right that people who have been born into the membership of the Church should be allowed to fall a prey to temptation. Finally, the Church must see to it that the whole nation shall hear the message of salvation, and that everyone shall have at least contact with divine salvation. Mercy requires it, and the absolute divine origin of the truth of salvation justifies this procedure. Here it is permissible to force people for their own good. This, however, demands the co-operation of the material power of the State, without which neither the inner uniformity of the Church, nor the building up of popular and territorial churches, would ever have come into existence. In all this the Church is only fulfilling its duty towards Divine Truth. This line of argument explains the rise of the complicated question of the relation between Church and State.

The point of view of the sects, however, is quite different. They do not wish to be popular churches, but Christian denominations composed of "saints." The sects are small groups which exist alongside of the State and Society. They also maintain that they possess the absolute truth of the Gospel, but they claim that this truth is far beyond the spiritual grasp of the masses and of the State, and therefore they desire to be free from the State. Further, since it is precisely this absolute Gospel which forbids them to use force, authority, or law, they also must renounce forcing their opinions upon anyone, either within or without their community. Hence they demand external toleration, the religious neutrality of the State. Within their own borders, however, they practise a spiritual discipline of doctrine and of morals. They possess the tolerance of an idealism which believes in its own cause, and they forbid their followers to deduce from the absolute character of Truth the right to use violence in order to enforce it upon others. They do not expect to see the Truth permeating the masses before the Last Day. Where various sectarian groups exist alongside of each other, they permit the exercise of purely spiritual controversy and merely ethical rivalry without losing faith in the absolute character of the truth they possess. This truth is not meant for the masses, or for humanity in general; and it will only attain its final consummation at the Last Day. Their conception of toleration and freedom of conscience is of a toleration extended to groups like their own by the churches and the ruling powers; within their own borders, however, they had very little idea of toleration, since here Scriptural law prevails. Since, however, in order to uphold this unity they renounce State aid, and at the most can exercise the method of social boycott, endless divisions arise among them. It is a fact that real conformity can only be secured with the aid of the State and the exercise of compulsion.

Finally, the point of view of spiritual idealism and mysticism differs entirely from that of the churches or the sects. From its standpoint the truth of salvation is inward and relative, a personal possession which is unutterable, and lies unspoken beneath all literal forms. The merely relative significance of the Biblical, dogmatic, or ritual form in which Truth is expressed makes mysticism independent of all historic forms, and the inner Unity of the Spirit quite naturally unites all souls in the common truth which is purely spiritual, and impossible to formulate. From this point of view, and from it alone, are toleration and freedom of conscience also possible within the religious community, since the organization becomes merely a method of ecclesiastical administration, while the religious life itself can move freely under various forms of expression which are relatively justified. This, however, led to difficulties, for from this point of view it was very difficult to decide by what authority it was possible to determine the standard of what constituted Christianity in general. The usual answer, "the Spirit recognizes the Spirit," was found to be useless in practice. Hence this standpoint easily led to the giving up of all and every kind of organized fellowship, or to a withdrawal

into private groups of a purely personal character composed of kindred souls. As well as conformity mysticism threatens to sacrifice fellowship altogether, and it easily falls into a comparative individualism. The problem of Christian toleration and liberty of conscience in relation to the conditions of the formation of religious fellowship belongs to this group of ideas. There is no escape from it. There are only varying practical suggestions of approximate utility which emerge out of this tragic interplay of forces.

Another result of this inquiry is the light which it throws upon the history of the Christian Ethos, a subject which, as is well known, presents extraordinary difficulties. The Ethos of the Gospel is a combination of infinite sublimity and childlike intimacy. On the one hand, it demands the sanctification of the self for God by the practice of detachment from everything which disturbs inward communion with God, and by the exercise of everything which inwardly binds the soul with God's Will. On the other hand, it demands that brotherly love, which overcomes in God all the tension and harshness of the struggle for existence, of law, and of the merely external order, while it unites souls in a deep spirit of mutual understanding, as well as in the most self-sacrificing love, which, even in its simplest expressions, gives a true hint of the nature of God Himself. This is an ideal which requires a new world if it is to be fully realized; it was this new world-order that Jesus proclaimed in His Message of the Kingdom of God. But it is an ideal which cannot be realized within this world apart from compromise. Therefore the history of the Christian Ethos becomes the story of a constantly renewed search for this compromise, and of fresh opposition to this spirit of compromise. The Church in particular, however, as a popular institution, is forced to compromise; this she effects by transferring to the institution the sanctity and the grace of forgiveness proper to it as an institution; the Church completed this compromise by making a covenant with the Stoic idea of the relative Law of Nature, which has prevailed since the Fall, which permits for the term of the earthly life the existence of law, might, tyranny, war, private property, and the desire to acquire possessions; it regards these things as the results of sin as well as means for the healing of sin.

When this compromise had been effected, however, within the Church, the average morality of the world and the strict morality of holiness then separated and went their different ways. The ethic of holiness became fused with the dualistic asceticism of late antiquity, and organized the monastic system, whence it once more influenced the world by permeating secular life with its higher ideals. Thus there arose a dualistic ethic which the classical Catholic theory worked into an ingenious system of evolution; the ascent from Nature to Grace.

Ecclesiastical Protestantism destroyed this dualism, and wove both its elements into the ethic of the "calling": Lutheranism carried this out with a careless acceptance of existing conditions, which are due to the presence of sin in the world, Calvinism and Ascetic Protestantism in an attempt to restore in a rational manner the holy community within the life of the world.

Alongside of these ecclesiastical compromises, however, there stood from the beginning the sect, which desired to realize the ideal of the Sermon on the Mount in all its purity; this view forced it into sharp opposition to the world. In the form of the passive and persecuted sect it realized the ideal with the fewest concessions in small and quiet groups, and comforted itself with the thought of the coming Kingdom of God, until, through its connection with Ascetic Protestantism, it also found a way of becoming incorporated with the life of this present world. In the form of the aggressive sect, when the End of the World seemed imminent, it felt justified in using force, and tried to establish the Christian order of life by violent methods; naturally, the experiment was never permanently successful; also such outbreaks always damaged the real Christianity of the sect, for then the Apocalypse and the Old Testament took the place of the Gospel.

Finally, untroubled by any of these questions of compromise, mysticism and "spiritual religion" went its own way, proclaiming the freedom of the Spirit and liberty of conscience, antinomian in the good, and also incidentally in the bad, sense; even where it was severely ascetic it maintained its spirit of freedom. This is the piety which acts or refrains from action as it is "moved by the Spirit," to use the language of the Quakers; that is, its action is controlled by its sense of inward communion with the living and holy God, and it expresses itself in a purely inward personal communion of individuals. This point of view certainly prevents its influencing the masses, or effecting any kind of organization of life on a large scale. But from the very outset this type of Christianity does not expect to influence the life of the world on a large scale; or if it does cherish such hopes it bases them purely on confidence in the interior "power of the Spirit." In the general way, it leaves to chance the question of the extension of its spirit into the general life of the world, and of a consequent inner transformation. In all these ethical movements, however, the impelling power is that of Christian hostility to the world. Today this fundamental Christian tendency has been sensibly weakened by the tendencies of modern life: with its Utilitarianism and its optimism, with its ideas of Immanence, its Naturalism, and its aesthetic glorification of Nature, often to the extent of being unable to interpret its own meaning. But it breaks forth anew from the fundamental ideas of religion and out of the self-destruction of every kind of purely secular optimism. In the midst of all the pleasures of civilization and of all mere sceptical pessimism, once again it summons the Christian ethic to face its task.

Today, therefore, the main problem of the Christian Ethos is still the problem of supernaturalism, and of its unavoidable result, asceticism, in the metaphysical-dualistic or in the disciplinary rigorist sense, an asceticism which is never merely a simple denial of the world and of self. On the other hand, its second main problem is how to supplement this religious onesidedness with an ethic of civilization which can be combined with it. The Church effected this supplement by drawing on the philosophy of late antiquity, and incorporating into its own ethic the idea of the moral Law of Nature. When the sect gave up this idea of a supplement of this kind altogether, it became uncultured and insignificant, while mysticism became complete and solitary resignation. Whenever both these movements rose to importance, they likewise introduced, each in its own way, a supplement. Today, however, in an entirely new state of civilization these earlier supplementary movements have become impossible. A new supplementary process, therefore, is necessary. In a permanent world the Christian Ethos cannot live and be entirely self-sufficing. The question is simply this: How can this supplement be shaped today? The answer to this question constitutes an imperative demand for a new Christian ethic.

H. Richard Niebuhr

THE SOCIAL SOURCES
OF
DENOMINATIONALISM

Christendom has often achieved apparent success by ignoring the precepts of its founder. The church, as an organization interested in self-preservation and in the gain of power, has sometimes found the counsel of the Cross quite as inexpedient as have national and economic groups. In dealing with such major

From The Social Sources of Denominationalism (1929), New York: 1957, pp. 3–6; 17–21; 25. By permission of Florence M. Niebuhr.

social evils as war, slavery, and social inequality, it has discovered convenient ambiguities in the letter of the Gospels which enabled it to violate their spirit and to ally itself with the prestige and power those evils had gained in their corporate organization. In adapting itself to the conditions of a civilization which its founder had bidden it to permeate with the spirit of divine love, it found that it was easier to give to Caesar the things belonging to Caesar if the examination of what might belong to God were not too closely pressed.

This proneness toward compromise which characterizes the whole history of the church, is no more difficult to understand than is the similar and inevitable tendency by which each individual Christian adapts the demands of the gospel to the necessities of existence in the body and in civilized society. It has often been pointed out that no ideal can be incorporated without the loss of some of its ideal character. When liberty gains a constitution, liberty is compromised; when fraternity elects officers, fraternity yields some of the ideal qualities of brotherhood to the necessities of government. And the gospel of Christ is especially subject to this sacrifice of character in the interest of organic embodiment; for the very essence of Christianity lies in the tension which it presupposes or creates between the worlds of nature and of spirit, and in its resolution of that conflict by means of justifying faith. It demands the impossible in conduct and belief; it runs counter to the instinctive life of man and exalts the rationality of the irrational; in a world of relativity it calls for unyielding loyalty to unchangeable absolutes. Clothe its faith in terms of philosophy, whether medieval or modern, and you lose the meaning of its high desires, of its living experience, reducing these to a set of opinions often irrelevant, sometimes contrary, to the original content. Organize its ethics—as organize them you must whenever two or three are gathered in the name of Christ—and the free spirit of forgiving love becomes a new law, requiring interpretation, commentary, and all the machinery of justice—just the sort of impersonal relationship which the gospel denies and combats. Place this society in the world, demanding that it be not of the world, and strenuous as may be its efforts to transcend or to

sublimate the mundane life, it will yet be unable to escape all taint of conspiracy and connivance with the worldly interests it despises. Yet, on the other hand, Christian ethics will not permit a world-fleeing asceticism which seeks purity at the cost of service. At the end, if not at the beginning, of every effort to incorporate Christianity there is, therefore, a compromise, and the Christian cannot escape the necessity of seeking the last source of righteousness outside himself and the world in the divine aggression, in a justification that is by faith.

The fact that compromise is inevitable does not make it less an evil. The fault of every concession, of course, is that it is made too soon, before the ultimate resistance "to the blood" has been offered. Even where resistance seems to have gone to the uttermost the loyal man remembers that it might have been begun earlier, that it might have been continued a little longer, and that any compromise of the absolute good remains an evil. At last men must continue to condemn themselves not only for their failure to do what they could, but also for their failure to perform what they could not, for their denial of the absolute good whose categorical demands were laid upon their incapable will. But compromises are doubly evil when they are unacknowledged, when the emasculation of the Christian ideal remains undiscovered and when, in consequence, men take pride, as in an achievement, in a defeat of the essential gospel. Such unconscious hypocrisy not only bars the way to continued efforts to penetrate the stubborn stuff of life with the ethics of Jesus but is the author of further compromises made all too early. So it produces at last a spurious gospel unaware of its departure from the faith once delivered to the saints.

Denominationalism in the Christian church is such an unacknowledged hypocrisy. It is a compromise, made far too lightly, between Christianity and the world. Yet it often regards itself as a Christian achievement and glorifies its martyrs as bearers of the Cross. It represents the accommodation of Christianity to the caste-system of human society. It carries over into the organization of the Christian principle of brotherhood the prides and prejudices, the privilege and prestige, as well as the humiliations and abasements, the injustices and inequalities of that specious order of high and low wherein men find the satisfaction of their craving for vainglory. The division of the churches closely follows the division of men into the castes of national, racial, and economic groups. It draws the color line in the church of God; it fosters the misunderstandings, the self-exaltations, the hatreds of jingoistic nationalism by continuing in the body of Christ the spurious differences of provincial loyalties; it seats the rich and poor apart at the table of the Lord, where the fortunate may enjoy the bounty they have provided while the others feed upon the crusts their poverty affords.

*   *   *

One element in the social sources of theological differentiation deserves especial attention. Max Weber and Ernst Troeltsch have demonstrated how important are the differences in the sociological structure of religious groups in the determination of their doctrine. The primary distinction to be made here is that between the church and the sect, of which the former is a natural social group akin to the family or the nation while the latter is a voluntary association. The difference has been well described as lying primarily in the fact that members are born into the church while they must join the sect. Churches are inclusive institutions, frequently are national in scope, and emphasize the universalism of the gospel; while sects are exclusive in character, appeal to the individualistic

element in Christianity, and emphasize its ethical demands. Membership in a church is socially obligatory, the necessary consequence of birth into a family or nation, and no special requirements condition its privileges; the sect, on the other hand, is likely to demand some definite type of religious experience as a pre-requisite of membership.

These differences in structure have their corollaries in differences in ethics and doctrine. The institutional church naturally attaches a high importance to the means of grace which it administers, to the system of doctrine which it has formulated, and to the official administration of sacraments and teaching by an official clergy; for it is an educational institution which must seek to train its youthful members to conformity in thought and practice and so fit them for the exercise of rights they have inherited. The associational sect, on the other hand, attaches primary importance to the religious experience of its members prior to their fellowship with the group, to the priesthood of all believers, to the sacraments as symbols of fellowship and pledges of allegiance. It frequently rejects an official clergy, preferring to trust for guidance to lay inspiration rather than to theological or liturgical expertness. The church as an inclusive social group is closely allied with national, economic, and cultural interests; by the very nature of its constitution it is committed to the accommodation of its ethics to the ethics of civilization; it must represent the morality of the respectable majority, not of the heroic minority. The sect, however, is always a minority group, whose separatist and semi-ascetic attitude toward "the world" is re-enforced by the loyalty which persecution nurtures. It holds with tenacity to its interpretation of Christian ethics and prefers isolation to compromise. At times it refuses participation in the government, at times rejects war, at times seeks to sever as much as possible the bonds which tie it to the common life of industry and culture. So the sociological structure, while resting in part on a conception of Christianity, reacts upon that conception and re-enforces or modifies it. On the other hand the adoption of one or the other type of consitution is itself largely due to the social condition of those who form the sect or compose the church. In Protestant history the sect has ever been the child of an outcast minority, taking its rise in the religious revolts of the poor, of those who were without effective representation in church or state and who formed their conventicles of dissent in the only way open to them, on the democratic, associational pattern. The sociological character of sectarianism, however, is almost always modified in the course of time by the natural processes of birth and death, and on this change in structure changes in doctrine and ethics inevitably follow. By its very nature the sectarian type of organization is valid only for one generation. The children born to the voluntary members of the first generation begin to make the sect a church long before they have arrived at the years of discretion. For with their coming the sect must take on the character of an educational and disciplinary institution, with the purpose of bringing the new generation into conformity with ideals and customs which have become traditional. Rarely does a second generation hold the convictions it has inherited with a fervor equal to that of its fathers, who fashioned these convictions in the heat of conflict and at the risk of martyrdom. As generation succeeds generation, the isolation of the community from the world becomes more difficult. Furthermore, wealth frequently increases when the sect subjects itself to the discipline of asceticism in work and expenditure; with the increase of wealth the possibilities for culture also become more numerous and involvement in the economic life of the nation as a whole can less easily be limited. Compromise begins and the ethics of the sect approach the churchly type of morals. As with the ethics, so with the doctrine, so also with the administration of religion. An official clergy, theologically educated and schooled in the refinements of ritual, takes the place of lay leadership; easily imparted creeds are substituted for the difficult enthusiasms of the pioneers; children are born into the group and infant baptism or dedication becomes once more a means of grace. So the sect becomes a church.

Religious history amply illustrates the process. An outstanding example is the "Half-Way Covenant" of the New England churches, which provided for the baptism of the children of second-generation, unconverted parents who had "owned the covenant" and submitted to the discipline of the church without being able to attain full membership because of their lack of the experience of salvation. The rise of "birth-right membership" in the Society of Friends shows the same process at work while the histories of Mennonites, Baptists, and Methodists offer further illustrations. Doctrines and practice change with the mutations of social structure, not vice versa; the ideological interpretation of such changes quite misses the point.

*   *   *

. . . For the denominations, churches, sects, are sociological groups whose principle of differentiation is to be sought in their conformity to the order of social classes and castes. It would not be true to affirm that the denominations are not religious groups with religious purposes, but it is true that they represent the accommodation of religion to the caste system. They are emblems, therefore, of the victory of the world over the church, of the secularization of Christianity, of the church's sanction of that divisiveness which the church's gospel condemns.

Denominationalism thus represents the moral failure of Christianity. And unless the ethics of brotherhood can gain the victory over this divisiveness within the body of Christ it is useless to expect it to be victorious in the world. But before the church can hope to overcome its fatal division it must learn to recognize and to acknowledge the secular character of its denominationalism.

Max Weber

CHURCH AND SECT

The Church

Four features characterize the emergence of a *church* out of a hierocracy: 1) the rise of a professional priesthood removed from the "world," with salaries, promotions, professional duties, and a distinctive way of life; 2) claims to universal domination, that means, hierocracy must at least have overcome household, lineage and tribal ties: we speak of a church in the full sense of the word only when ethnic and national barriers have been eliminated, hence after the levelling of all non-religious distinctions; 3) dogma and rites *(Kultus)* must have been rationalized, recorded in holy scriptures, provided with commentaries, and turned into objects of a systematic education, as distinct from mere training in technical skills; 4) all of these features must occur in some kind of compulsory organization. For the decisive fact is the separation of charisma from the *person* and its linkage with the institution and, particularly, with the *office*: from this fact derive all the above features, which we find developed in

From Max Weber, Economy and Society (1922), Guenther Roth and Claus Wittich, eds. Totowa, N.J.: Bedminster Press, 1968, pp. 1164–66; 1207–10. Copyright © 1968 Bedminster Press Incorporated. Reprinted by permission.

different degrees of typicality. Sociologically, the church differs from the sect by considering itself the trustee of a "trust fund" of eternal blessings that are offered to everyone; as a rule, it is not joined voluntarily, like an association, but its members are born into it; hence even those who lack religious qualification, who are heretical, are subject to its discipline. In one word, the church is the bearer and trustee of an office charisma, not a community of personally charismatic individuals, like the sect. In the full sense of the term, churches have arisen only in Islam and Lamaist Buddhism, apart from Christianity; in a more restricted sense —because of the national delimitation— churches were also created by Mahdism, Judaism and, apparently, the ancient Egyptian hierocracy.

Hierocratic Reglementation of Conduct and Opposition to Personal Charisma

The church advances its demands toward the political power on the basis of its claims to office charisma. This charisma is used for a radical elevation of its bearer's dignity. For its officials the church secures immunity from secular jurisdiction, exemption from taxation and all other public duties, and protection, through heavy penalties, against any show of disrespect. In particular, the church establishes a distinctive way of life for its officials. This requires a specific course of training and hence a regular hierocratic education. Once it has created the latter, it also gains control over lay education and, through it, provides the political authorities with officials and subjects who have been properly brought up in the hierocratic spirit.

By virtue of its power, the hierocratic church also establishes a comprehensive ethico-religious reglementation of all spheres of conduct; in principle, this system has never tolerated any substantive limitations, just as today Catholic doctrine cannot recognize any limits for its claims upon the *disciplina morum*. For the enforcement of its claims hierocracy disposes of very considerable means of power, even beyond the support of the political authorities. Excommunication, the exclusion from the church service, has the same effect as the strictest social boycott, and in one way or another all hierocracies resort to economic boycott by means of the injunction against social intercourse with those ostracized. Insofar as this reglementation of conduct is determined by hierocratic power interests—and that, after all, is true to a large extent—, it is directed against the rise of competing powers. This has several consequences: The "weak"—those subject to non-hierocratic power—are defended; hence slaves, serfs, women and children are championed against the arbitrariness of their master, and petty-bourgeois strata and peasants against usury; the rise of economic powers that cannot be controlled by hierocratic means is impeded, especially that of new powers alien to tradition, such as capitalism; in general, any threat to tradition and the belief in its sanctity is opposed, since this is the inner basis of hierocratic power;

therefore, the established and traditional authorities are strongly supported.

In this manner hierocracy leads to typification just as much as its very opposite, especially in its most characteristic features. The rational organization for administering divine blessings is an institution (*Anstalt*), and charismatic sanctity is transferred to the institution as such; this is typical of every church. Hence fully developed office charisma inevitably becomes the most uncompromising foe of all genuinely personal charisma, which propagates and preaches its own way to God and is prophetic, mystic and ecstatic. Office charisma must oppose it, in order to preserve the dignity of the organization. Whoever works miracles on his own, without an office, is suspect as a heretic or magician. (An early example can be found in the inscriptions of the period of the Sutras, and one of the four deadly sins of the Buddhist monastic order is the claim to personal supernatural powers.) The miracle is incorporated into the regular organization, as for example the miracle of the sacraments. Charismatic qualification is depersonalized; it adheres to the ordination as such and is, in principle, detached from the personal worthiness of the officeholder *(character indelebilis)*—this was the subject matter of the Donatist controversy. In accordance with the overall scheme, the incumbent is distinguished from the office; otherwise his unworthiness would compromise the office charisma. The position of the charismatic prophets and teachers in the old church declines as the church administration is bureaucratized in the hands of the bishops and presbyters, again in accordance with the familiar scheme of depersonalization. The structure of the apparatus is adapted, in technical and economic respects, to the conditions of everyday operations. This results in an office hierarchy with delimited jurisdictions, regular channels, reglementation, fees, benefices, a disciplinary order, rationalization of doctrine and of office-holding as a "vocation"—in fact, these features were first developed, at least in the Occident, by the church as the heir to ancient traditions, which in some respects probably originated in Egypt. This is not at all surprising, since the typically bureaucratic policy of distinguishing the unworthy incumbent from the holy office had to be carried through consistently as soon as the development toward the charisma of office had gotten under way. [. . . .]

Sect, Church and Democracy

. . . By virtue of the dictum that "We must obey God rather than men" [Acts, 5: 29], hierocracy claimed an autonomous charisma and law of its own, secured obedience and firmly restrained the political power. With its office charisma, hierocracy protects those over whom it claims domination against encroachment from other authorities, whether the interfering person be the political ruler, the husband or the father. Since both the mature political and hierocratic power raise universalist demands, that is, since they both want to define the extent of their control over the individual, their adequate relation is a compromise or an alliance for the sake of joint domination in which their spheres of influence are mutually delimited. The formula of the separation of church and state is feasible only if either of the two powers has in fact abandoned its claim to control completely those areas of life that are in principle accessible to it.

In contrast to hierocracy, the sect opposes the charisma of office. The individual can exercise hierocratic powers only by virtue of his personal charisma, just as he can become a member only by virtue of a publicly established qualification, the most unambiguous symbol of

which is the "rebaptism" of the Baptists, in reality, the baptizing of qualified adults. The services of the Quakers are a silent waiting in order to see whether the Divine spirit will overcome a member on this day. Only he will speak up to preach or pray. It is already a concession to the need for regulation and order if those who have proven their qualification to preach the Word of God are put on special seats and are now compelled to help along the coming of the spirit by preparing sermons; this is done in most Quaker congregations. However, in contrast to all consistent churches, all rigorous sects adhere to the principle of lay preaching and of every member's priesthood, even if they establish regular offices for economic and pedagogic reasons.

Moreover, pure sects also insist upon "direct democratic administration" by the congregation and upon treating clerical officials as servants of the congregation. These very structural features demonstrate the elective affinity between the sect and political democracy. They also account for its peculiar and highly important relationship to the political power: The sect is a specifically anti-political or at least apolitical group. Since it must not raise universal demands and endeavors to exist as a voluntary association of qualified believers, it cannot enter into an alliance with the political power. If it concludes such an alliance, as the Independents did in New England, the result is an aristocratic rule by the ecclesiastically qualified; this leads to compromises and to the loss of the sect character—witness the so-called Halfway-Covenant [of the Congregational churches in 1662]. The greatest experiment of this kind was the abortive rule by Cromwell's Parliament of Saints. The pure sect must advocate "tolerance" and "separation of church and state" for several reasons: Because it is in fact *not* a universalist redemptory institution for the repression of sin and can suffer political as little as hierocratic reglementation; because no official power can dispense grace to unqualified persons and, hence, all use of political force in religious matters must appear senseless or outright diabolical; because the sect is simply not concerned with outsiders; because, taking all this together, the sect just cannot be anything but an absolutely voluntary association if it wants to retain its true religious identity and its effectiveness. Therefore, consistent sects have always taken this position and have been the most genuine advocates of "freedom of conscience."

Other communities, too, have favored freedom of conscience, but in a different sense. It is possible to speak of this freedom and of tolerance under the caesaropapist regimes of Rome, China, India and Japan, since the most diverse cults of subjected or affiliated states were permitted and since no religious compulsion existed; however, in principle this is limited by the official cult of the political power, the cult of the emperor in Rome, the religious veneration of the emperor in Japan, and probably also the emperor's Cult of Heaven in China. Moreover, this tolerance had political, not religious reasons, as did that of William the Silent or, much earlier, Emperor Frederick II, or manorial lords who used sect members as skilled labor, and the city of Amsterdam, where the sectarians were major agents of commercial life. Thus, economic motives played an important role. But the genuine sect must demand the non-intervention of the political power and freedom of conscience for specifically religious reasons—there are transitional forms, but we leave them aside deliberately.

A fully developed church—advancing universalist claims—cannot concede freedom of conscience; wherever it pleads for this freedom, it is because it finds itself in a minority position and demands something which, in principle, it cannot grant to others. "The Catholic's freedom of conscience," Mallinckrodt said in the Reichstag, "consists in being free to obey the pope," that means, in following *his own* conscience. However, if they are strong enough, neither the Catholic nor the (old) Lutheran Church and, all the more so, the Calvinist and Baptist old church recognise freedom of conscience for *others*. These churches cannot act differently in view of their institutional commitment to safeguard the salvation of the soul or, in the case of the Calvinists, to protect the glory of God. By contrast, the consistent Quaker applies the principle of the freedom of conscience not only to himself but also to others, and rejects any attempt to compel those who are not Quakers or Baptists to act as if they belonged to his group. Thus the consistent sect gives rise to an inalienable personal right of the governed as against any power, whether political, hierocratic or patriarchal. Such freedom of conscience may be the oldest Right of Man—as Jellinek has argued convincingly; at any rate, it is the most basic Right of Man because it comprises all ethically conditioned action and guarantees freedom from compulsion, especially from the power of the state. In this sense the concept was as unknown to Antiquity and the Middle Ages as it was to Rousseau's social contract with its power of religious compulsion. The other Rights of Man or civil rights were joined to this basic right, especially the right to pursue one's own economic interests, which includes the inviolability of individual property, the freedom of contract, and vocational choice. This economic right exists within the limits of a system of guaranteed abstract rules that apply to everybody alike. All of these rights find their ultimate justification in the belief of the Enlightenment in the workings of individual reason which, if unimpeded, would result in the at least relatively best of all worlds, by virtue of

Divine providence and because the individual is best qualified to know his own interests. This charismatic glorification of "Reason," which found a characteristic expression in its apotheosis by Robespierre, is the last form that charisma has adopted in its fateful historical course. It is clear that these postulates of formal legal equality and economic mobility paved the way for the destruction of all patrimonial and feudal law in favor of abstract norms and hence indirectly of bureaucratization. It is also clear that they facilitated the expansion of capitalism. The basic Rights of Man made it possible for the capitalist to use things and men freely, just as the this-worldly asceticism—adopted with some dogmatic variations—and the specific discipline of the sects bred the capitalist spirit and the rational professional *(Berufsmensch)* who was needed by capitalism.

Max Weber

STATE
AND HIEROCRACY

The bourgeoisie depends economically on work which is continuous and rational (or at least empirically rationalized); such work contrasts with the seasonal character of agricultural work that is exposed to unusual and unknown natural forces; it makes the connection between means and ends, success and failure relatively transparent. The product of the potter, weaver, turner and carpenter is much less affected by unpredictable natural events, especially by organic reproduction that involves the mystery of "creation" for which only phantasy can provide an explanation. The resulting rationalization and intellectualization parallel the loss of the immediate relationship to the palpable and vital realities of nature, because the work is done largely within the house and is removed from the organically determined quest for

From *Max Weber*, Economy and Society (1922), *Guenther Roth and Claus Wittich*, eds. Totowa, N.J.: Bedminster Press, 1968, pp. 1178–81; 1185–88; 1190–91; 1193–95; 1196–1200. Copyright © 1968 Bedminster Press Incorporated. Reprinted by permission.

food; perhaps it is also relevant that the largest muscles of the body are not used. The forces of nature become an intellectual problem as soon as they are no longer part of the immediate environment. This provokes the rationalist quest for the transcendental meaning of existence, a search that always leads to religious speculation. Ecstatic frenzy or dreaming are replaced by the paler forms of contemplative mysticism and of common-sense contemplation. At the same time, the steady professional nature of the artisan's work for his customers easily suggests the conception of duty and reward as the basis of conduct, and since the social context of his work requires a relatively rational order, religiosity tends to be imbued with moralistic considerations.

By contrast, a feeling of sinfulness, which developed from the older idea of ritual purity, is incompatible with the feudal lord's sense of dignity, and for the peasant, "sin" is even today difficult to understand. These agricultural strata do not seek redemption, in fact, they do not quite know from what they should be redeemed. Their gods are strong beings, whose passions resemble those of man; they may be brave or treacherous, friendly or hostile to one another and to man; at any rate, like man they are completely amoral, amenable to bribery through sacrifices and subject to magic influence, which may make the human manipulator even stronger than they are. At this stage there are as yet no incentives to construe a theodicy or to pursue any type of ethical speculation about the cosmic order. In a directly utilitarian fashion, the priesthood and strict adherence to ritual prescriptions serve as means of magical control over nature, especially as a defense against demons, whose ill will might bring bad weather, attacks by predatory animals and insects, diseases and animal epidemics. The internalization and rationalization of religiosity usually develops parallel to a certain degree of handicraft production, most of the time to that of the urban trades. This involves the projection of ethical criteria and commandments, and the transfiguration of gods into ethical powers which will reward good and punish evil; now the gods themselves must conform to moral expectations and the individual's sense of sinfulness and his desire for redemption can emerge. It is impossible to reduce this parallel development to an unambiguous relation of cause and effect: Religious rationalization has its own dynamics, which economic conditions merely channel; above all, it is linked to the emergence of priestly education. Although we do not know much about Mahdism, it appears that it lacked any economic basis. It is very doubtful that it was an hierocratic outgrowth of the old Islamic religion, the work of the founder of a sect who was driven across the border into a remote region. However, it seems certain that the rational-moralistic evolution of the religion of Yahwe was influenced by the great

centers of civilization; yet prophecy and, even more so, the older moralism arose when the city and the trades were still undeveloped, at any rate in comparison with contemporary Mesopotamia and Egypt. However, the hierocracy was established by the city priests of Jerusalem in their struggle with the countryside, and the elaboration of the Law and its imposition were the work of the exiles living in the city of Babylon. The ancient Mediterranean polis, on the other hand, did not rationalize religion, in part because of Homer's influence as the accepted means of literary education, but primarily because of the absence of a priesthood that was hierocratically organized and clerically educated.

In spite of all these differences, it is quite clear that there is an elective affinity between priesthood and urban petty-bourgeois strata. Above all, the opponents are typically the same in Antiquity and the Middle Ages—the great feudal families; in their hands was both the political power and the usurious loan business. For this reason bourgeois strata have often tended to support every move of an hierocracy in the direction of autonomy and rationalization. Thus, the urban population in Sumeria, Babylonia, Phoenicia and Jerusalem supported the hierocratic claims, and the Pharisees (i.e., Puritans) drew their following against the Sadducaic patricians from the cities, just as all emotional cults of Mediterranean Antiquity had an urban base. The early Christian church was made up of petty-bourgeois congregations; the papal autonomy claims, just as the medieval Puritan sects, found their strongest support in the cities; certain trades produced heretic movements as well as religious orders, such as the *Humiliati*—both tendencies border on one another. In the long run, ascetic Protestantism in the broadest sense of the term (Calvinist and Baptist Puritans, Mennonites, Methodists and Pietists) drew the core of its following from the middle and lower ranks of the bourgeoisie, just as the unshakable religious law consciousness of Judaism began only with its urban entrenchment and depended on it.

This does not mean that religious movements have usually been class movements. Nothing is as wrong as the idea that Christianity, which for compelling political and cultural reasons had to be unacceptable to the ruling strata of Antiquity, was a "proletarian" movement. Buddhism was founded by a prince and imported into Japan with the active support of the nobility. Luther addressed the "Christian nobility" (i.e., the highest nobles, the princes). At the height of their great struggles, the French Huguenots and the Scottish Calvinists were led by nobles, but the Puritan Revolution was successful because of the cavalry provided by the rural gentry. These examples show that, by and large, religious cleavage cuts vertically through all strata. This remains true for the period of enthusiastic devotion to transcendental interests, a devotion that almost always has an eschatological orientation.

In the long run, however, an elective affinity between spiritually prescribed conduct and the socially conditioned way of life of status groups and classes asserts itself, as the eschatological expectations recede and the new religious beliefs are routinized. Horizontal stratification increasingly displaces vertical divisions. Thus, the Huguenot and Scottish nobility later stopped fighting for Calvinism, and everywhere the further development of ascetic Protestantism became the concern of the bourgeois middle classes. We cannot pursue these problems in detail, but we can at least consider it certain that the evolution of hierocracy into a rational means of domination, and the related rational-ethical development of religious thought,

usually finds strong support in the bourgeois classes, especially their lower strata, despite the conflicts between hierocracy and bourgeoisie with which we must deal in a different context. [. . . .]

The Impact of Hierocracy on Economic Development

. . . Hierocracy is the most important typifying power in existence. The *ius divinum*, the Islamic *sharî'ah*, the Torah of the Jews are inviolable. On the other hand, in those areas not regulated by the *ius divinum* hierocracy is the least rationally predictable power: Charismatic justice in the form of the oracle, ordeal, *fetwa* of a *mufti* or judicature of an Islamic ecclesiastic court is irrational and at best decides a given case according to considerations of equity. These formal elements of adjudication, which we have mentioned several times before, had an anti-capitalist impact, but in addition hierocracy necessarily felt a deep antipathy toward the non-traditional power of capitalism, even though it occasionally collaborated with it. This antipathy is rooted in the natural community of interest with all traditionally sanctified authorities whose monopoly appears to be threatened by the domination of capital.

However, another reason for this antipathy is inherent in capitalism. It is true that only Occidental hierocracy, which was more rationalized than all the others, developed a rational trial procedure—in its own interest, to be sure—, in addition to a rational canon law; moreover, it threw its full weight to the side of the reception of a rational law: Roman law. Nevertheless, the intervention of the ecclesiastic courts has been barely tolerated, evaded or openly rejected by the capitalist bourgeoisie. [The reasons for this mutual antipathy must be sought in the fact that] the domination of capital is the only one which cannot be ethically regulated, because of its impersonal character. Most of the time this domination appears in such an indirect form that one cannot identify any concrete master and hence cannot make any ethical demands upon him. It is possible to advance ethical postulates and to attempt the imposition of substantive norms with regard to household head and servant, master and apprentice, manorial lord and dependents or officials, master and slave, or patriarchal ruler and subject, since their relationship is personal and since the expected services result therefrom. Within wide limits, personal, flexible interests are operative here, and purely personal intent and action can decisively change the relationship and the condition of the person involved. But for the director of a joint-stock company, who is obliged to represent the interests of the stock-holders as the masters proper, it is very difficult to relate in this manner to the factory workers; it is even more difficult for the director of the bank that finances the joint-stock company, or for the mortgage holder in relation to the owner of property on which the bank granted a loan. Decisive are the need for competitive survival and the conditions of the labor, money and commodity market; hence matter-of-fact considerations that are simply non-ethical determine individual behavior and interpose impersonal forces between the persons involved. From an ethical viewpoint, this "masterless slavery" to which capitalism subjects the worker or the mortgagee is questionable only as an *institution*. However, in principle, the behavior of any *individual* cannot be so questioned, since it is prescribed in all relevant respects by objective situations. The penalty for non-compliance is extinction, and this would not be helpful in any way. More important is that such economic behavior has the quality of a *service* toward an *impersonal* purpose.

In all ethically rationalized religions, these conditions conflict perennially with the most elementary social postulates of the hierocracy. Every ethically oriented religiosity begins with eschatological hopes and hence rejects the world. These beginnings are directly antieconomic, also in the sense that they lack the notion of a specific dignity of work. However, insofar as the adherents of a religious community cannot live from patronage or begging, or do not live under warrior communism, as in the case of militant Islam, exemplary members live from their own work—Paulus as well as Saint Aegidius. This was recommended by the early Christian church as well as by Saint Francis, but not because work as such was esteemed. It is simply a fairy tale that work received any greater dignity in the New Testament. The exhortation "to abide in the same calling" [Corinth. 7: 20] expresses complete eschatological indifference, just as the prescription "to render unto Caesar the things that are Caesar's" [Luke 20: 25]. This is not, as it is often alleged today, an inculcation of duties toward the state, but the expression of absolute indifference toward anything that happens in the political sphere—this exactly constitutes the difference from the Judaic parties. Work attained dignity much later, beginning with the monastic orders who used it as an ascetic means. During the charismatic period of a religion, the perfect disciple must also reject landed property, and the mass of believers is expected to be indifferent toward it. An expression of this indifference is that attenuated form of the charismatic communism of love which apparently existed in the early Christian community of Jerusalem, where the members of the community owned property "as if they did not own it." Such unlimited, unrationalized sharing with needy brothers, which forced the missionaries, especially Paulus, to collect alms abroad for the anti-economic central community, is probably what lies behind that much-discussed tradition, not any allegedly "socialist" organization or communist "collective ownership." Once the eschatological expectations fade, charismatic communism in all its forms declines and retreats into monastic circles, where it becomes the special concern of the exemplary followers of God (*Gottesgefolgschaft*). But even there we always find the tendency toward prebendalization. It becomes necessary to advise against abandoning one's vocation and to warn against missionary parasites — Paulus' famous saying: "Whoever does not work shall not eat" [2 Thess. 3:10] is addressed only to them. The maintenance of the indigent and unemployed brothers becomes the task of a regular officer, the deacon. Some ecclesiastic revenues are set aside for them (in Islam as well as Christianity). For the rest, poor relief becomes the concern of the monks. As a remnant of the charismatic communism of love, Islam, Buddhism and Christianity equally consider the giving of alms as pleasing to God, despite their greatly different origins.

However, the churches always retain some distinctive, more or less articulate attitude toward the economic order. It is true that they can no longer denounce it as a Satanic creation, since they must use it and ally themselves with it. Just like the state, the economic order appears either as a concession to the world's sinfulness, which God permitted to arise and hence must be accepted as inevitable, or even as a divinely ordained means for the subduing of sin, and then it is important to imbue the bearers of an economic order with an ethic that will make them use their power for this purpose. However, this attempt meets difficulties in all capitalist relationships, even in their most primitive forms. For *caritas,* brotherhood and

ethically imbued personal relations between master and servant remain the foundation of every ecclesiastic ethic, from Islam and Judaism to Buddhism and Christianity; they are the residues of the old ethos of love of the charismatic brotherhood. In the economic realm the rise of capitalism makes these ideas just as meaningless as the implicit pacifist ideals of early Christianity have always been in the political realm in which all domination ultimately rests on force. For under capitalism all patriarchal relationships are divested of their genuine character and become impersonal; in principle, a person can practice *caritas* and brotherhood only outside his vocational life. [. . . .]

With regard to the theory of *iustum pretium* [teaching of the "just price"], late medieval doctrine had already made great concessions.

In general, it appears scarcely admissible to say that the church had an economic program. The church did not decisively influence basic institutions. In Antiquity as well as the Middle Ages, for example, it had no major share in the waning of such a fundamental institution as slavery. Insofar as it took a stand in modern history, it lagged behind the economic facts and later behind the protest of the Enlightenment. And insofar as religious influences were important, they emanated from the sects, especially the Quakers, although in practice even they often ignored their hostility to slavery. In all other respects, too, the church endorsed, if it intervened at all, the traditionalist and "minimum subsistence" measures of the cities and princes. Nevertheless, the influence of the medieval church was not insignificant but extraordinarily great. But it did not make or unmake institutions as much as it molded attitudes, and even then its influence was essentially negative. Against the forces of capitalism, the church has reinforced all personal patriarchal authority and all peasant and petty-bourgeois traditionalist interests—fully in accordance with the rationale of all hierocracy. The mentality furthered by the church is non-capitalist, and partly anti-capitalist. The church does not condemn the acquisitive drive *Erwerbstreib*—a concept, by the way, which is wholly imprecise and better not used at all); rather, the church condones it, as it does all worldly things, in those who do not have the charisma necessary for adhering to the *consilia evangelica*. However, the church cannot bridge the gap between its highest ethical ideals and a rational, methodical orientation toward the capitalist enterprise which treats profit as the ultimate goal of a vocation and—this is the main point—regards it as a measure of personal virtue. The church outbids secular morality in marriage, state, vocation and business through the monastic ethic as the higher principle, and thus reduces everyday life, especially in the economic sphere, to an ethically inferior level. Only for the monk did the church create a methodical ascetic way of life oriented toward a unified goal. This applies to the church of the Occident just as much as to Buddhism, which in its beginnings was a religion purely for monks. The church looks at the layman's doings with a certain tolerance if he bows to its authority and, in Buddhism, presents it with gifts. Most importantly, the church lets the layman periodically relieve himself of his sins in the aural confession, the clergy's most impressive power instrument, which only in the Occidental Christian church was developed with full consistency. But through the confession, and by stressing to the layman its own role as a charismatic institution of salvation, the church inevitably weakens the believer's motivation for living his worldly and occupational life methodically and exclusively on his own responsibility: The highest

religious ideals could not be followed in this manner anyway, for they are not of this world.

It is true that, all in all, the conduct of the medieval Catholic in his secular vocation was much less bound by tradition and law than that of the Jew, about whom we will have to say more below, and in some respects even that of the Mohammedan or Buddhist. Yet whatever seemed to be gained thereby for capitalist development was lost again because of the lack of incentives for the methodical fulfillment of a secular vocation, especially in business. There was no psychic premium on work in one's secular vocation. *Deo placere non potest* remained, in spite of all attenuation, the last word for the believer with regard to the idea that his economic conduct should serve a rational, impersonal, profit-oriented enterprise. Thus persists the dualism between the "world" and ascetic ideals that can be realised only by leaving it. [. . . .]

Hierocracy in the Age of Capitalism and of Bourgeois Democracy

The rise of modern bourgeois democracy and of capitalism has greatly changed the preconditions of hierocratic domination. At first sight it appears that hierocracy did not benefit from this development. Capitalism advanced triumphantly in spite of the protest and frequently the direct resistance of the clergy. The *grande bourgeoisie* increasingly outgrew the historical connections between bourgeoisie and hierocracy. The carriers of magic gifts of grace and, in particular, those hierocratic claims that were most authoritarian and backed the traditional authorities, suffered from their own attempts to regulate social conduct and from their own objections to modern science, the technical basis of capitalism; they were also adversely affected by the growing rationalism that made social life less opaque and more amenable to reconstruction. It would be wrong to assume that anti-ethical or non-ethical, libertarian tendencies of the rising bourgeois strata played a major role in this process; after all, by means of the confessional, the church went far to compromise with the kind of ethical laxity that has always been characteristic of entrenched feudal strata. Rather, it is the rigoristic ethics of bourgeois rationalism that is ultimately bound to clash with the hierocratic claims, for it endangers the ecclesiastic Power of the Keys and the value of dispensing grace and absolution. Therefore, the hierocracy has always treated such rigoristic ethics as a stepping stone to heresy if it did not conform to clerically controlled asceticism.

As capitalism and the bourgeoisie advanced, all traditionalist strata sought the protection of the church: the petty-bourgeoisie, the nobility, and even the monarchy, after the age of alliance between securely established princes and capitalism had passed and the political aspirations of the bourgeoisie had become dangerous. The bourgeoisie has done the same, wherever its position has been endangered by the assault of the working class. But the church, too, accommodates itself to established capitalism; this can easily be demonstrated by looking at the development of the German Center Party from Bishop Ketteler [1811–1877] up to the present. It is true that for a time the hierocracy put economical eschatological hopes into "Christian," that means, hierocratically dominated "socialism," by which diverse, mostly petty-bourgeois utopias were understood; it is also true that the hierocracy helped undermine the belief in the bourgeois economic system, but the typical and almost inevitable hostility of the labor movement to authority changed its attitude. The modern pro-

letarian is not a petty-bourgeois. He is threatened not by demons and natural forces that must be magically checked, but by social conditions that can be rationally understood. The economically strongest strata of the working class often reject any guidance by the hierocracy or accept it merely as a gratuitous interest representation—provided the hierocracy actually represents their interest. The more certain the indestructibility of the capitalist order becomes, the more do hierocratic interests require compromises with the new authorities. In accordance with its natural ethical interests, hierocracy endeavors to transform the capitalist dependency of the working class into a personal authoritarian subordination amenable to *caritas;* in particular, the hierocracy recommends those "welfare institutions" which restrict the workers' anti-authoritarian freedom of mobility; it also furthers as much as possible the home industry, which seemingly favors family bonds and patriarchal work relations, as against the concentration of the workers in factories, which promotes anti-authoritarian class consciousness. With deep distrust the hierocracy views an anti-authoritarian weapon such as the strike and all organizations which facilitate it; it opposes these most when they threaten to result in interdenominational solidarity. [. . . .]

The Reformation and Its Impact on Economic Life

The Reformation, which greatly changed the position of hierocracy, was certainly codetermined by economic factors. On the whole, however, their influence was indirect. To be sure, the peasants were interested in the new doctrine primarily because they wanted their land to be freed from the payments in kind and the services that were not justified by the Bible, just as is true today of the Russian peasants. But the immediate interests of the bourgeoisie clashed only with the monastic crafts; everything else was secondary. Nowhere is the prohibition of usury mentioned as an issue. Decisive for the transformation was the weakening of papal authority through the Great Schism [1378–1417], which in turn had political reasons, and through the resulting conciliar movement, which further reduced papal authority in the remote Northern countries where it had been less strong than in the South. Papal authority was also diminished by the persistent and successful struggle of the princes and Estates against its interference with the granting of domestic benefices and against its tax and fee system; it lost ground because of the caesaropapist inclinations and secularizing tendencies of the princes who had strengthened their power tremendously through administrative rationalization, and after the ecclesiastic tradition became discredited in the eyes of the intellectual circles and the noble and bourgeois strata.

However, these tendencies toward emancipation were almost completely unrelated to any desires for an emancipation from a religious way of life, and connected only slightly with a desire for diminishing the hierocratic restraints. It would be completely wrong to assume that a society longing for an affirmation of worldly life, "freedom of the individual," or even beauty and sensual enjoyment felt fettered by ecclesiastic hostility to these aspirations. In practice, the church left nothing to be desired in this respect. The very opposite is true: The reformers believed that the religious penetration of worldly life through the hierocracy did *not go far enough,* and this was believed especially by bourgeois groups. The church never dared to demand the self-control, asceticism and ecclesiastic discipline that the great

ideological opponents of the papacy, the Anabaptists and related sects, imposed upon themselves to a degree sheerly incomprehensible for us today. It was precisely the unavoidable compromise of the hierocracy with the secular powers and with sin which provoked them. The ascetic varieties of Protestantism have prevailed wherever the bourgeoisie was a social power, and the least ascetic churches of the Reformation, Anglicanism and Lutheranism, wherever the nobility or the princes had the upper hand. It was the peculiar piety of the intensely religious bourgeois strata that made them side with the reformist preachers against the traditional ecclesiastic apparatus, just as they had sided earlier with the hierocracy against the Empire and with the mendicant orders against the secular clergy; their piety was characterized by a relatively rational ethic, by the nature of bourgeois occupations and by a relatively strong preoccupation with self-justification before God, features which corresponded to a mode of life that was less determined by organic natural events than peasant life. These strata would have much preferred an internal reform of the church to an ecclesiastic revolution, if the former would have satisfied their ethical demands. However, the hierocracy was confronted with certain difficulties that it could not resolve in time, since they were rooted in the historical legacies of its organization and connected with concrete power interests. The massive impact of specific economic and, especially, political constellations on the course of the religious split is well-known, but must not be allowed to blur the great importance of the ultimately religious motives.

Lutheranism

The Reformation in turn strongly affected economic development, but its impact varied with the peculiarities of the new creeds. The attitude of the Lutheran churches toward the two capitalist classes, bourgeoisie and proletariat, differs from the Catholic only in degree. Luther's views on economic affairs were strictly traditional and far less "modern" than those of the Florentine theoreticians. His church was founded explicitly upon the office charisma of the minister, whose calling was the preaching of the Gospel; his church was bluntly hostile to any rebellion against the God-given authorities. The most important innovation, also in economic respects, was the elimination of the *consilia evangelica,* which had surpassed the standards of secular morality and social order; thus, the monasteries and monastic asceticism were abolished as a useless and dangerous expression of seeking salvation through good works—a measure to which at first Luther was not at all committed. Henceforth, the Christian virtues could be pursued only within the secular social order, in marriage, state and vocation. The duty of safeguarding the primary task, the propagation of the pure Gospel, fell in Lutheranism to the political power, since the hierocracy as well as the attempt at forming autonomous religious communes had failed —the latter, of course, in part for political and economic reasons—and since the office charisma of the church, as a redemptory institution for the obligatory preaching of the Word, was retained. The resulting caesaropapism was tremendously strengthened through the great secularizations of the Reformation period.

Ethics and Church in Calvinism

An anti-capitalist ethos and welfare orientation is, in effect, a common characteristic of all religions that promise

salvation. However, there are two exceptions, differing from one another: *Puritanism* and *Judaism*. Only one of the Puritan communities (in the broad sense that comprises all essentially ascetic Protestant groups) is not a sect, but a church in the sociological meaning used here, that means, an hierocratic institution: Calvinism.

The character of the Calvinist church differs from that of all other churches, Catholic, Lutheran and Islamic. In view of the limited space available to us, we will, perforce, summarise our theory of Calvinism in a purposively accentuated manner. The basic dogma of strict Calvinism, the doctrine of predestination, makes it impossible for the church to administer sacraments whose reception can have any significance for eternal salvation. Moreover, the actual behavior of the believer is irrelevant to his fate, which has been determined from eternity through God's inscrutable and immutable will. The elect need no church for their own sake. Its very existence, and largely also its organization, rests exclusively upon God's commandment, just like all other political and social institutions and all social duties of the believers. The reasons for this commandment are unknown to the believers, but it has been definitively revealed in the Bible; its details can be supplemented and interpreted by human reason, which exists for this purpose. By no means does the church exist for the salvation of souls and the sinners' community of love; its sole purpose is the augmentation of God's glory and honor, thus a cold Divine *raison d'état*. The church exists not only for the blessed but also the condemned, so that, for the greater glory of God, it can suppress sinfulness, which is common to all men and separates all beings irremediably from God: The church is a scourge and not a vehicle of salvation. Every attempt at resorting to magic sacraments is a foolish infringement on God's established order; the church does not dispose of such means. Thus the church has here been completely divested of its charismatic character and has become a mere social institution. However, its establishment is a duty *divini iuris;* its dignity surpasses that of all other institutions and its form of organization is the only one prescribed by God. Yet apart from this feature, the duty to maintain the church is ultimately not different from the social obligation to support the equally God-willed state and from the duties in a worldly calling. In contrast to all other churches, these duties cannot consist in the endeavor to attain a specific state of grace, in the manner of the monks, by surpassing secular morality, for such attempts are meaningless in the face of predestination; rather, these duties consist in serving God's glory within the given order and within a "calling."

The notion of a "calling" derives in all Protestant countries from the Bible translations, and among the Calvinists it explicitly includes the legal profit from capitalist enterprises. With the consistent development of Calvinism—which is not identical with Calvin's own attitudes —such profit and the rational means of its realization received an ever more positive evaluation. The inscrutability of predestination to either salvation or damnation was naturally intolerable to the believer: he searched for the *certitudo salutis,* for an indication that he belonged to the elect. Since otherworldly asceticism had been rejected, he could find this certainty, on the one hand, in the conviction that he was acting according to the letter of the law and according to reason, repressing all animal drives; on the other, he could find it in visible proofs that God blessed his work. "Good works" of the Catholic variety were meaningless in the face of God's unchangeable decree; however, for the believer and his community,

his own ethical conduct and fate in the secular social order became supremely important as an indication of his state of grace. A person was considered elect or condemned as an entity; no confession and absolution could relieve him and change his position before God and, in contrast to Catholicism, no individual "good deed" could compensate for his sins. Therefore, the individual could only be sure of his state of grace if he felt reason to believe that, by adhering to a principle of methodical conduct, he pursued the sole correct path in all his action—that he worked for God's glory. Methodical conduct, the rational form of asceticism, is thus carried from the monastery into the world. The ascetic means are in principle identical: Rejected are all vain glorification of the self and of all other things of the flesh, feudal pride, the spontaneous enjoyment of art and life, "levity," all waste of money and time, eroticism or any other activity that detracts from the rational orientation to God's will and glory, that means, from rational work in one's private vocation and within the God-willed social order. The curtailment of all feudal ostentation and of all irrational consumption facilitates capital accumulation and the ever-renewed utilization of property for productive purposes; this-worldly asceticism as a whole favors the breeding and exaltation of the professionalism needed by capitalism and bureaucracy. Life is focused not on persons but on impersonal rational goals. Charity becomes an impersonal operation of poor-relief for the greater glory of God. And since the success of work is the surest symptom that it pleases God, capitalist profit is one of the most important criteria for establishing that God's blessing rests on the enterprise.

It is clear that this style of life is very closely related to the self-justification that is customary for bourgeois acquisition:

profit and property appear not as ends in themselves but as indications of personal ability. Here has been attained the union of religious postulate and bourgeois style of life that promotes capitalism. Of course, this was not the purpose of the Puritan ethic, especially not the encouragement of money-making; on the contrary, as in all Christian denominations, wealth was regarded as dangerous and full of temptation. However, just as the monasteries time and again brought this temptation on themselves by virtue of the ascetic rational work and conduct of their members, so did now the pious bourgeois who lived and worked ascetically.

IV

RELIGION
IN
TRANSFORMATION

Discussion of the Present Situation

SECTION ONE

Substantive Studies on the Changing Structure of Religious Beliefs and Practices

T. W. Adorno

NEUTRALIZED RELIGION AND ITS FUNCTIONS

Although religion may no longer stimulate open fanaticism against those who do not share one's own belief, we are led to suspect that on a deeper, more unconscious level the religious heritage, the carry-over of old belief and the identification with certain denominations, still make themselves felt.

Our approach was guided by certain theoretical considerations inherent in our general frame of reference. In order to give relief to the focus of our observations, it is appropriate to indicate the more fundamental of these theoretical reflections.

It was expected from the very beginning that the relations between religious

From T. W. Adorno et al., The Authoritarian Personality, New York : 1950, pp. 728–738. Copyright 1950 by the American Jewish Committee. Reprinted by permission of Harper & Row, Publishers, Inc.

ideology and ethnocentrism would be complex. On the one hand the Christian doctrine of universal love and the idea of "Christian Humanism" is opposed to prejudice. This doctrine is doubtless one of the major historical presuppositions for the recognition of minorities as sharing equal rights with majorities "in the sight of God." The Christian relativization of the natural, the extreme emphasis on the "spirit," forbids any tendency to regard natural characteristics such as "racial" traits as ultimate values or to judge man according to his descent.

On the other hand, Christianity as the religion of the "Son" contains an implicit antagonism against the religion of the "Father" and its surviving witnesses, the Jews. This antagonism, continuous since St. Paul, is enhanced by the fact that the Jews, by clinging to their own religious culture, rejected the religion of the Son and by the fact that the New Testament puts upon them the blame for Christ's death. It has been pointed out again and again by great theologians, from Tertullian and Augustine to Kierkegaard, that the acceptance of Christianity by the Christians themselves contains a problematic and ambiguous element, engendered by the paradoxical nature of the doctrine of God becoming man, the Infinite finite. Unless this element is consciously put into the center of the religious conception, it tends to promote hostility against the outgroup. As Samuel has pointed out, the "weak" Christians resent bitterly the openly negative attitude of the Jews toward the religion of the Son, since they feel within themselves traces of this negative attitude based upon the paradoxical, irrational nature of their creed—an attitude which they do not dare to admit and which they must therefore put under a heavy taboo in others.

It is hardly an exaggeration to say that many of the usual rationalizations of anti-Semitism originate within Christianity or at least have been amalgamated with Christian motives. The fight against the Jews seems to be modeled after the fight between the Redeemer and the Christian Devil. Joshuah Trachtenberg has given detailed evidence that the imagery of the Jew is largely a secularization of the medieval imagery of the Devil. The fantasies about Jewish bankers and money-lenders have their biblical archetype in the story of Jesus driving the usurers from the Temple. The idea of the Jewish intellectual as a sophist is in keeping with the Christian denuciation of the Pharisee. The Jewish traitor who betrays not only his master but also the ingroup to which he has been admitted, is Judas. These motifs are enhanced by more unconscious trends such as are expressed in the idea of the crucifix and

the sacrifice of blood. Although these latter ideas have been more or less successfully replaced by "Christian Humanism," their deeper psychological roots have still to be reckoned with.

In attempting to evaluate the influence of such elements of religion upon the existence or absence of prejudice today, one has to take into consideration the position in which Christianity presently finds itself: it is faced with an "indifference" which often seems to make it altogether unimportant. The Christian religion has been deeply affected by the process of Enlightenment and the conquest of the scientific spirit. The "magical" elements of Christianity as well as the factual basis of Christian belief in biblical history have been profoundly shaken. This, however, does not mean that Christian religion has been abolished. Although largely emasculated in its profoundest claims, it has maintained at least part of the social functions acquired throughout the centuries. This means that it has largely become *neutralized*. The shell of Christian doctrine, above all its social authority and also a number of more or less isolated elements of its content, is preserved and "consumed" in a haphazard way as a "cultural good" like patriotism or traditional art.

This neutralization of religious beliefs is strikingly exemplified by the following statement of *M109,* a high-scoring Roman Catholic who attends church regularly. He writes on his questionnaire that he considers religion a "thoroughly important part of existence, perhaps it should occupy 2 to 5 per cent of leisure time."

The relegation of religion, which was once regarded as the most essential sphere of life, to "leisure," as well as the time allotment made for it and, above all, the fact that it is subsumed under a calculated time schedule and referred to in terms of per cent is symbolic of the profound changes which have taken place with regard to the prevailing attitude towards religion.

It may be assumed that such neutralized residues of Christianity as that indicated in *M109's* statement are largely severed from their basis in serious belief and substantial individual experience. Therefore, they rarely produce individual behavior that is different from what is to be expected from the prevailing patterns of civilization. However, some of the formal properties of religion, such as the rigid antithesis of good and evil, ascetic ideals, emphasis upon unlimited effort on the part of the individual, still exercise considerable power. Severed from their roots and often devoid of any specific content, these formal constituents are apt to be congealed into mere formulae. Thus, they assume an aspect of rigidity and intolerance such as we expect to find in the prejudiced person.

The dissolution of positive religion and its preservation in a noncommittal ideological form are due to social processes. While religion has been deprived of the intrinsic claim of truth, it has been gradually transformed into "social cement." The more this cement is needed for the maintenance of the *status quo* and the more dubious its inherent truth becomes, the more obstinately is its authority upheld and the more its hostile, destructive and negative features come to the fore. The transformation of religion into an agency of social conformity makes it fall in line with most other conformist tendencies. Adherence to Christianity under such conditions easily lends itself to abuse, to subservience, overadjustment, and ingroup loyalty as an ideology which covers up hatred against the disbeliever, the dissenter, the Jew. Belonging to a denomination assumes an air of aggressive fatality, similar to that of being born as a member of one particular nation. Membership in any particular religious group tends to be reduced to a fairly abstract ingroup-outgroup relationship within the general pattern brought out by the foregoing discussion of ethnocentrism. . . .

There is much in the interview material to support the view, suggested by findings from the questionnaire, that the more religion becomes conventionalized, the more it falls in line with the general outlook of the ethnocentric individual. An illustration of this point is afforded by the following excerpt from the interview of *F5054*, a woman who scored high on the ethnocentrism scale.

The subject seems to have accepted a set of rather dogmatic moral codes which makes her regard people, especially "youngsters who call themselves atheists" as falling outside the circle in which she wants to move. She made a point of admitting (confidentially) that one of the main reasons she was looking forward to moving away from Westwood was that she could thereby get her youngest daughter away from the influence of the neighbor's boy, who is an atheist because his father tells him "religion is a lot of hooey." She is also distressed, because her eldest daughter "just won't go to church."

From the above it is evident that she is quite in agreement with organized religion and tends to be a conformist in religious matters. Christian ethics and its moral codes are regarded as absolutes, and deviations are to be frowned upon or punished.

This account suggests that there is a connection between conventional religious rigidity and an almost complete absence of what might be called personally "experienced" belief. The same holds for the high-scoring man *5057*, a person who sticks to the Church although he "does not believe in a personal God."

The subject believes that most Protestant religions are very much the same. He selected Christian Science because "it is a quieter religion than most." He started going to Unity Sunday school while living with his grandparents and liked the Unity Church, which, in his estimation, presents a mild form of Christian Science. He joined the Christian Science Church when he married, inasmuch as his wife's family and his wife are all Christian Scientists. "Religion should not be allowed to interfere with the ordinary essentials. However, religion should restrain you from overindulgences of any kind, such as drinking, gambling, or anything to excess."

A high-scoring young woman, *F103*, says, "My parents let us make our own choice; just so we go to church." There we see the lack of any interest in the content of religion; one goes to church because "it's the thing to do" and because one wants to please one's parents. A final example is afforded by another prejudiced young woman, *F104*, who remarks, "I have never known any people who were not religious. I have known one fellow who was wavering, and he was a very morbid person." The idea here seems to be that one goes to church in order to express one's normality or at least to be classed with normal people.

These examples help us to understand why persons or groups who "take religion seriously" in a more internalized sense are likely to be opposed to ethnocentrism. What proved to be true in Germany, where "radical" Christian movements, such as the dialectical theology of Karl Barth, courageously opposed Nazism, seems to hold good beyond the theological "élite." The fact that a person really worries about the meaning of religion as such, when he lives in a general atmosphere of "neutralized" religion, is indicative of a nonconformist attitude. It may easily lead toward opposition to the "regular fellow," for whom it is as much "second nature" to attend church

as it is not to admit Jews to his country club. Moreover, the stress on the specific content of religion, rather than on the division between those who belong and those who do not belong to the Christian faith, necessarily accentuates the motives of love and compassion buried under conventionalized religious patterns. The more "human" and concrete a person's relation to religion, the more human his approach to those who "do not belong" is likely to be: their sufferings remind the religious subjectivist of the idea of martyrdom inseparably bound up with his thinking about Christ.

To put it bluntly, the adherent of what Kierkegaard, a hundred years ago, called "official Christianity" is likely to be ethnocentric although the religious organizations with which he is affiliated may be officially opposed to it, whereas the "radical" Christian is prone to think and to act differently.

However, it should not be forgotten that extreme religious subjectivism, with its one-sided emphasis on religious experience set against the objectified Church, may also under certain conditions fall in line with the potentially fascist mentality. Religious subjectivism that dispenses with any binding principles provides the spiritual climate for other authoritative claims. Moreover, the sectarian spirit of people who carry this outlook to an extreme sometimes results in a certain affinity for the aggressive ingroup mood of movements generally condemned as "crack-pot," as well as for those underlying anarchical trends which characterize the potentially fascistic individual. This aspect of religious subjectivism plays an important role in the mentality of fascist agitators who operate in a religious setting.

Among those who *reject* religion, a number of significant differences may be noted. As our quantitative results have shown, no mechanical identification of the non- or anti-religious person with the "low scorer" can be made. There are, to be sure, "agnostic" or "atheistic" persons whose persuasions are part and parcel of a universally progressive attitude which holds for minority questions. The actual meaning of this "progressiveness," however, may vary widely. Whereas anti-religious progressives are definitely opposed to prejudice under present conditions, when it comes to the question of susceptibility to fascist propaganda, it makes all the difference whether they are "ticket thinkers" who subscribe wholesale to tolerance, atheism, and what not, or whether their attitude toward religion can be called an autonomous one based on thinking of their own.

Moreover, it may turn out to be an important criterion of susceptibility whether a person is opposed to religion as an ally of repression and reaction, in which case we should expect him to be relatively unprejudiced, or whether he adopts an attitude of cynical utilitarianism and rejects everything that is not "realistic" and tangible, in which case we should expect him to be prejudiced. There also exists a fascist type of irreligious person who has become completely cynical after having been disillusioned with regard to religion, and who talks about the laws of nature, survival of the fittest and the rights of the strong. The true candidates of neo-paganism of the fascist extreme are recruited from the ranks of these people. A good example is the high-scoring man *5064*, the Boy Scout leader. Asked about religion, he confesses to "worshiping nature." He exalts athletics and camp collectivity, probably on the basis of latent homosexuality. He is the clearest example we have of the syndrome involving pagan pantheism, belief in "power," the idea of collective leadership, and a generally ethnocentric and pseudo-conservative ideology.

It is against the background of these general observations on the structure of the relationship between religion and

modern prejudice that the following, more specific observations may be understood.

Specific Issues

THE FUNCTION OF RELIGION IN HIGH AND LOW SCORERS

Evidence in support of our hypothesis concerning "neutralized" religion is offered by a trait which seems to occur rather frequently in our interview material. It is the disposition to view religion as a means instead of an end. Religion is accepted, not because of its objective truth, but on account of its value in realizing goals that might also be achieved by other means. This attitude falls in line with the general tendency toward subordination and renunciation of one's own judgment so characteristic of the mentality of those who follow fascist movements. Acceptance of an ideology is not based upon understanding of or belief in its content but rather upon what immediate use can be made of it, or upon arbitrary decisions. Here lies one of the roots of the stubborn, conscious, and manipulative irrationalism of the Nazis, as it was summed up by Hitler's saying: *"Man kann nur für eine Idee sterben, die man nicht versteht."* (One can die only for an idea which one does not understand.) This is by its intrinsic logic tantamount to contempt for truth *per se*. One selects a *"Weltanschauung"* after the pattern of choosing a particularly well advertised commodity, rather than for its real quality. This attitude, applied to religion, must necessarily produce ambivalence, for religion claims to express *absolute* truth. If it is accepted for some other reason alone, this claim is implicitly denied and thereby religion itself rejected, even while being accepted. Thus, rigid confirmation of religious values on account of their "usefulness" works against them by necessity.

Subordination of religion to extrinsic aims is common in both high and low scorers; by itself, it does not appear to differentiate between them. It seems, however, that prejudiced and unprejudiced subjects do differ with respect to the kinds of goals that are emphasized and the ways in which religion is utilized in their service.

High scorers, more often than low scorers, seem to make use of religious ideas in order to gain some immediate practical advantage or to aid in the manipulation of other people. An example of the way in which formalized religion is adhered to as a means for maintaining social status and social relationships is afforded by the highly prejudiced young woman, *F201*, who is very frankly interested in "a stable society" in which class lines are clearly drawn.

"I was brought up in the Episcopalian Church through going to a school for girls. It's nice. My friends go. It's more of a philosophy (than Christian Science); it raises your standards. The philosophy of the Episcopalian Church follows the pattern of all Protestant churches. It takes in the upper classes and gives them a religion or makes it a little nearer."

Ethnocentric subjects frequently think of religion as a practical aid in the mental hygiene of the individual. The statement of *F109* is characteristic.

"I don't understand religion. It's like a fairy tale to me. I don't know if I believe in God. There must be one but it is hard to believe it. Religion gives you something to hold on to, to base your life on."

If religion only serves the need for something "to hold on to," this need may also be served by anything which provides the individual with absolute authority, such as the fascist state. There is a strong probability that fascism played exactly the same role with German womanhood which was formally exercised by their belief in positive religion. Psychologically, fascist hierarchies may function largely as secularizations and substitutes of ecclesiastical ones. It is not accidental that Nazism arose in Southern Germany with its strong Roman-Catholic tradition. . . .

The approach to religion for extraneous reasons is probably not so much an expression of the subject's own wants and needs as an expression of his opinion that religion is good for others, helps to keep them content, in short, can be used for manipulative purposes. Recommending religion to others makes it easier for a person to be "in favor" of it without any actual identification with it. The cynicism of the central European administrators of the nineteenth century who taught that religion is a good medicine for the masses, seems to have been to a certain extent democratized. Numerous members of the masses themselves proclaim that religion is good for the masses, whereas they make for themselves, as individuals, a kind of mental reservation. There is a strong similarity between these appreciations of religion and a trait which played a large role in Nazi Germany. There, innumerable persons exempted themselves privately from the ruling ideology and talked about "they" when discussing the Party. The fascist-minded personality, it seems, can manage his life only by splitting his own ego into several agencies, some of which fall in line with the official doctrine, whilst others, heirs to the old superego, protect him from mental unbalance and allow him to maintain himself as an individual. . . .

It must now be pointed out that low scorers also often accept religion, not because of any intrinsic truth that it may hold for them, but because it may serve as a means for furthering human aims. An example of such practical religion is the following excerpt from the interview with a woman student of journalism, *F126,* who obtained extremely low scores on both the A-S and the E scales.

Family were moderate church-goers. She rarely goes now. However, she has much respect for religion and seems to feel that it might be developed into something that would give people that faith and understanding for each other that is lacking. "I don't know what else could give people something to hold onto, some purpose in life. They seem to need something to believe in. Some of us seem to have a love for people without that, but not very many."

In one sense this way of looking at religion has something in common with the externalized attitudes described above. However, it is our impression that when the practical approach to religion appears in the thinking of the low scorer its content, or its context, can usually be distinguished from what is found in the thinking of the high scorer. Thus, although the young woman just quoted believes that religion is good for people, gives them "something to hold onto," she seems to mean that they need it at least for a humane and ideal purpose, that is, so that they may have more "understanding for each other," not simply in order to get along better or to function more efficiently. Low as well as high scorers are likely to consider that religion contributes to the mental hygiene of the individual; but whereas the high scorers characteristically indicate that it is good for other people because they are chronically weak, and possibly good for themselves in times of acute external stress ("fox-hole religion"), the low scorers are more likely to think of religion in internalized terms, as a means for reducing hatred, resolving inner conflicts, relieving anxiety, and the like. Practically never do we encounter a low scorer who conceives of religion primarily in terms of external practical utility—as an aid to success, to status and power, or to a sense of being in accord with conventional values.

BELIEF IN GOD, DISBELIEF IN IMMORTALITY

The neutralization of religion is accompanied by its dissection. Just as emphasis on the practical uses of religion tends to sever religious truth from religious authority, so the specific contents of religion are continually submitted to a process of selection and adaptation. The interview material suggests that the tendency to believe selectively in religion is a distinguishing feature of our prejudiced subjects. A fairly common phenomenon among them is belief in God accompanied by disbelief in immortality. Two examples follow. In the case of *5009,* a devout Baptist, the interviewer reports:

sincerely feels deeply religious, believes in God, but has, as an educated man, occasional doubts concerning the life after death.

And in the case of *5002:*

still is a "Christian," believes in God, would like to believe in life after death, but has doubts and thinks that a sincere religious revival or a new religious myth would be a good thing for the world.

Particularly common are statements to the effect that interviewees regard themselves as religious, as followers of the church, but disagree with "some of its teachings," which sometimes refers to miracles, sometimes to immortality. This outlook seems corroborative of an underlying pattern of considerable significance the elements of which have been established in our psychological analyses. The abstract idea of God is accepted as an expansion of the father idea, whereas general destructiveness makes itself felt in a reaction against the hope for the individual expressed by the dogma of immortality. Subjects with this point of view want a God to exist as the absolute authority to which they can bow, but they wish the individual to perish completely.

The concept of God underlying this way of thinking is that of the absolute essence of punitiveness. It is therefore not astonishing that religious leanings of this particular brand are frequent in the high scorers among our group of prison inmates.

M627, who is serving a life sentence for rape, is "having trouble with religion" and does not believe that "there should be a set way of worship." But he believes, in spite of an undertone of religious rebelliousness,

"that every man should have his own way of worship as long as he believes in a power greater than himself."

This power has the form of external authority, but remains completely abstract, nothing but the projective concept of power as such.

"Well, I have heard so many fellows talk about the powers they believed in . . . and I tried to recognize the power in myself and just couldn't . . . read all kinds of religious books . . . but still kind of foggy."

The same line of thought is expressed by *M656A*, who is serving a term for forgery.

"Well, I'm not a man to discuss religion a great deal, because I don't know a lot about it. I believe in the Bible, I believe there is someone a lot bigger and stronger than anyone on this earth. . . . I don't attend church often but . . . try to live the right way."

For this man all specific religious content is negligible compared with the idea of power and the closely related rigid, moralistic stereotypes of good and bad:

"The Catholic religion, for example, is just as good as the one I believe in. They all are patterned after the same type of living, right or wrong. I'm the type of person that

doesn't believe in any particular denomination."

This "abstract authoritarianism" in religious matters easily turns into cynicism and overt contempt for what one professes to believe. *M664C*, asked about his religious views, answers:

"Oh, I don't pay much attention . . . I believe in God and all that stuff but that is about all."

The choice of the word "stuff" refutes the statement in which it occurs. One effect of neutralization in such cases is that little is left of God but the object of swearing.

The nihilistic aspect of the configuration here under consideration is clearly indicated in the case of the murderer *M651*.

"The part I like about it is the fact that it makes other people happy, though it doesn't concern me, and you see so much hypocrisy. . . ."

Asked what is most important in religion, he says:

"Belief, I think that belief is everything. That is the thing that holds you together."

When this is pursued by the interviewer who wants to find out something about the subject's own religious feelings, he answers:

". . . I believe when you die you are through. . . . Life is short and eternity is forever. How could God send you to Hell for eternity, just on the basis of a short lifetime's record . . . it doesn't seem to be either merciful or just."

This material is indicative of relationships among abstract belief in power, rejection of the more concrete and personal aspects of religion, particularly the idea of an eternal life, and thinly veiled impulses toward violence. As this violence is taboo within the individual, particularly in situations such as a prison, it is projected upon a Deity. Moreover, it should not be forgotten that an entirely abstract idea of the almighty Deity, as it prevailed during the eighteenth century, could be reconciled much more easily with the "scientific spirit" than could the doctrine of an immortal soul, with its "magical" connotations. The process of demythification liquidates traces of animism earlier and more radically than it does the philosophical idea of the Absolute.

It may be noted, however, that just the opposite tendency can be observed among addicts of astrology and spiritualism. They often believe in the immortality of the soul, but strongly deny the existence of God, because of some kind of pantheism which ultimately results in exaltation of nature. Thus, case *M651*, not quite consistently with his previous confession of religiousness for extraneous reasons, comes out with the statement that he:

believes in astrology because he doesn't believe in God.

There is reason to believe that the ultimate consequence of this attitude is sinister.

Will Herberg

THE CONTEMPORARY UPSWING IN RELIGION

No one who attempts to see the contemporary religious situation in the United States in perspective can fail to be struck by the extraordinary pervasiveness of religious identification among present-day Americans. Almost everybody in the United States today locates himself in one or another of the three great religious communities. Asked to identify themselves in terms of religious "preference,"[1]

From Protestant-Catholic-Jew: An Essay in American Religious Sociology. Garden City, N.Y.: 1955, pp. 59–60, 64–66, 68–75. Copyright © 1955, 1960, by Will Herberg. Reprinted by permission of Doubleday & Company, Inc.

[1]The use of the term "preference" to indicate religious identification is itself of considerable significance; it reflects the feeling of Americans that somehow they *choose* ("religious preference") their *status* ("religious community"). Actually, no more than 4 per cent of Americans leave the religious community (Protestant, Catholic, Jewish) of their birth.

95 per cent of the American people, according to a recent public opinion survey, declared themselves to be either Protestants, Catholics, or Jews (68 per cent Protestants, 23 per cent Catholics, 4 per cent Jews); only 5 per cent admitted to no "preference."[2] Some differences,

[2]"Who Belongs to What Church?", *The Catholic Digest*, January 1953. This is a report of a survey conducted by Ben Gaffin and Associates. (Only adults over 18 are considered. It is also worth nothing that the category "other religions" proved too small for analysis and is included under "no preference.") As will appear in the sequel, the results of this survey agree remarkably well with the conclusions of other recent surveys on religion at points where comparison is possible. A survey of churches in 23 metropolitan districts, made by the Committee for Cooperative Field Research some years ago, indicated that "in none of them did more than 7 per cent of the people fail to give themselves a religious classification, not merely by faith but generally by

one or two perhaps of real significance, are indicated when these figures are broken down according to race, age, sex, education, occupation, income, region, and degree of urbanization; but, by and large, the conclusion seems to be that virtually the entire body of the American People, in every part of the country and in every section of society, regard themselves as belonging to some religious community. The results of the survey are fully borne out by the reports of informed observers of the American scene.

Such information as that which this survey provides is unfortunately not available for earlier times, and so direct comparison is impossible. But it seems safe to assume that these figures, reflecting the situation in the early 1950s, represent an all-time high in religious identification. Through the nineteenth century and well into the twentieth America knew the militant secularist, the atheist or "free-thinker," as a familiar figure in cultural life, along with considerably larger numbers of "agnostics" who would have nothing to do with churches and refused to identify themselves religiously. These still exist, of course, but their ranks are dwindling and they are becoming more and more inconspicuous, taking the American people as a whole.[3] The "village atheist"

is a vanishing figure; Clarence Darrow and Brann the Iconoclast, who once commanded large and excited audiences, have left no successors. Indeed, their kind of antireligion is virtually meaningless to most Americans today, who simply cannot understand how one can be "against religion" and for whom some sort of religious identification is more or less a matter of course. This was not always the case; that it is the case today there can be no reasonable doubt. The pervasiveness of religious identification may safely be put down as a significant feature of America that has emerged in the past quarter of a century.

The figures for church membership tell the same story but in greater detail. Religious statistics in this country are notoriously inaccurate,[4] but the trend is so well marked that it overrides all margins of error. In the quarter of a century between 1926 and 1950 the population of continental United States increased 28.6 per cent; membership of religious bodies increased 59.8 per cent; in other words, church membership grew more than twice as fast as population. Protestants increased 63.7 per cent, Catholics 53.9 per cent, Jews 22.5 per

---

denominations." (*Information Service* [National Council of Churches of Christ], January 21, 1950.) See also the Gallup poll of the "religious preference" of adult Americans made early in 1955, according to which 96.9 per cent were found to identify themselves religiously (70.8 per cent Protestants, 22.9 per cent Catholics, 3.1 per cent Jews) and only 3.1 per cent gave answers that placed them in the "other, none" category (See *Public Opinion News Service,* March 20, 1955).

[3]Herbert W. Schneider speaks of the "dwindling band of radical secularists" and the "few remaining militant atheists and freethinkers" (Herbert Wallace Schneider, *Religion in 20th Century America* [Harvard, 1952], pp. 32, 31).

[4]There are many reasons for the confusion in religious statistics. Not all churches calculate membership on the same basis: Roman Catholics, Greek Orthodox, and latterly some Lutheran and Episcopal groups include all baptized persons, infants as well as adults; Protestant groups generally report only those over 13 years of age; "Jewish congregations" usually take in all Jews in communities having synagogues or temples. Then there are also the vague and imprecise ways of reporting at every level. To this must be added the fact that statistics after 1926 are strictly not comparable with those before that date, since a new basis of calculation was introduced with the 1926 Census of Religious Bodies. See *Yearbook of American Churches,* 1953 edition, ed. by Benson Y. Landis (National Council of Churches Christ, 1953), sec. 3. Williams believes that "the total number of church members is underreported by the United States Census" (Robin M. Williams, *American Society: A Sociological Interpretation* [Knopf, 1951], p. 322 note).

cent. Among Protestants, however, the increase varied considerably as between denominations: Baptist increase was well over 100 per cent, some "holiness" sects grew even more rapidly, while the figure for the Episcopal Church was only 36.7 per cent, for the Methodist Church 32.2 per cent, for the Northern Presbyterians 22.4 per cent, and for the Congregationalists 21.1 per cent.[5] In general, it may be said that "practically all major types of American religion have staged what is vulgarly called a "comeback".[6]

*　　*　　*

The enhanced standing of churches and religion among the American people is strikingly indicated by the enhanced status of religious leaders. According to surveys conducted by Elmo Roper, Americans, in answering the question, "Which one of these groups do you feel is doing the most good for the country at the present time?" placed religious leaders third, after government leaders and business leaders, 1942, but first in 1947. In the former year (1942), 17.5 per cent thought religious leaders were "doing the most good," as against 27.7 per cent who put more trust in government leaders, and 18.7 per cent in business leaders (6.2 per cent trusted most in labor leaders and another 6.2 per cent in Congress). Five years later, however, in 1947, 32.6 per cent of the people chose religious leaders as those who were "doing most good"; 18.8 percent chose business leaders; 15.4 per cent, government leaders; 10.6 per cent, labor leaders; and 6.7 per cent, Congress.[7] A similar survey, conducted by Mr. Roper in 1953, found that 40 per cent of the American people picked religious leaders as the group "doing the most good" and most to be trusted. "No other group—whether government, Congressional, business, or labor—came anywhere near matching the prestige and pulling power of the men who are the ministers of God."[8] The picture of the clergyman that Americans have may not be without its ambiguous aspects, but there can be little doubt that the "minister of God" ranks high, and is rising rapidly, in the American scale of prestige. This rise of public confidence in clergymen no doubt reflects the rising status of religion and the church in American social life.

Much the same may be said about the high and growing repute of religion in American public mind. "Religion is given continued public and political approval . . . "Godless" is a powerful epithet. . . . At least nominal public acceptance of religion tends to be a prerequisite to political success . . ."[9] It was not always so; there was a time when an atheist or agnostic like Robert G. Ingersoll, who went around the country defying God and making anti-religious speeches, could nevertheless occupy a respected and influential position in American politics.[10] Today that would be quite inconceivable; a professed "unbeliever" would be anathema to either of the big parties and would have no chance

---

[5]*Information Service,* March 8, 1952.

[6]Schneider, *Religion in 20th Century America,* p. 16.

[7]See Elmo Roper, "What People Are Thinking," *New York Herald Tribune,* July 3, 1947. It is interesting that in 1942 more people (7.4 per cent) thought religious leaders were "doing the *least* good" than business leaders (5.9 per cent) or government leaders (3.3 per cent); in 1947,

only 3.9 per cent thought religious leaders were "doing the least good," far less than the figures for the other groups.

[8]Roper, NBC "Newsweek Documentaries," December 27, 1953; see also *Information Service,* April 3, 1954.

[9]Williams, *American Society,* pp. 326, 336.

[10]Robert Graves Ingersoll (1833–99), Civil War colonel, was known in his day as "the great agnostic." His anti-Christian lectures and writings were notorious. Yet he was an influential Republican leader, and at the national Republican convention in 1876 was designated to nominate James G. Blaine for the Presidency.

whatever in political life. The contrast between the days of Ingersoll and our day, when every candidate for public office is virtually required to testify to his high esteem for religion, measures the position that religion as a "value" or institution has acquired in the American public mind. Only one of 95 Senators of the 83rd Congress reported no religious affiliation; 94 declared themselves members of some religious denomination, even though five could find nothing more specific to say than "Protestant."[11]

That public opinion is markedly more favorable to religion today than it has been for a long time is recognized by all observers. "A hostile attitude toward religion as such," Schneider notes, "gets less of a hearing today than a century ago, or even half a century ago."[12] Foreign visitors are almost without exception amazed at the extreme deference paid to religion, religious leaders, and religious institutions in present-day America.[13] It is probably true that "in

no other modern industrial state does organized religion play a greater role" than it does in the United States.[14]

With institutional growth and enhanced public status has come a notable increase in the self-assurance of the spokesmen of religion, who no longer feel themselves defending a losing cause against a hostile world. "It [has become] clear that, contrary to what many . . . leading historians and sociologists asserted early in the century, religion has not declined in America since 1900,"[15] very much to the contrary. Spokesmen of religion are now beginning to speak with the confidence of those who feel that things are going their way and that they are assured of a respectful hearing. Indeed, there have lately arisen voices among the "ir-religious" minority who profess to see their "freedom *from* religion" threatened by the increasingly proreligious climate of our culture and the new aggressiveness of the churches.[16] It is a far cry indeed from the 1920s, when religion and the churches were in retreat, faith was taken as a sign of intellectual backwardness or imbecility, and the initiative had passed to the "emancipated" debunkers of the superstitions of the "Babbitts" and the "Bible Belt." That age has disappeared almost without a trace, and the generation that has arisen since finds it well-nigh impossible to imagine what those days were like, so remote from our consciousness have they become.

Particularly significant as reflecting a reversal of trend is the new intellectual prestige of religion on all levels of cultural life. On one level, this means the extraordinarily high proportion of so-

---

[11]See *Information Service,* December 27, 1952.

[12]Schneider, *Religion in 20th Century America,* p. 32.

[13]*The Catholic Digest* notes a marked trend "for the better" in the public relations enjoyed by religion in the past twenty years: "Two decades ago, almost any editor would have dropped dead if someone had predicted what is happening today: newspapers publishing Fulton Oursler's books on page one; magazines practically never coming out without an article on religion; book companies searching for religious titles; four or five of the ten best sellers on religion; Bishop Sheen leading the TV pack; Conrad Hilton putting copies of *Guideposts* in every one of his hotel rooms; chapels being built in industrial plants and in airports, and such like" ("The Religious Press," *The Catholic Digest,* February 1954). And, according to *Time,* "praying dolls" have now joined walking dolls, talking dolls, and dolls who drink their bottles and wet their diapers: "In response to the resurgence of religious feeling and practise in America today," the Ideal Toy Co. is putting on sale a knee-jointed doll that can be made to "kneel in praying position" (*Time,* September 20, 1954). Note also religion's "capture of the juke box"

(Hutchinson, "Have We a 'New' Religion?" *Life,* April 11, 1955, pp. 138–40).

[14]Williams, *American Society,* p. 304.

[15]Schneider, *Religion in 20th Century America,* p.16.

[16]See, e.g., Schneider, *Religion in 20th Century America,* p. 33.

called "religious books" on the best-seller lists,[17] on another, the remarkable vogue in intellectual circles of the more sophisticated religious and theological writing of our time. Kierkegaard (rediscovered in this generation), Maritain, Reinhold Niebuhr, Buber, Tillich, Berdyaev, Simone Weil: these writers have standing and prestige with the intellectual elite of today in a way that no religious writers have had for many decades. Religious ideas, concepts, and teachings have become familiar in the pages of the "vanguard" journals of literature, politics, and art. "It is certainly true," a recent English survey of religion in America concludes, "that the intellectual climate for religious thinking and the social climate for religious living are much more congenial than they were in the twenties and thirties."[18]

* * *

Though we are obliged to note the qualifications and ambiguities of the current turn to religion, among the intellectuals as among other sections of the population, it would be a gross

error to ignore or deny the genuine personal faith and commitment to be found in American religion at all levels. "It is probably true," Schneider concludes, "that . . . Americans take religion more personally than other peoples do." He mentions "an Anglican visitor to the United States recently [who] reported that there prevails a 'shocking personal religiosity among Americans.' "[19] This "personal religiosity" has many sides, which we shall attempt to examine later in the discussion, but its existence cannot be denied, nor its importance in subtly transmuting much of the externalism of the religious institutions and activities to which we have devoted our attention so far.

That there has in recent years been an upswing of religion in the United States can hardly be doubted; the evidence is diverse, converging, and unequivocal beyond all possibilities of error. It is another matter, however, when we come to assess the factors that have made, and are making, for this notable shift in the social attitudes and cultural climate of our time. When we try to isolate these factors or reveal their mode of operation, we begin to sense the inadequacy of all sociological "explanation" of phenomena that in their very nature transcend the sociological. Nevertheless, it seems to me that certain significant things may be said about the present religious situation which might contribute to an understanding of the current turn to religion in America.

We may proceed with our analysis on various levels. Most generally and comprehensively, the rise in religious identification, membership, and attendance would seem to be closely related to the change in social structure of the American community we have described in earlier chapters. America, it was there

[17]See *Publishers' Weekly,* January 23, 1954: "The theme of religion dominates the non-fiction best sellers in 1953, as it has in many of the preceding years." Discussing religious book publishing in America in 1953, a writer in *The Times Literary Supplement* states: "As a classification, they [religious books] stood third, ranking below fiction and juvenile, and just above biography. . . . Of the ten bestselling fiction titles, the two most in demand were books with religious themes. . . . In the non-fiction category, seven out of the ten best-selling titles were religious titles" (*The Times Literary Supplement,* No. 2746, September 17, 1954, Supplement, p. lxiv). It is, perhaps, also of some significance that "Christmas cards with a religious motive have 'more than doubled' during the past five years, according to the National Association of Greeting Card Publishers. One in every five cards sold last year had a spiritual theme as against one in ten about five years ago" (*Christopher News Notes,* No. 62, November 1954).

[18]*The Times Literary Supplement,* No. 2746, September 17, 1954, Supplement, p. lxiv.

[19]Schneider, *Religion in 20th Century America,* pp. 166.

pointed out, has changed from the "land of immigrants," with its thriving ethnic groups, to the "triple melting pot," in which people tend more and more 'to identify and locate themselves socially in terms of three great subcommunities—Protestant, Catholic, Jewish—defined in religious terms. To find a place in American society increasingly means to place oneself in one or another of these religious communities. And although this process of self-identification and social location is not in itself intrinsically religious, the mere fact that in order to be "something" one must be either a Protestant, a Catholic, or a Jew means that one begins to think of oneself as religiously identified and affiliated. *Naming* oneself a Protestant, a Catholic, or a Jew carries with it a distinctive attitude to "one's" church, an attitude that is definitely favorable. Since one "is" a Protestant, a Catholic, or a Jew, and recognizes oneself as such, one tends to think of oneself as somehow part of a church and involved in its activities and concerns. Whether one actually joins or not, the inclination is to think of oneself as a member: hence the significant fact that many more people report themselves as members of churches than are on church rolls.[20] And increasingly one does actually become a member and join in the activities of the church; increasingly too the children are sent to church and church school— for many reasons, not least, however, because "the church supplies a place where children come to learn what they are."[21] There does not seem to be any real question that the restructuring of American society that emerges with the third generation has been a major factor

in the turn to religion so characteristic of our time.

Another factor of prime sociological importance has worked toward the same end, and that is the basic change in character structure that seems to be under way among certain sections of the American people. The reference here is to the shift from inner-direction to other-direction, which David Riesman has analyzed and documented so impressively.[22] Riesman, it will be recalled, distinguishes three types of character structure—tradition-directed, inner-directed, and other-directed—which he finds predominating at different times in different societies yet also entering in different degrees into contemporary American life. Tradition-direction, in which each generation receives from its predecessor and internalizes for itself a fairly fixed pattern of folkways, is characteristic of primitive and stable peasant societies; it has never really been part of the ongoing life of a dynamic society such as ours, although the collapse of tradition-direction upon the peasant immigrant's first encounter with the New World has had repercussions into our own time. American society has hitherto been, and still is, predominantly inner-directed; each succeeding generation internalizes not a traditional pattern of folkways but a set of "goals" or "principles," to which the individual is kept true by a powerful inner drive. Borrowing a figure from Gardner Murphy, Riesman pictures the inner-directed man as operating with a kind of built-in gyroscope which holds him steadily, sometimes ruthlessly, to his course, driving ahead for the fulfillment of his purposes. The inner-directed man is work-conscious, intent upon achievement, not afraid to

---

[20]See above, pp. 61–62.

[21]Oscar Handlin, *The American People in the Twentieth Century* (Harvard, 1954), p. 222; the tenses have been changed to the present.

[22]See David Riesman, *The Lonely Crowd* (Yale, 1950); *Faces in the Crowd* (Yale, 1952); *Individualism Reconsidered* (Free Press, 1954).

stand on his own feet and if necessary against the crowd, interested in "results" not in "personalities." It is the inner-directed man who has been characteristic of American life and achievement so far.

Lately, however, for reasons that are still obscure though we are beginning to get some inkling of them, there has been emerging on certain levels another character type, described as other-directed. Instead of possessing a built-in gyroscope to keep him true to his course, the other-directed man operates with a kind of built-in radar apparatus which is ceaselessly at work receiving signals from the person's "peer group" and adjusting him to the situation indicated by these signals. The other-directed man is a man who is concerned with adjustment rather than with achievement; he is personality-conscious rather than work-conscious, bland, tolerant, co-operative, "civilized"—but dreadfully afraid of being too "different," of getting too much out of line with his "peer group." Indeed, the greatest horror of the other-directed man, that which renders him so acutely uncomfortable, is to feel "unadjusted" and "unsociable" ("anti-social"); whereas the inner-directed man, as we have seen, is always ready to stand up against his environment and indeed seems to get a kind of grim satisfaction out of doing so. The "morality" of the inner-directed type becomes "morale" for the other-directed; "character" becomes "personality"; moral indignation and intolerance give way to a kind of all-embracing tolerance—tolerance of everything and everybody except the "unadjusted" and the "anti-social". The operative law of life of the other-directed man is conformity and adjustment; the built-in radar that characterizes other-direction sees to it that such adjustment to a fluctuating environment is generally achieved quite unconsciously

and is therefore invested with the emotional power of unconscious motivation.

In America today, though inner-direction remains dominant, other-direction has already become prevalent in the new suburban middle-class society consisting of professionals and junior executives, and seems bound to spread upward and downward in the social hierarchy. The emergence of this type, and its growing prominence in the community, bring with it a number of farreaching consequences for the social and cultural life of our time.

In particular, it is not difficult to see the current turn to religion and the church as, in part at least, a reflection of the growing other-directedness of our middle-class culture. The people in the suburbs want to feel psychologically secure, adjusted, at home in their environment; the very character structure that makes this so urgent a necessity for them also operates to meet the need. Being religious and joining a church is, under contemporary American conditions, a fundamental way of "adjusting" and "belonging"; through the built-in radar apparatus of other-direction it becomes almost automatic as an obvious social requirement, like entertaining or culture. The vogue of Van Gogh and Renoir reproductions in the suburban home and the rising church affiliation of the suburban community may not be totally unconnected; both may, without disparagement, be interpreted, in part at least, as the consequence of the craving for adjustment and conformity involved in other-direction. The right kind of art reproductions testify to one's being adjusted to the culture of one's "peer-group"; belonging to the church is experienced as the most satisfactory form of social "belonging." The trend toward religious identification and church affiliation may thus to an extent be a reflection of the growing need for conformity and sociability that the drift to other-direction brings with it.[23]

The operations of other-direction fall in rather neatly with the over-all effects of the restructuring of American society in terms of religious community. To identify and locate oneself in the social context is a requirement under all conditions; it becomes particularly pressing and urgent under conditions of other-direction, since other-direction craves conformity and adjustment as a veritable necessity of life. On the other hand, the other-directed need for "belonging" finds its most direct and appropriate expression in present-day America in identifying oneself with a religious community and joining a church. Whether we approach it from one direction or the other the result seems to be the same: a marked trend toward religious identification and church affiliation.

These more obviously sociological factors ought not, however, to obscure other, perhaps less definable, forces operating at other levels of human life. The contemporary crisis of Western civilization, which has brought a sense of total insecurity to men everywhere, is surely one of the most significant of these. The utter predicament of human existence is no longer simply a philosophical or theological proposition; it is the most patent of everyday facts. The hydrogen bomb, on which our survival depends, yet which threatens us with destruction, is the sinister symbol of our plight. Confronted with the demonic threat of Communist totalitarianism, we are driven to look beyond the routine ideas and attitudes that may have served in easier times. On every side insecurity assails us, and yet security is becoming more and more the urgent need of our time.

In this situation of pervasive crisis and danger, religion appeals to many as "synonymous with peace," indeed as offering the "best hope of peace in the world today"[24]—"peace of mind" for the individual amid the anxieties and confusions of contemporary existence, peace for the nation in the life-and-death struggle with Communism. Particularly in this latter conflict religion commends itself as our greatest resource and most powerful "secret weapon." In the week in which I write this three outstanding clerical leaders of the three religious communities of the nation made eloquent pleas for religion on this ground: one called religion the "shield of the nation"; the other proclaimed it as "more powerful than the H-bomb"; the third recommended it as "America's strongest weapon against atheistic Communism." Even erstwhile secularists are beginning to see things in a new light; the *Zeitgeist* has not been without effect among them, nor the urgencies of the present world situation. They are beginning to show a growing appreciation of the social utility of religion for Western culture, especially in fighting Communism. Quite a few old-time secularists are no longer so sure that religion is on its way out; nor for that matter are they so sure that they would be happy to see religion go, for when religion goes (many secularists now ruefully admit), it is only too often replaced not by "reason" and "enlightenment" but by one or another of the wild superstitions and demonic cults that the modern age has spawned. Religion has suddenly emerged as a major power in the "hundred years of Cold War" that appears to confront mankind.

On another, more personal, or rather

---

[23]Curiously, in his own account of the present-day rise in religious identification and church membership in the United States, David Riesman does not make use of his valuable insights into the changing character structure of the American people; see *Individualism Reconsidered,* chap xxiv.

[24]Roper, in NBC "Newsweek Documentaries," December 27, 1953; see report in *Information Service,* April 3, 1954.

more domestic, level, too, religion has been found to serve the need for security. On this level the turn to religion is to be linked, many think, with the sensational reversal of long-time population trends and the sudden rise of birth rates among college graduates and professional people in the United States. Since 1946 these rates have been increasing every year, and in 1954 married graduates of the class of 1944, ten years our of college, already averaged more children than the class of 1921 when it had been out twenty-five years in 1946, the year the study we are citing was initiated.[25] This demographical fact would seem to confirm the impression many observers have had in recent years that, amid the mount-

ing insecurities of our time, increasing numbers of younger people are turning to the security to be found in the enduring, elemental ways and institutions of mankind; in the family, they feel, they can find the permanence and stability, the meaning and value they crave amid a world falling into chaos. Religion, like the family, is one of the enduring, elemental institutions of mankind; indeed, the two have been closely linked from the very earliest times. The search for meaning and security in what is basic and unchanging, rather than in the fluctuating fortunes of social or political activity, is one of the major factors in the upswing of religion among the American people today.

Gerhard Lenski

RELIGIOUS ORIENTATIONS

Embedded in the institutional structure of both Judaism and Christianity are a variety of religious orientations which have, to some degree, competed and contended with one another. As noted previously, we have limited our analysis here to two of the more important of them: doctrinal orthodoxy and devotionalism.

Doctrinal Orthodoxy

For our measure of doctrinal orthodoxy we have relied on the responses of

From The Religious Factor: A Sociological Study of Religion's Impact on Politics, Economics, and Family Life. Garden City, New York: 1961, pp. 50–55; 288– 293; 295–297. Copyright © 1961 by Gerhard Lenski. Reprinted by permission of Doubleday & Company, Inc.

[25]See report of the Population Reference Bureau, *Boston Daily Globe,* June 10, 1954.

Detroiters to six questions. These were:

1. Do you believe there is a God, or not? (Q. 42)
2. Do you think God is like a Heavenly Father who watches over you, or do you have some other belief? (Q. 43)
3. Do you believe that God answers people's prayers, or not? (Q. 44)
4. Do you believe in a life after death, or not (Q. 45); if so, do you also believe that in the next life some people will be punished and others rewarded by God, or not? (Q. 45a)
5. Do you believe that, when they are able, God expects people to worship Him in their churches and synagogues, *every* week, or not? (Q. 46)
6. Do you believe that Jesus was God's only Son sent into the world by God to save sinful men, or do you believe that he was simply a very good man and

teacher, or do you have some other belief? (Q. 52)

Because the Jewish group was too small for intragroup analysis of this type, these questions were designed for classifying Christians only. Christians were classified as orthodox if they asserted that they believed in a God who watched over them like a Heavenly Father, who answered prayers, and who expected weekly worship, if they believed that Jesus was God's only Son, and if they believed in punishments and rewards in a life after death. If an individual expressed uncertainty or unbelief with respect to *any* of these items he was classified as unorthodox. In many of the preliminary tabulations distinctions were made between the more unorthodox and the less unorthodox, but in the end we decided that the size of the sample made it impractical to extend the analysis to more than a simple dichotomy between the orthodox and unorthodox.

The reader may wonder why we used such a rigorous definition of orthodoxy. We generally decided on strict definitions *whenever* we were faced with the problem of where to divide such basic variables, and the reasoning behind this decision was as follows. If there are differences between people with more or less of a given characteristic, the most meaningful difference is likely to appear between a small elite of highly committed persons and the larger mass of less committed or indifferent persons. Furthermore, it is when individuals are strongly committed to something that we can best judge the influence of the commitment on their lives. It therefore seemed wiser to define our more orthodox category so as to include only those who took the orthodox position on *all* items.

As might be expected, doctrinal orthodoxy proved more frequent among Catholics than among Protestants. Sixty-two per cent of the Catholic respondents took an orthodox stance on all items, compared with only 38 per cent of the Negro Protestants and 32 per cent of the white Protestants. Most of the heterodox accepted the majority of the six basic doctrines. Only 10 per cent of the white Protestants, 4 per cent of the white Catholics, and 2 per cent of the Negro Protestants rejected more than half of them.

Devotionalism

The second basic religious orientation we sought to isolate was that which values direct, personal communication with God through prayer and meditation, and which seeks divine direction in daily affairs. To establish an index of devotionalism, we utilized answers to two questions: Question 44b on the frequency with which the respondent engaged in prayer, and Question 55 on the frequency with which he sought to determine what God wanted him to do when he had important decisions to make.

Detroiters were ranked high in devotionalism if (a) they reported praying more than once a day, plus asking what God would have them to do either *often* or *sometimes,* or if (b) they reported praying once a day, but *often* asking what God would have them to do. Using this measure, 68 per cent of the Negro Protestants were ranked high in devotionalism. The comparable figures for white Catholics and Protestants were 47 and 29 per cent respectively. It may be noted that doctrinal orthodoxy was somewhat more common than the devotional orientation among Catholics, while the reverse proved true among Negro Protestants. In the case of the white Protestant group these two orientations were more nearly balanced in strength.

One of the striking findings of this study was the limited nature of the relationship between these two orientations. Using the Taub measure of association, a coefficient of only .05 was obtained. In terms of the more familiar Pearsonian r, this same relationship would produce a coefficient of approximately .23. Both measures indicate the modest character of the relationship, and emphasize the necessity for differentiating between the various elements of what is so often subsumed under the single heading, "religiosity."

Trends in Orthodoxy and Devotionalism

Earlier in this chapter we sought to discover whether the communal and associational aspects of religious group organization are gaining or declining. The same question should also be raised about our two important religious orientations.

Among white Catholics, the evidence suggests a trend toward increased devotionalism and increased doctrinal orthodoxy. Comparing more recent immigrants with those who were more Americanized, the latter were more often active devotionally *and* doctrinally orthodox than the former. Class data suggest that devotionalism increases the farther up the social scale one goes; but orthodoxy is not affected by changes in status. Thus the transformation of the class system should increase the general measure of Catholic devotionalism, but have little effect on Catholic orthodoxy. The data on education suggest that the rising level of education will have little or no effect on either orientation.

Among white Protestants, current social trends should have the effect of somewhat weakening both orientations. The doctrinally orthodox were more numerous among the southern-born, first-and second-generation immigrants, working-class people, and the less well educated. Since all of these groups are

likely to decline in the future, heterodoxy is likely to increase, barring some major change originating in the churches themselves. It looks as though white Protestant devotionalism will also decline, but the differences between the classes suggest that the transformation of the class system might be a force counteracting this trend.

Earlier in this chapter we found that attendance at white Protestant churches will probably increase, but we are now saying that there may be a decline in the proportion of those same congregations committed to such basic orientations as orthodoxy and devotionalism. On first inspection this combination of developments may seem improbable. Surely such trends cannot move in opposite directions.

This, however, is very close to what Herberg had in mind when he stated his now familiar paradox that Americans are becoming more religious while at the same time becoming more secular. Despite attending the churches more frequently, their thoughts and values are less often derived from distinctly religious (in the sense of associational) sources and more often derived from secular sources. In short, a transcendental faith is gradually being transformed into a cultural faith. Contrary to Herberg, our data do not suggest that such a fate is likely to overtake American Catholicism in the foreseeable future, but they do suggest that American Protestantism has already moved far in this direction, and is continuing to move further.

In the Negro Protestant group, just as in the white Protestant group, there is likely to be a decline in both doctrinal orthodoxy and in devotionalism in the next generation. Every indicator, without exception, points to a decline, and in all but one instance (out of six), to a rather pronounced decline. Throughout this discussion of future trends we have spoken entirely of trends resulting from changes in the structure of American society, ignoring changes which might originate from ferment within the churches themselves. Obviously, however, organizations, like organisms, change in response to both external and internal forces. For example, a powerful movement of spiritual revitalization might suddenly sweep through one of our groups in response perhaps to internal stresses created by the numerous contradictions between the ideals and practices of the churches. We cannot rule out this possibility. However, movements of this nature are not common, and if they should develop in the Protestant churches, they would be confronted with secular social trends pushing powerfully in the opposite direction. Hence, even if such movements were to develop, the probabilities of their success are not impressive. Detroit Protestantism seems in some danger of becoming what Richard Niebuhr and others have referred to as a "cultural religion." That is to say, it is in danger of becoming a religion which has lost its transcendental character. Perhaps this is too sweeping an inference to draw from our limited data on orthodoxy and devotionalism, but the fact remains that Protestant church attendance is increasing while at the same time *both* orthodoxy and devotionalism are declining. This strongly suggests that such a trend is under way. We might add that the pages of history are replete with the ruins of cultural religions which have had the misfortune of subsequently encountering transcendental religions.

* * *

Summary of Findings

To begin with, it seems clear that, contrary to the expectations of the nineteenth-century positivists, religious organizations remain vigorous and influential in contemporary American society. Only in the case of the Jewish group is there any evidence of serious organizational weakness, and this is limited entirely to the associational aspects of the group. In fact, the vigor of Jewish communalism more than compensates for the weakness of the religious associations. In the case of the two largest groups, the white Protestants and Catholics, the evidence indicates considerable associational and communal vitality at present, especially among the Catholics.

Second, and more important, are our findings relevant to probable future trends. Most signs point to *gains* in associational vigor and vitality in the foreseeable future. Most of the changes now occurring in the structure of American society are weakening and reducing in relative size those elements in the population least involved in the churches (e.g., first-generation immigrants and members of the working class), and strengthening and enlarging those elements most involved in the churches (e.g., third-generation Americans and members of the middle classes). There are indications that the next twenty or thirty years will see a weakening of the Negro Protestant churches, but since most members of the other major groups are unwilling to establish primary-type relations with Negroes, it seems unlikely that this development will seriously weaken the internal solidarity of the group.

Third (and this is the central finding of our study), from our evidence it is clear that religion in various ways is constantly influencing the daily lives of the masses of men and women in the modern American metropolis. More than that: through its impact on individuals, religion makes an impact on all the other institutional systems of the community in which these individuals participate. Hence the influence of religion operates at the social level as well as at the personal level.

Depending on the socio-religious group to which a person belongs, the probabilities are increased or decreased that he will enjoy his occupation, indulge in installment buying, save to achieve objectives far in the future, believe in the American Dream, vote Republican, favor the welfare state, take a liberal view on the issue of freedom of speech, oppose racial integration in the schools, migrate to another community, maintain close ties with his family, develop a commitment to the principle of intellectual autonomy, have a large family, complete a given unit of education, or rise in the class system. These are only a few of the consequences which we have observed to be associated with differences in socio-religious group membership, and the position of individuals in these groups.

In analyzing these relationships we constantly sought to determine whether religion is a *causal* factor, itself increasing or decreasing the probabilities of various patterns of action, or whether it is merely a factor *correlated* with them but having no influence on them. As a first step in this direction we repeatedly applied controls of various types to our data to make sure that a given relationship was not merely a by-product of other factors such as class, region of birth, or immigrant generation. In the majority of instances such controls did not appreciably affect the relationship in question, and when they did have a more substantial effect, they were almost as likely to strengthen the relationship as to weaken it.

As a second step in our effort to test the causal hypothesis we tried to establish the existence of a temporal sequence in which religious differences existed *before* differences in secular behavior appeared. For example, in examining the relationship between religion and vertical mobility we found that individuals raised in devout white Protestant families are more likely to become upwardly mobile in their adult years than are individuals raised in less devout white Protestant families or in Catholic families. Similarly, we were able to demonstrate that individuals raised in white Protestant families are more likely to shift their political affiliation to the Republican Party in later years than are individuals raised in Catholic families. Although our evidence in connection with this problem is hardly definitive, it tends to support the hypothesis of causality and contradict the hypothesis of mere correlation or association.

Third, and finally, we checked the causal hypothesis by making intragroup comparisons to see if those who are more highly involved in the religious groups display patterns of action peculiar to their groups more often than those who are less involved. This required comparisons among laymen and also between the laity and the clergy. As a general rule we found that when there are differences of any magnitude *between* two socio-religious groups, *internal* differences are also present, suggesting that the differences between groups reflect the influence of the groups, and are not merely a statistical correlation.

On many of the variables analyzed, the four major socio-religious groups split into two divisions: white Protestants and Jews on the one hand; Negro Protestants and Catholics on the other. This pattern is most evident in encomic behavior. White Protestants and Jews have a positive attitude toward work more often than Negro Protestants or Catholics, especially in upper-middle class jobs. They are likelier to believe that ability is more important than family connections; to be self-employed; to believe in intellectual autonomy; and to have small families. However, in some respects members of the Jewish group resemble Catholics more nearly than white Protestants. This is especially true of party preference and of attitudes toward the kin group.

The Negro Protestant group was especially interesting. With no controls for socio-economic factors, it resembles the Catholic group far more closely than the white Protestant group. However, we usually found that the more carefully one controls for these socio-economic factors, the more nearly Negro Protestants resemble white Protestants. In short, our findings suggest that the similarities between the Negro Protestant and Catholic groups are largely induced by the highly unfavorable social and economic situation in which the great majority of Negro Protestants find themselves.

In our examination of these differences among the major socio-religious groups, we repeatedly sought to determine whether they are declining in importance, holding their own, or gaining in strength. The classical theory of urbanism stresses the importance of those forces which increase contact and communication among people and thus have a homogenizing effect. On the basis of this theory one would expect the differences between groups to decline. While it is difficult to ascertain social trends on the basis of data gathered in a single survey at any one point in time, we were able nevertheless to make some estimates of trends. We based these estimates on comparisons between third-generation Americans and more recent immigrants, middle-class Detroiters and `working-class Detroiters, Detroiters of urban origin and those of rural origin. These comparisons were based on the assumption that the third generation, the middle class, and people of urban origin represent the "wave of the future," or those segments of the population destined to expand, while the first and second generations, the working class, and the rural element represent those segments of the population destined to decline in relative numbers. On the basis of such comparisons we can only conclude that differences among the socio-religious groups are *not* declining and are not likely to decline in the foreseeable future. They are, at the very least, as sharply drawn as ever, and there are numerous indications that they may become more pronounced in the future. This possibility is especially suggested by data based on interclass comparisons, which generally reveal that socio-religious differences are greater among members of the middle class than among members of the working class.

Not only is the behavior of men influenced by the socio-religious groups to which they belong; our evidence also indicates it is influenced by their *religious orientations*. Repeatedly throughout this study we found that the orthodox and the devotional orientations are linked with differing and even opposed behavior patterns. In general, the orthodox orientation is associated with a compartmentalized outlook which separates and segregates religion from daily life. By contrast, the devotional orientation is linked with a unified *Weltanschauung,* or view of life, with religious beliefs and practices being integrated with other major aspects of daily life. In particular, the devotional orientation is linked with a humanitarian orientation.

In a review such as this it would be a mistake to overlook the fact that on some of the variables examined no appreciable differences were observed within or between groups. For example, this was evident in the case of most of the questions concerning foreign policy (though even here devotionalism seemed to influence attitudes appreciably). Clearly there are some matters on which socio-religious group membership has little influence, or at least little *differentiating* influence.

In those instances where religion did appear to be an active factor, the *magnitude* of its influence on patterns of thought and action was highly variable. Sometimes the differences between groups ranged up to 40 or 50 percentage points; sometimes they were so small that it was difficult to decide whether or not the difference was due merely to sampling error. In any sociological analysis, one of the problems which inevitably arises is that which is sometimes called the "fully-only" problem. A difference of 15 percentage points between two groups may be described as "fully 15 percentage points," or "only 15 percentage points." Obviously the qualifying word a writer uses depends to a great extent upon his previous expectations.

To avoid such subjective criteria, some kind of objective criterion has to be substituted. One which has been suggested many times is the "criterion of perfection." In other words, if one is comparing two groups with respect to a certain characteristic, such as party preference, and all the members of one group are Republicans while all the members of the other group are Democrats, one is justified in using the qualifying word "fully," but if the difference departs far from this standard of perfection, one should use the word "only."

For those familiar with the findings of modern sociological research, it is clear that the criterion of perfection is most unrealistic. Almost every human action reflects the influence of countless forces, so that the degree of influence exercised by any single factor normally falls far short of that which would be determinative. Hence, a much more realistic measure of the influence of any single factor is a comparison with the influence of some other single factor generally recognized to be of major importance.

In this study we have repeatedly compared the differences associated with socio-religious variables with the differences associated with class position. Among the many variables which sociologists customarily employ to account for behavioral differences, there is probably none which is generally regarded to be of as great importance with respect to as wide a range of variables as class position. Hence it provides a realistic (and therefore meaningful) standard for judging the magnitude and importance of the differences uncovered in this study.

Using such a standard, it seems clear that the differences associated with religion are substantial. In general they are of a magnitude comparable to the differences associated with class on the same questions. What is even more important, the *range* of variables affected by religion seems to be fully as great as that affected by class.

*　　*　　*

With a different set of dependent variables (or comparable diversity) one might get a somewhat different result, but the main point seems clear: *socio-religious group membership is a variable comparable in importance to class, both with respect to its potency and with respect to the range, or extent, of its influence.*

This is not to say that religion is such a powerful factor in the modern metropolis that knowledge of a man's socio-religious group and his position in the group is sufficient to predict accurately how he will vote, whether he will be upwardly mobile, whether he will migrate from his native community, how often he will visit with relatives, and so forth. This is simply not the case; but it is well to remember that no single variable exists which permits predictions of this type for any significant range of phenomena. Despite the fond hopes of the economic determinists, there are no "magic keys" that open all doors. Human beings and the social organizations which they create are far more complex phenomena than the determinists credit them with being.

A fourth major finding of this study concerns the utility of our conceptual distinction between the communal and the associational aspects of socio-religious groups. The evidence uncovered in this study makes it clear that this is not only a useful, but also a necessary, distinction if one is to understand the role which religious groups play in modern society, and the means by which they play it.

We found that contrary to common sense, there is only a very limited relationship between the degree to which individuals are involved in the formal association and the degree to which they are involved in the corresponding subcommunity. Hence, the subcommunity is a vehicle by means of which large numbers of persons are effectively indoctrinated with the norms of the group. This is especially important in the case of groups such as the Jewish and white Protestant where associational ties are often quite weak. Thus the subcommunity becomes an important instrument for extending the influence of religious groups in the life of the community.

However, as we noted on numerous occasions in the discussions of economics, politics, and family life, the subcommunity is something more than an instrument for reinforcing the influence of the association. It is a distinct social system in its own right, and only imperfectly coordinated with the religious association. At times, in fact, it exercises an influence which brings it into conflict with the formal association.

By and large, our evidence leads us to the conclusion that religious subcommunities tend to *foster and encourage a provincial view of the world.* We noted that unfavorable images of other groups are consistently linked with a high level of communal involvement, but not with a high level of associational involvement.

In fact, there was some evidence that a high level of associational involvement among Protestants at least, had the opposite effect. A high level of communal involvement was also linked with a heteronomic intellectual orientation, a high valuation of the kin group, and low rates of vertical mobility (both up and down). In short, involvement in socio-religious subcommunities seems to promote many of the virtues and vice which Tönnies and others have identified with *Gemeinschaft,* the folk community or the little community as it has been variously designated. However, what is startling about our present study is the finding that communalism survives, and even thrives, in the heart of the modern metropolis, though admittedly in a guise which makes its recognition difficult for those accustomed to associating communalism with geographically isolated and numerically small populations.

The discovery of socio-religious subcommunities is also significant from one other standpoint. Many of the critics of the churches have often charged them with promoting intolerance, narrow mindedness, and similar characteristics. Our findings suggest that these critics have been a bit wide of their mark, since it is the subcommunities rather than the churches which seem to foster these traits. This is a subtle, but important distinction. Obviously, if there were no churches, there would be no subcommunities, and hence this particular source of intolerance would disappear. However there seems good reason for believing that the development of subcommunities is a phenomenon which may not be dependent solely on the existence of churches in the strict sense of this latter term. For example, there is some reason for believing that there is a secularist subcommunity in America today which fosters its own distinctive brand of intolerance and narrow-mindedness.

While this is a highly speculative judgment, we feel safe in asserting that our findings demonstrate that the concept of communalism is one which is essential to an adequate understanding of intergroup hostility and tension.

Fifth, and finally, our findings provide ample justification for the further investigation of the consequences of those religious orientations, such as doctrinal orthodoxy and devotionalism, which transcend socio-religious group boundaries. The two which we selected for preliminary investigation in this study have clearly emerged as linked with distinctive patterns of action in the secular world. On the whole, doctrinal orthodoxy appears to be a type of religious orientation which is linked with (and we suspect fosters) *a compartmentalized view of life*. It seems to foster the view that one's religious commitments are irrelevant to one's political and economic actions and other aspects of secular life—except, of course, that in interpersonal relations one should be honest and fair. Devotionalism, by contrast, seems linked both with the spirit of capitalism and with a humanitarian outlook when confronted with problems of social injustice. This interesting combination of attributes seems to create a dilemma for persons committed to this orientation when faced with proposals for humanitarian activity by agencies of government. Our evidence indicates that such persons prefer humanitarian action by private individuals and agencies, distrusting, as they appear to, the welfare state.

Our evidence concerning these orientations is far from satisfactory. We have no information concerning the important question of when and how such orientations are acquired by the individual. Hence, it proved impossible to deal effectively with the difficult problem of causality. Furthermore, orthodoxy and devotionalism are but two among a much larger number of religious orientations which deserve to be explored. Although we gathered data on certain other important orientations, our resources were too limited to analyze these data at this time. Hence, our major conclusion on this point must be that the limited investigation undertaken up to this point fully justifies further work in this area.

Berndt Gustafsson

THE ESTABLISHED CHURCH
AND THE DECLINE
IN CHURCH ATTENDANCE IN SWEDEN

The established Lutheran churches of Scandinavia occupy a special position among other Lutheran churches in Europe, in so far as the disproportion between the number of their nominal members and the number of those who regularly take part in the life of the church is extremely great. In Sweden, barely 1% of the population has left the church, but on average only 3% of church members attend an ordinary Sunday service. In Norway, 3.8% are not church members, and the first and so far only count of church attendance in Norway, made in 1956, revealed that only 2.7% of church members attend divine service. In view of this the existence of established churches may appear paradoxical. In order to interpret this phenomenon, that process must be analysed which may be summed up in the concept of *Entkirchlichung* (decline in church attendance). For this decline is no straightforward process, but rather is made up of numerous variations and different aspects.

I. The Church, as Seen by Those Who Left It.

In any attempt to analyse this decline in church attendance as an historical

and contemporary process, the important question arises as to which church is meant by those who feel themselves to be outside the church and estranged from it. That image of the church must be ascertained from which those who left the church took their bearings at the time of their "falling off." In the course of this investigation several typical variations will be discovered, with the result that we have to speak, not of one, but of several forms of this "decline in church attendance." In Sweden indeed the constellations of reasons and causes for the processes of this decline at that time have been by no means fully investigated. Yet there are a few indications, with reference to the social environment of the church as seen by those who have left it. Naturally, the image of the church changes; in the second or third generation it often becomes a stereotype which at the same time splits up and becomes individualized. But the "objective" effect of the formation of this stereotype remains: the falling off of church attendance. This question of the church image among ex-members is of special interest today as a result of contemporary signs of slackening in this process of decreasing attendance in Sweden, without any perceptible basic change in the religious beliefs of the population. One conclusion from this might point to a change in the church-image on a mass scale. When this anti-church movement

" Staatskirche und Entkirchlichung in Schweden" in Probleme der Religionssoziologie. *Köln and Opladen: 1962, pp. 158–65. Translated for this anthology by Ann Harding. By permission of Westdeutscher Verlag.*

began, in the sense of a perceptible decrease in participation in church life, especially service attendance, the Swedish church was a church for peasants and townsfolk, with here and there completely farcical expressions and severe church discipline. The peasants and working people of the towns were only converted to Christianity in so far as it was necessary to get them to church every Sunday. Church attendance was seen as an exercise in Christianity, which was necessary because the existence of men was threatened on all sides by "evil powers." The church was the protecting sentry and the watchful eye, and it was dangerous not to be allowed to go to church. It was dreadful punishment of old to be prevented from attending church, for example criminals or un-churched women. It was a dramatic, dualistic outlook which came down heavily on the exercise of church attendance: belief in a never-ending battle between Christianity and heathendom, between good and evil powers. In order to resist the attacks of the Evil One, one had to be reached by the sound of the church bells.

It was the rising cultured middle class which was the first to neglect public church services, because it did not desire to mix with the masses. Just as the cultured middle class dissociated itself in social life from the lower classes, in preferring its own salons to communal activities with the illiterate, so also it went its own way in religious life. The cultured middle class sought a more personal and, in its eyes, "purer" religion. This process was already beginning in the 17th century and accelerated in the course of the 18th.

During the 19th century new factors came into play and the falling-off process now affected all classes of society. One new factor was the large number of pietist revival movements, which led to the formation of free churches and free communities; the other was the growth of an indigenous proletarian culture through which countless new groups were moved to dissociate themselves from the established church.

The image of the church in pietist revival movements is well known. Most of all the revivalists left themselves to be better and "truer" Christians than the—indeed often honest and loyal—Sunday church-goers. The marked cultural ambitions of the revivalists justified their wish to dissociate themselves from the primitivism of the masses. Since the outbreak of the revivalist movements, a noticeable regrouping has taken place in the free churches. The Baptist movements, above all the Pentecostal movements, have come to the fore. Taken together the free church groups still occupy today a striking and constant position in Swedish society.

STRENGTH OF THE FREE CHURCHES IN SWEDEN 1900–1960

	No. of Members	% Population over 18
1900	133,000	4.0
1910	164,000	4.6
1920	212,000	5.4
1930	260,000	5.9
1940	253,000	5.2
1950	264,000	5.3
1960	280,000	5.3

The trust which the free churches enjoyed from the growing national movements—those movements which were of basic importance for the democratic rising in Sweden (1910–1921)—was connected with the image of the

Swedish church as a national church. This image was shared by the free churches and the democratic movements. In this respect the free churches had for a long time an indirect influence on a broad social front and thereby contributed also to a decline in church attendance outside their own church ranks, above all by furthering the crisis of loyalty between the established church and the people. The church was no longer an unquestioned Christian power; its Christian legitimacy was disputed and it lost in social and political strength.

Whilst the members of the free churches set themselves apart from the "church Christians" because of their special revival experience, the proletarians felt themselves to be shut out of the official church because of their social position. Until towards the end of the 19th century the landed peasants in the villages and the estate-owning townsmen had their own pews. Even before the formation of the social democracy the workers regarded the church as a creation of the "higher" classes. In 1850, workers in Stockholm complained that they could no longer understand the sermons. Part of the working classes turned to the free churches, but the majority turned to the Marxist-inspired social democracy.

Other factors which promoted the depopulation of the church in the 19th century were the growing education of the masses and school reform. The old superstitious fear of the powers against which the church was once the only protection received ever decreasing nourishment in proportion as the unknown and the dangerous became familiar and controllable. This growing popular enlightenment contributed to the emptying of the churches in the same measure as religious piety and popular primitivism flourish together.

A special problem in the interpretation of this development in the church is

posed by the extension and foundation of communities and towns. Often her churches were not built until the third or even fourth generation, so that it i rightly questioned whether this falling off process can seriously be discusse here, since these cases lack a precedin build-up in church-going (*Verkirch lichung*). What is certain is that in man new towns the church appeared rathe as a rural idyll.

Since 1950, however, this drift awa has eased off. The available material is no sufficient to give a comprehensive pic ture and interpretation of the position Some new studies of individual case seem to show, however, new element in the church image of some socia groups. Among these is that the churcl is seen to show a greater openness to wards everyone, regardless of his socia status, and that one does not need to "serve" the church, without being im mediately accused by it of being un Christian. To this image of the churcl corresponds the attitude of showin; oneself open to church practices, withou personally committing oneself too strongly to the community. This nev image of the church in the popular min needs further detailed investigation.

II. From Church Attendance to Private Religion.

Several investigations have shown tha the Swedes generally attend church only sporadically. The statistical basis for a estimation of this process (the waverin; frequency of church attendance) i relatively good for Sweden, since representative popular census was hel in 1942, 1948, and 1955–56, and sinc counts of church attendance have bee made in every diocese for the last twent years.

At the turn of the century 17% of th Swedish population attended churche of the established church, in 1927, 5.7% and in 1960, 3%. These figures represent the number of church-goers on an average Sunday in all the churches of the established Swedish church.

However, since decreasing attendance also implies a fall in the *individual frequency of attendance,* the figure of 3% does not mean that 97% of the population never enter a church. If one calculates church attendance per individual, one finds that 19% of the population go to church at least once a month, but only 2% every Sunday. About 30% of the population attend church at least once per six months.

On the other hand, most Swedish people also make use of the church for ceremonial purposes. More than 85% have their children baptised and confirmed in church. More than 90% of weddings take place in church. The percentage of civil weddings of the total has remained fairly constant at 6–7% during the last 50 years. More than 95% of burials are conducted by the church. Civil interments are extremely rare.

These figures correspond in many respects to those of other countries. They point perhaps to the fact that the church still has the function of providing people with a position and opinion at certain times in life. How far the ties to these rituals have any religious meaning is more difficult to estimate. On the other hand, in a census of church non-attenders in the country, the majority declared that they had their children baptised so that they might "become Christians and receive God's blessing." People are, one might say, church-minded in certain situations, in others not—not only formally or externally, but also in concept and desire. This church-mindedness is conditioned by the situation, which means also that church non-attendance is conditioned by situation. Certain times of life seem to be more non-church-minded than others. This is also true of the working life. Work itself seems to be "de-churched" even for church attenders. Few of regular Sunday church attenders were of the opinion that they received real help for their daily work from a church service, indeed from religion at all. This is perhaps connected with the fact that the total and individual frequency of church attendance is least in those age groups capable of earning their living. Perhaps we have here a reason why men and women who go to work so rarely go to church.

Public life, too, has no contact with the church. Since the middle of the 19th century, society has gradually emancipated itself more and more from the church. The social services, school and law are now almost completely divorced from the church. The religious law of 1951 and its provisions have removed the old identity of middle class and membership of the church of Sweden. Until 1951, all members of the government had to belong to the Swedish church; today, only the minister for church affairs. The system of the established church is almost the only respect in which public life has not lost contact with the church. In 1958, a commission was set up to examine the relations between church and state. It was not given the task of preparing a break. But the way is leading, perhaps of necessity, to a separation of church and state, although it seems that the people do not desire it.

Social relations for the most part are also divorced from the church. Even church attenders believe in no real help from religion for their community or for the understanding of other people. Such help is as rare a part of their image of the church as for those who do not take part in the organised life of the church. On the other hand, religion and church have a greater importance for the personal life of church attenders. They believe that the greatest and most effective help which they have received from religion concerns life in God and help in overcoming personal problems. In social questions church attenders take the same humanitarian attitude as non-attenders. On the whole, their attitudes reflect the usual modes of thought of the social milieu to which they belong.

In other words, this movement away from the church goes with a form of religion which has become individualized and private. Investigations have shown us that this element of the private is implied in the very beginning of the whole process, perhaps equally as cause and as result. The final result is, however, quite clearly this, that even in church-going families the exercise of religion is often seen only as the affair of the individual. The old family worship and the custom of mealtime prayers have become rare, and religion seems to have become totally private. Only within the walls of the church itself is Christianity practised before the eyes of others.

III. The Present National Church System as an Ambivalent Connection With the Church.

It is especially difficult in analysing declining church attendance to draw a sharp division between "church-loyalists" and non-church-loyalists. *In the past one could talk about a wealth of marginal relations with the church.* Those who attend the established church regularly (every Sunday) are an extreme group, 2% of the whole population. A further extreme group is formed by the Sunday service attenders in the free churches, likewise 2% of the population. In different respects even these two extreme groups are not rarely non-church-minded: their norms and concepts in social, political and ethical questions are partly taken from other spheres than those of the church.

In addition to these two extreme

groups is the group of those who less regularly, but at least once a month attend a church service (17% of the total population in the established church, 6% in the free church). A further 25% of the population are "Christians off their own bat": they go to a service every so often. At times they think more of the church than those loyal to it. 23% of the population claim to be non-Christians, but not infrequently, however, have their children baptised and confirmed without any hesitation. 19% of the population are indifferent and at the end of the scale there is a further extreme group of 6% of the population who are declared atheists.

The centre of this religious opinion profile of the Swedish population is formed by the so-called "Christians off their own bat" and those who are indifferent. But both groups seem to have at least some relationship with the church: they value the church, like some of those loyal to it, as a moral institution. They believe, however, that they, themselves, fulfil the demands of the church by attempting to live as decently and respectably as possible. The pathos of this uprightness is often exaggerated and the named groups of non-attenders often display it demonstratively. It seems that social uprightness, for which e.g. the Swedish working class declares it fights, is conceived by most of those belonging to this class as a kind of Christianity, indeed as a kind of church piety. Though the workers made violent attacks on the church during the Marxist epoch of the Swedish national movement, today, long since conquered by revisionism and neo-Kantianism, they wish to claim the church and Christianity almost as *their* territory and their ideology, together with the claim that, as "practical Christians" they only need to be minimally practising members of the church to qualify as loyal to it.

This dimension of non-churchism

presents a wealth of theological problems. Above all, there is the necessity of interpreting this strong element of uprightness in combination with a minimum of church activity in the light of religion. From a pastoral-theological point of view, this uprightness must have a religious meaning: man is upright before God and tries to protect himself from God with good works and intentions. Every second one in this attitude group thanks religion that he is as upright as he thinks himself to be. *One takes the norms of uprightness from religion,* AND *uses these norms again to circumvent religion itself in the claims of its institutional ties.*

To sum up, the essential attitudes of the named groups are that they:

(a) want to be regarded as Christians;

(b) believe that they take their norms and ethical principles from Christianity (above all with reference to the Sermon on the Mount and the general commandment of Love Thy Neighbour); and,

(c) they wish to participate in the institutional life of the church—referring to their general Christian attitude—only at overwhelming times in life.

In Sweden, we are only at the beginning of an investigation into this "popular piety." Whereas, in 19th century society people were anxious to expound their faith in God, now they seem to want to hide it. Religion has been driven out of general consciousness and plays its role in secret. Here, in secret, the church seems to direct and prohibitively to determine the religious attitudes of many people—from afar—in that certain moral directions are taken over from the church, which are used to live uprightly, not only before others, but also before God. One also wants to defend his private existence from God. With a naive Pharisaism man

attempts to defend himself against religion as a personal life in God.

To this protective disguise there belongs also a certain positive attitude against the church as an institution and the preservation of an established church system, which gives the church very little support. Large communities can only be divided when the number of inhabitants exceeds 45,000, and then only after a difficult procedure. There is a concealed lack of priests which the state does not recognize. Although the population has doubled since 1860, the number of priests has not risen since then; it has, rather, decreased. In 1860, to 1,278 people there was one priest; in 1960, however, one priest to 2,790 people. In no other previous decade has this relationship worsened more than between 1950–60. Even in 1860, the number of priests to 10,000 inhabitants (namely 8) was too small, if the church was to be really effective. Today there are 3.5 priests to every 10,000 inhabitants and it is no exaggeration to talk of a great undisclosed lack of priests. The Lutherans in the United States are less numerous than those in Sweden, but they have four times as many priests.

This movement away from the church has taken place with great declarations of respect, of which the subjective uprightness in the individual case can scarcely be doubted. My hypothesis is that man is protecting himself by means of the church against the church. This situation is a multifarious result of this general drift, and the ambivalence which is expressed in it must be investigated more closely. Sociology of religion in Sweden must, in the first place, devote itself to the development of suitable methods for investigations thus oriented.

Emile Poulat

THE FUTURE
OF THE WORKER PRIESTS

Much has been written about the worker-priests in France and much more said about them. But there were only one hundred of them after ten years' existence when the Vatican caused them to be disbanded. This extraordinary enterprise falls within two dates, one of which was propitious and the other ill-fated. On July 1, 1943, Cardinal Suhard, Archbishop of Paris, resolved to found the *Mission de Paris*; on March 1, 1954, the period within which the worker-priests had to give up their work expired.[1]

I shall not dwell much on the past, although much might still be said from the sociologist's, if not from the journalist's, point of view. But the past will not repeat itself: history never takes the same road twice. The reflections which follow are made with an eye on the future.

"The Future of the Worker Priests," The Modern Churchman, June 1959, pp. 191–199. *Reprinted here in its entirety by permission of author and publisher.*

[1]Two books appeared respectively on these dates: Henri Godin and Yvan Daniel, *La France, pays de mission?* Lyon-Paris, ed. du Cerf, 1943, 161 pp. (The French edition reached 100,000 copies. A very accurate adaptation in English was made by Maisie Ward, "France pagan?" London: Sheed & Ward.) *Les prêtres ouvriers,* Paris, ed. de Minuit, 1954, 290 pp. (A collection of documents published by the worker-priests who remained at their post. English translation: *The Worker Priests,* London: Routledge & Kegan Paul, 1956, 204 pp.) In addition, I would refer to my "Notes sur la psychologie réligieuse des prêtres ouvriers," *Journal de Psychologie normale et pathologique,* 1957, I, pp. 51–66.

It is necessary first to make several preliminary observations. In the first place let us recall the atmosphere prevailing at the start of the experiment. The war was not yet ended, but Nazism was in its last months: men were secretly preparing for the end, united together without any distinctions, and standing together shoulder to shoulder. It was plain that the liberation would not be accomplished without many profound changes. A quasi-prophetic enthusiasm prevailed, and it was by no means confined to young, inexperienced priests. A Jesuit who was a well-known preacher at retreats for priests proclaimed, "The old forms are going to fall into dust." The eminent preacher before the war at Notre Dame, Mgr. Chevrot, who was also the curé of an important parish in Paris, wrote to the Abbé Godin, "The rechristianization of France, and especially of the lower classes, must begin with a radical reform of society. First of all, the slave-status of the proletariat must be completely destroyed. . . . The Church of France will have to accommodate itself to this revolution. The part which it will be called upon to play is no mean one, but is commensurate with its share of responsibility for the social abuses resulting in the dechristianizing of our country. It is doubtful if the hierarchy of its own accord will have the courage to embark on these reforms. God will have to come to the Church's aid or compel it to act. . . ." Thus men voluntarily surrendered themselves to the enthusiasm of the Holy Spirit instead of placing their trust in the proved solidity of traditional forms and institutions.

The Abbé Godin, who was pioneer in the undertaking, expressed on January 17, 1944, his acute sense of the material and moral misery of the dechristianized masses. "The work," he wrote, "would demand patience and persistence." But at the same time he reckoned that the deserted masses were malleable material, hungry for the gospel, provided that it was presented to them in simple and concrete language; all that was required was to let down the net and there would be a miraculous catch.[2] But this evangelistic optimism faced a tough obstacle in the middle-class outlook of the traditional parish, which was no more able to absorb new converts from the working-classes than to understand a Chinaman or an Eskimo. Consequently a priest was almost condemned to choose between two social strata which cannot mix, and involving separate cultures and different ways of living and thought. The choice is radical and definite. "A Missionary usually cannot adapt himself to a new environment. In the Mission to Paris, if you give it your complete loyalty, you may possibly find that later on you cannot undertake something else," he told his first recruits. If you become a barbarian with the barbarians, you cannot return to being a Greek with the Greeks.

The missionary envisaged by the Abbé Godin would be, above every thing else, the herald of the pure Gospel to the poorest of the poor. It is a conception laden with memories for the historian[3]

and bristling with problems for the theologian: it is disturbing and even aggressive regarded from an orthodox point of view, and yet one which no one thinks of worrying himself about.[4] Superficially transparent, it is really ambiguous. In short, the Gospel is not only discourse but life, the needs of which cannot be discovered from the written word, but only from contact with concrete reality. The poverty demanded by the Beatitudes has assumed many varied forms throughout the ages; it could be canonized by the monastic rule, but this is not the kind of poverty which authentically proclaims the gospel to the proletariat of our large industrialized cities. The poverty, which will be understood in a system organized continually to increase production and in a collective environment, is not some ideal voluntary privation. The pure gospel is not the fruit of a new interpretation, but a veritable *kenosis;* the priest must in his turn deprive himself of his cultural environment; he must give up the social position with which his priestly vocation has become identified in order to live with the poor and share their fate.

Authentically, to preach the gospel is not therefore in its essence to prune it with commentaries which are themselves open to question and cannot be assimilated by the masses: it is primarily to restore to it its power of fermentation long quenched by attitudes which have become so dear to us. The missionary should be the first one to be converted: he does not proclaim a truth for which he has the formula, but the transformation

---

[2]The Abbé Godin had more experience of youth than of adults; also, under the German occupation, all labour organizations were proscribed and many of their leaders were arrested or driven underground.

[3]There comes to mind the mediaeval movement of the *Spirituals.*

[4]*France, pays de mission?* caused a considerable conflagration among French Catholics, but it was a shot with a narrow field of fire. Its criticism was spectacular, but very limited in range: it is confined to the level of teaching, in spite of the efforts of Catholic Labour Action, and to a small sociological field, treating the parish as a closed social environment: it never takes a wider sweep.

of the whole man. Of this he must be the proof which has slowly matured. That is where the ambiguity which I have previously mentioned is so plain. The spiritual ideal put out by the Abbé Godin is defined by a rejection of inferior realities, and at the same time by an appeal to the *whole* man[5]: it is like an angel who has been compelled to become incarnate and finds himself caught up in the tension of two conflicting logics.

The Abbé Godin died on the very day the Mission to Paris began, and never saw the first worker-priests. The plan had been submitted to him, did it not meet with his approval. Perhaps he would not have been able to resist it for long: while it did not come within his perspective, it was clearly a result of his action. In the same way we meet here the source of the ecclesiastical difficulties with which the worker-priests were subsequently faced. But before the difficulties between them and the Catholic hierarchy came to a head, they always had the feeling that they were being drawn in different directions or, to put it less dramatically, they saw before them a chain of demands following one upon the other with their own inexorable logic, which had not been foreseen at the start. How can one seriously share the lot of the poorest of the people by living on air or on subsidies provided by the middle-class? These people have their own concrete character: they are not down-and-outs to whom charity has been given to bring them within the reach of a church; they are workmen involved in the mechanistic set-up of big industry, organized to defend their rights, struggling for a better world with greater comradeship, and in their French environment under the powerful influence of communism.

[5]The spiritual which Catholicism opposes to the temporal should rather be defined as a *compromise*: this has created a historical dialectic of a different kind.

In this way two novel steps were taken. The first was to become detached from every kind of service associated with the classical pattern of the ministry in order to plunge into the life of the masses; the second was to share without any reservations the life of the working-man, with the inevitable result of becoming involved in the communist system. These decisions were made slowly and painfully, with much hesitation and uncertainty after heated argument and without any preconceived ideas.

Not only were the priest-workmen involved: there was heated opposition to them and heated support for them. In 1945, on the basis of strong denunciations, the Holy See expressed grave anxiety to Cardinal Suhard. Ten months later the Holy Office asked for replies to a precise questionnaire. Interventions of this kind were periodically renewed until in August 1953 it was learnt that Rome was going to take drastic measures. The French bishops, who were interested, defended their priest-workmen: they only managed to save a semblance of manual labour, i.e. three hours a day. More than half of the priest-workmen refused these terms: the rest submitted in the hope that the measures would be repealed and, while they waited, many refused offers to take ministries of a regular type.

Since then five years have passed, and the storm created by this affair is far from dying down. According to one's point of view, a great hope has been dashed or a dangerous threat avoided; the problem, however, remains alive in its entirety. What chance have we of seeing a renewal?

As soon as the priest-workmen had been suppressed, it was announced that the idea of "Priests for the Mission to Labour" was being broached. All that could be learnt showed that the authorities had not succeeded in going beyond the blue-print stage or making administrative arrangements. Gradually, with the good-will of their bishops, a number of these priests returned to full duty, and so seemed to become "lost men" while waiting for a ruling which did not come. It was said at the time that as long as Pope Pius XII was alive there was no hope. The advent of his successor has perhaps opened the way: he has, however, as yet given no solution to the problems raised.[6]

Thus it is shown that, if the worker-priests have not been pliable material in the hands of the bishops, the decisions made at Rome have only complicated their task: perhaps that is due to the fact that the Vatican, whose hostility to the experiment has never wavered, has drawn the attention of the French bishops to aspects of the problem which they had ignored. It is well known that three cardinals went to Rome in November, 1953, and they returned to make it plain that they were convinced by Pius XII's point of view.

It is tempting to think that these difficulties were primarily political. This idea has been maintained: in my estimation it does not reveal the real nature of the problem. It is true that the worker-priests were noted for their left-wing views, and particularly for what is perhaps a somewhat surprising attitude

towards communism. Truth compels me to say that their attitude was, generally speaking, much more covert than was stated; in the realm of political struggles, this reserve may appear to be formal: in the realm of religious psychology it is essential. Further, Pius XII never condemned the worker-priests for philo-communism, but because in his view they compromised the purity of the Catholic priesthood. Also, it is possible that in the politics of the Vatican anti-communism plays a much more positive part than appeared in France: it should be observed that anti-communism cannot be divorced from a theology and ecclesiology much older than communism. Communism has given the conflict between the Church and the "modern world" a much sharper turn: it did not create the conflict; it has shown itself to be a particularly efficacious catalyst: it does not appear to have created specific religious problems. It does not look as if there was any difficulty here to prevent the new "Mission to Labour" from making a start.

It must then be recognized that these difficulties are at bottom religious.[7] I can only mention them briefly, though each could fill a book by itself. I will make use of a metaphor borrowed from space-rockets, and suppose that there are three stages. The first consists of the formal status to be given to those priests who will embark on a new experiment on the basis of the experience provided by the first one. The second derives from the calls which have come to the worker-priests from the very heart of their

---

[6]Cardinal Feltin, Archbishop of Paris, said after the conclave to an Italian hebdomadary: 'I am certain that a *missionary apostolate* to the working-classes is needed just as much as missions to distant lands, as the workers are far removed from us. Pius XII considered that the worker-priest movement was not the best way to attain this end, and asked us to think out other ways and means. His Holiness John XXIII is fully aware of the problem with which we are faced and knows the difficulties. My predecessor, Cardinal Roncalli, never gave any opinion. Later on, then, we shall ask John XXIII what we can do; we shall tell him of our experiences and inform him of our intentions. If he does not approve of them, we shall begin our studies afresh, and with better ideas shall go on looking for the best approach" (*Epoca*, November 9, 1958).

[7]The relationship between politics and religion, the temporal and the spiritual, is the Gordian knot of Roman theology and strategy. It is the root of every crisis and conflict. There is an urgent need not for a fresh historical study, but for a sociological analysis: this is the only way to bring a little light on to what has never appeared to be anything but a succession of discussions between different interests and debates about abstractions.

condition as workmen; the third comes from the forces of resistance, which were not created by any formal status, but to which they were all more or less related. (1) At first sight, in strict logic, it would appear as if the problem of their formal status ought to come last after the appeals and resistances which I have just mentioned have been analysed. This may be the way the worker-priests who have declined to submit look at things: it cannot be that of the Catholic hierarchy, who mean to keep a control on the new venture which they failed to do on the first one, and who, while they will make the minimum concessions for adaptation, mean to hold fast to the traditional methods of Roman strategy and the principles inspiring it.

The Catholic priest is a social type well defined by his clothes, his daily pursuits and occupations, his manners and relationships; he is caught up in a close net of customs and obligations, and knows what he must do and say every hour of the day. At least, he ought to know! There is little difference in his behaviour whether he is with students, women, children or working men: the only difference for him between the various types lies in their *occupation*. Looked at in this light, the Catholic industrial chaplain represents perhaps a new type of *pastor* unknown to previous generations; he certainly does not represent a new type of *priest* in spite of his specialized work; neither—if we take a step further—is he the factory chaplain or missionary[8]: all are known as "ecclesiastics," received or rejected as agents of an ecclesiastical institution. The idea of the worker-priest creates some ambiguity. From the very name he would appear to be a hy-

brid creature endowed with a certain lack of balance. It is asked what he is or what he will want to be, because the difference between the worker-priest and the ordinary secular grows wider as time goes on. At first he seems to be a somewhat bold pastoral type of priest who is troubled by clericalism: "Why," it is asked, "does this cleric disguise himself as a layman except to take the place of a layman in laymen's business?" Then gradually he becomes aware that he is primarily engaged in looking for a new type of priest: in his daily life all the outward symbols associated with a priest disappear. Which vanishes, his *priestly* character or a *historic* and *temporary* form of the priesthood? This was the sense and drift of the debate which ended in their suppression by Rome.

This explains the difficulties felt when successors to them were set up, protected by being given a satisfactory formal status. There was a desire, to quote from Claudel's *Le Soulier de Satin,* to create a novelty which was really nothing new at all. Furthermore, the idea of a worker priest not only possesses a strong attraction for the younger clergy, but also carries with it logical implications and consequences following upon laws from which there is no escape and which are beyond the power of any pope, however liberal, to modify.

(2) The worker-priests answered a profound call—a *missionary* call, it has been said, to use what has become a blessed word. Let us rid ourselves of the magic of the word. The Abbé Godin had just this intuition, that the word of God is conveyed to those who failed to grasp it at the beginning not through preaching by human words, but by human living and then not by the example of a life which is in accord with the canons of hagiography, but by sharing in the kind of life the concrete conditions of which the Church knows nothing. Once that is assumed, the rest follows: the worker

---

[8]The difference between the dispenser of charity and the factory chaplain may be wide, as is to be seen from the various countries where they exist. France, which has also known Protestant worker-pastors, has escaped formulations of this kind.

priest is a worker, a trade-unionist, a fighter, and should his mate's confidence demand it, a shop-steward. To share a particular kind of life involves a sharing of interests, struggles, and destiny.

By one and the same movement the worker-priests broke down two barriers, one which, owing to unforeseen associations, separates the Church and the proletariat, and the other which, owing to a secular tradition, separates clergy from laity.[9] Deprived of his social superiority, the priest ceased to belong to a body and play a definite part; he is no longer in a position of superiority. He is an equal, creating fraternal relationships with those over whom he has charge and, like them, completely *absque peccato,* as they said of their own accord, at the beginning of the Mission to Paris with a reference to the Epistle to the Hebrews.

It is then a mistake to speak here of clericalism: it is not a matter of some superficial adaptation but an internal assimilation, just as Fr. Lebbe wished to become a Chinaman with the Chinese. The worker-priest represents a new priestly type which he is trying to create rather than a new pastoral method, a transitional being if you like, anticipating the worker who is also a priest (not as he sees himself to-day, a priest who is also a worker), as well as the priest who is also a peasant. Is this a utopian ideal, or is it heresy? The latter, if we identify the priesthood with the clergy in the sense that the latter is a social and professional body. It will at any rate be noticed that this venture calls for a new sociology concerning the priesthood, but not necessarily for a new theology. This idea of a lay priesthood, if it may be so described, has nothing to do with the doctrine of the priesthood of believers and congregationalism; it is associated with a

radical transformation of the conditions of the priest's life, not with any surrender of a priest's peculiar powers and responsibilities; it implies a renunciation of his social caste-marks, not of his sacramental character. Finally, it calls for new methods of social contact and encounter, concerning which enquiry must be made as to the form and urgency with which the Church needs them.

(3) When the problem is viewed in this light,[10] it is understandable why the Church hesitates; its present structure is completely bound up with a clerical hierarchy. But apart from the *institutional problem,* the worker-priests present a strategic problem which calls in question what have usually been taken for granted as unquestionable certainties. They were commissioned on an evangelistic mission. Now they are told that they have very quickly become "dumb dogs." It must be pointed out that the problem exists on two planes. As a piece of apparatus within the organization and activity of the Roman Church (activities, movements, organizations, parties, etc.), the worker-priests are recognized as sharpshooters, a reconnaissance-commando troop which has become a bridgehead. This quickly caused a sharply-felt tension on all sides. According to the teaching of papal encyclicals, the whole of this powerful apparatus has been patiently built up with the aim of making society Christian again and establishing a new Christen-

[9]Such had been the condition of the soldier-priest from temporary circumstances during the war.

[10]*Traductor, traditor?* I am analysing here past tendencies, for the worker-priests never evolved a theory concerning their position; rather they allowed themselves to be guided by events and what they revealed as circumstances changed and not by the fulfilment of any coherent plan. That was why they were divided by the decisions of Rome in March 1954. It is worth noting that since the Apostolic Constitution *Provida Mater Ecclesia* (1947), "Secular Institutes" have grown in number for religious orders, consisting not of priests but of men and women who are living a completely lay life.

dom; consequently for the unbeliever this means conversion to Catholicism, i.e. not just encounter with Christ of the Gospel and Word of God, but integration within the framework of the Church and the acceptance of its age-long outlook on the world. Furthermore, this conception, as it condemns socialism *altogether* and only the *abuses* within capitalism, ends in hallowing the present structure of society under the cloak of Christianity. Must then the proclamation of the Word of God be tied up with the notion that a Christian society must be more or less hierarchical in form, an ideal which has come down from the Middle Ages and is impregnated with nostalgia? This is a question which French Catholics have long debated and which has been answered by the worker-priests with a definite and radical negative. Thus, by explicitly rejecting the "social thinking" of the Church and accepting the prospect of a socialized society, they not only weakened their position as sharpshooters, but found themselves faced with difficult questions. What becomes of the Church's part in a world which means to dispense with its protection? What significance is left to the traditional Christian notions in a technological world which has shaken off its ancestral traditions? And what is to be said in the name of God to men who oppose a religious criticism of society with a sociological criticism of religion? This religion, purified of obsolete temporal elements, is in the process of searching for a new look to meet the times, and no one has any idea as to what form it should take. The unavoidable task of evangelism is set in a situation which has not been mapped out. It seems foolish to proclaim from outside a message of which the social elements, such as brotherhood and peace, has already been assimilated by the best elements of the working-classes, while Christian circles more often than not have given a contrary

witness. It seems foolish to wish to pour new wine into old bottles; it is first necessary to discover for oneself what in the forms of a nascent civilization might be of Christian significance and what are the concrete demands of the Gospel. The task is found to be not preaching, but being born afresh—all together, clergy and laity closely associated together as Christians in the same quest and in close contact with all those outside the Church who yesterday were strangers, to-day are fellow-workmen living together, and to-morrow perhaps will be brothers in a faith expressed in their tongue.

After reading through this article, I feel profoundly dissatisfied at the almost cavalier fashion in which I have had to treat problems, each one of which demands a book to itself. The question of evangelism in particular calls for separate treatment. All the experiences of evangelism which have met the same obstacles—there is no shortage of them—should be collected and compared.[11] At any rate, I have wanted to point out that a powerful spiritual drive still animates the worker-priests, in spite of what outside observers may think. We may not agree with their choice of methods; we may criticize them, although I have not done so for the same reason that I have not given them unstinted praise. We may think that everything in their experiment has not equal value and that there are other paths to explore. All this is true. But two obvious conclusions cannot be avoided, (1) the reality, depth, and pressing nature of the problems raised by their very existence cannot be denied; (2) the Church does not seem to have

[11] The writer of this article would be glad to hear from Anglicans, since in their country he considers that there has been a long period of a large number of very diverse experiments in evangelism which would provide an infinitely greater wealth of material than we know of in France.

seriously tackled these problems in any way at all. Hence, while it is admitted that in the end a status may be accorded to the worker-priests which allows them to make a fresh start, there is a danger that they may take refuge in one of the following alternatives. Either they will evade the problems which will continue to press upon them because they are afraid of losing their status, if they tackled them; or their ordered status will canalize the movement away from problems which are too searching, as has happened to many other movements in the past from that of St. Francis onwards.

M. N. Srinivas

SANSKRITIZATION AND WESTERNIZATION

The first use of the term Sanskritization in this sense occurs in my book, *Religion and Society among the Coorgs of South India* (Oxford, 1952, p. 30):

The caste system is far from a rigid system in which the position of each component caste is fixed for all time. Movement has always been possible, and especially so in the middle regions of the hierarchy. A low caste was able, in a generation or two, to rise to a higher position in the hierarchy by adopting vegetarianism and teetotalism, and by Sanskritizing its ritual and pantheon. In short, it took over, as far as possible, the customs, rites, and beliefs of the Brahmins, and the adoption of the Brahminic way of life by a low caste seems to have been frequent, though theoretically forbidden. This process has been called "Sanskritization" in this book, in preference to "Brahminization," as certain Vedic rites are confined to the Brahmins and the two other "twiceborn" castes.

The structural basis of Hindu society is caste, and it is not possible to understand Sanskritization without reference to the structural framework in which it occurs. Speaking generally, the castes occupying the top positions in the hierarchy are more Sanskritized than castes in the lower and middle regions of the hierarchy and this has been responsible for the Sanskritization of the lower castes as well as the outlying tribes. The lower castes always seem to have tried to take over the customs and way of life of the higher castes. The theoretical existence of a ban on their adoption of Brahminical customs and rites was not very effective, and this is clear when we consider the fact that many non-Brahminical castes practise many Brahminical customs and rites. A more effective barrier to the lower castes' taking over of the customs and rites of the higher castes was the hostile attitude of the locally dominant caste, or of the king of the region. In their case there was physical force which could be used to keep the lower groups in check.

The point which is really interesting to note is that in spite of the existence of certain obstacles, Brahminical customs and way of life did manage to spread not only among all Hindus but also among

From Caste in Modern India and Other Essays, Bombay: 1962, pp. 44–55, 60–61. By permission of Asia Publishing House.

some outlying tribes. This is to some extent due to the fact that Hindu society is a stratified one, in which there are innumerable small groups each of which tries to pass for a higher group. And the best way of staking a claim to a higher position is to adopt the customs and way of life of a higher caste. As this process was common to all the castes except the highest, it meant that the Brahminical customs and way of life spread among all Hindus. It is possible that the very ban on the lower castes' adoption of the Brahminical way of life had an exactly opposite effect.

Though, over a long period of time, Brahminical rites and customs spread among the lower castes, in the short run the locally dominant caste was imitated by the rest. And the locally dominant caste was frequently not Brahmin. It could be said that in the case of the numerous castes occupying the lowest levels, Brahminical customs reached them in a chain reaction. That is, each group took from the one higher to it, and in turn gave to the group below. Sometimes, however, as in the case of the Smiths of South India, a caste tried to jump over all its structural neighbours, and claimed equality with the Brahmins. The hostility which the Smiths have attracted is perhaps due to their collective social megalomania.

Occasionally we find castes which enjoyed political and economic power but were not rated high in ritual ranking. That is, there was a hiatus between their ritual and politico-economic positions. In such cases Sanskritization occurred sooner or later, because without it the claim to a higher position was not fully effective. The three main axes of power in the caste system are the ritual, the economic, and the political ones, and the possession of power in any one sphere usually leads to the acquisition of power in the other two. This does not mean, however, that inconsistencies do not occur—occasionally, a wealthy caste has a low ritual position, and contrariwise, a caste having a high ritual position is poor.

The idea of hierarchy is omnipresent in the caste system; not only do the various castes form a hierarchy, but the occupations practised by them, the various items of their diet, and the customs they observe all form separate hierarchies. Thus, practising an occupation such as butchery, tanning, herding swine or handling toddy, puts a caste in a low position. Eating pork or beef is more defiling than eating fish or mutton. Castes which offer blood-sacrifices to deities are lower than castes making only offerings of fruit and flower. The entire way of life of the top castes seeps down the hierarchy. And as mentioned earlier, the language, cooking, clothing, jewellery, and way of life of the Brahmins spreads eventually to the entire society.

Two "legal fictions" seem to have helped the spread of Sanskritization among the low castes. Firstly, the ban against the non-twice-born castes' performance of Vedic ritual was circumvented by restricting the ban only to the chanting of *mantras* from the Vedas. That is, the ritual acts were separated from the accompanying *mantras* and this separation facilitated the spread of Brahminic ritual among all Hindu castes, frequently including Untouchables. Thus several Vedic rites, including the rite of the gift of the virgin (*kanyadan*), are performed at the marriage of many non-Brahminical castes in Mysore State. And secondly, a Brahmin priest officiates at these weddings. He does not chant Vedic *mantras,* however, but instead, the *mangalashtaka stotras* which are post-Vedic verses in Sanskrit. The substitution of these verses for Vedic *mantras* is the second "legal fiction."

The non-Brahminical castes adopt not only Brahminical ritual, but also certain Brahminical institutions and values.

I shall illustrate what I mean by reference to marriage, women, and kinship. I should add here that throughout this essay I have drawn on my experience of conditions in Mysore State, except when I have stated otherwise.

Until recently, Brahmins used to marry their girls before puberty, and parents who had not succeeded in finding husbands for daughters past the age of puberty were regarded as guilty of a great sin. Brahmin marriage is in theory indissoluble, and a Brahmin widow, even if she be a child widow, is required to shave her head, shed all jewellery and ostentation in colthes. She was (and still is, to some extent) regarded as inauspicious. Sex life is denied her. Among Hindus generally, there is a preference for virginity in brides, chastity in wives, and continence in widows, and this is specially marked among the highest castes.

The institutions of the "low" castes are more liberal in the spheres of marriage and sex than those of the Brahmins. Post-puberty marriages do occur among them, widows do not have to shave their heads, and divorce and widow marriage are both permitted and practised. In general, their sex code is not as harsh towards women as that of the top castes, especially Brahmins. But as a caste rises in the hierarchy and its ways become more Sanskritized, it adopts the sex and marriage code of the Brahmins. Sanskritization results in harshness towards women.

Sanskritization has significant effects on conjugal relations. Among Brahmins for instance, a wife is enjoined to treat her husband as a deity. It is very unusual for a wife to take her meal before the husband has his, and in orthodox families, the wife still eats on the dining leaf on which her husband has eaten. Normally, such a leaf may not be touched as it would render impure the hand touching it. Usually the woman who removes the dining leaf purifies the spot where the

leaf had rested with a solution of cow-dung, after which she washes her hands. There is no pollution, however, in eating on the leaf on which the husband has eaten.

Orthodox Brahmin women perform a number of *vratas* or religious vows, the aim of some of which is to secure a long life for the husband. A woman's hope is to predecease her husband and thus avoid becoming a widow. Women who predecease their husbands are considered lucky as well as good, while widowhood is attributed to sins committed in a previous incarnation. A wife who shows utter devotion to her husband is held up as an ideal, as a *pativrata*, i.e, one who regards the devoted service of her husband as her greatest duty. There are myths describing the devotion and loyalty of some sainted women to their husbands. These women are reverenced on certain occasions.

While polygyny is permitted, monogamy is held up as an ideal. Rama, the hero of the epic *Ramayana,* is dedicated to the ideal of having only one wife (*ekapatnivrata*). The conjugal state is regarded as a holy state, and the husband and wife must perform several rites together. A bachelor has a lower religious status than a married man, and is not allowed to perform certain important rites such as offering *pinda* or balls of cooked rice to the manes. Marriage is a religious duty. When bathing in the Ganges or other sacred river, the husband and wife have the ends of their garments tied together. A wife is entitled to half the religious merit earned by her husband by fasting, prayer, and penance.

In the sphere of kinship, Sanskritization stresses the importance of the *vamsha*, which is the patrilineal lineage of the Brahmins. The dead ancestors are apotheosized, and offerings of food and drink have to be made to them periodically by their male descendants. Absence of these offerings will confine the manes to a hell called *put*. The Sanskrit word for son is *putra*, which by folk etymology is considered to mean one who frees the manes from the hell called *put*.[1] In short, Sanskritization results in increasing the importance of having sons by making them a religious necessity. At the same time it has the effect of lowering the value of daughters because, as said earlier, parents are required to get them married before they come of age to a suitable man from the same subcaste. It is often difficult to find such a man, and in recent years, the difficulty has increased enormously owing to the institution of dowry.

Among the non-Brahmins of Mysore, however, though a son is preferred, a daughter is not unwelcome. Actually, girls are in demand among them. And there is no religious duty to get a girl married before puberty. The code under which a woman has to live is not as harsh among them as among the Brahmins. The non-Brahmins are also patrilineal, and the patrilineal lineage is well developed among them. The dead ancestors are occasionally offered food and drink. But it could be said that in the lineage of the non-Brahmins the religious element is less prominent than among the Brahmins.

Sanskritization means not only the adoption of new customs and habits, but also exposure to new ideas and values which have found frequent expression in the vast body of Sanskrit literature, sacred as well as secular. *Karma, dharma, papa, maya, samsara* and *moksha* are examples of some of the most common Sanskritic

theological ideas, and when a people become Sanskritized these words occur frequently in their talk. These ideas reach the common people through Sanskritic myths and stories. The institution of *harikatha* helps in spreading Sanskrit stories and ideas among the illiterate. In a *harikatha* the priest reads and explains a religious story to his audience. Each story takes a few weeks to complete, the audience meeting for a few hours every evening in a temple. *Harikathas* may be held at any time, but festivals such as Dasara, Ramanavami, Shivaratri, and Ganesh Chaturthi are considered especially suitable for listening to *harikathas*. The faithful believe that such listening leads to the acquisition of spiritual merit. It is one of the traditionally approved ways of spending one's time.

The spread of Sanskrit theological ideas increased under British rule. The development of communications carried Sanskritization to areas previously inaccessible, and the spread of literacy carried it to groups very low in the caste hierarchy. Western technology—railways, the internal combustion engine, press, radio, and plane—has aided the spread of Sanskritization. For instance, the popularity of *harikatha* has increased in the last few years in Mysore City, the narrator usually using a microphone to reach a much larger audience than before. Indian films are popularizing stories and incidents borrowed from the epics and *puranas*. Films have been made about the lives of saints such as Nandanar, Potana, Tukaram, Chaitanya, Mira, Thyagaraja and Tulasidas. Cheap and popular editions of the epics, *puranas,* and other religious and semi-religious books in the various vernaculars are available nowadays.

The introduction by the British of a Western political institution like parliamentary democracy has also contributed to the increased Sanskritization of the country. Prohibition, a Sanskritic value,

[1]See M. Monier-Williams, *A Sanskrit-English Dictionary,* 2nd edition, Oxford, 1899, p. 632: "*put* or *pud* (a word invented to explain *putra* or *put-tra,* see Mn. ix, 138, and cf. Nir. ii, 11) hell or partic. hell (to which the childless are condemned)"; and "*putra,* m. (etym. doubtful . . . traditionally said to be a comp. *put-tra* 'preserving from the hell called Put,' Mn. ix, 138) a son, child . . . "

has been written into the Constitution of the Republic of India, and the Congress Governments in all the States have introduced it wholly or partly in their respective areas.

In Mysore State, the local Congress party is busy conducting a campaign against offering blood-sacrifices to village deities. The Congress in the South is dominated by non-Brahminical castes, the vast majority of whom periodically sacrifice animals to their deities. In spite of this, the leaders of the Congress are advocating the substitution of offerings of fruit and flower for animals. This is again a triumph for Sanskritic, though post-Vedic, values against the values of the bulk of the population.

So far, I have mentioned only the ways in which the Westernization of a group has helped its Sanskritization. In another sense, however, there is a conflict between Sanskritic and Western values. For instance there appears to be a conflict between the world-view disclosed by the systematic application of scientific method to the various spheres of knowledge and the world-view of the traditional religions.

No analysis of modern Indian social life would be complete without a consideration of Westernization and the interaction between it and Sanskritization. In the nineteenth century, the British found in India institutions such as slavery, human sacrifice, suttee, thuggery, and in certain parts of the country, female infanticide. They used all the power at their disposal to fight these institutions which they considered barbarous. There were also many other institutions which they did not approve of, but which, for various reasons, they did not try to abolish directly.

The fact that the country was overrun by aliens who looked down upon many features of the life of the natives, some of which they regarded as plainly barbarous, threw the Indian leaders on the defensive.

Reformist movements such as the Brahmo Samaj were aimed at ridding Hinduism of its numerous "evils."[2] The present was so bleak that the past became golden. The Arya Samaj, another reformist movement within Hinduism, emphasized a wish to return to Vedic Hinduism, which was unlike contemporary Hinduism. The discovery of Sanskrit by Western scholars, and the systematic piecing together of India's past by Western or Western-inspired scholarship, gave Indians a much-needed confidence in their relations with the West. Tributes to the greatness of ancient Indian culture by Western scholars such as Max Muller were gratefully received by Indian leaders (see, for instance, appendices to Mahatma Gandhi's *Hind Swaraj*).[3] It was not uncommon for educated Indians to make extravagant claims for their own culture, and to run down the West as materialistic and unspiritual.

The caste and class from which Indian leaders came were also relevant in this connection. The upper castes had a literary tradition and were opposed to blood-sacrifices, but in certain other customs and habits they were further removed from the British than the lower castes. The latter ate meat, some of them ate even pork and beef, and drank alcoholic liquor; women enjoyed greater freedom among them; and divorce and widow marriage were not prohibited. The Indian leaders were thus caught in a dilemma. They found that certain customs and habits which until then they had looked down upon obtained also among their masters. The British who ate beef and pork and drank

[2]See "Brahmo Samaj" in the *Encyclopaedia of Religion and Ethics,* Vol. II, pp. 813–14.

[3]Ahmedabad, 1946. See the Appendices which contain "testimonies by eminent men" to the greatness of Indian culture. Among the eminent men are Max Muller, J. Seymour Keay, M.P., Victor Cousin, Col. Thomas Munro and the Abbé Dubois.

liquor, possessed political and economic power, a new technology, scientific knowledge, and a great literature. The Westernized upper castes began acquiring customs and habits which were not dissimilar from those they had looked down upon. Another result was that the evils of upper caste Hindu society came to be regarded as evils of the entire society.

The form and pace of Westernization of India too varied from one region to another, and from one section of the population to another. For instance, one group of people became Westernized in their dress, diet, manners, speech, sports, and in the gadgets they used, while another absorbed Western science, knowledge, and literature remaining relatively free from Westernization in externals. It is clear that such a distinction cannot be a hard and fast one, but one of relative emphasis. It has to be made, however, in order to distinguish different types of Westernization which obtained among the different groups in the country.

In Mysore State, for instance, the Brahmins led the other castes in Westernization. This was only natural as the Brahmins possessed a literary tradition, and, in addition, many of them stood at the top of the rural economic hierarchy as landowners. (Formerly, it was customary to give land to Brahmins as an act of charity. Distinguished Brahmin administrators were also given gifts of land.) They were the first to sense the arrival of new opportunities following the establishment of British rule, and left their natal villages for cities such as Bangalore and Mysore in order to obtain the benefit of English education, and indispensable passport to employment under the new dispensation.

Though the scholarly tradition of the Brahmins placed them in a favourable position for obtaining the new knowledge, in certain other matters they were the most handicapped in the race for Westernization. This was especially so in the South where the large majority of them were vegetarians and abstained from alcoholic liquor. Also, the fear of being polluted prevented them from eating cooked food touched by others, and from taking up occupations considered defiling. To orthodox Brahmins the Englishman who ate pork and beef, drank whisky, and smoked a pipe, was the living embodiment of ritual impurity. On the other hand, the Englishman had political and economic power, for which he was feared, admired, respected, and disliked.

The net result of the Westernization of the Brahmins was that they interposed themselves between the British and the rest of the native population. The result was a new and secular caste system super-imposed on the traditional system, in which the British, the New Kshatriyas, stood at the top, while the Brahmins occupied the second position, and the others stood at the base of the pyramid. The Brahmins looked up to the British, and the rest of the people looked up to both the Brahmins and the British. The fact that some of the values and customs of the British were opposed to some Brahminical values made the situation confusing. However, such a contradiction has always been implicit, though not in such a pronounced manner, in the caste system. Kshatriya and Brahminical values have always been opposed to some extent, and in spite of the theoretical superiority of the Brahmin to all the other castes, the Kshatriya, by virtue of the political (and through it the economic) power at his disposal, has throughout exercised a dominant position. The super-imposition of the British on the caste system only sharpened the contrast.

The position of the Brahmin in the new hierarchy was crucial. He became the filter through which Westernization reached the rest of Hindu society in Mysore. This probably helped Westernization as the other castes were used to imitating the ways of the Brahmins. But while the Westernization of the Brahmins enabled the entire Hindu society to Westernize, the Brahmins themselves found some aspects of Westernization, such as the British diet, dress, and freedom from pollution, difficult to accept. (Perhaps another caste should not have found them so difficult. The Coorgs, for instance, took quite easily to British diet and dress, and certain activities like dancing, hunting and sports.)

The Brahmins of Mysore are divided into *vidikas* or priests, and *laukikas* or the laity, and a similar distinction seems to obtain among the Brahmins in other parts of India. It is only the *vidikas* who follow the priestly vocation while the *laukikas* follow other and secular occupations. Ritually, the priests are higher than the laity, but the fact that the latter frequently enjoyed economic and political power gave them a superior position in secular contexts. British rule widened further the gulf between the two, for it provided the laity with numerous opportunities to acquire wealth and power. And one of the long-term effects of British rule was to increase the secularization of Indian life. The secularization as well as the widening of the economic horizon pushed the priests into a lower position than before. Also traditional Sanskrit learning did not have either the prestige, or yield the dividends, which Western education did. The priests began by being aggressive towards the Westernized laity, but gradually, as the numbers of the latter increased, they were thrown more and more on the defensive. Worse was to follow when the priests themselves started becoming Westernized. They wanted electric lights, radios, and water taps in their houses. They began riding cycles. The leather seat of the cycle was considered defiling, and so it was at first covered with the pure and sacred deerskin. In course of time the deerskin was discarded and the "naked" leather seat was used. Tap water was objected to at first as the water had to pass through a leather washer, but in time even this objection was set aside. Finally, the priests started sending their sons to Western-type schools, and this frequently meant that there was none in the family to continue the father's occupation.

There is, however, another tendency in modern India which is buttressing the position and authority of the priests. Educated and Westernized Indians are showing some interest in Sanskrit and in ancient Indian culture, and in the country at large, politicians are frequently heard stressing the importance of Sanskritic learning. Pandit Nehru's *Discovery of India* has started many a young man on a similar journey into the country's past. Also, many Westerners have suddenly begun discovering new virtues in India, Indians, and Indian culture, and this has resulted in more Indians wanting to seek a better acquaintance with their culture.

The Westernization of the Brahmins of Mysore brought about a number of changes in their life. There was a change in their appearance and dress. The tuft gave way to cropped hair and the traditional dress gave place, at least partially, to Western-type dress and shoes. The change in dress marked a gradual weakening of ideas regarding ritual purity. For instance, formerly, eating was a ritual act, and a Brahmin had to wear ritually pure robes while eating or serving a meal. This meant wearing either a freshly-washed cotton dhoti, or a silk dhoti, and a pure upper cloth. Wearing a shirt was taboo. But as Western clothes became more popular Brahmin men sat to dinner with their shirts on. And today, dining at a table is becoming common among the rich.

Formerly, the morning meal was offered to the domestic deity before being served to the members of the family, and all the male members who had donned the sacred thread performed a few ritual acts before beginning the meal. Nowadays, however, many Brahmins have discarded the sacred thread, though the *upanayana* ceremony at which the thread is donned still continues to be performed. And it is only at formal dinners where the orthodox are present that certain ritual acts are performed before eating. Where people eat at a table, purification with a solution of cowdung is no longer done.

The Brahmin dietary has been enlarged to include certain vegetables which were formerly forbidden, such as onion, potato, carrot, radish, and beetroot. Many eat raw eggs for health reasons and consume medicines which they know to be made from various organs of animals. But meat-eating is even now rare, while the consumption of Western alcoholic liquor is not as rare. Cigarettes are common among the educated.

The Brahmins have also taken to new occupations. Even in the thirties, the Brahmins showed a reluctance to take up trade or any occupation involving manual work. But they were driven by the prevalent economic depression to take up new jobs, and World War II completed this process. Many Brahmins enlisted themselves in the army and this effected a great change in their habits and outlook. Before World War II, young men who wanted to go to Bombay, Calcutta, or Delhi in search of jobs had to be prepared for the opposition of their elders. But the postwar years found young men not only in all parts of India, but outside too. There was a sudden expansion in the geographical and social space of the Brahmins. Formerly, Brahmins objected to becoming doctors as the profession involved handling men from all castes, including Untouchables, and corpses. This is now a thing of the past. A few educated Brahmins now own farms where

they raise poultry. One of them even wants to have a piggery.

Over seventy years ago, the institution of brideprice seems to have prevailed among some sections of Mysore Brahmins. But with Westernization, and the demand it created for educated boys who had good jobs, dowry became popular. The better educated a boy, the larger the dowry his parents demanded for him. The age at which girls married shot up. Over twenty-five years ago it was customary for Brahmins to marry their girls before puberty. Nowadays, urban and middle class Brahmins are rarely able to get their girls married before they are eighteen, and there are many girls above twenty who are unmarried. Child widows are rare, and shaving the heads of widows is practically a thing of the past.

There has been a general secularization of Hindu life in the last one hundred and fifty years, and this has especially affected the Brahmins whose life was permeated with ritual. The life of no other caste among Hindus was equally ritualized. One of the many interesting contradictions of modern Hindu social life is that while the Brahmins are becoming more and more Westernized, the other castes are becoming more and more Sanskritized. In the lower reaches of the hierarchy, castes are taking up customs which the Brahmins are busy discarding. As far as these castes are concerned, it looks as though Sanskritization is an essential preliminary to Westernization. . . .

In the case of some festivals only the name is common all over India and everything else is different—the same name connotes different things to people in different regions. Similarly each region has its own body of folklore about the heroes of the *Ramayana* and *Mahabharata,* and not infrequently, epic incidents and characters are related to outstanding features of local geography. And in every part of India are to be found Brahmins who worship the local deities which preside over epidemics, cattle, children's lives, and crops, besides the great gods of all-India Hinduism. It is not unknown for a Brahmin to make a blood-sacrifice to one of these deities through the medium of a non-Brahmin friend. Throughout Indian history Sanskritic Hinduism has absorbed local and folk elements and their presence makes easier the further absorption of similar elements. The absorption is done in such a way that there is a continuity between the folk and the theological or philosophical levels, and this makes possible both gradual transformation of the folk layer as well as the "vulgarization" of the theological layer.

In the foregoing essay I have stated that it looks as though for the non-Brahmin castes of Mysore, Sanskritization is an essential preliminary to Westernization. I wish to stress here that this is a matter of empirical observation only, and does not refer to any logical necessity for Sanskritization occurring prior to Westernization. It is possible that Westernization may occur without an intermediate process of Sanskritization. This may happen to groups and individuals living in the cities as well as to rural and tribal folk; and it is especially likely to happen under the swift industrialization contemplated by the Five-Year Plans. Increasing Westernization will also mean the greater secularization of the outlook of the people and this, together with the movement towards a "classless and casteless society" which is the professed aim of the present government, might mean the disappearance of Hinduism altogether. To the question of whether the threat to religion from Westernization is not common to all countries in the world and not something peculiar to

Hinduism, the answer is that Christianity and Islam are probably better equipped to withstand Westernization because they have a strong organization whereas Hinduism lacks all organization, excluding the caste system. If and when caste disappears, Hinduism may also disappear, and it is hardly necessary to point out that the present climate of influential opinion in the country is extremely hostile to caste. Even those who are extremely sceptical of the effectiveness of the measures advocated to do away with caste consider industrialization and urbanization to be effective solvents of caste in the long run. The question is, how long is the run going to be? A warning must, however, be uttered against the facile assumption that caste is going to melt like butter before Westernization. The student of caste is impressed with its great strength and its capacity to adjust itself to new circumstances. It is salutary to remember that during the last hundred years or more, caste became stronger in some respects. Westernization has also in some ways favoured Sanskritization. The assumption of a simple and direct opposition between the two and of the ultimate triumph of Westernization, I find too simple a hypothesis, considering the strength of caste as an institution and the great complexity of the processes involved.

It is necessary to underline the fact that Sanskritization is an extremely complex and heterogeneous concept. It is even possible that it would be more profitable to treat it as a bundle of concepts than as a single concept. The important thing to remember is that it is only a name for a widespread social and cultural process, and our main task is to understand the nature of these processes. . . .

Kiyomi Morioka

CONTEMPORARY CHANGES IN JAPANESE RELIGION

I.

According to the latest statistics (1962), there are 402 religious groups in Japan. These can be ordered into four major categories: 153 Shinto, 175 Buddhist, 43 Christian, and 31 miscellaneous groups. The largest among them, Shrine Shinto, claims 79 thousand local bodies and 52 million parishioners; the smallest, by contrast, Tenshin-kyo, is reported to have but 5 local units and 43 adherents. Shinto is the indigenous religion of Japan, whilst Buddhism came to ancient Japan through China and Korea. Christianity was also brought from the outside, in the latter half of the sixteenth and again in the latter half of the nineteenth centuries. The miscellaneous groups have syncretistic doctrines which contain elements derived from two, and sometimes more, religious traditions.

During the Second World War, the Japanese government compelled amalgamations between religious groups; it granted official approval only to 13 Shinto, 28 Buddhist, and 2 Christian bodies. After the war, however, the removal of governmental control over religion led to a rapid increase in the number of independent religious groups, most of which had been forcibly organ-

Written especially for this anthology.

ised into larger ones or had gone underground. The postwar confusion, deprivation, and inflation induced anxiety and frustration in the Japanese. The need for new religious movements was met by the development of a great number of bodies of different kinds.

How large is the religious population of Japan? The latest governmental statistics (1962) record 78 million Shintoists, 65 million Buddhists, 5 million miscellaneous, and 900 thousand Christians, a total of *circa* 148 million. This total is more than one and one half times the estimated national population of 1962. How can we account for this great discrepancy?[1]

One cause is that each religious group tends to include even "dormant"[2] and hypothetical adherents[3] in its estimate of the faithful, especially when it publishes its statistics—despite its awareness of the

[1]According to the Japanese National Character Survey (1961) by the Institute of Statistical Mathematics, only 35% of Japan's adult population are estimated to hold a religious faith. If we take this fact into consideration, the discrepancy becomes much greater.

[2]Joseph H. Fichter, *Social Relations in the Urban Parish,* University of Chicago Press, 1954.

[3]By hypothetical adherents we mean members of a shrine community or the household members of a believer who are not believers themselves but presumed to convert soon by the authority of a religious body.

fairly exact number of its active members. For example, the Sôka-gakkai, the largest of the tightly organised contemporary Japanese religious associations, claims 4 million households in 1964, but is estimated to have 2 million active members. Another significant factor is dual or multiple membership. If an individual belongs to two or more different religious groups at the same time, the national total of adherents is likely to exceed the total actual population, even if reports to the Ministry of Education (which deals with religious statistics) are entirely accurate.

Dual membership is most typically and widely observed between Buddhism and Shrine Shinto. The state formerly regarded Shrine Shinto not as a religion but as the Japanese national ideology, with rituals to be observed by every citizen regardless of his own religious creed. The special position given to Shrine Shinto accentuated its religiosity, which culminated in the Emperor Cult. After the war, the institutional tie between the state and Shrine Shinto was abolished, overnight. We can now treat Shrine Shinto as a religion in competition with the others; affiliation with Shrine Shinto and another religion concurrently constitutes dual membership in the full sense of the term.

II.

The national union of Shrine Shinto consists of nearly 80 thousand local shrine communities each of which has a shrine as its center.[4] The deities enshrined there are believed to protect the community; it follows that all residents of the community are regarded as parishioners of the shrine. At the same time, however, virtually all the residents are affiliated

with particular Buddhist temples. The temples in question are not necessarily located within the community. Further, all Buddhists in the same community do not belong to the same temple; rather, neighbours belong separately to a number of different temples, whose parishioners are not confined to the one community.[5] A Buddhist temple has no territory, whereas a Shinto shrine does. Temple affiliation contains an element of choice. Although both are tradition-bound, and the membership unit is a household rather than an individual, they differ in group structure. The shinto shrine—to follow Joachim Wach's terminology—is based on a natural (territorial) principle and the Buddhist temple is a specifically religious group.[6] This significant difference between a shrine community and a temple parish suggests that dual membership means much more than mere duplication.

It now seems reasonable to ask why most Japanese hold dual membership in Shinto and Buddhism. Put differently, why do these two religions co-exist peacefully? First, there is little possibility of doctrinal conflict. Shrine Shinto, based upon traditional folk belief, has no doctrinal system worthy of the name. Buddhism, on the other hand, has created a special doctrine which proclaims the ultimate identity of Shinto deities and Buddhist holy figures. Japanese history does contain a few cases which are exceptions to this generalisation. Shin-Buddhism, which is monotheistic, during a period of rapid growth and extension came into serious conflict with Shinto in the seventeenth century. Shinto, as an integral part of community life, could not be abolished by Shin-Buddhism. During

[4]In Japan, "shrine" means always a Shinto building, while "temple" means its Buddhist counterpart.

[5]The sect affiliation of temples rarely reflects the class structure of the community, but often the existence of several lineage groups and other forms of sectional differentiation.

[6]J. Wach, *Sociology of Religion,* University of Chicago Press, 1944.

the opening years of the Meiji period, additionally, aggressive Shintoists persecuted Buddhist priests and temples. This persecution on the level of the elite (and the state) was hardly followed by popular antagonism; the common people needed both temple and shrine, Buddhism and Shinto, in either a mixed or separate form.

Second, the functions of Shrine Shinto and Buddhism are generally co-ordinated and complementary. Buddhism was accepted by the people at large in a way which involved no conflict with their traditional religion; the division of labour or harmonious co-existence of the two produced no doctrines which could legitimate any antagonism. How, then, are their functions differentiated? As John F. Embree has shown,[7] the festival calendar of the Shinto shrine reflects community concerns for social value and community welfare and maintains the solidarity of the local group and its common beliefs and sentiments. By contrast, a Buddhist priest deals with the ultimate frustration and social dislocation caused by death; he helps his parishioners to a sense of security and protection by conducting funeral services and the subsequent rituals of ancestor worship. The ritual of the shrine is for the whole community; the Buddhist service is for parishioner households. The former is for this-worldly prosperity; the latter is of other-worldly concern. The sense of security fostered by the former invokes the interdependence of living neighbours, that afforded by the latter rests on the continuity of the family over generations.

Conflict can occur among Buddhist groups or between Buddhist priests of the same or different sect affiliation,

particularly in the course of proselytization. The impracticability of a division of labour among the Buddhists accounts for this sort of conflict. However, a group like Shugen in the Edo Period (1603–1867), and some famous temples like Narita-san near Tokyo, have functioned in the intermediate area between Shinto shrines and ordinary Buddhist temples. Their main aim has been prayer for the prosperity in this world of the individual household. In these cases, a certain division of labour between the temples is apparent; the one organises funeral services and the other prayer. (The tie between a prayer temple and its worshippers is loose, contact is infrequent and rather impersonal; we excluded the prayer temple from our discussion of dual membership.) It is among funeral temples, therefore, that a division of labour is impracticable, not between funeral temples and prayer temples, or even between prayer temples each specialising in different prayers. In view of the open and covert conflict among funeral temples, the Tokugawa Shogunate prohibited priests from competing for more adherents. In order to eliminate Christianity, the priests were made registrars, the officials who registered birth, marriage and death for the parishioners; this made a change of temple affiliation extremely difficult. After the Meiji Restoration (1868), governmental protection and interference were withdrawn, and the Buddhist groups themselves agreed to refrain from competing with one another.

Lack of competition, and the efforts to avoid possible conflict, reflects the high evaluation of personal harmony which is one of the characteristics of Japanese culture. This is not a reflection of that sort of tolerance which could emerge after centuries of brutal warfare among religions. By maintaining the boundaries of their domains, the groups

[7]John F. Embree, "Some Social Functions of Religion in Rural Japan," *American Journal of Sociology* 57 (Sept., 1941), 184–189.

and priests escaped the possible consequences of excessive competition, but there ensued, necessarily, a compartmentalisation and rigidification on the level of both doctrine and organisation. The universalistic elements in Buddhism were excluded, and Buddhism's peculiar vitality—its ability to free people from community and tradition—was almost totally lost. A Buddhist ethic did not develop; instead, Buddhism became a mere prop to the existing social order and to the traditional value system.

Dual membership, observable everywhere in rural and traditional Japan, can be seen in the religious objects found in individual households. A household keeps a family Buddhist altar, where Buddha and the family's ancestral spirits are enshrined, and a family Shinto altar for charms distributed by the local shrine and the Ise Grand Shrine; meanwhile, charms issued by prayer temples are posted on the walls and pillars of the house. It is clear that these three sorts of religious object have different meanings. On the whole they do have a protective role in the household and they support the traditional Japanese family system.

III.

New elements entered the scene in the course of Japan's modernisation, since the 1870's. One was Christianity. The propagation of Catholicism began again, mainly in Kyushu, and Protestant missions from the U.S.A. developed vigorously in the cities. The spread of Christianity created serious tensions with Shinto and Buddhism. Although it was assumed in the 1880's that the whole country would be converted to Christianity before long, the transcendent idea of God was quite foreign to the Japanese and prevented a widespread acceptance of Christianity. It was limited to a small number of intellectuals, professionals and students.

Another new element was constituted by the new religions which appeared at the end of the Edo Period and were approved by the Meiji government as independent groups under the category of Sectarian Shinto. They claimed the right to officiate at the burial services for their converts, and came into conflict with the Buddhist clergy. They did meet the growing need for salvation in this world, which both a community-bound Shinto and a frigidified Buddhism failed to satisfy. A leading Sectarian Shinto group, Tenri-kyo, won converts rapidly from the lower class, especially in the periods of depression following the 1890's. The founders of Sectarian Shinto were attributed by their followers, under the stress of conflict, poverty and illness, with charismatic powers. In the course of the growth and stabilisation of these groups, bureaucratisation took place; so did an ethical emphasis which included the new value of public service as well as the more traditional one of filial piety.

IV.

After the Peace Treaty of 1956, a marked increase in industrialisation and urbanisation changed some aspects of Japanese religious life. In the cities, the notion that a Shinto shrine has a territory of its own is still held only by the old-timers who have lived in their neighborhood over generations and who participate in the shrine's annual festivals. The majority of immigrants to the neighborhood, who commute for work outside it, are generally indifferent towards the shrine; all that can be asked of them is a modest financial contribution. The old-timers are affiliated with particular

Buddhist temples which perform funeral services; immigrants, especially newcomers, have no temple affiliation except in their place of origin. The shrine community does not make much sense for those whose loyalty has been shifted from the community to the work place; similarly, the temple is meaningless for those who lack ancestors requiring priestly services. Buddhist priests both in cities and in the countryside, despite the minimal possibility of conflict, do not approach the migrants—chiefly due to their (the priests') lack of experience of active proselytization. Cities and even suburbs with their rapidly growing populations have become religious deserts; it was in this vacuum that new postwar religions were successful in making converts.

Risshôkôsei-kai and Sôka-gakkai, offshoots of Buddhism, may be considered representative of the new postwar religions, in the sense that they have expanded astonishingly since 1950. They provide a doctrine of salvation which is considered a modern interpretation of Buddhism. The values they assert appeal to the ordinary Japanese who suffered the loss of long-cherished values at Japan's surrender in 1945. As a result of rapid expansion, they have a huge organisation from which a believer can derive a sense of security. They also provide small face-to-face discussion groups which satisfy psychological needs for expression and response. These organisational characteristics are particularly significant for those who are uprooted from their native places and who do not belong to large organisations like business corporations or labour unions. It is not surprising that these new religions are thought to cater to housewives, and to owners and employees of middle and small scale business who are easily disturbed by economic fluctuation.

In the course of their expansion, these groups necessarily disturbed the vested interests of existing Buddhist groups. Sôka-gakkai and Risshôkôsei-kai represent, respectively, two contrasting attitudes in this situation. The former is condemnatory of other religions and demands of its converts that they discard their earlier religions completely. The latter manifests a compromising attitude and allows its followers to keep their ties with their earlier religions. This last attitude is continuous with Japanese tradition, and the more exclusive one is rather atypical, if not entirely new. It should be noted that the success of Sôka-gakkai has been most marked in the religious desert, where religion has come to mean hardly more than outmoded ritual practices and an obsolete form of entertainment.

Martin E. Marty

SECTS
AND CULTS

ABSTRACT: Sects and cults constitute a third Christian force, in addition to Protestantism and Roman Catholicism, in contemporary America. Sects are particularist groups with a basically negative orientation. Cults tend to be positively oriented and to be organized around a charismatic leader. Any discussion of the various religious groups in the United States must take into account the differences in context, rather than the differences in content, between them. Religious context largely determines whether or not religious groups are in the mainstream of historical development. The principal distinction between sects or cults and denominations is that sects or cults are established to achieve the spatial and psychic context of isolation. The denominations currently adapt to middle-class beliefs and values. The sects and cults are uneroded, unexposed, intransigent, and withdrawn. They provide a haven from social interpenetration and complexity. They do not wish to be assimilated into the mainstream of religious thought and practice. The sects and cults, in almost every particular, provide a counter current in the mid-twentieth century religious revival—Ed.

The conventional tripartite division of American religion into Protestant, Roman Catholic, and Jewish has been widely criticized for its neatness and its limitations. The Eastern Orthodox churches obviously do not fit into any of the divisions. There are millions of Americans who either adhere to a great world religion other than Christianity or Judaism or profess a secular religion of humanism or ultimate devotion to democratic processes. This sixfold division still does not do justice to the inclusiveness of organized religion in America. A large and growing cluster of denominations and forces, most of them of Christian orientation, do not find recognition within Protestantism nor do they wish to be numbered with classic reformed churches.

Reprinted from The Annals of The American Academy of Political and Social Science, CCCXXXII (November 1960), pp. 125–134. By permission of author and publisher.

Third Force

This cluster, which we here refer to without derogation as sects and cults, has assumed sufficient proportions for the president of a large interdenominational seminary to call national attention to them as being a "third force" in Christianity in America. The first two forces, of course, are Protestantism and Roman Catholicism. President Henry Pitney Van Dusen—in the interest of a theology centered on witness to the Holy Spirit—is surprisingly positive in his regard for this force. He finds it primarily in the "Spirit-centered" churches, that is, the Pentecostal and Holiness bodies.

The current growth and fluidity of pattern among these sects and cults runs counter to many of the major trends in the revival of religion which has followed the Second World War. These groups have made it necessary to alter the conventional ways of thinking about churches as institutions in order to understand the appeal and classification of religious feeling to which the sect is a response. Traditional categories still are useful but they fail to account adequately for the context in which sects and cults appear today.

The Mainstream

The first and most obvious observation about the sects and cults is that they do not conform. A survey of the twelve major histories of American religion or American Protestantism—from Robert Baird in 1844 to Jerald C. Brauer in 1953 —confirms suspicions garnered from less disciplined reading: historians and sociologists as well as laymen have evolved certain ways of classifying American religious groups according to whether or not they belong to the mainstream of the nation's experience. The categories do not always follow the lines one would expect. "Stream" is not a static category, and groups once in the mainstream at another time may be out of it. "Mainstream" is Ralph Henry Gabriel's term, but it is matched by Leonard Bacon's distinction between groups only "incidentally connected" with the history of American Christianity and others which are organically connected. William Warren Sweet, the dean of modern historians in this field, speaks of "indigenous" and of "typically American" churches. Andrew Drummond speaks of "Americanized" and "definitely American" churches. Each lacks precision in defining the mainstream, but all twelve remarkably agree on what belongs in it.

Statistical data, for example, do not explain the place of denominations in the mainstream. Many mainstream groups are no larger than the Pentecostals, but the Pentecostals do not belong. Never

in American religious history has size, that most American form of measurement, explained the national significance of a religion. Roman Catholicism, Lutheranism, and continental Reformed groups were of relatively immense size before they came to be accepted in the mainstream. Similarly, attempts on the basis of polity to distinguish denominations that belong from sects and cults which do not belong have been unsatisfactory. Episcopalianism has been considered by many historians, particularly in the past, to have a nondemocratic polity. Methodism also has been seen in this light. But both were considered to be as much a part of the American scene as were the Baptist and Congregational bodies.

Class distinctions provide some explanation, just as they have in classic writing on sects. But while membership in denominations might vary along classic economic and social lines from Episcopalian to Unitarian affiliation among the wealthy and influential classes to Methodist and Baptist affiliation among the lower classes, lower class identification did not by any means exclude a body from the mainstream, certainly not since the age of Jackson. The churches which historically served the disinherited and uninfluential elements in society might still be in the mainstream. Theological generalizations, references to the substance and the content of the faith, provide almost no help in forming a generalization, although a century ago the evangelical bodies were squarely in the mainstream and the bodies which were not evangelical—Roman Catholic, Universal, Shaker, socialist—were insecure.

Context, not Content

The approach which this article takes to the position of sects and cults in the present scene is that factors other than those which classically have determined ecclesiastical institutional life are operative in America. Internal conditions, matters of content, are of secondary importance. The degree of religious comprehension in the lives of adherents, the claims made on their devotion, the tenacity with which they hold the church's tenets, the theological acumen, the richness of worship, all factors that are important in generalizing about most of historical Western Christendom, are secondary in American life. Instead, certain external conditions, matters of context, are of primary importance.

In this light, new distinctions emerge which help in the present task of understanding sects. There have been historic transformations. Until the modern period of realized pluralism, national origin was significant; to be of Anglo-Saxon provenance was of great help. Thus, a review of American churches in 1836 by Reed and Matheson provides the clue:

Blot out Britain and America from the map of the world, and you destroy all those great institutions which almost exclusively promise the world's renovation; but unite Britain and America in energetic and resolved cooperation for the world's salvation; and the world is saved.

Conversely, less than a century ago historian Daniel Dorchester could speak of Germans and Irish immigrants as having . . . low habits and ideas, retaining supreme allegiance to a foreign pontiff, or controlled by radical, rationalistic, materialistic, or communistic theories. . . . Can religion and morality endure the severe strain and the virtue and intelligence of the people be preserved?

Needless to say, these ethnic distinctions have largely disappeared.

Other almost mystic accidents of national history contribute to uncritical historical generalizations on the location of denominations. Historic identifica-

tion with the religion of New England guaranteed a place to bodies like the Congregationalists which saw their relative size diminish but their symbolism on greeting card covers offer a guarantee of security. Identification with the struggles of religious liberty and voluntarism stood Baptists, Quakers, and some others in good stead. Participation in the major movements of national religious life—expansion through the frontiers, the involvement in successive great awakenings or revivals of religion—enhanced denominational claims.

The result of the foregoing for the discussion of sects is this: Americans tend to classify denominations in relation to their typical or mainstream status by a set of subtle contextual norms. Most of them revolve around the dialogue of American churches with their environment. The more exposed a group has been or becomes, the more its claims are eroded by its place in a pluralist society, the more it has been seen in harmony with main themes of national history, that much more does it belong. The more isolated, intransigent, withdrawn, the less exposed and eroded a group has been, no matter what its size and influence, the less it has come to be regarded as a normative religious expression for America. The largest remaining body of unexposed believers belong to what is known as sects and cults, and they can best be accounted for and located by this approach.

Particularism

Why are sects and cults of third-force Christianity and its fringes growing so rapidly today? What is their reason for existence? What part will they play in the future? These questions raise theologically and sociologically perplexing problems. The widespread observation that ideologies are being diffused and even buried today—as argued by Daniel Boorstin and Daniel Bell—in politics, philosophy, and religion, is countered by the spurts of energy and growth of religious groups who make much of their different and, sometimes, completely esoteric systems of belief. The tendencies to homogenize religious beliefs and groups, so ably chronicled by Will Herberg, William Lee Miller, Stanley Rowland, G. Roy Eckardt, and others, seem relevant until one encounters the growing sects and cults. The temptation of Americans to cancel the varieties of religious experience and institutional options with apathy—probably as a reaction against bewildering evidences of pluralism and competition of claims—is evident and can be documented. People are identified with religious institutions, but they lack apparent conviction or passion. Yet the sects and cults refuse to participate in this oversimplification of a pluralist heritage. They noisily assert their particularities even at the sacrifice of participation in inclusive American religious institutional *Gestalten*.

These basically religious considerations disturb those who try to classify nonmainstream sects and cults, but sociological factors further complicate the picture. Social historians depict the affluent society as one in which the masses have attained the historic status and have acquired the historic values of the middle classes. America has become, in its prosperity, a pan-middle class society. Its religions, no matter what their historic origins, tend to take on appropriate characteristics. The obvious examples would be the lavish institutional outlays of the large urban Southern Baptist churches in which a plush setting and the current technological devices serve groups which derive their historic warrant for existence

from their disinherited positions. Yet the sects and cults are not dependent on middle class inclusiveness, and even where they succeed amidst relative prosperity, they do so without vital contact with the culture. Since World War II, the normative growth of American denominations has come about through their easy and uncritical identification with suburban value systems. Yet the sects and cults are not dependent on the situations which make mere belonging to a religious organization so attractive.

Thus, paradoxically, the sects and cults show most remarkable growth in a period during which most documented social and theological factors and events seem to contradict their claims. This necessitates revision not only of historical observation but also of sociological classification. So significant an exception to the rule, while it may prove the rule, may also enlarge the definition of the rule. The late twentieth century conceptions of mainstream American denominations must be related to nontypical sects and cults.

Sect and Denomination

"Sect," in this context, is obviously not a translation of "denomination." One guide in the perplexing problem of locating sects today has been that "sect" has become a less satisfactory term for denoting what should be called, neutrally, "denominations." When the obsolete terminology appears it tends to be used by organized antiorganized-religion fronts or is used thoughtlessly. When *Life* magazine in 1957 referred to the Congregational Christian and Evangelical and Reformed bodies as sects, reaction was instant and significant. In our classification, the term is used without any sense of patronization or derogation. It is used in relation to groups which would readily accept some term to set themselves off from the typical or mainstream denominations which desire to be part of the nation's *mores* and its *ethos*. This does not mean that the sects in question want to be thought of as partial; ordinarily they do assert catholicity or wholeness; their witness is seen to be the hope of a rejecting world. But asserting this witness necessarily involves separation from other witnesses, and this separation is at the basis of the term "sect."

Dramatic Growth

It is not important or possible here to shed new light on the quest for statistical precision in discussing the non-mainstream groups. Statistics are, at best, relative; they are notoriously slippery when provided by religious groups. The quest is further complicated by the dynamism of sect growth and change—the process of fissiparation seems to be part of the essence of sect life—and by the fact that many sect and cult statistical summaries are kept secret. Finally, for strategic reasons, sects may feel called upon to exaggerate their size at moments when growth enhances a claim or to exaggerate their diminutiveness at moments when smallness seems to substantiate the theological and ethical correctness of a group's concerns. Suffice it here to say that the smaller sect-type bodies are, for the most part, experiencing dramatic growth against the pattern of middle class church identification. And economic support for the isolated groups is disproportionately higher than is that of the more prosperous, settled churches. Yet the marked and perhaps nervously exaggerated growth of Dr. Van Dusen's third force is not a necessary factor in the need to account for

its presence: the mere fact of survival would occasion this quest.

Sects and Cults

The thesis here is that negatively-oriented sects gain their current attractiveness from their attempt and relative success at isolating people from competing value systems; and that positively-oriented cults, usually gathered around charismatic persons or clans, succeed to the extent that they provide surrogates for interpersonal relations or attachment to significant persons in an apparently depersonalizing society. To the first group would belong sects like the historic Adventist bodies, some of the Churches of God, the primitive bodies, the Jehovah's Witnesses, the Pentecostals, the Assemblies of God, and other eschatological groups; to the second would belong the cults which offer substance in place of meaning. Among them would be the Peace Mission Movement of Father Divine; the "I Am" Movement, in some respects, the Oxford Group Movement; Unity School of Christianity; Theosophy; New Thought; and others.

The sects with an essentially negative orientation to the world were originally and in a different society organized around charismatic leaders, but they are not dependent on charisma for survival. A philosophy of history and an anti-world context are basic for them. The cults with an essentially positive orientation to the world and to material or substantial values need the presence of the charismatic leader, and they often flounder in the absence of charisma. Since the latter group, apart from fanatic devotion to the person of the founder, takes on characteristics of mainstream American religion in its substantial offers to a prosperous society, it is not necessary to account for them as an exception, and they will receive further consideration only when they illustrate the quest for surrogates for personality. It is the sect, then, that concerns us, and the cult concerns us only as it partakes of the character of the sect.

The Sect Phenomenon

"Sect" is etymologically closely related to what we are here calling "cult." That is, it does not derive from the Latin *secare, sectum,* to cut, as is commonly thought, but from the positive *sequi,* to follow. It should refer to "a group having in common a leader or a distinctive doctrine . . . a following," according to Webster's *New International Dictionary.* But origins do not explain present significance, and history and sociology displace etymology. The dictionary continues, "In religion, the believers in a particular creed, or upholders of a particular practice; . . . a party dissenting from an established church. . . . " This definition is of some use if we recall that establishment can belong as much to *ethos* and *mores* as it can to legal sanction.

The amiable neutrality of this definition has been displaced by attempts to establish "sect" as a distinct and distinctive category from "church" or even "denomination." The decisive and still most creative work in this respect, whatever its present-day limitations, has been done by Ernst Troeltsch and Max Weber. They describe the sect as essentially a society established by contract as opposed to the institutional and "natural" or organic ecclesiastical body. As they point out, success is one of the hazards of sectarian life, and many historic sects, in this sense, tend to take on the character of churches as they establish themselves in society. This

is true of Baptist and Congregational bodies in the Old World which came to predominance in the mainstream of the New. Weber and Troeltsch account for this in part by the quieting of religious fervor in the second generation, although a variety of political factors also play their part in post-Revolutionary developments. Troeltsch and Weber leave us in their debt for their attempt at isolating the meaning and historic purposes of sects. H. Richard Niebuhr produced the classic American work, *The Social Sources of Denominationalism,* written at a time when economic and social considerations played a much larger part than they currently do in theological setting. He stressed genesis and entry. One is born into the church, a "natural social grouping," but he must join the sect. The church is the automatic way for the individual to be located in religious society; the sect is the outlet for self-determination against the grain of religious or secular society. There are limitations to Niebuhr's distinction. People constantly are joining churches, and members of sects bear children into the sect. This led Niebuhr to point out that in the decisive sense a sect lasts only one generation. The deficiencies of Niebuhr's helpful work are apparent in the prolonged image of certain sects across the centuries and in the resuscitation and revivification of certain undying sectarian impulses whether they be of the classically negative sectarian or normatively positive cultic varieties. The Montanists illustrate the negative and the Gnostics illustrate the positive aspects of the tendency to recur. Ellsworth Faris, in *The Nature of Human Nature,* pointed beyond these definitions, but he did not fully develop the perceptive notion that the contemporary significance of such groups is their isolation in a modern world. A fourth useful and illuminating approach was Howard Becker's designation of the "ecclesia" as a compulsory group and the sect as a voluntary group. A denomination, according to Becker, is a sect in its later generations, and cult is personal, quasi-mystical religion. Joachim Wach made original contributions to the study of sects, particularly in the development of the idea that sects originate during times of change or collapse in old orders. Finally, Dietrich Bonhoeffer, in his sociological study of religion, made a point that in content there was no essential difference between church and sect. This leads us to pursue the contextual question for the illumination sect and cult bring to settled denominationalism. Rather than concentrate on many of the enduring features—charisms, emotions, positive and negative aspects, and so on—it is profitable in this limited context to stress one factor that accounts for sect importance today.

To isolate this factor it is necessary to develop a construct by which our whole society can be viewed.

Sectarian Isolation

One fruitful approach is the distinction between a society which can be described in diagrammatic terms and one dialogically defined. Or, to borrow the acute observation of the Jesuit scholar Walter J. Ong: spatial metaphors are largely obsolete for depicting current forms of community and communication; interpersonal metaphors are decisive. The importance of the sect in what Faris calls its isolation will emerge against this setting.

All the spatial pictures—ward, ghetto, sector, valley, and, in its static sense, parish—are obsolete or becoming obsolete as approaches to the nurture of religion in a free society. Only a coercive society can depend upon spatial images and the realities to which they

point for nurture of ideology. The sect can be seen as a quasi-voluntaristic reaction against the erosion of spatial settings. What accounts for the change? When "inner direction" and "tradition direction" were real possibilities, the diagrammatic way of looking at the human community was feasible. People lived in physical and psychical independence of one another. Truth could be sustained and perpetuated by reference to the whole, local, undisturbed community.

Almost every documented feature of what it means to live in the modern world militates against perpetuation of the spatial relation. Population growth has removed both actual and psychic distance between peoples who hold to different ultimate or even proximate value systems. The extreme mobility of modern life brings people into new contact both in their geographical, horizontal movements and in vertical class adjustments. Men have long known nomadism, but nomads of today move not as clans but as individuals; they do not carry community religious patterns with them. Transportation advances, the juxtaposition of ideologies, and, most of all, the interruption of all spatial illusions and realities by instantaneous, efficient, and total means of mass communication render the diagrammatic approach impossible as a permanent strategy. That this interruption has obvious assets is clear. Few modern men would ignore or undo these factors of modernity. At the same time, much restlessness, rootlessness, and anxiety have come to light in recent years.

Religious groups in America, particularly the mainstream groups, provide little buffer against the jostling which the interpersonal world has brought. Denominations which adapt and conform to the value systems of a middle-class society become the captives of it: their distinctiveness erodes and their particularity is muffled. This means that anyone who seeks refuge from easy identification with a casually this-worldly religiousness must move in one of two directions.

One possibility is for him to accept a religious constellation which in part affirms the world and tells him that not all the stimuli he receives from his environment are harmful to his religious development. This amounts to agreeing that his milieu is, after all, God's workshop. And that dialogue with the environment can be a revelatory and redemptive experience. Many of the most noted Christian theologians are seeking to prove the truth, or Biblical warrant, of this position. Nurture, however, remains complicated in such a setting; theology must be transferable and almost, we might say, portable. It is easy in such a conjunction of religion and world to see rapid dissipation of religious energies and relapse into unsatisfying identification with the restless contemporaneity which the individual sought to escape.

The sectarian possibility is for the individual to seek a group whose philosophy of history contradicts the existing values so dramatically that the group sustains itself at least through a generation. The comfort, the appeal, and the sanction of the sect, in this instance, are that it provides surrogates for insularity through apparent psychic if not always possible physical distance from worldliness and competing systems. The sect provides the illusion and sometimes the reality of a buttress against encroaching and eroding forces which contradict personal beliefs. The sect organizes itself, if not in physical spatial contradistinction from other groups, at least in psychological distinction and distance.

Thus, modern sects remain segregated in varying degrees with little contact beyond their own organization. This is unlike almost all other social groupings today where a mass society creates an apparent availability of prosperity to all. The sects sometimes actually are nomadic, preserving community by moving. A Milwaukee fundamentalist group followed its pastor to the southwest. Some sects achieve isolation by walling themselves in. An extreme apocalyptic cult in Arizona did this. Ordinarily, mass media of communication are criticized and motion pictures, picture magazines, and television barred by a sect because of their dialogical interruption of temporarily sustained barriers. The consciousness that the group's philosophy of history runs counter to all that the world and established religious groups offer helps cultivate the feeling of isolation.

Authentic Simplification

One of the obvious appeals of the sect in the modern world is comparable to the appeal of monasticism. Despite the fact that both set high standards and that the calling makes demands of discipline, rigor, or Puritan zeal which would be unattractive to the hedonistic escapist, both sectarianism and monasticism provide authentic simplifications of an overly complex society. In this sense, sectarianism is a form of escape from complication. For some sects this may eventuate in a prideful relation to those outside; for others it develops an authentic humility and spirit of service which motivates missionary activity and seeks to serve those who do not and will not conceivably become part of the nurtured system of values. One thinks here of the historic peace churches insofar as they retain characteristics of the sect type. The cult in our usage differs in that it depends upon some withdrawal and isolation in order to offer not less but more in the middle of the world. Through esoteric and mystic approaches, substance is proffered instead of sacrifice being solicited. The cult offers some escape through attachment to the charismatic person at a time when a dialogical, interpersonal society tends to level and plane personality.

No attempt has been made here to account for the authentic religious vision in sects or even in cults. This is not because the vision is to be downgraded, but because it falls beyond the scope of social analysis. One authentic appeal of the sect is that it provides authority and usually a coherent system of beliefs and hopes, an attraction that cannot be denied in a time of confusion. But this appeal becomes important here only for the way in which it is sustained and nurtured: in prolongation of relative isolation.

Three Contexts

In the period before Christendom emerged as the entity which expressed interpenetration and interpermeation of church and world, symbolically until 313 A.D., the sect provided Christian distance from a pagan world, as in Montanism. In the period of Christendom, symbolically until the later eighteenth century, the sect provided Christian distance from establishment and complaisance, as in Waldensianism and Albigensianism. In the period of post-Christendom, the sect provides religious distance from religion. It displaces all philosophies of history and all leaderships but one. It is not difficult for the sect, as it relates to the Christian doctrine of the Holy Spirit, to claim primitive warrant for what it is doing. Most sects do this. It can point to an authentic prototype in early Christian disci-

pline. The theological question as to whether or not the sect is adequate in the post-Christendom constellation is basic to the choice people in a Christian culture make between church and sect.

Will the pressures of life in a society where the spatial metaphor seems doomed by the factors essential to modernity also doom the sects? If the factors themselves dissipate, sectarian impulses may be prolonged. If the ideologies of the sects prevail, the impulse will be transformed, perhaps into churchliness. If a sect could attain coercive powers in a community, it could nurture life based on the diagrammatic assumption. None of these three possibilities seems worthy of serious speculation to anyone outside the sects. Yet the sectarian impulse, having survived in the West in at least three basic concatenations of circumstance, would, no doubt, erupt in surprising and durable new ways. There seems to be a need in the hearts of many religious people for the preservation of distance from the world. In the present situation, the failure of communication between the sects and the churches doubtless contributes to the detriment of both. Yet the sects, with a calculation that goes beyond the rational to the profoundly instinctive, recognize that authentic communication means the beginning of the end of the diagrammatic or spatial construct they have succeeded in establishing or preserving in the contemporary world. Actual communication, in other words, could mean the death of the sect. The contribution of the sect to the larger society is, therefore, made best through the sympathetic observer who carries with him a picture of the advantages of particularity and assertiveness back to the world of dialogical complexity. It is, no doubt, through the publicists of the third force that its force might be felt on Christians and other religious people who easily accommodate themselves to an existing culture. On this level of interaction the sects and cults become socially important to those they do not directly attract and serve. It is on this level, the level of the sect in the culture of a world where spatial and psychic barriers have been removed for most people, that the discussion of sect and cult could move beyond Weber, Troeltsch, Niebuhr, and Wach. The resulting discussions of nurture and discipline could be meaningful in the study of education, politics, and the arts and sciences in a democratic society.

SECTION TWO

Implications of These Changes
for the Sociology of Religion

Charles E. Glock

THE RELIGIOUS
REVIVAL
IN AMERICA ?

Recent assessments of the state of religion in America appear curiously inconsistent. Some observers, a preponderance of them perhaps, perceive a major post-war revival in American religion.[1] Others, while agreeing that interest in religion has heightened in recent years, argue that the increase does not represent a revival so much as the continuation of a long term upward trend in the religiosity of Americans.[2] Still others contend to the contrary that the long term trend is towards the increasing secularization of American life.[3] And, most recently, the idea has been expressed that the remarkable quality of American religion over the last century and more has been its stability; there has been a propensity neither towards greater religiousness nor towards greater secularization.[4]

Not all of these assessments can be correct—or can they? The purpose of the present paper is to cast a critical eye on the attempts being made to assess the state of religion in America and hopefully, in the process, to afford some new perspectives for studying religion's place in American life.

Reprinted from Religion and the Face of America. Berkeley: 1958, pp. 25–42. By permission of the University of California.

[1]Will Herberg, *Protestant, Catholic and Jew,* Doubleday, 1955, 59–84.
[2]Michael Argyle, *Religious Behavior,* Routledge and Kegan Paul, 1958.

[3]William H. Whyte, Jr., *The Organization Man,* Simon and Schuster, 1956.
[4]Seymour M. Lipset, "Religion in America: What Religious Revival?" *Columbia University Forum,* II, 2, Winter, 1959.

These disagreements over whether or not a revival has in fact occurred and concerning the nature of the long term trend in American religiosity may simply be a result of some observers being mistaken and others being correct. This would appear to be a plausible conclusion, given the overtly contradictory assessments which have been made. On reflection, however, disagreement may stem from other factors. Religion is not necessarily the same thing to all men; perhaps, therefore, the source of the disagreement is that different observers are defining religion in different ways. Some may equate it with belief, others with practice, and still others with experience. If it should turn out that there has been an increase in one, a decline in the second, and no change in the third, much of the disagreement would be explained if not resolved.

A further possibility is that the observers agree on definitions but still disagree on what has happened because they adopt different criteria or indicators in making their assessments. Some may base their judgment on how many people go to church and others on how many so-called blue laws are still on the statute books. But even agreement here would not assure consensus, for there is still the evidence to consider, and different observers may turn to different evidence of the same indicator or interpret the same evidence in different ways. To sort out the pieces, some effort to order definitions, indicators, and evidence seems an obvious prerequisite.

Religiousness: Definitions, Indicators, and Evidence

Religion, religiousness, and religiosity are of a *genre* of words which appear almost to defy definition, at least in a way to which everyone will agree. One is tempted to suggest that there are as many definitions as there are people offering them. Yet, if we carefully examine the imagery which the words stimulate, it is not that people disagree on definitions so much as that they use these words, which are multidimensional in meaning, in a unidimensional way. They tend to equate religion with belief *or* with practise *or* with experience without recognizing consciously that the other dimensions exist. While it may not be possible to secure agreement on the importance of the dimensions, it is possible so specify what they are and, in so doing, to make manifest the different frames of reference within which the religiousness of an entity—whether it be a person, a religious group or some larger collective such as a nation or a society—may be observed and assessed.

For present purposes, it seems helpful to think of religiousness as a concept which is divisible into four dimensions: dimensions which we shall call the experiential, the ritualistic, the ideological and the consequential. Classifiable under the experiential dimension are all of those feelings, perceptions, and sensations which are experienced by an actor or defined by a religious group or a society as involving some communication, however slight, with a divine essence, i.e., with God, with ultimate reality, with transcendental authority. It is, in effect, spirituality—emotional experience defined as religious which in its extreme forms would be represented by conversion, the visitation of the Holy Spirit, mysticism.

The ideological dimension is constituted, in turn, by what people believe along religious lines rather than by what they feel. It includes all of those ideas which represent what is believed about the nature of divine or ultimate reality and its purpose. The designation of beliefs as religious may be made by an individual, by a religious group, by a society, or, if you will, by a social scientist.

The designations of one, to be sure, may not and probably will not always jibe with the designations of another. While these differences cannot be ignored, they need not concern us here. Our present interest is to indicate that belief is a dimension of religion, not to establish what makes a belief religious.

The ritualistic dimension bears on what people do of a religious nature rather than on what they feel or think. It comprises that group of activities which generally fall into the category of religious practice: worship, prayer, scripture reading, church membership and attendance, and the like.

The consequential, the last of our four dimensions, is different in kind from the first three. It deals with what people do and with the attitudes they hold as a consequence of their religious beliefs, practices and experiences. The notion of "works" in the theological meaning of the term is what is connoted here. The consequential dimension also differs from the others in that it deals with how man relates himself to man rather than with how he relates himself to God.

These dimensions, it is proposed, are the principal frames of reference which may be adopted in assessing religion or religiousness. The dimensions are interrelated rather than independent of one another and an assessment made within one dimension often implies an assessment in another. The dimensions are nevertheless a useful heuristic device for examining religious behavior.

It is not always possible to tell from the observation or assessment itself what dimension the observer has in mind. For example, we cannot tell the observer's frame of reference from his simple observation that "America is in the midst of a religious revival." He may be thinking along a single dimension or using some combination of the dimensions we have identified. Any attempt to be scientific about assessing the religious state of an individual or collective of some kind obviously requires that the observer make clear the dimension(s) that he is talking about. Any discussion of the religious revival, for example, requires that the discussants clarify whether they perceive the revival as occurring on one, several, or all of the four dimensions.

A further requirement is that the criteria or indicators of religiousness within a dimension also be cited. Indicators are simply the means used to locate objects within a dimension, i.e., to order them according to some degree of religiousness. The specification of the indicators constitutes, in effect, the observer's defining what he means by "religious" within a given dimension.

Two types of indicators may be distinguished: indicators of degree and indicators of kind. The notion of a religious revival implies a distinction in degree, namely, that America is more religious today than in the immediate past. Distinctions in kind may also be made within any dimension, though these are less relevant to a discussion of the so-called revival than are distinctions in degree. The statement, "Pentecostalists adhere to a fundamentalist theology (belief) whereas Congregationalists subscribe to a liberal theology (belief)," represents a distinction in kind made within the ideological dimension.

In our everyday conversation, we constantly use indicators to make distinctions within concepts. Some of the indicators which we use—feet and inches to represent height, pounds and ounces to represent weight, and miles per hour to represent speed—have the quality of being accepted virtually universally, at least in our society. Indicators of other concepts, on the other hand, are not universally agreed upon; in some instances, they may almost be private to an individual.

Friendliness, for example, is a concept

for which the indicators are neither precise nor widely agreed upon. It would be much easier to obtain consensus on how tall a person is than on how friendly he is. Actually, it is one of the functions of science—physical and social—to systematize the process of developing indicators and to develop a means—in the form of measuring instruments—for applying indicators. The measuring stick, the scale, and the speedometer are good examples of instruments developed to allow the uniform application of indicators for such concepts as height, weight, and speed. . . .

In the development of indicators of religion, we are at a stage much closer to where we stand with respect to developing indicators of friendliness than that of developing indicators of height. The problem has not been approached in a scientific way. Yet, underlying any observation about the religiousness of an entity are indicators which the observer implicitly, if not explicitly, has in mind. This is true of those with scholarly interests in religion as well as those who comment on religion in the course of ordinary conversation.

What, then, are some of the indicators commonly used? In pursuing an answer, we must deal separately with each of the dimensions, distinguish between indicators of degree and of kind, and consider how indicators may shift depending upon whether the referent is an individual, a religious group, or some large collective.

Indicators are most likely to be developed and to become agreed upon for those aspects of behavior which are directly observable. It is not surprising, therefore, that it is relatively easier to think of indicators for making distinctions within the ritualistic dimension than to conceive of indicators for the other dimensions. What people do ritually is more likely to be observable than their religious experiences or their beliefs.

On the consequential dimension, what people do may be observable but it is difficult to identify whether or not this is religiously motivated.

In turn, within the ritualistic dimension, it is around those practices which are the more observable that indicators are more likely to be developed. There are indicators on this dimension to tell us whether or not a person is religious, how religious he is, and also the way in which he is religious. Membership in a church is perhaps the most visible indicator of his ritual behavior and the one most commonly used to differentiate the religious from the non-religious person. Whether a person prays or not, reads scripture, participates in religious sacraments constitute other indicators for making judgments of religiousness. These same indicators are used to make distinctions in degree. Here, however, the judgment is likely to be based not only on what practices a person engages in but also how frequently.

It is more difficult to think of commonly used indicators of kind on this dimension. Whether a person attends a liturgical or non-liturgical church, prays in a kneeling or standing position, genuflects or not are possible indicators for making such distinctions, but they are not commonly used. On the individual level, distinctions in kind, as we shall shortly see, are more likely to be made on the ideological than on the ritualistic dimension.

The indicators used to make distinctions in the religiousness of collectives may be derived from accumulating information on individual behavior or from other sources. Religious groups may be distinguished by the degree to which their members adhere to the ritual practices laid down by the denomination. How religious a nation is on the ritualistic dimension may be indicated by what proportion of its population are church members. In both examples, the indicators are derived from accumulating information on individual behavior. Distinctions may also be made without attending to individual behavior. For example, churches tend to be distinguished, particularly within denominations, with respect to how high or low church they are in their religious practices.

Except in extreme cases, there is no direct way to observe what people are feeling religiously. Consequently, examples of indicators commonly used to make distinctions on the experiential dimension do not come to mind readily. Whether or not a person has had a conversion experience is a possible indicator. Some religious groups place great emphasis on this indicator, believing that only those who have been "born again" can be included in the elect. In some primitive tribes, epileptic seizures are interpreted as indicating religious experience and those having them are perceived as being peculiarly endowed with mana (spirit).

On the level of religious groups, the distinction we sometimes make between sect and church implies, among other things, that sect members experience or feel their religion in contrast to church members who are more prone to practice it. The indicators implicit in such distinctions are outward signs of emotional religious expression such as are frequently manifested at revival meetings. These, it is claimed, are much more characteristic of so-called sects than churches. The indicators, however, are admittedly crude and do not allow for making fine distinctions.

For larger collectives, we have no information on the religious experiences of each member of the population and consequently no basis for developing indicators through accumulating information on individuals who are members of the collective. Such facts as that more prominent people are experiencing conversions or that a Billy Graham is capable of winning so many people to a religious commitment are sometimes interpreted as indicating spirituality.

On the ideological or belief dimension, it seems obligatory that we make distinctions in kind before we proceed to consider distinctions in degree. What constitutes belief in one religious tradition may not do so in another. Within a tradition, distinctions in degree may be based on indications of what the individual believes and how strongly.

At the group level, there is a tendency to think of more fundamentalist groups as stronger believers than non-fundamentalists, using as an indicator the degree to which the members of each group subscribe in a common way to an expressed set of religious beliefs. We may also use as an indicator of belief the amount of suffering which the individual or the members of a religious group are willing to undergo in upholding their beliefs. Thus, the Jehovah's Witnesses are frequently perceived as highly religious because they are willing to suffer major deprivations rather than give up their beliefs.

Judgments to the effect that one nation has stronger religious beliefs than another, or that Americans are more believing today than they were in the past, necessarily have to be based on indicators which obscure variations in religious traditions. Distinctions may be made on the proportion of the population which at different times profess a belief in God or in immortality. The indicators, once again, are not highly developed and not commonly agreed upon.

The difficulties which we have been experiencing in locating indicators used for making distinctions along the experiential and ideological dimensions are multiplied when we consider the consequential dimension. The problem is to find indicators to distinguish the ways and the degree to which a person's actions or attitudes are religiously motivated. The great religions all include ethical proscriptions and presumably these may serve as a standard against which individual behavior may be measured and distinguished. However, ethical behavior is not necessarily religious, so we require additional indicators to distinguish the religiously from the non-religiously motivated act. This leads us back to looking for indications of religiosity on our other three dimensions.

When we hear someone referred to as a truly religious person, it is possible that the observer has no more in mind than that the individual has been saved, believes, or is a good church member. The chances are, however, that something more is also implied, that the individual acts out his religiousness in some way. The acting out may be classifiable as ethical behavior but not necessarily so. The behavior of the missionary or the monk cannot be described as ethical except in a partial sense. What is common in these examples, perhaps, is that the actors are all perceived as acting out of selfless rather than selfish motivations, the selfless motivations being those which grow out of religious experience and belief. We have no systematic idea, however, as to what constitutes selfless as over against selfish behavior.

At the group level, the admiration with which many view the Quakers is closely related perhaps to the "good works" with which they are associated. Indications of the religiousness of larger collectives on the consequential dimension may be the degree to which the ethical proscriptions of the churches permeate the secular institutions of society. Another indicator may possibly be the amount of destructive deviant behavior which exists within the society.

For an indicator of any concept to be developed and to be universally adopted, an obvious and necessary requirement is that evidence be available or easily accumulated on which the indicator may be applied. The two—indicators and evidence—are closely interrelated. Unless the indicators are well formulated, it is not clear what evidence is needed. And, unless a means to collect the evidence is readily at hand, the incentive to construct the indicator is likely to be lacking.

The relative absence of precise indicators to make religious distinctions is, in some measure then, a function of the lack of available evidence and the difficulty of obtaining it. That we can think of more indicators within the ritualistic dimension than within other dimensions results from the fact that, as we have indicated before, ritual behavior and religious practice are more likely to be visible and conspicuous and therefore readily measurable.

What we have done thus far is to provide a framework for examining the claims and counterclaims concerning the state of religion in America. In such an examination, we shall want to consider the frame(s) of reference which different observers adopt in making their assessments, the indicators or religiousness which they use to make distinctions within dimensions, and the kind of evidence to which they turn in applying their indicators. Doing so will probably not enable us to reach conclusions about which everyone will agree. In the last analysis, conclusions in this area will always vary depending upon individual commitments to different conceptions of religion. But we can hope to clarify the current confusion and perhaps establish some new perspectives for assessing the religiousness of entities in the future.

The Religiousness of Americans: Past and Present

The current controversy about religion in America revolves about several issues rather than a single one. First, has there or has there not been a post-war increase in the religiousness of Americans? Secondly, does the post-war increase, if such there has been, represent a revival of religious interest, or is it rather the accelerated continuation of a long term upward trend in the religiosity of Americans? Third, and in a sense countervailing both of these questions, has there or has there not been an increasing secularization in American life? Let us first consider the proposition that there has been a substantial post-war increase in religiosity, leaving aside, for the moment, whether this is more appropriately labeled a revival or an acceleration of a long term upward trend.

Judging from the indicators of religiousness adopted and the evidence cited, the supporters of this proposition give greatest weight to the ritualistic dimension of religion. Some of their indicators touch on the ideological and experiential dimensions but none on the consequential dimension. The principal ritual indicators used are the proportion of Americans who are church members, the proportion who attend church on any given Sunday, the investment in church buildings, and contributions to religious institutions. On the belief dimension, indicators are almost exclusively limited to the proportion of Americans who hold to certain religious beliefs, most especially a belief in God. A further indicator, also classifiable as indicating belief, is constituted by the degree to which religion and religious institutions are subjected to criticism in the mass media and among intellectual elites. Indicators such as the amount of interest expressed in religious books and music and in commodities having a religious motif, are somewhat more difficult to classify, but we shall place them in the experiential dimension on the assumption that they represent spiritual concern in some undefinable way.

The claim is made that on each of these indicators, America has become increasingly more religious over the last few decades. Perhaps the most frequently cited evidence to this effect is statistical information on the proportion of Americans who belong to the nation's churches. Such information, compiled regularly by the Bureau of Research and Survey of the National Council of Churches in the U.S.A., is reported annually in the *Yearbook of American Churches*. Church membership as a percentage of the population for the period 1940 to 1957 is reported to have been as follows:[5]

1940	49%
1950	57%
1955	60.9%
1956	62%
1957	61%

The evidence on the proportion of Americans who attend church on a typical Sunday does not show as consistent nor as great an increase as these statistics on church membership. But they do indicate that Americans, on the average, were more likely to attend church in the 1950's than in the 1940's. The data are the results of national public opinion polls conducted at irregular intervals by the American Institute of Public Opinion (Gallup Poll) since 1939.[6]

Reflecting the increases in church membership and attendance are the increases in investments in church buildings and in per capita donations to congregational expenses and benevolences. In 1946, $76,000,000 was invested in church construction; by 1953 the figure had risen to $474,000,000.[7] Donations to eighteen Protestant denominations,

[5]Benson Y. Landis, ed., *Yearbook of American Churches for 1959*, National Council of Churches of Christ in the U.S.A., 1958.

[6]Reported in Landis, *op. cit.*, p. 297.

[7]Anonymous, "Construction of Religious Buildings," *Information Service*, National Council of the Churches of Christ in the U.S.A., May 8, 1954.

| | Percent of Adults Attending Church in |
| *Date* | *Week Preceding Interview* |
| February, 1939...41% |
| November, 1940 ....37% |
| May, 1942...36% |
| May, 1947...45% |
| April, 1950 ....39% |
| July, 1954 ....46% |
| December, 1955 ....49% |
| April, 1957 ....51% |
| December, 1957 ....47% |

computed as per capita contributions as a proportion of per capita income, declined between 1940 and 1943 but have increased almost steadily thereafter through 1952, the date of the last available statistics.[8]

The evidence on the proportion of Americans who identify themselves with a religious denomination and who express a belief in God suggests an increase on these indicators though comparable data over the last decade and a half is not available. However, the fact that in March, 1957, 96.4 percent of the American population fourteen years and over identified themselves with a religious denomination[9] and that a number of recent polls have shown that over 95 percent believe in God[10] is taken as corroborating the trend data available on other indicators in the sense that earlier figures could scarcely have been any higher.

When it comes to such indicators as the amount of criticism of religion which exists and the degree to which religious subjects occupy attention in the mass media and popular arts, the evidence, while partly impressionistic, shows an increasingly favorable attitude towards religion over the last two decades.[11]

All of this evidence is by now well known and to elaborate on it further can only be repetitive. Does it justify the claim that there has been a major postwar increase in religiousness in America? The claim may be questioned at several levels. First, the definition of religiousness which is implied in the indicators used omits any consideration of the consequential dimension. There is no authoritative way to decide whether or not the omission is a serious one. What contribution each of the dimensions makes or should make to the total concept—religion—is still a matter of judgment rather than fact. That the omission has been made, however, does reflect on the comprehensiveness of the claim.

More serious than this omission, however, is the inadequacy of the indicators to represent religiousness on any one or a combination of dimensions. Here, again, the point might be made that one must decide for himself how satisfactory the indicators are. Yet, to accept the indicators used as adequate representations of the concept is to ignore most of the issues which have maintained religion as a central feature of human life throughout time. On the other hand, there is also the possibility that there is little more to contemporary religion than what the indicators measure.

Leaving such issues for the reader to decide for himself, what about the evidence—how satisfactory is it? None of it actually is completely reliable although it is impossible to judge just

[8]Argyle, *op. cit.*, p. 30.
[9]Landis, *op. cit.*, p. 302.
[10]Figures quoted in Herberg, *op. cit.*, p. 59.
[11]See Herberg, *op. cit.*, for a summation of this evidence, pp. 59–84.

exactly how reliable it is. The statistics on church membership are perhaps most suspect, judging from a perceptive critique of church statistics by W. H. Hudson.[12]

Hudson makes two crucial points. One, he notes that many of the denominations submitting the reports from which the over-all figures are compiled invariably report their membership in round numbers and report increases from year to year in round numbers. On logical grounds Hudson questions, for example, that the membership of the Church of Christ actually increased from 1,500,000 to 1,600,000 between 1955 and 1956 as the *Yearbook* reports. His second point is perhaps even more damaging. He indicates that the statistics make no provision for taking account of denominations which furnish membership reports for the first time in any given year. He cites the case of the Christ Unity Science Church which reports a membership of 682,172 in the 1952 *Yearbook,* the first year in which figures for this denomination ever appeared.[13] He claims that much of the increase from year to year can be accounted for by new denominations submitting membership reports for the first time.

Hudson is also concerned about the source of the so-called increase. He discovers, by looking at the statistics for the same denominations over time, that the largest increases are reported for the more fundamentalist denominations. The old line Protestant churches show no greater increase in membership from 1940 to 1952 than might have been expected given the general increase in population.

While casting considerable doubt on the reliability of the statistics, Hudson does not attempt to correct them in any systematic way. In general, he indicates that the method of compilation and reporting contributes to inflation rather than deflation.

To his observations may be added the additional one that congregations are notably lax in maintaining accurate reports on membership. Individuals are often retained on church rolls long after they have discontinued membership whether because of loss of interest or because of mobility. Given the high degree of mobility in the last decade and a half, there seems no doubt that some of the reported increase in church membership is a consequence of some indeterminate proportion of persons being counted more than once.

The Gallup poll data reporting an increase in church attendance, taken at face value, would appear less subject to criticism on reliability grounds. The method used to collect the data at different points in time was consistent and logically, therefore, the changes observed would appear to be reliable. The data on contributions and on investments in church buildings is, in part at least, a reflection of the general prosperity but there seems no doubt about the increases reported. About contributions, however, Seymour Lipset makes the point that the per capita contributions in 1952 were lower than they were at the height of the depression.[14] The impressions, and the limited statistics underlying them, of increased interest in ideas and commodities with religious content cover so many aspects of popular culture, and the trend is so consistently upward, that one is convinced in the final analysis of their general reliability.

The evidence, then, while perhaps exaggerating the growth, appears reliable enough to justify a conclusion that, within the limitations of the indicators

---

[12]W.H. Hudson, "Are Churches Really Booming?" *Christian Century,* LXXVII, 51, December 21, 1955.

[13]It is of incidental interest that this denomination does not appear in the *Yearbook* for 1959.

[14]*Op. cit.*

used, some post-war growth in religiousness has occurred.

The growth has been explained as a result both of the state of anxiety created by the "cold war"[15] and of the need for third generation Americans to use religion to obtain some sense of identity to replace their rejection and subsequent loss of ethnic identity.[16] There is no evidence on which to check such interpretations or to offer alternative ones. However, as a further hypothesis, we would suggest that the increase may be, in part, the result of a self-fulfilling prophecy.

The earliest reports of the increase were based on the statistics of church membership issued by the National Council of Churches. These were given rather wide publicity in the late 1940's without any question being raised as to their reliability. It is conceivable that the publicity may have generated a commercial interest in producing and promoting religious literature, songs and plays with a religious motif, and commodities having religious connotations. The sudden flooding of the market with this material may have contributed to the impression that "religion was again in style," so to speak. This is how fads are generally created and there is some reason to believe, given the current belief that the religious resurgence has reached its peak,[17] that it may also have been no more than a fad.

Whether the increase represents a revival or an acceleration of religious interest has become an issue primarily because of a dispute over the accuracy of the historical statistics on church membership. These are also reported in

[15]Reinhold Niebuhr, "Is There a Revival of Religion?" *The New York Times Magazine,* November 10, 1950.

[16]Herberg, *op. cit.*

[17]Based on the statistic that there was a slight decline in church membership in 1957. Landis, *op. cit.*

the *Yearbook* with, however, the *caveat* that ". . . the figures in the table for 1920 and prior years are not on the same basis as those for 1930 and following years."[18] The statistics are:

Church Membership as Percentage of Population

1850	16%
1860	23%
1870	18%
1880	20%
1890	22%
1900	36%
1910	43%
1920	43%
1930	47%
1940	49%
1950	57%
1955	60.9%
1956	62%
1957	61%

Taken at face value, the figures appear to show that the long term trend in America has indeed been towards increased religious affiliation, thus supporting the contention that the current increase is more appropriately labeled an acceleration of a long term trend than a revival. Will Herberg, for example, holds this view though arguing for its support on slightly different grounds. Noting that 95 per cent of the American people in the 1950's regard themselves as belonging to some religious community, he comments:

Such information as that which this survey provides is unfortunately not available for earlier times, and so direct comparison is impossible. But it seems safe to assume that these figures, reflecting the situation in the early 1950's, represent an all-time high in religious identification. Through the nineteenth century and well into the twentieth America knew the militant secularist, the atheist or "free-thinker" as a familiar figure in cultural life, along with considerably larger numbers of "agnostics" who would have

[18]Landis, *op. cit.*

nothing to do with the churches and refused to identify themselves religiously. These still exist, of course, but their ranks are dwindling and they are becoming more and more inconspicuous, taking the American people as a whole. . . . The pervasiveness of religious identification may safely be put down as a significant feature of the America that has emerged in the past quarter of a century.[19]

The claim that recent increases represent an acceleration of a general upward trend rests solely on grounds of religious affiliation and identification. Lipset argues against the claim both by attacking the reliability of the statistics on religious affiliation and by pointing to other indications that there has been no long term religious trend in any one direction.[20] Since Lipset agrees basically that a post-war increase in religiosity has occurred and disagrees that this represents the continuation of a long term trend, his article "Religion in America: What Religious Revival?" seems to be peculiarly titled. However, it is probably intended to reflect his proposition that religious affiliation and observance in America is better characterized by its stability than by its undulations over the last century and a half.

In support thereof, Lipset first of all points out that, from the time of de Tocqueville in 1830, foreign observers have been struck consistently by the evidence of great religiosity which they have found in America. He cites early estimates that, in 1832, well over 90 per cent of the population were church members. He questions the reliability of the historical statistics on the grounds that the definition of a church member has gradually grown more inclusive and, citing Argyle, he notes that when this is taken into account church membership is found to decline between 1906 and 1940

rather than to have sharply increased as the *Yearbook* figures indicate. He also presents evidence that the ratio of clergymen to the total population has been strikingly constant between 1850 and 1950.

Lipset also refers to more recent data showing that *per capita* contributions to churches were higher in the 1920's than in the 1950's, that the religious activity of business executives declined sharply between 1925 and 1950, and that among college students the proportion believing in God also declined between World War I and 1952. As we have already indicated, he does acknowledge that the trend since 1940 has been towards increased religiosity, citing about the same evidence as we have presented before. He disagrees, however, that the increase is a substantial one.

Lipset's adroit questioning of the historical statistical evidence on church affiliation and identification casts reasonable doubt on the claim of a long term upward trend. However, his counter-evidence to support his contention of stability is also not entirely convincing. There simply are no reliable historical statistics on church membership and it is extremely doubtful that accurate statistics can be produced through manipulating the unreliable ones. Lipset's statistics on the stability of clergy to the total population, as he himself points out, do not take into account the possibility that the contemporary clergyman may be serving larger congregations than his historical counterpart. What he has to say about shifts in contributions and in religious activity in the 20th century do not wholly reflect stability nor can they reasonably be extended to represent the long term situation back through the 19th century. To these observations must be added the further one that Lipset deals almost exclusively with the ritual dimension of religion. He gives some slight

[19]Herberg, *op. cit.*, pp. 59–60.
[20]*Op. cit.*

attention to the ideological but none to the experiential and consequential dimensions.

This exploration into the long term evidence on the religiousness of Americans does not lead us to any firm conclusions even within the limited perspectives of the observations discussed. Perhaps the confusion may be dissipated as we now go on to examine the alternative proposition that the long term trend in America has been toward the increasing secularization of religion.

The spokesmen for this view are not all of one mind in the sense that they adopt the same frame of reference in making their observations. In general, however, they are more prone to emphasize the ideological and/or consequential dimensions than the experiential or ritual ones. And, where they adopt the same frame of reference as those who perceive a religious revival, they are likely to disagree with the "revivalists" on the acceptability of given indicators.

Perhaps the most important attribute of those who perceive secularization to be going on is their commitment to a particular view of what religion means. Those who perceive the belief dimension as paramount, for example, are likely themselves to be committed to a set of beliefs. If these are transcendental beliefs, indications of a watering down of belief—the trend toward ecumenicity, for example, or the increasing propensity to see all religions as equally good—are cited as evidence of secularization.

It is not uncommon for ideological commitment to include secular beliefs which are accepted as sacred—the belief in the free enterprise system, for example. For those who have such a commitment, indications of an increasing trend toward a welfare state would be offered as *prima facie* evidence of secularization.

In some instances, those committed to a notion of secularization emphasize the consequential rather than the belief dimension. Their ideological commitment may be to a religion which has ethical consequences for those who experience, believe, and practice it. They want a religion which will intrude itself into all phases of the life process and make its weight felt in national affairs. Indications that religion is playing less and less of a role in family life, in education, in social welfare, and in economic life would be cited as evidence of secularization. At the same time, indications of increases in religious belief, practice, and experience would be rejected as meaningless without concomitant indications of increased religiosity on the consequential dimension.

Actually, there is nothing in the literature, so far as we can find, which would constitute a serious and systematic defense of the secularization hypothesis. Its advocates are likely to be clergymen, church administrators, theologians, or journalists, and where they have been social scientists they have tended to be oriented to qualitative rather than quantitative observation. The evidence which they cite tends to be neither systematic nor thoroughly documented. Their view of religion, as the examples indicate, is likely to be a circumscribed one, though in a different way from the views of the "revivalists."

In his paper, Lipset parallels his argument that there has been no long term increase in religious affiliation and observance with the additional one that American religion is not becoming increasingly secularized. He does not deal systematically with all advocates of the secularization hypothesis but rather focuses his attention on those who see the process as manifested in the decline of transcendental belief. He acknowledges that the evidence is limited but argues that the secularization advocates ignore two things: one, the fact that evangelical re igions are growing much faster than the traditional ones; and two, the possibility that "the secularized religion which these observers see as distinctively modern may have been characteristic of American believers in the past." In support of this possibility, he notes that the same 19th-century foreign observers who were impressed by the religiosity of Americans also commented on its lack of depth and the unusual willingness of Americans to accept all religions as equally valid.

One may question whether the strength of transcendental belief constitutes a sufficient basis for testing the secularization hypothesis. But, even accepting it as such, some doubt may be cast on Lipset's implication that the two points he makes prove that secularization has not occurred.

The denominationalism which typified the 19th century is being slowly replaced by the ecumenicity of the 20th. An interpretation of the shift is far too complex to be attempted in short compass. Yet, that church mergers are increasingly occurring suggests that their clergy and laity are willing to compromise somewhat on their beliefs in pursuit of other values and ends perceived as more important. Too, while it appears to be the case, as Lipset points out, that the evangelical churches are gaining in strength, it is not altogether clear that their belief systems are quite as rigid as they were before. The indications are that even in a church as rigidly doctrinal as the Lutheran Church–Missouri Synod, liberalizing tendencies are making increasing headway.

Lipset ignores what has been happening in the traditional Protestant churches. Yet, the impression is that the authority of transcendental belief is being increasingly whittled away; the same may be said, but at a different level, for the Roman Catholic Church in America. There are indications that this is the trend, but solid evidence, to be sure, is lacking.

Commentary and Prospectus

A general conclusion to be drawn from all that has been said is that none of the work done to assess the state of religion in America currently or historically meets even the minimum standards of scientific inquiry. Investigators and commentators have not given adequate attention to conceptualizing religion or religiousness in a comprehensive way. Consequently, they have been considerably less than thorough in their selection of indicators of religiousness. And, in applying the indicators they have selected, they too often have relied upon evidence of dubious quality. Their work, as a result, does not provide a satisfactory basis for assessing either the state or the meaning of religion in America.

What can be concluded, at least tentatively, is that there has been a post-war growth in religious affiliation and observance. This has been accompanied by an increase of interest in ideas and commodities having a religious content. It is not possible, given the evidence, to decide just how great the increase has been, to predict whether it could be confirmed using a more comprehensive set of indicators or to understand the significance and meaning of the particular changes which have been observed. Furthermore, we cannot say authoritatively whether the increase constitutes a revival or merely an acceleration of an historical trend towards increased church membership and religious interest.

There are certain indications that the qualitative character of American religion has been changing in at least two respects. One, there appears to be a decline in doctrinal rigidity. Americans seem more inclined to interpret scripture in the light of history and to accept the validity of faiths other than their own. Two, it seems that the church as an institution is playing a proportionately smaller role today than in the past in some of the aspects of American culture with which it has been traditionally identified —in education, for example, in family life, and in social welfare. However, even these trends cannot be accepted as demonstrated. The evidence of a revival in the strength of evangelical religion, as Lipset points out, casts some doubt on the notion of a decline in transcendental belief. And, there are some areas of our culture—politics, for example—where it is impossible to say whether the influence of religion has declined, increased, or remained the same.

It is problematical whether consensus can ever be achieved on the state and meaning of religion in America or, for that matter, anywhere else. Ideological commitments to different conceptions of what it means to be religious cannot be resolved scientifically. However, while ultimate resolutions may not be possible and the horizons may not be limitless, the challenge remains and it is doubtful that man will be satisfied with the limited understanding he has achieved.

What this author would like to see as a next step is an attempt to deal systematically with the assessment to the state and meaning of religion in America. This would involve, to begin with, elaborating the conceptualization of religion outlined earlier, followed by an attempt to develop a comprehensive set of indicators for locating entities along each dimension. Instruments enabling the application of the indicators would then need to be developed after which the collection of evidence might be undertaken. Such a procedure seems eminently feasible for studying the contemporary religious situation, but in a modified and less thorough way it should also be possible to apply it historically as well. Not everyone, to be sure, would agree on the meaning of the results of such a far-reaching research endeavor. Yet, to know how indications of religiousness on different dimensions are interrelated and the conditions under which different degrees of religiosity arise would inevitably enhance our understanding of religion, still perhaps the most perplexing aspect of our culture.

Peter Berger

Thomas Luckmann

SOCIOLOGY OF RELIGION AND SOCIOLOGY OF KNOWLEDGE

Religion is both an important and an ambivalent phenomenon in contemporary

From Sociology and Social Research, XLVII, No. 4, July, 1963. By permission of the authors and publisher.

western society. This is true on both sides of the Atlantic, despite significant differences between America and Europe with regard to the social situation of religion. In America, religion continues to occupy an important position in public life and, on a quite voluntary basis, continues to enlist the formal allegiance of well over *half* the population in its organized bodies. In Europe, despite the survival of various degrees of legal establishment in various countries, popular participation in organized religion lags considerably behind the conspicuous piety of the cis-Atlantic masses. This lag, however, is compensated by the political prominence of organized religion as best exemplified by the political parties identified with one or both of the two major Christian confessions. In both Europe and America religion plays an important part in the overall ideological posture *vis-à-vis* the Communist world. Moreover, again in both sectors of the emerging north-Atlantic civilization, there is widespread popular interest in religion, strongly reflected by the mass media but also visible on more intellectually sophisticated levels. Both Protestantism and Catholicism have given birth to intellectual movements strong enough to be called a theological revival. Interestingly enough, it is precisely among the theologians that there are to be heard severe criticisms of the sort of religion that is prominent in the society and doubts as to whether this prominence may not be profoundly deceptive. Among some theologians there has been blunt mention of a "post-Christian era" only thinly veiled by the continuing busy-work of the religious organizations. The ambivalence of the religious phenomenon is thus present in the consciousness of the religious world itself, prior to any sociological imputation from without.

The ecclesiastical authorities of the two major confessions have commonly stopped short of these extreme diagnoses. Nevertheless it is a commonplace even in the inner circles of the religious bureaucracies that things are not what they ought to be and that there is something not quite real about the Christian rhetoric of public life. Minimally this ecclesiastical uneasiness can be seen in an awareness of certain obvious trouble spots on the religious scene, such as the persistent alienation of much of the working class in Europe or the problem of racial segregation within the churches of America. One of the rather surprising consequences of this uneasiness has been a turning towards sociology on the part of the churches.

In the period since World War II there has been a remarkable development of sociologically oriented research carried on under ecclesiastical auspices, to the point where today a sizable body of literature has been produced by this enterprise.[1] In this country, Protestant agencies have been engaging in this sort of research since the 1920's, largely in connection with the strategic planning of denominational and interdenominational offices, but the overall research enterprise has greatly expanded and also become more formalized in the wake of the postwar "religious revival." Catholic agencies in America have been influenced by this Protestant research-happiness as well as by the booming Catholic "religious sociology" in Europe, while Jewish organizations have been engaging in widespread research activities of their own. The most spectacular inroad of sociological techniques, however, has occurred in European Catholicism. It began in France, but today has spread to every country with a sizable Catholic population. Under various headings ("religious sociology," "parish sociology," "pastoral sociology," and others) a considerable number of research institutes, brought together in an interna-

---

[1] *Cf.* the extensive international bibliography in Dietrich Goldschmidt and Joachim Matthes, *Probleme der Religionssoziologie* (Cologne: Westdeutscher Verlag, 1962).

tional federation, is carrying on investigations under the direct sponsorship of the Catholic authorities.[2] European Protestants have not quite caught up with this development, but strenuous efforts are well under way to emulate the Catholic example.[3] This is not the place to evaluate these research enterprises, some of which have unquestionably yielded valuable data for the sociology of religion in contemporary society. However, a few comments ought to be made about the general character of this sociological activity.

This character is determined by the economic base of the enterprises in question. Generally speaking, the latter constitute a religious variety of market research. They are financed by ecclesiastical organizations facing pragmatic problems and seeking pragmatic solutions to these problems. It should not surprise anyone that this research is employer-oriented in its motivations. What is more important to see is that its conceptual framework is also determined by this employer-orientation. The focus of interest is church-affiliated religiosity, its presence or absence, constituting respectively a "good" or a "bad" situation from the management point of view. Needless to say, research carried on under ecclesiastical auspices shares this problem with the activities of sociologists employed by other types of bureaucratic management, for example in industry or government. It should also not be too surprising, consequently, that this ecclesiastically based research has borrowed its methodology from other branches of bureaucratically functional sociology. This methodology is narrowly

sociographic, a fact which is both technically and ideologically functional. It avoids questions that go beyond the immediate pragmatic concerns of the employer (since such questions are not amenable to treatment by the methods utilized) and it legitimates the "scientific" respectability of the enterprise (since these methods are acceptable precisely to the most rabidly positivistic scientism outside the churches).

There is something precious in this unexpected liaison between archbishops and pollsters. What concerns us here, however, is the enormous discrepancy between this latter-day sociology of religion and the place that religion occupied in classical sociological theory. It is hardly necessary in this context to amplify this statement in terms of the theoretical systems of Weber, Durkheim or Pareto, only to mention three crucial ones. One might recall, however, that none of the theorists just mentioned were personally "religious." They were concerned with religion for sociological reasons. Religion was perceived by them as a central phenomenon of social reality, therefore necessarily central for sociological understanding in general. Weber's recognition of religion as a prime factor in the historical process, Durkheim's insistence on the ultimately religious character of all human solidarity and Pareto's analysis of the place of religion in the perennial human pastime of self-deception—whatever one may want to do with these positions in one's own theorizing, it is clear that they are a long way, as starting points of sociological research, from the headaches of ecclesiastical bureaucrats.

This is not to say that, at any rate in American sociology, there is not some continuity with these classical sociological approaches to religion. Thus one can find strong Weberian undertones in the works on religion of Howard Becker and Gerhard Lenski, or a definite Durk-

---

[2]*Cf.* the principal international periodical published under these Catholic auspices, *Social Compass* (Brussels and The Hague).

[3]*Cf.* the report on the European Colloquium on the Sociology of Protestantism, held in Strasbourg in May 1959, in *Archives de sociologie des religions,* 8 (July-December 1959), 3–157.

heimian flavor in those of Lloyd Warner and Milton Yinger. The influence of both Weber and Durkheim on Talcott Parsons' treatment of religion is evident. It remains true that the sociology of religion is marginal in terms of the sociological enterprise proper (as distinguished from the ecclesiastical research enterprise discussed before), both in terms of its practice and in terms of its thought. Whatever may be the historical reasons for this segregation of the sociology of religion into a somewhat eccentric preserve, the implication is quite clear:— Religion is not a central concern for sociological theory or for the sociological analysis of contemporary society. Religion can, therefore, be left in the main to the social historians, to the ethnologists or to those few sociologists with an antiquarian interest in "the classics"—and, of course, to that fairly alienated group of colleagues employed by religious institutions.

Is this implication defensible? We would say that it is—but *only* if the field of the sociology of religion is defined in ecclesiastical terms, that is, if its focus is to be church-affiliated religiosity and its various degrees of presence or absence. The obvious next question is whether this definition makes sense from the standpoint of sociological theory. Our answer here is resoundingly negative. The reason for this answer is based on our understanding of the nature of the sociological enterprise.

We would say, first of all, that the sociologist who operates exclusively with an ecclesiastically oriented definition of religion has an altogether too narrow and, as it were, juridical concept of institution.[4] The latter must, of

course, be taken into account by the sociologist, but it does not exhaust the pertinent social reality of this or any other phenomenon. The juridical or other "official" versions of society invariably distort sociological perspective if taken at face value. The sociologist who so takes them simply adopts the viewpoint of "management" on the matter at hand. He is well on the way from that point on towards becoming a conservative ideologist, as is best illustrated by the positivistic school of jurisprudence which became precisely that with respect to the institution of law. What happens in this case is that the "official" or "management" viewpoint comes to delimit the area of sociological relevance. Or, speaking empirically, it is not the sociologist but his employers (be they archbishops or admirals, welfare officials or business executives) who define the proper objects of his investigations. Whatever does not fall within his definition of what is relevant is either relegated to an allegedly "subjective" and "scientifically inaccessible" domain or is courteously conceded to some other academic discipline. The former solution is that of the positivists, the latter of those sociologists who are anxious not to infringe on the territory of the psychologists. A pragmatic solution somewhere between the positivistic and the psychologistic alternatives is the one that would leave these institutionally undefined phenomena to such research on "opinions" or "attitudes" as dwells in the antechambers of the temple of sociology. We would contend that none of these options is viable for a sociologist who understands and respects his own universe of discourse.

Sociology must be concerned with everything which, already on the commonsense level, is taken as social reality, even if it does not fit into the "official" definition of what the institutions

---

[4]We would like to see a broader concept, but will not argue the point here. For a very suggestive development of the sociological concept of institution *vide* Arnold Gehlen, *Urmensch und Spaetkultur* (Bonn: Athenaeum, 1956).

of society are.[5] There is a wide range of human phenomena that are socially objectivated but not institutionalized in the narrow sense of the word. Not only is it methodologically inadmissible to exclude these phenomena from the perspective of sociology, but any concept of institution hangs theoretically in mid-air if it is not grounded in a sociological understanding of objectivation as such. The basic form of social objectivation is language. Language analyzes, recombines and "fixes" biologically based subjective consciousness and forms it into intersubjective, typical and communicable experiences. The metaphorical and analogical potential of language facilitates the crystallization of social values and norms by which experience is interpreted. It is this edifice of semantic fields, categories and norms which structures the subjective perceptions of reality into a meaningful, cohesive and "objective" universe. This universe, "reality as seen" in a culture, is taken for granted in any particular society or collectivity. For the members of a society or collectivity it constitutes the "natural" way of interpreting, remembering, and communicating individual experience. In this sense it is internal to the individual, as his way of experiencing the world. At the same time it is external to him as that universe in which he *and* his fellow-men exist and act.[6]

[5]This understanding of the scope of sociology has been strongly influenced by the sociological theories of Alfred Schutz. *Cf.* Alfred Schutz, *Collected Papers, 1—The Problem of Social Reality* (The Hague: Nijhoff, 1962).

[6]In addition to Schutz we would point here to the classic formulations of the character of this *conscience collective* in the works of Durkheim and Maurice Halbwachs. For more recent interpretations, *cf.* Eric Voegelin, *The New Science of Politics* (Chicago: University of Chicago Press, 1951); Robert Redfield, *The Primitive World and Its Transformations* (Ithaca: Cornell University Press, 1953); Claude Lévi-Strauss, *La pensée sauvage* (Paris: Plon, 1962).

Such a universe is fundamentally legitimated by the fact that it is there, confronting the individual from the beginning of his biography as the self-evident external reality which exercises unremitting constraint upon his individual experiences and actions. Nevertheless, this universe *as* a coherent configuration of meaning requires reiterated and explicitly formulated legitimation. The individual already learns in his primary socialization the fundamental formulas of this legitimation. Socialization, however, is never totally successful and never completed. The legitimating formulas must be reiterated in the ongoing life of the adult, especially in the great crises of this life (as in rites of passage). One can put this a little differently by saying that all universes, as meaning structures, are precarious. The individual's "knowledge" of the world is socially derived and must be socially sustained. Using Alfred Schutz's expression, the individual's world-taken-for-granted must be legitimated over and over again.[7] Normally this legitimation will occur in specific institutional forms. Yet one must be careful not to confound "knowledge" (i.e., the meaning configuration of the universe) with the formal institutions of learning or legitimation (i.e., the explicit—and symbolic—"explanation" of the coherence of that universe) with institutionally organized ideologies. This theoretical distinction is especially important in terms of the religious dimension of this socially constituted universe.

Throughout human history religion has played a decisive part in the construction and maintenance of universes.[8]

[7]For the phenomenological analysis of the "natural" way of looking at the world and its social relativity *cf.* Max Scheler, *Die Wissensformen und die Gesellschaft* (Bern: Francke, 1960).

[8]The classic sociological formulation of this is, of course, to be found in the works of Durk-

This statement does not necessarily imply an extreme Durkheimian position that religion has done nothing else or is nothing else apart from this social function, but it does imply that this function is sociologically central. In any case, while this function of religion can be discovered crossculturally, the institutionally specialized location of religion in churches or similar bodies is relatively rare in history. It is, of course, characteristic of the development of Christianity. But it is generally absent in ancient civilizations and is almost totally unknown in primitive societies. *Ergo*, for the purposes of a general sociology of religion, this institutional specialization cannot be used as the defining criterion of religion. The ecclesiastically oriented definition of the field of the sociology of religion betrays then, at the very least, a marked historical and cultural parochialism.

There is, indeed, a sociological problem in the relationship of institutionalized religion, where it exists, with the more general religious business of universe building. But this is not the only problem. The recent history of secularization in western and westernizing societies indicates, on the contrary, that the part of institutionally specialized religion in the fundamental processes of legitimation is on the wane. This development is of great sociological importance in itself and there already exist various theories seeking to explain it.[9] Another interesting

problem lies in what has been described as the "emigration" and subsequent "privatization" of even traditionally Christian religiosity from the churches, a phenomenon especially significant in Europe.[10] Yet another sociological problem is posed by the transformation of the traditional religious meanings within the churches themselves, something to be observed very clearly in America but also present in varying degrees in Europe.[11] From our viewpoint, however, another problem is sociologically the crucial one:—What are the characteristics of the legitimating processes actually operative in contemporary society?

No human society can exist without legitimation in one form or another. If it is correct to speak of contemporary society as increasingly secularized (and we think that this is correct), one is thereby saying that the sociologically crucial legitimations are to be found outside the area of institutionally specialized religion. To say this, however, is only the beginning of the sociological analysis that must now take place. One must now ask what forms these legitimations take, to what extent they are institutionalized and where they are so institutionalized (since there is no longer

---

heim and his school. For important corroboration from the fields of the phenomenology and history of religion *cf.* the works of Mircea Eliade (e.g. *Cosmos and History,* New York: Harper and Brothers, 1959) and Eric Voeglin (*Order and History,* vols. I-III, Baton Rouge: Lousiana State University Press, 1956–1957). For a recent sociological interpretation *cf.* W. Lloyd Warner, *The Living and the Dead* (New Haven: Yale University Press, 1959).

[9]*Cf.* Helmut Schelsky, "Ist die Dauerreflektion institutionalisierbar?" *Zeitschrift fuer*

evangelische Ethik, 4 (1957), 153–74; Talcott Parsons, *Structure and Process in Modern Societies* (New York: The Free Press of Glencoe, 1960), 295–321; Sabino Acquaviva, *L'eclissi del sacro nella civiltà industriale* (Milan: Comunità, 1961); Goldschmidt and Matthes, *op. cit.,* especially 65–77.

[10]*Cf.* Eberhard Stammler, *Protestanten ohne Kirche* (Stuttgart: Kreuz, 1960).

[11]*Cf.* Louis Schneider and Sanford Dornbusch, *Popular Religion* (Chicago: University of Chicago Press, 1958); Rose Goldsen *e.a., What College Students Think* (Princeton: D. Van Nostrand Company, 1960), 153–95; Peter Berger, *The Noise of Solemn Assemblies* (Garden City, N.Y.: Doubleday and Company, 1961); Hans-Otto Woelber, *Religion ohne Entscheidung* (Goettingen: Vandenhoeck & Ruprecht, 1959).

any reason to fixate one's attention on the traditional religious institutions). At this point, needless to say, one has arrived at some of the central questions of a sociological understanding of modern society.

Before we venture on some statements concerning the implications of this for the sociology of religion in this modern society we would return for a moment to more general theoretical considerations. Legitimation cannot be discussed apart from the universe that is being legitimated. Such a universe, as we have briefly tried to indicate, is a socially constituted reality, which the individual member of society learns to take for granted as "objective" knowledge about the world. This "objectivity" (what Durkheim called the "thing-like" character of social reality) is determined by the fact that socialization is not simply individual learning of cultural items but also social constraint in the formation of the most fundamental categories of experience, memory, thinking and communication. This means that knowledge, in the broadest sense, is socially derived. The task of the sociology of knowledge is the analysis of the social forms of knowledge, of the processes by which individuals acquire this knowledge and, finally, of the institutional organization and social distribution of knowledge. It will be clear that we are here giving to the sociology of knowledge a considerably broader meaning than has hitherto been given to it. We conceive the sociology of knowledge as being properly concerned with the whole area of the relationship of social structure and consciousness.[12]

[12]The authors of this article, in cooperation with several colleagues in sociology and philosophy, are currently engaged in the preparation of a systematic treatise in the sociology of knowledge that will seek to integrate with what is now known as the sociology of knowledge three other streams of sociological thought hitherto largely left outside this discipline—the phenomenological analysis of the life-world (especially

The sociology of knowledge thus understood ceases to be an idiosyncratic activity of sociologists with a penchant for the history of ideas and is placed squarely at the very center of sociological theory.[13]

The consequence for the sociology of religion as a discipline is clear:—The sociology of religion is an integral and even central part of the sociology of knowledge.—Its most important task is to analyze the cognitive and normative apparatus by which a socially constituted universe (that is, "knowledge" about it) is legitimated. Quite naturally, this task will include the analysis of both the institutionalized and the non-institutionalized aspects of this apparatus. This will involve the sociology of religion in the study of religion in the sense in which this term is commonly understood in western civilization (that is, as a Christian or Jewish interpretation of the world and of human destiny). But the sociology of religion will also have to deal with other legitimating systems, whether one wishes to call these religious or pseudo-religious, that are increasingly important in a secularized society (such as scientism, psychologism, Communism, and so forth). Indeed, only if the latter is also done will it be possible to obtain an adequate sociological understanding of

in the opus of Alfred Schutz), the Durkheimian approaches to the sociology of knowledge and those of American social psychology as derived from the work of G. H. Mead.

[13]The problem of ideology in its relationship to social strata and their conflicts, the original impetus and subject matter of the sociology of knowledge, remains an important area within such a broader definition of the discipline. In addition to the well-known works of Karl Mannheim *cf.* Robert Merton, *Social Theory and Social Structure* (New York: The Free Press of Glencoe, 1957), 439–508; Werner Stark, *The Sociology of Knowledge* (New York: The Free Press of Glencoe, 1958); Kurt Wolff, ed., "The Sociology of Knowledge," *Transactions of the Fourth World Congress of Sociology,* IV (Louvain: International Sociological Association, 1959).

the phenomena that persist within the traditional religious systems and their institutional manifestations.

What results can be expected from this re-interpretation of the task of the sociology of religion for empirical research? First of all, such a re-interpretation leads to a detachment of the sociologist (*qua* sociologist, that is) from the ideological interests of all, not only of the traditional religious legitimating systems. This includes an emancipation from the "management" point of view within the churches, and also from any scientistic ideology that may exist within the field of sociology itself. In terms of research practice, there will be an obvious broadening in scope of the sociology of religion. This broader scope is especially important in a modern pluralistic society in which different legitimating systems compete for the patronage of potential consumers of *Weltanschauungen*. Indeed, we strongly believe that this market character of legitimating systems is in itself an important characteristic deserving of sociological analysis. The sociology of religion here finds itself in close proximity to the problems already investigated by the sociology of mass culture and mass communications.

This leads to further important problems. We think that the relative freedom of the consumer *vis-à-vis* the various legitimating systems influences personality structure.[14] Compared with the obligatory and unambiguous internalization of any one legitimating system in traditional societies, the consumer status of the individual *vis-à-vis* competing legitimating systems in modern society provides, if nothing else, at least

the illusion of freedom. We think that the collision of this private "freedom" with the strict controls of functionally rational and bureaucratic institutions over the public conduct of the individual represents one of the central problems of the social psychology of modern society. There is a significant sociological problem involved in the loss of monopoly status incurred by the major legitimating systems of western civilization. We believe that this process is one of the social causes of the "privatization" of belief, that is, of the withdrawal of religious commitments from their traditionally designated locations in society into that curious area which German sociologists (not too happily) have called the "sphere of the intimate." The same global processes may well be related to the legitimating functions of psychoanalysis and other forms of psychologism in modern society, functions that can be said to be paradigmatic in terms of "privatization." The sociological analysis of contemporary sexuality, its myths and its rituals, would belong in the same area.

The market character of legitimation (a central aspect of what one likes to call pluralistic society) is very likely to have important consequences for the content of legitimating systems. It is one thing to preside in the role of Brahman over the metaphysical cravings of an isolated and fairly homogeneous peasant population which has no choice in the matter. It is quite another matter to try and market one legitimating system (even if it is Vedanta!) to an affluent and sophisticated clientele of suburbanites, Midwestern housewives, metropolitan secretaries, etc. A certain similarity between these social types may remain in the domains of emotion, sex, consumption, etc.—in short, in the "intimate sphere" which is relatively less dependent on class and institutional factors. The social as well as economic imperative of appealing immediately to the changeable taste of the

[14]*Cf.* David Riesman, *The Lonely Crowd* (New Haven: Yale University Press, 1950); Arnold Gehlen, *Die Seele im technischen Zeitalter* (Hamburg: Rowohlt, 1957); Thomas Luckmann, *Zum Problem der Religion in der modernen Gesellschaft* (Freiburg: Rombach).

largest possible number of "privatized" consumers may account for the importance of psychoanalysis, a legitimating system tailored to the "intimate sphere" *par excellence*. This, of course, does not preclude the success of Zen Buddhism or political chauvinism in narrower special segments of the mass market. It must not be overlooked that Presbyterianism and Reform Judaism are not exempt either from the mechanism of marginal differentiation called into play in this situation.

These considerations probably point to a comprehensive analysis of legitimation in modern society on the basis of a non-monopolistic market model. Special attention must be given here to the function of the mass media in the socialization of these consumer attitudes. The mass media are further significant in the direct, anonymous and, as it were, non-institutionalized transmission of a synthetic universe with its appropriate pre-fabricated legitimations. Another important area of investigation in this connection is the place of the family, the consuming entity *par excellence* with reference to all

marketable commodities from television sets to "peace of mind." The ideological constellation of "familism," with its broad institutional base in contemporary society ranging from child-centered church programs to the "kiddy-korners" of the suburban shopping centers, is to be analyzed as another aspect of the overall process of "privatization."

Some of these problems have been investigated by sociologists in various sub-disciplines of the field. The re-interpretation of the sociology of religion here undertaken thus in no way pretends that the task indicated above must begin from some sort of *tabula rasa* as far as empirical data are concerned. There is already existent a wealth of data both within and without the area of research more narrowly called the sociology of religion. However, we would contend that the conception of the sociology of religion here formulated would place these data in a more comprehensive theoretical frame of reference. Beyond that it can bring into focus as yet unexplored avenues of empirical research.

Helmut Schelsky

CAN CONTINUAL QUESTIONING BE INSTITUTIONALIZED?

The sociology of religion, such as that of Max Weber, Troeltsch, Sombart, and including that of Scheler, Dempf, etc.

"Ist die Dauerreflektion institutionalisierbar?" Zeit- schrift für evangelische Ethik, I (July 1957), 153–74. *Translated and slightly abridged for this anthology by Ann Harding. By permission of the author.*

which is now regarded as almost "classical," took as its main theme the evolution of the modern world from Christianity, the disclosure of the religious basis of rationalism in the monetary system, in the capitalist striving after financial gain, in works management and industrial organisation, in the conception of the state and the legitimisation of human rights, and so on; but today it seems that a counter-theme—the breakthrough of the sociology of religion—is holding its own: the signs that religion, or Christianity, is adapting itself to modern society. . . .

By this adaptation of religion and Christianity to modern society we understand the following: society at the turn of the century and therefore also its scholarship was already confronted by the rise of these new social structures in politics and government, in commerce and industry, in family and everyday life, but was still so tied to the continuity of the past that it responded intellectually to the change-over which was making itself known primarily with an interest in its origins, in a factual elucidation of the rise and growth of these new world and social structures within the framework of the history of ideas. During the epoch of the two world wars these structures of modern society have rapidly and radically become the natural pillars of our world. But the world today can scarcely be adequately conceived by reference to its origins. The change of function and independence of the results of these developmental processes have made the modern world into an autonomous, self-deriving fact, whose autonomy and brutally permanent everyday existence can be perceived or affected neither by pessimistic nor optimistic speculations about the future, neither by historical derivations nor by conservative desires and efforts to preserve. All forms of life, its groups and its institutions, whose existence and legitimacy depend upon a maintained continuity of time, face a new beginning in which the wisdom of the centuries carries no more weight. That is particularly relevant for the Christian faith and the Christian church. Today they can no longer explain the modern world as a result of its secularity

and interpret it as a mere fall from Christian times—"the godless century"—; they face the autonomy of this world as an undeniable fact, a world which arose through and beyond Christianity, but which is essentially no longer Christian. The attempt has often been made to characterise this situation by the formula that modern Christianity is confronted by a new paganism in the modern world, and especially in its society; this parallel however overlooks the fact that today Christianity brings no new truth into an old world, but has to assert an old truth in a new world.

This seems to me to indicate the change which has been taking place in our society since the thirties, in the relationship between the modern social and world structure on the one hand and the Christian faith and the Christian church on the other. The temporal element in faith and church, based on a social structure which was continuous and homogeneous for almost two thousand years, despite all developments, can no longer be preserved defensively by means of a few concessions to the courses of time—to attempt this is a forlorn hope—; church and faith must recognise and take for granted the incompatibility and independence of the state of the present-day world and society. The fact that this worldly, autonomous world, emancipated from centuries of Christianity and just "come of age," was recognised and described for the first time on behalf of the church by no other theologian than Dietrich Bonhoeffer, who struggled against the acceptance of modern society as a concrete historical fact with no regard for the personal consequences, casts aside any possible misconception that "recognition" expresses a resigned and opportunist "laissez-faire" attitude. But in face of the structure of modern society and the way in which it lives and moves, Christianity and its churches have no longer a sure historical reservoir in their past, from which and by which they can maintain and preserve their faith in secular institutions and forms of life and defend them socially, since they have had to accept the "emancipation of the world" into their own social structure. Christianity and the churches are confronted rather by the task of *re-establishing* their eternal truth in changed social structures which have become secularly autonomous. For the individual this may always have included taking the step of conversion and giving oneself to God; for Christianity and the churches as social phenomena, as they are discussed here, this is surely a new situation. In order to find among incompatible world and social structures, which must now be recognised as independent, a new social formulation of the truth necessary for salvation, it must come to terms with these social forms, assimilate them into its own social life, even if this means that Christianity and the churches must make a break with their own *social* past. This very process seems to me to have been taking place for some decades; sociologically it may be described as an "adaptation on the part of Christianity and religion to modern society. . . ."

If Christianity wishes to proclaim its saving truth to modern man, then it must participate in the social rules of conduct of this modern world as a *social* phenomenon, as it has always been, as an institution, an organisation, a communication with society, etc. and assimilate these independent, emancipated social forms. This process of the *transformation of the social form of appearance* of Christianity is what we designate as adaptation. How its saving truths are to become active in this changed social form and pattern of behaviour in Christianity, what they are to be called and how they are to be effective as faith, to answer this question as to the *content* and vitality of his faith in conflict with the modern world, which to the

Christian is probably the most important question, is not the affair of the sociologist. . . .

This adaptation, limited to its sociological context, of the socially conditioned forms of appearance of Christianity, to the structures of the modern world and society, seems to me to proceed on three planes of religious and social conduct: 1. As a change in the forms and methods of organisation of the church and Christian communities. To this group belong first of all those changes which may be called *passive adaptations* in the social structure of the church community, its increasing detachment from its traditional identification with the communal village society, and a sociological shrinking into a denominational congregation, in addition to the phenomenon of formal confessional allegiance, etc. But last not least, all the *active adaptations* on this plane stem from this perceptible shock to the parochial principle in the religious community: the organisational acquiescence in the forms of modern mass-democracy and politics, in the world of industrial labour and in the modern forms of leisure conduct, entertainment, social life and mass communication (conferences, radio, etc.). We would call this kind of structural change in religious life its *institutional or socio-tactical adaptations,* even if they occur on this plane with the full knowledge that there is merely taking place an assimilation of the forms of organisation and methods of the church community and gospel, which leaves untouched the basic belief and doctrine of Christianity. Thus here it is only a case of "which new ecclesiastical methods are acceptable to the changed world," as Eberhard Müller put it in his article "The World Has Changed," which is so important for and symptomatic of these tendencies.

2. On a second, higher level, *adaptations* are to the modern, changed world clearly

manifesting themselves, not only in the form, but also in the *content of Christian doctrine itself,* among which the attempts to permeate concrete modern social structures with *Christian ethics* are especially interesting sociologically. Basically the cause of all these adaptations may be seen in the fact that today an objective world has appeared, which is new in principle, confronting the revelation-content of the world. In this way, on the one hand the universal meaning of holy writ vanishes in the distance of historical and symbolic understanding, on the other hand these new universal facts must be "woven into" the content of Christian doctrine. Since today it is not the social conditions and forms, which in the first place reveal this novelty and incompatibility in comparison with those mentioned and laid down in the Bible, this adaptation-process too can largely be considered from sociological criterion.
3. A further level of adaptation of religion to the modern world, which in my opinion has been neglected until now, lies in the *changes in the form of belief,* which may be regarded as changes in the consciousness and in the form of the inner life of man. The form of consciousness of man is itself subject to historical influences, developments and structural changes, which can be diagnosed in the change of attitude in and to the world. The kind of religious faith, as a form of conscious life, which at the same time, as Christianity itself emphasises, represents also a social, communal consciousness and experience, takes part in these secular changes in the forms of consciousness, without involving *de facto* a change in the content or in the facts of faith. These adaptations of faith to the form of consciousness of modern mankind cannot indeed be diagnosed by sociological methods alone; in addition comparative-cultural and philosophical-anthropological considerations are

needed to recognise them, but, independent of the theological interpretation of knowledge of salvation itself, they can be fully perceived by empirical analysis.

It is at this level that I think these processes of the "modernisation" of Christianity take place, which have a directing and commanding function superior to the adaptation processes of the other planes. In any case it is from this plane that a principal basic theme for a modern sociology of religion can be formulated, which contains within itself the other adaptation processes of religion which have been mentioned as dependent and derivative processes. We shall therefore limit our further discussion to this adaptation of the *form* of belief and its social *consequences.* Let therefore the following questions lead us on from there: has the modern world produced another *form* of belief in religious truths, other than the faith of earlier times, and what results and possibilities derive from such a changed form of belief with regard to the social form of religion in the present?

Modern scientific industrial society today has in the first place undermined, disturbed, and in many cases put on one side a form of belief which we generally describe as *traditional community Christianity,* i.e. the close interweaving of religious life and the total social and private existence of man in traditional custom and inherited practice. "The Christian village community" or "the Christian family" of pre-scientific, pre-industrial society represented, in many respects, a very secularised form of Christianity. Its form of belief was that of unreflecting recognition of what is culturally self-evident.

Even the "religious struggles" of the Reformation represented decisions in matters of belief, but an actual change in the form of belief was first reached when the *choice between truths, to which one confesses* was made the decisive act of faith, i.e. when "belief" as a confession to definite truths, partly bound up in the details of the formulation, became the *object of consciousness.* This situation however becomes *socially* significant only when conscious doubt in the truth of religious assertions becomes comparatively general and widespread. This has been the case since the elucidation and examination of religious assertions, dogma and traditions, etc. on a rational basis, or rather since the popularisation of this situation in the 19th century, with the advance of atheism, scientific and pseudo-scientific Biblical criticism, etc. over a large area. The turning away of different social groups from their ties to traditional Christianity—from the intellectuals to the working class and the nationalised middle class of "ideologies"—has mostly been connected with the acceptance of such critical standpoints of enlightenment. In this situation "Christianity" becomes a confession of defined, consciously objective assertions, Christian doctrine is formulated as "counter-truth"; it must as such be consciously chosen, and therefore very easily becomes itself an "ideology," i.e. a counter-theory to explain the universe, to formulate action, etc. in a rational way, in opposition to the other rational ideologies. This level of belief is however that of conscious confession to a system of unshakable truths, in the form of concrete, unconsciously objective assertions.

As in philosophy or in the theory of the state, this firm and objective assertion of truth has also been of relatively short duration in the religious sphere. In making religious truths—as also philosophical or political ones—the objects of the consciousness, one was delivering them to the *medium of reflexion.* In philosophy the change in the structure of truth connected with this was very quickly attained: the straightforward assertions

of "rational truths" by Locke, Hume, Wolff, Thomasius, etc. were very soon destroyed by the increased reflexion of later idealism. Even with Fichte or Hegel it was clear that there are no firm maxims called truths; "truth is the whole," that is to say reflexion, which moves in a circle or in continual reiteration, continually struggling through the truth of the contradictions. It is likewise with the truths of social life and politics: the relativism of the sociology of knowledge was the last to fight for the recognition of contradictions in this field. "Natural rights," however much they ought to be re-asserted today, can no longer be drawn together in a catalogue of maxims. The situation where there are pairs or systems of opposing truths, in which the one side can simply be labelled true, the other false, is past. To call this kind of intellectual decision-making "belief" has become inferior, even in religion. *Continuous self-questioning,* the continual intensification of consciousness within oneself, has replaced this form of truth. This is also true of religious truths, in so far as they have assumed the character of objective assertion. . . .

From a philosophical point of view there would be much to say about the higher spirituality of the subjective ego, gained by continual self-examination, which can no longer be finally identified with any objectivised truths which have become concrete and unequivocal. During this reflective process the ego rejects these truths in order to turn with renewed vigour of reflexion into its inexhaustible and bottomless inmost depths. It is this very inwardness in reflexion, which cannot be sounded out, which cannot congeal to any final objective image or assertion, which confronts God today, i.e. the modern relationship of the ego to itself is to be sought there.

The epoch-making form of prevailing rationalism, that level and intensity of consciousness reached at that time, represented the existing highest form in which "revelation" enters the consciousness. "Revelation" today asserts its claim to be recognised in the form of continual self-questioning. Thus it comes about that the religious truths of the Bible, the Fathers of the church, and reformers —without the saving content of revelation, which is independent from the form of consciousness of their perception, being questioned—can be realised today only by way of elevated and permanent reflexion—historical, philosophical, anthropological, existential, dialectic, analytic, etc. This continual self-examination, in which modern faith exists and which is continually practised by the most penetrating Christians and even theologians who are closest to reality— for not one of them still believes the assertions of the Bible as simple facts or directly as objective meaning, all "interpret" through the medium of reflexion— has been little taken into account until now. . . .

The results of the reflective spirituality of modern consciousness, as they affect

the Christian faith and which can only be mentioned briefly here, can be easily shown from present-day religious writings, perhaps less from theological works than from the autobiographies of modern religious lives, which are still regarded by theology as "outsiders." They go as far as a radical rejection of religion in its traditional form altogether. Hammelsbeck, a pupil of Bonhoeffer, speaks even of an "end of the Christian religion," emphasising that very split between the religious maxims and relics of religion, which are objectively exhibited in the world, and the gospel of continual direct and ever-present encounter with Jesus Christ. Simone Weil, a believer of no fixed confession, writes: "Every belief which fills the empty spaces, which allays the bitterness, must be rejected. That in immortality. That in the usefulness of sins: etiam peccata. That in an order of events, determined by providence—in short the 'comforts,' which one usually looks for in religion" and "The supernatural is light; if one objectifies it, one debases it."

Talcott Parsons

FAMILY AND CHURCH AS "BOUNDARY" STRUCTURES

It has been suggested that however fragmented in particular cases, a religious tradition is inherently part of a culture

From "Mental Illness and 'Spiritual Malaise': The Role of the Psychiatrist and of the Minister of Religion," Social Structure and Personality. New York and London: 1964, pp. 305–13. By permission of Association Press.

and that this in turn is in the first instance integrated with a society rather than the personality of an individual. With reference to the theme of values, it is closest to the level of value-commitment which is institutionalized in the society—it is the highest level in the general scale of "ultimacy."

Given this very fundamental difference between the involvement of values in the personality of the individual in the genetic sequence on the one hand, in the culture and from it the society on the other, can there be said to be any analogy between the duality of involvement in the individual in two families, and his involvement in religious organization? I should like to suggest that there is, but that the sense in which this is the case must be very carefully formulated.

There is a critical sense in which the pre-oedipal child is not yet "in the society"; he is in his family. The family is the borderline structure between the roots of the personality of the individual and his beginning participation in the society. As an adult he is a full participant in the society, but through his family of procreation he still participates in this "presocietal soil" of his being as a human personality. There is an analogous sense in which, in all the higher religions, but notably Christianity, the religious collectivity is not fully "in the society." It is in an important sense "set apart," a field of participation which, to use the old phrase, is "in the world but not of it." The way in which this is the case may of course vary immensely, but I should like to postulate an essential element of constancy in this respect.

In the case of a church or denomination in the modern sense, however, its typical member is, in his other roles, very much a member of society. But the church is a partially segregated area where the concerns of secular life can, within limits, be held in abeyance. This would seem to be an important aspect of the more general phenomenon of the "set-apartness" of the realm of the sacred.

Churches, in their symbolic and ritualistic traditions, utilize a set of references of meaning which are particularly "set apart" even from intelligibility in the context of secular life. My general hypothesis here is that these references

are to what may be called metaphorically the "childhood of the culture." They do not refer primarily to stages in the life history of the individual, but to the "foundations" on which the present stage of religious commitment, particularly with reference to "the world," have been built up. In the Christian case, this reference is to the basic constitution of the early Christian church. There are four basic references, involved in all Christian ritual from this point of view, to God the Father as the transcendental reference of the ultimate ground of meaning; to the Christ figure as the mediator between Divinity and humanity and hence as the symbolic head of the church; to the church itself as the brotherhood of Christians imbued with the Holy Spirit, and to the individual Christian as participant in the church and, through it, in Divine grace.

From the point of view of adequate adjustment to and involvement in a society of the modern type, the early church was clearly "archaic." It was quite literally not "of" this world, particularly a modern world. Modern churches are the product of a complex process of evolution from the early church, but they of course still perpetuate this same fundamental complex of belief and symbolism and make it the focus not only of their ritualistic practices but in some sense of their organization as collectivities. In the "middle" period of this evolution the church became a very elaborate organization, which in a sense commanded jurisdiction over something approaching a half of life in society. Since the Reformation there has been a process of social differentiation in the course of which the church has become a more specialized agency to the point where, in the modern Protestant denomination, it has become predominantly a private association which has "lost" many of the functions of the earlier, particularly the mediaeval, church, notably with respect to jurisdiction over secular culture, education, and family life, whereas the political and economic spheres had earlier been predominantly institutionalized in secular terms. The pattern of the denomination has, particularly in the United States, profoundly influenced the religious organization of Judaism, and even considerably that of the Catholic church in that through its minority position and the separation of church and state the religious collectivity is deprived of many of the prerogatives it had traditionally enjoyed and still does where it is the established church.

The most important point for present purposes is that churches as social organizations constitute only a small fraction of the framework of organization of a complex modern society while the rest of the society is specifically categorized as secular. There is a certain parallelism to the fact that the family has, in the course of recent social evolution, also become a more differentiated, specialized agency, less diffusely embedded in larger social structures, such as the nexuses of extended kinship and local community.

This differentiation does not, as it is often contended, imply that either or both have lost most of their "importance" in modern society. It means that the influence they do exert is not through organizational jurisdiction over certain spheres of life now structurally differentiated from them, but through the value-commitments and motivational commitments of individuals. In spheres outside their families and their churches, then, individuals have come to be by and large free of organizational control and in this sense to act *autonomously,* on their own responsibility. But this is by no means to say that their behavior in these "external" spheres is uninfluenced by their participation in the family and the church respectively.

In modern society, then, the family and the church are "boundary-structures" vis-à-vis, respectively, the motivational and the value components of the individual personality. Let us try to sum up how these are related to each other. The axis on which I have tried to relate them is that defined on the one hand by the series of steps in the specification of orientation of value, from the highest religiously grounded level, down through the value system institutionalized in the society, to the levels which can become meaningful in the orientation of the particular individual, faced with a particular life situation within the society. The other series is grounded in the most general exigencies of the organization of the motivational system of the personality, starting in the earliest attachment to the mother, going up through the oedipal stage, through latency and adolescence to adulthood.

The latter series may, from one point of view, be regarded as a series of internalizations of value-patterns, of their "combination" with motivational components. But it starts with highly specific values, and only gradually works up to more and more generalized levels. Conversely the "religious" series is in the first instance one of the specification of values. It, however, starts at the *most* general level and must work "down" from there. Moreover, this process also, to be effective in conduct, must include the *institutionalization* of the values, and one major component of this process of institutionalization is the motivational commitment of individual personalities to them.[1] The church or churches have been the primary social agencies of this process of *institutionalization.*

For the given individual there must of

[1]On the general nature of this process, see "Christianity and Modern Industrial Society," by Talcott Parsons, in *Sociological Theory, Values, and Sociocultural Change,* Edward A. Tiryakian, ed., New York: The Free Press of Glencoe, 1963.

course be a process by which the religious values are internalized in his personality; various aspects of religious education are involved here, but we cannot take space to go into them. Once internalized, however, their reinforcement and maintenance operate through mechanisms which are analogous to those operating in the family of procreation. This is universally the process of religious observance and teaching, perhaps notably observance, on the ritualistic level. The most important point is that in both cases the stabilization functions operate mainly through institutionalized mechanisms which do not require any elaborately specific attention to the problems of the particular individual. It is rather that he normally participates in a nexus of social relationships and the attendant activities, and this participation normally regulates his pattern of commitments.

Now we may raise the question of where and how these two series meet in the structure of the society and the life-pattern of the individual. Looking at the problem from the life-cycle point of view the evidence seems to be that a specially crucial point is adolescence. There are certainly normally what we would call religious components in the orientations internalized throughout the life cycle, and certainly in the pre-oedipal and latency periods. But it is in adolescence that the child first comes to play a more highly differentiated set of roles in a variety of different contexts of participation. Furthermore it is here that he first, in a sense implying real commitment, faces the formation of the basic pattern of his adult life, notably with respect to choice of occupation and of marriage partner. Late adolescence brings both these commitments and also the first formal admission to participation in community responsibility, in modern societies especially symbolized by the right to vote. Finally, most modern religious groups institutionalize full religious participation through ceremonies such as confirmation sometime during this period.[2]

We may thus say that it is typically in adolescence that the individual enters into full participation in his society; that he becomes a contributor through occupational performance to its functioning, and thereby economically self-supporting; that he assumes his share of collective responsibility; and that he begins to participate in the socialization function through marriage. Here for the first time he is really confronted with the problem of the nature and extent of his value-commitments as an adult member of the society.[3]

We have emphasized that this extent and nature of societal commitment is in

[2]Particularly illuminating observations on the significance of adolescence for the religious orientations of the individual are presented in Robert N. Bellah, "The Place of Religion in Human Action," *Review of Religion,* March, 1958.

[3]An important, relatively new factor seems to have entered into this situation, the implications of which are far from clear. This is the increasing participation of the population in higher education even beyond the college level through advanced professional training. Just what are the limits of adolescence is a moot question, but certainly the middle twenties are beyond them. Anyway the effect is to postpone the full assumption of occupational roles and the attendant responsibilities and rewards to a much later point than has been typical of most of the population for most periods. It may well be that this is an important factor in the ferment about problems of meaning in our own time, since there is a certain conflict between the general emphasis on early independence and responsibility on the one hand, and the kind of tutelage in which persons in the system of formal education generally, and of professional training in particular, tend to be kept. One possible tendency may be to treat the higher commitments of meaning as even more tentative than before, since only the fully "mature" person should enter into them. But if this is the tendency, one would expect much conflict in the process of the working out of the new pattern, and that certain groups should feel a particularly urgent need to have firm "answers" almost immediately.

the nature of the case problematical on cultural—that is, eventually religious—levels. Somehow societal interests must be balanced against others, notably those of the individual's own personality itself, and the balance grounded in some orientation defining the meaning of *his* life.

Our very broad conclusion is that the problems of the groundwork of the motivational structure of the personality come to a head in relation to the oedipal stage of personality development, and to the relation between the individual's participation in his family of procreation, as spouse and parent, as an adult. The problems of value-commitment and its grounding in the individual's relation to the deeper layers of the cultural tradition of his society come to a head in his life history in adolescence, and in principle in terms of the current social structure, in his relation to the organized religion in which he was brought up or toward which he may be drawn.

Social Differentiation as Affecting the Statuses of Family and Church

Let us now attempt to look at the problem from the point of view of the social structure. Here the salient fact about modern society is the high development of structural differentiation, and the rapidity with which processes of structural change at the requisite levels have gone on. It has already been noted how the family has become a substantially more specialized agency, more fully differentiated from other agencies. By virtue of this fact its members are placed in a position of far greater autonomy in their relations outside the family, and these spheres constitute an increasingly large share of their life-interests. For the child of course this increasing autonomy centers in his schooling, and the relations to his age peers which are

closely associated with the school, but are also in important respects independent of it.

At the other end of our scale, the church in the denominational pattern has also become a more specialized agency and by virtue of this fact has lost many of its former functions. Its organizational involvement in the "things of this world" has in one important sense steadily receded. It has certainly lost notably in political power, relative to the situation in which established churches existed. It takes far less of a role in the control of economic production, and most notably perhaps it has renounced much of its formal jurisdiction over secular culture and education, and over family relations. By the same token as the family, it has tended to come to exert influence increasingly through its "moral" hold on individuals rather than through the more "massive" societal means of exerting influence.

Like marriage for the adult, church affiliation has become a voluntary matter. This is closely associated with the system of religious toleration, separation of church and state, and denominational pluralism. Religious adherence has become "privatized."

The fact that both institutional complexes have been so involved in the process of differentiation means that a gap has been created between them, which did not previously exist to the same extent. The "wedge" which symbolizes and has in part created this gap is, above all, secular education—in the United States, the public school system. But it is also clearly signalized by the tendency to deny to *organized* religion even directly moral, to say nothing of legal, jurisdiction over marriage and divorce and many of the problems of private morality, particularly those associated with the family.

It is in our opinion this process of structural differentiation in the society which underlies the emerging salience of the problem with which the discussion of this paper started. Our general thesis here is that the problems of mental health and illness root in the motivational organization of the personality of the individual. This in turn genetically is primarily concerned with the process of socialization down through the oedipal period, and in terms of the problem of adjustment of the individual, in the first instance with his roles in marriage and cognate relations and his role as a parent. Since mental illness ramifies into the personality as a whole, it affects all the behavioral contexts in which he is involved, but its structural core rests in the areas designated.

What has been referred to above as "spiritual malaise" is empirically often associated with psychopathology, but must be considered to be analytically independent of it. It concerns above all the individual's commitments to the values of his society and the various subsectors of it with which he is or potentially might be associated, and, from this point of departure, his involvements in problems of meaning. This is in turn genetically associated with his experience in the religious groups with which he and his parents and associates have been affiliated, an experience the personal significance of which has very generally come to a head in adolescence. It leads over into acute problems of the meaning of his life commitments.

Both sets of problems are closely related to strains which are inherent in the structure of a rapidly developing and differentiating society. The family itself has been rapidly changing its character. It is furthermore an important "residual legatee" of strains generated in other parts of the society and hence may often become disorganized under the impact of these strains. On the other side of the picture the religious organization is necessarily deeply involved in the struc-

ture of the society as a whole. Hence any major changes of the latter have a strong impact on organized religion. For these reasons, attitudes toward organized religion and its symbol-systems understandably play a major part in the impact on personalities of all the strains which are operative in a changing society.

Perhaps the most generalized formulation of the common factor in these two problem areas which is current in sociological thinking is the concept of *anomie*. This may be said to be the disturbance of the state of internalized expectations of persons occasioned by the processes of change in the normative components of the institutionalized culture, and hence in the definition of what can legitimately be expected of individuals and classes of them. The most essential point is that in the process of such change, what is expected often over wide areas becomes seriously indeterminate. Anomic components of the situation may, we feel, be propagated in both directions. On the one hand, they may raise questions on the more religiously based level of meaning. Where the normative structure involves serious anomic elements in particular, the balances between performance and sanction, between what is felt to be earned and the actual available rewards in fact forthcoming, will be upset. (The upset, it may be noted, may result from excessive as well as from inadequate reward.) In the other direction, looking to the motivation of the personality, life simply becomes more complex and there are problems of how far individuals are capable of "taking it" from the point of view of their own characters, particularly with respect to their "tolerance of ambiguity" and their capacity to handle risks.

This discussion has stressed the differentiation between the personality and religious contexts, between family and church. Before closing this structural analysis something should be said about one very important context of connection between them. Both the problem of mental health and that of religious commitment involve matters of intimate personal significance to individuals, what in a certain sense are highly "private" affairs. It is not fortuitous, therefore, that both center in the life of the local residential community and that by and large it is as family members that people are associated in churches. Both are hence somewhat withdrawn from the larger economic and political affairs of the society, and are associated together in this withdrawal. This situation has much to do with the sense in which the church has tended to maintain, and even develop further, a set of functions as a diffuse center of association at the first level beyond the household. It is a kind of substitute for the undifferentiated neighborhood, a place where "like-minded" people can get to know each other and be made to "feel at home" in contexts not specifically connected with religion.

It is not uncommon to suggest that this set of functions has in fact become primary, that modern churchgoers are "not really" religious at all, but are only interested in sociability. In my opinion this is a misinterpretation. This associational aspect of the modern denominational parish is a predictable feature of the general pattern of the development of modern society when the fact is taken into account that family and church have such intimate intrinsic relations to each other. The sociability pattern is the primary mechanism by which family and church are brought together with each other. Each, in its own specialized way, involves the "whole person." Unless they are to be, not merely differentiated, but *dissociated,* there must be some adequate mechanism of linkage. My hypothesis is that the church as a "social center" provides this mechanism, and that, as a result of the structural differentiation of modern society, this has become more rather than less important.

Concluding Statement

Gabriel Le Bras

SOME PROBLEMS
OF THE
SOCIOLOGY OF RELIGION

Travellers and scholars have always been fascinated by religious societies, but the scientific analysis of these societies, of their components and their relationships goes back no further than a hundred years. Max Weber was its main pioneer through his studies of the relationship between Calvinism and Capitalism, and especially through his researches into Eastern religions. Whilst Weber concentrated on the economic aspects of religion, his friend Ernst Troeltsch deepened the study of its social aspects, concentrating almost exclusively on Christian conceptions of society. At this same epoch of bold synthesis, Emile Durkeim constructed a philosophical

From " *Problèmes de la sociologie des Religions* " in G. Gurvitch, ed., Traité de sociologie, II, pp. 79–102. Paris : 1960. Translated for this anthology by Gareth Stedman Jones and Ann Duncan. By permission of Presses Universitaires de France.

interpretation of religion, which he conceived as a creation of society, some sort of sublime projection of the secular community. The school which he founded, and which Marcel Mauss was to follow, relied mainly on the systematic study of primitive groups. The researches of Lucien Levy-Bruhl on primitive mental attitudes took up a similar but original interpretation in repudiating the evolutionist thesis. In the twentieth century, study has been concentrated rather on contemporary religions. The school of Le Play had begun a series of monographs whose basic ideas have been applied with new criteria to religious societies, restricting themselves first of all to Catholicism, but ending in a comprehensive study of parishes. Protestantism is also examining its machinery and inquiries into Islam have begun. All these specific studies provide the material for re-assessment of the essential characteristics of religious societies which is inspired by the mass of documentation up to date.

The first problem of the sociology of religion is that of terminology. How can one define religion and the sociology which it may have motivated? If the links with the sacred are taken to constitute the essence of religion, this produces a gulf between religion and philosophy. But it remains to define the notion of the sacred; if it is admitted that the sacred inspires fear and awe, another gulf is opened between religion and magic which implies boldness and compulsion.

There is no difficulty in recognising religion in Christianity and Islam; but the role of religion in the broad Eastern conceptions of life and death, in the manifestations and practices of "primitive peoples," are subject to discussion; indeed would not even more scientific distinctions show us what remains of magic in the most purified religions, and that philosophy is concealed in those of "primitive peoples"? The definition of a sect is another difficult problem. Through dissent or imitation the sect can acquire sufficient originality, sufficient size and sufficient firmness of structure to become equivalent to the mother religion.

The most superficial glance at religions would reveal the profound differences between them: their link could be determined by its nature: family, clan or tribal; or by political geography: village, city, nation; or by the founder who preached a universal doctrine. The sociologist may wonder what might be the functional links between these variegated types. Provisional hierarchy? Progressive extension?

The *numina* of concentric or superimposed groups in the case of the "primitives" have their place in a system of double dimension. And it is the transition from the elementary form to enlarged forms which is part of the key to the mystery. The collapse of civil barriers favours the growth of religions: the gods of federated towns surrender to the gods of a nation and empires provide the ideal conditions for universal religions. This succession of forms raises the problems of the development of each religion, of each type of religion in time, and the relationship between these changes and the changes in secular society. It raises the historical and contemporary problem of mixtures—as in the case of the Afro-Brazilians—or cases of simple contamination as in the case of Islamic or Christian missions; or finally the result of the imposition of successive religions on the masses, one on top of the other. In the course of the long centuries of enthusiasm and apathy the sociologist, after periods of decline, comes across some growth of individual religion (we have studied an example at the end of the Roman republic). The problems of the sociology of religion stretch back to the dawn of history and cover the whole globe. We do not intend to give more than a partial and significant cross section.

Religion creates collective as well as individual connections with the sacred. It creates a society which, to a debatable degree, goes towards creating it. There is a continuous exchange between the human group which constitutes the religious society and the system of beliefs and rites. We have thus suggested the three aims of the sociology of religions. The record of fundamental disagreements of sociologists, and the large differences in emphasis between every one of them constrains us to present this modest essay merely as one of the interpretations of the recently discovered field of the sociology of religions. We will give our readers some appraisal of the program which we have just sketched on its methodological rules, and lastly on the limitations on the subject which certain epistemologists have suggested and the applications or extensions which might attract men of action.

Religious Society

Religions create societies similar to all types of society: they perpetuate themselves by their rules of incorporation; they divide their members up into categories and these members coordinate with each other either through necessary obedience or through voluntary association.

Each society determines the demands and the process of incorporation. Progressive initiation in the case of "primitive peoples" or in early Christianity, provided simple and immediate entrance through baptism in medieval and modern Catholicism, and automatic admission in certain natural groups. Once the preliminary problem of methods of entry into the group has been resolved, the demographers will have to assess the number of entrants: an easy task in the case of Catholics only during the last four centuries because of the existence of baptismal registers, and in some states straightforward institution of official census from the nineteenth century onwards. Whether a census exists or not, a third problem remains: that of true affiliation either by education or example: mothers play an immensely important role in this task. But through a strange omission there is little information on methods of instruction, the cultivation of emotional ties and the prerequisites of attachment to religious society. It is an important gap in our knowledge which needs to be filled.

The faithful form a mass, which gives to each religion its size and importance. The sociologists will, at a later stage, attempt to discern its form. This will be determined by territorial divisions, conditions of life, natural and social distinctions. It may be coherent or dis-

persed; geography will show us entities, diaspora and divisions: the homogeneity of Mohammedan or Hindu India, of South America or of the Mediterranean; the dispersion of Christian missions in the heart of Catholicism, and finally the divisions in Germany and in the United States.

In each enclave authority, austerity and prestige constitute the distance between the crowd and the priesthood, the ascetics or the elders who tend to differentiate their roles in the course of time. The mass sometimes dissolves and reconstitutes itself in the form of religious movements: the divisions between the sexes, the pyramid of ages, divisions of class and occupation.

This subdivision would result in anarchy if the two principles of coordination did not maintain unity and cohesion. Corporations founded on affinity cement the bonds between equals: hierarchies moulded through jurisdiction, magistracy or prestige maintain the ladder to power. What problems are raised by each of these words! The priesthoods of classical antiquity are more familiar than those of "primitive peoples" today: the priests of the Fijians and the priestesses of the Desuns have just been revealed to us. What did we know of the medieval lower clergy, before the recent studies on small incumbents? What do we know of the upholders of Islam from the great "Ulemas" until the masters of the schools of the Koran? We have not paid nearly enough attention to the authorities who did not necessarily possess spiritual power but who nevertheless were the cadres of religious societies.

More attention is paid to religious brotherhoods. They continue to occupy pride of place in recent works where their religious and secular importance is demonstrated through their recruitment and their function.

We have now considered the shapeless bulk, the homogeneous elements and the vertical and horizontal ties of religious society: this moving image with its dissections and measurements draws attention to the structure.

The forms of a religious society vary with the idea it has of its functions and aims and with the conditions of its spiritual and temporal life. It is known how the hierarchial principal has developed in Catholicism, and how the religious orders have created their side chapels. It is also known how the once egalitarian *samgha* have been transformed into the aristocratic *hinayana* within the hierarchial *mahayana*. Once we have studied the anatomy of a religious society, our curiosity ranges over every other aspect of its life. First a word on organisms. A jurist might content himself with the functional rules of a society; the sociologist observes how they actually function: at each level of Catholicism he scrutinises the actions of the head and his helpers (or competitors), the closed gathering of elders and the general assembly of the people. Even at basic tribal level he examines the nexus of forces, the rivalry or the differences between the traditional authorities and the public or secret associations that constitute the mass of the community.

The sociologist is not only interested in the workings of the law, but also the life of men. He searches for the many different signs of their apparent devotion to the religion which they have accepted. Practice of religion is only one of these signs, although for the sociologist the easiest to discover and the most necessary: for it shows us immediately the social division of true adherents and the frequency of their participation. Another important aspect is the psychology of collective practices: what meaning do the agents bestow upon their acts? An attentive semiology can reveal probabilities which intelligent enquiry can turn into certainty. The equipment, the attitude and even the punctuality of persons present at a ceremony allows the enquirer to assess the strength of their attachment to the group (and as we shall soon show, to the system).

The purpose of such curiosity will be the examination of the health of religious bodies. Can it resist the ravages of time, can it maintain its proper shape, and its constitutional balance? How much flexibility and strength does it show, adapting itself through its reforms and its triumphs? Or, on the other hand, do stagnation and decline show inflexibility, narrow conservatism and losses? The progress of Islam in Black Africa, the retreat of primitive religions, and the collapse of all religions especially in Communist countries provides the sociologist with an immense program of observation and research.

Relationship with the External World

Religious society is situated in the world. It has a general conception of the world and the powers which dominate it, and finally of the social structure.

The range of contrasts and nuances stretches from detachment through radical pessimism, cultivated asceticism, or an ecstatic love of God, involvement through the hope of a happy transformation, acceptance of the world by a compromise or by denying evil. Or again, the same society has been able, as in the case of Christianity to reverse its options or, as in the case of Hinduism, to bring them into harmony.

Every religious society makes judgments on each of the sources of Power: authority, riches and prestige. In its attitude towards political power, for instance, Christianity preaches submission, Buddhism indifference, some sects and ascetics, hostility. The same variety of opinions surrounds the question of wealth (which is sometimes taken as a sign of blessing, sometimes as a snare) and the economic system with which the majority of religions manage to co-exist, taking sporadic care to keep their distance from it. Finally, prestige—titles, honors, precedence—has been gradually accepted in all religious societies, either with reserve, or on the contrary, with refinements of their own: we have always insisted on the importance of this element in all societies. It is of especial importance in the case of religion because of the reverence accorded to the sacred, to the mediators between men and the supernatural powers, and to the priesthood often deprived by its rules of life from familiar and worldly pleasures, thus leaving the field clear for other vanities.

Religion has its official or academic doctrines on all forms of secular society. One conception of asceticism ends—as in the original Hinayana, or in several sects stemming from Christianity—in depreciating, or even condemning, marriage; on the other hand Catholicism raises marriage to the dignity of a sacrament. The elements and the aims of marital union are defined by religions; whether monogamous, polygamous or polyandrous; whether they teach the indissolubility of marriage, or divorce, separation of the bodies or the duty of procreation. It is important to distinguish between fundamental principles and popular preaching. The whole religious system of personal relationships and even patrimonies between husband and wife, parent and child, is given force by sacred or canonical texts, by traditions and customs.

Nearly everywhere religion justifies, accepts or supports the social order. In India, the "caste system" founded on the hierarchial opposition between the pure and the impure, is essentially religious. According to the code of Manou the four castes are of divine origin. Christianity has long conceded or desired that each man should remain in the station of his birth. On the other hand, Mazdaism, Hinayana (in India) and the prophets of Israel have repudiated traditional structures. In the great movements of this century, all religions have been called to make a standpoint on the class system. Taking account both of fundamental principles and of the temporal interests of the group, leaders and elders defend or abandon to its fate a tottering regime. A subject worthy of concentrated study.

The social ethic of every religion awaits new historians. How was the scale of sins against one's neighbor constructed and modified? Or even the very notion of pure and impure? By what phases was the link between religion and morality accomplished in ancient societies?

Religious society tends to govern intellectual life. Its ideal is to forbid, indeed repress all instruction contrary to its dogma and its morality; to mould and to direct people's minds. Nothing conforms more to its mission than the maintenance of a strict orthodoxy.

Its role in maintaining moral health brings it within the sphere of economics. Just usages, just weights and measures, the keeping of promises, good faith in acquiring wealth, prohibition of usury and respect for property: all these requirements of religious society tend to create an economic order.

The study of these conceptions is relatively easy. The study of the reality behind them is much more difficult. How much influence does secular society have on religious society and vice versa?

It sometimes happens that secular society suggests to or even imposes on religious society its own web of administrative forms: in France, most dioceses, deaneries and parishes correspond to the department, the canton and the township. The structure of the ecclesiastical hierarchy sometimes imitates or copies secular hierarchies: Catholicism was inspired by the Roman empire and religious authority is confused with civil authority in many societies both living and dead.

Not only the structures but also the life of religious communities depend on movements in secular societies. They pass through the same mutations which result from the legal regime: favor of public authorities allows religious societies to establish themselves and hold their sway; a fall from grace exposes them to decline, or else strengthens the adherence of passionate minorities and fanatical crowds.

Religious society is affected by every shock or change felt by civilisation: the substitution of the factory for the workshop, of public education for family instruction, the growth of contact with the outside world, the movement from the countryside to the town or from one country to another, the advance of sciences, all the new developments of a century shake beliefs, religious practices and traditional customs. Inevitably this produces ruptures, influences and adhesions which we can see today, just as much in "primitive societies" as in those which have reached a high degree of civilisation. Religious societies may have so much influence on secular societies that they may be said to absorb them. In the case of primitive peoples, of the sacred monarchies of antiquity, or of traditional Islam, as in the primitive family, it is not possible to talk of a secular society. In complete contrast, secularised societies seem free from all attachment to positive religion. However, one of the problems of religious sociology is to discover what remains of religious influence in states which supposedly make a distinction between the two Powers, and even those nations whose governments profess themselves alien or hostile to all religion.

This influence is difficult to assess in detail: it becomes apparent in global observations which could usefully be multiplied. Thus the comparison of the number of free unions, divorces and births amongst numerous groups of the faithful belonging to different religions, or between religious and irreligious groups, enables the sociologist to discover significant and sometimes enormous differences.

The role of religious societies in the political field has always obsessed States. Religions preserve the obedience of the subject or provoke his will to revolt; they favour or fight different parties and have a significant effect on international relations. The social structure depends to a large extent upon this arrangement, as much as upon the hierarchial or democratic conceptions of the dominant religion.

Even the economy is affected by the action of religious societies: production, by the feast days; consumption habits, by duties of fast and especially abstinence; distribution, by the principles relating to property.

The World Beyond

The essential characteristic of a religious society is that its ultimate end lies beyond this world: it claims to communicate with the hidden forces which reside either in a definite place which is not situated physically, or in a precise place like a tree or a stone but not in the manner of visible things. The sociologist attempts to understand these manifestations of the metaphysical and the mechanics of relationships with the supernatural world.

Even representations of the supernatural gain inspiration from familiar objects; without going as far as to find in them a projection of terrestial powers or a sublimated image of secular society, it is nevertheless undeniable that the heavenly courts bear a strong resemblance in popular imagination to royal palaces. Dealing between the two worlds can be conceived as a civil contract, and its reduction to this vulgar level is one of the perils which the representatives of deeply religious societies have to avert.

In the religions which can be called theist, the hidden forces compose a society in which the hierarchy tends to become increasingly elaborate. This ascending scale can be drawn up for the great religions: beneath the divine throne Catholicism has its increasingly differentiated and more specialized ranks of angels and saints. In the case of "primitive" religions, these gradations are no less distinct. In former African religions lesser gods are like servants of greater gods. The one god of Siberian tribes reigns over a host of master-spirits. In imperial China precedence was determined by the size of the group which protects the god. A similarly well-defined order reigns in the pantheons of the dead religions of antiquity.

Primitive religions which are closely associated with magic only suggest images and myths which are accepted by the whole social group; but in highly developed religions, thought progresses or deteriorates in very distinct stages which must not be confused. The totality of fixed truths constitutes Dogma; commentators on sacred texts construct Doctrine, with varying degrees of authority; instruction is handed down by the doctrinal authority and produces a diffusion of pure or corrupt forms of belief.

The sociologist is concerned with each of these stages. He studies the collective beliefs of different groups, natural, social or geographical, the contents, the proportions and the strength of these reserves of popular or aristocratic faith. He observes the teachers of the masses; he goes back to the theological schools to understand the structure and terminology of these dogmas (even those of the religion he professes); he studies their

development in a closed society which has demanded or accepted the formulation conveyed in specific circumstances through the intermediary of a language.

The pyramid of Powers is undoubtedly established to give the supernatural a coherent form, but it is also constructed to bind earthly society, through a chain of intercessions, to the Supreme God who reigns over it. The relationship between the two societies—one visible, the other invisible—is the chief preoccupation of all religious societies. They are particularly interesting from the point of view of the sociologist.

Official relations with the hidden forces are defined through fundamental rites; the liturgy, which may be considered both as a science and as an art, clarifies and varies actions. The cult organises these and the laity have their own customs. This creates many problems for sociology. It is a logical necessity and a condition of their survival that the authorities, when organising ceremonies, take account of the structure and the spirit of the group. It is the fate of all religions, that the faithful interpret and sometimes distort official or traditional procedures. Superstition attributes quasi-divine powers to some intermediaries between God and man. Magic even penetrates strictly defined religions in various ways: the hidden forces are conjured up and sometimes chastised; there is really only a vague frontier between established ritual and scattered and individual customs.

Many of these customs continue to survive and even thrive when religion declines. The abandonment of liturgies and dogmas by no means implies a move to atheism; it can result in or even be caused by a proliferation of beliefs and borrowed or invented customs. A fundamental chapter of contemporary religious sociology is that dealing with the transformation of declining religions where it is difficult to uncover the survival of religious feeling. The roads that lead to total atheism are diverse and fall within the scope of this science. Need we add that atheism itself encompasses varied forms and attitudes and we might well wonder whether certain disciplines, certain dogmas and forms of belief do not constitute churches without heavens, and certain affirmations of the sacred.

The delicate and conjectural yardstick of the strength and firmness of religious beliefs belongs initially to religious psychology. This reveals collective attitudes, the main source of the inspirations and the ecstasies of religious societies, and so the sociologist becomes involved in this type of inquiry. He observes the signs of participation, which are often illusory but more often significant, of the degree of adherence. If the religious faith is incommensurable, it is surely not surprising for it to be manifest in sacrifices, the enthusiasms and actions common to the groups concerned; conversely, its weakness would appear in huge desertions, submissions and fearful silences.

For academic purposes we have separated the problems of internal organisation of the three societies; the religious, the secular, and the supernatural. It is clear that the links between them depend on the organisation since worship and doctrine have a great capacity for assimilation, both in religious and secular societies. In the case of "primitive" societies, any analysis would have to take account of the relationship between rite and myth, in the case of great religions the relationship between cult and beliefs. Once the Australian aborigine has identified his gods, he may organise the ritual of the hunt, and penetrate the inviolable, but as techniques change, beliefs, on this account, may be changed. In Catholicism ritual is determined by dogma, but also shapes the meaning of certain definitions.

The size and variety of the problems necessitate the complex methods which we will suggest.

Method

There is as much agreement on the basic question of approach, scale and method of research as there is subtle difference of emphasis. We suggest that research should progress gradually from the most concrete aspects to the heights of abstraction; that the framework of reference of time and space should be steadily enlarged; that the necessary material should be got together carefully and sympathetically.

Every religious society is an organised group of men of which we can find out the exterior characteristics and workings by an inquiry which will take us from the most elementary unity to the point where we may survey all world religions, living and dead.

The sociologist's inquiries will, initially, be only superficial. He will observe what can be counted, weighed and measured only taking care to be accurate and exhaustive. At this stage "sociography" would be an apter name for his work. But this is an essential phase and not merely a preliminary: sociology is initially a descriptive science.

Sociology describes structures and movements. It attempts to discover all about the constitution or customs of a village or a clan. Failure to take account of one subdivision or one significant would falsify the whole picture. In other words we want a complete monograph, a profound and meticulous examination of each small society. The sounding we take is an act of resignation; a confession we have often had to make of the impossibility of encompassing the vast tracks of what is secret or unknown. One can neither get within a million homes, nor probe the innermost depths of a single soul; one has to choose the place and the instruments for scrupulous research: and to attain this correct methods of sampling and judicious questionnaires are necessary.

Once all the elements of a society are known, then sociology—in the common accepted use of the term—begins, by analysing and comparing realities, to deduce generalisations of incontestable scientific value.

The deductions are first based on types. We substitute for the ideal type, the type suggested by an examination of the institutions and the ways of life. Take the case of Christianity. The practice of asceticism draws our attention to the monks and hermits who constitute primary types. Amongst the Cenobites differences depend on the occupation which the community's rule primarily prescribes: manual labour, liturgy, teaching, the rigour of the cloister or the skill with which they influence the outside world. These secondary types guard against the type of inflexibility to which we would expose ourselves by constructing some form of invariable dichotomy or trichotomy. Nothing would be more dangerous than to reduce this mass of clerics, monks and laymen to a unity, when each form of life contains so many primary and secondary types within it. The simplified typology of the knight and the cleric, both in the Middle Ages and down to modern times, has tended to preserve a spirit of conflict; but a complex typology of clerks and knights reveals the diversities, the influences and the antagonisms which would tend to produce a more harmonious co-existence.

The differentiation of types seems to me to be the immediate introduction into the discovery of causes. When we have determined all the types of hierarchies and companies, of the priesthood and the communicants or rites and laws, of the characteristics and number of each type, then the problems of the interdependence between phenomena are brought into sharper focus. By dependence it is necessary to understand that we will not slip into confusing exterior circumstances with the true links or associations. In the case of phenomena, it is rare that one phenomenon encompasses the birth of an institution or the distribution of those who preach to its devotees. The causes, whether distinct, concurrent or coordinated, can only be found by a logical plan. General causes signify the history of the civilisation; national causes, the attitude of the political power, religious vicissitudes, the psychology of the people; local causes, the influence of ecclesiastical and secular cadres, the organisation of groups, the circulation figures of the press, traditions and historical hazards.

"Sociography" in some religions like Catholicism contains such an abundance of material that it is superfluous to accumulate more. For France, we know the normal number of communicants in each social group and in each region: the problem is to explain the mass evolutions and present state of mind regarding such.

When the nature of several religious societies is well-known, one can compare them to uncover identities or analogies between their structures, methods of explanation and developments.

Several religions contain nearly all types, a few of which are found in a great number of religions. The most striking example is that of organised asceticism. Those of us who have stayed in Buddhist monasteries or lamaseries or in Benedictine or Cistercian houses will know that monasticism everywhere has some invariable characteristics. A comparative study of foundations amongst different races produces the same results.

Analogies can be found all over the

world even where imitation plays the smallest part; the principal cause is the identity of aspirations. They lead to types of worship and institutions which seem to be the universal response of nature to the call of the sacred. Comparative studies on different religions will show us how society favours or handles these inventions and choices: why the structures and the lives of religions are affected in the same way by economic changes, movements of population, from isolation or contact with the outside world. There are local, regional and also general causes for the birth, the growth and the decline of all religious societies. This statement of causes will help us to discover a constant relationship which we might term laws, were they not open to a combined coefficient of surprise. We might be thought too prudent, for we meet such regular links that we can hardly doubt that they stem from some unavoidable logic. Is it not the normal fate of sects as of brotherhoods to make themselves into small churches; of ascetic protests to become powerful communities? Is the move from the countryside into the town, and of the peasant into the factory, in any circumstance an occasion for religious progress? What defeat of customary religion has not resulted in the appearance of a personal religion of an intellectual or social elite? Extreme care must prevent us from making too many generalisations. We must remember not to confuse frequency with universality: certain working class populations are more attached to religion than their bourgeois counterparts (in Germany and Poland for example). Nor must we confuse tradition with eternity: the unchangeability of men is problematic. But we can, however, draw attention to the normal conjunction of events, social conditions and men's attitudes to religion, all of which merit at least as much considera-

tion as the equally changeable laws of natural sciences.

Space and Time

To study a religious society as a closed world and only at the present point of time would be to abdicate any attempt to understand its dimensions, its bonds of attachment, its roots and its development.

Every society exists in space. A religious society cannot be subjected to an academic isolation since it is immersed in the whole of society. For "primitive" peoples there is only one society; until the last few years, the fusion was just as complete in Islam. The situation is completely reversed in the secularised countries of our time; but even the most radical of breaks cannot destroy all links.

The logical consequence of this is that the main focus of research (where they are not completely confused) should be centred on secular and not on religious society. We should consider not the parish and the diocese but the township and the region. Nothing will be considered irrelevant: the countryside and the men will compose a microcosm in which we will situate our religious society. Even bishops follow this method today. The handsome atlases which they have compiled contain as many secular as religious maps: place of abode, demography and movements of population occupy more place in them than religious practice.

Until the fifteenth century everywhere people were naturally placed in religious setting. Today the essentials of religious society are more often disseminated within secular society. Remoteness and contact, dispersion and coagulation, now take on an importance previously unsuspected or minimal.

Every religious society exists in time. We cannot resolve, nor even state, its problems except with reference to the past. The size and shape of religious societies change continually under our eyes; many lose adherents, some gain them. Demographic curves represent the progress of these movements: they allow us to follow the rise of Islam in black Africa, the fall in baptisms in France and the retreat of primitive religions.

A worry in all religions is the difficulty of preserving hierarchical cadres. It is well known what troubles are caused by the crisis in the number of priestly or pastoral callings in the case of Christian beliefs. But also amongst primitive peoples, priests and even the people who agree to represent the gods in the main ceremonies become rarer. These facts betray a decrease in fervour, and reveal a general decline in religion through the lack of priests and dedicated auxiliaries. It is necessary for us to get back to the origins of the crisis to understand its meaning and its breadth.

The first function of history is thus to clarify the present situation. It is clear that the corpus of beliefs, rites and laws in every religion is formed very gradually. In which societies did each of the positive religions arise, prosper and decline? It is not the role of sociology to follow in minute detail the development of religions; this belongs to the history of religions. It is for sociology to highlight the constituent traits of the group, its individual structure, its beliefs and its collective practices, to reveal the continuity or discontinuity of its existence—revivals and acculturation, substitutions, and inventions. The types of development raise problems of the awakening of latent traditions, of the slow regeneration that accompanies a change of civilisation, of the substitution of an urban for a rural religion and of strong and compelling creations.

Although recourse to history is too often limited to lazy generalizations, it is indispensable for the investigation of causes. To explain the weak religious observance of the Auxerrois by Jansenism, or Vendean Catholicism by the "chouannerie" is a puerile simplification. Jansenism and Chouannerie are amongst numerous causes which one would suppose to be a work: the organisation and activities (positive or negative) of ecclesiastical and secular authorities, of the abbeys, dislocation through war and a variety of external factors.

Finally the sociology of religions takes as known the whole of history of dead and living religions. Egypt and Babylon provide valuable examples for a typology of the priesthood. And no typology could be complete without examining all the vicissitudes of Buddhism, Christianity, Islam. It is the whole experience of religious societies since the beginning of time that makes possible a sketch of types, causes and regularities.

Means and Alliances

To undertake such a vast task, religious sociology uses every means; it employs all the aids that science—and not solely human science—can provide.

Religious sociology uses modern techniques and especially two amongst them: statistics and cartography.

"A discipline," wrote Paul Montel, "does not really merit the status of a science until the time when mathematics have penetrated it." Lord Kelvin can be used in support of such a strong maxim: "if you can measure something you are talking about and express it in numbers, then you know something about it; but if you cannot measure it or express it in numbers, then your knowledge is vague and unsatisfactory." We have given many proofs of this truth in examining several religions. According to the point of view of the author, France has either long been wholly Catholic (deduction made from the minority of Protestants and Jews) or a country completely detached from the church (deduction resulting from eccentric cantons, or from some biased bourgeois writers). In the Islamic countries, we have found statements less clear cut but just as contradictory about presence at prayer on Fridays or about the strength of brotherhoods. One can imagine the imprecision and the uncertainty of the figures provided by populations who attach importance only to sacred numbers.

Yet all religious societies provide statistical evidence since all of them prescribe or forbid public acts. It is evident that the more they assume legal forms the more statistics they provide. Catholicism provides a particularly useful instance especially in the classical age. Without halting at the five pillars of Islam let us look at the customs of the "primitive" peoples. Is it impossible to find out how many Zunis carry out the duty of throwing a fist-full of flour in the air every morning (as they recite a prayer) in front of their doors (with their faces to the east)?

Indispensable and enlightening as they are, statistics must be handled with the greatest of prudence. Care must be taken not to put into fractions anything except homogeneous figures. It is already something to know that 30% of the adults in Nantes are regular attendants at Sunday mass; that 30% of the men of an Arabian town go regularly to Friday prayers, and that 80% of the Zunis throw their morning flour into the air every day. These figures provide a useful indication, especially if one knows that the top of the curve was 100% a century ago. But the sociologist cannot content himself with raw figures. He will assess the proportion for each of the categories we have distinguished: age, sex, profession, locality, denominator; only those committed can be shown, the lapsed will

have to be deducted. In this way both peak percentages and false averages will be eliminated.

Handled with extreme attention to accuracy and caution, statistics must not blind us to the fact that the quantitative draws all its value from the qualitative. It is important to know the proportion of those attending Sunday mass, and of Zunis performing morning worship; it is even more important to understand the meaning of such observance. Mathematics is important and necessary; but only to count acts whose meaning is revealed, or at least suggested and estimated, through psychology. Our own experience has constantly turned us towards this master science of man. What is important in the interpretation of such acts is to know whether they stem from obedience to custom, or personal devotion, disinterested homage or fear of magic.

Graphs illustrate the results of calculations. It is desirable that people should be agreed on the scale of maps, the use and variety of colours and of the indications made. In this way our confused impressions of a diocese or a region become perfectly clear. The making of an atlas of religions will be the crowning triumph of "sociography."

Religious sociology needs the assistance of all the human sciences. We have encountered almost all of them: geography, history, psychology, and ethnology, law and ethics, theology and liturgy. It is not surprising that there were some demarcation disputes, or that there should have been some controversy concerning the relationship between religious sociology and psychology or history, or upon the preserves of human geography or phenomenology. But the spirit of cooperation has definitely cast these fruitless quarrels into oblivion.

There are fields common to several sciences, pursued by each with original preoccupations and methods. It is thus with collective psychology, phenomenology and human geography.

Other fields appear separate: but investigation into them would be impossible without the cooperation of neighbouring sciences. Geography, physics, law and history, have aims, methods and characteristics completely different from religious sociology. Thus law makes permanent the generally sanctioned rules of life in society, whilst religious sociology makes no normative or vindicating claims: but the structure of a hierarchy and the life of a parish are subordinated to prescriptions and taboos which the sociologist needs to know.

So religious sociology is a science of synthesis which harmoniously collates all the findings of individual sciences in connection with the structure and life of religious societies. Within the immense field of the science of religions, it is limited to considering the social to the exclusion of the purely individual or technical, but nothing which concerns the collective relationships of men with the sacred lies outside its range of interest.

Limits and Uses

We have revealed the justification of a human science through its program and methods. Not all sociologists are agreed upon the dimensions and functions of religious sociology. We have propounded them from our own standpoint without raising controversies. It is relevant here to state the main differences of opinion concerning its limits and uses.

The greatest scientific ambition is to discover the essence of religion. Emile Durkheim nurtured this ambition. "The principal aim of the science of religions," he wrote, "is to reach the point of grasping what constitutes the religious nature of man, the product of social causes." By going back to the most ancient

societies one would discover the primitive taboos of the clan, which are made into totems and made sacred to ensure their permanence. It is well known what objections have been raised against the joining of the taboo to the sacred, to the notion of the totem, to the evolutionary and organicist theory of the master of the "French School." It seems certain to us that no science will reach all the depths of religious sentiment. The most personal experiences which are the essence of religion elude us: we only perceive superficial manifestations of it, and can only make guesses at their meaning.

A radical opposition to the views of Durkheim would result in excluding from the program all approaches to the sacred. Certainly no religion can reasonably admit that the corpus of its dogma and ethics should be considered as a "secretion" of human societies. The interdictions observed by the adherents of each religion can arouse the sympathy of every student and even appeal to the reason. Every belief has its element of mystery. But we consider that no religion can deny the place of the community in the terminology of its definitions and the demands they make in the conditions and adaptions of worship, the preoccupations and the strictness of its morality.

Whether bold or constrained the sociologist assigns limits to his own research and sometimes to all research. He sometimes places these limits in time. The school of Durkheim at first concentrated on tribes and clans where the essential had not yet been obscured by the accessory and the secondary. Several people have suggested a practical reason rather than this argument of principal for this limitation in time: the impossibility of really knowing about dead religions of the past or the difficulty of observation would invalidate historical sociology. The excessive hopes of Durkheim have faded, and objections against history, besides only having a relative value—since observation is not the only means to knowledge—would reduce the field of religious sociology to contemporary societies.

Those who would reduce this vast field which we have described, do so in widely varying proportions. Excellent authors who have often influenced our thought exclude from religious sociology "the objective principles of religious life: worship, law and morality; the relation of these values with secular realities," and limit study to the forms or social structures of religious life, and the relationship of these structures with each other and with secular structures. We share their anxiety to avoid the enclopaedic approach: religious sociology has no reason to encroach on canon law, or to embody the examination of social Christianity. It has no need to study the reciprocal influences between canon and civil law, or religious and secular music. We might add that canon law and religious music only interest it directly when they are an expression or a rule of the religious society. On the other hand, it seems to us that the relationship between religious life and demography or economy lies properly in the realm of sociology. It is the structure, the teaching and the influence of the religious society which help to determine the curves of population and economy.

These reductions which we have seen made at the highest level of the subject are also made at the base. Some authors would assign purely theological foundations to religious sociology. The natural differences between the sacred and the profane would keep out the encroachments of an empirical phenomenological science. Without Revelation the structure and life of Christianity would be incomprehensible. Similar examples can be found amongst the philosophers of

Islam and other religions. Does this signify that dogma cannot be explained by the pressures and instruments of secular society? The believer, as we have already said, cannot renounce this profession of faith without making it meaningless. Do, however, dogma and its interpretation take pride of place in the vast field we have explored? Can the typology of religious orders or the structure of society of bishoprics, parishes and brotherhoods be explained by Revelation? The denunciations made by the Mohammedan or the Christian—and these are not even easily accessible to the agnostic—become reduced to the deepest meaning of his faith.

On the question of these differing opinions about the dimensions of religious sociology, we would concur with all that clears the way for a reasonable extension of the subject. We agree with the theologians that knowledge of dogmas and doctrines is essential to an understanding of a religious society and that belonging to that society, far from obscuring understanding, gives the extra knowledge of personal experience. Again we can agree with those, who, believers or non-believers, put emphasis on the outer forms of religious or irreligious solidarity. We would give a very important place to popular religion, to collective disagreements and to atheism itself as an expression of collective denial and as the motivating force of real groups (sometimes organised) of the indifferent, of moderate opponents or of the declared enemies of religion. We also agree with more ambitious colleagues, that sociology, if it cannot grasp the essence of religion, can at least show us forms of collective experience and can throw some light on communal inspiration.

Thus, there are many opinions on the scope of programs and we have only put forward the broadest imaginable of them, with the promise that one must never lose sight of the essence, forms and manifestations of religious society. Are there the same disagreements about the scientific and practical use of the subject?

That it should arouse some mistrust is to be expected from its aims. We have come across that of religious writers who fear the lowering of the sacred to the level of the profane. This is an ephemeral difficulty previously encountered by exegesis and anthropology.

Also natural is the mistrust of specialists who cast a disparaging glance upon new methods and foreign types of approach. Their scepticism is really directed at sociology in general and not just at one if its branches. It is justified when levelled against excess. We would hope to show that it is excessive in itself.

Religious and secular sciences receive in exchange for their invaluable discoveries one major return.

Liturgy, canon law and even theology and sacred arts have benefited from sociology and particularly religious sociology. A few examples can be cited. We have studied religious sociology for more than thirty years in order to gain a better understanding of the history of the law and institutions of the church. We now find the parish, the dioceses, and even Christianity more intelligible because, in place of an analytical table of juridical rules, we have substituted in our programs a vision of parish diocesan and Roman society with its rivalries, its tensions, its conflicts maintained by corporative interests; with the cooperations, moments of relaxation and alliances, inspired by the common ideal. The rule and the institution, whilst losing nothing of their technical character, appear both as the products and the regulators of social life. Do we forsake canon law by considering the government of the parish, the dioceses or Christianity as the meeting place of a head, a senate or an assembly? Or

because we consider the laws as the result of social experience rather than the product of authoritarian will—or the authorities themselves sacred? Sacred arts also benefit from the findings of sociology. So does music. Is it not obvious that the inspirations, the forms and even the techniques evolve according to the demands, the structures and the instruments of religious society? Sociology explains neither religion nor genius: but it does explain the conditions in which musical activity arises and flourishes. Is it likely that the careers of great musicians, the *genres* which they have exemplified, the rhythms and harmonies with which they have charmed us would be unrelated to the societies in which they lived?

What secular science would repudiate the insights and illuminations which can be provided by religious sociology? Ethnology, psychology, geography and economics, history and politics admit their support. Let us just take the examples of these two last sciences. Are not the structure and life of religious societies part of the subject matter of history? The study of the development of these powerful bodies, their relationships with each other and with civil societies, is an aim shared with religious sociology, which brings its own preoccupations and methods to bear on a field where exact chronology, the succession of events and research into economic and political causes could absorb the attention of the historian attempting to understand or explain an epoch.

Political science, though it appears completely secular, has close relations with religious sociology. These are apparent in societies initially subjected to religious law like "primitive" clans and Islamic states, and also in societies officially separated from all churches like the United States and popular democracies. Religious groups are in fact amongst the most coherent of national forces, and in certain states, the only organised forces with a minimum or maximum of independence, depending on whether it is a popular or bourgeois democracy.

Pure science has benefited greatly from religious sociology and this explains its success in uinversities and research centres. Nevertheless it is its practical usefulness that has stimulated the most energetic research both in religions and in States.

Different religions gain advantages from sociology, since it provides them with a balance sheet of their strengths and weaknesses, an insight into the dangers that threaten them, and means (often disproportionate) by which they can maintain themselves. At the heart of Catholicism, sociology is being used for the aid of the clergy and has stimulated both in men and works a remarkable effort at understanding which has resulted in investigations of real value and in a comprehensive cartography. Protestantism is also increasing its inquiries and pondering over the proofs as well as the mysteries of the mobility of religious societies. A newborn curiosity in Islam and in Buddhism strengthens our hope of a similar impulse: thus the upheavals of the twentieth century will be of great use to science in all religious societies and will benefit secular societies through the use religious societies make of science.

What we have said about political science makes it easy to understand why States should be interested in religious sociology. Precise and scientific knowledge of the structure and the life of Christian confessions and Islamic communities has always preoccupied the USSR and neighbouring countries; misunderstanding of the structures and life of Catholicism and Protestantism was one of the avowed weaknesses of the Third Republic at the beginning of the twentieth century. One of the aims of political science would be to provide statesmen with adequate means of information on which to base their actions; this could not be fulfilled without drawing upon the useful conclusions of religious sociology.

Thus the many interests of religious sociology have been recognised by States and Churches and by those involved in research. Chairs have been created, periodicals and study groups have been set up. We think that, far from engendering unwelcome clashes as we feared, religious sociology allows various religions to examine and purify themselves and to esteem each other; it enables secular societies to rid themselves of dangerous myths; it allows all educated men to consider dispassionately the social facts and the collective aspirations which bear witness to the universal and permanent need for the sublime.

SELECTED BIBLIOGRAPHY *

I Works of Reference: Bibliographies, Guides, Periodicals, Anthologies

"Sociology of Religions. A Trend Report and Bibliography." *Current Sociology,* V, 1, 1956.

Carrier, Hervé and Emile Pin, *Sociologie du Christianisme, Bibliographie Internationale/Sociology of Christianity, International Bibliography*. Rome, 1964.

The Oxford Dictionary of the Christian Church, ed. F.L. Cross. London, 1958.

Die Religion in Geschichte und Gegenwart. 3rd ed., 6 vols., Tübingen, 1957–1962.

Archives de Sociologie des Religions. Paris, 1956 to date.

Social Compass. (Index, 1953–63, vols. 1–10.) Den Haag, 1953 to date.

International Yearbook for the Sociology of Religion, ed. Joachim Matthes, vols. I and II. Köln-Opladen, 1965, 1966. (Continuing.)

Journal for the Scientific Study of Religion. Washington, 1960ff.

Fürstenberg, Friedrich, ed., *Religionssoziologie*. Neuwied and Berlin, 1964.

Lee, Robert, ed., *Cities and Churches: Readings in the Urban Church*. Philadelphia, 1962.

Lessa, William A., and Evon Z. Vogt, eds., *Reader in Comparative Religion. An Anthropological Approach*. Evanston, Ill., and Elmsford, NY., 1958.

Schneider, Louis, ed., *Religion, Culture and Society*. New York, London, Sydney, 1964.

Yinger, J. Milton, *Religion, Society and the Individual*. New York, 1957.

II Representative Texts in the Development of the Sociology of Religion

Becker, Carl L., *The Heavenly City of the Eighteenth-Century Philosophers*. New Haven, 1932.

Bergson, Henri, *Two Sources of Morality and Religion*. New York, 1935. (*Les deux sources de la morale et de la religion*. Paris, 1932.)

Borkenau, Franz, *Der Übergang vom feudalen zum bürgerlichen Weltbild*. Paris, 1934.

Bradley, Francis Herbert, *Ethical Studies*. 2nd ed., Oxford, 1927; first 1876.

Burckhardt, Jakob, *The Age of Constantine the Great*. New York, 1949. (*Die Zeit Konstantins des Grossen*. 1853.)

Comte, Auguste, *Cours de philosophie positive*. 6 vols., Paris, 1830–1842. (Abridged and condensed: *The Positive Philosophy of Auguste Comte*. London, 1868.)

Coulanges, Numa Denis Fustel de, *The Ancient City*. Boston and New York, 1882; Anchor ed., n.d. (*La cité antique*. Paris, 1864.)

Durkheim, Emile, *The Elementary Forms of the Religious Life*. London, 1915. (*Les formes élémentaires de la vie religieuse*. Paris, 1912.)

——, "De la définition des phénomènes religieux," *L'Année sociologique,* II, 1899.

——, *Suicide* (especially book II, chapter 2, "Egoistic Suicide"). Glencoe, Illinois, 1951. (*Le suicide*. Paris, 1897.)

* Note: When an entry in the following bibliography represents a translated text, the title of the English translation is given first and is then followed, in parentheses, by the original title and date of original publication.

446

Feuerbach, Ludwig, *The Essence of Christianity*. London, 1854. (*Das Wesen des Christentums*. Leipzig, 1841.)

Frazer, James G., *The Golden Bough: A Study in Magic and Religion*. 12 vols., 3rd ed., revised and enlarged, London, 1911–1915.

Freud, Sigmund, "Obsessive Actions and Religious Practices," vol. IX, *The Standard Edition of the Complete Psychological Works of Sigmund Freud*. London, 1959. ("Zwangshandlungen und Religionsübungen," Zeitschrift für Religionspsychologie, I, 1, 1907.)

———, *Totem and Taboo*, vol. XIII, *Standard Edition*. London, 1955. (*Totem und Tabu*. Vienna, 1913.)

———, *The Future of an Illusion*, vol. XXI, *Standard Edition*. London, 1961. (*Die Zukunft einer Illusion*. Leipzig, Vienna and Zurich, 1927.)

———, *Moses and Monotheism*, vol. XXIII, *Standard Edition*. London, 1964. (*Der Mann Moses und die monotheistische Religion: Drei Abhandlungen*. Amsterdam, 1939.)

Groethuysen, B., *Die Entwicklung der bürgerlichen Welt- und Lebensanschauung in Frankreich*, I, II, Halle, 1927–1930.

Halévy, Elie, "Religion," part III, ch. 1, *England in 1815*. London, 1949. (First published in French, 1913.)

Haller, William, *The Rise of Puritanism*. New York, 1938.

Hegel, Georg Wilhelm Friedrich, *Early Theological Writings*. Chicago, 1948. (*Hegels theologische Jugendschriften*. Tübingen, 1907.)

———, *Lectures on the Philosophy of Religion, Together With a Work on the Proofs of the Existence of God*. 3 vols., London, 1895. (*Vorlesungen über die Philosophie der Religion, nebst einer Schrift über die Beweise vom Dasein Gottes*, 1840)

———, *Lectures on the Philosophy of History*, 1858. (*Vorlesungen über die Philosophie der Geschichte*, 1837.)

Heine, Heinrich, *Religion and Philosophy in Germany*. Boston, 1882. (*Zur Geschichte der Religion und Philosophie in Deutschland*. Hamburg, 1835.)

Hume, David, *The Natural History of Religion*. 1757.

———, *Dialogues Concerning Natural Religion*. 1779.

James, William, *The Varieties of Religious Experience*. London, 1902.

Lévy-Bruhl, Lucien, *How Natives Think*. 1926. (*Les Fonctions mentales dans les sociétés inférieures*. 1910.)

———, *Primitive Mentality*. 1923. (*La Mentalité primitive*. 1922.)

Lough, John, ed., *The Encyclopédie of Diderot and D'Alembert (1751–65), Selected Articles*. Cambridge, 1954.

Lowie, Robert H., *Primitive Religion*. New York, 1924.

Löwith, Karl, *From Hegel to Nietzsche. The Revolution in Nineteenth-Century Thought*. New York, 1964. (*Von Hegel zu Nietzsche. Der revolutionäre Bruch im Denken des neunzehnten Jahrhunderts*. Zurich, 1941.)

Malinowski, Bronislaw, *Magic, Science and Religion and other Essays*. Boston, 1948.

Mannheim, Karl, *Ideology and Utopia*, enlarged ed. London, 1936. (*Ideologie und Utopie*. Bonn, 1929.)

Marx, Karl, and Friedrich Engels, *On Religion*. Moscow, 1957.

Mauss, Marcel, *Sociologie et anthropologie*. Paris, 1950.

Mill, John Stuart, *Nature, the Utility of Religion, Theism, Being Three Essays on Religion*. London, 1874.

Newman, John Henry, *An Essay on the Development of Christian Doctrine*. 1845.

Niebuhr, H. Richard, *The Social Sources of Denominationalism*. New York, 1929.

Nietzsche, Friedrich Wilhelm, *The Genealogy of Morals*. Edinburgh and London, 1910. (*Die Genealogie der Moral*. 1887.)

Radcliffe-Brown, A.R., *The Andaman Islanders*. Cambridge, 1922.

Rank, Otto, *The Myth of the Birth of the Hero*. New York, 1914. (*Der Mythos von der Geburt des Helden*. 1909.)

Rauschenbusch, Walter, *Christianity and the Social Crisis*. New York, 1907.

Saint-Simon, Claude Henri Comte de, *Nouveau Christianisme*. 1825, vol. III, new edition of *Oeuvres*, Paris, 1966.

Simmel, Georg, *Sociology of Religion*. New York, 1959. (*Die Religion, in Die Gesellschaft*, Sammlung Sozialpsychologischer Monographien, vol. II, 2nd ed., Frankfurt, 1912.)

Smith, William Robertson, *The Religion of the Semites*. 1889.

Spencer, Herbert, *Principles of Sociology*. 3 vols., London, 1876–1896.

Strauss, David Friedrich, *The Life of Jesus*. 3 vols., London, 1846. (*Das Leben Jesu*. 1835.)

Tawney, R. H., *Religion and the Rise of Capitalism*. London, 1926.

Tocqueville, Alexis de, *Democracy in America*. 2 vols., New York, 1945. (*De la démocratie en Amérique*. Paris, 1835, 1840.)

Troeltsch, Ernst, *The Social Teaching of the Christian Churches*. New York, 1960. (*Die Soziallehren der christlichen Kirchen und Gruppen*. Tübingen, 1912.)

———, *Aufsätze zur Geistesgeschichte und Religionssoziologie*, vol. IV, *Gesammelte Schriften*, ed. Hans Baron. Tübingen, 1925.

Tylor, Edward Burnett, *Primitive Culture: Researches Into the Development of Mythology, Philosophy, Religion, Language, Art, and Custom*. 2 vols., London, 1891; first ed. 1871.

Weber, Max, *The Protestant Ethic and the Spirit of Capitalism*. London, 1930. (*Die protestantische Ethik und der Geist des Kapitalismus*, in *Archiv für Sozialwissenschaft and Sozialpolitik*, vols. XX and XXI, 1904–05. Reprinted in revised form in *Gesammelte Aufsätze zur Religionssoziologie*, 3 vols., Tübingen, 1920–21.)

———, *The Sociology of Religion*. Boston, 1963. (*Religionssoziologie*. [*Typen religiöser Vergemeinschaftung*.] ch. 5, *Wirtschaft und Gesellschaft*, 4th ed., Tübingen, 1956, first 1922.)

———, *The Religion of China: Confucianism and Taoism*. Glencoe, Illinois, 1951. *The Religion of India: The Sociology of Hinduism and Buddhism*. Glencoe, 1958. *Ancient Judaism*. Glencoe, 1952. (*Gesammelte Aufsätze zur Religionssoziologie*. 3 vols., Tübingen, 1920–1921.)

———, "Die charismatische Herrschaft und ihre Umbildung," *Wirtschaft und Gesellschaft*, 4th ed., ch. 9, section 5. Tübingen, 1956.

———, "Politische und hierokratische Herrschaft," *Wirtschaft und Gesellschaft*, 4th ed., ch. 9, section 6. Tübingen, 1956.

Westermarck, Edvard Alexander, *Origin and Development of Moral Ideas*. 2 vols., London, 1906–1908.

Wundt, Wilhelm, *Elements of Folk Psychology*. London, New York, 1916. (*Elemente der Völkerpsychologie*. Leipzig, 1912.)

III Introductory and General Works

Argyle, Michael, *Religious Behaviour*. Glencoe, Illinois, 1959.

Becker, Howard, *Through Values to Social Interpretation*. Durham, 1950.

Bellah, Robert N., "Religious Evolution," *American Sociological Review*, XXIX (June, 1964), 358–74.

Berger, Peter, "Charisma and Religious Innovation: The Social Location of Israelite Prophecy," *American Sociological Review*, XXVIII, 1963, 940–950.

Berger, Peter, and Thomas Luckmann, "Sociology of Religion and Sociology of Knowledge," *Sociology and Social Research,* XLVII (July, 1963).

Carrier, Hervé, *Sociology of Religious Belonging.* New York, 1965. (*Psycho-sociologie de l'appertenance religieuse.* Rome, 1960.)

Desroche, Henri, "Areas and Methods of a Sociology of Religion, The Work of Gabriel Le Bras," *Journal of Religion,* XXXV (January, 1955), 34–47.

———, "Socialisme et sociologie du christianisme," *Cahiers Internationaux de Sociologie,* vol. XXI (July-December, 1956), 149–167.

———, *Socialismes et sociologie religieuse.* Paris, 1965.

———, *Marxisme et religions.* Paris, 1962.

Goddijn, W., and H.P.M. Goddijn, *Kirche als Institution. Einführung in die Religionssoziologie.* Mainz, 1963.

Goldschmidt, Dietrich, and Joachim Matthes, *Probleme der Religionssoziologie,* Sonderheft 6, *Kölner Zeitschrift für Soziologie und Sozialpsychologie.* Köln und Opladen, 1962. (Extensive bibliography.)

Homans, George C., "Anxiety and Ritual: the Theories of Malinowski and Radcliffe-Brown," *American Anthropologist,* XLIII (1941), 164–72.

Leach, Edmund, *Rethinking Anthropology.* London, 1961.

Le Bras, Gabriel, *Etudes de sociologie religieuse.* I: *Sociologie de la pratique religieuse dans les Campagnes Françaises.* Paris, 1955. II: *De la morphologie à la typologie.* Paris, 1956.

———, "Problèmes de la sociologie des religions," Georges Gurvitch, ed., *Traité de Sociologie,* II, Paris, 1960, 79–102.

Van der Leeuw, G., *Religion in Essence and Manifestation.* 2nd ed., London, 1964. (*Phänomenologie der Religion.* Tübingen, 1933.)

Lévi-Strauss, Claude, *Structural Anthropology.* New York, London, 1963. (*Anthropologie structurale.* Paris, 1958.)

———, *Totemism.* Boston, 1963. (*Le totémisme aujourd'hui.* Paris, 1962.)

———, *The Savage Mind.* London, 1966. (*La pensée sauvage.* Paris, 1962.)

Mehl, Roger, *Traité de sociologie du Protestantisme.* Neuchatel, 1965.

Parsons, Talcott, "The Theoretical Development of the Sociology of Religion," *Journal of the History of Ideas,* V (1944), 176–219. (Reprinted as chapter 10, *Essays in Sociological Theory.* Glencoe, Illinois, 1954.)

———, *Religious Perspectives of College Teaching in Sociology and Social Psychology.* New Haven, 1951.

———, "Mental Illness and 'Spiritual Malaise': The Role of the Psychiatrist and of the Minister of Religion," in *Social Structure and Personality.* Free Press of Glencoe, Collier Macmillan, New York and London, 1964.

Wach, Joachim, *Sociology of Religion.* Chicago, 1944.

IV Studies of Religion in Contemporary Industrial Society

Acquaviva, Sabino S., *Untergang des Heiligen in der industriellen Gesellschaft.* Essen, 1964. (*L'Eclissi del sacro nella civiltà industriale.* Milano, 1961.)

Adorno, Theodor W., et al., *The Authoritarian Personality.* 2 vols., New York, 1950.

Clark, S. D., *Church and Sect in Canada.* Toronto, 1948.

Coutrot, Aline, and François G. Dreyfus, *Les forces religieuses dans la société française.* Paris, 1965.

Fichter, Joseph, *Social Relations in an Urban Parish.* Chicago, 1954.

Garaudy, Roger, *From Anathema to Dialogue*. New York, 1966. (*De l'anathème au dialogue*. Paris, 1965.)

Glock, Charles E., "The Religious Revival in America," in papers of the conference: *Religion and the Face of America*. Berkeley, 1958, 25–42.

―――, and Rodney Stark, *Religion and Society in Tension*. Chicago, 1966.

Goldschmidt, D., F. Greiner, H. Schelsky, eds., *Soziologie der Kirchengemeinde*. Stuttgart, 1960.

Greeley, A. M., *Religion and Career: A Study of College Graduates*. New York, 1963.

Gustafsson, Berndt, "Staatskirche und Entkirchlichung in Schweden," in *Probleme der Religions-Soziologie,* Dietrich Goldschmidt and Joachim Matthes, eds.; Sonderheft 6, *Kölner Zeitschrift für Soziologie und Sozialpsychologie*. Köln und Opladen, 1962, 158–165.

Herberg, Will, *Protestant, Catholic, Jew*. New York, 1955.

Kellner, Erich, ed., *Christentum und Marxismus Heute*. Vienna, 1966.

Lenski, Gerhard, *The Religious Factor*. New York, 1961.

Luckmann, Thomas, *Das Problem der Religion in der modernen Gesellschaft*. Freiburg i.B., 1963.

Marty, Martin E., "Sects and Cults," *The Annals of the American Academy of Political and Social Science,* CCCXXXII (November 1960), 125–134.

Matthes, Joachim, *Die Emigration der Kirche aus der Gesellschaft*. Hamburg, 1964.

Pin, Emile, *Pratique religieuse et classes sociales dans une paroisse urbaine, Saint-Pothin à Lyon*. Paris, 1956.

Pope, Liston, *Millhands and Preachers*. New Haven, 1942.

Poulat, Emile, "The Future of the Worker Priests," *The Modern Churchman* (June 1959), 191–199.

―――, *Naissance des prêtres-ouvriers*. Tournai, Paris, 1965.

Schelsky, Helmut, "Ist die Dauerreflektion institutionalisierbar? Zum Thema einer modernen Religionssoziologie," *Zeitschrift für evangelische Ethik,* I (July 1957), 153–174.

Siefer, Gregor, *The Church and Industrial Society. A Survey of the Worker-Priest Movement and its Implications for the Christian Mission*. London, 1964. (*Die Mission der Arbeiterpriester. Ereignisse und Konsequenzen*. Essen, 1960.)

Sklare, Marshall, *Conservative Judaism*. Glencoe, Illinois, 1955.

Visser T'Hooft, W.A., and J.H. Oldham, *The Church and its Function in Society*. Chicago, 1935.

Ward, C.K., *Priests and People: A Study in the Sociology of Religion*. Liverpool, 1961.

Wilson, Bryan R., *Sects and Society: a Sociological Study of the Elim Tabernacle, Christian Science, and Christadelphians*. London, 1961.

V Historical and Comparative Studies

Balandier, Georges, *Sociologie actuelle de l'Afrique Noire*. Paris, 1955.

Bellah, Robert N., *Tokugawa Religion*. Glencoe, Illinois, 1957.

Berger, Peter, "Charisma and Religious Innovation: The Social Location of Israelite Prophecy," *American Sociological Review,* XXVIII (1963), 940–950.

Birnbaum, Norman, "The Zwinglian Reformation in Zürich," in *Sociology and History: Theory and Research,* W. Cahnmann and A. Boskoff, eds. (New York and London, 1964), pp. 328–339.

Bloch, Ernst, *Thomas Münzer.* Berlin, 1960.

Chenu, M.D., *La théologie au douzième siècle.* Paris, 1957.

Cohn, Norman, *The Pursuit of the Millennium.* New York, 1957.

Erikson, Erik H., *Young Man Luther.* New York, 1958.

Evans-Pritchard, E.E., *Nuer Religion.* Oxford, 1956.

Francis, E.K., "Toward a Typology of Religious Orders," *American Journal of Sociology,* LV (March 1950), 437–449.

Gellner, Ernest, *Thought and Change.* Chicago, 1965.

Geertz, Clifford, *The Religion of Java.* Glencoe, Illinois, 1960.

Goldmann, Lucien, *The Hidden God.* London, 1964. (*Le dieu caché.* Paris, 1955.)

Goode, William J., *Religion Among the Primitives.* Glencoe, Illinois, 1951.

Granet, Marcel, *Chinese Civilisation.* London, 1930. (*La civilisation Chinoise.* Paris, 1929.)

Heer, Friedrich, *The Medieval World.* London, 1962. (*Mittelalter von 1100 bis 1350.* 1961.)

Hill, Christopher, *Puritanism and Revolution.* London, 1958.

———, *Society and Puritanism in Pre-Revolutionary England.* London, 1964.

Hobsbawm, E.J., *Primitive Rebels.* London, 1959.

Huizinga, J., *The Waning of the Middle Ages.* 1924.

Horkheimer, Max, and Theodor W. Adorno, *Dialektik der Aufklärung.* Amsterdam, 1947.

Inglis, K.S., *Churches and the Working Classes in Victorian England.* London, 1963.

Isambert, François-André, *Christianisme et classe ouvrière, Jalons pour une étude de sociologie historique.* Tournai, 1961.

Lanternari, V., *The Religions of the Oppressed. A Study of Modern Messianic Cults.* New York, 1965.

Littell, Franklin Hamlin, T*he Anabaptist View of the Church.* Boston, 1958.

Lüthy, Herbert, *Le passé présent, Combats d'idées de Calvin à Rousseau.* Monaco, 1965.

Merton, Robert K., "Puritanism, Pietism and Science," *Social Theory and Social Structure.* 2nd ed., New York, 1957, pp. 574–606.

Mühlmann, W.E., *Chiliasmus und Nativismus: Studien zur Psychologie, Soziologie und historischen Kasuistik der Umsturzbewegunge.* Berlin, 1961.

Nelson, Benjamin, *The Idea of Usury. From Tribal Otherhood to Universal Brotherhood.* Princeton, 1949.

Poulat, Emile, *Histoire, dogme et critique dans la crise moderniste.* Tournai, Paris, 1962.

Queiros, Maria Isaura Pereira de, *La guerre sainte au Brésil: Le mouvement messianique du Contestado.* São Paulo, 1957.

Richter, Melvin, *The Politics of Conscience: T.H. Green and His Age.* New York, 1965.

Sarkisyanz, E., *Russland und der Messianismus des Orients.* Tübingen, 1955.

Smith, W.C., *Islam in Modern History.* Princeton, 1957.

Srinivas, M.N., *Caste in Modern India and Other Essays.* Bombay, 1962.

Sundkler, B.G.M., *Bantu Prophets in South Africa.* London, 1948.

Swanson, G.E., *The Birth of the Gods: The Origin of Primitive Belief.* Ann Arbor, 1960.

Talmon, Yonina, "Pursuit of the Millennium: the Relation Between Religious and Social Change," *European Journal of Sociology,* III (1962), 125–148.

Thapar, Romila, "Aśoka and Buddhism," *Past & Present,* 18 (1960), 43–51.

Thompson, E.P., *The Making of the English Working Class.* London, 1963.

Vernant, Jean-Pierre, *Mythe et pensée chez les Grecs. Etudes de psychologie historique.* Paris, 1965.

Watt, W. Montgomery, *Islam and the Integration of Society.* London, 1961.

Werner, Ernst, *Pauperes Christi. Studien zu sozial-religiösen Bewegungen im Zeitalter des Reformpapsttums.* Leipzig, 1956.

Wertheim, W.F., *Indonesian Society in Transition.* 2nd ed., Den Haag, 1959.

Wearmouth, Robert F., *Methodism and the Working-Class Movement of England, 1800–1850.* London, 1937.

Worsley, Peter, *The Trumpet Shall Sound.* London, 1957.

This anthology utilizes historical materials to illuminate the urgent contemporary problem of the relationship of religion to society. The selections have been chosen to illustrate the development of modern thought about religion as a social force. They date from the eighteenth century and include both classical and contemporary writings. A number of pieces have never before been translated into English; these include Borkenau's famous analysis of the social basis of early Calvinism and Schelsky's essay on contemporary religiosity. The anthology is intended to serve the needs of sociological students of religion and of a general public. It complements both recent publications of classical texts in the sociology of religion and current discussions of the present situation of religion, including the debate on "the death of God."

Both philosophical reflection and substantive empirical inquiry are represented in the texts. Among the classical thinkers included are: Hume, Hegel, Feuerbach, Marx, Comte, Spencer, Nietzsche, Freud, and Weber. Important modern theorists like Mannheim, Adorno, Desroche, and Parsons are represented, and the selections from contemporary sociological research and thought present the writings of scholars of the capacity of Erik-son, Glock, LeBras, Lenski, and H. Richard Niebuhr. The anthology treats the analysis of change in religion and society as the central problem for the sociology of religion, and is designed to situate the sociological analysis of religion at the very center of the main tradition of sociological thought. In an extensive introduction, the confluence of the development of sociology itself with the development of the modern sociology of religion is depicted.

The anthology includes much material relevant to the problem of primitive and non-western religions. The current debate between "functionalists" and "Marxists" or "Weberians" is depicted as a reflection of the larger problem of the interpretation of the historical evolution of religion in modern society. Much of the present discussion of secularization is found anticipated in nineteenth-century texts. Equally, much of the present emphasis on religion as a factor in "development" is traced to its intellectual sources, while other texts included in the anthology depict the present situation of religion in societies like Japan and India. Above all, the text enables American students and readers to enlarge their intellectual and historical horizons.